OPERATIONS MANAGEMENT
Theory and Problems

McGRAW-HILL SERIES IN MANAGEMENT
Keith Davis and Fred Luthans, Consulting Editors

Allen Management and Organization
Allen The Management Profession
Argyris Management and Organizational Development: The Path from XA to YB
Beckett Management Dynamics: The New Synthesis
Benton Supervision and Management
Bergen and Haney Organizational Relations and Management Action
Blough International Business: Environment and Adaptation
Bowman Management: Organization and Planning
Brown Judgment in Administration
Buchele The Management of Business and Public Organizations
Campbell, Dunnette, Lawler, and Weick Managerial Behavior, Performance, and Effectiveness
Cleland and King Management: A Systems Approach
Cleland and King Systems Analysis and Project Management
Cleland and King Systems, Organizations, Analysis, Management: A Book of Readings
Dale Management: Theory and Practice
Dale Readings in Management: Landmarks and New Frontiers
Davis Human Behavior at Work: Organizational Behavior
Davis Organizational Behavior: A Book of Readings
Davis and Blomstrom Business and Society: Environment and Responsibility
DeGreene Systems Psychology
Dunn and Rachel Wage and Salary Administration: Total Compensation Systems
Dunn and Stephens Management of Personnel: Manpower Management and Organizational Behavior
Edmunds and Letey Environmental Administration
Fiedler A Theory of Leadership Effectiveness
Finch, Jones, and Litterer Managing for Organizational Effectiveness: An Experiential Approach
Flippo Principles of Personnel Management
Glueck Business Policy: Strategy Formation and Management Action
Hampton Contemporary Management
Hicks and Gullett The Management of Organizations
Hicks and Gullett Modern Business Management: A Systems and Environmental Approach
Hicks and Gullett Organizations: Theory and Behavior
Johnson, Kast, and Rosenzweig The Theory and Management of Systems
Kast and Rosenzweig Experiential Exercises and Cases in Management
Kast and Rosenzweig Organization and Management: A Systems Approach
Knudson, Woodworth, and Bell Management: An Experiential Approach
Koontz Toward a Unified Theory of Management
Koontz and O'Donnell Essentials of Management
Koontz and O'Donnell Management: A Book of Readings
Koontz and O'Donnell Management: A Systems and Contingency Analysis of Managerial Functions
Lee and Dobler Purchasing and Materials Management: Text and Cases
Levin, McLaughlin, Lamone, and Kottas Production/Operations Management: Contemporary Policy for Managing Operating Systems
Luthans Contemporary Readings in Organizational Behavior
Luthans Introduction to Management: A Contingency Approach
Luthans Organizational Behavior
McNichols Policy Making and Executive Action
Maier Problem-solving Discussions and Conferences: Leadership Methods and Skills

Margulies and Raia Organizational Development: Values, Process, and Technology
Mayer Production and Operations Management
Miles Theories of Management: Implications for Organizational Behavior and Development
Monks Operations Management: Theory and Problems
Mundel A Conceptual Framework for the Management Sciences
Newstrom, Reif, and Monczka A Contingency Approach to Management: Readings
Petit The Moral Crisis in Management
Petrof, Carusone, and McDavid Small Business Management: Concepts and Techniques for Improving Decisions
Porter, Lawler, and Hackman Behavior in Organizations
Prasow and Peters Arbitration and Collective Bargaining: Conflict Resolution in Labor Relations
Ready The Administrator's Job
Reddin Managerial Effectiveness
Richman and Copen International Management and Economic Development
Sartain and Baker The Supervisor and His Job
Schrieber, Johnson, Meier, Fischer, and Newell Cases in Manufacturing Management
Shore Operations Management
Shull, Delbecq, and Cummings Organizational Decision Making
Steers and Porter Motivation and Work Behavior
Sutermeister People and Productivity
Tannenbaum, Weschler, and Massarik Leadership and Organization
Wofford, Gerloff, and Cummins Organizational Communication: The Keystone to Managerial Effectiveness

OPERATIONS MANAGEMENT Theory and Problems

Joseph G. Monks
Oregon State University

McGraw-Hill Book Company

New York St. Louis San Francisco Auckland
Bogotá Düsseldorf Johannesburg
London Madrid Mexico Montreal
New Delhi Panama Paris São Paulo
Singapore Sydney Tokyo Toronto

OPERATIONS MANAGEMENT
Theory and Problems

34567890 DODO 7832109

This book was set in Times New Roman. The editors were William J. Kane and Matthew Cahill; the designer was Joseph Gillians; the production supervisor was Charles Hess. The drawings were done by ANCO/Boston. R. R. Donnelley & Sons Company was printer and binder.

Library of Congress Cataloging in Publication Data

Monks, Joseph G.
Operations management.

(McGraw-Hill series in management)
Includes index.
1. Production management. I. Title.
TS155.M67 658.5 76-42193
ISBN 0-07-042718-6

To
Jack Keeley
of
Westinghouse

Contents

Preface

This book covers material professionally recognized as belonging to the field of production and operations management. It is based on the concept that managers are decision makers and that the ability to make better managerial decisions is something that can be learned. The operations we speak of involve industrial plants, hospitals, airlines, government agencies, and others, in locations that are both domestic and foreign. All these activities face systems design, resource allocation, work scheduling, inventory, quality, and other control problems which have common theoretical bases.

The text is intended for a first course in production or operations management at the undergraduate or graduate level. The objective of the book is to present the theory and applications of operations management in a framework that is particularly suitable for student learning, with the ultimate goal of producing better decision makers. It is not packed with verbal intricacies and second-order equations designed to impress those who already understand the material. As a result, statements of theory are intentionally basic, relatively concise, and, hopefully, even simple. Examples, solved problems, and skill-building exercises are probably more numerous than in most texts. I am convinced that applications, including a liberal number of single-answer problems, are the key to driving home important concepts to the user. Special effort has been made to set forth solutions to problems in a clear and logical manner so as to facilitate self-learning on the part of the student. This is simply a recognition of the gradual movement of today's educational systems from teacher-dominated prescriptive approaches to inquiry-centered student study.

Readers interested in teaching or learning psychology may recognize the influence of Maslow, Bloom, Rogers, Wales, and others in the approaches used in this text. These educators suggest that intellectual activities are at the highest level of a human being's need hierarchy. At this highest level, the human being is most fully realized by the acquisition of knowledge and/or skills which, when combined with values, enable rational, humane decisions to be made. Decision making thus merges facts, concepts, and methodologies with an understanding and appreciation of human value systems. The result is informed judgment.

We shall not attempt to cover every remotely related principle of knowledge in this book, nor shall we demand a reorientation of the reader's own value system. But we shall focus on fundamentally important concepts, practice relevant problem-solving skills, and hopefully bring to light an awareness of the role of values in the decision-making process. Contrary to the beliefs of many traditional approaches to education, business decisions are not value-free. It is time that we, as educators, recognize this.

Operations management courses have gradually incorporated an increasing amount of quantitative methodology because quantitative techniques improve management's decision-making ability. In some cases, however, theory has far outpaced practice. This text concentrates upon theory that has the potential to be applied in a meaningful way. It does make frequent use of the mathematical and statistical preparation normally acquired at the collegiate freshman and sophomore levels. However, years in the classroom have convinced me that students occasionally "forget" their statistics. Thus, the necessary concepts are reviewed herein as we progress. Quantitative methodologies are introduced in an applications context when first appropriate rather than concentrated at the start of the text or isolated in an appendix.

The material throughout the text is integrated within the structure of a conceptual model developed in the first chapter and summarized in the last. Nevertheless, the topics are packaged to allow maximum discretion over coverage on the part of the instructor. The chapters (except Chapters 8 and 9) are individual units of study and can be handled in a different order from that in which they are here presented, or a unit can even be bypassed without significant loss of continuity. In addition, within Chapter 11 the maintenance and cost control topics can be handled independently without jeopardizing coverage of the other material in the chapter.

In a sense, the book is somewhat akin to a reference manual in that the relatively brief, primary text materials are usually followed by numerous solved problems that solidify operations management concepts and illustrate how the theory is applied in a decision-making context. The problems are grouped under the same subheadings as are used in the theory sections. They can be included or omitted depending on the time available and the emphasis placed on the chapter by the instructor. Each solved problem emphasizes a slightly different perspective or a more advanced aspect of the theory. There are also a few starred (*) problems which offer a challenge of extending beyond the basic material that lies in the body of the chapters; these problems should be considered optional.

The solution to unsolved problems at the end of the chapters can often be facilitated by reference to the examples and solved problems. Answers to the odd-numbered problems are given in Appendix A.

Finally, a note of appreciation is offered to the individuals and organizations who helped in one way or another to produce this book. First, I wish to thank my students at Oregon State University for their patience, understanding, and constructive criticism as they worked through the preliminary drafts of the manuscript. I am also indebted to the operations management faculty at Oregon State (particularly Bill Forstrom, Cliff Gray, and Chuck Dane) for their reviews and comments. My good friend and international colleague, Art Stonehill, did much to help me internationalize the text in line with the most recent AACSB standards. Along those same lines, I would like to express my appreciation to Professor David O'Mahony of University College Cork (Ireland) and to the University of Manchester Business School (England) for making research facilities available to me when I needed them. I am particularly indebted to Oliver Wight and Walt Goddard of Oliver Wight, Inc., Harlow Loucks and Leroy Reinhart of Tektronix, Inc., and the American Production and Inventory Control Society (APICS) in general for opening my eyes as to what some firms are really doing in the way of production control. For years the academic world has substantially lagged behind industry in some areas, and I hope this work will make some contribution toward closing that gap. APICS has quickly become one of the most useful and effective professional societies in the world, and I strongly encourage students interested in operations management to become affiliated with it early and to participate actively.

A special thanks goes to my reviewers for their constructive criticism while the manuscript was in preparation. I am particularly indebted to Bruce Caldwell, Henry Hays of North Texas State, Ken Ramsing of the University of Oregon, Chan Hahn of Bowling Green, and Bill Boore of Portland State University.

Sheryl Wagner and Shirley Exon handled the typing in an admirable fashion. To these, to my wife Clara, and to all others who contributed, thanks.

Joseph G. Monks

PART

1

Planning and Organization of Operations

CHAPTER

1

Operations Management Concepts

INTRODUCTION

DEFINITION OF OPERATIONS MANAGEMENT

RESOURCES

SYSTEMS: DESIGN AND CONTROL

TRANSFORMATION AND VALUE-ADDED ACTIVITIES

MANAGERIAL POLICY

DECISION-MAKING FUNCTIONS: FRAMEWORK, ENVIRONMENT, AND METHODOLOGY

KNOWLEDGE AND VALUE BASE

ANALYTICAL FRAMEWORK FOR DECISIONS

ENVIRONMENT OF DECISIONS: CERTAINTY-UNCERTAINTY

METHODOLOGY OF DECISIONS

MODELS FOR OPERATIONS ANALYSIS

ECONOMIC BREAK-EVEN ANALYSIS

UTILITY-BASED DECISIONS

PRODUCTION SYSTEM SCHEMATIC

CLASSIFICATION OF OPERATIONS MANAGEMENT DECISION AREAS

INTRODUCTION

Two hundred years ago, the field of operations management did not exist. So if you had been fortunate enough to be enrolled in a university at the time of the Revolutionary War, you would not have had the opportunity (or perhaps you prefer the words "have been required") to learn the type of material that lies ahead in this text. Compared to some arts and sciences, operations management is a newcomer, born of an industrial and managerial revolution, and nurtured by scientific inquiry and technological innovation.

As a matter of fact, the term "operations management" has come into popular use only during the past few years. It has evolved from factory-oriented terms like "manufacturing management" and "production operations," but it conveys a broader meaning which now fully embraces service industries and nonprofit activities as well. Thus our textual material may find just as much application in the management of hospitals or airline operations as it does in the manufacture of automobiles. This is because the underlying theory of operations management is the same in each case. Inventory, scheduling, quality control, and other managerial activities have much in common from one industry to the next.

Our objective lies in developing a comprehensive theoretical framework for better managing the wide range of operations activities that make up much of our economic and social environment. But theory without practice is empty, so we shall be careful to develop the corresponding skill of application by frequent illustrations and example problems.

In this first chapter we lay the groundwork for an approach to operations management that will serve us throughout the remainder of the text. We begin with a definition of operations management and set forth a framework for managerial decisions that rests heavily upon systems and modeling concepts. Then we consider how this framework can accommodate the spectrum of real-world operational problems that range from some situations where the facts are all known for certain to others where everything is highly subjective or absolutely uncertain. Several types of analytical techniques, or models, are described and the key role of mathematical and statistical models is noted. We focus upon three representative types of models: (1) a traditional economic break-even analysis which assumes conditions of certainty; (2) a more sophisticated utility-based model that applies to highly subjective, uncertain situations; and (3) a more general schematic model which summarizes the operations management definition that is developed throughout the chapter. The chapter concludes by decomposing the general definition into major topic areas that will constitute the subjects of successive chapters.

With this brief introduction, let us turn to some perhaps terse but necessary definitions. They form the basis of much of what follows, so a clear understanding of them is important.

DEFINITION OF OPERATIONS MANAGEMENT

Operations managers may be found working under various organizational titles, such as vice president of operations, general manager, production manager, and others. They are usually executives who play a major role in managing the productive activities that manifest the objectives of an organization. We may define *operations management* as that activity whereby resources, flowing within a defined system, are combined and transformed in a controlled manner to add value in accordance with policies communicated by management.

Whereas the term "production," in a narrow sense, is often associated with a quantity of goods, or with an assembly or perhaps a chemical process, "production management" has always been concerned with the productivity of the transformation process. In a very real sense the above definition of operations management also encompasses production management. Indeed many authors would argue that the two terms are interchangeable. We shall recognize this understanding, using the word "production" to connote the vital concepts of transformation and value added. But we shall not necessarily restrict transformations to physical processes, nor assume that value added represents only material values that can be expressed in monetary terms (as opposed to human and immaterial values).

The production activity is dynamic and takes place in an uncertain economic and social environment that changes over time. Management has the task of acting upon and reacting to the environment by making decisions which direct productive efforts toward the achievement of organizational objectives. Key elements in the definition of operations management are the concepts of (1) resources, (2) systems, (3) transformation and value-adding activities, and (4) managerial policy. Let us examine each of these concepts in more detail.

RESOURCES

An organization's resources are the material and nonmaterial assets available to achieve desired objectives. Resource inputs to the production system may be conveniently classified into material and equipment, human, and capital resources.

Material and Equipment

These are the physical facilities and equipment such as plant, inventories, and supplies. Included are operating and control equipment like computers and the physical energies (for example, electrical, mechanical) used in operations. In an accounting sense, the material and equipment usually constitute the major assets of an organization.

Human

The human input is both physical and intellectual. Early production efforts relied heavily upon human physical labor, but as production technology and methodology advanced, a higher proportion of the human input became devoted to planning, organizing, and controlling efforts. By using the intellectual capabilities of people, labor inputs are magnified many times, resulting in increased productivity as well as a much closer worker-machine interface. This closer integration of human and physical systems has in turn presented new challenges in job design to achieve worker satisfaction.

The labor resource, although it is often the key asset of an organization, is typically not accounted for in the balance sheet of the organization. Some embryonic attempts are now under way to deal with human resource accounting but the problems are many and the rate of progress has been slow. Nevertheless, it is the human resource, in the form of managerial talent, engineering skill, employee cooperation, and the like, that has provided the primary impetus for the growth and development of the large-scale organizations that flourish today.

People bring human values into an organization, and some of these values are essentially institutionalized into the resulting organizational society. They become traditions, standards, and ethical guidelines, both for internal operations and for dealing with "the public." These values often play a strong but difficult to define role in the organizational decision process.

Capital

Funds are essentially an immaterial store of value which can be applied to establish and regulate the amount of material and human inputs. In an aggregate sense they help to determine the level of technology and the tradeoff between the use of labor versus equipment. As more capital is allocated to a given phase of a production process, the level of technology typically rises and, via automation, equipment replaces human labor.

In free enterprise organizations, capital becomes available in the form of equity (stock) or debt (bonds) funds and is replenished via profits. In nonprofit organizations, taxes or contributions are a continuing source of funds to finance operations deemed to be in the group or public interest. However, whether an organization is profit- or nonprofit-oriented, efficient and effective use of resources rests heavily upon fundamental principles of operations management.

SYSTEMS: DESIGN AND CONTROL

A *system* is an arrangement of components designed to achieve a particular objective (or objectives) according to plan. The components may be either physical or conceptual or both, but they all share a unique relationship with each other and with the overall objective of the system. A health care delivery system, for example, has doctors and physical facilities plus conceptual operating policies which combine to ultimately provide patients with a specified level of medical care.

Our cultural environment includes a multitude of economic and social systems, many of which are interrelated and function simultaneously for the benefit of society as a whole. For example, we have a national monetary system which facilitates the exchange of goods and a transportation network which can move these goods quickly and efficiently to any part of the country.

The individual business and government organizations are essentially subsystems of larger social systems. They, in turn, are typically composed of their own subsystems, which theoretically function for the good of their individual organizations. The production, marketing, and finance functions are traditional subsystems of the formal organization of a firm. However, many firms are now reorganizing their formal structure to better account for the interdependency of such subsystems. As a result, business systems are emerging which are based more upon information flows and decision responsibilities than upon strict functional lines.

A systems approach to operations management problems places strong emphasis upon the integrative nature of management responsibilities, recognizing both the interdependence and the hierarchical nature of subsystems. Some authors have characterized it as macro-micro-macro cycle [7] and others as an analysis-synthesis approach [**12**: 53]. In essence, systems theory stresses the understanding and relationships of the whole system, recognizing that a combined effect of components can be greater than the sum total of individual effects, that is, can be *synergistic*. Problems must first be abstracted from the overall (macro) environment, then they can be broken down into parts (micro), analyzed, and solutions proposed. But ultimately the components must again be restructured or synthesized (macro) to discover and evaluate the impact of new interrelationships that arise from proposed changes in the system.

The ability of any system to achieve its objectives depends upon (1) the *design* of the system and (2) the *control* exercised by the system.

Systems Design

Most managers realize that the independent optimization of individual subsystems, such as marketing or production functions, does not necessarily result in optimization of the objectives of the total system. Production may favor a steady manufacturing rate and low inventories while marketing is anxious to meet highly seasonal demands. If any form of total system optimization is to be achieved, the subsystem objectives must be integrated and coordinated in light of overall system goals. It makes sense to start with a clearly delineated set of overall system objectives and to develop a hierarchy of subsystem goals which, when consistently pursued, will most effectively facilitate the overall objectives.

Unfortunately this is more easily said than done. We, as a nation, have not yet succeeded in establishing a clear-cut set of national objectives. Many top corporate managers refuse to face up to the task of clearly defining organizational goal policy. In these cases, the second-level managers or systems designers are forced to interpret the objectives as best they can. They must make full use of what data are available, including their knowledge of the value systems and behavioral characteristics of the members of the organizations affected by the design.

A *design* is simply a predetermined arrangement of components or operating parameters, such as the set of drawings for a plant expansion or the plans and procedures for enforcing statewide air pollution controls. One of the first tasks faced by systems designers, after they have identified their objectives, is to abstract their particular problems from the maze of intertwined problems that usually constitute the design environment. The systems design process thus involves identifying and bounding the relevant parameters so as to isolate them from numerous irrelevant variables. Following this, many considerations enter into the analysis and design (or redesign) stage of a systems design, such as the economics of use of available resources, level of technology to be used, safety and reliability of the system itself, and impact of the system upon the environment outside the organization.

One of the most vital inputs to systems design comes from the consumers or users. They embody the service objectives of the organization and are also the ultimate source of funds for the operations. Since the system functions to serve the consumers, their quantity and cost requirements, as well as quality and other technological desires, should be incorporated into the production systems design. Business history has vividly proved that orientation to the consumers is a key element in an organization's success. This holds true for public and nonprofit organizations as well as profit-making firms.

The more structured the design is, the less planning and decision making will be involved in the operation of the system. Similarly, a highly structured design, although suitable for high-volume production of standardized products, is inherently less adaptable to meeting competitive pressures of broader product lines in smaller volumes upon shorter notice from the customer. An increasingly important consideration in modern systems design arises from the need for flexibility and adaptability of the system to meet new and unexpected demands. Fortunately, both physical equipment and human components can be geared to accept change, especially if the system has been designed with this inevitability in mind.

Production systems are often categorized as *continuous* or *intermittent*, although many systems are a combination of the two. In continuous designs, the physical flow of products is continuous and production is usually in high volumes accomplished by means of line-type operations. Plant layout is arranged to accommodate the product, such as paper, and specialized equipment is used. In intermittent designs, the physical flow of products is intermittent and production is on a batch or job-order basis. Layout is arranged according to process, and general-purpose equipment is used.

Figure 1-1 shows a simplified theoretical model of a production system design. Note that the essential elements are *inputs*, *transformation activities*, and *outputs*. We shall expand upon this basic model as we progress through this chapter.

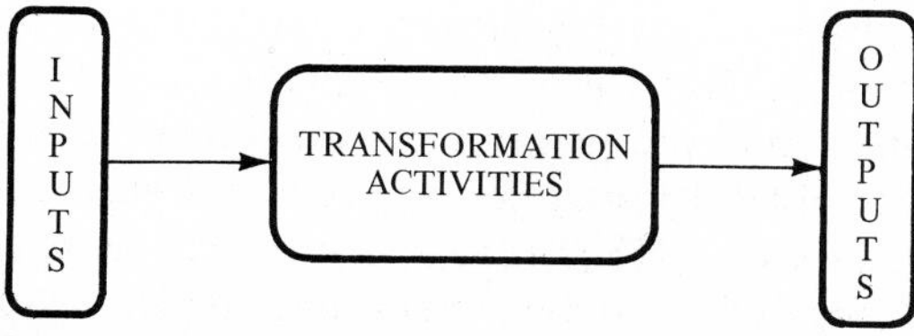

FIGURE 1-1 Simplified production system

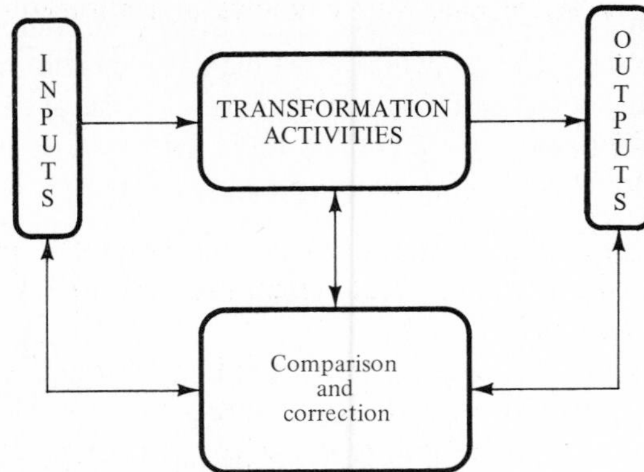

FIGURE 1-2 System with feedback

Systems Control

Systems control consists of all actions necessary to ensure that activities conform to preconceived plans or goals. Control involves *measurement*, *feedback*, *comparison with standards*, and *corrective action.*

Figure 1-2 adds a control mechanism to the production system of Fig. 1-1. (The classic example is a home thermostat.) The measurement function must be accomplished by some appropriately accurate sensory device. Data are then fed back for comparison and correction, with the feedback activity depending heavily upon the physical or organizational communication network. An effective information system having appropriate response times is essential to the operation of an effective control system. Standards for comparison are based upon historical or engineered criteria and may be in the form of physical measurements, control limits, cost variances, and the like. Finally, corrective action implies both an authority to change the system and the ability to implement those changes.

The system described in Fig. 1-2 is a *closed-loop* arrangement because it can automatically function on the basis of data from within its own system to ensure that the outputs will continuously meet control standards. *Open-loop* control systems do not have sufficient internal feedback with automatic control to maintain desired standards for they are influenced by "outside" information. Any system that interfaces with the environment is open to the extent that it receives stimuli from outside its own control. For example, a spaceship that depends upon navigational information from computers on earth would be operating (at least partly) as an open system.

TRANSFORMATION AND VALUE-ADDED ACTIVITIES

The objective of combining resources (that is, factors of production) under controlled conditions is to transform them into goods or services having a higher (material or immaterial) value than the original inputs. The effectiveness of the use of the factors of production to produce goods and services is commonly referred to as *productivity*. Basically, productivity connotes a relationship of output to input such that:

$$\frac{\text{Value of output}}{\text{Cost of input}} > 1$$

This concept of value added is in contrast to the notion of engineering efficiency where energy losses within any physical system prohibit the ratio of output to input from being greater than one.

We all know that the values placed on a good or service differ from one consumer to the next. But as a large volume of output enters a competitive market, monetary amounts typically emerge as indicators of value. However, many outputs from a production system, such as employee satisfactions, social and environmental impacts, and so forth, are unique, and are difficult to value on a monetary basis. In the past, such intangible values and side effects of production decisions were often overlooked. Today we recognize the reality of these outputs and managers are forced to deal with them in terms of different individual and group value systems.

Measures of physical productivity serve as means of comparison for two or more individual units or organizations, as well as for whole industries and even nations. In the United States, despite recessions and inflation, productivity has increased at an average rate of about 3 percent per year over several decades. The resource base, population growth, ethic of the people, and existing level of technology all contribute to this economic growth rate. Our productivity of labor is high relative to some other countries because of (1) the level of training and education of the workers and (2) the substantially higher capital investment in automated production equipment.

Since organizations operate in a dynamic environment that changes over time, the inputs and outputs are best described as flows of inputs and outputs. In the physical sense, production (as a noun) results from maintaining the system flows. For a given level of inputs, improvements in the design or control of the system will increase productivity and the value of the outputs will be greater.

Production operations managers are concerned with both the technology of the transformation process and the methodology of managing the process. The technology is often unique to given industries, such as steel or paper processing, and is not the central focus of this text. However, the methodology of planning, organizing, directing, and controlling activities has a theoretical base which is common to most, or perhaps all, production activities. The development and use of this type of analytical base is the concern of this text.

MANAGERIAL POLICY

Modern management techniques have developed from a unique history of practical and theoretical effort. As a result of ideas expressed about 200 years ago, such as Adam Smith's philosophy of division of labor and James Watt's steam engine, the machine-powered factory system became well established by the early 1900s. At that time Frederick Taylor came on the scene to suggest that the scientific method be applied to all management problems. More specifically, he proposed (1) scientific selection and training of workers, (2) definition of each worker's tasks, and (3) cooperation and division of work between labor and management. Taylor's ideas were installed as "scientific management systems" by colleagues, such as Henry Gantt, who also made outstanding contributions of their own. As the "father of scientific management," Taylor's work opened the door to many others who followed, including Frank and Lillian Gilbreth (time and motion study), F. W. Harris (mathematical models for inventory control), W. Shewhart (statistical quality control), and L. H. C. Tippett (work sampling).

As corporations grew, a larger financial base was required and stock ownership became more widespread. Owners soon turned to professional managers to run their organizations. Several theories have developed to explain the role of managers; the most noteworthy approaches to management are the following.

1 *Functional approach* This widely held approach holds that management has traditionally been charged with the role of planning, organizing, directing, and controlling the activities of an organization. It stems from early writings of Henri Fayol, Chester Bernard, and other classical theorists. Followers of this approach regard management as a universal process which is readily understood in terms of these fundamental functions which must be performed regardless of the type of organization.

2 *Behavioral approach* This human relations approach recognizes that managers are people who work through other people to lead the activities of an organization. In viewing the individual as a sociopsychological being, it concentrates upon behavioral and motivational forces and stresses the art of interpersonal relationships. The manager is a leader of individuals or groups and the human element of organization receives paramount attention. This emphasis on the behavioral aspects of management has arisen primarily from Elton Mayo's studies at the Western Electric plant in the late 1920s.

3 *Decision-making–systems approach* This approach views a manager basically as a decision maker within an operating system. Management is concerned with the methodology and implementation of decisions that facilitate system goals. The decisions may well relate to both functions (such as planning, organizing, directing, and controlling) and to people, for these subgoals and resources both exist within a systems context. Furthermore, scientific methods of modeling and systems analysis can be followed to help reach decisions.

Whereas some management theorists would separate the decision-making and systems approaches, we have chosen to emphasize decision making in a systems context because of its theoretical basis and applied usefulness. Other approaches also exist, but we shall not explore them in any depth. For our purposes, then, we shall refer to *management* as the process of making decisions and taking action relative to functions and behavior which direct the activities of people in organized systems toward common objectives.

DECISION-MAKING FUNCTIONS: FRAMEWORK, ENVIRONMENT, AND METHODOLOGY

Certainly each of the above approaches to management has some validity and something to offer practitioners. So even though the decision-making–systems approach has particular scientific and analytical suitability, we shall freely use selected concepts from other perspectives.

KNOWLEDGE AND VALUE BASE

The idea of management as a science is founded upon several observations. *First*, the "principles and methodology of management" form an organized body of knowledge. Organization theory, for example, is concerned with tenets of formal and informal organization, line and staff relationships, span of control, authority and responsibility concepts, and so on. Moreover, much of the current decision methodology has advanced to a logically rigorous state. *Second*, real-world data are available for analysis. The business world is essentially a laboratory to the management scientist. *Third*, an objective systematic analysis of the data can often be made. This analysis relies largely upon modern mathematical and statistical techniques. *Finally*, another experimenter (decision maker) could use the same data and arrive at consistent results.

The association of management with the scientific method involves drawing objective conclusions from facts, and facts come from analysis of data. Therefore, the idea of quantification of data is an important element in viewing management as a science. Computers and management information systems are now providing such a data base for decisions. By means of mathematical modeling and simulation, this decision-making process also allows for experimentation and for testing of hypotheses.

Viewing management from the standpoint of a science, one must conclude that the decision-making methodology can be both taught and learned as can other sciences. People need not be "born managers" to do the job. Education, training, and experience can improve managers' abilities to make optimal decisions. They can learn ways of identifying relevant system parameters, collecting data, and analyzing data that will lead to better courses of action. As decision making becomes more scientific, the importance of clearly defined objectives and systematic analysis also becomes more apparent.

If managers were nothing more than mechanistic robots operating in a computerized laboratory, we might uncompromisingly argue for the full-fledged classification of management as a science. But management decisions are not always based upon an "objective systematic analysis of the data." For example, a production planner may have difficulty deciding whether to cope with a weak demand by laying off workers or by keeping them on and building up an inventory in expectation of a stronger demand in the future. It may be less costly to lay off the workers than to carry excess inventory, but the planner may feel an obligation to provide steady employment if it is at all possible.

The same humanistic element of concern for others exists in the engineering, medical, and other professions which we commonly associate with the scientific method. Professional decisions are not always value free—the choice of an "appropriate action" often rests, at least partly, upon an individual or an institutionalized value system.

The incorporation of values into business decisions does not necessarily brand the decision process as nonscientific—nor the results as invalid or unpredictable—for several reasons. First, many business decisions can legitimately be based upon facts that do not carry value-laden implications. This is especially true for numerous routine decisions related to micro, or subsystem, operations. An example of this would be the choice an operations manager must make between two similar pieces of capital equipment with differing initial costs and lifetimes. The chances are that this decision can be made in a fairly objective, systematic manner.

Second, existing legal or environmental controls may accurately reflect individual or organizational ethics. For example, production cost auditors may believe that the intent of the tax laws accurately reflects what their firms "should" pay in federal taxes. Thus they neither overlook legitimate cost deductions nor attempt to capitalize on tax "loopholes." In this case, the applicable laws provide a satisfactory guide to action.

Third, values can be made known and accepted as an underlying standard. Many organizations have identified and adhere to sound values (such as codes of ethics) that are applied in a consistent and predictable manner. In this sense, a broadly based value system acts much like an organized body of knowledge and facilitates a scientific approach to decisions.

Of course, many (perhaps most) value-based decisions are complex. Problems arise when "the law" is an inadequate guideline or when values are not commonly or consistently held. Individual decision makers sometimes narrow organizational concerns to their own self-interests. Others have little sense of distributive justice and their allegiance wavers among the conflicting interests of themselves, employees, stockholders, consumers, society, and the like. Decision making in such situations cannot be construed as being truly "scientific." Nevertheless there is even hope for eventually moving these situations a little closer toward a scientific basis through proper education and training of the decision makers. As decision makers gain an improved awareness of the value systems of others, the reasons for differences become explored, some differences are resolved, and others perhaps are more willingly accommodated.

Recognizing that despite value differences a scientific framework for business decisions does have wide applicability, we now go on to examine the analytical framework for decisions in greater detail. As we proceed through the steps we shall note the areas where value system differences come into play.

ANALYTICAL FRAMEWORK FOR DECISIONS

An analytical and scientific framework for decisions implies several systematic steps for the decision maker. These steps are summarized in Table 1-1.

The *systems approach to defining the problem* (step 1) helps to ensure that the final decisions are as nearly optimal as possible. A system defined too broadly may include many tangential aspects of a problem, making it extremely difficult to establish the complex relationships among the variables. Similarly, a narrowly defined problem might omit relevant variables. The inclusion or exclusion of variables depends upon the system goals; if variables have a significant effect on the goals, they should be included as parameters of the system.

In some cases, skilled systems analysts can facilitate the solution of problems by providing the operating manager with specific systems design and programming skills. However, the model user must almost inevitably become actively involved in defining the problem and formulating the relationships (that is, model building) if the solution is to be truly a useful user-oriented one. This requires close communication and interchange of information between the systems analyst and the decision maker.

The *establishment of decision criteria* (step 2) is of paramount importance for they stem directly from objectives which give purpose and direction to work efforts of the organization. For many years, profits served as a convenient and accepted goal for most free enterprise organizations. Perhaps this was because early models of firm behavior were based almost wholly on economic theory. Today, empirical research reveals that organizations have sets of goals rather than single goals and that profits are only one of many possible objectives. One early study of 1,072 businesses revealed the data shown in Table 1-2 [**4**] which identify eight types of goals. There is reason to suggest that social welfare goals have gained more importance as environmental concerns have become more prominent during the past few years. Social pressures are now strongly limiting the exploitation of resources solely for economic gain and instead are focusing upon the greatest good for the most people over the longest period. Nevertheless, for many organizations within our free enterprise society, profits continue to be a key source of motivation, rewards, and investment capital that underlies a good deal of our nation's economic progress.

Numerous ways exist for classifying objectives, such as economic, social, and political, or individual and organizational, and so forth. The goals in Table 1-2 have been classified into: (1) *general efficiency*, which are specific and largely quantifiable criteria and include organizational efficiency, high productivity, and profit maximization; (2) *associative status*, which sometimes results as a by-product of action toward general efficiency goals and includes organizational growth, industrial leadership, and

TABLE 1-1 FRAMEWORK FOR DECISIONS

1	Define the system and its parameters.
2	Establish the decision criteria (i.e., the goals).
3	Formulate a relationship (model) between the parameters and the criteria.
4	Generate alternatives by varying the values of the parameters.
5	Choose the course of action which most closely satisfies the criteria.

TABLE 1-2 BUSINESS ORGANIZATION GOALS

Type of goal	% rating goal as highly important
Organizational efficiency	81
High productivity	80
Profit maximization	72
Organizational stability	58
Employee welfare	65
Organizational growth	60
Industrial leadership	58
Social welfare	16

organizational stability; (3) *employee welfare*; and (4) *social welfare* classifications. The study referenced found relatively strong correlations between associative goals and personal or organizational characteristics suggesting that differences in firm behavior may be due more to associative status goals than to general efficiency goals, and that actual goals of a business may be related more closely to personal characteristics of the managers than to broad characteristics of the business.

The personal characteristics and activities of managers are, in a very real sense, reflections of their individual value systems. So too are organizational characteristics a reflection of institutionalized values. Thus, as organizations place different emphasis upon efficiency, status, and welfare goals, they are essentially expressing institutionalized values in the form of a unique mix of operational goals.

The decision criterion (or set of criteria) flows directly from organizational objectives and should be as specific as possible. A criterion of "maximizing profits" may be adequate as one (economic) organizational goal, but too broad and inadequate for much decision making on an operational level. Figure 1-3 depicts the hierarchical structure of goals by comparing it to the familiar upside-down planning pyramid which begins with broad objectives that are ultimately operationalized into specific rules. The figure illustrates the necessity of specific directives such as "Rotate workers among 3 jobs" in order to fulfill broader objectives such as "Increase profits." Note that subsystem criteria must be consistent with the higher-level goals. If inconsistencies exist in the goal structure, some of the organization's resources are probably being wasted by the pursuit of contradictory objectives. An example of this would be a power company with vague profit and service objectives. If its marketing group were to promote the distribution of air conditioners while the production capacity was inadequate, neither profit nor service objectives would be achieved.

In some cases system criteria, such as "good customer service," are so difficult to quantify that substitute criteria, such as "number of customer complaints," must be used. One should clearly recognize and label such measures as indicators, or surrogate criteria. Otherwise, the substitute criteria may be satisfied, even though the intent of the system criteria is not. For example, a pressured office manager might "reduce the number of customer complaints by 50 percent" by simply instituting a tedious 10-page customer complaint form. Unfortunately, this is not likely to help

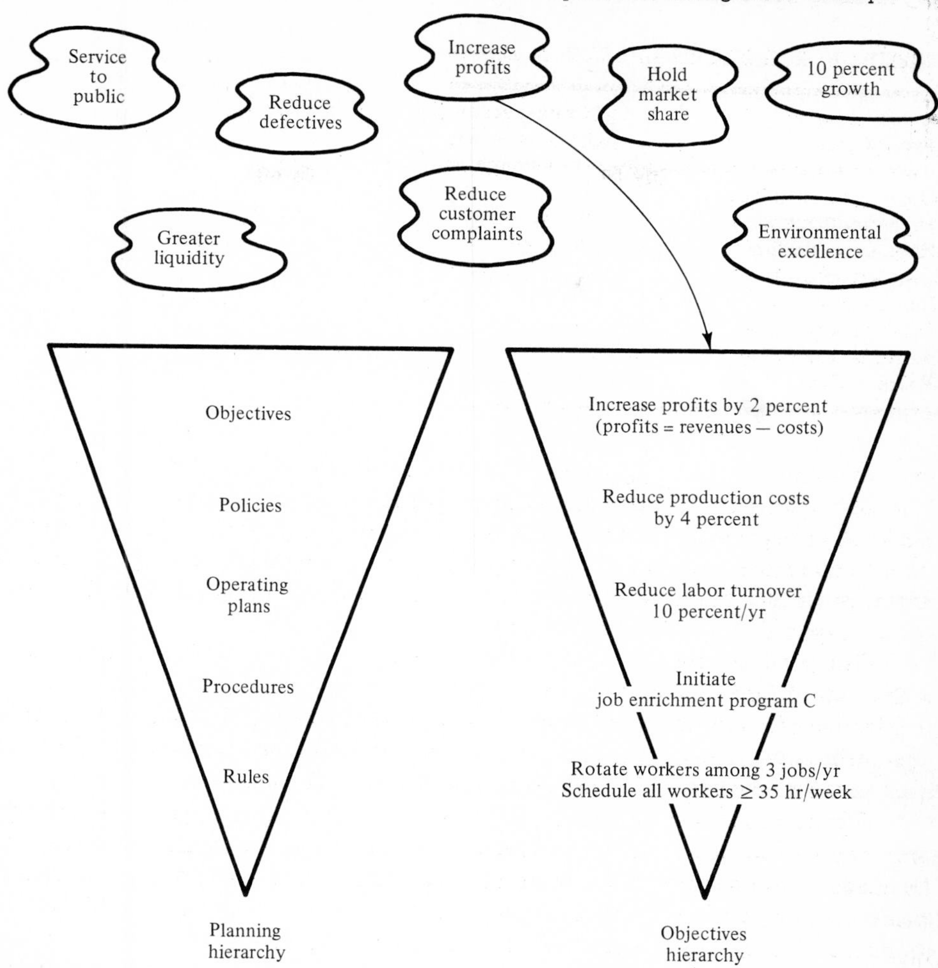

FIGURE 1-3 Decision criteria hierarchy

achieve the organizational objective of better customer service even though the office manager will have satisfied the substitute criteria. Large bureaucracies are often faced with such problems of using substitute criteria because system objectives become institutionalized in terms of formal policies and impersonal regulations. For this reason decision criteria should be reviewed frequently to ensure that surrogate criteria are being used in a manner consistent with total system criteria.

The *formulation of a relationship, or model,* for experimentation (Table 1-1, step 3) lies at the heart of the scientific decision-making process. Models may be verbal, pictorial, schematic, physical, scale, numerical and statistical, or mathematical. In general, they attempt to describe the essence of a situation or activity by abstracting from reality so the decision maker can study the relationship among relevant variables in isolation. They do not attempt to duplicate reality in all respects, for models that do this reveal nothing. Instead, they are limited approximations of reality. If, for example, the system boundaries were defined in a wide and inclusive manner, the problem situation would perhaps be more realistic, but the problem itself would remain just as difficult to solve. The key to model building lies in abstracting only the relevant variables that affect the criteria and expressing the relationships in a testable form.

As management scientists tackle more complex problem situations, they find that statistical and mathematical models become especially useful. They are typically more abstract than pictorial or scale models, but they also offer the potential of dealing with factors that cannot readily be visualized. These models, aided by computers and simulation techniques, can essentially extend one's thought processes into the realm of the fourth and higher dimensions even though one can visualize reality only in terms of three dimensions at best.

A generalized mathematical or statistical model might take the form:

$$\text{Objective criteria} = \text{function of}\begin{pmatrix}\text{controllable} & \text{uncontrollable} & \\ \text{variables,} & \text{variables,} & \text{error}\end{pmatrix}$$

or symbolically

$$\text{Obj} = f(X, Y, \varepsilon) \tag{1-1}$$

A full description of any model should also include a statement of its assumptions and constraints. All models need not have controllable X, uncontrollable Y, and error terms ε, but these are convenient classifications. The error term often represents a statistical factor which accounts for our use of sample rather than census data. Of course we attempt to keep the amount of error as small as possible.

As an example of a more specific mathematical model we might express a proposed production quantity Q as:

$$Q = f(F, D, I)$$

where

F = forecast or budgeted production rate
D = actual demand rate
I = current inventory level

Note that the forecast production rate F is a controllable variable, actual demand D is largely uncontrollable, and current inventory level I has elements of both. By relating the parameters F, D, and I, via appropriate equations and assigning values to these parameters, the model builder can arrive at proposed values for Q.

Figure 1-4 shows the mathematical modeling process in the form of a schematic model [**1**: 72 (modified)]. Note that it is an abstraction which begins and ends with the real world. The validity of a model should, of course, be judged relative to what it is supposed to do. If, for example, a forecasting model accurately predicts real-

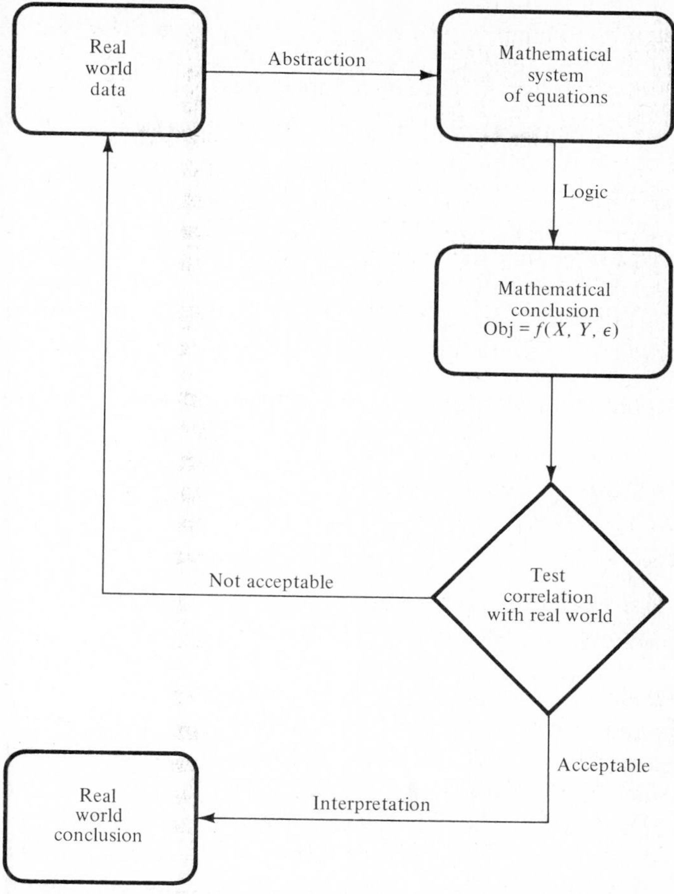

FIGURE 1-4 Mathematical models. Reprinted by permission of the publisher from Carl Brown, Joseph G. Monks, and James R. Park, *Decision Making in Water Resource Allocation*, Lexington Books, Lexington, Mass., 1973.

world demand, a manager would consider it to be a "good" model. Techniques are available to evaluate the validity of models, some of which we shall discuss later in the text.

One of the most difficult aspects of model building lies in incorporating experience, human values, and subjective or less-tangible factors into the relationship in a mathematical or statistical manner. Although this is certainly not a new problem, the renewed emphasis on human and social values has generated increased efforts along these lines. Techniques of Bayesian analysis, utility theory, and some other experiential models show a good deal of promise here.

Another difficult aspect of model building involves the problems of accommodating multiple goals, such as those mentioned in Table 1-2. Whereas goal identification is still largely a subjective undertaking, the quantitative approaches of utility theory and goal programming offer some objective potential in this realm.

Any decision problem implies that alternatives exist. The relationships formulated between the parameters and the decision criteria permit the *generation of alternative solutions* (Table 1-1, step 4) by varying the values of the parameters. Mathematical and statistical models, again, are particularly suitable for generating alternatives because they are so easily modified. The model builder can "experiment" with the model by substituting different values for controllable variables (such as employment levels) as well as uncontrollable variables (such as actual demand).

We noted earlier that the goals and decision criteria had a strong value base. The generation of alternatives also has important value connotations. Just as goals are an end, the alternatives are a means to that end. Both individuals and institutions are sometimes faced with the question of whether or not a given means is morally acceptable.

Our society generally upholds the conviction that the end does not justify the means. For example, the courts have said that a legitimate goal of profits or market share does not justify price fixing or collusion as a means of obtaining it. In some cases, legislation (such as antitrust laws) may constitute a satisfactory behavioral guide for managers. But laws do not anticipate every situation and managers must generally rely upon their individual and institutional value systems. In these situations values play an important role in the decision process by ruling out (as infeasible) any alternatives that are not consistent with behavioral standards.

The final step in the decision process (Table 1-1, step 5) is to *choose the best course of action*, that is, the one that best satisfies the criteria. Some models, such as linear programming, are inherently of an optimizing nature and automatically seek out a maximizing or minimizing solution. If the system boundaries are clearly defined, and all the model assumptions are satisfied, these methods will generate optimal solutions to the specific situations. Other models are more suitable for use in situations that are so complex, uncertain, or subjective that optimal solutions cannot be guaranteed. In these cases, various heuristics and statistical techniques can be used to suggest the best course of action, or at least a preferred course, on the basis of the information and resources available to make the decision. We shall explore this question of model applicability to different information environments in a moment. But first a few words of caution and follow-up.

The best course of action or solution to a problem determined via use of a model is just that—a solution to the model! The true test of the decision process comes when the theoretical solution is applied to the real-world situation. Decision-making processes should therefore incorporate follow-up procedures to ensure that the action is appropriate in the real world. These procedures should include an analysis and evaluation of the solution plus any recommendations for changes or adjustments.

ENVIRONMENT OF DECISIONS: CERTAINTY-UNCERTAINTY

We focus now upon the knowledge and information base that provides the data which are so essential to the scientific decision-making process. With better information, a decision maker can be expected to make decisions that more effectively move

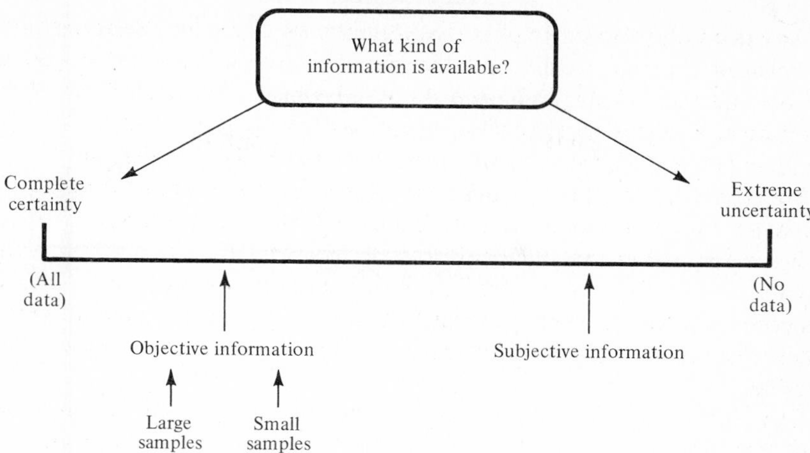

FIGURE 1-5 Information environment

an organization toward its goals. Figure 1-5 depicts the information environment of decisions as one ranging from a situation where the decision maker has (or assumes he or she has) complete information about the decision variables to the other extreme where he or she has no information about them. Operations management decisions are in fact made at numerous points along this continuum from complete certainty to extreme uncertainty.

As can be seen, complete certainty requires census data on all elements in the population. Lacking this, large samples lend more certainty than do small samples. Beyond this, subjective information is very likely better than no data at all.[1]

METHODOLOGY OF DECISIONS

The kind and amount of information available about the decision criteria and variables help determine which type of analytical methods are most appropriate for a given decision situation. Figure 1-6 shows some useful quantitative methods currently available to operations managers. These analytical techniques often serve as the basis for formulating models to help reach decisions. Illustrative problems in this text make wide use of these and other quantitative methods. The text material is, however, applications-oriented, and organized according to subject matter rather than to quantitative method. Thus, in many cases, more than one methodology may be suitable for a given problem. A brief description of some of these analytical methods would include the following.

Complete Certainty Methods

A condition of certainty does not necessarily imply that decision making is easy, for a problem may be ill-defined, decision criteria unclear, or there may be too

[1] I am indebted to Professor Steven Archer of Willamette University for this approach to the information environment.

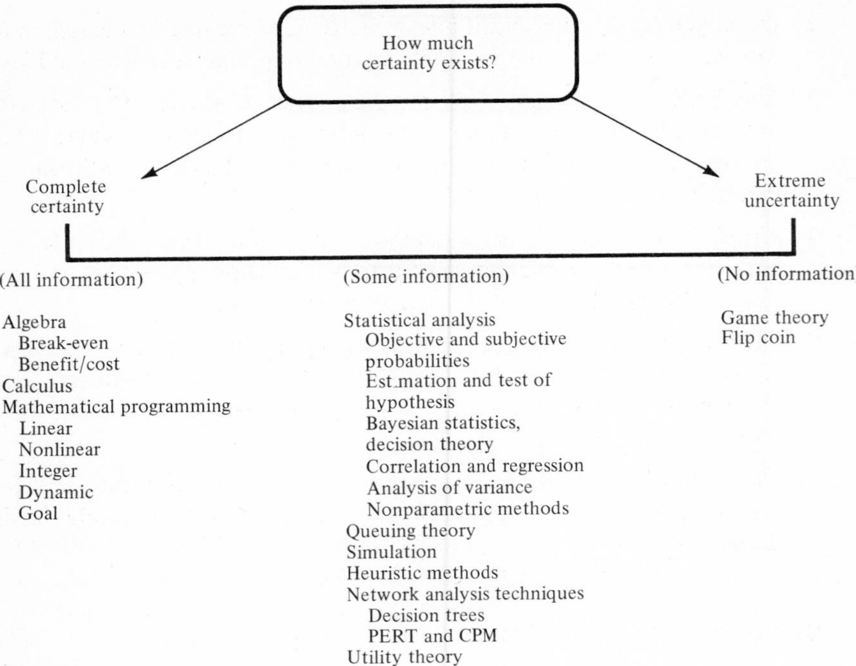

FIGURE 1-6 Decision certainty

many variables to accommodate economically, even though the model is theoretically feasible. For many situations, however, the following methods are useful.

1 *Algebra* This basic mathematical logic is useful in both certainty and uncertainty analysis. Given valid assumptions, algebra provides a deterministic solution in situations such as break-even and benefit-cost analysis.

2 *Calculus* This branch of mathematics provides a useful tool for determining optimal values (limits) where functions are to be maximized or minimized, such as inventory costs.

3 *Mathematical programming* Programming techniques have found extensive applications in product-mix decisions, minimizing transportation costs, planning and scheduling production, and numerous other areas.

Partial Information Methods

1 *Statistical analysis* Classical estimation and testing techniques as well as Bayesian methods have proven increasingly valuable as means of better using operating information for decisions. Some of the widespread applications include the setting of labor standards, forecasting, inventory and production control, and quality control.

2 *Queuing theory* Analysis of queues in terms of waiting-line length and mean waiting time is particularly useful in analyzing maintenance activities.

3 *Simulation* Simulations duplicate the essence of an activity or system without actually achieving reality. Computer simulations are valuable tools for analysis of investment outcomes, production processes, scheduling, and maintenance activities.

4 *Heuristic methods* Heuristic methods are sets of rules which, though perhaps not optimal, do facilitate solutions of scheduling, layout, and distribution problems when applied in a consistent manner.

5 *Network analysis techniques* Network approaches include decision trees, CPM, and PERT methods. They are particularly helpful in identifying alternative courses of action and controlling research, investment, and a multitude of project activities.

6 *Utility theory* Utility or preference theory allows decision makers to incorporate their own experience and values into a relatively formalized decision structure.

Extreme Uncertainty Methods

1 *Game theory* Game theory helps decision makers to choose courses of action when there is absolutely no information about what state of the environment will occur.

2 *Flip coin* In spite of the "unscientific" nature of flipping a coin, random measures such as this are widely used in situations where the decision makers are wholly indifferent.

The extent of use of selected quantitative techniques is illustrated in Fig. 1-7. The figure reports on three studies of members of the American Production and Inventory Control Society (APICS) over a 12-year period. The earliest survey includes 453 responses, the next 626, and the last 1,846. The data reveal significant growth in some of the inventory management techniques (ABC classification and economic order quantity approaches) with only very limited use of other techniques, such as game theory. The same study also confirmed that only 13 percent of small firms (with less than 500 employees) had formal operations research (OR) departments, whereas approximately 47 percent of large firms (with over 5,000 employees) had some group performing an OR function.

MODELS FOR OPERATIONS ANALYSIS

We illustrate some decision-making aids by reviewing three models useful for operations analysis: (1) economic break-even analysis, (2) utility-based decisions, and (3) a production system schematic.

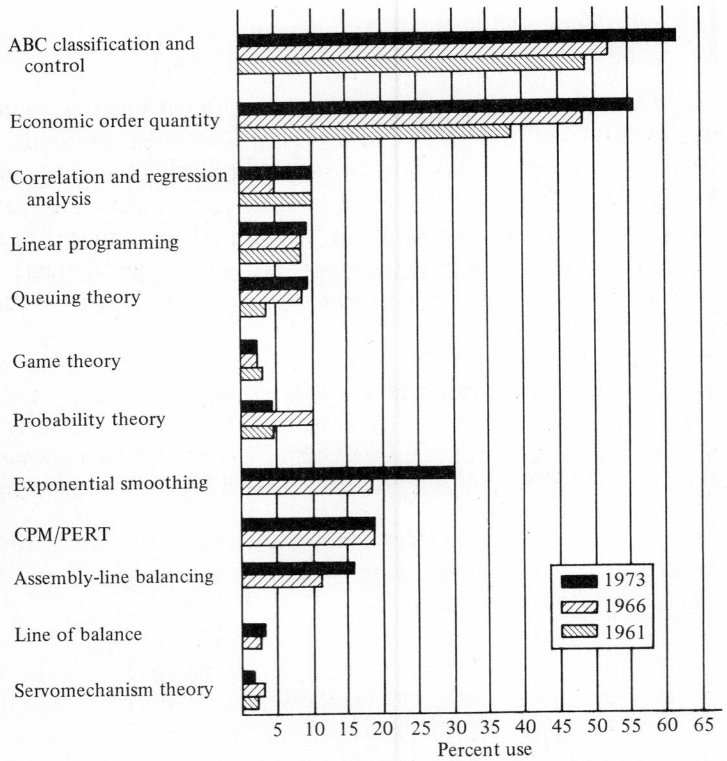

FIGURE 1-7 Past use of selected quantitative techniques. **Source**: Edward W. Davis, "A Look at the Use of Production-Inventory Techniques: Past and Present," *Production and Inventory Management*, vol. 16, no. 4, 1975.

ECONOMIC BREAK-EVEN ANALYSIS

Traditional economic theory views human beings as rational creatures seeking economic gain, a perspective in keeping with the Protestant ethic of many early settlers of this country. The productive activities of individuals have been appropriately housed in an impersonal bureaucratic structure where rules are formalized and organizational objectives are paramount. This economic model has facilitated industrial development by providing organizations with a simplified profit-oriented goal structure that favors innovation, efficiency, and growth.

Profits, of course, arise from the excess of total revenues (TR) over total costs (TC). Recognizing that total costs are composed of both fixed costs (FC) and total variable costs (TVC), we can express the profit function as:

$$\text{Profit} = \text{TR} - \text{TC}$$

$$\text{Profit} = \text{TR} - (\text{FC} + \text{TVC}) \tag{1-2}$$

Major cost categories often include direct labor, direct material, and overhead (or indirect production expenses). The direct labor and direct material, plus some other items such as factory supplies, are usually classified as variable costs because they typically change with the volume of production. Supervision, taxes, office salaries, building depreciation, and so forth, are usually of a more fixed or semi-variable nature. Fixed costs are essentially constant over a given range of output, but admittedly do change over the long run as plant expansions are made, taxes change, and the like.

A *break-even chart* is a convenient way of graphically describing the relationship between costs and revenues for different volumes of output. Figure 1-8 depicts this relationship over a range of volume where total revenue increases linearly with each unit sold, and total cost reflects both an unavoidable fixed cost plus a per unit variable cost. The *break-even point* (BEP) is that volume of output where the fixed and variable

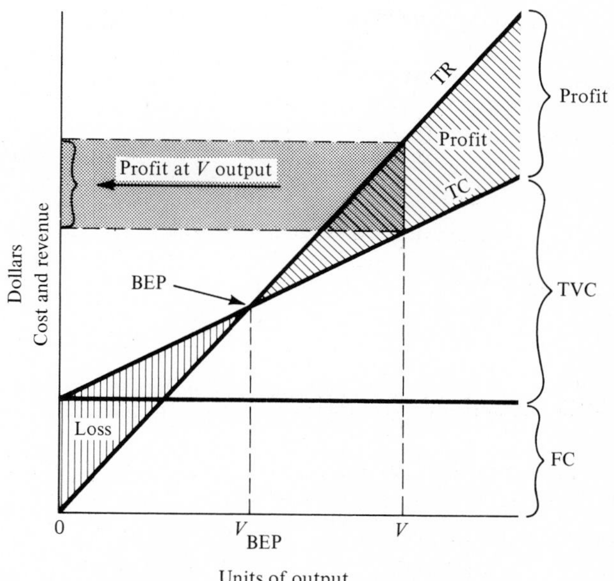

FIGURE 1-8 Break-even chart

costs are just covered, but no profit exists. Thus at the BEP, the total revenues equal the total costs (TR = TC). Recognizing that revenues reflect the price P charged per item times the volume V sold, we can restate the TR = TC expression as:

$$P(V) = \text{FC} + \text{VC}(V) \tag{1-3}$$

and derive an expression for the break-even volume as:

$$V_{\text{BEP}} = \frac{\text{FC}}{P - \text{VC}} \tag{1-4}$$

Break-even analysis is simple and easy to visualize, and it condenses decision information into a form that is readily understandable by almost anyone. Also, it is concerned with a vital aspect of free enterprise of organizations—profitability. However, it is a technique based wholly upon economic factors. It assumes one has complete knowledge about all the economic parameters, for the price, cost, and demand data must either be known for certain or assumed. Viewed in this perspective, it is an algebraic technique that resides on the complete certainty end of the spectrum described in Fig. 1-6. Furthermore, the relationship between these variables is assumed to follow a simple linear function which may be acceptable over short ranges but often is really not satisfactory for longer-range decisions. Extrapolation to high outputs involves an increasing amount of risk, for the model fails to account for any effects of decreasing returns to scale as facilities become overloaded or markets become saturated.

Example 1-1

A producer of electronic calculators has fixed costs of $120,000, variable costs of $30 per unit, and the calculators sell for $50 each. What is the break-even point in number of units?

Solution

$$V_{\text{BEP}} = \frac{\text{FC}}{P - \text{VC}} = \frac{\$120{,}000}{\$50/\text{unit} - \$30/\text{unit}} = 6{,}000 \text{ units}$$

Break-even analysis is particularly suitable for single-product applications but it can also be applied to multiproduct situations. In this case, the fixed and variable components of a product mix can be estimated by the method of least squares using the "normal equations," which we shall review in a later chapter. Upon solution, the intercept value a of the standard linear equation $Y = a + bx$ constitutes the fixed-cost component and the slope value b constitutes the variable cost per unit.

A companion measure of economic value, which has many of the same advantages and disadvantages of break-even analysis, is the contribution ratio. *Contribution* C of a product tells how much the sale of one unit will contribute to cover fixed costs, with the remainder going to profits. It is determined by subtracting variable unit costs VC from the unit price P:

$$C = P - \text{VC} \tag{1-5}$$

The *contribution ratio* CR is:

$$\text{CR} = \frac{P - \text{VC}}{P} \tag{1-6}$$

Note that the denominator in the break-even volume expression [Eq. (1-4)] is simply the per unit contribution [Eq. (1-5)]. The BEP occurs when the contribution per unit times the number of units sold just equals the total fixed costs.

Example 1-2

A food processing firm has \$64,000 fixed costs plus variable costs of \$3.75 per unit. The plant manager proposes to sell the product for \$7.75 per unit (in contrast to a competitor's brand that sells for \$8 per unit).

(*a*) What is the contribution?

(*b*) How many units must be sold to break even?

Solution

(*a*) $C = P - \text{VC} = \$7.75/\text{unit} - \$3.75/\text{unit} = \$4/\text{unit}$

(*b*) $V_{\text{BEP}} = \dfrac{\text{FC}}{P - \text{VC}} = \dfrac{\text{FC}}{C} = \dfrac{\$64{,}000}{\$4/\text{unit}} = 16{,}000 \text{ units}$

Contribution ratios are useful for comparing the profitability of several products within a product line. Then the ones that contribute most can be emphasized. Of course, a product line as a whole should have sufficient contribution to cover all its fixed costs, but individual products in a line often cover differing shares of the total fixed costs.

Additional and more complex examples of break-even and contribution analysis will be found in the solved problems section at the end of this chapter. Let us move on now to a slightly more sophisticated decision model which incorporates some features for handling uncertain and subjective factors. It lies in the "some information" section of Fig. 1-6.

UTILITY-BASED DECISIONS

Although utility theory dates back to the early 1800s, modern utility theory stems largely from the pioneering work of von Neumann and Morgenstern published in 1947 [**14**] and concentrates upon decision making under conditions of uncertainty. *Utility* is the measure of preference that individuals have for various choices available to them. The utility value of a given alternative is unique to individual decision makers and, unlike a simple monetary amount, can incorporate intangible factors or subjective standards from their own value systems.

Utility functions typically describe the relative preference value (in *utils*) that individuals have for a given amount of the criterion (such as money, goods). They are often determined by proposing a situation to the subjects whereby they must choose between receiving a given amount (for example, \$20,000) for certain versus a 50:50 chance of gaining a larger amount or nothing (such as \$60,000 or zero). The gamble amount (the \$60,000) is then adjusted upward or downward until the individual is indifferent to whether he or she receives the certain amount (\$20,000) or the gamble. This indifference point then establishes one experimentally determined value on the individual's utility curve and other points are similarly determined. The end-point values for the curve (say 0 and 100 utils) are arbitrarily assigned to extremes of the individual's normal decision range.

Example 1-3

An individual is indifferent as to whether she receives a certain \$20,000 or a 50:50 chance of \$50,000 or nothing. Assuming end-point values of 100 and 0 utils for the \$50,000 and \$0, respectively, what is the utility of the certain \$20,000 (that is, $U[\$20{,}000]$)?

Solution

The utility of the \$20,000 can be equated to the utility of the gamble, which is a 50 percent chance of 100 utils plus a 50 percent chance of 0 utils:

$$\begin{aligned} U[\$20{,}000] &= 0.50(U[50{,}000]) + 0.50(U[0]) \\ &= 0.50(100) + 0.50(0) = 50 \text{ utils} \end{aligned}$$

The above process would have to be repeated for perhaps five or six additional certainty values (for example, using \$10,000, \$15,000, \$30,000, and other amounts) by varying the probabilities and/or using previously determined values as a base until the shape of the resultant function was fully described. This example simply illustrates the determination of one point.

Once derived, a utility function can be used to convert a decision criteria value into utils so that a decision can be made on the basis of maximizing the expected utility value (EUV) rather than, say, the expected monetary value (EMV). The reader will recall that a mathematical expectation is the sum ($\sum$) of products obtained by multiplying each possible event's value X by the probability P with which it occurs. In symbols, the expected value (EV) is:

$$\text{EV} = P_1X_1 + P_2X_2 + \cdots + P_nX_n = \sum_{i=1}^{n} P_iX_i \tag{1-7}$$

When X represents monetary units, we designate the EV as an expected monetary value (EMV) and can choose the action that yields the highest EMV. Similarly, when utility values are used, we designate the EV as EUV and the decision maker can choose that alternative with the highest sum of probability times utility values. The following example illustrates the potential difference in outcome from an EMV and an EUV approach.

Example 1-4

A manager must choose between investments *A* and *B* which are calculated to yield net profits of $1,200 and $1,600, respectively, with probabilities subjectively estimated at 0.75 and 0.60. Assume the manager's utility function reveals that utilities for the $1,200 and $1,600 amounts are 40 and 45 utils, respectively. What is the best choice on the basis of (*a*) EMV and (*b*) EUV?

Solution

(*a*) $$\text{EMV} = \sum P_i X_i \tag{1-8}$$

where

P_i = probability of outcome i
X_i = monetary value of outcome i

$$\text{EMV}_A = P_A X_A = (0.75)(\$1{,}200) = \$900$$

$$\text{EMV}_B = P_B X_B = (0.60)(\$1{,}600) = \$960$$

∴ Best choice = investment *B*.

(*b*) $$\text{EUV} = \sum P_i U_i \tag{1-9}$$

where

U_i = utility value of outcome i

$$\text{EUV}_A = P_A U_A = (0.75)(40 \text{ utils}) = 30 \text{ utils}$$

$$\text{EUV}_B = P_B U_B = (0.60)(45 \text{ utils}) = 27 \text{ utils}$$

∴ Best choice = investment *A*.

In the example above, utility values played a role similar to monetary values. Note that they are not probabilities and there is no requirement that they sum up to 100. Utility values can be established on the basis of criteria other than monetary income (such as asset value, capacity, environmental factors) and the criteria can represent multiple objectives. A slightly more sophisticated questioning technique is sometimes used to establish a comparative utility value for a package of effects evaluated as a unit. Another approach involves the development of individual utility functions for the respective criteria and then combining them into a multiattribute utility function [**8**].

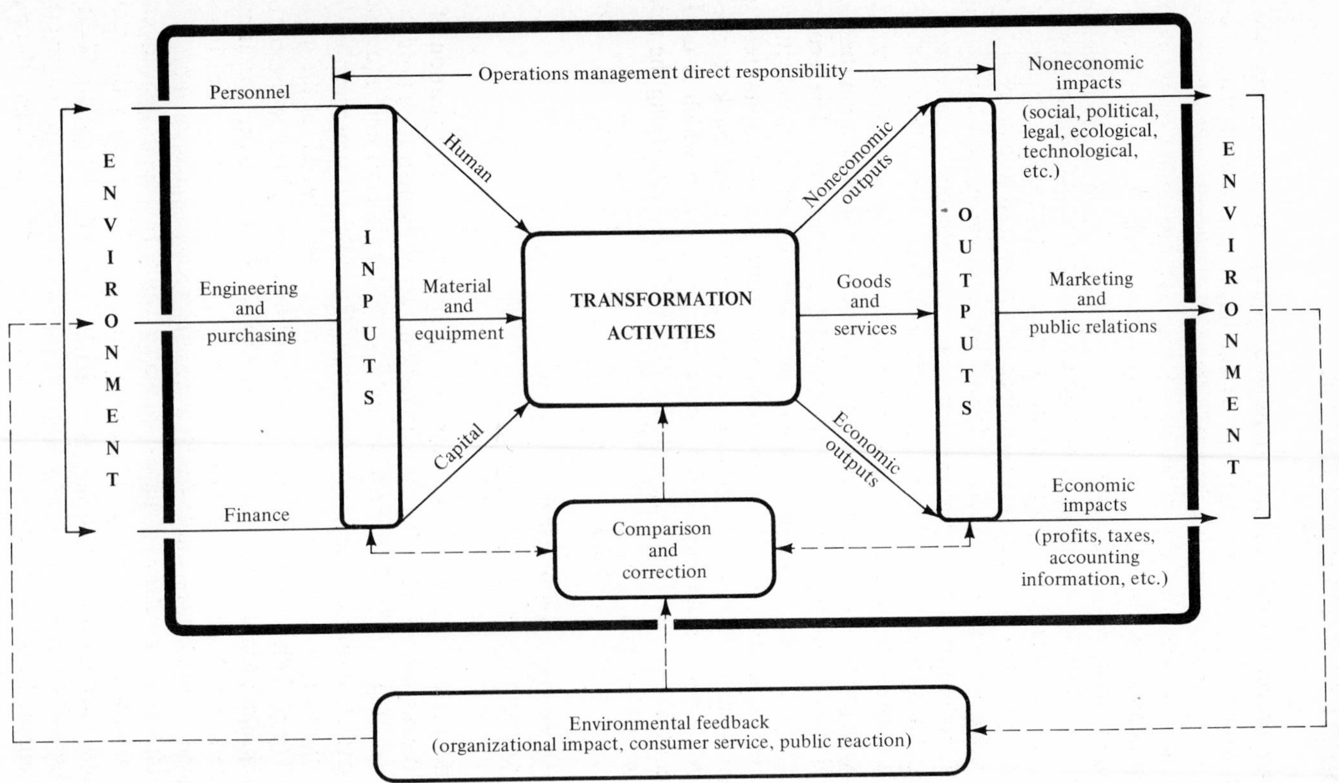

FIGURE 1-9 Schematic model of a production system

PRODUCTION SYSTEM SCHEMATIC

We have previously defined operations management as that activity whereby resources, flowing within a defined system, are combined and transformed in a controlled manner to add value in accordance with policies communicated by management. Having discussed the key concepts of resources, systems, transformation activities, and managerial policy, as well as the concept of models, let us now visualize this definition in terms of a schematic model.

Figure 1-9 presents a schematic representation of an operating production system. As shown, operations management is directly responsible for the transformation activities whereby inputs are combined and converted into outputs. It also exercises an influence over the human, material and equipment, and capital inputs by virtue of functioning within a total system where the personnel, engineering and purchasing, and finance activities exist but are under the direct responsibility of others. Similarly, the outputs are not only tangible goods and services which are managed by the marketing group. Production operations also exert an impact upon the social, political, ecological, and technological environment of the firm. The economic results which flow to the public are another direct reflection of the production activities. In essence, the model depicts flows of human, material, and capital resources from the environment, through the transformation activities, and back to the environment. All flows are accompanied by data and information which is used internally for control purposes and externally for describing and modifying the role of the firm in its environment.

CLASSIFICATION OF OPERATIONS MANAGEMENT DECISION AREAS

A glance at the table of contents of this text will reveal that the organization of the remainder of the material is related to the schematic model of the operating production system shown in Fig. 1-9. It is convenient to classify the material and equipment, human, and capital resource decisions primarily as planning and organization decisions. They relate largely to the design, or modification of the design, of the production system. The process analysis, forecasting, inventory control, production control, quality control, maintenance and cost control decisions all relate to the operation of the production system. These decisions have been broadly classified as direction and control decisions. Finally, an increasingly important decision area pertains to environmental factors. This classification is shown in Table 1-3. Each item included in the table is illustrated and discussed in more detail in the chapters that follow (chapter numbers are shown in boldface type). In most cases, a discussion of theory is followed by solved problems which illustrate applications of the management decision-making methodology that is suitable for given problem situations. Problems preceded by an asterisk contain additional or more advanced methods that go beyond the basic material in the chapters. These problems may be included on an optional basis.

TABLE 1-3 MAJOR OPERATIONS MANAGEMENT DECISION AREAS

Planning and Organizing Decisions

1 Operations modeling
Systems definition
Objectives
Modeling methodology
Alternative generation
Choice activities

2 Materials and equipment
Plant capacity
Plant location
Plant layout
Product standards
Process methods
Material handling
Make vs. buy

3 Human resources
Job design
Work methods
Motion economy
Labor standards
Labor relations
Employee safety
Employee incentives

4 Capital
Sources and uses of funds
Cost of funds
Depreciation method
Tax effects
Evaluation technique
Handling uncertainties in cash flow

Direction and Control Decisions

5 Production and process analysis
R & D effort
Product design
Product mix
Process planning
Process selection
Line balancing

6 Forecasting
Uses of forecasts
Response to demand
Forecasting methodology
Validity and control

7 Inventory control
Uses of inventories
Quantity to order
Quantity to produce
Handling uncertainties in demand and lead time
Deriving stock-out costs
Control system to use

8 Aggregate planning
Objectives and criteria
Variables to control
Learning curve effect
Planning methodology

9 Scheduling and control
Scheduling philosophy
Scheduling methodology
Control methodology

10 Quality control
Quality objectives
Acceptance sampling
Control charts to use

11 Maintenance and cost control
Maintenance objectives
Reliability required
Service rates
Budget type and use
Cost standards
Cost variances

Environmental Interface Decisions

12 Production environment
Goods and services
Economic impacts
Noneconomic impacts
Social responsibilities

SUMMARY

Operations managers are decision makers responsible for using human, material, and capital resources to create valuable goods and services. Their work can be greatly facilitated by adopting a decision-making–systems approach to managerial activities. This approach requires (1) a clear definition of the system, (2) the establishment of criteria, (3) a formulation of relationships, (4) the generation of alternatives, and (5) the choosing of a course of action based upon the criteria.

The key element of a decision-making activity often involves formulation of a model so that the alternative courses of action can best be analyzed and evaluated. The actual structure of the model, of course, depends upon the kind of information available and the prevailing level of certainty in the real world. Techniques for making decisions under the various certainty-uncertainty conditions will be used as relevant topics arise within the text. Three analytical aids for operations analysis were discussed in this chapter. Break-even analysis assumes certainty and is generally limited in scope to economic factors, but it is widely used. Utility theory is a newer and promising technique for uncertain situations, but it is not yet widely accepted. It is one of the more formalized methods of incorporating human values into the decision process. The production system model described in this chapter is essentially a schematic "visualization" of the definition of operations management.

In general, the sequence of topics for the remainder of the text follows an input-transformation-output format. Planning and organization inputs are discussed first, followed by various direction and control activities, such as inventory and quality control. We will conclude the text with an integrated summary and a discussion of how organizational activities interface with the environment.

SOLVED PROBLEMS

MODELS FOR OPERATIONS ANALYSIS

1 If fixed costs are $20,000 and variable costs are estimated at 50 percent of the unit selling price of $80, what is the BEP?

Solution

$$V_{\mathrm{BEP}} = \frac{\mathrm{FC}}{P - \mathrm{VC}} = \frac{\$20{,}000}{\$80/\mathrm{unit} - \$40/\mathrm{unit}} = 500 \text{ units}$$

2 Process A has fixed costs of $10,000 per year and variable costs of $8 per unit, whereas process B costs are $4,000 per year and $20 per unit, respectively. At what production rate are the total costs of A and B equal?

Solution

$$\begin{aligned} A &= B \\ FC_A + VC_A(V) &= FC_B + VC_B(V) \\ 10{,}000 + 8V &= 4{,}000 + 20V \\ 12V &= 6{,}000 \\ V &= 500 \text{ units/year} \end{aligned}$$

3 Given the break-even chart shown, answer the following questions.

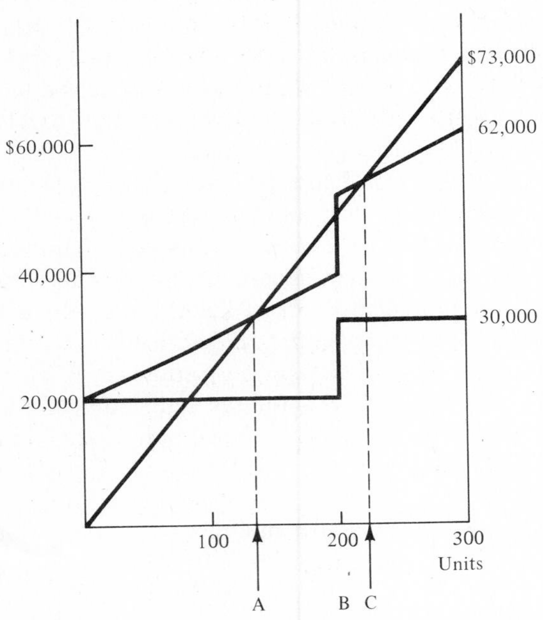

(*a*) For a 300-unit output, what is the appropriate FC, TVC, and profit?
(*b*) What is the BEP?
(*c*) How would you explain the step increase in the TC line?

Solution

(*a*) FC = \$30,000; TVC = \$62,000 − \$30,000 = \$32,000;
Profit = \$73,000 − \$62,000 = \$11,000
(*b*) There are two BEP's, one at volume *A*, the other at *C*.
(*c*) To produce more than 200 units per year, additional FC of \$10,000 must be incurred. These costs are not reflected in the VC but do cause an incremental increase in the FC.

4 A firm has annual fixed costs of \$2.1 million and variable costs of \$6 per unit. It is considering an additional investment of \$900,000 which will increase fixed costs by \$180,000 per year and will increase the contribution by \$1 per unit. No change is anticipated in the sales volume or the sales price, which is \$10 per unit. What is the break-even volume if the new investment is made?

Solution

The \$1 increase in C will decrease VC to \$6 − \$1 = \$5/unit. The addition to FC makes them \$2.1 million + \$180,000 = \$2,280,000

$$V_{\text{BEP}} = \frac{\text{FC}}{P - \text{VC}} = \frac{\$2{,}280{,}000}{\$10/\text{unit} - \$5/\text{unit}} = 456{,}000 \text{ units}$$

5 An automated production operation produces 1, 2, 5, or 10 percent defective items depending upon a random machine adjustment which occurs with respective probabilities of 0.6, 0.2, 0.1, and 0.1. If the reject costs associated with the fraction defectives are \$2, \$10, \$30, and \$70 per hour, respectively, how many hours per day of a mechanic's time would be justified, on the average, in order to maintain the adjustment at 1 percent defective? The mechanic's labor cost is \$15 per hour.

Solution

$$\text{EMV} = \sum P_i X_i$$

where

P_i = probability of i percent defective
X_i = monetary cost of i percent defective

$$\begin{aligned}\text{EMV} &= (0.6)(\$2) + (0.2)(\$10) + (0.1)(\$30) \\ &\quad + (0.1)(\$70) \\ &= \$13.20/\text{hr}\end{aligned}$$

$$\text{Expected cost/day} = \left(\frac{\$13.20}{\text{hr}}\right)\left(\frac{8\text{ hr}}{\text{day}}\right) = \$105.60/\text{day}$$

$$\text{Cost/day at 1 percent defective} = \left(\frac{\$2}{\text{hr}}\right)\left(\frac{8\text{ hr}}{\text{day}}\right) = \$16/\text{day}$$

$$\text{Net cost justified} = \$105.60 - \$16 = \$89.60/\text{day}$$

$$\text{Hours justified at }\$15/\text{hr} = \frac{\$89.60/\text{day}}{\$15/\text{hr}} = 6\text{ hr/day}$$

***6** Cleveland Plating Company (CPC) is developing a bid for 20,000 air-conditioner parts which are estimated to have direct material and labor costs of \$0.50 and \$1.50 per unit respectively. In addition, the job, if received, should be expected to cover \$20,000 fixed costs.

(*a*) Assuming CPC bids \$6 per unit, what is the break-even volume?

(*b*) CPC management feels they have a 90 percent chance of obtaining the job if they bid \$5 per unit but only a 70 percent chance if they bid \$6.

* An asterisk indicates the problem involves an extension or integration beyond what is in the chapter.

Under which bid price is the expected value of the contribution the highest? Calculate both amounts and show your comparison.

(*c*) Comment on the advisability of applying expected-value concepts to sales and variable-cost figures versus fixed-cost figures.

Solution

(*a*) $P(V) = \text{FC} + \text{VC}(V)$

$$\$6V = \$20{,}000 + (\$0.50 + \$1.50)\,V$$

$$V = \frac{\$20{,}000}{\$4/\text{unit}} = 5{,}000 \text{ units}$$

(*b*) $C = S - \text{VC}(V)$

where

$$\begin{aligned} C &= \text{contribution (total)} \\ S &= \text{sales revenue (total)} \\ \text{VC}(V) &= \text{material cost} + \text{labor cost} \\ &= \$.50(20{,}000) + \$1.50(20{,}000) \\ &= \$10{,}000 + \$30{,}000 = \$40{,}000 \end{aligned}$$

At $P = \$5$: $S = \$5/\text{unit (20,000 units)} = \$100{,}000$
$C = \$100{,}000 - \$40{,}000 = \$60{,}000$
Exp. value $= C\text{ (probability } C) = \$60{,}000(0.9) = \$54{,}000$

At $P = \$6$: $S = \$6/\text{unit (20,000 units)} = \$120{,}000$
$C = \$120{,}000 - \$40{,}000 = \$80{,}000$
Exp. value $= C\text{ (probability } C) = \$80{,}000(0.7) = \$56{,}000$

The expected value of the contribution is highest with a bid price of $6 per unit.

(*c*) The notion of an expected value implies that a probabilistic element is involved. In this case, the probabilistic element is the uncertainty of selling the product and the uncertainty of incurring variable costs. There is no uncertainty associated with fixed costs; they continue regardless of whether the bid is favorable or not.

QUESTIONS

1-1 Define operations management.

1-2 What do you consider to be the central and most essential concept in the definition of operations management?

1-3 What is a system?

1-4 The usefulness of a system depends upon how it is designed and controlled. What does systems design and control entail?

1-5 A firm makes a $50 profit on its motors (sale price = $250) which convert 90 percent of their input electrical energy to mechanical power. In what sense are "transformation" activities involved? Use this example to distinguish between productivity and efficiency.

1-6 Distinguish between technology and methodology. Which do you consider more closely related to the objectives of the text?

1-7 In what way did Frederick Taylor contribute to the development of the field of operations management?

1-8 Distinguish between the functional, behavioral, and decision-making–systems approaches to management.

1-9 In what sense is the decision-making–systems approach to management a "scientific" approach?

1-10 Explain the role of values in the decision-making process. Does the existence of values negate the validity of the decision-making process? Why or why not?

1-11 Select a business decision situation or an appropriate hypothetical one and trace through the analytical framework for decisions as given in the chapter. Write out each step and the corresponding element in your business or hypothetical example.

1-12 What is model building and how does it relate to the scientific decision-making system?

1-13 Is decision making under complete certainty always preferred to decision making using sample or subjective information? Illustrate your answer with an example.

1-14 How does the break-even model differ from the utility-based model with respect to (*a*) applicability in certainty versus uncertainty situations, (*b*) the scope of decision variables that can be accommodated, and (*c*) the extent of actual use in industry?

PROBLEMS

1 Nationwide Survey Company has fixed costs of $20,000 per year, variable costs of $3 per survey, and charges $5 per survey for a certain type of work. What is the break-even point in number of surveys?

2 A manufacturer is producing 60,000 units which sell for $2.10 per unit. The fixed costs are $54,000 and at that volume the total variable costs are $90,000. What is the break-even point?

3 If the sales price of a product is $8 and the variable cost is $2, what is (*a*) the contribution and (*b*) the contribution ratio?

4 A firm has the capacity to manufacture 25,000 relays per year. They have annual fixed costs of $45,000 and the contribution from each relay is 75 percent of the $3 per unit sales price. What is the break-even volume?

5 A travel agency has an excursion package that sells for $125 each. Fixed costs are $80,000 and, at a volume of 1,000 customers, variable costs are $25,000 and profits $20,000.
   (*a*) What is the break-even point volume?
   (*b*) Assuming fixed costs hold as is, how many additional customers are required to increase profit by $1,000?

6 A Jolly Giant plant has fixed costs of $80,000 and sells all 10-oz. cans of corn wholesale at $10 per case. A typical supermarket retails them at $0.20–$0.25 per can. Variable costs in the plant are estimated at $8 per case and the production line has a capacity of 60,000 cases per season.
   (*a*) What is the product's contribution to the fixed cost and profit?
   (*b*) What sales are required to break even?
   (*c*) What is the plant's profit (or loss) if it operates at full capacity for the season?

7 A cost analyst has prepared the break-even chart shown for a management meeting. The analyst points out that at the present volume of 500 units per year the firm makes a $2 profit on each unit. During discussion, the analyst is asked:
   (*a*) What is the contribution *per unit* at a volume of 500 units?
   (*b*) By how much can annual production be reduced before incurring a loss?

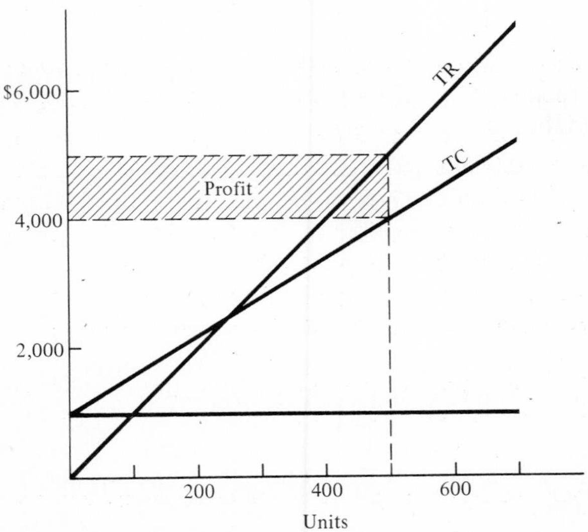

8 Timber Products Company is currently operating at 70 percent of its capacity of 40,000 units per year. At current volume fixed costs are $220,000, variable costs are $9 per unit, and annual revenue is $448,000.

(*a*) Determine the current annual profit or loss.

(*b*) Find the break-even volume in units.

(*c*) What profit would the firm earn at 90 percent of capacity?

9 A nonprofit municipal water department has variable costs (direct labor) of $5 million per year. Current revenue, based upon the service of 200,000 accounts, is $20 million. The water production manager wishes to add equipment that will raise the yearly fixed costs by $1 million and reduce current and future direct labor costs by 20 percent. What volume of account services would be required to justify the change economically? The price paid per customer is to be held constant.

10 Management is concerned with a possible recession this year and seeks to cut production in one of its flour mills. The plant is currently producing 4,000 tons per year and operates 300 days of the year, bringing in $200,000 in revenue. It has fixed costs of $90,000 per year and its total costs are $150,000 per year. There are only five employees in the plant.

(*a*) How much does each ton contribute to fixed costs and profit?

(*b*) To what rate can production be reduced before the firm starts to lose money?

11 The Dever Furniture Company produced 200 maple dressers pattern 427 last year which sold for $210 each. The company incurred labor costs of $42 per unit, material costs of $18 per unit, and allocated $80 per unit of overhead costs to each dresser. Cost records reveal that overhead costs are 60 percent fixed and 40 percent variable. What was the total annual contribution from pattern 427?

***12** A metals firm operating at 100 percent capacity produces 1,000 ingots per year for sales of $10 million per year. Their operations have a fixed cost of $5 million per year and variable costs of $2 million per year. A study has shown that an investment of $500,000 in material handling equipment would reduce variable costs by 25 percent, although it would not increase plant capacity. The firm must pay a 10 percent interest cost on funds used for the new investment.

(*a*) Would the investment be worthwhile?

(*b*) By how many ingots will the BEP change?

(*c*) By how much will the contribution per unit change?

13 Frozen Pizza Company is considering whether they should allocate funds for research on an instant freeze-dry process for home use. If successful (and the

* An asterisk indicates the problem involves an extension or integration beyond what is in the chapter.

R&D manager feels there is a 75 percent chance they will be), the firm could market the product at a $4 million profit. However, if the research is a failure, the firm would incur a $6 million loss. What is the expected monetary value (EMV) of proceeding with the research?

14 A textile company worker produces from 8 to 10 finished items per 8-hour day depending upon "how things go," as described by the probability distribution shown.

Number X	Probability $P(X)$
8	0.4
9	0.5
10	0.1

If the worker's wage cost is $4 per hour and the net value added by the work (before deducting wage cost) is $7 per item, what is the net expected monetary value to the company per day?

15 Two forest supervisors must decide upon the size of a fire crew required to provide adequate fire protection for timber and wildlife resources in a given area at minimum cost. Even though they have definite budget limitations, they know they bear some social and perhaps "political" responsibility for the decision, in addition to their organizational objective and budget responsibilities.

The supervisors' major controllable variable is crew size and they wish to decide between a 20- and a 40-worker fire crew. Their major uncontrollable variable is the weather, which the experts tell them will likely be "normal" (50 percent chance), with a slightly greater chance of being dry (30 percent chance) than being wet (20 percent chance).

Letting *A* and *B* represent the crew size alternatives of 20 and 40 workers, respectively, and θ_1, θ_2, and θ_3 the weather condition probabilities of dry, normal, and wet, the alternative outcomes are summarized as shown.

	Weather condition		
Crew size	**Dry $\theta_1 = 0.3$**	**Ave. $\theta_2 = 0.5$**	**Wet $\theta_3 = 0.2$**
A (20 workers)	Weak coverage over wide area at low cost	Moderate coverage over wide area at low cost	Strong coverage over moderate area at low cost
B (40 workers)	Moderate coverage over wide area at high cost	Strong coverage over small area at high cost	Strong coverage over wide area at high cost

Using a questioning technique, the supervisors' utility values for the alternative outcomes shown were determined:

	Derived utilities		
	θ_1	θ_2	θ_3
A	10	40	90
B	5	30	98

Determine the expected utility of each course of action and indicate which size fire crew would be selected on an expected utility basis.

16 Dakota Mining Company management must decide how to respond to a proposed partnership offer with another firm. They have an opportunity of owning $A = 0$ percent, $B = 40$ percent, or $C = 80$ percent interest in the partnership, and have estimated their chances of finding no ore, low-grade ore,

	Profits ($)		
	θ_1 = no ore	θ_2 = low grade	θ_3 = high grade
A	$0	$0	$0
B	(40,000)	30,000	150,000
C	(80,000)	60,000	300,000

or high-grade ore at $\theta_1 = 0.1$, $\theta_2 = 0.7$, and $\theta_3 = 0.2$, respectively. Profits (and losses) from the venture depend both upon the degree of ownership and the grade of ore found and are given in the above table. In addition, since the mining activity involves environmental impacts, an analyst has been engaged to derive utility values for the various outcomes and these are as shown.

Outcome	Utils
$A\theta_1$	30
$A\theta_2$	15
$A\theta_3$	12
$B\theta_1$	10
$B\theta_2$	50
$B\theta_3$	71
$C\theta_1$	0
$C\theta_2$	52
$C\theta_3$	80

(*a*) Determine the best course of action on an EMV basis.
(*b*) Determine the best course of action on an EUV basis.
(*c*) Explain why the utility value for outcome $A\theta_3$ could be different from that for $A\theta_1$ even though the monetary payoff is the same in each case.

CASE: MOUNTAIN AIRLINES

Mountain Airlines is a small southwestern carrier with a top management group consisting of the president, vice president of operations, marketing and traffic manager, financial manager, legal counsel, and comptroller. The company is committed to providing customers in their area with good flight service so long as it is profitable to do so. They carry about 50,000 passengers per year an average of 300 miles each and earn a revenue of $0.40 per passenger mile. Fixed costs for the company are $2 million per year and their variable costs are currently running $0.10 per passenger mile.

The management group is currently considering three alternative proposals to improve operations:

1 Invest in new capital equipment which will increase fixed costs by $300,000 per year and variable costs by $0.01 per passenger mile but will bring in additional revenue of $0.05 per passenger mile. Traffic volume would not be expected to change.

2 Adopt a proposed advertising program and promote it at a cost of $200,000 per year. The new program is expected to generate an additional 3 million passenger miles per year while in effect.

3 Undertake a cooperative venture with Plains Airlines which will give Mountain customers better flight connections and increase profit (before taxes) by an estimated $550,000 to $600,000 per year.

Alternative 1 would bring the customers the latest in traffic control and safety equipment, although the existing facilities do meet current FAA safety requirements. The company can raise the necessary capital for this alternative if its president and operations vice president personally guarantee the necessary loan. Both are willing to do so, although the president is somewhat reluctant and has asked that other members of the top management group join them in the guarantee. All have agreed to do so except the comptroller, who is quite wealthy.

Capacity is (just barely) adequate to handle the increased volume expected under alternative 2. However, the operations vice president has written an internal memorandum to the marketing manager indicating a feeling that the proposed advertising slogan is "discriminatory, in bad taste, and contrary to company policy of not using liquor or suggestive materials in our advertising." The memo was forwarded (without comment) to the firm's legal counsel who advised that although they too had some personal reservations, the "chances of our firm being sued for anything like $1 million over this are probably less than 10 percent."

Several members of the management group mentioned the antitrust implications of alternative 3. All are agreed that the type of cooperative venture proposed would not violate the intent of the antitrust statutes, but the legal counsel feels the details of the arrangement would have to be "checked out thoroughly" with the justice department before any contractual arrangements could be finalized.

The president has asked the vice president of operations to handle this decision. Analyze the situation and propose a course of action based upon the data given.

BIBLIOGRAPHY

[1] BROWN, CARL, J. G. MONKS, and J. R. PARK: *Decision Making in Water Resource Allocation*, Lexington Books, Lexington, Massachusetts, 1973.

[2] BUFFA, ELWOOD S.: *Modern Production Management*, John Wiley & Sons, New York, 1973.

[3] EDWARDS, W.: "The Theory of Decision Making," in W. EDWARDS and S. TVERSKY (eds.), *Decision Making*, Penguin Books, Middlesex, England, 1967.

[4] ENGLAND, G. W.: "Organizational Goals and Expected Behavior of American Managers," *Academy of Management Journal*, vol. 10, no. 2, 1967, pp. 107–117.

[5] HULL, J., P. G. MOORE, and H. THOMAS: "Utility and Its Measurement," *Journal of the Royal Statistical Society, A.*, vol. 136, 1973, pp. 226–247.

[6] JOHNSON, R. A., F. E. KAST, and J. E. ROSENZWEIG: *The Theory and Management of Systems*, McGraw-Hill, New York, 1967.

[7] KAST, F. E., and J. E. ROSENZWEIG: "Systems Concepts: Pervasiveness and Potential," *Management International Review*, vol. 7, 1967, pp. 4–5.

[8] KEENEY, R. L.: "A Decision Analysis with Multiple Objectives: The Mexico City Airport," *The Bell Journal of Economics and Management Science*, vol. 4, no. 1, Spring 1973, pp. 101–117.

[9] MONKS, JOSEPH G.: "A Utility Approach to R & D Decisions," *R & D Management*, Manchester Business School, vol. 6, no. 2, 1976, pp. 59–66.

[10] OLSEN, R. A.: *Manufacturing Management: A Quantitative Approach*, International Textbook, Scranton, Penn., 1968.

[11] PAIN, N. R.: "A Useful Approach to the Group Choice Problem," *Decision Sciences*, vol. 4, no. 1, January 1973, pp. 21–30.

[12] STARR, M. K.: *Production Management: Systems and Synthesis*, Prentice-Hall, Englewood Cliffs, N.J., 1964.

[13] VOLLMAN, T. E.: *Operations Management*, Addison-Wesley, Reading, Mass., 1973.

[14] VON NEUMANN, J., and O. MORGENSTERN: *Theory of Games and Economic Behavior*, Princeton University Press, Princeton, N.J., 1947.

CHAPTER

2

Material and Equipment Inputs

The material and equipment inputs to a production operation consist primarily of raw materials and supplies, plus the physical plant and the processing and materials handling equipment. In the United States, plant and equipment expenditures alone now average slightly over $100 billion per year [**17**: 12]. Material and equipment assets may represent a greater proportion of the total worth of manufacturing firms than they do of service organizations, but their astute management is vital to both. The major operations management concerns are related to plant capacity, plant location, plant layout, product standards, process and material handling methods, and decisions to make versus decisions to buy components. We shall discuss these topics in this order, in an effort to gain an understanding of management's decision responsibilities in this area and to develop some facility in the use of analytical methods that are useful in carrying out those responsibilities.

PLANT DESIGN AND CAPACITY

Plant capacity is one of the first major decisions faced by a new firm or one that is modifying its facilities. Like most other management decisions, though, it cannot be made independently of other considerations—especially the market. The design capacity of a plant should be derived from knowledge of current and expected consumer demand. This may come from past experience in the industry, knowledge of supply-demand characteristics, research data on existing and potential markets, and a number of other sources.

Once the capacity requirements and other relevant characteristics are determined, these parameters are conveyed to plant architects and design engineers. Plant design and construction is a specialized field outside the scope of this text. The lighting, heating and ventilation, and other systems can best be designed by professional engineers. However, the systems concepts discussed in Chap. 1 strongly suggest that if the plant design is to be truly user-oriented, the user should become intimately involved in the evolution of the design. Close cooperation is usually fostered by questions that arise with respect to plant requirements, work-flow patterns, and inspection and testing procedures.

With this brief introduction, we now focus attention upon the important managerial decisions related to capacity.

CAPACITY UNDER UNCERTAIN DEMAND

If management knew that the demand for their firm's products was going to be absolutely constant and also knew precisely what the amount of demand would be, the capacity problem would be greatly simplified. But this is hardly ever the case for two reasons: (1) seasonal and cyclical factors often generate long-term swings in demand, and (2) random events usually cause short-term fluctuations. As a result, demand over time may appear as depicted in Fig. 2-1.

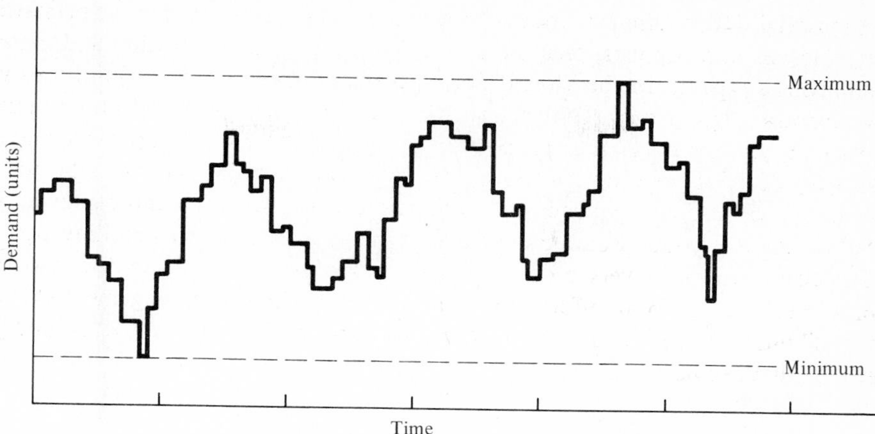

FIGURE 2-1 Demand-capacity relationships

Figure 2-1 shows both some regular swings and some sharp short-term fluctuations. Many products are seasonal, but the uncertainties are compounded when irregular or random effects are superimposed upon seasonal peaks or troughs. Managerial decision makers must take into consideration both these present demand characteristics as well as projected future demand levels when they are making a plant capacity decision.

In a simplified sense, the plant capacity may be designed for *maximum* demand, *minimum* demand, or some intermediate *average* level. If the plant had sufficient capacity to meet an infrequently occurring peak demand, the result would be an inefficient use of capital equipment (and probably a highly fluctuating labor force). On the other hand, although a design for minimum demand would result in high utilization of facilities and little or no fluctuation in labor, inadequate capacity might result in inferior service and dissatisfied or lost customers.

Many firms content themselves with some in-between level of capacity and follow various overtime, inventory, back-order, or other strategies to adjust to demand fluctuations. Even though most firms are not sure how future demand will fluctuate, they must continually face the capacity question—and it is just as relevant for a hospital as it is for an auto parts supplier.

In most cases some historical data on demand or some experienced judgments can be assembled to provide a data base for decision, even though it may be very rough. The expected value of demand $E(X)$ is one "average" estimate that provides about as good a measure of central tendency as we can get. As we saw in Chap. 1 it can be obtained by weighting the various estimates of the variable (that is, demand) by their probabilities of occurrence. Once this estimate is made, other factors, such as financial constraints, workpower capabilities, and so forth, can be brought into consideration to determine whether a capacity for average demand (or greater or less than average) will best facilitate organizational objectives.

Example 2-1

Directors of the Cork City Hospital Board have subjectively estimated the demand for beds for a new hospital as follows:

50 to under 100 beds	10 percent chance
100 to under 150 beds	30 percent chance
150 to under 200 beds	50 percent chance
200 to under 250 beds	10 percent chance

They wish to establish the capacity at a base level that will accommodate 120 percent of the estimated average demand and add a 10 percent allowance to that for growth. What should be the final capacity?

Solution

Number of hospital beds		Probability	
Interval	Midpoint (X)	$P(X)$	$X \cdot P(X)$
50 < 100	75	0.10	7.5
100 < 150	125	0.30	37.5
150 < 200	175	0.50	87.5
200 < 250	225	0.10	22.5
		Total	155.0

$$\text{Expected value of demand} = E(X) = \sum XP(X) = 155 \text{ beds}$$

$$\text{Base level} = 120\%(155) = 186$$

$$\text{Final capacity} = 186 + 10\%(186) = 204.6, \text{ say } 205 \text{ beds}$$

Assume that a firm has designed its capacity to accommodate some given expected value of demand plus an allowance for growth. Chances are the firm will operate within that capacity constraint for some time—perhaps a year or more. The firm then has several alternatives available to help meet the shorter-term fluctuations in demand. One course of action is to adjust to the demand as closely as possible by going to overtime or time off, hiring or firing employees, and the like. Another approach is to make no attempt to have production respond to fluctuations but rather to level production by producing for inventory during slack periods and delivering from inventory during periods of heavy demand. Management may also choose to make a partial response to demand by using moderate shifts in personnel, varying inventory levels, and extending delivery times—that is, making customers wait for their product. This aspect of managing operations will be one of our major concerns when we take up the subject of scheduling and production control later on in the text.

UTILIZATION OF CAPACITY

Although the initial plant design usually specifies a certain capacity, firms modify their facilities to accommodate changes in business. For example, airports are continually expanding to meet an ever increasing demand for air travel, and manufacturers are constantly adding new products to their line. But increased capacity is seldom available in the incremental units so commonly encountered in economic theory. Economies of scale dictate that capacity increases are typically in increments of 20 percent, 50 percent, and the like. The same holds true for capacities of individual machinery and equipment. The larger increments often mean that fixed costs of overcapacity must be borne without immediate revenue to cover them, even though some temporary idle capacity may be justified from a longer-term perspective.

For operations management purposes, capacities should be stated in terms of physical units or machine hours rather than in dollar volume of sales. To equalize the capacities of various equipment within the plant, the analyst must deal with the total production capabilities and actual production rates. Whereas the plant design and layout may include components with differing individual capacities, the system capacity limits what can be produced. The *system capacity* is that maximum output of a specific product that the total system of workers and machines is capable of producing as an integrated whole.[1] It is specified relative to a specific product because the output capability varies depending upon the characteristics or configuration of the product produced.

System capacity is always less than or equal to the design capacity of the individual components that make up a production line. The capacity of a system is often the capacity of the limiting machine or work group that constitutes an integral part of the system. Design capacity may be constrained due to imbalance of equipment or labor, the specific nature of a product mix, or very exacting specifications for selected products. In general, these system constraints are attributable to design, policy, or market considerations.

Suppose, for example, that a firm producing laundry detergents has a plant designed to produce 1,200 tons per week of a regular white detergent. However, due to competitive pressures, some of the output is soon produced in the form of a "new improved" blue detergent. Later the firm diversifies again to produce an attractive green crystalline version as well as a red soap to be marketed specifically for baby laundry. All production is still done on the same production equipment, but each time the line is used for a different-colored product the equipment must be shut down for adjustment and cleaned out so that no color contamination will result. And whereas the original design capacity is still 1,200 tons of regular white detergent per week, the capacity of the system to produce colored detergents is now only 1,000 tons per week. System capacity will continue to be designated as 1,000 tons of colored

[1] Activities aimed at balancing the equipment (and/or labor) at various work stations in order to get maximum use from these resources are referred to as *line-balancing* activities. We shall defer consideration of line-balancing techniques until we take up the subject of process analysis.

detergent per week until some ingenious person steps forward with the idea of eliminating the lost production during changeover by simply segregating the color-contaminated changeover production and marketing it as another "new and improved" detergent with "powerful fast-acting white, blue, green, and red crystals."

The relationship between system (or subsystem) capacity and an individual component capacity is expressed as the potential use factor (PUF). The *potential use factor* tells how effectively an individual component could be used if the system always produced at full system capacity.[2]

$$\text{PUF} = \frac{\text{system capacity}}{\text{individual unit capacity}} \tag{2-1}$$

Unfortunately, few systems operate at their full system capacity. This inefficiency is largely attributable to machine or worker performance and day-to-day managerial efforts. Work may be improperly scheduled, the facilities inadequately staffed, or an unexpected breakdown or maintenance activity may result in inefficient use of workers or equipment. The relationship between the actual measured output of goods or services and the system capacity is referred to as the *system efficiency* (SE).[3]

$$\text{SE} = \frac{\text{actual output}}{\text{system capacity}} \tag{2-2}$$

Example 2-2

A plastics firm has two production sections, A and B (in series), with individual and system capacities for the given product mix as shown. The actual output is 306 units per day. Find (*a*) the potential use factors for sections A and B and (*b*) the system efficiency.

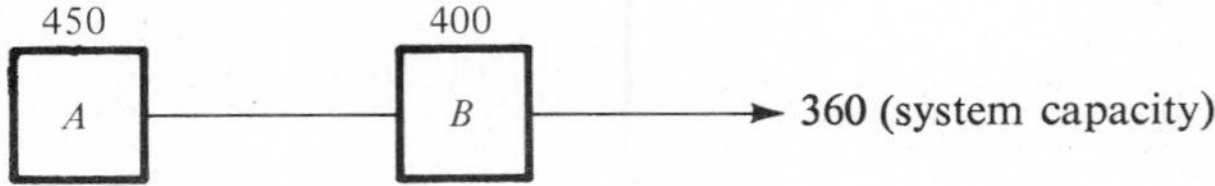

Solution

(*a*) Potential use factor $= \text{PUF} = \dfrac{\text{system capacity}}{\text{individual unit capacity}}$

$$\text{For } A = \frac{360}{450} = 80\%$$

$$\text{For } B = \frac{360}{400} = 90\%$$

[2] Some analysts also refer to an "actual" use factor of individual components (AUF) as distinct from the (system-related) potential use factor (PUF) referred to here. The actual use factor could be determined simply by replacing system capacity in Eq. (2-1) with actual output.

[3] As the *Survey of Current Business* points out, "The concept of capacity is not unambiguous" [**14**: 4]. The Federal Reserve refers to this ratio of actual output to system capacity as "utilization rate" of capacity. On an industry basis, the utilization rate may range from 85 to 95 percent or even higher, depending largely upon investment levels and national economic conditions.

(*b*) System efficiency $= \text{SE} = \dfrac{\text{actual output}}{\text{system capacity}} = \dfrac{306}{360} = 85\%$

This solution tells us that the firm is producing at only 85 percent of system capacity and that even if it were operated at full system capacity sections *A* and *B* would be used at only 80 percent and 90 percent, respectively, of their individual capacities.

DETERMINATION OF EQUIPMENT REQUIRED

The amount or size of equipment required to produce a specified output can be calculated from estimates of the potential use factor and system efficiency. This calculation is made by "working backward" from the required output to allow for inefficiencies and nonuse of the equipment. Efficiencies are usually given in terms of equipment efficiencies or the amount of quantity loss (scrap) or both. If, for example, a scrap-loss estimate can be made, the required system capacity can be determined by dividing actual output by SE (see Eq. [2-2]). Equipment use is often measured in terms of percent of individual capacity used or percent of time used. If use data are not available, one can assume 100 percent use or can base calculations on some other assumed (and stated) value.

Example 2-3

A metals processing firm wishes to install enough automatic molders to produce 200,000 good parts per year. The firm operates 2,000 hours per year but the molding equipment is part of a production line which will be used only 60 percent of the time, and its output is about 3 percent defective. A molding operation takes 90 seconds per part. Allowing for temperature adjustments and maintenance downtime, the molders are about 80 percent efficient. How many molders are required?

Solution

The solution here lies in finding the system capacity (in parts per hour) needed to supply the required output and dividing this by the actual output (in parts per hour) that can be obtained from each molder. This will tell us how many molders are required.

We begin with the output requirement and work backward to first determine the required system capacity. Since 3 percent of the total parts are defective, only 97 percent are good, so SE = 0.97.

$$\text{Required system capacity} = \frac{\text{actual (good) output}}{\text{SE}}$$

$$= \frac{200{,}000}{0.97}$$

$$= 206{,}186 \text{ parts/yr}$$

Since the firm operates 2,000 hours per year, this can be restated as:

$$\text{Required system capacity} = \frac{206{,}186 \text{ parts/yr}}{2{,}000 \text{ hr/yr}} = 103.1 \text{ parts/hr}$$

The actual output that can be obtained from each molder depends upon the individual unit capacity, its use factor, and its individual efficiency.

$$\begin{aligned}
\text{Individual unit capacity} &= \frac{3{,}600 \text{ sec/hr}}{90 \text{ sec/part}} = 40 \text{ parts/hr-machine} \\
\text{Molder subsystem capacity} &= (\text{individual unit capacity})(\text{PUF}) \\
&= (40)(0.60) = 24 \text{ parts/hr-machine} \\
\text{Actual molder output} &= (\text{molder subsystem capacity}) \\
&\quad \cdot (\text{molder subsystem efficiency}) \\
&= (24 \text{ parts/hr})(0.80) \\
&= 19.2 \text{ parts/hr-machine} \\
\therefore \text{ number of molders required} &= \frac{\text{required system capacity}}{\text{actual molder output per machine}} \\
&= \frac{103.1 \text{ parts/hr}}{19.2 \text{ parts/hr-machine}} \\
&= 5.4 \text{ machines}
\end{aligned}$$

Note that the problem involved two levels of efficiency, one on the system level (that is, the 97 percent) and one on a subsystem level (the 80 percent). We found that to overcome the system efficiency, the firm must produce 103.1 parts per hour. But because of the molder use factor (0.60) and molder subsystem efficiency (80 percent), each machine could actually average only 19.2 parts per hour, resulting in a requirement of 5.4 machines. The firm should probably plan for installation of six machines. However, with careful scheduling of maintenance activities, it might be able to improve efficiency enough to get by with five machines.

PLANT LOCATION

Plant location should be an early and continuing consideration for a new or expanding organization. Many firms are continually growing and decentralizing operations, so locational methodology is vitally important to them. As a matter of fact, few firms can really afford to overlook relocation opportunities—even those that are "well established."

For most firms, many locations would probably be "satisfactory," or equivalently good. On the other hand, some locations would be exceptionally bad, or even disastrous. Unfortunately there is no method of analysis which guarantees a firm it has selected an "optimal" site, desirable as that may be. A generalized procedure for developing a good location can be developed from our framework for decisions discussed in Chap. 1. This procedure would be (1) to clearly define the organizational unit to be located (along with its relevant characteristics), (2) to delineate the criteria for making the location decision, (3) to obtain relevant data on potential locations for the new facilities, (4) to evaluate the alternative locations in light of the criteria, and (5) to select the best location.

Numerous attempts have been made to quantify the location analysis procedure, but so many individual and institutional value judgments enter into this type of decision that a totally objective analysis is usually impossible. We must rely, at least partly, on subjective judgment. Fortunately, the human mind is capable of intuitively processing numerous beliefs and judgments, for mathematical procedures are not the only way of knowing the truth or making decisions [**12**]. Nevertheless, where possible, we shall bolster the intangible and subjective elements with whatever quantitative data are available and relevant to the decision and shall try to describe the procedure in as systematic a manner as possible.

A MODEL OF LOCATIONAL FACTORS

The system definition and characterization (step 1 above) is an important first step for it identifies the problem according to industry, type of organization, product lines, market, and so forth. A useful method of delineating the relevant criteria (step 2 above) is to systematically analyze the inputs, processing, and outputs of the newly proposed facility in relation to both the internal and environmental factors that will affect them. The schematic model of the operating production system of Chap. 1 provides a convenient framework for such an analysis. Referring to the model, we might cite the considerations given in Table 2-1. A systematized review such as this, or a standardized checklist of some kind, is extremely worthwhile to ensure that some potentially critical factors are not overlooked.

In reviewing the factors listed, which are by no means exhaustive, certain considerations assume more importance than others, depending upon the product, firm, industry, and so on. An accurate definition of the system in the initial step is helpful in isolating key factors. Also, some factors lend themselves to quantitative analysis more readily than do others.

One method of systematically evaluating alternative locations (step 4 above) is to first evaluate those important factors that can be quantified and then to allow the less-tangible factors to influence the selection by using the best available experience and judgment of management. Quite often, economic factors are a useful preliminary quantifying medium. But this must be followed with equally or perhaps more important considerations of the work force and community attitude, environmental impact, and so forth. In these days of extreme concern with ecological, social, and other environmental issues, an increasing number of plant location studies include a comprehensive environmental-impact study clearly projecting the long-range effects a new plant will have upon the proposed locations.

TABLE 2-1 PLANT LOCATIONAL FACTORS

Input Considerations
Human resource
Availability and total supply
Skills available
Wage levels and fringe benefit practices
Union activity and contract history
Housing suitability
Educational, recreational, and cultural facilities
Materials and equipment
Site availability and costs
Construction costs
Utility supply and rates (gas, electric, water)
Raw material supply
Transport facilities
Capital
Banking and monetary exchange facilities
Equity and debt capital potential
Processing Considerations
Production and process analysis
Educational facilities and research organizations
Engineering and management consultants
Forecasting, scheduling, and various control activities
Data sources for forecasting, scheduling, etc.
Data processing capabilities
Inventory storage and future expansion availability
Environmental affects on product quality
Maintenance and cost control
Service and repair facilities
Accounting and auditing facilities
Output Considerations
Noneconomic impacts
Ordinances, zoning, and building codes
Environmental standards (air, land, water)
Community services
Presence of related industries
Marketing and public relations
Community attitude toward industry and company
Present and future market potential (local and international)
Storage and distribution facilities
Transportation facilities and costs
Economic impacts
Stockholder interests and profit distribution
Organizational decentralization policies
Local, state, and federal taxes

LOCATIONAL BREAK-EVEN ANALYSIS

In comparing several potential locations on an economic basis, the only costs that need be considered are the relevant costs that vary from one location to another. Many of these costs may, in turn, vary with the production volume. If the expected volume for a new plant is likely to vary, as it often is, the economic comparison can be made by identifying the fixed and variable costs and graphing them for each location. This method is sometimes referred to as locational break-even analysis. The graphic approach has an advantage over a simple tabular approach in that one can easily identify ranges over which one location is preferable to another.

The methodology for locational break-even analysis may be summarized as follows:

1 Determine all relevant costs that vary with the locations under consideration.
2 Categorize the costs for each location in terms of annual fixed costs (FC) and variable per-unit costs (VC).
3 Plot the costs associated with each location on a single chart of annual cost versus annual volume.
4 Select the location with the lowest total annual cost (TC) at the expected production volume (V).

Once the economic preference of various locations has been established and the locational feasibility confirmed, the less-tangible criteria (Table 2-1) should be considered before making the final selection (step 5). If economic criteria are a determining consideration, the selection may be simplified. If the net result of numerous other criteria is not clear, and the choice is still not obvious, a system of weighting the criteria may be desirable. (We will take up qualitative factor analysis a little later.)

Example 2-4

Potential locations A, B, and C have the following cost structure. Find the most economical location for an expected volume of 1,850 units per year.

Site	Fixed cost/year	Variable cost/unit
A	$20,000	$50
B	40,000	30
C	80,000	10

Solution

For each site, plot the fixed costs (costs at zero volume) and total costs (fixed costs + variable costs) at a volume in the vicinity of the expected output, say 2,000 units.

$$\begin{array}{ll} & \text{TC} = \text{FC} + \text{VC}(V) \\ \text{Site } A & \text{TC} = \$20{,}000 + \$50(2{,}000) = \$120{,}000 \\ \text{Site } B & \text{TC} = \$40{,}000 + \$30(2{,}000) = \$100{,}000 \\ \text{Site } C & \text{TC} = \$80{,}000 + \$10(2{,}000) = \$100{,}000 \end{array}$$

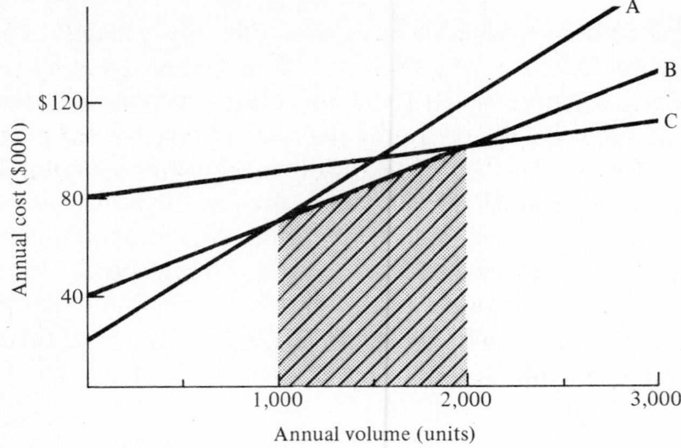

FIGURE 2-2 Locational break-even chart

From the graph, the most economical location for a volume of 1,850 units is site *B*. Note that for volumes $< 1{,}000$ units, site *A* would be preferred. For volumes $> 2{,}000$ units, site *C* would be preferred.

Locational break-even analysis is a means of comparing all relevant costs for several alternative locations and selecting a plant location that will minimize costs for a given volume. It is desirable that the "relevant costs" include transportation and/or distribution costs if they vary from one location to another, which is usually the case. When transportation costs are especially significant or when the same product can be produced at more than one plant and/or transported to more than one distribution point, a detailed analysis of transportation costs is warranted.

TRANSPORTATION COST MINIMIZATION USING DISTRIBUTION LINEAR PROGRAMMING

Assume that the management of a national baking company feel they can justify another new plant to produce their standard line of breads and bakery goods. They wish to give specific consideration to transportation costs since they have a relatively bulky, low unit value product to distribute. Before reaching their final plant location decision they will want to anticipate how the addition of another plant will affect their existing production-distribution patterns. Which plants will ultimately be used to produce what quantities and to which distribution warehouses should the various quantities be shipped?

If the problem can be formulated (modeled) as one of minimizing some given cost, such as transportation expense, the methods of distribution linear programming are useful techniques for minimizing the cost function subject to supply and demand constraints.

Distribution linear programming methods are widely used for minimizing transportation costs and are indeed useful in numerous other maximization or minimization situations, such as maximizing revenues available from various alternative locations, minimizing unit production costs, and minimizing materials handling costs. The demand requirements and supply availabilities (demand-supply constraints) are typically formulated in a rectangular arrangement (matrix) with the transported amounts (cell loadings) being governed by the cost or profit for the particular supply-demand route. Several methods of obtaining initial and final solutions have been developed, some of which include the following.

I Initial Solutions
- **A** Northwest corner method
- **B** Minimum matrix method (minimum cost)
- **C** Vogel's approximation method

II Optimal Solutions
- **A** Stepping-stone method
- **B** Modified distribution method (MODI)

The following example will illustrate the use of an initial allocation via the northwest corner method and a final solution via the stepping-stone method. These are not usually the most expedient methods to follow when the problem has any degree of complexity, but they have intuitive value and quickly convey the basic methodology. An optional problem in the solved problem section at the end of this chapter illustrates the use of the minimum cost method.

The solution procedure necessitates that only unused transportation paths (vacant cells) be evaluated, and there is only one available pattern of moves to evaluate each vacant cell. This is because moves are restricted to occupied cells. Every time a vacant cell is filled, *one* previously occupied cell must become vacant. The initial (and continuing) number of entries is always maintained at $R + C - 1$, that is, number of rows plus number of columns minus one.[4] When a move happens to cause fewer entries (for example, when two cells become vacant at the same time but only one is filled), a "zero" entry must be retained in one of the cells to avoid what is termed a "degeneracy" situation. The zero entry should be assigned to an independent cell, that is, to one that cannot be reached by a closed path involving only filled cells. The cell with the zero entry is then considered to be an occupied and potentially usable cell.

A second potentially troublesome situation may arise when supply and demand are unequal. In this situation a "dummy" supply plant or absorption location can be created either to produce the additional needed supply or to absorb the excess supply:

If demand > supply: Create a dummy supply and assign zero transportation cost to it so excess demand is satisfied.

If supply > demand: Create a dummy demand and assign zero transportation cost to it so excess supply is absorbed.

[4] This corresponds to a fundamental linear programming rule which holds that the number of variables in solution must equal the number of constraints that are binding.

The example below does not require the use of a dummy location because supply and demand capacities are equal.

Example 2-5

The Milltex Company has production plants in Albany, Bend, and Corvallis, all of which manufacture similar paneling for the housing market. Their products are currently distributed through plants in Seattle and Portland. They are considering adding another distribution plant in San Francisco and have developed the following transportation costs in dollars per unit.

Production Plants	Cost to ship to distribution plant in: Seattle	Portland	San Francisco
Albany	$10	$14	$ 8
Bend	12	10	12
Corvallis	8	12	10

The production capabilities at the Albany, Bend, and Corvallis plants are 20, 30, and 40 unit loads per week, respectively. Management feels that a San Francisco plant could absorb 20 units per week, with Seattle and Portland claiming 40 and 30 units per week, respectively. Determine the optimal distribution arrangement and cost if the San Francisco site is selected.

Solution

We will use the northwest corner method for the initial allocation and the stepping-stone method for the final solution. This requires that the data be arranged in a matrix. Figure 2-3 shows supply on the horizontal rows, demand on the columns, and unit transportation costs ($) in the small boxes in the matrix.

The initial allocation via the northwest (NW) corner method is made as follows.

1 Assign as many units as possible to the NW corner cell A1 from the total available in row A. Given the 20 units available supply in row A, and the 40-unit demand in column 1, the maximum number of units that can be assigned to cell A1 is 20. This is shown as (20), indicating an initial allocation.

2 Assign additional units of supply from row B (or additional rows) until the demand in column 1 is satisfied. This requires 20 additional units in cell B1 and leaves 10 units of B's unassigned.

3 Assign remaining units in the subject row to the next column, continuing as above until its demand requirements are satisfied. This means the 10 units left in B are assigned to cell B2. Since this does not satisfy demand in column 2, an additional 20 units are allocated from row C.

Distribution plants

(Demand)

Production plants (Supply)	(1) Seattle	(2) Portland	(3) San Francisco	
A	10 (20)	14	8	20
B	12 (20)	10 (10)	12	30
C	8	12 (20)	10 (20)	40
	40	30	20	90

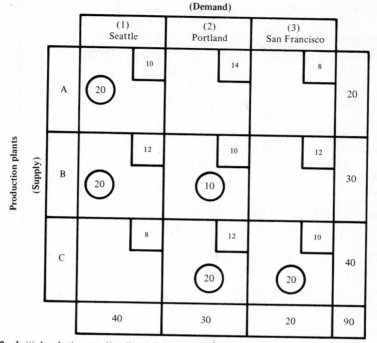

FIGURE 2-3 Initial solution to distribution linear programming matrix

4 Continue down from the NW corner until all supply has been allocated to demand. The initial assignment is completed by assigning the 20 units remaining in row C to cell C3.

5 Check allocations to verify that all supply and demand conditions are satisfied. Since all row and column totals agree, the initial assignment is correct. Also the number of entries is five, which satisfies the $R + C - 1$ requirement for $3 + 3 - 1 = 5$.

The initial solution is, perhaps obviously, not an optimal (or least-cost) allocation scheme. The transportation cost for this arrangement is:

20 units	A to Seattle @ $10/unit	=	$200
20 units	B to Seattle @ $12/unit	=	240
10 units	B to Portland @ $10/unit	=	100
20 units	C to Portland @ $12/unit	=	240
20 units	C to San Francisco @ $10/unit	=	200
		Total	$980

An optimal solution can be obtained by following a stepping-stone approach, which requires calculation of the net monetary gain or loss that can be obtained by shifting an allocation from one supply source to another. The important rule to keep in mind is that every increase (or decrease) in supply at one location must be accompanied by a decrease (or increase) in supply at another. The same holds true for demand. Thus there must be two changes in every row or column that is changed—one change increasing the quantity and one change decreasing it. This is easily done by evaluating reallocations in a closed-path sequence with only right-angle turns permitted. Of course, a cell must have an initial entry before it can be reduced in favor of another, but empty (or filled) cells may be skipped over to get to a corner cell. To be sure that all reallocation possibilities are considered, it is best to proceed systematically, evaluating each empty cell. When any changes are made, cells vacated earlier must be rechecked.

The criterion for making a reallocation is simply the desired effect upon costs. The net loss or gain is determined by listing the unit costs associated with each cell (which is used as a corner in the evaluation path), and then summing over the path to find the net effect. Signs alternate from + to − depending upon whether shipments are being added or reduced at a given point. A negative sign on the net result indicates a cost reduction can be made by making the change. The total savings are of course limited to the least number of units available for reallocation at any given cell on the path.

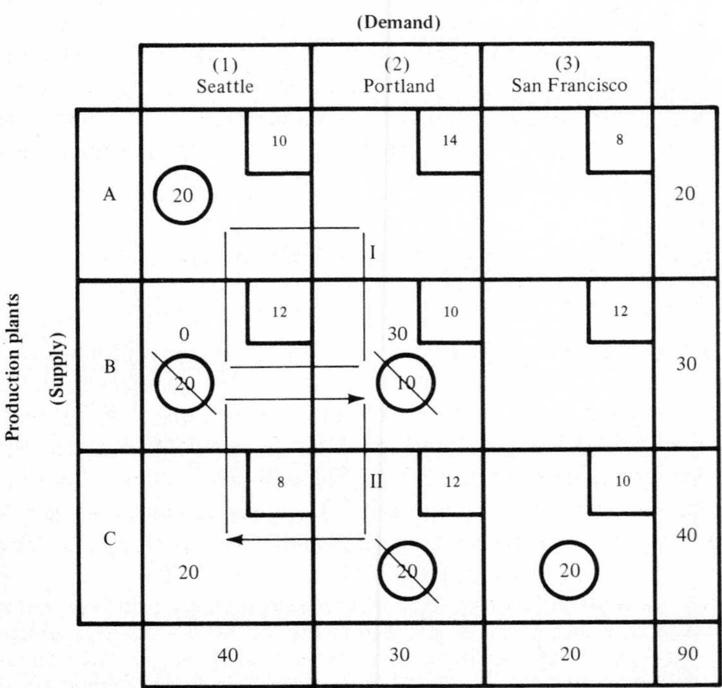

FIGURE 2-4 Revision of matrix

1 *Evaluate cell* A2
Path A1 to A2 to B2 to B1 (designated I in Fig. 2-4)
Cost $-10 + 14 - 10 + 12 = +6$ (cost increase)
∴ make no change.

2 *Evaluate cell* C1
Path C2 to C1 to B1 to B2 (designated II in Fig. 2-4)
Cost $-12 + 8 - 12 + 10 = -6$ (cost savings)
∴ this is a potential change. Evaluate remaining empty cells to see if other changes are more profitable.

3 *Evaluate cell* A3
Path A1 to A3 to C3 to C2 to B2 to B1 (not shown in Fig. 2-4)
Cost $-10 + 8 - 10 + 12 - 10 + 12 = +2$ (cost increase)

4 *Evaluate cell* B3
Path B2 to B3 to C3 to C2 (not shown in Fig. 2-4)
Cost $-10 + 12 - 10 + 12 = +4$ (cost increase)

Cell C1 presents the best (only) opportunity for improvement. For each unit from C reallocated to Seattle and from B reallocated to Portland, a $6 savings results. Change the maximum number available in the loop (20) for a net savings of ($6)(20) = $120. (The maximum number will always be the smallest number in the cells where shipments are being reduced, that is, cells with negative coefficients.) The crossed circles and arrows on loop II in Fig. 2-4 show that transformations have been made. Note that cells B1 and C2 have both become vacant (a degenerate situation) so a zero has been assigned to one of the vacant cells (B1) to maintain the $R + C - 1$ requirement of 5. Since a reallocation was made, the empty cells are again evaluated for further improvement:

1 Cell A2 A1 – A2 – B2 – B1 = +6 no change

2 Cell C2 B2 – C2 – C1 – B1 = +6 no change

3 Cell A3 A1 – A3 – C3 – C1 = –4 a possibility

4 Cell B3 B1 – B3 – C3 – C1 = –2 a possibility

Cell A3 has the greatest potential for improvement. (Note that the loop evaluating cell B3 has zero units available for transfer from cell B1 so no reallocation could take place without first locating another route to B3. This would be done by relocating the zero.[5] However, in this example cell A3 offers the best improvement so we capitalize upon the opportunity to load cell A3.)

[5] If a cell evaluation reveals an improvement potential in a given cell but no units are available because of a zero entry in the path to that cell, the zero (zero units) should be transported to the vacant cell just as any other units would be shipped. Then the matrix should be reevaluated. Improvements may still be possible until the zero entries are relocated to where evaluations of all vacant cells are ≥ 0.

Distribution plants

(Demand)

Production plants (Supply)	(1) Seattle	(2) Portland	(3) San Francisco	
A	10	14	8	
			20	20
B	12	10	12	
	0	30		30
C	8	12	10	
	40		0	40
	40	30	20	90

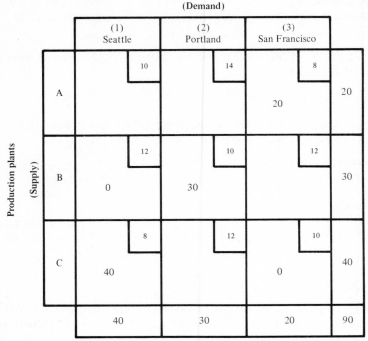

FIGURE 2-5 Optimal solution

A reallocation of 20 units to cell A3 results in the matrix shown in Fig. 2-5. Note that a zero has again been retained in one of the vacated cells (C3) to satisfy the $R + C - 1$ constraint.

Further evaluation of the cells reveals that no additional savings can be achieved. The optimal solution is as shown in Fig. 2-5. The transportation cost for this arrangement is:

40 units	C to Seattle @ \$8/unit =	\$320
30 units	B to Portland @ \$10/unit =	300
20 units	A to San Francisco @ \$8/unit =	160
	Total	\$780

Net savings over the initial allocation: \$980 − \$780 = \$200/week.

QUALITATIVE FACTOR ANALYSIS

In the discussion on locational break-even analysis we suggested that if economic criteria were not sufficiently influential and the net result of numerous other criteria was unclear, a system of weighting the criteria might be a useful means of arriving at a plant location decision. This approach is referred to as qualitative factor analysis and is another means of allowing the decision maker to inject values into a decision-making structure in a relatively formalized manner. It is described in the following procedure.

1 *Develop* a list of the relevant factors. (This might be derived from a check-list, or Table 2-1.)

2 *Assign* a scale to each factor and designate any minimums.

3 *Weight* the factors relative to each other in light of their importance toward achievement of system goals.

4 *Score* each potential location according to the designated scale and multiply the scores by the weights.

5 *Total* the points for each location and either
   (*a*) use them in conjunction with a separate economic analysis, or
   (*b*) include an economic factor in the list of factors and choose the location on the basis of maximum points.

Example 2-6

The Milltex Company with distribution plants in Seattle and Portland is considering adding a third assembly and distribution plant in either San Francisco, Boise, or Spokane. They have collected the following economic and non-economic data.

	San Francisco	Boise	Spokane
Transportation cost/wk	$ 780	$ 640	$ 560
Labor cost/wk	1,200	1,020	1,180
Selected criteria scores (based on scale of 0–100 points)			
Finishing material supply	35	85	70
Maintenance facilities	60	25	30
Community attitude	50	85	70

Company management has preestablished weights for various factors and they include a standard of 1.0 for each $10 per week of economic advantage. Other weights applicable are 1.5 on finishing material supply, 0.80 on maintenance facilities, and 2.0 on community attitudes. Maintenance also has a minimum acceptable score of 30. Develop a qualitative factor comparison for the three locations.

Solution

1 The relevant factors are (*a*) relative economic advantage, (*b*) finishing material supply, (*c*) maintenance facilities, and (*d*) community attitude.

2 Evaluation scales are all 0–100 points.

3 Factor weights for (*a*), (*b*), (*c*), and (*d*) are 1.0/$10 weekly advantage, 1.5, 0.8, and 2.0, respectively.

4 Weighted scores = $\sum$ (score)(weight). First we must determine the relative economic advantage score:

	San Francisco	Boise	Spokane
Cost/wk (transportation + labor)	$1,980	$1,660	$1,740
Relative economic advantage (highest cost − cost/wk)	0	320	240
Economic advantage score in $10 units	0	32	24

Factors	San Francisco (score)(weight) = weighted score	Boise (score)(weight) = weighted score	Spokane (score)(weight) = weighted score
Economic	(0) (1.0) = 0	(32) (1.0) = 32.0	(24) (1.0) = 24.0
Material supply	(35) (1.5) = 52.5	(85) (1.5) = 127.5	(70) (1.5) = 105.0
Maintenance	(60) (0.8) = 48.0	(25) (0.8) = 20.0	(30) (0.8) = 24.0
Community	(50) (2.0) = 100.0	(85) (2.0) = 170.0	(70) (2.0) = 140.0
Total	200.5	XXX	293.0

The Boise site does not meet the maintenance minimum criterion of 30. Spokane has the highest total points and so would be recommended on the basis of this limited analysis (even though Boise has a lower cost structure).

INTERNATIONAL CONSIDERATIONS

Foreign locations often offer some unique advantages to a firm, but each location should receive a thorough analysis for there are also numerous pitfalls.

From a human resources standpoint, production skills are much more broadly based throughout Europe, Asia, South America, and the world in general than they were 30 years ago. Wage rates often appear, on the surface, to be a plus factor, but the advantages of "cheap foreign labor" are not necessarily sufficient reason for establishing foreign plants. *First*, many industrialized countries, such as West Germany, Sweden, and Switzerland, now have wage rates that are equal to or even greater than those in the United States. *Second*, many foreign countries have substantially higher social costs of medical care, welfare, and so on, than is currently paid by firms in the United States. *Third*, the productivity of workers in most foreign countries lags behind that of United States workers. This is not because the workers are inferior or do not work as hard, but because of the level of capital equipment and technology used. As a result, the production output per worker-hour is typically less.

Although we tend to feel that highly mechanized and automated production equipment is most desirable, this is not always true in foreign locations. One study, financed by the Ford Foundation, of automation as applied to plants in developing countries revealed that governments of those countries saw advanced technology as a cause of their perplexing problems of massive unemployment. The study concluded that "contrary to the accepted idea, it is more difficult in many cases to run an automated plant in a developing country than a more labor-intensive operation [**15**: 112]." Sometimes an intermediate level of technology using secondhand and labor-intensive equipment is more profitable to both the company and the community.

Foreign investment accounts for about 15–20 percent of the total plant and equipment investment by United States-based firms. Many firms attempt to raise capital for foreign ventures in the foreign location in order to (1) preserve their own supply of domestic capital, and (2) give them some protection against loss in the event of expropriation (or takeover) of the facility by the foreign government. However, some countries, particularly developing nations, restrict the availability of long-term capital to their own firms to prevent profits from flowing off to stockholders in other countries.

Production processing differences also present multinational firms with unique problems. Research and development facilities vary from extremely good to nonexistent. Language and cultural differences can present operating, control, and even policy problems. Units of measure (for example, metric versus English) differ. Some countries, such as India, Mexico, and Brazil, even dictate what a foreign plant will produce by virtue of tax laws and local "sourcing" requirements. *Sourcing* requires that firms producing a given product must also obtain or produce a specified percentage of the components for that product within the host country as well.

These, and a myriad of other considerations with respect to inventories, tariffs, markets, the political environment, and so forth, confirm that the foreign location decision can be a very complex one. As in a domestic situation, a systematic analysis is essential, for the costs of overlooking something crucial appear to far outweigh the benefits of hurriedly capitalizing on something that makes an attractive first impression.

PLANT LAYOUT

Plant layout decisions are concerned with the arrangement of facilities wherein the labor and material inputs are combined or transformed to produce the outputs. To a large extent the layout determines the flow patterns for future work efforts, so operations managers are highly interested in developing efficient layouts. Most plants are arranged either according to the product, or according to the production process, or both. The type of layout is generally determined by the

1 *Type of product*, that is, whether the product is a good or service, the product design and product standards

2 *Type of production process*, that is, the physical process and type of materials handling equipment, or the means of providing the service

3 *Volume (capacity) of production*, that is, the plant design and capacity requirements and facilities utilization and efficiency

TYPES OF LAYOUTS

The basic types of plant layouts used in industry can be classified as (1) *product* or line layout, (2) *process* layout, and (3) *fixed-material* layout. Product layouts typically have equipment sequenced to produce a single type of product, often in a continuous manner. Material flow is largely dictated by the structured nature of the equipment arrangement. This type of layout is particularly useful for high-volume production of standardized products which can be assembled with interchangeable parts. Work is often routine and highly repetitive, so it commands a comparatively low wage rate and does not appeal to all workers. The scheduling and control activities are generally simpler than for process layouts.

Product layouts are sometimes referred to as line layouts and usually deliver a product at a relatively low cost per unit. (See Fig. 2-6.) They lend themselves to the use of conveyors and automated equipment which minimizes any manual material handling and reduces the need for in-process inventories. On the other hand, since all equipment is specialized and sequenced to produce one type of product, a breakdown in one component can idle much of the equipment and reduce or stop the total production output.

Process layouts consist of equipment designed to perform similar functions being grouped together, as shown in Fig. 2-7. This is sometimes referred to as a job

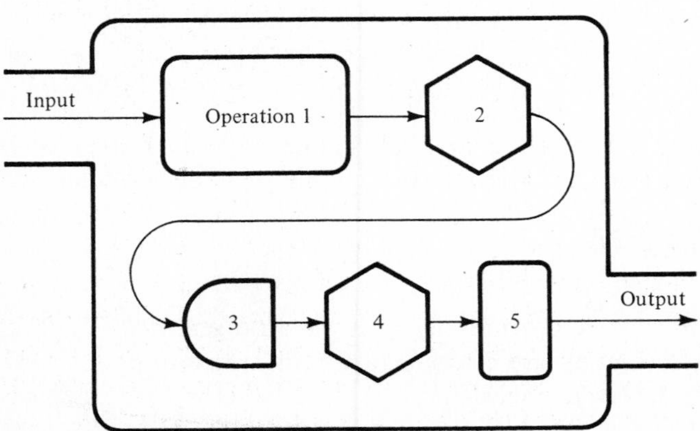

FIGURE 2-6 Product layout

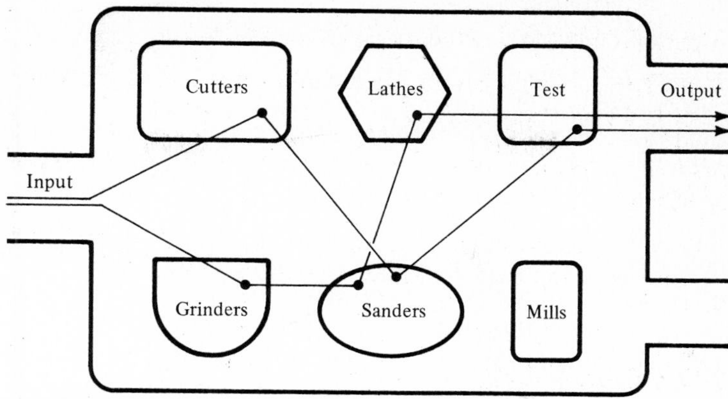

FIGURE 2-7 Process layout

shop or functional layout, where specialized activities, such as milling, electroplating, or x-raying, are performed in one location for various products. Hospitals often have process layout characteristics.

The process layout is relatively flexible and an individual machine or facility breakdown need not affect the whole production system. However, substantial in-process inventories may be required, and labor, materials handling, and inspection costs can be significant. Routing, scheduling, and cost accounting of production becomes more complex as the number of jobs and functions to be performed increases.

A third type of layout is sometimes referred to as a fixed-material or project-type layout. In it, the materials and processing are brought to the project location where work is done largely on a custom basis. Examples of this are homebuilding, shipbuilding, and dam construction projects.

SELECTION OF OPTIMAL LAYOUT

Whereas the types of layout can be conveniently classified as product, process, and fixed-material, most layouts include elements of more than one type and in reality are combinations. This makes the job of managing operations a little more difficult, for some problems tend to be more common in one type of layout than in another. For example, a manager scheduling production may be faced with both assembly line balancing problems (which are primarily of concern in product-line layouts) and establishing decision rules to designate which jobs take priority in processing (which are of more concern in process layouts.)

Although there is no general theory for optimizing the numerous interdependent factors that enter into plant layout decisions, many of the specific layout problem areas lend themselves to analysis. In some cases, where the problems are primarily technological, they can best be handled by engineers on the operations staff or in conjunction with plant engineering. Other situations may require direct managerial attention. Many large firms, like Westinghouse Electric Corporation, have specialized departments for layout activities. Planners in these groups typically use small-scale physical models and computer models to evaluate existing layouts and develop layouts for new plants.

Two important criteria for selecting and designing a layout are worker effectiveness and materials handling cost. Specific consideration of work methods will be taken up in the chapter on human resource inputs. Let us simply note here that the effectiveness of labor-intensive processes is largely determined by (1) the level of performance and (2) the productive time of the worker. The layout should be designed to facilitate satisfaction of the workers in their jobs and to use the workers at the highest skill level for which they are being paid. This applies just as much to an office layout, where an engineer may spend half of a working day delivering memos, as it does to a factory layout, where a machinist travels long distances for tools. The communications system layout and tool crib locations are obviously relevant plant layout considerations in these cases. Similarly, if the machinist is forced to be idle for long periods because of the lack of a nearby quality inspection center, productive time is further diminished.

Materials handling cost is the second important criterion. Desirable layouts are arranged so that product flow is automated (as much as practical) and flow distances are minimized. The extent of automation is, of course, a function of the level of technology and location of the particular industry, the capital available in the individual firm, and behavioral considerations of employees. Flow distances and times are usually minimized by attempting to locate sequential processing activities in adjacent areas.

Several analytical methods have been developed to facilitate plant layout by minimizing materials handling costs, including techniques of operations sequence analysis and CRAFT (Computerized Relative Allocation of Facilities Technique).

Operations sequence analysis consists of designating the various work centers as circles on a rectangular sheet of graph paper. Lines between the circles represent loads transported during a given time, such as 50 units per month. Departments next to each other, or diagonally across from each other, are regarded as adjacent and take on a distance factor of 1; others take on successively higher integer values depending on the number of rows or columns they are from each other. Departments are then shifted in an effort to minimize the sum of the (load) × (distance) for the entire matrix. Selection of which departments to shift is done by visual inspection and the result is not necessarily a mathematically provable optimum, but it can result in substantial improvement over more arbitrary methods of layout.

CRAFT is a more systematic method of selecting a plant layout on the basis of minimizing materials handling costs [**3**]. The process is an iterative heuristic method whereby data are fed into a computer which calculates costs, exchanges departments, calculates more costs, and ultimately issues a printout of its best solution.

The CRAFT program can handle the exchange of up to three departments at a time for up to 40 activity centers. It has some other limiting assumptions concerning material flows and cost linearity, but they are sufficiently loose to make the program usable on a practical basis.

PRODUCT DESIGN AND STANDARDS

We observed earlier that plant layout decisions are concerned with the arrangement of facilities to produce the outputs. Obviously, the rationale for plant layout stems directly from the good or service being produced. It should appropriately reflect the desires of the consumer, for the plant layout is justified only by virtue of creating a good or service which has value to the consumer. The product design and quality standards should therefore reflect the potential market in terms of an engineering design. In this design stage, engineering and production concerns should be directed toward facilitating production by product simplification and standardization, while at the same time keeping consumer desires in mind. The simplification efforts are aimed at reducing costs by eliminating nonessential activities or components and the product standardization activities seek to define the optimal material, dimensions, and the like, for the product. In larger firms some of these tasks are done by specialized value engineering personnel.

PROCESS METHODS AND MATERIALS HANDLING

The plant layout provides a system for efficiently combining various resources so that the output is of greater value than the total cost of the inputs and processing. Value is added in numerous ways, many of which represent the application of existing technology. Of primary importance are mechanical, electrical, chemical, and nuclear transformations. Thus we see value added in terms of mechanical construction and assembly, electrical generation, control, and electrolytic processing, chemical combinations for numerous products, and the controlled release of nuclear energy. In all these activities the process method lies at the heart of the value-added function. So we find that the final assemblage of automobile parts is of much more value than the component parts, and a beautiful nylon carpet is a welcome transformation from the chemicals which were blended to produce it. Technology has been a key source of value added.

The level of technology also provides a basis for offering consumers increased value in terms of their use of the environmental resources of time and space. Airlines and telephone companies produce services which effectively reduce transportation time and distance. Hospitals offer a controlled environment to those in need. In every case the process method is a function of the level of technology and it is justified in terms of providing a value to a consumer. Goods are typically valued in terms of their physical worth, and services in terms of the personal or environmental needs they fulfill.

One activity which adds little or no value per se but is absolutely essential to many production processes is that of materials handling. Most process methods are highly dependent upon the physical flow of materials. Furthermore, this transportation cost often averages about 20 percent of the total cost of production [**11**: 75]. It is not surprising then that many large organizations have specialized materials handling engineers who report to the production or operations manager. These analysts assist in planning the flow of materials, conduct feasibility and cost studies for alternative types of handling equipment, and make recommendations concerning the selection, use, and maintenance of equipment.

Some basic guidelines have been developed [**11**: 75] to facilitate good materials handling practice:

1. *Plan handling as a system*, with flow from supplier, through process, to consumer.

2. *Minimize handling* as much as possible, mechanizing it where economically justified.

3. Fully *evaluate alternate methods and select proper equipment* for the job. Relatively straight, rapid, steady flows are often best.

4. *Use equipment properly* for the job it is designed to do.

Equipment selection involves many considerations, such as the type and volume of material to be handled, distance to be moved, type of production system, and so forth. Often a basic economic analysis provides a satisfactory decision criterion. In view of the numerous types of fixed-path equipment (belt conveyors, pneumatic conveyors, cranes, elevators) and variable-path equipment (hand trucks, fork lifts, tractors) careful consideration should be given to the selection of equipment at the time a plant is being designed. Some firms realize this too late and are unable to take advantage of the best method without extensive, and costly, modification to their plant.

The use of automated systems for storing work in process as well as raw materials and finished goods inventory is one example of a technological advancement that has become widely adopted in both the United States and Europe. These computer-controlled systems minimize individual handling to the point where one operator can control all the incoming and outgoing flow of materials from and to a multitude of large steel storage racks. The systems have automated storage-retrieval machines (stackers) which travel several hundred feet per minute (and elevate while moving) to do the work equivalent of 8 or 10 workers with fork lift trucks. In addition, the data control system keeps accurate records of inventory amounts, locations, and use patterns.

PURCHASING: MAKE VERSUS BUY DECISIONS

Materials handling activities can be viewed as one component of a larger materials management system which encompasses purchasing, receiving, traffic, inventory flows and physical distribution activities. In some firms, many of these activities are coordinated under a materials manager who reports directly to the general manager or to the chief executive. More commonly, however, materials management activities are segregated or incorporated within other components of the organization.

Purchasing is a key concern of operations and of the total organization, for material and equipment purchases from outside suppliers normally consume from one-quarter to three-quarters of a firm's sales revenue. In some organizations the purchasing agent reports directly to the operations manager, but many large firms have more autonomous purchasing departments. Whatever the case, the purchasing activities, like engineering and personnel procurement, must be closely coordinated with the production operations. This close relationship was illustrated in our schematic model of Chap. 1.

To obtain needed materials and equipment on time, operations personnel must provide full and accurate information to their firm's buyers. This should include complete specifications of items desired (type, style number, and so forth), quantities, delivery dates required, expected costs (if available), and possibly recommended suppliers. The buyers, in turn, may be expected to analyze the purchase requisitions carefully, questioning the specifications and quantities, and investigating whether substitute or less costly materials are acceptable.

The close cooperation and full exchange of information between purchasing and production facilitates organizational goals in many ways. For example, with annual requirement information from operations, purchasing may be able to take advantage of quantity discounts for volume purchases, or of long-term contracts such as "blanket" purchase orders that firm up a price but leave the delivery dates open for shipments as needed. Similarly, when operations is forewarned of expected delays in the receipt of much-needed material, work can be rescheduled more efficiently than if the absence of material comes as a surprise. This type of information is essential for the smooth functioning of material requirements planning systems which we shall discuss in later chapters of the text.

Many firms are faced at some time, perhaps often, with decisions as to whether to make or buy items or components. There is no simple answer to these problems, for a number of considerations come into play. One approach is to first establish economic feasibility and then follow with consideration of the more value-based, "less-economic" factors.

If the production of a proposed item is profitable, it is economically feasible. The situation is somewhat more complex, however, when we begin to consider the extent to which a product will be using capacity that could be used to produce other products; that is, the opportunity cost of producing the product rather than buying it. If the firm has excess capacity, and the component value is sufficient to cover all the variable costs that go into it as well as make some contribution to fixed costs, it is probably a good candidate for production. Often the fixed costs of plant and equipment depreciation are effectively irrevocable ("sunk" costs) so that the extent to which the product covers a share of these costs is somewhat less significant. However, as capacity becomes more fully utilized, the decision to make the product should be reviewed again, for other alternative products may offer a higher contribution.

Some of the important "less-economic" factors influencing a decision as to whether to make an item or buy it are the following:

1. Availability of supply
2. Alternative sources of supply
3. Control of trade secrets
4. Desire to specialize or expand into the area
5. Delivery security
6. Employee preferences and employment stability
7. Flexibility impact
8. Goodwill effects
9. Quality and reliability effects
10. Research and development facilities
11. Reciprocity impact

Each situation is, of course, different. A soft drink producer may put extreme importance upon controlling its secret mix formula, whereas a missile manufacturer may be unable to obtain the necessary quality in components from an outside supplier. After economic feasibility is established, the above factors (and any other relevant ones) should be given careful consideration before one reaches a final decision. If the number of relevant factors turns out to be large, and the constraining considerations vague, the decision maker may wish to devise a weighting system for the qualitative factors as we saw illustrated in Example 2-6 for the plant location problem.

SUMMARY

The capacity, location, and layout of a facility are far-reaching decisions which can be very instrumental to the organization's long-run success or failure. Capacity is usually sized for some intermediate level of demand, with perhaps an allowance for growth. Many firms do not fully use their individual equipment capacities because the components are not exactly balanced, or the product mix has limiting characteristics. Thus the system capacity is often less than the individual unit capacities. The ratio of the two is the potential use factor. Actual output is, however, usually below system capacity and the ratio of output to system capacity is expressed as system efficiency.

There is no optimizing theory for plant location. One approach is to first establish some economically feasible sites and then follow a systematic method of evaluating the less-tangible factors. Every location study should follow some systematic method of analysis so as not to overlook crucial factors that might compromise the success of a new venture. International locations are particularly vulnerable to unique and unexpected problems in all three areas of input, processing, and output.

Locational break-even analysis is a method of evaluating relevant costs. It provides a graphic aid which gives the analyst some appreciation of the sensitivity of a given site to a change in volume.

If transportation costs are particularly relevant, distribution linear programming methods are useful for locating sites in a manner that will minimize costs. Several methods exist to solve such problems; the text example used was the northwest corner method for the initial allocation and the stepping-stone method for the final solution. The solution method is an iterative procedure that progressively approaches an optimum by reallocating supply and demand to lower-cost transportation routes.

The plant layout depends largely upon the type of product, type of process, and volume of production. Product-line layouts have equipment sequenced to produce a single type of product, whereas process layouts have equipment grouped according to the functions it performs. There is no universal technique for obtaining an optimal layout, but major considerations are worker effectiveness and materials handling cost. The operations sequence analysis and CRAFT are examples of heuristic approaches designed to find satisfactory arrangements with low materials handling cost. Materials handling guidelines stress the advantage of a systems approach to material flow, indicating that the proper selection and use of equipment is an important step toward minimizing handling costs.

When excess capacity exists, a firm may wish to produce (rather than buy) certain components. The decision to make versus buy should come only after thorough evaluation of the economic as well as the "less-economic" factors and should be reevaluated periodically.

SOLVED PROBLEMS

PLANT DESIGN AND CAPACITY

1 A forest ranger in charge of constructing a new campground has been instructed to provide enough campsites to accommodate 10 percent more than the average summer weekend demand at the nearby Fall Creek site. The ranger obtains the following estimate from an employee who patrols the Fall Creek area. For what capacity should the ranger design the new campground?

Campsite demand	Percent of time
0 to 10	5
10 to 20	30
20 to 50	50
50 to 80	10
80 to 100	5

Solution

The employee has provided the ranger with a distribution which has unequal class sizes and overlapping class limits—that is, we do not know into which class the "20" (and 50 and 80) fall. Nevertheless, if this is the best information available we should use it.

Midpoint (X)	$P(X)$	$XP(X)$
5	0.05	0.25
15	0.30	4.50
35	0.50	17.50
65	0.10	6.50
90	0.05	4.50
		33.25

$$E(D) = \sum XP(X) = 33.25 \text{ campsites}$$

$$\text{Add } 10\% \quad \underline{3.32} \text{ campsites}$$

$$\text{Design capacity } 36.57 \text{ campsites}$$

Best estimate = 37 campsites

2 A common stock transfer operation of a large New York brokerage firm has been "automated" so that each of four workers (A = Alice, B = Bob, C = Carol, and D = Dan) performs a sequential task, such as typing names on certificates, recording ownership, and the like. The maximum number of certificates per hour that each worker is capable of handling is 75, 50, 70, and 60, respectively. However, workers A and D operate at 70 percent efficiency and workers B and C at 90 percent efficiency relative to the system capacity. (Assume workload is greater than capacity.)

(*a*) What is the effective capacity of the system?
(*b*) What is the potential use factor for worker C?
(*c*) What is the expected output of the system?

Solution

A schematic representation of the system is shown in the accompanying sketch.

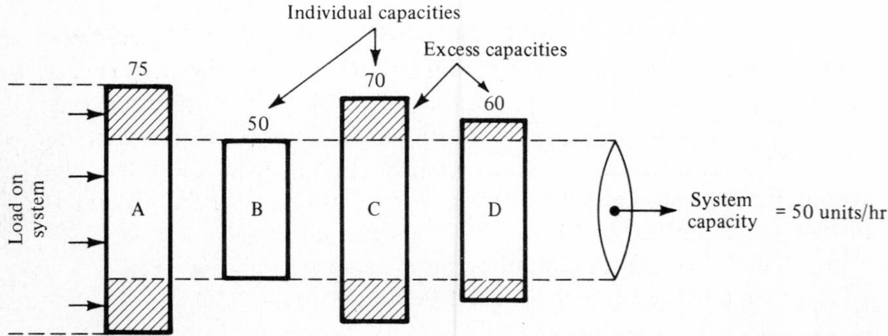

(*a*) Effective capacity of the system: System is inherently limited by individual capacity of B. Therefore, system capacity = 50 units/hr

(*b*) Potential use factor for worker C:

$$\text{PUF} = \frac{\text{system capacity}}{\text{individual capacity}} = \frac{50}{70} = 71\%$$

(*c*) Expected output of the system: Each worker's efficiency relative to the system capacity is given. If the workers have an "informal understanding" that the effective capacity of the system should not exceed 50 units per hour and they operate at 70 percent and 90 percent rates relative to this system capacity, the expected output from the system would be that output processed by the most limiting unit in the system:

$$\text{For A} = (50)(0.70) = 35 \text{ units/hr}$$

$$\text{B} = (50)(0.90) = 45 \text{ units/hr}$$

$$\text{C} = (50)(0.90) = 45 \text{ units/hr}$$

$$\text{D} = (50)(0.70) = 35 \text{ units/hr}$$

Limiting outputs are A and D at 35 units/hr

Many firms, sometimes unknowingly, operate with an informal quota system such as in this example, which results in compounding any existing inefficiency. If, in this entirely human subsystem, each worker's efficiency were judged relative to his or her own individual capability, the expected output would be raised to 42 units per hour, as limited by worker D:

$$\text{A} = (75 \text{ units/hr})(0.70) = 52.5 \text{ units/hr}$$

$$\text{B} = (50 \text{ units/hr})(0.90) = 45.0 \text{ units/hr}$$

$$\text{C} = (70 \text{ units/hr})(0.90) = 63.0 \text{ units/hr}$$

$$\text{D} = (60 \text{ units/hr})(0.70) = 42.0 \text{ units/hr}$$

3 Rocket Propulsion Company is considering expansion of a solid-propellant manufacturing process by adding more one-ton-capacity curing furnaces. Each batch (one ton) of propellant must undergo 30 minutes of furnace time, including load and unload operations. However, the furnace potential use factor is only 80 percent due to flow restrictions in other parts of the system. Required output for the new layout is to be 16 tons per shift (8 hr). Plant (system) efficiency is estimated at 50 percent of system capacity.

(*a*) Determine the number of furnaces required.

(*b*) Estimate the percent of time the furnaces will be idle.

Solution

(*a*) $$\text{Required system capacity} = \frac{\text{actual output}}{\text{SE}} = \frac{16 \text{ tons/day}}{0.50} = 32 \text{ tons/day}$$

$$= \frac{32 \text{ tons/day}}{8 \text{ hr/day}} = 4 \text{ tons/hr}$$

$$\text{Individual furnace capacity} = \frac{1 \text{ ton}}{0.5 \text{ hr}} = 2 \text{ ton/hr-furnace}$$

$$\begin{aligned}\text{Furnace subsystem capacity} &= \text{(individual unit capacity)(PUF)} \\ &= (2 \text{ ton/hr})(0.80) = 1.6 \text{ tons/hr-furnace}\end{aligned}$$

$$\begin{aligned}\text{Actual furnace output} &= \text{(furnace subsystem capacity)} \\ &\quad \cdot \text{(furnace efficiency)} \\ &= (1.6 \text{ tons/hr-furnace})(\text{assume } 100\%) \\ &= 1.6 \text{ tons/hr-furnace}\end{aligned}$$

$$\begin{aligned}\text{Number of furnaces required} &= \frac{\text{required system capacity}}{\text{actual output/furnace}} \\ &= \frac{4 \text{ tons/hr}}{1.6 \text{ tons/hr-furnace}} \\ &= 2.5 \text{ furnaces (say 3)}\end{aligned}$$

Alternatively, another way of formulating the problem is:

$$\text{Output required/day} = 16 \text{ tons}$$

$$\text{Time available} = (8 \text{ hr})(80\%) = 6.4 \text{ hr}$$

$$\text{Output required/hr} = \frac{16 \text{ tons}}{6.4 \text{ hr}} = 2.5 \text{ tons/hr}$$

For each furnace:

$$\text{Time required/ton} = 0.5 \text{ hr}$$

$$\text{Output/hr @ } 50\% \text{ efficiency} = \frac{(50\%)}{0.5 \text{ hr/ton}} = 1 \text{ ton/hr}$$

$$\begin{aligned}\text{Number of furnaces required} &= \frac{\text{output required/hr}}{\text{output/hr-furnace}} \\ &= \frac{2.5 \text{ tons/hr}}{1 \text{ ton/hr-furnace}} \\ &= 2.5 \text{ furnaces (say 3)}\end{aligned}$$

(*b*) Percent idle time:

$$\begin{aligned}\text{Total hr available/shift} &= 3 \text{ furnaces @ } 8 \text{ hr} = 24 \text{ furnace hr}\\ \text{Total hr actual use/shift} &= 16 \text{ tons } (0.5 \text{ hr/tons}) = \underline{\ 8 \text{ furnace hr}}\\ &\qquad\qquad \text{Idle time} = 16 \text{ furnace hr}\end{aligned}$$

$$\% \text{ time} = \frac{16 \text{ hr idle}}{24 \text{ hr total}} = 67\% \text{ idle time}$$

PLANT LOCATION

4 A manufacturer of farm equipment is considering three locations (A, B, and C) for a new plant. Cost studies show that fixed costs per year at the sites are \$240,000, \$270,000, and \$252,000, respectively, whereas variable costs are \$100 per unit, \$90 per unit, and \$95 per unit, respectively. If the plant is designed to have an effective system capacity of 2,500 units per year and is expected to operate at 80 percent efficiency, what is the most economic location, based on the actual output?

Solution

$$\begin{aligned}\text{Actual output} &= (\text{system efficiency})(\text{system capacity})\\ &= (0.80)(2{,}500) = 2{,}000 \text{ units/yr}\end{aligned}$$

$$\begin{aligned}\text{Cost/site} &= \text{FC} + \text{VC}(V)\\ \text{A} &= \$240{,}000 + \$100(2{,}000) = \$440{,}000\\ \text{B} &= 270{,}000 + 90(2{,}000) = 450{,}000\\ \text{C} &= 252{,}000 + 95(2{,}000) = 442{,}000\end{aligned}$$

Most economical location is A. Note that the actual output is specified and a locational break-even chart is not necessary for the solution.

5 A firm is considering four alternative locations for a new plant. They have attempted to study all costs at the various locations and find that the production costs of the following items vary from one location to another. The firm will finance the new plant from bonds bearing 10 percent interest.

	A	*B*	*C*	*D*
Labor (per unit)	0.75	1.10	0.80	1.00
Plant construction cost (million \$)	4.6	3.9	4.0	4.2
Materials and equipment* (per unit)	0.43	0.60	0.40	0.55
Electricity (per yr)	30,000	26,000	30,000	28,000
Water (per yr)	7,000	6,000	7,000	7,000
Transportation (per unit)	0.02	0.10	0.10	0.05
Taxes (per yr)	33,000	28,000	63,000	35,000

* This cost includes a projected depreciation expense, but no interest cost.

Determine the most suitable location (economically) for output volumes in the range of 50,000 to 130,000 units per year.

Solution

Costs	*A*	*B*	*C*	*D*
Fixed costs (per yr)				
10% of investment	$460,000	$390,000	$400,000	$420,000
Electricity	30,000	26,000	30,000	28,000
Water	7,000	6,000	7,000	7,000
Taxes	33,000	28,000	63,000	35,000
Total	$530,000	$450,000	$500,000	$490,000
Variable costs (per unit)				
Labor	$0.75	$1.10	$0.80	$1.00
Materials and equipment	0.43	0.60	0.40	0.55
Transportation	0.02	0.10	0.10	0.05
Total	$1.20	$1.80	$1.30	$1.60
Total costs	$530,000+ $1.20/unit	$450,000+ $1.80/unit	$500,000+ $1.30/unit	$490,000+ $1.60/unit

Points for plant location break-even analysis chart are as follows. At zero units of output, used fixed-cost values. At 100,000 units of output,

$$\begin{aligned}
A &= \$530{,}000 + 100{,}000(\$1.20) = \$650{,}000 \\
B &= \$450{,}000 + 100{,}000(\$1.80) = \$630{,}000 \\
C &= \$500{,}000 + 100{,}000(\$1.30) = \$630{,}000 \\
D &= \$490{,}000 + 100{,}000(\$1.60) = \$650{,}000
\end{aligned}$$

The graph (see page 79) of these linear functions shows that for minimum cost, use site B for volume 50,000 to 100,000 units; use site C for volume 100,000 to 130,000 units.

(*a*) The market research department of this firm has developed the following estimate of the market volume for the product per year over the next 10 years.

Volume (*X*)	**Probability** (*X*)
50,000 units	0.40
75,000 units	0.20
100,000 units	0.10
200,000 units	0.30

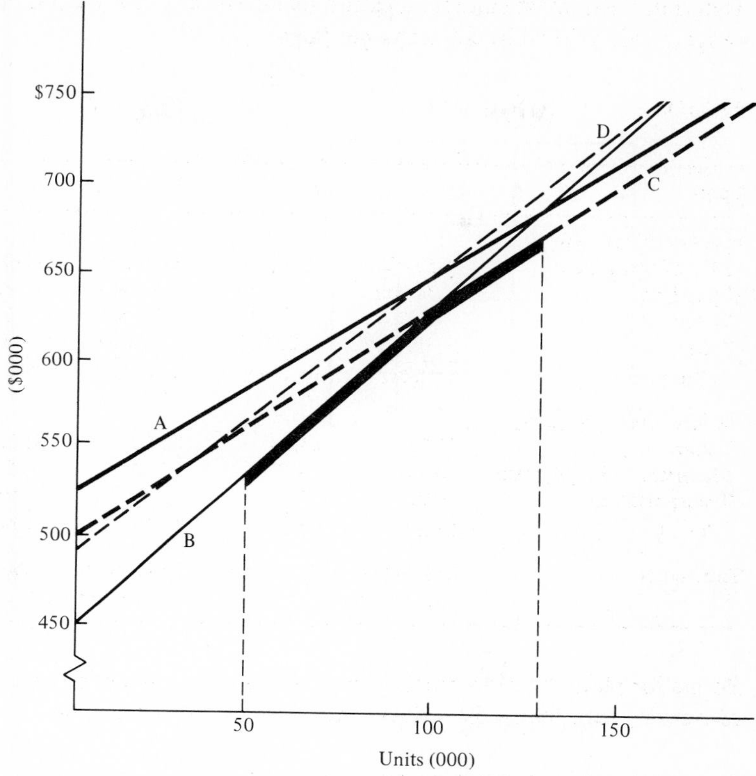

Using an expected value criterion based upon the above volume estimates, what is the most suitable location?

Solution

(*a*)

Volume (X)	Probability $P(X)$	Expected value $XP(X)$
50,000	0.40	20,000
75,000	0.20	15,000
100,000	0.10	10,000
200,000	0.30	60,000
	Expected demand	105,000

Select site C.

6 A firm producing tires is considering locating two warehouses capable of absorbing 80 units (total) per day from the firm's plants. If unit transportation costs are as shown ($), what is the total transportation cost for an optimal allocation? Use the northwest corner and stepping-stone methods.

Warehouse site

Production plant	**SF**	**SL**	
1	10	12	40
2	12	15	40
	30	50	80

Solution

(*a*) Beginning in the NW corner we assign 30 units to 1 SF and the remaining 10 to 1 SL. This exhausts our supply from Plant 1.

(*b*) Going to row 2 we assign all 40 units to 2 SL. This completes the initial allocation. All row and column totals agree and we have $R + C - 1 = 2 + 2 - 1 = 3$ entries.

(*c*) Evaluate cell 2 SF:

Path 2 SL–2 SF–1 SF–1 SL
Cost $-15 + 12 - 10 + 12 = -1$ ($1 cost decrease)

∴ change 30 units.

(*d*) No other changes can be made to improve the allocation. Cost of the optimal solution is:

40 units	1 to SL @ $12 =	$480
30 units	2 to SF @ 12 =	360
10 units	2 to SL @ 15 =	150
	Total cost =	$990

Warehouse site

Production plant	**SF**	**SL**	
1	10 (30)	12 (10) 40	40
2	12 30	15 (40) 10	40
	30	50	80

7 Plastic Cabinet Supply Company (PCS) is a wholly owned subsidiary of an international conglomerate firm which has major interests in the housing industry. PCS has cabinet plants located in Boston, Seattle, and Miami. The plants produce prefabricated housing components which are delivered to other company assembly plants in Chicago, Denver, and Nashville. Demand has grown to the point where PCS can justify construction of another plant. Their immediate problem is determining a location that will minimize production and transportation costs to the existing assembly plants. In order to be close to raw material supply and to service other potential markets, the alternative plant locations have been narrowed down to Omaha and Phoenix. Cost, demand, and production data on the various alternatives are as shown.

PCS production data			**Assemblies demanded**	
Plants	**Units per month**	**Cost per unit**	**Plant**	**Units per month**
Boston (B)	2,000	$7.00	Chicago (C)	6,000
Seattle (S)	6,000	7.08	Denver (D)	5,000
Miami (M)	5,000	6.90	Nashville (N)	6,000
Omaha (O)	4,000	6.90 (anticipated)		
Phoenix (P)	4,000	6.20 (anticipated)		

Transportation cost, $/unit

	from				
To	**Boston**	**Seattle**	**Miami**	**Omaha**	**Phoenix**
Chicago	$5.00	$7.00	$5.00	$4.00	$6.00
Denver	6.00	4.00	7.00	3.00	4.50
Nashville	5.50	7.00	3.00	5.00	5.00

Which of the two plant locations (Omaha or Phoenix) is more desirable from an economic standpoint?

Solution

It makes no difference whether supply is on the horizontal or vertical axis. The major concern is that row and column totals agree. Since the data are given with demand on the horizontal axis, let us use it that way.

Solution (using Omaha)

Allocating via the northwest corner method and making adjustments by the stepping-stone method we arrive at the following matrix (omitting any zero adjustments).

	Boston	Seattle	Miami	Omaha	Demand
Chicago	\$5.00 2,000	\$7.00	\$5.00	\$4.00 4,000	6,000
Denver	6.00	4.00 5,000	7.00	3.00	5,000
Nashville	5.50	7.00 1,000	3.00 5,000	5.00	6,000
Supply	2,000	6,000	5,000	4,000	17,000

Transportation cost calculation:

2,000 × 5.00 = \$10,000
4,000 × 4.00 = 16,000
5,000 × 4.00 = 20,000
1,000 × 7.00 = 7,000
5,000 × 3.00 = 15,000
\$68,000 ⟶ \$68,000

Add production costs (Omaha): \$6.90/unit × 4,000 = 27,600
\$95,600

Solution (using Phoenix)

	Boston	Seattle	Miami	Phoenix	Demand
Chicago	\$5.00 2,000	\$7.00 1,000	\$5.00	\$6.00 3,000	6,000
Denver	6.00	4.00 5,000	7.00	4.50	5,000
Nashville	5.50	7.00	3.00 5,000	5.00 1,000	6,000
Supply	2,000	6,000	5,000	4,000	17,000

Cost calculation:

2,000 × 5.00 = \$10,000
1,000 × 7.00 = 7,000
3,000 × 6.00 = 18,000
5,000 × 4.00 = 20,000
5,000 × 3.00 = 15,000
1,000 × 5.00 = 5,000
\$75,000 ⟶ \$75,000

Add production costs (Phoenix): \$6.20/unit × 4,000 = 24,800
\$99,800

Conclusion: Omaha location is least-cost situation per month.

*8 Use the data from Example 2-5, except make the initial allocation via the minimum cost method and the final solution via the stepping-stone method.

Solution

The minimum cost method is simple: the lowest cost cell is located and as many units as possible are assigned to it. The next-lowest cost cell is then located and again filled up. This continues until all supply and demand conditions (that is, rim conditions) are satisfied. In the case of two boxes having equally low costs, the best choice is to fill the one which can absorb the most units. Then fill the other if possible.

Distribution plants (demand)

Production plants (supply)	**(1) Seattle**	**(2) Portland**	**(3) San Francisco**	
A	[10]	[14]	[8] (20)	20
B	[12] 0	[10] (30)	[12]	30
C	[8] (40)	[12]	[10] 0	40
	40	30	20	

(*a*) Cells C1 and A3 both have equally low costs of \$8/unit. First put 40 units into C1 to meet its supply and demand conditions of 40 and 40. Then fill A3 with 20 units to meet its requirements of 20 and 20.

(*b*) The next-lowest transportation cost is \$10/unit which occurs in cells A1, B2, and C3. However, the supply conditions of rows A and C have already been satisfied (exhausted), so only B2 need be considered. Put 30 units in B2 to meet its rim conditions.

(*c*) The initial solution appears to be correct, but the normal checks of row and column totals must be made.

Row A	$20 = 20$, OK	Col. 1	$40 = 40$, OK
Row B	$30 = 30$, OK	Col. 2	$30 = 30$, OK
Row C	$40 = 40$, OK	Col. 3	$20 = 20$, OK

(*d*) The initial solution is now complete. (It is, however, degenerate in that (no. rows) + (no. cols.) $-$ 1 $\neq$ (no. of entries); that is, $3 + 3 - 1 \neq 3$. Zeros may be assigned to two empty cells, say B1 and C3, so that the constraint is satisfied.)

Note that the initial solution happened to be the same as the final optimal solution as arrived at in Example 2-5 via the stepping-stone method. This will not necessarily always be the case, although the initial solution is likely to be better than the initial solution as arrived at via the northwest corner method. Since the optimal solution has already been achieved, no additional stepping-stone method calculations will be carried out.

***9** Paul's Hamburgers, Incorporated, plans to build four new plants, two in the 11 Western states, one in the 6 Middle Atlantic states, and one in Maine, Hawaii, or Alaska. If they wish to analyze each possible combination of locations, how many combinations would they have to study?

Solution

$$\text{Number combinations} = C_x^n = \frac{n!}{x!\,(n-x)!} \qquad (2\text{-}3)$$

From 11 Western states choose two. Therefore, C_2^{11}. And for each of those combinations, there are C_1^6 ways to choose the next. And C_1^3 ways to choose the last.

$$\therefore C_x^n = \binom{11}{2}\binom{6}{1}\binom{3}{1} = \left(\frac{11!}{2!\,9!}\right)\left(\frac{6!}{1!\,5!}\right)\left(\frac{3!}{1!\,2!}\right) = 990$$

PLANT LAYOUT

***10** Shown at left in the accompanying diagram is an initial solution in a plant layout operations sequence analysis. The numbers shown on the lines connecting work centers (circles) represent the number of loads transported between centers (in either direction). Develop any improvements in the layout that you can, and show your improved layout by lettering the work centers. Note that work centers F and G are fixed.

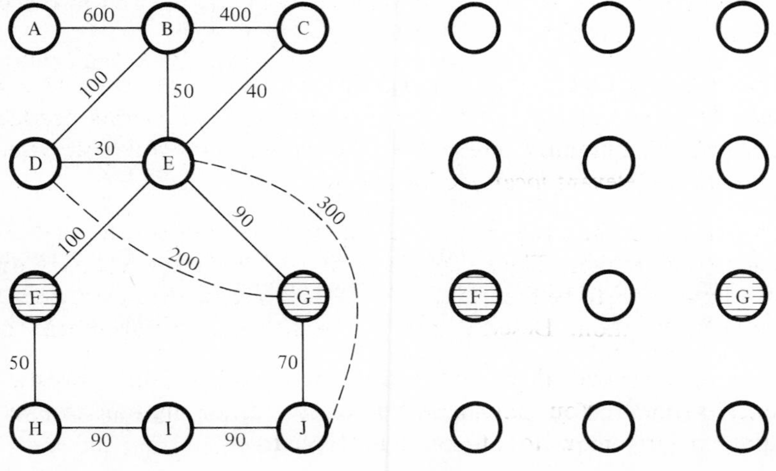

Solution

(*a*) Regard departments as adjacent if they are next to each other or diagonally across from each other.

(*b*) Minimize the nonadjacent (distance) × (load). This layout has two nonadjacent loads, each going to two columns (or rows) beyond the starting point:

$$2(200) + 2(300) = 1{,}000 \text{ unit distances}$$

(*c*) Improve the layout by visual inspection and calculation check. Some solutions are shown below. (There are additional layouts that are equally optimal.) Note that all solutions given are equally satisfactory and cannot be improved upon because no loads are transported to nonadjacent work centers.

A	B	C	A	B		C	B	A		A	
	E	D	C	E	D		E	D	C	B	D
F	J	G	F	J	G	F	J	G	F	E	G
	H	I	H	I		H	I		H	I	J

QUESTIONS

2-1 Should a firm always design a plant with sufficient capacity to handle future demand? Explain why or why not.

2-2 How might an organization approach the problem of designating capacity when its future demand level is very uncertain?

2-3 Explain the difference between (*a*) individual unit capacity, (*b*) system capacity, and (*c*) output. How are the concepts of potential use factor and efficiency related to these terms?

2-4 Four different organizations are considering your home town as a potential plant location: (*a*) a medical research center, (*b*) a soft drink producer, (*c*) a steel mill, (*d*) a uranium mining firm. Select one of the four and systematically evaluate the relevant locational factors.

2-5 You are given the assignment of developing an economic evaluation of four potential plant sites. The analysis is to be applicable to a relatively wide range of volume. It is to be presented to the board of directors in summary form for their consideration. Describe how you would develop and present the data.

2-6 How do international location considerations differ from domestic location considerations? You may answer by briefly identifying four or five problem areas that are unique to international locations.

2-7 An equipment supplier has collected the following data on possible plant locations. Costs are in $/yr.

	Site A	Site B	Site C
Rent and utilities	$ 10,000	$ 12,000	$ 15,000
Taxes	2,000	1,500	1,000
Labor	95,000	80,000	90,000
Materials	130,000	132,000	127,000
	$237,000	$225,500	$233,000
Community services	Good	Poor	Average
Community attitude	Indifferent	Indifferent	Favorable

If you were responsible for making the decision on the basis of the information given, which site would you select, and why?

2-8 In what way is distribution linear programming useful as a means of minimizing transportation costs? Answer the question by describing what data are required, what constraints exist, and the concept underlying revisions in an original demand-supply matrix.

2-9 Distinguish between a product and a process layout.

2-10 To what extent do analytical methods solve the problem of determining optimal plant layouts?

2-11 What are the basic guidelines to good materials handling practice?

2-12 An automobile manufacturer has always purchased its coolant system fluid from DuPont Chemical Company. However, a recent model change has vacated a large portion of one factory and a member of the board of directors has suggested the firm begin producing their own antifreeze coolant in the vacated area right away. Your assignment is to draft a brief recommendation that will convince the board to wait for a detailed study before making a decision on this matter. (The board will not read any recommendations greater than one page in length.)

PROBLEMS

1 A transistor manufacturer uses 3 type XSR7T3 transistors in each radio produced. Demand estimates for the number of radios that could be sold next year are:

Demand	Probability
10,000	0.10
11,000	0.70
12,000	0.20

Assuming the firm decides to produce on an expected-value basis, how many transistors should it plan to make for next year's radio sales?

2 A research foundation is considering expanding its facilities in order to bid on a government contract. The new facilities would cost \$700,000. If the foundation expands and receives the contract, it will realize a \$500,000 net gain. In the event that it does not get the contract, it could recover about \$400,000 of the \$700,000 cost by doing some subcontracting work and using some of the equipment elsewhere. If the foundation does not decide to expand, it definitely will not be awarded the contract, but it is guaranteed subcontract work (from other bidders) that will net a \$150,000 gain. The director of operations feels there is a 60 percent chance the foundation would obtain the contracts if it went ahead and expanded the facilities first.

(*a*) What is the best course of action to take on an economic expected-value basis?

(*b*) Is "expected value" an adequate basis for decision?

3 The individual component capacities (in units/day) for a line layout which consists of five activities are as shown in the accompanying diagram.

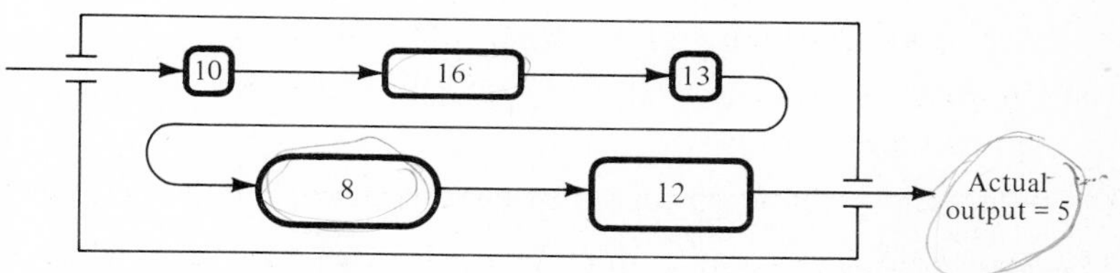

(*a*) What is the system capacity?

(*b*) What is the potential use factor for the second component in the system?

(*c*) What is the efficiency of the system?

4 An automatic drive-in teller at American National Bank has the capacity of handling 2,000 entries per regular banking day (according to the firm which sold it to the bank). However, because of limitations imposed by automobile access, the potential use factor (percent of time available) is 60 percent. It is actually being used for about 800 entries per day. What is the system efficiency?

5 An existing factory has the equipment arrangement shown in the accompanying diagram. Manufactured fittings must be processed through each of three operations in sequence, but it does not matter which lathe or mill is used. Each lathe

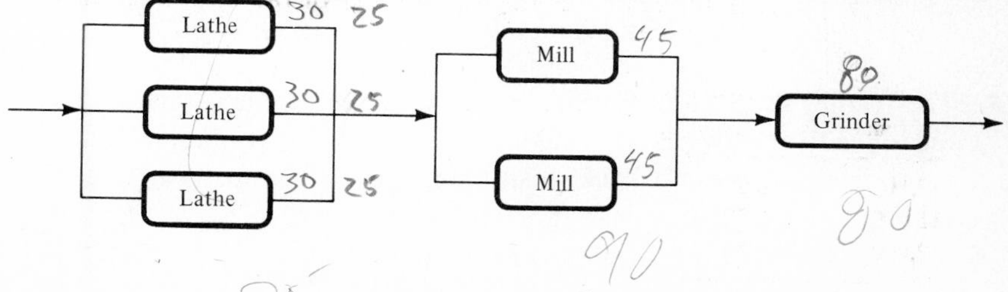

is capable of handling 30 fittings per hour, each mill can handle 45 per hour, and the grinder can handle 80 per hour. A different operator runs each group of machines and, due to the workload, the lathe operator can handle an output of 25 fittings per hour from each lathe when they are all operating. The mill and grinder operators can produce 45 per hour (per mill) and 80 per hour (per grinder), respectively. During the past 40-hr week, actual production from this department was 1,000 fittings. Find the

(*a*) system capacity
(*b*) potential use factor for the lathes (machines, not the operators)
(*c*) system efficiency

6 A new plant is being equipped to produce 720 electronic components in an 8-hr day shift of work. Each component requires 25 min testing time in an automatic testing machine. Included in this time are 3 min for loading and unloading and another 2 min for adjustment. If the plant (system) efficiency is expected to be 90 percent, how many testing machines should be installed to fully handle the load? (Assume 100 percent use factor.)

7 Tractorboy Products Company is evaluating three different cities for a new plant designed to produce garden tractors which will sell for $145 each. The economic portion of a plant location study shows the following cost and market data.

Cost data	City A	City B	City C
Fixed costs/yr	$300,000	$200,000	$75,000
Variable costs/unit	30	45	70

Market data

Volume (X)	6,500	5,500	4,500
Probability $P(X)$	0.60	0.30	0.10

(*a*) On the basis of maximizing an economic expected value, graph the plant location cost-curve using appropriate scales.
(*b*) On the basis of your graph, which city should be selected on the basis of the given volume estimate?
(*c*) What is the break-even volume for the city selected?

8 The Hadley Steel Tank Company has conducted a cost study of three potential locations for a new plant. They plan to construct the plant, sell it to an investment firm, and lease it back. Estimated costs are shown in the accompanying table.

	Boise	Denver	Sacramento
Plant rental (per yr)	$90,000	$100,000	$160,000
Tank materials (per unit)	7,900	7,500	7,000
Utilities (annual cost)	24,000	28,000	30,000
Labor cost per tank	1,700	2,200	2,400
Taxes (per yr)	12,000	12,000	15,000
Transportation (per unit)	1,400	800	600

Management's best-researched estimate of the market is:

No. of tanks/yr	Percent chance
500	0.20
800	0.50
1,000	0.30

Based on the number of tanks expected to be sold, which plant location is best from an economic standpoint? (Graphing the solution is optional.)

9 A large copper producer has refineries in Magna, Utah; Yuma, Arizona; and Grants, New Mexico, all of which receive ore from mines identified as MX-1, MX-2, MX-3, and MX-4, located in the Four Corners Area. The mine supply and mill capacities (units/day) and shipping cost ($/unit load) data are shown.

	Refineries			
	Magna	Yuma	Grants	Supply
MX-1	3	5	5	400
MX-2	5	7	8	500
MX-3	2	9	5	200
MX-4	10	7	3	700
Capacity	500	500	800	1,800 units/day

The vice president of operations has requested that you analyze the transportation costs and determine an optimal distribution.

10 Suppose that in problem 9, MX-4 is closed because of low-grade ore and MX-5, which has the same capacity (700 units/day), is opened. It has shipping costs to Magna, Yuma, and Grants of $4, $8, and $12, respectively. What is the optimal distribution now?

11 Suppose that in problem 9 the variable production costs ($/unit load) for mines MX-1, MX-2, MX-3, and MX-4 are $2, $1, $3, and $1, respectively. What is the optimal distribution, taking production as well as distribution costs into account?

12 A firm producing automobile components has the following production capacities (units/month), assembly requirements, and transportation costs ($).

	Assembly location			
Prod. plant	**Memphis**	**Newark**	**San Jose**	**Capacity**
Atlanta	5	7	10	160
Boston	11	6	12	240
Chicago	7	8	10	200
*				200
Requirement	220	280	300	800

The asterisk in the box under "Chicago" indicates a new plant with 200 units/month capacity to be located in either Dallas or Denver.

	Fixed costs/mo	Variable costs/unit	Cost to ship to Memphis	Newark	San Jose
Denver	$6,000	$5.70	6	8	6
Dallas	5,100	5.50	5	9	11

From a cost standpoint, which is the better site for the fourth plant, Denver or Dallas? Structure your answer in such a way as to show the total relevant costs under each alternative.

***13** Dayfresh Bakery has plants at A, B, and C which have capacities of 20, 30, and 40 truckloads of bread per day, respectively. Production costs are the same at each plant but the bread must be trucked to distribution centers at X, Y, and Z and trucking costs per load (dollars) vary as shown in the table. The distribution centers currently absorb most of the capacity with X, Y, and Z taking 30, 30, and 20 loads per day, respectively. Use the distribution method of linear programming.

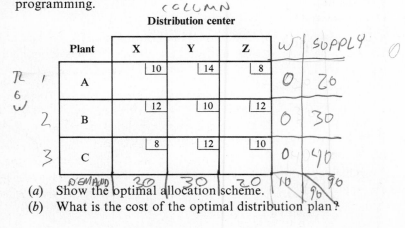

	Distribution center		
Plant	**X**	**Y**	**Z**
A	10	14	8
B	12	10	12
C	8	12	10

(*a*) Show the optimal allocation scheme.
(*b*) What is the cost of the optimal distribution plan?

***14** A luggage manufacturer using a CRAFT layout program has 28 departments and wants to check materials handling costs after each switch of three departments. How many combinations of layouts can be obtained from 28 departments by changing three at a time? *Hint:* The equation for combinations of n things taken x at a time is

$$C_x^n = \frac{n!}{x!\,(n-x)!}$$

***15** In the operations sequence chart shown, circles represent work centers and numbers represent the units of load transported. Develop improvements in the layout and show the best one you can.

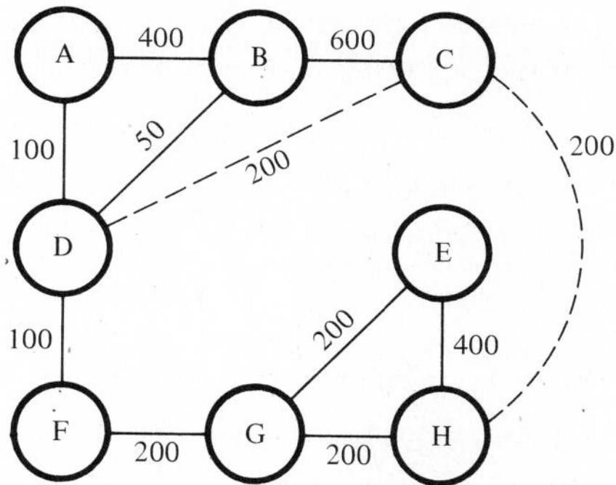

16 Lakeview Lumber Company uses Hysten fork-lift trucks to move lumber from the mill to a storage warehouse 0.3 km away. The lift trucks can move three loaded pallets per trip and travel at an average speed of 6 km/hr (allowing for loadings, delays, and travel loaded and unloaded). If 420 pallet loads must be moved during each 8-hr shift, how many lift trucks are required to handle this material?

CASE: ROCKY FLATS POWER COMPANY

Rocky Flats Power Company (RFP) is an investor-owned electric utility which has exclusive rights to serve a wide area including parts of Wyoming, Nevada, Idaho, and eastern Oregon. Along with these monopolistic "rights" comes the legal "obligation" to provide adequate power to meet the demand of customers in the area. The rates the company can charge, and certain other operational activities, are regulated by the Federal Power Commission (FPC). The firm also has coal properties in Montana and land holdings in Canada. RFP's demand pattern has evidenced a fairly consistent growth pattern in the past, as shown in the accompanying figure. Demand is now adequately being met by their seven generating plants, three of which are hydro (H),

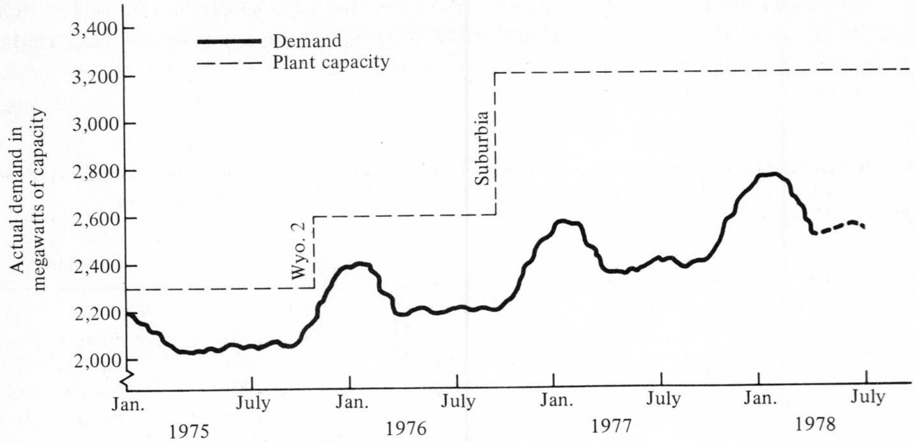

three coal-fired (C), and one nuclear (N). The plant design capacities in megawatts (MW) are as follows:

1	Wyo 1 (H)	100 MW	**5**	Rocky 2 (N)	1,000 MW
2	Rocky Flats 1 (H)	200 MW	**6**	Wyo 2 (C)	300 MW
3	Dexter (C)	800 MW	**7**	Suburbia (C)	600 MW
4	Canyon Point (H)	200 MW	**8**	Falls River (H)	—

The company's eighth plant (Falls River) will be completed next year (1979) and will add another 600 MW of capacity to the system. Company policy calls for overhauls and servicing of individual units to be done regularly on a year-round basis by the shutting down of portions of one or two units at a time. This reduces system capacity to about 90 percent of the design capacity. But while in normal operation, each individual unit is fully used and delivers its full rated capacity.

During last month's board meeting, Ken Curtis, manager of long-range planning, reiterated an earlier plea for approval to proceed with planning and engineering for another "probably coal-fired" plant immediately, emphatically pointing out that it would take about five years to get such a plant "on line." Keith Jackson, one of the newer members of the board, again got the action delayed by making a convincing speech noting that (1) with Falls River, RFP's capacity "will be more than adequate for years to come," (2) coal was a pollutant and he was not sure it was the most economical choice of fuel anyway, and (3) he had not seen any evidence of a "really thorough" location study for the new plant. "How about the geothermal potential in eastern Oregon, and what about all that potential hydro power on our lands in Canada?" he questioned.

In preparation for this month's meeting, Mr. Curtis called his assistant, James Bell, into his office and handed him the bulging file on the proposed Plant 9. "See if you can come up with something that will get Jackson off our backs, will you Jim?" he asked. "I think all we've got to do is convince him we know what we're doing. But if we don't convince him soon, I'm afraid RFP is going to be short of kilowatts in five years and you and I are going to be out of a job."

As Jim read through the stack of papers in the file, he came across data which had been collected from a wide range of sources, including some correspondence from Mr. Jackson.

SHEET 1

ROUGH ESTIMATE OF COSTS AT GENERATION SITE FOR 500-MW PLANT (ALL $ IN 000)

	Hydro	Coal	Nuclear	Geothermal
Fixed cost/yr	4,000	4,000	5,000	?
Variable cost/MW-yr	32	54	60	36 est.
Feasibility	Best sites in service area are used up	Good supplies in Montana	Need good supply of cooling water. Idaho?	R&D work needed; limited capacity anyway
Estimated construction time (years)	4	5	7	10

SHEET 2

POWER DISTRIBUTION COST COEFFICIENTS FOR EXISTING PLANTS (AND FALLS RIVER)

Generating plant location	For power delivered to geographical area				Plant capacity
	Wyoming	Nevada	Idaho	Oregon	
Wyo. 1	20	80	40	80	100
Rocky Flats	50	30	10	40	200
Dexter	60	40	20	30	800
Canyon Point	90	10	60	80	200
Rocky 2	20	70	40	90	1000
Wyo. 2	30	60	50	100	300
Suburbia	80	50	30	10	600
Falls River	100	20	20	40	600
Plant 9					(?) 500
MW capacity demanded by geographical area (as of Jan.)	500	700	1200	400	

ESTIMATED POWER DISTRIBUTION COST COEFFICIENTS FOR POTENTIAL SITES FOR NEW 500-MW COAL-FIRED PLANT

Generating plant location	For power delivered to geographical area			
	Wyoming	Nevada	Idaho	Oregon
Paris, Idaho	30	40	10	50
Coalton, Mont.	20	70	40	80
Casper, Wyo.	10	60	50	90

SHEET 3

Things to check:

1 Check with EPA on impact study requirements for an Idaho nuclear site.

2 Canada? How about the FPC and border problems?

3 Status of R&D on geothermal. What really are the costs? Feasible?

4 Phone Tom Burke on overhaul scheduling. Is it iron-clad or can we adjust?

5 Have Watson look into Amer. Petrol. Inst. reports on oil from Montana coal deposits.

6 Get updated nuclear fuel cost estimate from Kale at Westinghouse.

7

SHEET 4

February 7

TO: K. Curtis, Planning

FROM: K. Jackson, Assistant to the President

SUBJECT: Your memo to President William Brunson concerning plans for plant 9

Re your memo 1/27. Bill asked me to react and I have been doing some checking on my own. Our average demand over the past two years has been only 2,440 MW. With the Falls River plant next year we will have 3,800 MW of capacity, an overcapacity of 55%. I'm surprised that one of your staff analysts hasn't got enough facts together to show that the "urgency" you referred to is probably more fictitious than real.

Second, when the time does come for building another plant I think we're all going to have to realize that times have changed. With the environmental pressures on air pollution and all, it seems to me we ought to stick to hydro power or get into geothermal. I've read where it will be the power source of the future and I understand we already have some natural steam properties in Eastern Oregon. With that, and our more than ample water supplies in Canada, I see no need to plan for more coal fired plants in the future. Of course, you're in a better position to analyze the situation than I am. But I do feel geothermal would be environmentally perfect for us and we'd get a lot of favorable publicity on it for nothing. That's a benefit we can't afford to overlook.

After spending four hours going through the file, Jim went back into Mr. Curtis's office. "I'm afraid I'm more confused now than ever," he admitted. "What is it you want me to do—pick a site?"

"Oh no!" replied Mr. Curtis. "Just outline some plan of attack on this problem to make sure we cover all the bases when we do grind out the detailed analysis later. I think coal is the right way to go, but I don't want to get shot down by Keith Jackson again in the next board meeting. I think that if we convince him we're taking a systematic approach to this location thing he'll stop being such a roadblock."

As an aid to analysis of this case, consider the following questions:

1 State the nature of the decision problem and outline a brief but systematic plan of analysis. (Simply indicate what steps should be taken but *do not actually perform the accompanying calculations.*)

2 In what way might the data on sheets 1 and 2 be used in the analysis?

3 What is the significance of the various items on the "things to check" note in the file?

4 Mr. Jackson's calculations revealed that RFP will have "an overcapacity of 55 percent" next year. How should Mr. Curtis respond to Mr. Jackson's observation that the urgency is "more fictitious than real"?

5 Why did Mr. Curtis think coal was the "right way to go"? [That is, (1) is additional capacity really needed, and (2) if it were needed why should the choice be a coal-fired plant?]

BIBLIOGRAPHY

[1] ABRAMOWITZ, I.: *Production Management*, Ronald Press, New York, 1967.

[2] BELLI, R. DAVID: "Plant and Equipment Expenditures by Foreign Affiliates of U.S. Corporations, 1971–73," *Survey of Current Business*, September 1972.

[3] BUFFA, ELWOOD S.: *Operations Management*, John Wiley & Sons, New York, 1976.

[4] DESIMONE, DANIEL V.: "Moving to Metric Makes Dollars and Sense," *Harvard Business Review*, January-February 1972.

[5] GARRETT, LEONARD J., and MILTON SILVER: *Production Management Analysis*, 2d ed., Harcourt, Brace & World, New York, 1973.

[6] GEORGE, CLAUDE S.: *Management in Industry.*

[7] GOOD, IRVING JOHN: *The Estimation of Probabilities—An Essay on Modern Bayesian Methods.*

[8] MASON, R. HAL: "The Multinational Firm and Cost of Technology to Developing Countries," *California Management Review*, Summer 1973.

[9] MAYER, RAYMOND R.: *Production Management*, 3d ed., McGraw-Hill, New York, 1975.

[10] MOORE, FRANKLIN G.: *Production Management*, 6th ed., Richard D. Irwin, Homewood, Illinois, 1973.

[11] RADFORD, J. D., and D. G. RICHARDSON: *The Management of Production*, Macmillan, London, 1968.

[12] ROSS, M. (ed.): *Operational Research, 1972*, North-Holland, Amsterdam; see particularly N. N. Moiseev, "Operations Research in the USSR."

[13] SCHERER, F. M.: "The Determinants of Industrial Plant Size in Six Nations," *Review of Economics and Statistics*, May 1973.

[14] *Survey of Current Business*, "The Business Situation," November 1973.

[15] WELLS, LOUIS T., JR.: "Don't Overautomate Your Foreign Plant," *Harvard Business Review*, January-February 1974.

[16] WINKLER, ROBERT L.: "The Quantification of Judgment: Some Methodological Suggestions," *Journal of the American Statistical Association*, vol. 62, 1967, pp. 1105–1120.

[17] WOODWARD, JOHN T.: "Capital Expenditure Programs and Sales Expectations for 1975," *Survey of Current Business*, March 1975.

CHAPTER

3

Human Resource Inputs

The labor inputs to a production operation consist of an extremely complex combination of physical and intellectual capabilities—human beings! Humans have an intrinsic value that no equipment can match and they have a diversity of skills, emotions, and levels of performance that cannot be found in any machine. As a group, workers largely control the productivity of an organization. As individuals, they are often its most valuable asset. In managing the work force, operations managers face one of their most responsible and challenging tasks.

Due to the widescale impact of the work force upon an organization, it is difficult to classify labor inputs into simple yet comprehensive categories. Nevertheless, it is necessary to systematically analyze and manage these inputs. We will find it convenient to structure our approach around the areas of responsibility of operations managers. We begin with a consideration of some of the philosophical and psychological aspects of the human resource, how jobs are designed, and methods of getting work done. The principles of motion economy and analytical procedures used in flow process charts are tools for improving work methods. After this background on jobs and methods, we turn to labor standards, exploring their purpose and use. Then we go on to consider other facets of labor relations and such factors as employee safety, wages, and benefits.

In short, the operations manager is concerned with what the job is, how it is done, and the welfare of those who do it. He must ensure that the total human resource effort is effectively managed so as to facilitate individual and organizational objectives.

HUMAN BEINGS IN THE WORK ENVIRONMENT

A good deal has been written about the nature of work and the behavior of human beings in the work environment. We can gain a better appreciation of job design if we begin with a brief review of the human characteristics of the labor resource, and then examine this resource in the context of the work environment.

THE HUMAN RESOURCE

Let us start with the simple observation that classes of beings share in existence but have different fundamental natures, or essences, as depicted in Fig. 3-1. And whereas humans, as a class of being, differ from rocks, plants, and other entities, all human beings share a common essence. In fact, it is the common intrinsic nature of "humanness" that provides the basis for fairness and equal rights under the law for everyone in our society. We hold that the intrinsic value of persons stems more from their human nature than it does from their accomplishments, position, or possessions. This essence of humanity in effect establishes a minimal level of behavior with respect to interactions with others of the same essence. You might say it suggests that man-

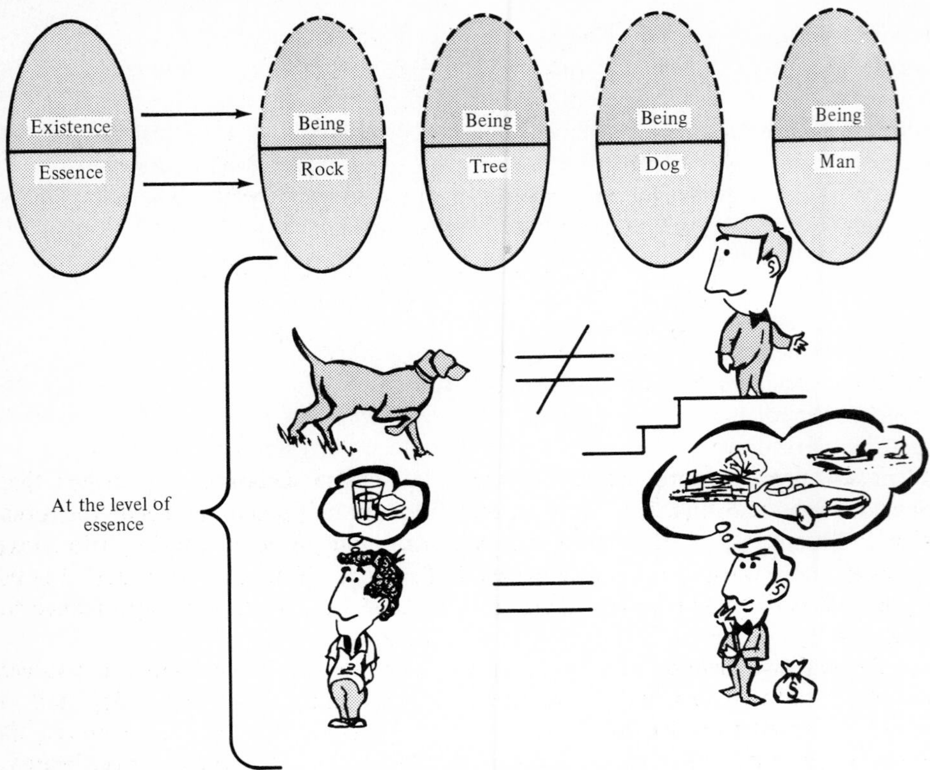

FIGURE 3-1 Existence and the different levels of essence

agers, workers, and all others associated with an organization should, at least as a bare minimum, *naturally* treat each other as humans—and not, for example, as "dogs."

Having set one cornerstone of human resource management policy firmly upon the concept of "humanness," let us turn our attention to the level of existence. The psychologist Maslow has suggested that human beings have a hierarchy of needs that ranges from a minimal level of existence to a fuller psychological state of self-actualization [**17**]. The need hierarchy is depicted in Fig. 3-2 and includes the following [cited in **24**: 2.9].

1 Self-preservation (air, food, water, comfort)

2 Safety (security, protection, freedom from anxiety)

3 Belonging (family or group, acceptance, love, friendship)

4 Respect (esteem, approval, self-respect, dignity)

5 Self-actualization (use of talents, capacities, potentialities)

The separate needs really form an integrated hierarchy, for each higher-level need depends upon a minimal level of satisfaction of the preceding (lower-level) need. But a full existence as a normal, healthy individual means that all five levels of need

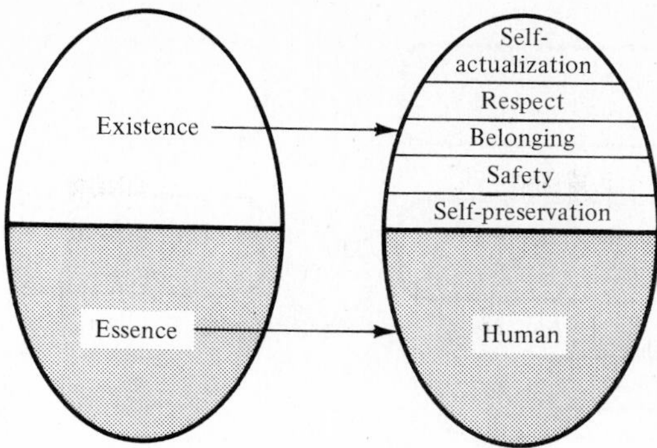

FIGURE 3-2 Maslow's hierarchy in the level of existence

must be satisfied to some extent. From a job design standpoint, it means that employees require adequate compensation to satisfy their economic needs for food, shelter, and clothing. Furthermore, they need a genuine sense of security, belonging, and respect. It also suggests that some level of self-actualization is necessary. Let us look at this need of self-actualization in more depth to ascertain its significance to job design.

The self-actualization need is a complex one related to the knowledge and values concepts introduced in Chap. 1. A schematic representation of this is depicted in Fig. 3-3 [adapted from **24** (modified)]. Here we see that the essential components are knowledge (of facts, concepts, methodologies, and so on), values (love, beauty, emotions, and the like), skills (productive, artistic, and so forth), and decision-making activities. Some psychologists refer to knowledge as the "cognitive domain" and values as the "affective domain." Figure 3-4 depicts, in brief form, the stages in the acquisition of human knowledge and values. *Knowledge* relies upon the senses and the intellect. *Values* relate more to inherent sensitivity and the will, although, as shown by the dotted-line path, they often have a rational basis. Examples are freedom,

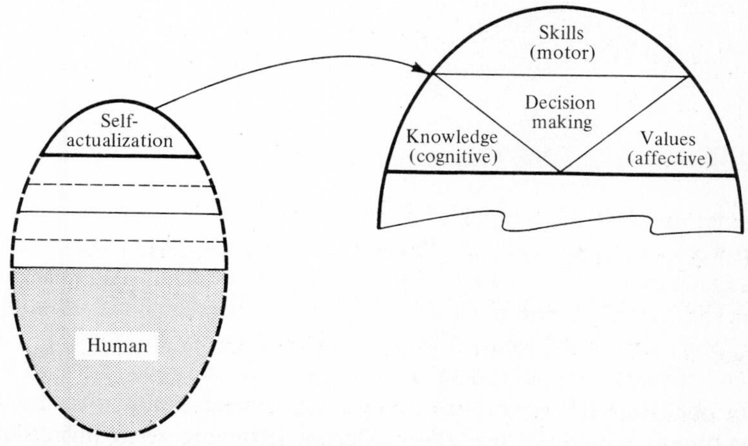

FIGURE 3-3 Components of self-actualization

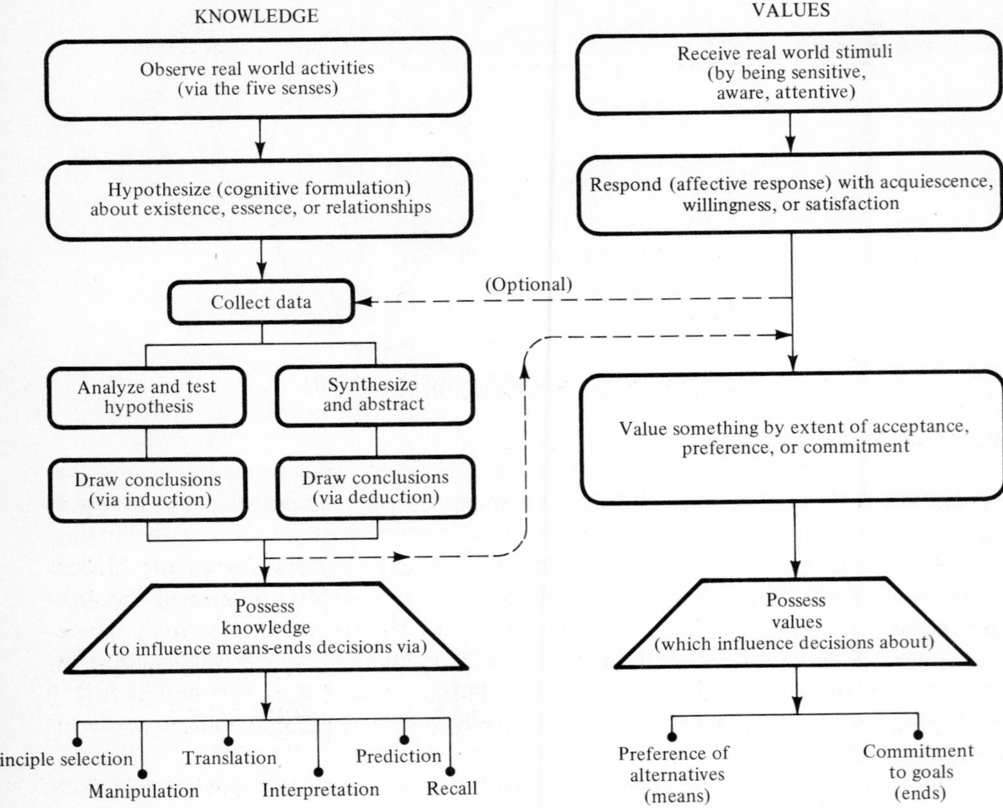

FIGURE 3-4 Stages in the acquisition of human knowledge and values. (Portions adapted and modified from the work of Bloom, Krathwohl, and Wales.)

justice, and environmental tranquility. The third component, *skill* development (not shown in Fig. 3-4), arises primarily from training and practice. The knowledge, value, and skill capabilities reflect a higher (spiritual) level of existence than simply a physical (material) presence.

WORK

Now let us relate the foregoing philosophical and psychological concepts more directly to work and organizations. Rettig [21] defines *work* as "any activity undertaken in a quest for extrinsic rewards," pointing out that the activity may be physical, mental, or some combination of both. Work is thus a means one takes to satisfy a need or to obtain a reward which is outside the activity itself.

When activities are undertaken in search of intrinsic rewards, such as playing a piano for one's own enjoyment only, they are nonwork. And of course there is a continuum of semiwork activities between the two extremes, where an activity may be

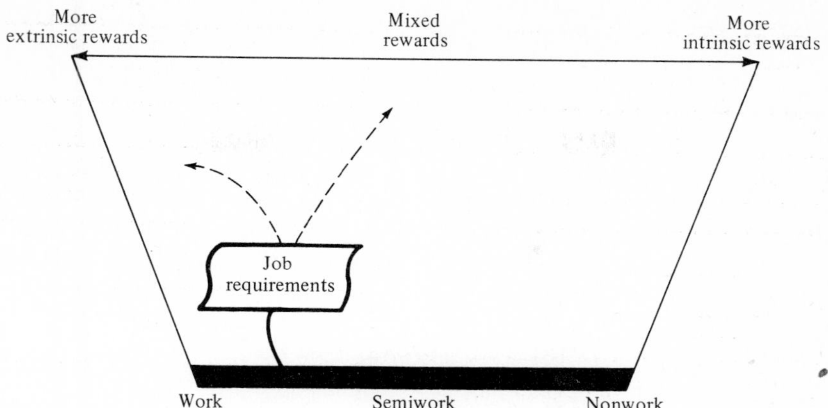

FIGURE 3-5 Jobs in the work-nonwork continuum

intrinsically satisfying and still hold some promise of extrinsic payoffs. Producing a play could be an example of this.

As one progresses from the basic level of Maslow's hierarchy to the higher levels, one's needs take on a more intrinsic flavor. Without minimizing the importance of extrinsic rewards (such as the paycheck) it seems reasonable to conclude that as the lower-level needs of a person become satisfied the intrinsic rewards of a job take on an increasingly significant role. Food and shelter are not enough; employees look to their oganization for acceptance or respect, and the opportunity to use their talents or to make decisions.

To the extent that these higher-level needs are intrinsic, individuals are in fact moving toward the nonwork end of the work-nonwork continuum shown in Fig. 3-5. At the start, the job satisfies their basic necessities and links them with an organization that gives them a sense of belonging. It also provides extrinsic rewards associated with status and position. Then, as the individuals grow to value their contributions for what they are to themselves, rather than for what they appear to be to others, the job shifts from being "work" per se to becoming a more absorbing and intrinsically satisfying reward package [**21**]. It begins to take on more of a professional flavor, where higher-order nonwage incentives such as competency goals replace the more materialistic goals of wages, status, and so forth. This intrinsic element can emerge from both physical and mental assignments. For example, a welder may gain as much satisfaction from completing a difficult weld on a new skyscraper as did the architect from designing the building.

Our second cornerstone of human resource management policy thus rests on the observation that employees have a hierarchy of needs, and jobs that provide intrinsic satisfactions are preferable to those that do not. With this background on humans in the work environment we now move on to some of the more specific aspects of job design.[1]

[1] To remain consistent with the generally accepted connotation of the word "work," we shall (loosely) refer to work as effort on the job, whether it is extrinsically or intrinsically satisfying (or neither).

JOB DESIGN AND ENRICHMENT

Job design is the consciously planned structuring of work effort. The design should delineate what task is to be performed, how it is to be done, and, if necessary, where and when to do it. Designers usually try to minimize the amount of physical human effort required for a work task, although this is not always the case—particularly in certain applications in developing countries. Years ago, employers searched for workers with the physical capabilities to suit a given task. Today, jobs are designed to suit an average worker and capability distinctions are more likely to be on the basis of education and experience.

JOB DESIGN REQUIREMENTS

A job design should be (1) in writing, (2) fully understood and agreed to by both employee and employer, and (3) consistent with organizational objectives. These simple requirements are often violated, with resulting misunderstandings, morale problems, and inefficiencies.

A written job description forces a clear definition of activities within the job and helps to ensure that they are designed, rather than "just happening."[2] Such clarity of definition is important to any viable organization; otherwise worker activity and management policy may be in conflict. But jobs should not be specified in such a manner as to imply that employee development and welfare interests are peripheral or illegitimate. The set of organizational objectives can and should reflect employee interests as well as stockholder and other interests. The written specification of a job is a crucial step in blending those interests into a unified organizational effort.

A properly designed job should be the product of many efforts, such as those of engineers, supervisors, and perhaps even the workers themselves. Studies have shown the value of worker participation in many aspects of operations management [7] and, of these, job design is certainly one of the most important. Some firms ask their workers to outline their "job" as they understand it and the manager or supervisor to do likewise. Then the two jointly discuss the similarities and discrepancies in order to reach a clear agreement. In other organizations, management defines the jobs and then encourages the workers to react by agreeing to or challenging the statement of content. Some managers take an approach which asks, "Are there any absolutely vital functions that would have to be performed if the subject position were abolished? If so, what are they?" This more drastic approach does not appear to be especially human-relations sensitive, but with full employee understanding and participation it, too, can be an effective approach. The important outcome is a fully understood written description which will serve as a standard of comparison for future activities.

[2] Actual surveys show that some firms have positions that were "filled simply because they had become an accepted part of the structure and the reason for their inception had been forgotten" [27:22]. Nevertheless, some employers feel a written description unnecessarily restricts performance, especially at the professional level.

Management by objectives (MBO) is a managerial technique closely related to job design. Under an MBO program, work objectives are clearly and quantitatively specified in advance and agreed to by both manager and employees. The planning period often covers a full year. Then, as the year progresses, the employees are evaluated against the specified objectives only—not unexpected disasters or windfalls over which they had no responsibility or control. In these and some other management techniques, the job objectives are of paramount importance, and work methods are intentionally supportive of the objectives.

As the future turns into the present, products change, new equipment becomes installed, and work methods are improved. Thus job design should be a continuing process rather than a one-shot activity. Job specifications should be reevaluated periodically to ensure that full advantage is taken of newly developed mechanized aids and that the worker's human capabilities remain effectively utilized and rewarded.

JOB ENRICHMENT

Many jobs, as originally designed, are difficult, boring, or inherently unappealing to workers. Employees tend to avoid such jobs, or perhaps do them reluctantly with a resulting low rate of productivity. Repetitive jobs, such as those on an automative assembly line, are examples of this. Yet these jobs must be done, so managers are faced with the problem of motivating their employees to do them.

In earlier days, employees were threatened or even ridiculed into doing some jobs. Today we see more positive inducements in the way of monetary rewards and organizational status symbols [**13**]. Thus many firms offer increased wages and fringe benefits, or decrease the on-the-job time requirement. Others have undertaken special communications and human relations training programs, and some have experimented with sensitivity training or more extensive employee counseling. A good deal of effort has gone into *job enlargement* programs, which are designed to increase the scope and complexity of a worker's job in order to make it more appealing.

Numerous studies of motivational efforts, especially of job enlargement, have been made in insurance companies, appliance producers, textile firms, computer manufacturers, and so forth. The study results attest to the difficulties of motivating employees but do suggest that productivity can be improved—at least in the short run. (The impact upon long-run productivity is still questioned by many researchers, however.) In an insurance firm, productivity was increased and the number of errors decreased after workers were given responsibility for preparing a complete insurance policy application rather than only one portion of it [**5**: 412]. In a worker-participation experiment involving an assembly line operation, productivity was increased by letting the workers set the line speed at their own (variable) rate rather than at the rate set by the firm [**5**: 417].

Although numerous types of positive incentive programs have been tried, Herzberg has observed that none are fully satisfactory [**13**]. He has concluded that the factors that contribute to job dissatisfaction are not the same as those that make for job satisfaction. In 12 investigations covering 1,685 employees, respondents were asked what job events led to extreme satisfaction and extreme dissatisfaction. The primary *causes of satisfaction*, in decreasing order of importance, were (1) achievement, (2) recognition, (3) work itself, (4) advancement, and (5) growth. Herzberg terms these "motivator factors." They are uniquely human in character and relate to an individual's ability to achieve, and through achievement to experience psychological growth. This achievement and growth is a result of the job content.

The primary *causes of job dissatisfaction* were (1) company policy and administration, (2) supervision, (3) relationship with supervisor, (4) work conditions, (5) salary, (6) relationship with peers, (7) personal life, (8) relationship with subordinates, (9) status, and (10) security. These "dissatisfiers" are termed "hygiene factors" by Herzberg and he identifies them more with the job environment than with the job content.

Unlike job enlargement, which deals with a horizontal expansion of the activities within a job classification, *job enrichment* is a systematic attempt to motivate employees by changing motivational factors. Job enrichment involves vertical job loading which gives employees an opportunity for growth and achievement beyond their current role. While it may not always be possible to provide employees with opportunities for development and greater responsibility in their jobs, this does seem to be most desirable from a motivational standpoint.

THE SOCIOTECHNICAL SYSTEM

Some analysts view a modern productive organization as having two functioning systems: a technical system and an accompanying social system [**6**: 418]. The *technical system* consists of the technological equipment or skills underlying a given transformation process. The *social system* relates to the formal and informal work-group organization. Although somewhat independent of the technology, the social system exerts a strong influence over production in the way it motivates workers and facilitates the coordination of work activities.

In reviewing studies of sociotechnical systems, Chase and Aquilano have derived three observations relevant to job design [**6**: 420–422].

- People's role in many systems is gradually changing from that of using direct productive skills to one of monitoring and controlling the variance of automatic equipment. This in turn dictates different aptitude requirements for the employee.
- A good task definition in terms of its technological attributes, location, and time factors can affect the success of the whole sociotechnical system. It helps to ensure that all relevant factors are included and that an appropriate supervisory structure for monitoring task performance can be developed.
- There is a need for individual and group autonomy because of the inherent variability in work situations. But even relatively autonomous work groups require some minimal control to ensure that they are self-maintaining and self-adjusting.

The work of Davis [**8**] and Emery et al. [**9**] has prompted Chase and Aquilano to offer some guidelines for job design at the individual and group levels [**6**: 422, drawn largely from **9**].

Individual-level Guidelines

1 Give workers an optimum level of variety of tasks within the job. Too great a variety is inefficient; too little results in boredom. The right amount gives workers a break from routine activity.

2 Arrange diverse but interdependent tasks into one meaningful pattern.

3 Give workers an optimum length of work cycle.

4 If feasible, give workers some responsibility in setting standards of quantity and quality, along with quick feedback knowledge of their job performance.

5 Include some auxiliary and preparatory tasks that extend the scope of the job and worker involvement in it.

6 Make the job tasks require sufficient skill, knowledge, or effort to generate respect within the workers' own work group.

7 Make the job show some contribution of value to the overall product or service being produced.

Group-level Guidelines

8 At the group level, it is desirable to provide for interlocking tasks, job rotation, or physical proximity of workers. This is especially important in three types of situations: (*a*) where there is a necessary independence of jobs (in which it helps to create cooperation and better understanding among members of the work group); (*b*) where the individual jobs involve a relatively high degree of stress (so that communication and interaction with others often lessen stress and reduces mistakes and accidents); (*c*) where individual jobs do not make an obvious, perceptible contribution to the end product.

9 Where the group has responsibility for a number of jobs that are linked together by interlocking tasks, its members should (*a*) have some perspective of the overall task to which they are contributing, (*b*) have some responsibility for setting standards and receiving feedback of results, and (*c*) have some control over "boundary tasks" (such as preparation and inspection activities).

The above guidelines are not necessarily appropriate for all circumstances, nor should they be implemented in a haphazard or arbitrary manner. Some firms, in Europe and elsewhere, have achieved what they consider to be successful results from stressing such things as worker autonomy. Volvo, the automobile manufacturer in Sweden, is a prime example. The Volvo experiments with automobile assembly done by work groups that took major responsibilities for the total effort have attracted worldwide attention and admiration. However, many organizations are not prepared to give work groups more decision-making responsibility, nor are the work groups prepared to accept it. Attempts to prematurely force changes by means of job redesign could do more harm to the organization than good.

On the other hand, guidelines such as those above do exist for integrating both individual and group tasks within the structure of a technical system. Some of the guidelines may prove useful in facilitating both individual and organizational goals by enhancing the meaningfulness of tasks; encouraging interest, responsibility, and respect for carrying them out; and fostering the cooperative and supportive benefits of work-group interaction. But the sociotechnical challenge cannot be met overnight and each organization's response must be tailored to its own circumstances and leadership style.

WORK METHODS AND MOTION ECONOMY

Work methods are simply ways of doing work. Sometimes they are specified as part of a job design, at other times they are left to the discretion or experience of the worker. They play a key role in adding value to a production operation (that is, to productivity) and so have been given continuous attention since the beginnings of industrial development.

HISTORICAL DEVELOPMENT

As early as 1776, Adam Smith was extolling the economic advantages of the division of labor into specialized operations. He pointed out that this division saved time, allowed for the use of specialized machines, and encouraged the development of higher levels of skill in employees. During the industrial revolution (early 1800s) the factory system developed and used some of these principles. By the early 1900s, countries like the United States and Great Britain became "mechanized," although not very effectively according to today's standards. During this period (the early 1900s), the foundations of methods study were developed by Frank and Lillian Gilbreth, a husband and wife team. The Gilbreths were interested in making human efforts more effective and performed extensive studies to define, classify, and economize work methods.

PRINCIPLES OF MOTION ECONOMY

As attention to work methods has continued, certain principles regarding body movement, work-place arrangement, and tool and equipment usage have been formulated [3]. Some of the more important principles are listed in Table 3-1.

TABLE 3-1 PRINCIPLES OF MOTION ECONOMY

Human Body

1 Begin and end motions of both hands at the same time.
2 Do not allow both hands to be idle at the same time except during rest periods.
3 Make sure that motions of arms are in opposite and symmetrical directions and at the same time.
4 Confine hand and body motions to the simplest movements that will do the work.
5 Use momentum to assist where helpful but reduce it if it must be overcome by muscular effort.
6 Use smooth, continuous curved motions in preference to straight-line motions that involve sudden changes in direction.
7 Remember that ballistic motions are faster, easier, and more accurate than controlled movements.
8 Arrange work to permit use of natural rhythm wherever possible.
9 Keep eye fixations as few and as close together as possible.

Work Place

10 Keep all tools and materials in a definite and fixed place.
11 Keep tools, materials, and controls close to the point of use.
12 Use gravity feed bins and containers to deliver material close to the point of use.
13 Use drop deliveries wherever possible.
14 Locate materials and tools to permit the best sequence of motions.
15 Provide proper illumination, heating, and ventilation.
16 Arrange the height of the work place and the chair so that alternate sitting and standing is easily possible.
17 Provide a chair that permits good posture for every worker.

Tools and Equipment

18 Relieve the hands of all work that can be done by jigs, fixtures, and foot-operated devices.
19 Combine two or more tools wherever possible.
20 Pre-position tools and materials to reduce motions of searching, finding, and selecting as much as possible.
21 Distribute the load on each finger in accordance with the inherent capabilities of the fingers.
22 Locate levers, crossbars, and handwheels so that the operator can manipulate them with the least change in body position and with the greatest mechanical advantage.

If, upon first reading, the principles appear trivial, take the list yourself and step into an industrial office, a cafeteria, or even your own work or study situation. A systematic check through the list is likely to reveal some potential improvements, even to an unskilled observer. And, of course, if a task is highly repetitive, the benefits of a single improvement are multiplied many times.

Note that many of the principles relate to tools and equipment. As technology advances, we tend to rely more and more upon machines for improvement in work methods.

WORKER-MACHINE SYSTEMS

Productivity was defined earlier as a relationship of output to input such that the value of the output exceeds the cost of the inputs. Although the physical capabilities of human beings tend to limit their productivity, their intellectual capabilities are constantly at work developing new methods to improve productivity. Much of this development has now gone beyond the physical limitations of an individual worker, or group of workers, to a worker-machine or machine-machine system. People have found that machines are far superior to them in applying large forces, in performing repetitive tasks quickly and accurately, and in handling information [**5**: 360]. So job designers have gradually shifted human efforts from strictly physical labor to more decision-making and equipment-control functions. This automation effect is largely responsible for maintenance of increased productivity over the past 50 years.

As people have come to use machines more and more, the interaction of worker and machine has merited special attention, both from a physical and a psychological standpoint. One method of describing the physical interface is in terms of a worker-machine chart. *Worker-machine charts* are graphic methods of depicting the simultaneous activities of workers and the machine, or machines, they operate. We shall reserve in-depth consideration of how to construct and use these charts for a subsequent chapter concerned with product and process analysis.

FLOW PROCESS CHARTS

Work methods are often described in terms of *flow process charts* which depict, in detail, the precise activities involved in a job. These charts show the time sequence of activities in terms of standardized symbols. See the accompanying diagram. An example of a flow process chart is shown in Fig. 3-6. Some versions of these charts do not include time or distance moved, whereas others include this as well as an elaborate form for a structured analysis of the method.

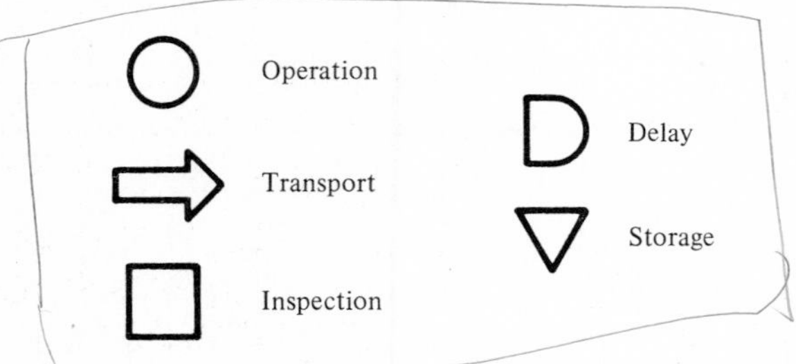

METHODS IMPROVEMENT STUDY

Since human resources constitute such a vital input to production activities, the methods of doing work should rightly undergo critical examination. A systematic

FLOW PROCESS CHART

Job C/R installation

[X] Existing method
[ ] Proposed method

Date July 18
Charted by L. J. Smith
Chart no. IF423

Details of Method	Activity	Time	Distance (ft)	Analysis Why? What?	Where?	When?	Who?	How?	Notes	Action Eliminate	Combine	Change sequence	Simplify	Other
In pit	○ ⇨ □ D ▽	8:10	–											
Inform supervisor	○ ⇨ □ D ▽	8:33	–					X	Eliminate signature – use intercom	X			X	
Wait for approval	○ ⇨ □ D ▽	8:45	–											
Lift C/R into cask	○ ⇨ □ D ▽	9:16	20											
To reactor	○ ⇨ □ D ▽	9:19	130											
Clear area	○ ⇨ □ D ▽	9:40	–			X			Need advance warning			X		
Quality inspection	○ ⇨ □ D ▽	9:47	–											
Install C/R	○ ⇨ □ D ▽	10:03	12											
In reactor	○ ⇨ □ D ▽	10:15	–											

FIGURE 3-6 Flow process chart

manner of making a methods improvement study is in wide use in industry today. The procedure consists of the following steps:

1. *Select* work to be studied.
2. *Record* present method.
3. Critically *analyze* present method.
4. *Develop* improved method.
5. *Install* improved method.
6. *Maintain* improved method.

Each of these steps is discussed below.

SELECT WORK TO BE STUDIED

Management consultants and work-study analysts have found that certain types of work offer more potential for cost reduction or improved labor relations than others. Some of these include jobs that:

Have a high labor content, that is, are time consuming.
Have a large demand, that is, are frequently occurring.
Present quality problems by rejects or rework required.
Are bottlenecks in the system, thus limiting output.
Are unsafe, unpleasant, or fatiguing.
Offer excessively low or high earnings (including overtime).
Have never before been studied.

Looking for these types of work often proves surprisingly effective in getting a methods study off to a good start. Of course, the selection procedure must take account of guiding economic and human limitations as well. Economically, capital must be available for improvements and the cost of any changes must be justified by the job life and the productive use of any time saved. From a behavioral standpoint it is preferable to begin methods improvement in work areas where labor relations are such that the employees will readily accept and participate in implementing well-managed changes. Word of success in these areas will hopefully increase the likelihood of acceptance in other areas.

RECORD PRESENT METHOD

The actual writing out of a step-by-step procedure describing the present method of work in full detail is important. A general sketch of the floor plan and flow of work is a good place to start. The details of the present method can often be very effectively recorded by using an appropriate chart, such as a worker-machine chart or a flow process chart. The starting and ending points of each component activity of the job should first be precisely defined. Then if, for example, a flow process chart is used, each step is identified in terms of an operation ○, transport ⇒, inspection □, delay D, or storage ▽ activity, and a time for each activity is determined. Many flow process chart forms also have a space in which the analyst can note any deviations in quality, quantity, sequence of operations, or tools used.

CRITICALLY ANALYZE PRESENT METHOD

Among the proven ways of examining the present method are the questioning technique and the checklist technique. In addition, photographic methods are often useful. The questioning technique is widely used and very effective, for the analyst is forced to probe *every step* of the work method, asking the questions:

1 What is its purpose?
2 Why is it necessary?
3 Can it be eliminated? Combined with another? Changed in sequence? Simplified in any way?

Some flow process charts have a series of columns listing these questions alongside the time column so that the analyst will automatically consider them in any examination. Both the questioning and the checklist approaches should take full advantage of inputs from the workers themselves.

The checklist technique simply consists of critically reviewing every activity with respect to a set of guidelines concerning material flow, work-place design, hand and body movements, and so on. The principles of motion economy (Table 3-1) comprise one of the most effective such check lists.

Photographic methods are advantageous ways of analysis if the cost is justified and employees do not object to being photographed. This kind of motion study depends, to some extent, upon the cycle of the work activity. For short-cycle operations, *micromotion* studies are made using high-speed cameras that take perhaps 50 to 100 picture frames a second. The analyst can then slow the film down for study purposes and analyze it in detail. For long-cycle operations, *memomotion* studies are made with slow-speed cameras. In analyzing these, the analyst speeds up the film to get a better overall perspective of the activity.

DEVELOP IMPROVED METHOD

From the critical analysis of the present method should come some suggestions as to what activities can be combined or eliminated, which hand motions can be changed, which tools added, and so forth, to make the operation better. All improvement suggestions, including those from the employees doing the job (especially those!), should be considered in developing new alternatives.

New flow process charts of alternative methods should be prepared in order to compare these methods with the existing method. The total time required and total number of operations are often good indicators of improvement. After time, quality, cost, personnel effects, and any other relevant criteria have been considered with respect to the alternative methods, the best method should be selected and described in a summary report that delineates and justifies the proposed change.

INSTALL IMPROVED METHOD

There are several important requirements for installing a new work method. Assuming that the study was thorough and the proposal carefully prepared, the changes must still be "sold" to both the appropriate line management and the employees. A major change may involve considerable planning and should include line supervisor and employee suggestions on implementation. Few changes work smoothly from the very start, so the analyst, supervisor, and employees should all be prepared to spend some effort in overcoming the usual "start-up" problems.

MAINTAIN IMPROVED METHOD

Any change worth doing is worth following up to ensure that the new method is functioning according to plan. This not only guards against unplanned changes but can also provide data and ideas for improvement elsewhere in the system.

LABOR STANDARDS

If the labor resource is to be effectively managed, labor standards are desirable. *Labor standards* are specific declarations of the amount of time that should reasonably be incurred in performing a specified activity under normal working conditions. Many firms make do with simple judgmental estimates based on past experience. Such estimates are inexpensive to derive, quickly and easily formulated, and may be sufficiently accurate. On the other hand, they are subjective, inconsistent, and susceptible to bias. Three of the more formalized methods of determining activity times upon which standards are based are (1) time study, (2) predetermined time standards, and (3) work sampling. We shall examine each of these methods after first justifying the need for labor standards.

NEED FOR LABOR STANDARDS

As new and improved work methods are developed, their time and performance characteristics should be incorporated into the formal labor standards of the organization. In the United States, job designers set standards such that about 95 percent or more of the qualified workers should be able to perform the job on a continuous basis within the specified time if they work according to prescribed methods.

As mentioned earlier, not all firms have recognized a need for formally derived labor standards. Some kinds of work activities, of course, do not readily lend themselves to measurement. In other cases the firms simply have not justified the use of formal standards, or perhaps have lacked the capability of implementing them. Nevertheless, organizations that do not have explicit documented standards often have informal ones—perhaps even established by the workers themselves. Informal standards may be better than none, but they usually do not rest on an organized data base and they can easily lead to incongruous and suboptimal action.

Standards facilitate management of operations in many ways. From the standpoint of the worker, standards specify an immediate goal in terms of an expected level of performance. When the standard is "reasonable" (as it should be), workers can gain a psychological satisfaction from knowing what is expected of them and that it is an attainable expectation. The standard can also provide a basis for discharging poor workers and for giving an incentive payment to workers performing above reasonable expectations.

In a similar manner, standards serve as surrogate goals for the organization by specifying levels of performance in terms of time or cost or number of units produced. Thus a second use of standards is as a measure of performance of the organization.

A third use of standards is to facilitate existing operations. For example, once standard labor times have been established, production scheduling can use this information to estimate production run times and derive schedules of the number of labor hours needed for a given job. The times required to build up specified inventory levels can also be estimated. From the time estimates, labor cost data can be derived for product pricing and bidding activities. The standards also serve as a basis for comparison of new production processes or work methods.

In summary, standards serve many purposes, including satisfying the needs of the worker, providing a measure of performance for the organization, and facilitating existing operations of the organization. We turn now to ways of obtaining standards.

TIME-STUDY METHODS

Time-study methods were originally proposed by Frederick Taylor and were later modified to include a rating-factor (RF) adjustment. They have now become one of the most widely used methods of work measurement. Basically, by using time study, an analyst is taking a small sample of one worker's activity and using it to derive a standard for the entire organization. The only equipment needed is a stopwatch plus paper and pencil. In brief, the procedure is as follows:

1 Select the job, inform the worker, and define the best method.

2 Time an appropriate number of cycles (such as 25–50).

3 Compute the average cycle time:

$$\mathrm{CT} = \frac{\sum \text{times}}{n \text{ cycles}} \tag{3-1}$$

4 Compute normal time:

$$NT = CT(RF) \tag{3-2}$$

5 Compute standard time:

$$ST = \frac{NT(100)}{100 - \%\ \text{allowance}} \tag{3-3}$$

Labor standards are developed for numerous activities, and almost any repetitive short-cycle labor activity may be a candidate for time study. But a prerequisite to any study is that supervisors and workers be fully informed about the purpose and procedures of the study.[3] An analyst should get acquainted with the operators and put them at ease as much as possible so that the study will be done under "normal" conditions. He or she will also want to assure himself or herself that the worker is using the best methods to do the job. As a first procedural step, the analyst should note the relevant details of the job and define it very precisely in elemental form. Each element should be a distinct operation and should be as short as possible—down to not less than 2 or 3 seconds in length.

The number of cycles to time actually depends upon how confident (statistically) the analyst wishes to be when inferring that the sample times are representative of actual on-the-job times. Since any operator's time may vary from one cycle to the next, the analyst must time enough cycles to obtain a valid estimate of the true average time. The sample size can be calculated from knowledge of the distribution of sample mean times, but numerous charts and graphs available make this unnecessary. We shall reserve the topic of calculating sample size and the precise meaning of statistical confidence until we take up work sampling later on in this chapter. But for the moment let us direct attention to Fig. 3-7, which permits us to read the time-study sample size directly from a chart, once a value of the coefficient of variation V has been estimated from a preliminary or partial sample. The *coefficient of variation* is simply an expression of the value of the sample standard deviation s divided by the sample mean $\bar{x}$. The sample standard deviation is the common statistical measure of dispersion of data points about their sample mean and is defined to include an adjustment for the fact that sample rather than population values are used.[4] (It may have to be estimated from a preliminary sample if historical data are not available.)

$$V = \frac{s}{\bar{x}} \tag{3-4}$$

[3] The author once unthinkingly walked into a large production area of a Pittsburgh plant carrying a clipboard and began collecting data. This immediately brought activities to a standstill until it was made clear that data was for a plant-location analysis and not for a time study.

[4] The uncorrected (and downwardly biased) definition of the sample standard deviation is

$$\sqrt{\frac{\sum (x - \bar{x})^2}{n}}$$

However, this form has little use in terms of statistical inference and this text follows the convention of assuming that sample standard deviations are calculated with an $n - 1$ in the denominator in order to obtain the best estimate of the population standard deviation (σ).

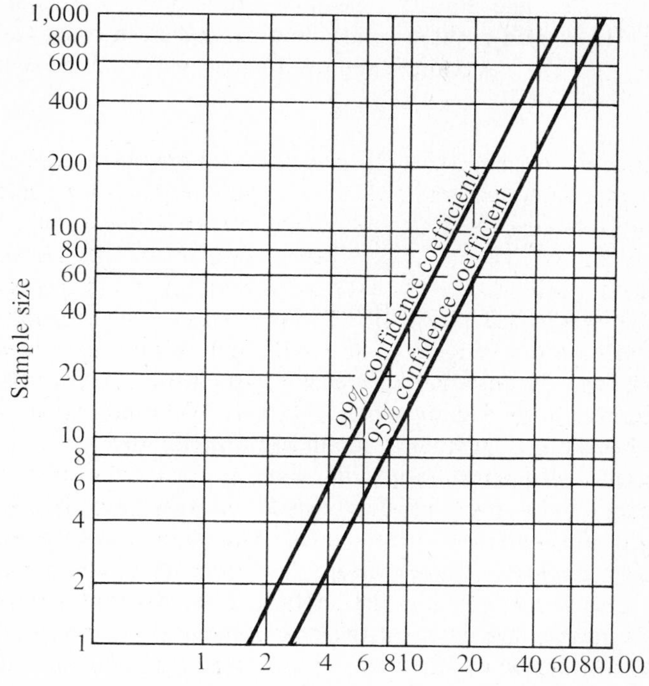

FIGURE 3-7 Time-study sample size chart. Chart is for ±5 percent accuracy for various coefficient of variation values. Source: [1]

where s = standard deviation of the sample

$$= \sqrt{\frac{\sum (x - \bar{x})^2}{n - 1}} \tag{3-5}$$

x = individual sample observation

$\bar{x}$ = sample mean

n = number in sample

Figure 3-7 provides sample sizes which offer the analyst 95 percent or 99 percent confidence that the sample mean will be within ±5 percent of the true population mean. Of course, the higher level of confidence requires a larger sample size. The chart is entered at the base with the value of the coefficient of variation. Proceed up to the curve depicting the desired confidence coefficient and read the required sample size on the left-hand scale.

Example 3-1

A preliminary sample showed a mean of 3.10 min and a standard deviation of 0.62 min. How many cycles should be time-studied in order to be 95 percent confident that the resultant standard time is within 5 percent of the true population value?

Solution

$$V = \frac{s}{\bar{x}} = \frac{0.62}{3.10} = 20\%$$

Therefore, time $n = 60$ cycles (from Fig. 3-7).

Note that for a 20 percent coefficient of variation and 5 percent accuracy, the sample size in this case is slightly more than the 25–50 cycles stated initially in the summary procedure for time studies. Confidence levels of 95 percent and accuracies of ± 5 percent and ± 10 percent are widely used.

The timing activity then consists of actually clocking each element of the work cycle with a stopwatch and recording the times. Continuous readings may be recorded or, by using a "snap-back" stopwatch, discrete times may be recorded. If readings are continuous, each reading must be subtracted from the subsequent reading in order to obtain incremental times for the cycle elements.

Before averaging the cycle times, the readings for any nonrecurring or foreign elements should be deleted. This adjusted average cycle time (CT) is sometimes referred to as the "select time."

Normal time (NT) is the product of the cycle time multiplied by a *rating factor* (RF) which adjusts the standard so that it is not geared to the skill or effort level of the particular worker being studied. Thus if the subject employee works at a faster pace than an average worker, for example, at 110 percent, the cycle time will be multiplied by 1.10 so that the resultant normal time will be longer and will still properly serve as a standard for an average worker.

Each element in a cycle should be rated with respect to performance during the time study. The rating factor is a subjective valuation by the analyst of how the individual worker compares to a concept of standard performance. Management has the right (and indeed the responsibility) to expect employees to complete assigned tasks at a high level of performance. Two measures of 100 percent performance are (1) walking at a steady pace of 3 mph and (2) dealing 52 cards into four piles in 0.5 minutes. Other appropriate working-activity standards have been filmed and are available throughout the United States and the rest of the world from lending libraries and some large firms. These films serve as a constant reference to ensure that analysts do not allow their perceptions of 100 percent performance to drift from recorded standards.

It may seem unreasonable to expect an analyst to tell whether a worker is performing at 110 percent or 115 percent. As a matter of fact, with practice, experienced analysts can rate workers within ± 5 percent about half the time and within

±10 percent perhaps 75 percent of the time [**20**: 113]. The farther a worker's performance is from 100 percent the more difficult it is to get an accurate rating. Ratings for machine-controlled times of a cycle are normally assumed to be at 100 percent.

The final computation of *standard time* (ST) makes allowances for personal time, fatigue, and unavoidable delays. Many firms have a specified personal-time allowance for employees, for coffee breaks and the like. Often, specific allowances, such as 10–15 percent, are negotiated into collective bargaining agreements.

Numerous experiments have been conducted on the actual energy consumption and heart rate of workers doing various jobs, and some fatigue allowances are set on this basis. The energy consumption of a worker varies from around 2 calories per minute for light clerical activities to around 10 or 12 calories per minute for very heavy work [**25**]. Similarly, the heart rate can be expected to double from its normal 70 beats per minute to over 140 beats per minute for strenuous physical labor. But even though this more-or-less scientific approach to fatigue allowances has been developed, most companies still set allowances on the basis of experience and subjective observation [**6**: 465]. The personal, fatigue, and unavoidable-delay allowances are computed as a percent of total on-the-job time, not as a percent of working time.

Example 3-2

A job design to be time-studied has fatigue and delay allowances of 10 min/day and 25 min/day respectively. The union contract further specifies that employees shall be allowed 25 min/day for personal time. Determine the percent allowance necessary to compute a standard time for this activity.

Solution

Personal time	25 min
Fatigue time	10 min
Delay time	25 min
Total	60 min

Assuming an 8-hr day (480 min), the 60 min as a percent of 480 min is:

$$\text{Allowance } \% = \frac{60}{480} = 12.5\%$$

Having discussed the procedure for a time study, let us conclude with a slightly more comprehensive example.

Example 3-3

A time study of a shop worker revealed the actual times shown. The standard deviation of the sample (with the 10.20 min cycle omitted) was $s = 0.21$ min. The analyst rated the worker at 90 percent RF and the company allows the following per 8-hr day:

Personal time	20 min
Delay time	30 min

Time in min/cycle		
Worker	Machine	Total
2.30	0.80	3.1
1.80	0.80	2.6
2.00	0.80	2.8
2.20	0.80	3.0
1.90	0.80	2.7
10.20[a]	0.80	11.0
2.20	0.80	3.0
1.80	0.80	2.6

[a] Unusual, nonrecurring situation

(*a*) Find the standard time.

(*b*) Determine whether the sample was of adequate size for the analyst to be 99 percent confident that the resultant standard time is within 5 percent of the true value. If not, how many cycles should have been time-studied to gain this level of confidence?

Solution

(*a*) Cycle time should omit the unusual situation of taking 10.20 min.

$$\text{Worker CT} = \frac{\sum \text{times}}{n \text{ cycles}}$$

$$= \frac{2.30 + 1.80 + 2.00 + 2.20 + 1.90 + 2.20 + 1.80}{7}$$

$$= 2.03 \text{ min}$$

$$\text{Machine CT} = 0.80 \text{ min}$$

$$\text{NT} = \text{CT(RF)} = \underset{\text{(worker time)}}{2.03(0.90)} + \underset{\text{(machine)}}{0.80(1.00)} = 2.63 \text{ min}$$

$$\text{ST} = \frac{\text{NT}(100)}{100 - \%\text{ allowance}}$$

$$\left(\text{where \% allowance} = 50 \text{ min as \% of } 480 = \frac{50}{480} = 10.42\%\right)$$

$$= \frac{2.63(100)}{100 - 10.42}$$

$$= 2.94 \text{ min/cycle}$$

(*b*) Coefficient of variation:

$$V = \frac{s}{\bar{x}} = \frac{0.21}{2.03} = 10.34\%$$

Using Fig. 3-7, $n \cong 40$ cycles would have been required. The 7 cycles were not adequate for 99 percent confidence.

PREDETERMINED TIME STANDARDS

A second method of setting labor standards is by using predetermined time values. This method consists of defining a job in terms of very small basic elements which have known (published) times. The times are then added until a total time value for the subject task is determined.

The advantages of this method are that (1) the standard can be determined from standard data which are universally available, (2) the standard can be completed before a job is done, (3) no performance rating is required, (4) it (the method) need not disrupt normal activities, and (5) it is widely accepted as a fair system of determining standards.

Several predetermined motion time systems have been developed, with two of the most popular being the *methods time measurement* (MTM) and the *work factor* systems. The MTM system uses times for basic motions referred to as "therbligs" (an anagram of Gilbreth's name) and consisting of such activities as search, select, grasp, transport loaded, and so on. Times are measured in time-measurement units (TMU), where one TMU equals only 0.0006 minute. Since it takes about 200 elements of motion to make up a minute of work, it requires considerable time and skill to set a standard. Although both the MTM system and a simplified MTM are widely accepted, some engineers question the accuracy of these systems, pointing out that the time taken to complete a therblig is not simply a function of distance moved or force overcome but also of the complexity of the task, direction of movement, eye-hand coordination needed, number of therbligs in the motion pattern, and so forth [**20**: 115]. The various systems attempt to take these factors into account. Even so, although some unions fully accept this system it is not always considered sufficiently accurate to be used for setting wage incentives.

Another form of standard which is sometimes predetermined is referred to as an *elemental time* (or synthesis) system. Element times are usually compiled from time-study data and often pertain to specific activities within the given organization. By keeping a record of common element times, a firm can conveniently set standards for jobs having similar component activities. Problems may result if the data are incomplete or require substantial interpolation. Table 3-2 provides a rough comparison of time study, MTM, and elemental time systems. Individual situations may, of course, differ from this.

TABLE 3-2 APPROXIMATE TIME STANDARD COMPARISON

	Approximate no. elements motion per min work	Approximate time to set 1 min of standard	Relative cost	Relative accuracy
Time study	3(±)	Varies	Most	Most
MTM	200(±)	60 min	Next	Next
Elemental	3(±)	10 min	Least	Least

WORK SAMPLING

The development of work sampling was a major advance in the techniques for establishing labor standards. The method was introduced by L. H. C. Tippett in 1934 for studying activities in the cotton industry. *Work sampling* consists of taking random observations of workers to determine the proportion of time they spend in specified activities. It is particularly useful for analyzing group activities, repetitive activities that take a relatively long time to complete, and activities that are not rigidly constrained from a time standpoint. Once data from a work-sampling study are available, they may be useful for methods analysis or cost analysis as well as for standards purposes.

Work-sampling methods have several advantages over time-study and predetermined time methods. By using statistical sampling techniques, sample sizes can be selected to provide the same specified level of confidence as with time studies. However, they can be used for a wider (less-structured) range of activities, they can be done by less-skilled (or part-time) observers, and they are less disturbing to workers. In general, work sampling has proved a very useful and economical technique and has found broad application in industrial plants, offices, hospitals, and other organizations.

The procedure for conducting a work-sampling study can be briefly summarized as follows:

1. Select the job or group to be studied and describe the operations in writing.
2. Inform the workers and prepare lists of their activities.
3. Determine the number of observations required and prepare a tour schedule.
4. Observe, rate, and record worker activities per schedule.
5. Record starting time, stopping time, and number of acceptable units completed during period.
6. Compute normal time:

$$\text{NT} = \frac{(\text{total time})(\%\ \text{working})(\text{RF})}{\text{number units completed}} \tag{3-6}$$

7. Compute standard time:

$$\text{ST} = \frac{\text{NT}(100)}{100 - \%\ \text{allowance}}$$

As with any employee-centered study, it is important to gain worker cooperation before embarking on the study. Discussions with the workers will prove helpful in charting the work flow pattern and classifying work activities into major categories. They also give workers a fuller sense of participation in setting standards and of having a stake in their operational success.

The number of observations required is, again, a function of the level of confidence desired by analysts when they infer that the sample observations are representative of the actual population of activities.

Suppose, for example, that an analyst wished to conduct a study to determine the proportion of time a worker is idle. Continuous observation of the worker would, of course, yield the exact proportion of idle time, but that would be too costly. The analyst would likely be willing to settle for a "close estimate" if there were assurance that it was within a few percentage points of the true figure, say 95 percent of the time (that is, a 95 percent confidence level). The analyst can get this assurance by applying some basic knowledge of statistical sampling to help in determining the appropriate sample size. Let us briefly review the theory involved in sample size determination, then we will summarize it in the form of a simple equation and go through an example of finding the sample size for estimating the proportion of time a worker is idle. The same theory (with a slightly modified equation) applies to estimation of measured time values (such as minutes) rather than proportions, and it is illustrated in Solved Prob. 4 at the end of the chapter.

First, the analyst would realize that different samples (for example, of 120 observations each) would likely suggest different values for the true proportion of idle time. We shall designate the true (but unknown) proportion as π and the proportion in a sample as p where:

$$p = \frac{\text{number of observations in the classification}}{\text{total number of observations}}$$

One sample proportion p_1 may show an 8 percent idle time whereas the next one p_2 may suggest 15 percent. The analyst is obviously not in a position to take all possible sample results into account but, from statistical theory, he or she can be assured that the sample proportions (p's) form a normal distribution about the true, but unknown, population proportion π if a sufficiently large number of samples of adequate size (say, 100 observations each) are taken.

The number of sample combinations possible can be determined by the combinatorial calculation C_x^n which we saw in Equation (2-3) and generally runs into the thousands or even millions. Although we seldom take more than one sample of a given size (for example, $n = 120$) the distribution of *all* the sample proportions for samples of a given size is theoretically useful. It is referred to as the *sampling distribution* of proportions and is shown in Fig. 3-8.

The mean of this distribution π is always equal to the mean of all the sample proportions

$$\pi = \frac{p_1 + p_2 + \cdots + p_{\text{last}}}{\text{number of samples}}$$

and the standard deviation of this theoretical distribution of sample proportions is referred to as the *standard error of proportion* σ_p. Of course the true value of σ_p is

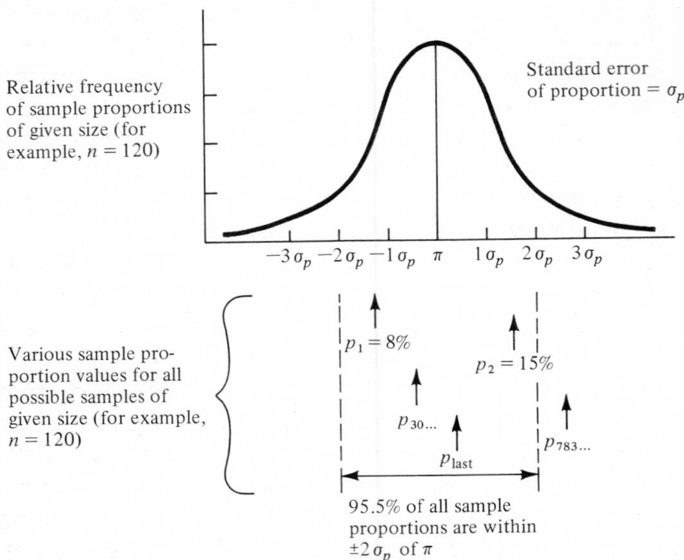

FIGURE 3-8 Sampling distribution of proportions

unknown (like π) but the sample standard error of proportion s_p is a good estimator of σ_p, even if it is computed on the basis of data from only *one* sample.

$$s_p = \sqrt{\frac{pq}{n}} \qquad (3\text{-}7)$$

where p = value of sample proportion
$q = (1 - p)$
n = number in the sample

Although the analyst does not know where his or her particular sample proportion (for example, p_1) lies, relative to the true parameter value π, by knowing that the sample values are normally distributed he or she can be assured that:

68.3 percent of the p's are within $\pm 1\sigma_p$ of π
95.5 percent of the p's are within $\pm 2\sigma_p$ of π
99.7 percent of the p's are within $\pm 3\sigma_p$ of π

Thus, for example, an interval of $\pi \pm 2\sigma_p$ would include 95.5 percent of the sample proportions as illustrated in Fig. 3-8. *Similarly, we can infer that if this same size interval were established around all the sample proportions*, 95.5 *percent of the intervals would include the true proportion*, π. (This is perhaps the most important concept underlying statistical inference!) These intervals of standard errors, when established about sample proportion values, constitute *confidence limits* (CLs).

$$\text{CL} = p \pm Zs_p \qquad (3\text{-}8)$$

The number of standard errors is normally referred to as the *standard normal deviate* Z. In addition to the Z values of 1, 2, and 3 for 68.3, 95.5, and 99.7 percent confidence respectively, other commonly used values are $Z = \pm 1.96$ for 95 percent confidence, and $Z = \pm 2.58$ for 99 percent confidence. These percentages are, of course, areas under the normal curve, and values for other levels of confidence can be obtained from any table of the normal distribution (see Appendix D). Note again that in the confidence interval expression we use the sample standard error of proportion s_p as an estimator of σ_p, since the latter is almost always unknown.

Using the interval about a sample proportion is a valid approach to finding a required sample size not because a given interval will definitely contain the population parameter π, but because the *procedure* being followed will ensure that the true population proportion is within the interval a specified percentage (that is, a confidence-level percentage) of the time. The analyst simply sets up an expression for the confidence-interval width about the sample proportion, equates it to the accuracy interval desired, and solves the expression for n, the sample size. Since the distribution of sample proportions is symmetrical, it is more convenient to work with half an accuracy interval h than with a whole interval. Thus, the analyst seeking an accuracy of ± 4 percent (that is, an 8 percent interval) would set up an expression stating that half the accuracy interval width (4 percent) must equal the Zs_p value, which is half the width of the confidence interval. An expression for sample size for proportions can be derived from this relationship, where:

$$h = Zs_p$$

where Z = the standard normal deviate for the desired confidence level

$$s_p = \text{the sample standard error of proportion} = \sqrt{\frac{pq}{n}}$$

Thus

$$h = \frac{Z\sqrt{pq}}{\sqrt{n}}$$

Solving for n yields the expression

$$n = \frac{Z^2 pq}{h^2} \tag{3-9}$$

Example 3-4

A data processing manager estimates that the key punch staff is idle 20 percent of the time and would like to take a work-sampling study that would be accurate within ± 4 percent. The manager wishes to have 95 percent confidence in the resulting study. How many observations should be taken?

Solution

Ninety five percent of the intervals $p \pm Zs_p$ will include the population value, π. We seek to find the value of n such that the number Z of standard errors multiplied by the value of each standard error s_p will equal one-half the accuracy interval (4 percent). That is:

$$h = Zs_p$$

where h = half the accuracy interval = 0.04
Z = 1.96 for 95% confidence

$$s_p = \sqrt{\frac{pq}{n}} = \frac{\sqrt{pq}}{\sqrt{n}}$$

where p is estimated at $p = 0.20$
$q = (1 - p) = 1 - 0.20 = 0.80$

$$s_p = \frac{\sqrt{(0.20)(0.80)}}{\sqrt{n}} = \frac{0.4}{\sqrt{n}}$$

$$0.04 = 1.96\,\frac{(0.4)}{\sqrt{n}}$$

$$\sqrt{n} = 19.6$$

$$n = 384 \text{ observations}$$

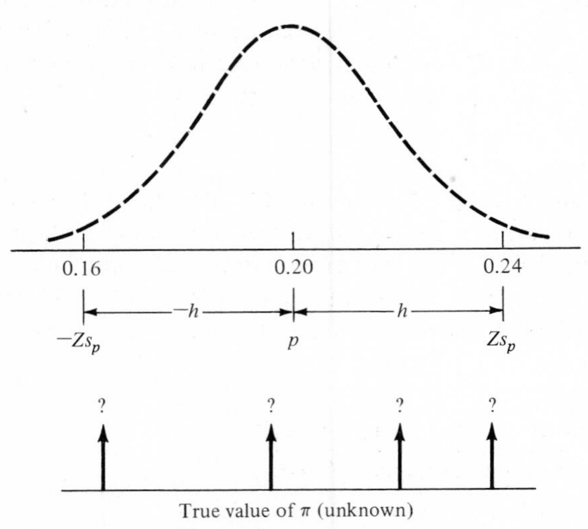

Alternatively, we can use Equation (3-9) directly:

$$n = \frac{Z^2pq}{h^2} = \frac{(1.96)^2(0.2)(0.8)}{(0.04)^2} = 384 \text{ observations}$$

Note that we have used the estimate of idle time (20 percent) to calculate n. If early study results indicate that p will be outside the range of 20 percent $\pm$

4 percent, then the number of observations may have to be adjusted as the study progresses.

Once the number of observations has been determined, a tour schedule should be prepared showing when each observation is to be made. A good method of ensuring that observations are random is to use a random number table (Appendix B). If, for example, a work-sampling study is to be conducted over a one-week period of five 8-hour work days, the number of minutes available would be 60 minutes per hour times 8 hours per day times 5 days per week = 2,400 minutes. A four-digit column of random numbers could be used to select numbers between 0,000 and 2,400. If, for example, 384 observations were required, then 384 random numbers would be chosen in this way (eliminating numbers greater than 2,400) and each would represent some minute of the 2,400-minute work week when an observation should be taken.

If few observations are required, or if they are taken only occasionally over an extended period, the observer may wish to use some form of alarm watch or other system to remind him or her to take the observations. In this way, the study data can be collected by part-time observers.

An advantage of work-sampling studies is that the observations need not disturb the workers. One quick glance at a worker will generally be sufficient to identify which activity he or she is engaged in. Many analysts simply walk through a work area, mentally noting what the subjects of the study are doing, and then later convert this to a written tally. As the analysts observe the activities, they also take note of the skill and effort level of their performance so that by the end of the period they have a representative performance rating RF for the subjects. Some analysts assume the RF is 100 percent unless it appears to be significantly above or below average.

After the data on times and units produced has been collected and tabulated, the normal time and standard time may be computed.

Example 3-5

A work-sampling study of customer service representatives in a telephone company office showed that a receptionist was working 80 percent of the time at 100 percent RF. This receptionist handled 200 customers during the 8-hr study period. Company policy is to give allowances of 10 percent of total on-the-job time. Find the normal time and the standard time per customer.

Solution

$$\text{NT} = \frac{(\text{total time})(\%\ \text{working})(\text{RF})}{\text{number units completed}}$$

$$= \frac{(480\ \text{min})(0.80)(1.00)}{200} = 1.92\ \text{min/customer}$$

$$\text{ST} = \frac{\text{NT}(100)}{100 - \%\ \text{allowance}}$$

$$= \frac{(1.92)(100)}{100 - 10} = 2.13\ \text{min/customer}$$

LABOR RELATIONS

Labor standards and performance measurement are topics of concern to workers because they influence the amount of work employees must do as well as the amount of pay they receive. As a result, individual workers and worker organizations are often very knowledgeable about standards and performance. An employee-conscious management should also be well informed about standards and performance as well as about other internal or external conditions that influence their work force.

As a matter of fact, any work place or environmental condition, bad or good, that influences the performance or satisfaction that workers receive from their jobs should be of interest to operations management. A number of these factors were mentioned when we considered the determinants for plant location; others pertain to the informal work groups and individual satisfactions that workers derive from within the formal structure of most large organizations. One of management's most important and perhaps most difficult tasks is to foster and preserve a favorable climate for employee relations within this total work and social environment.

To the layman, labor relations may seem to be almost wholly concerned with negotiating union contracts or settling strikes. These can be time-consuming and frustrating experiences, as many union leaders and industrial relations personnel will attest. But the results are not as bad as one might assume from reading the local press. In the United States there are approximately 150,000 collective agreements in force and about 98 percent of them are successfully negotiated without any work stoppage taking place. An average of about 300 collective bargaining agreements are concluded every day [**2**: 15].

Although operations managers may not be totally responsible for the conduct of contract negotiations, they often participate in negotiations or exert a strong influence upon them. After all, it is really the manager that must live with the agreements and make them work. The negotiations are typically characterized by a "give and take," with labor and management gradually moving closer together. The employer's greatest power is the threat of curtailing or relocating operations, which could put labor out of work. Labor's power is closely related to its potential ability to strike and cause economic damage to the employer.

The issues which divide labor and management often penetrate to the very purpose of the organization. And the problems are numerous. But in labor negotiations, as in many other aspects of managing operations, a respectable and systematic approach can be useful. This suggests that a prerequisite to bargaining is some broad agreement concerning organizational objectives, plus a thorough and factual knowledge of existing levels of performance. It is perhaps obvious that performance measures rely heavily on labor standards, so it is important that they be accurate and up to date. In addition, however, data on the organization's performance should be made available to employees in a way that will permit them to identify their own interests within the pursuit of organizational objectives.

The importance of a broad knowledge base on the part of all involved cannot be overstressed, if management wishes to build solid bonds of cooperation among the rank-and-file workers. To strengthen these bonds many firms in the United States and abroad have moved toward an increasing amount of worker participation in operating decisions. In Germany, trade union and worker representatives are not only on the supervisory board of nationalized industries but on the board of all public companies [**7**: 131]. Some reports indicate the Yugoslavs have gone to the extent of allowing trade unions to:

> intervene when it is judged that things are going wrong. They can propose the recall of members of the worker's management or the dismissal of the enterprise director. The distribution of income within the enterprise must also meet with trade union approval both as to its equity and to ensure that the workers are not overpaying themselves [**7**: 130].

However, this level of worker autonomy does not appear to be fully confirmed throughout the country or in all situations.

Participation by workers in management of firms in most other countries has not reached the stage reported in the Yugoslav situation, and is not expected to—at least in the foreseeable future. Yet the level of social support for more widescale participation is strong, as evidenced by the papal encyclical "Mater et Magistra," 1972.

> We . . . are convinced that employees are justified in wishing to participate in the activity of the industrial concern for which they work. . . . We are in no two minds as to the need for giving workers an active share in the business of the company for which they work—be it a private or public one. Every effort must be made to ensure that there is indeed a community of persons concerned about the needs, the activities, and the standing of each of its members [from translation in **26**: para. 91, as cited in **7**: 10].

British researchers predict that in English and American organizations, small and gradual changes will provide a combination of means of participation in the future [**7**: 192]. Certainly a number of the changes that will be most significant can be expected to arise from the sociotechnical environment. As brought out earlier in the chapter, the worker's role is already gradually changing from one of personally producing goods to one of controlling machinery and product variability. In some cases (but not all) these control activities move the worker to a higher level of decision making and participation. In others, they challenge the job designer to make the job more humanly satisfying, both from the individual (labor) and organizational (labor relations) standpoints.

The dangers of unplanned or unmanaged participation are perhaps obvious. But, in this context, it is worth reiterating that *managers have the prime responsibility* for planning, organizing, directing, and controlling the activities of the organization. They are leaders, specially skilled in making decisions, who direct the activities of the organization. In addition, their perspective of operations, if truly a systems approach, represents the interests of stockholders, consumers, and other units of society, as well as those of the employees. Managers, and the entire organization, can benefit from an appropriate level of worker participation. But the benefits will quickly be lost if the organization gets out of control and individual managers fail to use their managerial talents and skills.

Unions were initially formed as a reaction against management. Now the concept of collective bargaining has done much to balance the power of labor and management so that freedom of contract prevails. Nevertheless, the forces of big business and strong unions (and governments) are difficult to control. Problems arise when the power is out of balance. Then the firm can place unfair demands on the workers or, alternatively, the union can force the firm into economic disaster. Management faces a continuing challenge of creating a work environment where an awareness of objectives, knowledge of current performance, and active participation by all members of the organization will move it toward mutually satisfactory goals in a climate of cooperation and respect.

EMPLOYEE SAFETY

Good labor relations cannot be legislated, but laws can help, and have helped, to improve the conditions that constitute the "work environment." Employee safety is one condition that has received significant attention over the years, from the early days of industrialization to the most recent federal health and safety laws.

One of the most influential pieces of safety legislation in the United States has been the Occupational Safety and Health Act (OSHA), passed in 1970. This on-the-job safety program covers approximately 50 million industrial, farm, and construction workers employed by firms that are engaged in interstate commerce and that have four or more employees.

The OSHA has proven effective in upgrading safety and health standards because it incorporates all the essentials of legal control, including sanctions for non-compliance. The law provides for plant safety inspections by government inspectors on a random basis as well as on a specific complaint or a catastrophic basis (that is, any death or any accident where five or more workers are hospitalized). Inspection results are recorded and deviations from safety standards are noted via a formal citation to the organization. This identifies the violations and specifies a deadline for correction of the hazard. Compliance is further enhanced by the fact that the law provides for monetary fines for violations. The amount of the fine depends on a number of factors, including the size of the firm, seriousness of the violation, and history of the firm's "good faith."

Operations managers usually carry a major responsibility for employee safety, but the slogan "Safety is everyone's job" certainly holds true. Accidents happen to unsuspecting individuals. By definition they are unplanned events, as illustrated by the following incident [**22**: 1] involving the shutdown of two large nuclear reactors which, at the time, were producing enough electric power to supply the needs of a city of a million people.

> On March 22, 1975, a fire occurred at the Browns Ferry Nuclear Plant, near Decatur, Alabama. The Browns Ferry Plant is a three-unit electric generating station owned by the Tennessee Valley Authority (TVA). At the time of the fire units 1 and 2 were

> in operation, each producing approximately 1,000 megawatts of electrical power. Unit 3 was still in the construction phase. The fire originated from a candle flame used to check for air leakage in an electrical cable penetration between the cable-spreading room—located beneath the control room for units 1 and 2—and the reactor building. The fire, which burned for several hours, spread horizontally and vertically from its point of origin to all 10 cable trays within the penetration, into the cable-spreading room for several feet, and along the cables through the penetration for about 40 feet into the reactor building. About 2,000 cables were damaged, causing the shutdown of both units 1 and 2. Some components normally relied upon for shutdown cooling of the reactors by design are also part of the emergency core cooling systems (ECCS). Because of the fire all normally used shutdown cooling systems and other components which comprise the ECCS for unit 1 were inoperable for several hours. TVA, however, used other installed equipment and maintained sufficient cooling capability to protect the nuclear fuel.

Some minor injuries occurred as a result of the fire, but no one was killed and plant operators were able to adequately cool the two reactor cores so that no unusual radiological impact resulted to plant personnel or the surrounding environment. An investigation by the U.S. Nuclear Regulatory Commission (NRC) revealed the following factors (among others) which were listed as contributing to the cause or severity of the fire:

1 Failure to evaluate the hazards involved in the sealing operation and to prepare and implement controlling procedures.

2 Failure of workers to report numerous earlier small fires that took place during the sealing operations, and failure of supervisory personnel to recognize the significance of those fires which were reported and to take appropriate corrective actions.

3 Use of an open flame without fire precautions specific to this activity.

4 Ineffectual leadership by TVA in firefighting activities.

5 Inadequate training of TVA personnel in firefighting procedures and equipment.

6 Delay in applying water to the fire.

7 Difficulties encountered in use of self-contained breathing apparatus, caused by inadequate training of personnel in its use, inadequate maintenance, and inability to recharge air bottles fully.

A broad classification of causes would show accidents to be due to either facility inadequacy or employee (or management) negligence. To counteract these causes, management efforts should be directed toward providing a safe working environment (by design) and encouraging employees to be safety-conscious in their work.

Many organizations have safety engineers and extensive safety programs. Safety analysts should be encouraged to conduct comprehensive studies of existing

TABLE 3-3 PROBABILITY RULES

Complement

$$P(A) = 1 - P(\bar{A}) \qquad (3\text{–}10)$$

Addition

$$\begin{aligned} P(A \text{ or } B) &= P(A) + P(B) - P(A \text{ and } B) \qquad (3\text{–}11) \\ &= P(A) + P(B) \quad \text{(if mutually exclusive)} \end{aligned}$$

Multiplication

$$\begin{aligned} P(A \text{ and } B) &= P(A)P(B \mid A) \qquad (3\text{–}12) \\ &= P(A)\,P(B) \quad \text{(if independent)} \end{aligned}$$

Bayes rule

$$P(A \mid B) = \frac{P(A \text{ and } B)}{P(B)} = \frac{P(A)P(B \mid A)}{P(A)P(B \mid A) + P(\bar{A})P(B \mid \bar{A})} \qquad (3\text{–}13)$$

facilities and programs so that potential hazards can be detected and work practices evaluated against industry safety standards. The systematic collection of safety and accident data can provide a useful basis for analysis aimed at improving conditions. Quantitative techniques particularly suitable for analysis of safety data include probability, chi-square, and regression methods.

Since accidents are regarded as chance occurrences, the probability of their happening is often analyzed on a statistical basis, using the standard rules of probability reviewed in Table 3-3. The complement rule would hold, for example, that the probability of an accident A equals one minus the probability of no accident. By the addition rule, the probability of either accident A or B occurring equals the total probability of the two minus the joint probability of their occurring together. The multiplication rule says that the joint probability of two accidents equals the probability of the first one times the probability of the second, given (the symbol is |) that the first has occurred.

By manipulation of the first three rules one can arrive at Bayes rule, which holds that the conditional probability of one accident, given that another has occurred, is equal to the joint probability of the two divided by the marginal probability of the latter. Bayes rule is useful in analyzing the prior existence of unsafe conditions given that some accident has occurred, such as an airplane crash or a refinery explosion. If we let θ represent the unsafe condition, and A the occurrence of an accident, then Bayes rule can be restated as:

$$P(\theta \mid A) = \frac{P(\theta)P(A \mid \theta)}{P(\theta)P(A \mid \theta) + P(\bar{\theta})P(A \mid \bar{\theta})}$$

Example 3-6

Let θ represent the probability of defective wiring and A represent an accidental fire. In a large old factory spot checks have established that $P(\theta) = 0.20$. Given that a plant has defective wiring, the probability of a fire occurring at some time during the year is 0.7 (that is, $P(A \mid \theta) = 0.7$), and if the wiring is not defective the chance of a fire is reduced to 0.1 (that is, $P(A \mid \bar{\theta}) = 0.1$). A recent fire burned one employee severely and caused $90,000 damage. Although evidence is destroyed, the operations manager has been asked by an insurance company to estimate the likelihood it was due to defective wiring.

Solution

$$P(\theta) = 0.2 \qquad \therefore P(\bar{\theta}) = 1 - 0.2 = 0.8$$
$$P(A \mid \theta) = 0.7 \qquad \therefore P(\bar{A} \mid \theta) = 1 - 0.7 = 0.3$$
$$P(A \mid \bar{\theta}) = 0.1 \qquad \therefore P(\bar{A} \mid \bar{\theta}) = 1 - 0.1 = 0.9$$

We wish to find the probability of defective wiring θ given the occurrence of the recent fire A.

$$P(\theta \mid A) = \frac{P(\theta)P(A \mid \theta)}{P(\theta)P(A \mid \theta) + P(\bar{\theta})P(A \mid \bar{\theta})}$$

$$= \frac{(0.2)(0.7)}{(0.2)(0.7) + (0.8)(0.1)} = 0.64 \qquad \therefore \text{64 percent chance}$$

EMPLOYEE INCENTIVES

Employee incentives can be broadly classified into wage incentives and fringe and other benefits. Both types of incentives are discussed below.

WAGE INCENTIVES

Wage and salary administration within an organization is usually the responsibility of the personnel division. Nevertheless, the operations manager often exercises an influence over the employee selection process and production personnel look to him for fair and equitable allocation of wages.

Wage levels depend upon both the industry (or technological skill classification) and locality (local, metropolitan, foreign, and so forth). A competitive firm must not only preserve an internal consistency within the various facets of its own organization and industry, but it must also meet the (external) wage level of the community. In many cases, this means conforming to nationwide union demands.

Several methods of setting and changing wages are in use, ranging from simple ranking systems to grading schemes (such as the "GS" ratings used by the U.S. government) and more sophisticated point and factor comparison plans. These plans are not generally administered by the production manager, and a detailed discussion of them is outside the scope of this text. However, a few comments on the use of incentives are in order.

History has shown that highest levels of output are obtained under incentive schemes and a number of firms have some type of financial incentives built into their wage systems. Most incentive programs have a minimum level, often established as part of the labor contract, with bonus payments arranged for by various methods. Some systems reward the worker on a per-unit basis for all units produced above the minimum; others pay a bonus on the basis of time saved. Some systems average the performance over a few months and make periodic adjustments in a regular wage rate.

The use of group incentives has also gained some popularity because all members tend to cooperate in order to share a bonus. Problems of measuring and recording individual performances are lessened. As with other incentive schemes, however, the rewards should be in direct relation to the output above a specified minimum. Also, plans that are easily understandable and relatively stable are favored over complicated, ever-changing plans. Employee stock plans are a widely used mechanism.

FRINGE AND OTHER BENEFITS

Employee desires for pleasant working conditions and job security have replaced some of the earlier emphasis on wages. We saw earlier in this chapter that employees naturally seek more intrinsic rewards once their basic needs are satisfied. For millions of workers, the work place has become an organizational home which profoundly influences their life style and even their value system. It is not surprising, then, that workers have come to look more and more to organizations to provide them with job security and a sense of belonging, in addition to such items as retirement benefits, health care, and paid vacations.

The implication of this trend to corporate management is that employee benefits should be structured into an organization's objectives, just as are other production and profit objectives. It is only by clearly identifying these objectives in conjunction with other corporate goals that the decision system of the firm can be made to function in a congruent, purposive, and responsive manner.

SUMMARY

The human resource is probably the most challenging input to manage. From the initial design of a job through the work methods and measurement of performance to the final reward for services, an infinite number of problems seem to arise. Perhaps this is because people differ so vastly from machines. Not only does human output and capability differ, but the essence of humanness demands that workers be "respected" as individuals and not simply "allocated" as another physical resource might be.

A well-designed job is described in writing, is fully understood, and is consistent with organization objectives. Job methods can often be improved by conducting a scientific study of present methods using well-developed questioning techniques and principles of motion economy.

Once the best method of doing a job has been determined, it is important to develop standards of performance. These should not be developed arbitrarily, but instead should use the cooperation and participation of the workers to whom they will apply. In addition to serving as a measure of performance for the organization, standards satisfy a need of the workers and provide data for scheduling, inventory control, pricing, and other activities.

Time study, predetermined time methods, and work sampling are all useful ways of developing standards. Basically, time study and work sampling consist of sampling a worker's activities and subjectively rating his or her performance level to determine a normal time NT. Allowances are then taken into consideration for personal, fatigue, and delay times, and a standard time ST is determined. Work sampling is particularly suitable for analyzing less-structured and group operations.

Every operations manager has numerous labor relations "opportunities." The manager should try to foster a favorable work climate on the basis of respect and concern for the workers as fellow human beings. Some managers are finding that wider worker participation in operations decisions has helped to create a better work environment. Nevertheless, it remains management's responsibility to plan, organize, and control the work efforts, for management is responsible to the owners, consumers, and society as well as to the employees. The organizational response to worker demands is vividly demonstrated by the continuing trend of accepting responsibility for workers' social and retirement benefits in addition to their wage compensation.

SOLVED PROBLEMS

LABOR STANDARDS

1 An analyst wants to obtain a cycle time estimate that is within $\pm$ 5 percent of the true value. A preliminary run of 20 cycles took 40 min to complete and had a calculated standard deviation of 0.3 min. What is the value of the coefficient of variation to be used for computing sample size for the forthcoming time study?

Solution

$$V = \frac{s}{\bar{x}}$$

where s = standard deviation of sample = 0.3 min/cycle

$$\bar{x} = \text{mean of sample} = \frac{\sum x}{n} = \frac{40 \text{ min}}{20 \text{ cycles}} = 2 \text{ min/cycle}$$

$$V = \frac{0.3}{2} = 0.15$$

2 How large a sample should be taken to provide 99 percent confidence that a sample value is within ± 5 percent of the true value if the coefficient of variation is estimated to be 15 percent?

Solution

From Fig. 3-7, for $V = 15\%$, $n \cong 80$

3 Past records of a certain work activity show it has a mean time of 60 sec and a standard deviation of 9 sec. How many time-study observations should be taken to be 95 percent confident that the sample mean is within 3 sec (± 3) of the true population value?

Solution

$$V = \frac{s}{\bar{x}}$$

where $s = 9$ sec
$\bar{x} = 60$ sec

$$V = \frac{9}{60} = 0.15$$

Figure 3-7 can be used because the 3-sec accuracy required corresponds to $3/60 =$ 5 percent accuracy.

$$\therefore n \cong 35 \text{ observations}$$

4 Suppose we make a preliminary estimate that the standard deviation of an activity is 9 sec. How many time-study observations should be taken to be 95 percent confident that the sample mean is within 3 sec (± 3) of the true population value?

Solution

Note the similarity between this and the previous problem. In this case we have no mean value available to estimate the coefficient of variation, so we must calculate the sample size instead of using Fig. 3-7. Our method is similar to that followed for the work-sampling Example 3-4 except in this case we are dealing with means ($\bar{x}$'s) rather than sample proportions (p's). Both situations rely on the fact that the sample means and proportions are normally distributed about the population parameters (that is, μ and π respectively) if the sample size is sufficiently large (say, 30 or more for means and 100 or more for proportions).

The distribution of all sample means of a given size (that is, one value of n) is as shown in the diagram atop page 137, with the mean of all the sample means, $\bar{\bar{x}} = \mu$, and the standard deviation of the sampling distribution (called the standard error of the mean):

$$\sigma_{\bar{x}} = \frac{\sigma}{\sqrt{n}} \tag{3-14}$$

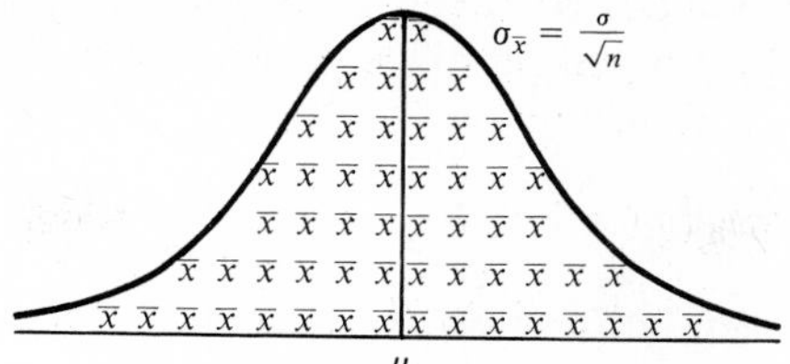

where

$$\sigma = \sqrt{\frac{\sum (x - \mu)^2}{N}} \tag{3-15}$$

Although analysts will not know where a given sample mean lies, relative to μ, they can be confident that 95 percent of the sample means will lie within 1.96 $\sigma_{\bar{x}}$ of μ. As with proportions, when working from sample rather than population data we use estimators:

$\bar{x}$ is an estimator of μ
s is an estimator of σ
$s_{\bar{x}}$ is an estimator of $\sigma_{\bar{x}}$

where

$$s_{\bar{x}} = \frac{s}{\sqrt{n}} \quad \text{and} \quad s = \text{SD of sample} \tag{3-16}$$

$$= \sqrt{\frac{\sum (x - \bar{x})^2}{n - 1}}$$

Solving this problem we wish to set one-half the accuracy interval width ($Zs_{\bar{x}}$) equal to 3 sec.

$$h = Zs_{\bar{x}} = Z\frac{s}{\sqrt{n}}$$

$$\therefore n = \frac{Z^2s^2}{h^2} \tag{3-17}$$

where $h = 3$
$Z = 1.96$
$s = 9$

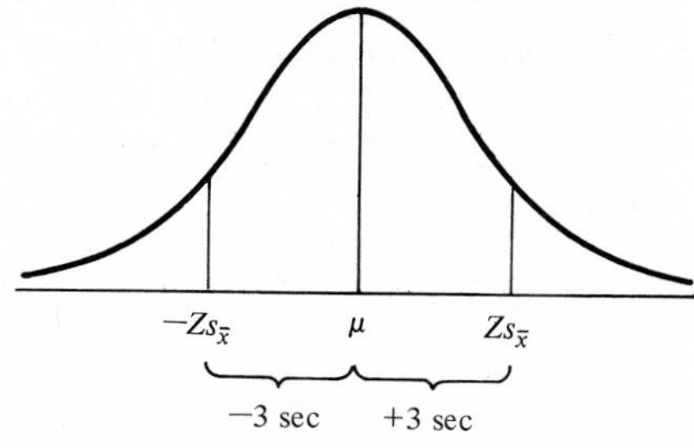

$$n = \frac{(1.96)^2(9)^2}{(3)^2}$$

$$n \cong 35 \text{ observations}$$

Note that the chart method (previous problem) and the calculation method (this problem) are essentially equivalent, but the chart is perhaps a little easier to use if V can be estimated.

5 A time-study analyst wishes to estimate the cycle time for an assembly operation within ± 0.03 min at a confidence level of 95.5 percent. If the cycle time standard deviation σ is known to be 0.08 min, how many observations are required?

Solution

$$n = \frac{Z^2\sigma^2}{h^2} \qquad \text{(Since } \sigma \text{ is known, we use it instead of } s.)$$

where $h = 0.03$
$Z = 2$
$\sigma = 0.08$

$$\therefore n = \frac{2^2(0.08)^2}{(0.03)^2}$$

$$= 28.4, \text{ say 29 observations}$$

Note that as the sample size gets below 30, the t is a more appropriate distribution than the normal. However, the normal approximation should be roughly adequate in this case.

6 A time study of a restaurant activity yielded a cycle time of 2.00 min and the waitress was rated at RF = 96 percent. The restaurant chain has a 20 percent allowance factor. Find the standard time.

Solution

$$\text{CT} = 2.00 \text{ min}$$

$$\text{NT} = \text{CT(RF)} = (2.00)(0.96) = 1.92 \text{ min}$$

$$\text{ST} = \frac{\text{NT}(100)}{100 - \%\text{ allowance}} = \frac{1.92(100)}{100 - 20} = 2.40 \text{ min}$$

7 An operator in a packing operation was clocked by a snap-back stopwatch with the results shown in the accompanying table. The allowance for this type of work is 15 percent. Find

(*a*) the normal time per cycle
(*b*) the standard time per cycle

Element	Cycle (min) 1	2	3	4	5	Performance rating
(1) Obtain 2 boxes	0.82	—	0.80	—	0.85	130
(2) Pack 4 items/box	0.44	0.42	0.46	0.40	0.41	110
(3) Set box aside	0.71	0.67	0.69	0.71	0.68	115

Solution

(*a*) NT = CT(RF)

For (1) Each box suffices for 2 cycles

$$= \frac{0.82 + 0.80 + 0.85}{6}(1.30) = 0.535$$

$$(2) \quad = \frac{0.44 + 0.42 + 0.46 + 0.40 + 0.41}{5}(1.10) = 0.469$$

$$(3) \quad = \frac{0.71 + 0.67 + 0.69 + 0.71 + 0.68}{5}(1.15) = 0.796$$

$$\text{Total} \quad = \overline{1.800}$$

$\therefore$ NT = 1.80 min/cycle

$$(b) \quad \text{ST} = \frac{\text{NT}(100)}{100 - \%\ \text{allowance}} = \frac{1.80(100)}{100 - 15} = 2.12\ \text{min/cycle}$$

8 The State of Oreida Mental Health Division has a health care activity that has a normal time of 8 min, but the activity seems to have been prolonged recently by an increasing number of unavoidable delays. D. R. Mix, a management analyst called in to determine a new standard, conducted a work-sampling study and obtained the results shown in the accompanying table.

Activity	Number of observations	Percent of observations
Working	585	78
Unavoidable delay	90	12
Personal time	75	10
Total	750	100

The Mental Health Division grants its workers a personal time allowance of 8 percent of total time and D. R. Mix wishes to retain that in the new standard.

(*a*) Incorporate the unavoidable delay time and determine a standard time for this activity.

(*b*) Determine how precise the estimate is of unavoidable time, assuming the analyst wishes to have 95 percent confidence in the estimate.

(*c*) State whether the same precision applies to the estimate of personal time.

Solution

(*a*) Allowances should now consist of:

Personal time	8 percent
Unavoidable delay	12 percent
Total	20 percent

$$ST = \frac{NT(100)}{100 - \%\text{ allowance}} = \frac{8(100)}{100 - 20} = 10 \text{ min}$$

(*b*) For 95 percent confidence interval $Z = 1.96$
Half the interval width is:

$$h = Zs_p$$

$$\text{where} \quad S_p = \sqrt{\frac{pq}{n}} = \sqrt{\frac{(0.12)(0.88)}{750}} = 0.011$$

$$h = 1.96(0.011) = 0.023$$

The interval is ± 2.3 percent—that is, the analyst could be 95 percent confident that the true unavoidable delay time is from 9.7 percent to 14.3 percent of total time.

(*c*) The precision interval for the personal time estimate would be slightly smaller (better) due to the use of 10 percent instead of 12 percent for the value of p. In general, for a given level of precision, the sample size required for various activities is governed by those activities with p values closest to 0.5.

LABOR RELATIONS

***9** In a union-management negotiation over a new two-year contract, the union leaders and management representatives each ranked the importance of 10 items (A through J) as follows:

Item	Union ranking	Management ranking
A (productivity)	5	1
B (insurance)	2	7
C (safety)	6	6
D (seniority)	8	10
E (vacation)	1	4
F (standards)	7	5
G (health care)	4	3
H (incentives)	9	8
I (wages)	3	2
J (work hours)	10	9

Is there significant agreement (at the 5 percent level of significance) among the representatives as to the relative importance of the items? *Hint:* Use the rank correlation coefficient to evaluate the significance of these rankings.

Solution

The rank correlation coefficient (r_r) is a nonparametric test and makes no assumptions about the statistical distribution of the variables. It is often a satisfactory measure of correlation for intangible qualities such as contract agreement, leadership abilities, environmental conditions, etc.

$$r_r = 1 - \frac{6 \sum d^2}{n^3 - n} \tag{3-18}$$

where d = difference between assigned ranks
n = number of items ranked

If this calculated value of r_r exceeds the tabled value (which can be obtained from any appropriate statistical reference text) the correlation is statistically significant:

Item	Union ranking	Management ranking	d	d^2
A	5	1	4	16
B	2	7	5	25
C	6	6	0	0
D	8	10	2	4
E	1	4	3	9
F	7	5	2	4
G	4	3	1	1
H	9	8	1	1
I	3	2	1	1
J	10	9	1	1
				$\Sigma = 62$

$$r_r = 1 - \frac{6(62)}{(10)^3 - 10} = 1 - 0.375 = 0.625$$

The table value of r_r (as given in a statistical reference text) for a significance level of $\alpha = 0.05$ is 0.564.

Since $0.625 > 0.564$, the agreement is significant at the 5 percent level; that is, this close agreement would occur by chance less than 5 percent of the time. (Note that it is *not* highly significant; that is, it is not significant at the 1 percent level.)

Note: Rank correlation methods are useful for measuring the general level of agreement on organizational goals. As indicated throughout Chaps. 1 and 3, the specification and congruency of goals is vital to the efficient management of any business system.

EMPLOYEE SAFETY

10 Company safety records show that 40 percent of all accidents occur when "new" employees (those with less than one year's service) are operating equipment, and 60 percent occur when the more experienced employees are operating it. The firm averages six accidents over a 300-work-day year. What is the chance that on any given day during the year an accident will happen to (*a*) a "new" employee, (*b*) an experienced employee?

Solution

$$P(\text{new} \mid \text{accident}) = P(N \mid A) = 0.40$$
$$P(\text{old} \mid \text{accident}) = P(O \mid A) = 0.60$$
$$P(\text{accident}) = P(A) = 6/300 = 0.02$$

(*a*) $P(A \text{ and } N) = P(A)P(N \mid A) = (0.02)(0.40) = 0.008$
(*b*) $P(A \text{ and } O) = P(A)P(O \mid A) = (0.02)(0.60) = 0.012$

QUESTIONS

3-1 What two cornerstones of human resource management policy are brought out in the chapter?

3-2 Distinguish between knowledge and values. Which is more important when it comes to making decisions?

3-3 What does "job design" entail and what are the requirements of a good job design?

3-4 While conducting a work-methods study, a production analyst observed the activities (and times) for processing a component that are shown in the accompanying table.

Classification	Time	Symbol
Cast component in mold	12 min	_____
Undergo inspection	2 min	_____
Wait for lift truck	13 min	_____
Transport component to warehouse	4 min	_____
Store; await shipment	3 days	_____

(*a*) What kind of chart could be used to show these activities and times?
(*b*) Supply the appropriate symbols for the activities described.

3-5 A consultant making a methods-improvement study has identified a problem and developed a written description of the present method of doing the job. What kinds of questions or principles would be most useful for analyzing the problem?

***3-6** Request permission to conduct a methods-improvement study from the industrial relations manager of a local firm. Instead of installing and maintaining new methods, provide the responsible manager (and your instructor) with a finished copy of your report and recommendations.

3-7 How are labor standards established and what are their principle uses?

3-8 Define (*a*) coefficient of variation, (*b*) sample standard deviation, (*c*) standard error of the mean, (*d*) standard error of proportion, and (*e*) level of confidence.

3-9 Distinguish between (*a*) cycle time, (*b*) normal time, and (*c*) standard time. Show the relationship between these times in your answer.

3-10 Under what circumstances would work sampling be preferable to time-study or predetermined time methods for developing labor standards?

3-11 As an assistant manager of operations, you have been assigned the task of formulating some "guidelines that will make the next contract negotiations run a little smoother." Recognizing that this could be an insurmountable task, are there any general principles you might recommend for consideration?

3-12 An operations superintendent has stated that "safety management is simply an extension of fringe benefits and should be the responsibility of the industrial relations manager, not me." Discuss this statement.

PROBLEMS

1 A textile workers' union in New York City has requested that a new time study be made of a skirt-sewing activity. Previous data indicate the activity has a mean time of $\bar{x} = 1.80$ min and standard deviation of 0.40 min. What is the best (preliminary) estimate of the sample size required in order to have 95 percent confidence in the result?

2 Fifty samples of a production cycle showed an average time of 3.60 min/piece. The performance rating was estimated at 90 percent and allowances are set at 20 percent of the total time available. What is the standard time in min/piece?

3 A time study of an Iowa City grain-elevator loading activity revealed a cycle time of 8.57 min for a worker rated at 107 percent. The allowances are: personal time = 25 min/day, fatigue = 84 min/day, delay = 35 min/day. Determine the standard time for an 8-hr/day operation.

4 The standard time for a telephone-installation activity was determined to be 8.40 min from a study of a worker who was rated at 120 percent. If this standard includes a 20 percent allowance factor, what was the actual (cycle) time of the worker studied?

5 An activity has a select time of 2.20 min/cycle and a calculated normal time of 2.64 min/cycle. Allowances are 10 percent. What was (*a*) the performance rating factor of the worker studied, and (*b*) the resultant standard time?

6 A time study of 25 cycles of a worker-machine operation shows these cycle times:

Hand time	0.40 min/cycle
Machine time	1.60 min/cycle

The worker was rated at 110 percent and allowances for the operation, based on an 8-hr workday, are: personal = 20 min/day, fatigue = 30 min/day, delay = 22 min/day. Calculate the standard time per cycle for the worker-machine operation (combined).

7 Time-study data taken of a bulk-filling activity in a cannery in Baltimore was recorded on a *continuous* basis as shown in the accompanying table.

	Cycle time (sec)					
	1	2	3	4	5	RF
Grasp bag	4	37	74	105	338	120
Locate for fill	16	51	84	117	352	120
Machine fill	26	61	94	127	362	
Set on conveyor	34	68	102	334[a]	369	110

[a] Bag broke open due to presence of a foreign object on the conveyor.

The firm's labor contract requires a 15 percent allowance for all workers on the bulk-filling line. Compute the standard time for this activity.

8 A work-sampling study is to be taken of an elevator system in a large metropolitan office building. The building manager feels the elevators are idle 40 percent of the time and wishes to have 95.5 percent confidence that the accuracy is within ± 2 percent. How many observations should be taken?

9 An analyst wishes to develop a labor cost standard for a manual computer-card-sorting activity. The elements consist of (1) collecting the cards, (2) sorting them, and (3) filing the sorted deck. For element (2), the standard deviation is estimated to be $\sigma = 2.25$. To determine the sorting time to an accuracy of within ± 0.5 min with 95.5 percent confidence, how large a sample should be taken?

10 A work-sampling study is to be taken of a metal shop operation for the purpose of developing standard costs. Estimates of the various element times, as provided by the shop manager, are as shown in the accompanying table. Management

would like a 95.5 percent confidence-level estimate of the true proportion of time of the various elements within an accuracy of ± 2.5 percent. How many samples should be taken to be sure the 95.5 percent confidence level holds for all elements?

Job element	Estimated time
Planning and layout	25%
Metal cutting	15
Fabrication	50
Delay	10
	100%

11 A work-sampling study was made of a cargo-loading operation for the purpose of developing a standard time. During the total 120 min of observation the employee was working 80 percent of the time and loaded 60 pieces of cargo. The analyst rated the performance at 90 percent. If the firm wishes to incorporate a 10 percent allowance factor for fatigue, delays, and personal time, what is the standard time for this operation in min/piece?

12 A soldering operation was work-sampled over two days (16-hr total) during which time the employee soldered 108 joints. Actual working time was 90 percent of total time and the performance rating was estimated to be 120 percent. If allowable time per union contract is set at 15 percent of the total time available, what is the standard time for this operation?

13 In a chemical plant, the probability of any given employee being injured from a fall is $P(F) = 0.005$ and from chemical inhalation is $P(C) = 0.020$. If a worker falls, the probability of injury from chemical inhalation increases to $P(C \mid F) = 0.100$. What is the probability that an employee will be injured (*a*) by both a fall and chemical inhalation, (*b*) by either a fall or chemical inhalation?

14 Data collected by a safety committee show that over 80 percent of the accidents in a plant are caused by 10 percent of the 400 employees, whom they classify as accident prone *AP*. The firm has 120 employees over 50 years of age and 6 of them are included in the *AP* classification.

An employee is selected at random for a potentially hazardous task. What is the probability that the employee is (*a*) an *AP* employee, (*b*) either *AP* or over 50? (*c*) If selection is restricted to those 50 years old or younger, what is the probability of selecting an *AP* employee?

15 Due to a purchasing error, 30 percent of the half-inch-diameter bolts in a stockroom bin are low-tensile steel (that is, $P(L) = 0.30$). Before any bolts are used in construction, they are supposed to be examined by an inspector to ensure that only high-tensile bolts are used. The bolts look very much alike and there is a 0.2 probability that the inspector will incorrectly identify any bolt. A bolt is withdrawn from stock, routinely inspected, and installed at a critical point in a guard rail five stories above ground. What is the probability that it was a high-tensile bolt?

Hint: Let I = incorrect identification and $\bar{I}$ = correct identification. The probability we seek is $P(\bar{L} \mid \bar{I})$.

***16** A study was made to determine whether the wages in a printing department really reflected the performance level of employees. All 10 employees were rated by the foreman, and these ratings corresponded as follows to their relative wages.

Employee	Performance ranking	Wage ranking
O'Sullivan	7	8
Monaghan	2	1
O'Connell	9	10
Keeley	1	3
Sweeney	4	2
Murphy	10	9
Fitzpatrick	3	6
O'Mahony	8	5
O'Shea	5	4
Hennessy	6	7

Is there a (statistically) significant relationship between performance and wages in this department? (Use the 99 percent level of significance).

CASE: FORMATION PLASTICS

Three years ago, President Phillip Osgood of Formation Plastics began implementation of a three-year productivity plan to "get this organization moving again!" As part of the effort, Osgood hired Vance Gruel as a special assistant and positioned him in the plant operations department under Operations Manager Toni Dahl but reporting directly back to Mr. Osgood. Gruel had a wide range of operating experience in four other larger plastics firms. He had also done some purchasing work for another firm and was known for driving a hard bargain. He was not especially diplomatic, but he was action oriented and got things done—and generally done his way.

By now things were moving, but not everyone agreed on the direction. Gruel and Osgood seemed to be spending most of their time convincing each other that the firm was on the verge of a great era and that the current situation was a "stabilizing period before takeoff." In contrast, the engineering manager characterized the situation (privately) as "Osgood's Follies" and the personnel manager, Kate Howard, referred to it as "the great motivational inversion."

The past three years had been characterized by the following:

Three years ago

Production output was high (demand was very strong) but prices were low and profits mediocre.

Employment level was at 200, with employees nonunion, receiving average wages, and reasonably content.

No job descriptions or labor standards were in use.

Two years ago

Production output, prices, and profits were all higher.

Employment level was up to 300, although some of the poor-performance employees had been laid off.

Work standards had been implemented in the extrusion, fabrication, and finishing (but not molding) departments.

One year ago

Production output began to level off, but prices climbed higher and profits held up fairly well.

Additional automated machinery was installed.

Employment level was 350, but some employees complained of being bored with their work and others began to resist the pressures for more output. Unionization efforts got under way.

Today

Production output and productivity are down slightly from last year.

Costs and wages are higher, prices are firm, but profits are down.

Employment level is at 370, but several grievances have been filed over "tight standards" and "inadequate safety programs." The company is unionized.

There are still no work standards in the molding department.

At the insistence of Toni Dahl, Mr. Osgood agreed to hold a top-level management meeting to review the situation. During the meeting the following discussion took place.

Osgood (president) After having nearly doubled our employment in the last three years, Toni and I thought it was appropriate to assess our progress to date, and perhaps lay plans for the future. Why don't we just throw the meeting open for discussion—feel free to say what you like.

Gruel (special assistant) Well, I for one would say the three-year plan has gone well, except for some bottlenecks like the supervisor (Tom Rowley) in the molding department. If I could convince Toni here to put some pressure on Tom Rowley I think we'd move a little faster.

Dahl (operations manager) Tom's got a fairly close group there with a couple of older men who have been around a long time—and are kind of nice to have around when those molders break down. I guess the guys kind of trade-off down there and Tom is afraid Gruel's standards will break up the group and force Harry Wheeler to retire early.

Gruel That's just the problem! There are no job descriptions, no specific duties, no standards—nothing! I bet the costs per unit in that department could be cut in half with some good, tight standards. Instead, I suspect they've probably doubled in the past three years.

Martin (accountant) I can speak to that, and they haven't doubled. We just finished an extensive analysis of unit cost data over the past three years and I'd say molding costs are very close to what they were three years ago—within 2-3 percent.

Gruel Anyway, it's holdouts like Tom that are causing our problems.

Howard (personnel) Well, they're not causing me the headaches that the extrusion and fabrication departments are. I'm getting more official grievances from them than I can keep track of. Cleanup and accidents, cleanup and safety—that's all I hear!

Gruel Safety is really engineering's problem, but I can straighten you out on the cleanup thing. Before we got some controls in this place they took about an hour a day for a leisurely "cleanup" break. That's $12\frac{1}{2}$ percent of the whole day! We set some reasonable standards of 5 percent—that's plenty of time.

Howard But they're saying it is not enough time! They say the standard is "arbitrary and too tight." They don't have enough time to collect their gear, they're losing tools, people are stumbling over their equipment . . .

Gruel (**interrupting Howard**) Arbitrary! Arbitrary my foot! I took work-sampling studies with one hundred on-the-spot observations in each of three departments myself. It was just a week after some of the deadwood had been fired two years ago. And it showed both extrusion and fabrication could get the cleanup part of the job done in an average of 28 minutes, plus or minus 2 minutes. I'm practically 100 percent sure it can be done. But we'll never convince those lazy do-nothings of it if you act like the standards are questionable yourself. I think you should reject grievances like that outright!

Howard Well, I certainly can't do that and I have no intention to. As a matter of fact, I have to agree with some of the scuttlebutt that's going around. I think maybe we'd be better off if we threw out the whole standards program—at least my job would be a lot simpler.

Gruel I'm afraid it's a little late for that now, Kate. Anyway, with costs in extrusion and fabrication going up so fast we need the controls more than ever now. Cost per unit is up 15 percent over last year but no one seems to worry about that except me.

Dahl I haven't opposed the implementation of standards and, as a matter of fact, I support the concept of standards. But it seems to me our approach may be doing more harm than good. How about some of us sitting down with the supervisors of the extrusion, fabrication, and molding departments and retracing our path over the past three years?

Howard Count me in!

Gruel Count me out! Why do that. It's a waste of time! I've argued with Tom Rowley lots of times about getting molding to move up with the rest of the company. I don't think a meeting will convince him.

Dahl That's not necessarily my intent.

Gruel Well then, what is? Do we want an efficient, moving organization here, or don't we?

Osgood Count me in. Let's set up the meeting for next Monday morning in my conference room. Vance will be out of town but we'll see that he gets a full report. And let's have someone from marketing and cost accounting sit in. Meeting adjourned.

QUESTIONS

1 Was President Osgood correct in giving Vance Gruel pretty much a free reign to work on productivity and standards?

2 Do you feel Gruel was technically competent?

3 How do you account for the cost-per-unit differences in the molding versus the extrusion and fabrication departments?

4 What are the roots of the safety grievances?

5 Why is Osgood going ahead with the meeting (and including accounting and marketing people) even though Gruel is going to be out of town?

6 How can Dahl support the concept of standards and yet not give full support to Gruel in implementing them?

BIBLIOGRAPHY

[1] ABRUZZI, A.: *Work Measurement*, Columbia University Press, New York, 1952.

[2] AFL-CIO: "Collective Bargaining—Democracy on the Job," publication 136, Washington, D.C., July 1965.

[3] BARNES, RALPH M.: *Motion and Time Study: Design and Measurement of Work*, 6th ed., John Wiley & Sons, New York, 1968.

[4] BLOOM, B. S., et al. (eds.): *Taxonomy of Educational Objectives: Cognitive Domain*, David McKay Company, New York, 1956.

[5] BUFFA, ELWOOD S.: *Modern Production Management*, 3d ed., John Wiley & Sons, New York, 1969.

[6] CHASE, RICHARD B., and NICHOLAS J. AQUILANO: *Production and Operations Management*, Richard D. Irwin, Homewood, Illinois, 1973.

[7] CLARK, R. O., D. J. FATCHETT, and B. C. ROBERTS: *Workers' Participation in Management in Britain*, Heineman Educational Books, London, 1972.

[8] DAVIS, LOUIS E.: *Job Satisfaction—A Socio-Technical View*, Report 575-1-69, University of California, Los Angeles, 1969.

[9] EMERY, F. E., E. THORSUD, and K. LANGE: *The Industrial Democracy Project*, report no. 2, Institute for Industrial and Social Research, Technical University of Norway, Trondheim, 1965.

[10] GARRETT, LEONARD J., and MILTON SILVER: *Production Management Analysis*, 2d ed., Harcourt, Brace & Jovanovich, New York, 1973.

[11] GAVETT, J. WILLIAM: *Production and Operations Management*, Harcourt, Brace & World, New York, 1968.

[12] HAMBURG, MORRIS: *Statistical Analysis for Decision Making*, Harcourt, Brace & World, New York, 1970.

[13] HERZBERG, FREDRICK: "One More Time: How Do You Motivate Employees," *Harvard Business Review*, January–February 1968.

[14] HOPEMAN, RICHARD J.: *Production*, Charles E. Merrill Books, 1971.

[15] KRATHWOHL, D. R., et al.: *Taxonomy of Educational Objectives: Affective Domain*, David McKay Company, New York, 1964.

[16] MAYER, RAYMOND R.: *Production and Operations Management*, 3d ed., McGraw-Hill, New York, 1975.

[17] MASLOW, A. H.: *Toward a Psychology of Being*, 2d ed., Van Nostrand, New York, 1968.

[18] NIEBEL, BENJAMIN W.: *Motion and Time Study*, 5th ed., Richard D. Irwin, Homewood, Illinois, 1972.

[19] OLSEN, R. A.: *Manufacturing Management: A Quantitative Approach*, International Textbook, Scranton, Pennsylvania, 1968.

[20] RADFORD, J. D., and D. B. RICHARDSON: *The Management of Production*, Macmillan, London, 1968.

[21] RETTIG, JACK L.: "On the Meaning of Work," working paper, Oregon State University, Corvallis, Oregon, 1975.

[22] UNITED STATES NUCLEAR REGULATORY COMMISSION: News Release, vol. 1, no. 26, August 5, 1975.

[23] VROOM, V. H.: *Work and Motivation*, John Wiley & Sons, New York, 1964.

[24] WALES, C. E., and R. A. STAGER: *Educational Systems Design*, 1974 (available from C. E. Wales and West Virginia University).

[25] WEBB, PAUL (ed.): *Biostatistics Data Book*, National Aeronautics and Space Administration, Washington, D.C., 1964.

[26] WINSTONE, H. E.: *New Light on Social Problems*, Catholic Truth Society, London, 1963.

[27] WOODWARD, JOAN: *Industrial Organization: Theory and Practice*, Oxford University Press, London, 1965.

CHAPTER

4

Capital Inputs

COMPARISON AND SUMMARY
SOLVED PROBLEMS
QUESTIONS
PROBLEMS
CASE: FACTHOMES, INCORPORATED
BIBLIOGRAPHY

Operations managers often have to make decisions about the use of capital in their operations. These decisions are primarily concerned with how best to allocate a limited amount of funds to facilities and equipment so that the organization's objectives will be most effectively facilitated.

In some cases, the capital allocation decisions involve a labor versus equipment tradeoff. However, labor costs are usually regarded as operating costs of a variable nature, whereas facilities and equipment are classified as "fixed." In this sense the capital allocation decisions have an extended impact on the organization, for the fixed costs are charged off against income over several years in the future.

This chapter concentrates upon methodologies that can help an operations manager make better decisions concerning the use of capital. We look first, and briefly, at the concepts of capital, interest, and depreciation. The major part of the chapter then deals with the methodology, advantages, and disadvantages of the various techniques. Numerous examples and solved problems are included to illustrate the wide range of applications and provide a comparative basis for selecting the appropriate technique for any given situation. We conclude the chapter with some observations regarding capital management in multinational operations.

CAPITAL AND INTEREST

Capital is a resource of funds owned or used by an organization. Since the total supply of funds is limited, the use of funds is usually carefully planned and controlled. A financial plan which shows the sources and allocations of funds for a given period in the future is called a *capital budget*. Sources and allocations of funds are discussed below.

SOURCES OF FUNDS

An organization may obtain funds from either or both of two major sources *external* to the operations: equity and debt. Equity capital comes from the funds paid in for capital stock ownership. Debt capital constitutes the funds borrowed via bonds, notes, and other liabilities. Should the organization fail to be self-sustaining, debt capital has prior claim to assets over equity capital. Nonprofit organizations are often financed by debt capital which is repaid through operating income or taxes levied against the public.

Internally, an organization may increase its available funds by retaining earnings from profits generated in the past. In profit-making organizations, some profits are typically distributed to stockholders, but those retained earnings not paid out as dividends become available for capital budgeting. (Depreciation is sometimes referred to as a source of funds, but it is actually no more of a source than are any other funds in the organization.)

The cost of capital depends on the mix of equity and debt which the firm holds. Debt financing is typically less expensive than equity financing, at least up to a point (say over 40 percent or 50 percent debt) where debt proportion is so high that the equity holders incur a significant risk that the firm will become insolvent. Then the equity investors are less willing to risk their funds (that is, or are not willing to pay as much for the capital stock) and the effective cost of equity capital increases.

METHODS OF ALLOCATING FUNDS

At the national level, government policies with respect to economic growth, employment, inflation, interest rates, and the like, exert a strong influence over the availability and allocation of funds. Within the organization, capital is channeled into those activities which best fulfill operating objectives. The organization's economic goals typically constitute an important criterion for allocation of funds. In addition, past decisions often obligate the organization to many current and future operating expenditures. For example, a plant expansion two years earlier may have already dictated a current machinery investment and future operating costs.

Since organizational goals must be sought within a complex economic and social environment, numerous factors influence allocation decisions. The problem examples that follow in this chapter are based primarily upon an economic criterion, with the intent that the decision maker will first want to examine those factors that are most readily quantifiable. For free enterprise organizations, economic profitability is perhaps the most comprehensive measure of performance available. Indeed, some writers claim that in the long run it is difficult to think of any managerial responsibilities that would not be reflected in profit performance [**2**: 11]. Nevertheless, as indicated in our framework for decisions in Chap. 1, the decision maker may also want to incorporate other relevant but perhaps less-tangible factors into the model before selecting from among all alternative courses of action.

Some techniques useful for evaluating uses of funds include:

1 Payback

2 Annual cost methods (average and equivalent)

3 Present value

4 Rate of return (unadjusted and adjusted)

5 MAPI

Of these techniques, the payback, present value, and adjusted rate of return probably receive most widespread use. Both the average annual cost and the unadjusted rate of return methods involve approximations which introduce varying degrees of inaccuracy. The equivalent annual cost is just as accurate as, and in fact is equivalent to, present value. We will see that present value can be extended to the concept of expected present value, when uncertainties regarding future cash flows must be taken into account. Payback is relatively crude but is widely used, and MAPI is relatively specialized and not as widely used.

INTEREST AND PRESENT VALUE CONCEPTS

In a capitalistic economy there are numerous sources of funds available. Similarly, there are many demands for funds from individuals, firms, government agencies, and the like. A given quantity of these capital funds is more valuable today than the same amount of funds would be at some time in the future. This is because the funds can be used to buy factors of production which, when properly combined and transformed, add value to the production system outputs. In other words, the funds have an earning power. Since they have this value over time and can be used to generate more funds, their use legitimately involves some cost.

Interest is the cost of money, or the rental rate for funds. This cost is determined by the availability of capital funds in the economy, the alternative opportunities investors enjoy to use those funds, and the risk of loss the lenders must take. Funds used in very safe investments involve little risk of loss and can usually be obtained at a more moderate cost. Funds used in more speculative ventures typically offer a greater potential earning power, but the borrower must compensate the lender for the greater risk of loss by paying a higher rate of interest. Thus the risk, along with economic conditions in general, helps establish a basic interest rate.

Given an interest rate, the total amount of interest charged a borrower is then proportional to the principal amount borrowed and the length of time until repayment.

$$\begin{aligned} \text{Interest} &= (\text{principal})(\text{rate})(\text{time}) \\ i &= prt \end{aligned} \qquad (4\text{-}1)$$

Example 4-1

Find the amount of interest due at the end of one year if \$1,000 is borrowed at a 6 percent rate.

Solution

$$\begin{aligned} \text{Interest} &= prt \\ i &= (\$1{,}000)(0.06)(1) = \$60 \end{aligned}$$

The total amount due at the end of a time period consists of the principal amount borrowed plus the interest on that principal. Symbolically, if we let P = present value amount of the principal, i = interest rate, and F = future sum due, we have, for one time period:

$$F_1 = P + P(i) = P(1 + i)$$

The total amount due at the end of two time periods consists of the amount due at the end of the first period, $P(1 + i)$, plus interest on that amount for the second period:

$$F_2 = P(1 + i) + P(1 + i)i = P(1 + i)(1 + i)$$
$$F_2 = P(1 + i)^2$$

Similarly, at the end of three years:

$$F_3 = P(1 + i)^3$$

And for n years, the future sum (F) is:

$$F = P(1 + i)^n \tag{4-2}$$

Example 4-2

Find the amount of principal and interest due at the end of 2 years if $1,000 is borrowed at a 6 percent rate. (See the accompanying diagram.)

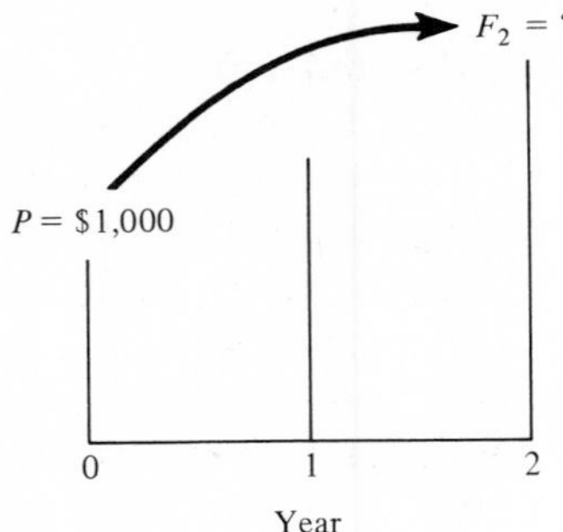

Solution

$$F = P(1 + i)^n$$
$$F_2 = \$1,000(1 + 0.06)^2 = \$1,123.60$$

Conversely, the present value P of future sum F discounted (reduced in value back to the present) at interest rate i for n periods is:

$$P = \frac{F}{(1 + i)^n} \tag{4-3}$$

Example 4-3

What is the present value of $1,123.60 received 2 years from now if the sum is discounted at 6 percent? (See the accompanying diagram.)

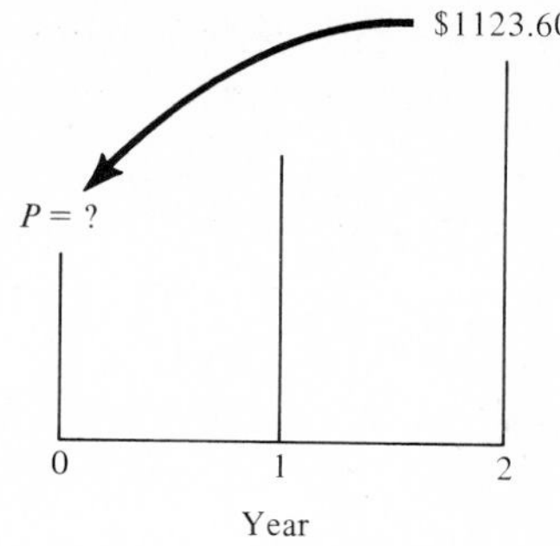

Solution

$$P = F\frac{1}{(1 + i)^n}$$

$$= \$1{,}123.60\,\frac{1}{(1 + 0.06)^2} = \$1{,}000$$

The above expression can be restated in the convenient form:

$$P = F\frac{1}{(1 + i)^n} = F(\text{factor}) = F(\text{PV}_{sp})_{i\%}^{n\text{yr}} \tag{4-4}$$

where PV_{sp} is a certain factor for the present value of *single payments* made in n years if the interest rate is i percent. This PV_{sp} factor, when multiplied by the amount of the future payment F will yield a discounted present value amount P. Appendix G contains PV_{sp} factors for payments of $1 over a commonly used range of interest rate i and period n values. Many electronic hand calculators are designed and programmed to produce and use these factors directly, once the i and n values are specified.

Example 4-4

What is the present value of the salvage on a piece of construction equipment if the salvage price 10 years from now is $8,000 and if the cost of funds is 8 percent?

Solution

$$\begin{aligned} P &= F(\text{PV}_{sp})_{8\%}^{10\text{yr}} \\ &\doteq \$8{,}000(0.463) \\ &= \$3{,}704 \end{aligned}$$

On many occasions one must determine the present value or future sum of a series of equal payments made over n years when they are discounted or compounded at an interest rate i. These equal *sums paid or received regularly are annuities* and are designated as R. Appendix H contains present value factors for annuities PV_a of $1.

Thus, the present value of annuities can be determined in a manner similar to that of single payments, except that the factor differs.

$$P = R(\mathrm{PV}_a)_{i\%}^{n\,\mathrm{yr}} \tag{4-5}$$

Example 4-5

Find the present value of $100 paid at the end of each of 5 years, when the interest rate is 6 percent.

Solution

$$P = R(\mathrm{PV}_a)_{i\%}^{n\,\mathrm{yr}} = \$100(\mathrm{PV}_a)_{6\%}^{5\,\mathrm{yr}}$$
$$P = \$100(4.212) = \$421.20$$

This means that the sum of $421.20 now is equivalent to annual payments of $100 at the end of each 5 years if the cost of capital is 6 percent. That is, if $421.20 were placed in a bank at 6 percent interest, sums of $100 could be withdrawn at the end of each of 5 years. With the fifth year withdrawal of $100, the balance would be exactly zero.

Since interest is the price paid for the use of funds, the cost of funds will vary as the interest rate varies. In the United States, the prime interest rate, which is the "favorable" rate charged by lending institutions to large borrowers, has fluctuated from around 6 percent to 12 percent during the past several years. The international rate has exceeded 12 percent in many nations. With a high interest rate, future incomes (or expenses) of cash have a lesser present value than when interest rates are lower. Thus, the relative economic advantage of one project over another may very well change as the interest rate changes domestically, or as evaluations take on an international dimension.

DEPRECIATION AND TAXES

Depreciation is a charge that reflects the decrease in value of an asset over time. Since most fixed assets have a limited useful life, their cost should be charged off gradually against the income they help produce during that useful life. No cash flows out of the organization when this accounting entry is made, but the use of any given asset must be reflected as an expense of doing business. Depreciation is an expense that must be deducted from the gross operating income of an organization.

The decline in value of an asset over time may be difficult to estimate and may take many different paths, depending upon the type of asset and the operating conditions. In many cases the best estimate of depreciation expense is obtained by subtracting an estimated salvage value from the cost of the asset and apportioning the remaining cost equally over the economic life of the asset. In other cases the asset may decline in value more in earlier years than in later years. Whatever the case, from a decision-making standpoint the economic value or service life of the asset is more important than an arbitrary book value. The rate of depreciation allowed by government regulations is of significance also, however, from a tax standpoint.

Since depreciation is a noncash expense that reduces gross income, the amount of depreciation charged off in a given period affects profits and taxes for that period. Because of the time value of (cash) money, many firms seek to charge off their depreciation expense as early as practicable. Although the total monetary amount of depreciation expense (and thus also the effect on gross income) would appear to be the same regardless of when the expense is incurred, some cash outlay for income taxes is deferred by using an accelerated depreciation method.

$$\text{Tax} = \text{tax rate (income} - \text{expense)} \tag{4-6}$$

Taxes on the deferred net income must obviously be paid in future periods, but in the meantime the firm has the use of cash that it would not otherwise have. This cash has a value consistent with the cost of capital to the organization.

During periods of sustained price inflation, the book value of depreciation charged against plant or equipment reflects an increasingly smaller proportion of the actual replacement cost of such resources. Similarly, accounting records may understate potential salvage values. In these as well as other uncertain circumstances, actual market values usually form a better basis for decision than do accounting book values. Nevertheless, the accounting records typically form the basis for income tax determination.

STRAIGHT LINE

Under straight-line depreciation the book value of an asset decreases at a constant rate over the life of the asset. If I represents the original investment value, S represents salvage, and n is the number of years of life, the depreciation is:

$$\text{Straight-line depreciation} = \frac{\text{investment} - \text{salvage}}{\text{life}} = \frac{I - S}{n} \tag{4-7}$$

Note that the depreciation represents capital recovery only and does not include any return on the investment.

Example 4-6

An investment of \$5,000 in new equipment is expected to have a salvage value of \$1,000 after a 4-yr life. Find the straight-line depreciation expense.

Solution

The depreciation schedule is shown in Fig. 4-1.

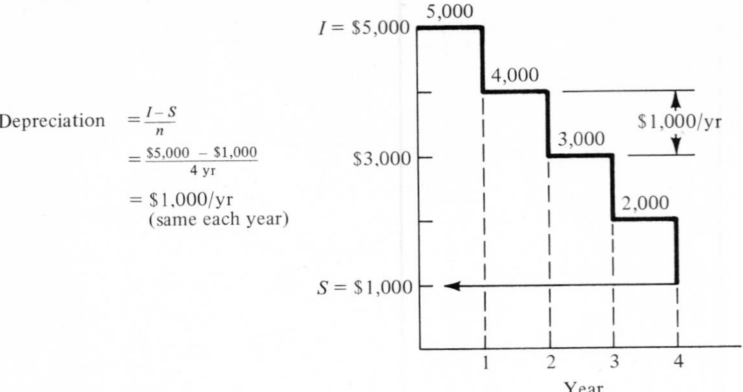

FIGURE 4-1 Straight-line depreciation

DECLINING BALANCE

Under declining-balance depreciation a fixed percentage of the book value of the asset is deducted each period (for example, each year) and the book value decreases at a decreasing rate. This accelerated depreciation method results in a most rapid decline in value in the early stages of an asset's life. The maximum rate allowed by the U.S. Internal Revenue Service has been twice that percentage allowed by straight-line depreciation, except that the rate is not allowed to exceed 20 percent.

Therefore, if

$$\text{Straight line \%} = \frac{1}{n}$$

$$\text{Declining balance \% (max)} = \frac{2}{n} \tag{4-8}$$

The amount of depreciation in any given year is then

$$\text{Declining-balance depreciation} = \frac{2}{n}\text{(asset book value)} \tag{4-9}$$

Example 4-7

An investment of $5,000 in new equipment is expected to have a salvage value of $1,000 after a 4-yr life. Find the declining-balance depreciation expense, if the maximum allowed by law is twice the percentage allowed by straight-line methods.

Solution

The depreciation schedule is as shown in Fig. 4-2. The maximum rate allowed is:

$$\text{Rate} = \frac{2}{n} = \frac{2}{4} = 50\%/\text{yr}$$

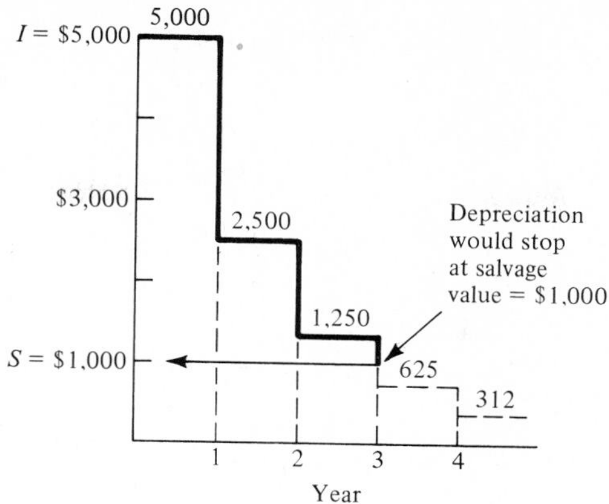

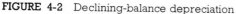

FIGURE 4-2 Declining-balance depreciation

Note that since this rate exceeds 20 percent, the firm would have to limit its rate to 20 percent if it were in the United States. However, depreciation regulations in foreign countries differ and we shall continue with the 50 percent rate for purposes of illustration and comparison.

Depreciation	= rate (book value)	
∴ 1st yr: depreciation	= 0.50(5,000) = $2,500	$2,500
2d yr: book value	= original I − 1st yr depreciation	
	= $5,000 − $2,500 = $2,500	
∴ depreciation	= 0.50(2500) = $1,250	$1,250
3d yr: book value	= previous book value − 2d yr depreciation	
	= $2,500 − $1,250 = $1,250	
∴ depreciation	= 0.50(1250) = $625	

Note: Depreciation expense would be terminated at the salvage value of $1,000. Thus the recorded depreciation for the third year would be $1,250 − $1,000 = $250. — $ 250

4th yr: depreciation = $0 — 0

Total $4,000

Since declining-balance methods do not usually deplete all the investment value, users sometimes convert to straight-line depreciation during the latter stages of asset life, or as soon as the straight-line method yields larger depreciation amounts than would occur by continuing the declining-balance method.

SUM-OF-YEARS DIGITS

Under the sum-of-years digits depreciation, the digits representing each year of life of the asset are summed and this total serves as the denominator of a fraction which is multiplied by the (investment-salvage) value. The numerator varies each

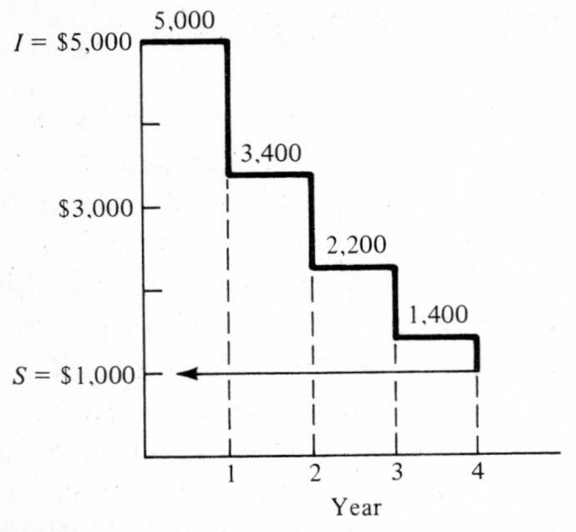

$$\text{1st year depreciation} = \frac{4}{\Sigma n}(I - S)$$
$$= \frac{4}{10}(\$5{,}000 - \$1{,}000)$$
$$= \frac{4}{10}(\$4{,}000) = \$1{,}600$$
$$\text{2nd year depreciation} = \frac{3}{10}(\$4{,}000) = \$1{,}200$$
$$\text{3rd year depreciation} = \frac{2}{10}(\$4{,}000) = \$\ \ 800$$
$$\text{4th year depreciation} = \frac{1}{10}(\$4{,}000) = \$\ \ 400$$
$$\text{Total} \quad \$4{,}000$$

FIGURE 4-3 Sum-of-years digits depreciation

period, beginning with the largest-year digit down to the smallest. Thus for the first year:

$$\text{Sum-of-years depreciation} = \frac{n}{\sum n}(I - S) \tag{4-10}$$

For the second year, the numerator is $n - 1$.

The sum-of-years digits is an accelerated depreciation method and the asset value decreases at a decreasing rate. It does not yield as rapid a depreciation schedule as the declining-balance method, however.

Example 4-8

An investment of $5,000 in new equipment is expected to have a salvage value of $1,000 after a 4-yr life. Find the sum-of-years digits depreciation expense.

Solution

The depreciation schedule is as shown in Fig. 4-3. The sum-of-years digits is:

$$n = 1 + 2 + 3 + 4 = 10$$

The depreciation amounts determined via the three depreciation methods discussed in the examples above are summarized in the accompanying table.

Year	Straight line	Declining balance	Sum-of-years digits
1	1,000	2,500	1,600
2	1,000	1,250	1,200
3	1,000	250[a]	800
4	1,000	0[a]	400
	4,000	4,000	4,000

[a] Depreciation expense terminated at salvage value of $1,000.

CAPITAL INVESTMENT EVALUATION TECHNIQUES

The decision problem associated with investment evaluation arises from the fact that the capital resource always has alternative uses. A quantitative evaluation of the economic gains and/or losses of different alternatives helps permit the decision maker to select the use which most closely conforms with the organization's objectives.

Since operations activities have time, rate, and magnitude dimensions, a decision criterion which focuses on one aspect of investment to the exclusion of others may be inadequate—or even misleading. Thus, for two alternatives requiring different investment amounts, one might favor a project that offers a 35 percent of return over one offering 30 percent—until one found that the total magnitude of return on the first is \$6,000, whereas the second is \$50,000. Similarly, a project that pays for itself in three years is not necessarily better than one that returns its cost in four years if the latter continues yielding a return over many more years in the future.

There are several criteria that are widely used to evaluate capital investments in production operations activities. While each method has its advantages and shortcomings, some are more appropriate than others in given situations. Many organizations have found that more than one technique of analysis is necessary to ensure that all dimensions of the decision alternatives are considered.

PAYBACK

Payback (payoff) tells the number of years for an investment to pay for itself.

$$\text{Payback} = \frac{\text{investment} - \text{salvage}}{\text{operating advantage/yr}} = \frac{I - S}{\text{OA/yr}} \tag{4-11}$$

The *operating advantage* (OA) reflects the improvement in cash flows either from increased income or decreased expenses, or both, but it does not yet have depreciation expenses deducted from it. On the contrary, payback measures how quickly the savings will recoup the investment amount. In its simplest form, payback does not consider salvage values, taxes, or the like. However, when salvage and tax considerations apply, they should be included in the analysis. The investment I should be reduced by the value of any salvage S expected[1] and the operating advantage should be the after-tax (AT) advantage, or net cash flow after tax:[2]

$$(AT)\ \text{Operating advantage} = \frac{\text{operating advantage}}{\text{yr}} - \frac{\text{tax}}{\text{yr}}$$

[1] When I is reduced by the *present value* of the expected salvage, and the operating advantage per year is a time-adjusted average, the payback is designated as being time adjusted by the notation: Payback TA.

[2] Note, however, that in calculating the tax per year, depreciation expenses should be deducted from the operating advantage before taxes are computed. In the following example, straight-line depreciation would be (\$20,000 − \$2,000) ÷ 10 yr = \$1,800-yr. Tax is levied against the savings less depreciation at a 50 percent rate. Therefore, tax = 0.50(\$4,000 − \$1,800) = \$1,100.

Example 4-9

The Lake City Bank is considering purchase of a data processing storage unit which will cost $20,000, last 10 years, and then have a guaranteed $2,000 salvage value. It will generate savings of $4,000/yr (before depreciation) but necessitates that $1,100 of the savings must be paid in taxes. If management insists on a 5-yr payoff period, does this investment qualify?

Solution

$$(AT)\quad \text{Payback} = \frac{I - S}{\text{OA/yr}} = \frac{\$20{,}000 - \$2{,}000}{\$4{,}000 - \$1{,}100} = 6.2 \text{ yrs}$$

The investment does not meet management criteria.

The operating advantage on an incremental investment to improve a process would thus be the net annual operating advantage minus the additional tax that will be incurred on this operating advantage

$$(AT)\quad \frac{\text{OA}}{\text{yr}} = \begin{pmatrix}\text{old} & & \text{new}\\ \text{operating} & - & \text{operating}\\ \text{cost} & & \text{cost}\end{pmatrix} - \text{tax}\begin{pmatrix}\text{old} & & \text{new operating}\\ \text{operating} & - & \text{cost and}\\ \text{cost} & & \text{depreciation}\end{pmatrix} \tag{4-12}$$

Advantages of payback are that it is (1) simple and quick to calculate, (2) easy to understand, and (3) a measure of time required to return an original investment. Disadvantages are that payback (1) does not consider the economic life of the investment, and (2) does not consider the total return on the investment (that is, life of equipment after payback is reached). In addition, (3) simple payback does not consider the time value of money or the imbalance of cash flows, that is, high inflow now and low inflow later, or vice versa. However, the imbalance shortcoming is sometimes circumvented by accumulating nonuniform cash flows on a cumulative basis until the investment is recouped. Despite these disadvantages payback is a very widely used method of investment evaluation. One survey of American firms indicated that 60 percent used payback and, of those, only 16 percent accepted a payback period of more than five years [**13**: 132].

ANNUAL COST METHODS

Two methods of evaluating capital investments on the basis of determining an annual cost are in use. The first, average annual cost, can usually be calculated without reference to any present value or annuity tables because it uses an approximation. As a result, although it is easy to compute, it is slightly less accurate than the equivalent annual cost method. Both methods are discussed below.

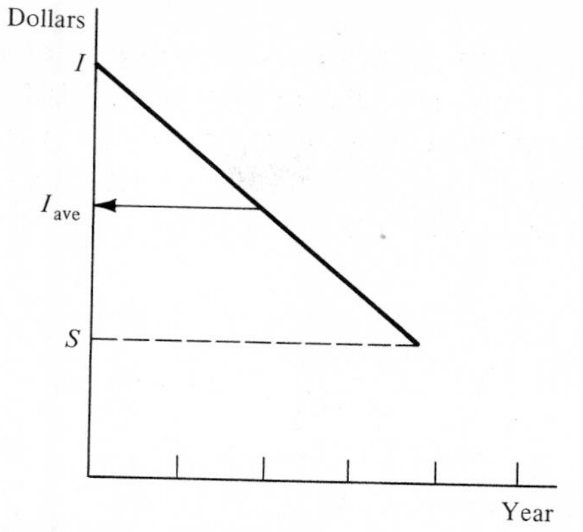

$$I_{ave} = \frac{\text{investment} + \text{salvage}}{2}$$

$$I_{ave} = \frac{I + S}{2} \qquad (4\text{-}13)$$

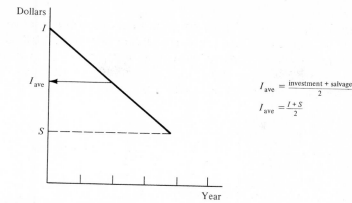

FIGURE 4-4 Average investment

Average Annual Cost

Average annual cost is an approximate method of calculating an equal annual cost over the life of an investment. The costs for various alternatives can then be compared on an annual basis. Average annual costs include three items:

Capital costs of depreciation or investment recovery (*CR*)
Return, or interest, on the average investment (*R*)
Other annual operating and maintenance costs (*OC*)

The capital costs are very often simply straight-line depreciation amounts, and when this is true the capital recovery *CR* is apportioned out equally over the life of the investment. The return *R* on average investment I_{ave} is a charge for the use of funds. If the funds used to buy equipment were borrowed, the lender would expect to recover the capital loaned *CR* plus interest *R* on that capital. Since some of the capital is "repaid" each period (the depreciation amount), the amount of the loan would decrease from a large value initially to a small (salvage) value ultimately. An approximation of the average value of the investment is shown in Fig. 4-4. From this, one can observe that I_{ave} is the mean of two points representing the initial *I* and final *S* investment amounts.

The return on I_{ave} depends upon the firm's cost of capital or borrowing rate (i).

$$R = (i)I_{ave}$$

The average annual cost is then:

$$\text{Average annual cost} = \text{capital recovery} + \text{return} + \text{other costs}$$

$$\text{Average annual cost} = CR + R + OC \qquad (4\text{-}14)$$

Example 4-10

An investment of $20,000 in an off-gas monitoring system will have a salvage value of $6,000 after an economic life of 5 yr. Maintenance and operating costs are $4,400/yr and the firm's cost of capital is 10 percent. What is the average annual cost of this investment?

Solution

Note that capital recovery is the straight-line depreciation amount.

$$CR = \frac{I - S}{n} = \frac{\$20{,}000 - \$6{,}000}{5 \text{ yr}} = \qquad \$2{,}800/\text{yr}$$

$$R = (i)I_{\text{ave}} = 0.10\left(\frac{I + S}{2}\right)$$

$$= 0.10\left(\frac{\$20{,}000 + \$6{,}000}{2}\right) = \qquad 1{,}300/\text{yr}$$

$$OC = M \text{ and } O \text{ costs} = \qquad 4{,}400/\text{yr}$$

$$\text{Total} \quad \$8{,}500/\text{yr}$$

Advantages of the average annual cost method are that (1) it is relatively simple and quick to calculate, (2) it is not difficult to visualize an investment as costing an equal amount each year, (3) alternatives with different lifetimes can be effectively compared, and (4) cost comparisons can be made without knowledge of income or considering the effect of taxes on incomes. Disadvantages are that (1) an approximation is used which ignores the timing of cash flows by computing interest on the average investment, (2) uniform, or straight-line, depreciation of assets is usually assumed, and (3) total costs are not explicitly considered.

Equivalent Annual Cost

Equivalent annual cost is a time-adjusted (more exact) method of calculating an equal annual cost over the life of an investment. This method, like the average annual cost technique, permits comparison of alternatives with different economic lives, but it is more exact than average annual cost in that it takes the compounding of interest into account. The equivalent annual cost includes three items:

Capital recovery and return (CR and R)
Interest on salvage $(i)S$
Other annual operating and maintenance costs (OC)

The capital recovery and return is basically an annuity amount derived from the present value investment amount. Thus the *CR* and *R* on a $1,000 investment at 10 percent over five years would be a given size annuity that could be withdrawn each year for five years to finally exhaust the sum. The total amount withdrawn would exceed $1,000 by the amount of interest accumulated on the declining capital amount. The annual *CR* and *R* amount can be determined from either the present value annuity factor (PV_a) or a factor called the capital recovery factor (*CRF*) by noting that the present value investment amount *I* must be the product of a PV_a factor times some appropriate annuity amount *R*:

$$I = R(PV_a)_{i\%}^{n\,yr}$$

Solving for

$$\begin{aligned} R &= \frac{I}{(PV_a)_{i\%}^{n\,yr}} \\ &= I\left[\frac{1}{(PV_a)_{i\%}^{n\,yr}}\right] \qquad (4\text{-}15) \\ &= I\,(CRF) \end{aligned}$$

For $n = 5$ yr, $i = 10\%$

$$CRF = \frac{1}{PV_a} = \frac{1}{3.791} = 0.264$$

The *CR* and *R* applies to the investment less salvage, $(I - S)$. Therefore, since funds are also tied up in the salvage amount during the life of the investment, the equivalent annual costs must include, as a second item, the interest on salvage. A convenient way to intuitively justify this cost is to imagine that funds are borrowed on a separate basis to cover the salvage amount. At the end of life of the investment, the salvage value is assigned to the lender and the only cost to the borrower is the annual interest charge on the amount borrowed. The equivalent annual cost is then:

$$\begin{aligned} \text{Equivalent annual cost} &= \text{capital recovery and return} \\ &\quad + \text{interest on salvage} + \text{other costs} \\ &= CR \text{ and } R + (i)S + OC \qquad (4\text{-}16) \end{aligned}$$

Example 4-11

An investment of $20,000 in an off-gas monitoring system will have a salvage value of $6,000 after an economic life of 5 years. Maintenance and operating costs are $4,400/yr and the firm's cost of capital is 10 percent.

(*a*) What is the equivalent annual cost of this investment?

(*b*) How does the equivalent annual cost compare with the average annual cost of Example 4-10?

Solution

(*a*) The equivalent annual cost consists of:

Capital recovery and return: CR and R = (investment − salvage)$\left(\frac{1}{\text{Pv}_a}\right)$

$$CR \text{ and } R = (I - S)\left[\frac{1}{(\text{PV}_a)^{5\text{yr}}_{10\%}}\right]$$

$$= (\$20{,}000 - \$6{,}000)\left(\frac{1}{3.791}\right) = \qquad \$3{,}693/\text{yr}$$

[Alternatively, $(I - S)(CRF)$ = \$14,000(0.264) = \$3,693]

Interest on salvage: $\text{Int}_s = (i)S = (0.10)(\$6{,}000) =$ 600/yr

Other: OC = maintenance and operation = 4,400/yr

Total \$8.693/yr

(*b*) This compares with an average annual cost of \$8,500/yr and is larger because the effect of compounding interest on the capital investment is taken into account in the equivalent annual cost method. As an approximate method, the average annual cost is within about 2 percent of the more exact method for this problem. In view of other assumptions often made, this error may be insignificant.

Advantages of the equivalent annual cost method are that (1) it is relatively exact in that it takes compounding of interest into account, (2) it is not difficult to visualize an investment as costing an equal amount each year, (3) alternatives with different lifetimes can be compared, and (4) cost comparisons can be made without knowledge of income or considering the effect of taxes on income. Disadvantages are that (1) total costs are not explicitly considered, and (2) the illusion of accuracy may be misleading in view of assumptions usually made about future costs, equipment lifetimes, salvage values, and interest rates.

In comparing average annual cost with equivalent annual cost, note that in the former method the interest charge, or return R, is on the average book value of the investment, which includes the salvage component. There is no need to make a separate calculation for interest on the salvage value since salvage is included in the book value. In the equivalent annual cost method, the annual annuity payment CR and R includes capital payment and compounded interest on the investment less salvage. Since interest on the salvage value is not included in the CR and R, a separate charge must be made for it.

PRESENT VALUE

Present value tells the worth of future income or expense flows in terms of present dollars. Whereas future values increase due to the *compounding* effect of interest on progressively larger amounts, the reverse of this, or reduction of future values to lesser present values, is what we have referred to as *discounting*. The present value technique of analysis discounts all relevant future cash flows to present value terms. These cash flows are typically the investment value, the maintenance and operation costs, and the income flows. The initial investment is usually already in present value terms and thus inherently includes future depreciation and interest charges (or capital recovery and return as it is referred to in the equivalent annual cost method). Maintenance and operation expenses, on the other hand, do involve cash outlays in the future and therefore must be discounted back to present value.

$$\text{Present value cost} = \text{PV investment} + \text{PV other costs} - \text{PV salvage}$$

$$\text{PV}_{\text{cost}} = I(\text{PV}_{sp}) + \sum OC(\text{PV}_{sp}) - S(\text{PV}_{sp}) \tag{4-17}$$

Example 4-12

An investment of $20,000 in an off-gas monitoring system will have a salvage value of $6,000 after an economic life of 5 years. Maintenance and operating costs are $4,000 the first year and increase by $200/yr thereafter. The firm's cost of capital is 10 percent. What is the net present value cost of this investment?

Solution

$$\text{Present value cost} = \text{PV investment} + \text{PV other costs} - \text{PV salvage}$$

$$\text{PV investment} = I(\text{PV}_{sp})^{0\text{yr}}_{10\%} = \$20{,}000(1.00) = \qquad \$20{,}000$$

$$\text{PV other costs} = OC(\text{PV}_{sp})^{n\text{yr}}_{10\%}$$

yr 1	($4,000)(0.909) =	$3,636
yr 2	(4,200)(0.826) =	3,469
yr 3	(4,400)(0.751) =	3,304
yr 4	(4,600)(0.683) =	3,142
yr 5	(4,800)(0.621) =	2,981
		$16,532

16,532

Total $36,532

$$\text{Less: PV salvage} = -S(\text{PV}_{sp})^{5\text{yr}}_{10\%}$$

$$= -\$6{,}000(0.621) = \qquad -3{,}726$$

PV cost $32,806

Advantages of the present value approach are that (1) it considers the total return (which is important when the amount of capital is limited), (2) it includes time-adjusting considerations, (3) it can easily handle fluctuations in costs or revenues, and (4) total cost comparisons can be made without knowledge of income or considering the effect of taxes, or, on the other hand, these factors can be considered if applicable. Disadvantages are that (1) it considers the total amount but does not explicitly consider the rate of return or number of years for an investment to pay for itself, and

(2) it inherently assumes that capital can be reinvested at the current cost of capital. The advantages of present value often outweigh the disadvantages and as a result it is one of the most widely used techniques for investment evaluation.

RATE OF RETURN

Rate of return expresses the percentage of profit to the investment. Simple rate of return is:

$$RR_s = \frac{\text{profit}}{\text{investment}} \tag{4-18}$$

and is expressed as an interest rate i. The assumption here is that time factors are not considered, or alternatively that the investment and profits all occur within the first time period (that is, are already in present value terms). Profits consist of the net operating advantage less depreciation (and taxes if applicable).

The words "rate of return" are often used loosely and convey different meanings to different people. We shall identify the two major types of rate of return calculations according to whether or not they have been adjusted to include the compounding effect of the time value of money. The unadjusted rate of return has not been so adjusted (and uses an approximation much like that used in the average annual cost method) whereas the adjusted rate of return does take interest compounding into account.

Rate of Return (Unadjusted)

Unadjusted rate of return RR_u refers to the fact that the calculations use average investment values which are not discounted to present value. Thus no compounding effect of interest is recognized. The RR_u connotes the same meaning as simple RR in that it depicts a profit as a percentage of the investment. However, the profit values are yearly, or periodic, so the relationship is one of profit per year over average investment. Since profit consists of the operating advantage per year (OA/yr) less depreciation (dep), the RR_u before tax is:

$$(BT) \quad RR_u = \left(\frac{\text{OA/yr} - \text{depreciation/yr}}{I_{\text{ave}}}\right) \tag{4-19}$$

We shall continue to refer to *operating advantage (or gross operating advantage)* as the incremental savings (increased income or decreased expenses) before depreciation and taxes are deducted. After deduction of only depreciation expense, we have a *net operating advantage BT*, and after deduction of both depreciation and taxes we have a *net operating advantage AT*. Where the analyst wishes to determine the RR_u after taxes, the above equation becomes:

$$(AT)\quad RR_u = \left(\frac{\text{OA/yr} - \text{depreciation/yr} - \text{tax/yr}}{I_{\text{ave}}}\right) \tag{4-20}$$

As usual, taxes are based upon the operating advantage less the tax allowed depreciation. In some cases, the depreciation schedule used for tax purposes will not be the same as the economic depreciation used for other decision purposes.

$$\text{Tax/yr} = \%\ \text{rate (OA} - \text{tax allowed depreciation)} \tag{4-21}$$

Example 4-13

A nuclear utility in Ohio has an opportunity to install an irradiation tube in its reactor during a forthcoming shutdown. The tube will cost $10,000 initially and will be of no value (highly contaminated) after use. During the 4-yr life of the project, the tube will be used to collect radioactive isotopes which can be sold to yield an operating advantage of $3,000/yr.

(*a*) Find the before-tax rate of return (unadjusted for interest compounding).

(*b*) If the utility claims an 8 percent before-tax cost on its debt-equity capital structure, is this a worthwhile venture from an economic standpoint?

Solution

$$(a)\quad (BT)\quad RR_u = \left(\frac{\text{OA/yr} - \text{depreciation/yr}}{I_{\text{ave}}}\right)$$

$$\text{where}\quad \text{depreciation} = \frac{\$10{,}000 - 0}{4\ \text{yr}} = \$2{,}500/\text{yr}$$

$$I_{\text{ave}} = \frac{\$10{,}000 + 0}{2} = \$5{,}000$$

$$(BT)\quad RR_u = \frac{\$3{,}000 - \$2{,}500}{\$5{,}000} = 10\%$$

(*b*) Yes, they have a 2 percent return above their capital cost. On the other hand, many firms would not be satisfied with this 2 percent advantage, especially if there were other opportunities for investment that would yield 5 percent, 10 percent, or 20 percent above their cost of capital.

Advantages of using the unadjusted rate of return are that (1) it defines a rate at which profits are earned and can thus be compared with similar rates from other projects, (2) it is a useful measure to compare against the cost of capital (if a rate of return does not equal or exceed the cost of capital, it is a losing venture), and (3) it can be interpreted either on the basis of a total project RR_s or on an annual basis RR_u.

Disadvantages are that (1) it does not adjust for the compounding value of income, (2) it does not consider the total magnitude of the project, (3) it does not allow for variance in the gross return per year, and (4) it requires estimates of return as well as costs.

A special note of caution is justified in view of the approximation made to determine average investment. When cash flows are equal and regular, such as with an annuity, the RR_u gives a reasonably close estimate of return which is satisfactory for many decision situations. However, if the cash flows are irregular (high in some years and low in others), or if the project life is very long or very short, this technique may yield a distorted value as compared to a time-adjusted rate of return RR_A.

Rate of Return (Adjusted)

The adjusted rate of return is the discount rate which equates an investment cost with its projected earnings. Some analysts refer to it as the *internal rate of return* (IRR) or as the *return on investment* (ROI). It is a time-adjusted method in that it equates the discounted present value earnings with the discounted present value cost and does not base the future earnings and costs on year-average values. In concept, however, it is similar to the simple and unadjusted rates of return. Whereas simple rate of return is the ratio or percentage of total profit to total investment, the adjusted rate of return is the same ratio except that profit and investment values are all in present value terms. It is thus a time-adjusted rate of return RR_A.

One of the difficulties in calculating RR_A is that the PV_{sp} factor for each year's earnings or expenses differs. Since the calculation technique is an attempt to determine at what interest rate i the cash inflow equals the cash outflow, the procedure is necessarily a trial-and-error process. The adjusted rate of return:

$$RR_A = (i) \text{ rate, where PV (cash outflow)} = \text{PV (cash inflow)} \tag{4-22}$$

If, for example, an initial trial at an arbitrarily selected i rate reveals that the present value of future earnings is less than the present value of the investment, this

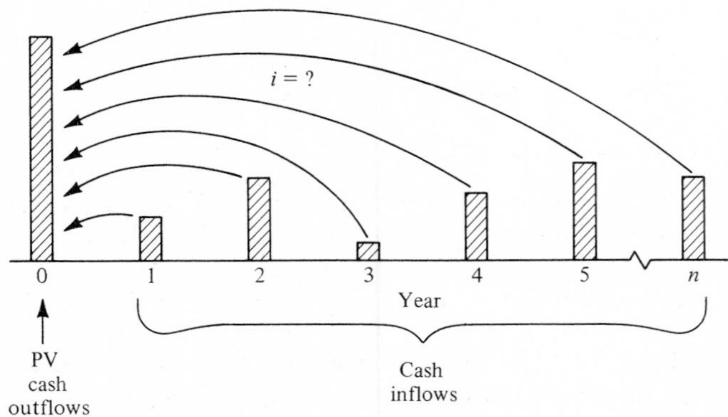

FIGURE 4-5 Rate of return

indicates that the true rate of return must be lower than that initially tried. With a lower i rate, the present value of a series of earnings will be more and will more closely approximate the present value of the investment. As we lower the i rate, the present value of earnings continues to increase to the point where, at 0 percent, the present value is a maximum which is simply the arithmetic sum of the series. The reverse also holds true so that as the i rate is increased, the present value of the series of cash flows decreases.

Example 4-14

(Similar to Example 4-13 but time-adjusted). A nuclear utility in Ohio has an opportunity to install an irradiation tube in its reactor during a forthcoming shutdown. The tube will cost $10,000 initially and will be of no value (highly contaminated) after use. During the 4-yr life of the project, the tube will be used to collect isotopes which can be sold to yield an operating advantage of $3,000/yr.

(*a*) Find the before-tax rate of return (adjusted for interest compounding).

(*b*) If the utility claims an 8 percent before-tax cost on its debt-equity capital structure, is this a worthwhile venture from an economic standpoint?

Solution

(*a*) $RR_A = (i)$ rate

where PV (cash outflow) equals PV (cash inflow)
given PV(cash outflow) = $10,000

PV(cash inflow) must now be set equal to $10,000. Solution method is to try various discount rates until the appropriate rate is determined.

Try 10 percent

Year	Operating advantage	PV_{sp} factor	PV amount
1	$3,000	0.909	$2,727
2	3,000	0.826	2,478
3	3,000	0.751	2,253
4	3,000	0.683	2,049
			$9,507

Note 1: Since each year's operating advantage was the same, the PV_a factor could have been used in this problem:

$$\text{PV amount} = R(PV_a)^{4yr}_{10\%} = \$3{,}000(3.170) = \$9{,}510 \text{ (rounding difference)}$$

Note 2: Since the PV amount of the operation advantage ($9,510) is less than the PV investment amount, the earnings have been discounted too much. The RR_A must be lower than 10 percent.

Try 8 percent

$$\text{PV amount} = R(\text{PV}_a)^{4\text{yr}}_{8\%} = \$3{,}000(3.312) = \$9{,}936$$

Try 6 percent

$$\text{PV amount} = R(\text{PV}_a)^{4\text{yr}}_{6\%} = \$3{,}000(3.465) = \$10{,}395$$

Interpolation

The actual RR_A is between 6 percent and 8 percent, the present value difference between these being \$10,395 − \$9,936 = \$459. The 8 percent figure (\$9,936) is \$10,000 − \$9,936 = \$64 low. The \$64 is \$64 ÷ \$459 = 14 percent of the 2 percent difference (of 8–6 percent). Therefore, the linear interpolated rate is (0.14) (2 percent) = 0.28 points below 8 percent.

$$\left.\begin{matrix} 6\% \\ \\ 8\% \end{matrix}\right\} 2\% \quad \begin{matrix} = \\ \\ = \end{matrix} \quad \$459 \left\{ \begin{matrix} \$10{,}395 \\ 10{,}000 \\ 9{,}936 \end{matrix} \right. \left.\begin{matrix} \\ \\ \end{matrix}\right\} \$64 = 14\%$$

$$(0.14) \text{ of } 2\% \text{ difference} = 0.28\%$$

$$\text{Therefore } (BT)\ RR_A = 8.00\% - 0.28\% = 7.72\% \cong 7.7\%$$

Note that comparing this 7.7 percent time-adjusted rate of return with the 10 percent unadjusted rate determined in Example 4-13, it is evident that the discounting effect can be significant, even for earnings received in the relatively near future. Had the same total earnings extended over a longer period, the adjusted rate would have been correspondingly less.

(*b*) On a time-adjusted basis the 7.7 percent return does not equal or exceed the firm's cost of capital and the venture is not worthwhile. In this situation, the firm would be using capital at a cost of 8 percent to invest in a project that would yield only 7.7 percent—a losing proposition.

Advantages of the adjusted rate of return technique are similar to the unadjusted rate of return except that the adjusted method considers the time of cash flows and discounts them accordingly. However, it also necessitates estimates of return in order to be useful and does not explicitly consider the total amount of return.

MAPI

During the late 1940s and 1950s a method of analysis for machine replacement was developed by George Terborgh and published by the Machinery and Allied Products Institute (MAPI). This MAPI formula yields essentially a next year's relative rate of return and compares this with alternatives of not investing now. The resultant is an urgency rating; the higher the rating the greater the profit. The urgency rating includes consideration of

1 Net investment (that is, cost less any amount avoided).
2 Next year operating advantage (that is, net change in operating costs and revenues—except capital costs and taxes).
3 Next year capital consumption:
   (a) *Avoided* (depreciation, and the like, avoided by not purchasing new equipment).
   (b) *Incurred* (depreciation, overhaul, and so forth).
4 Next year income tax adjustment (the net effect on income taxes).

The urgency rating *UR* developed is essentially a tax-adjusted first year rate of return.

$$UR = \frac{\text{amount available for return on investment}}{\text{average net investment}} \tag{4-23}$$

MAPI is based upon empirical evidence of replacement life and takes various depreciation schedules and tax rates into account in its structured calculation method. On the other hand, it evaluates alternatives only one year in advance and does not examine future earnings streams.

INVESTMENT EVALUATION UNDER UNCERTAINTY

Capital investment evaluations typically assume that the amount of the future cash flows is well known and that these flows are certain to occur. This degree of certainty is usually not justified by conditions that prevail in the real world. Demand levels, equipment lifetimes, salvage values, and other factors that affect cash flow are usually uncertain and can be considered probabilistic in nature.

The uncertainty of future cash flows can be handled in a number of ways. One way is to go ahead with the evaluations as if a state of certainty did exist and then subjectively allow for the uncertainties associated with each alternative. This can easily result in different choices by different individuals because the allowance for uncertainty is totally subjective. Another frequently used (but not highly recommended) method is to inject additional conservatism to compensate for the uncertainty, for example, to require an estimated 25 percent rate of return rather than a 20 percent rate before any investment is authorized.

More analytical methods of incorporating the uncertainty of future cash flows into capital investment evaluations have recently been developed. Some of the methods we shall consider briefly are (1) computer simulation, (2) various decision-theory approaches, and (3) expected value analysis using decision trees.

RISK ANALYSIS VIA COMPUTER SIMULATION

By means of simulation, a wide range of cash flows and/or rates of return that could result from following a given investment policy can be modeled on a computer. The models are basically mathematical and statistical statements of possible future cash flows. As different assumptions are made about costs, sales price, and so forth, the resultant cash flows change and the computer computes and prints out these results. The relative frequencies with which the outcomes occur and their dispersion of values provide the analyst with descriptive measures of the distribution of outcomes, such as the mean and standard deviation. The mean then is a measure of the central tendency of the outcome and the standard deviation is a measure of the precision of the estimate. With these and other summary statistics (such as the coefficient of variation) a manager can more confidently choose from among alternatives.

Suppose, for example, that a firm's top management is considering a major investment in new plant equipment. Some factors which could affect the success of such an investment include (1) market size, (2) selling prices, (3) market growth rate, (4) share of the market, (5) investment required, (6) residual value of the investment, (7) operating costs, (8) fixed costs, and (9) useful life of the facilities [**6**]. To determine values for each of these factors, knowledgeable executives are asked for a range of values for each factor and the probabilities that those values will be achieved. For example, a simulated rate of return may require estimating the useful life of a chemical plant. Estimates may range from less than 5 years to perhaps over 30 years, with the most likelihood that it will be around 10 to 15 years. Probability values may be attached to the various estimates resulting in a distribution, perhaps like that shown in Fig. 4-6.

The distributions of values for the useful life and various other factors are then combined to estimate the return. Any method of rating the return which is suitable to management may be used, such as an adjusted rate of return. The firm's computer is programmed to select a value at random from each of the input distributions (nine, in this case) and to compute an adjusted rate of return for the combination of values

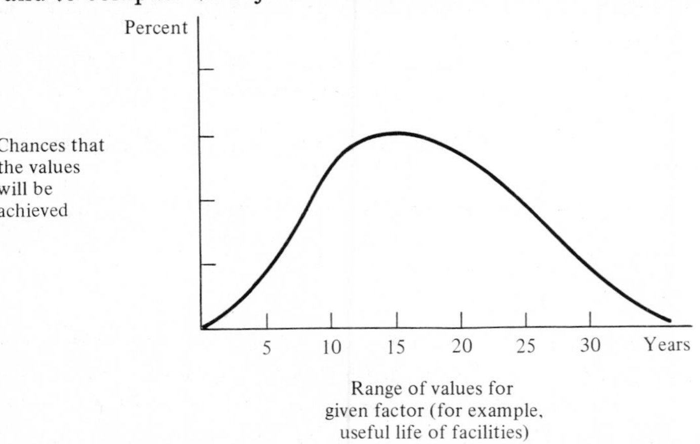

FIGURE 4-6 Estimated lifetime

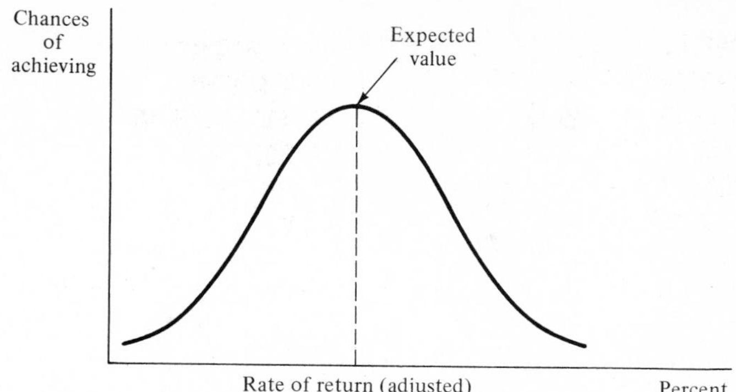

FIGURE 4-7 Probability distribution of rates of return

selected. Several thousand such calculations are done in two or three minutes for a nominal $15–$25 cost. The computed values are then reported in the form of a probability distribution, as shown in Fig. 4-7.

As can be seen, this method makes good use of the available data, permits experience and judgment to be incorporated into the calculations, and provides the decision maker with a measure of dispersion (risk) as well as an expected value. The chances that a given rate of return will be achieved can be determined and used in the decision-making process.

DECISION-THEORY CRITERIA

The computer simulation methodology just described relies heavily on the idea of an average or expected value. In the long run, where an event occurs repeatedly the expected value is a good, unbiased limit of the relative frequency of occurrence of an event. However, many capital investment decisions are "one-time" decisions, and in many cases the risk-taking attitude of management or the asset position of the firm mitigates against using an expected value approach. Some other possible (legitimate) courses of action in addition to expected value are shown below.

1 *Expected value* Choose the act with the highest expected monetary value (EMV).

2 *Maximax* Choose the act that will maximize the maximum possible profit.

3 *Maximin* Choose the act that will maximize the minimum possible profit (or minimize the maximum possible cost).

4 *Maximum probability* Choose the act that will maximize profit under the most likely state of the environment.

The maximax criterion is optimistic whereas the maximin is pessimistic. Other strategies can also be identified but they are beyond the scope of this text.

The main point is that decision makers should recognize their own organization's attitude toward risk and act accordingly. They should not blindly accept an expected value criteria when the situation dictates otherwise.

EXPECTED VALUE ANALYSIS VIA DECISION TREES

A simple yet effective way of incorporating probabilistic events into a decision framework is via the use of decision trees. Decision trees depict alternative outcomes in schematic form, as branches of a tree. The value of each outcome times its probability of occurrence represents an expected value which is compared to the expected value of other alternatives so that the alternative with the highest expected value may be selected—assuming expected value is a satisfactory criterion.

Many types of investment decisions lend themselves to modeling via a decision tree [**8**]. The tree is constructed from left to right using, along its branches, a sequence of boxes for controllable (decision) points and circles for uncontrollable (chance) events. The tree is analyzed backwards (from right to left) by first stating the payoff value associated with each branch on the extreme right. Then the payoffs are multiplied by their respective probabilities (which may be noted under the payoff values). The highest expected value may be entered on the schematic at the preceding decision point. This then becomes the payoff value for the next higher-order expectation, as the analyst continues to work back to the trunk of the tree.

Example 4-15

A glass factory specializing in crystal is developing a substantial backlog and the firm's management is considering three courses of action: (A) arrange for subcontracting, (B) begin overtime production, and (C) construct new facilities. The correct choice depends largely upon future demand which may be low, medium, or high. By consensus, management ranks the respective probabilities as 0.10, 0.50, and 0.40. A cost analysis reveals the effect upon profits that is shown in the accompanying table.

	Profit ($000) if demand is		
	Low (P = 0.10)	**Medium** (P = 0.50)	**High** (P = 0.40)
A = Arrange subcontracting	10	50	50
B = Begin overtime	−20	60	100
C = Construct facilities	−150	20	200

(a) State which course of action would be taken under a criterion of: (1) maximax, (2) maximin, (3) maximum probability, (4) maximum expected value.

(b) Show this decision situation schematically in the form of a decision tree.

Solution

(*a*) *Maximax* Maximize the maximum profit. Choose C in hopes demand will be high.

Maximin Maximize the minimum profit. Choose A where the least profit is \$10,000.

Maximum probability Maximize under the most likely state. Choose B as the highest payoff under medium demand where $p = 0.50$.

Maximum expected value Choose the act with the highest expected value.

$$
\begin{aligned}
E(X) &= \sum XP(X) \\
E(A) &= 10(0.10) + 50(0.50) + 50(0.40) = 46{,}000 \\
E(B) &= -20(0.10) + 60(0.50) + 100(0.40) = 68{,}000 \\
E(C) &= -150(0.10) + 20(0.50) + 200(0.40) = 75{,}000
\end{aligned}
$$

Therefore choose C with expected value of \$75,000 profit.

(*b*) As shown in Fig. 4-8, for a decision tree the controllable (choice) decision variables are A, B, and C and the uncontrollable variable is demand. We begin on the left by showing the decision choices first, followed by the chance alternatives of demand. The payoff values under each

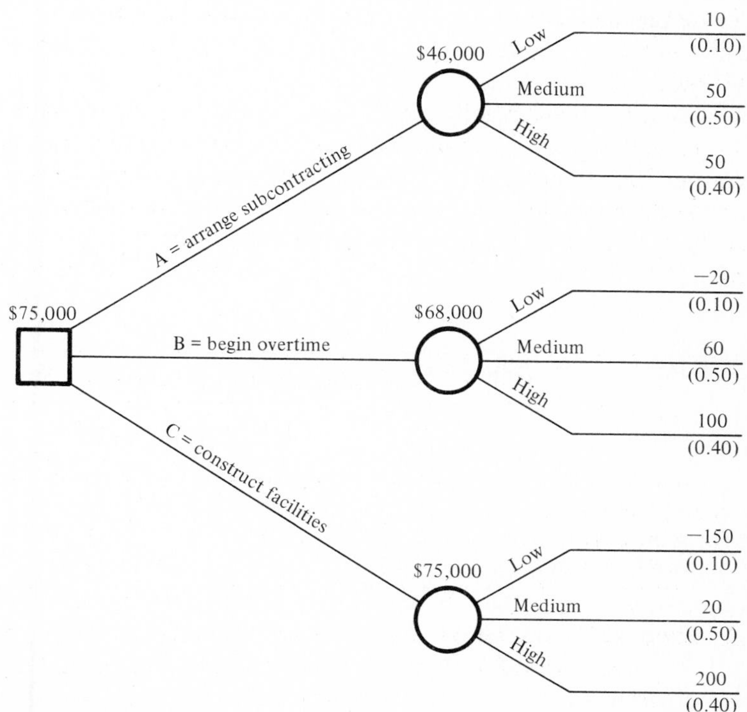

FIGURE 4-8 Decision tree

alternative are shown at the right with associated probabilities below each value. The expected value of each branch is then computed by summing the profit times probability for each. For example, for A

$$10(0.10) + 50(0.50) + 50(0.40) = \$46{,}000$$

These values (such as $46,000) are entered at the nodes and the choice at the preceding node is dictated by the highest respective values. In this example our choice to construct new facilities (C) for the expected value of $75,000 is higher than that of the other two alternatives.

Advantages of a decision tree approach are that (1) it helps one structure a decision in an objective way, (2) it forces an explicit identification of alternatives, (3) it helps one distinguish between controllable and uncontrollable variables, and (4) it permits one to incorporate uncertainty in a systematic, objective way. Disadvantages are that (1) probabilities and monetary values must still be estimated, (2) not all variables are easily quantified, and (3) expected value may not be the most desirable approach in a given situation.

Although the disadvantages can pose real obstacles, decision trees are a graphically revealing technique and some extensions are being made to overcome their limitations. For example, considerable work is being done to make use of an expected utility value rather than an expected monetary value for situations where intangibles play a significant role or where the decision maker's utility for monetary increments does not follow a linear pattern.

Because decision trees so conveniently lend themselves to analysis of cash flows sequenced over time, the incorporation of present value concepts is an easy and very useful extension. The time value of money is included simply by compounding or discounting all monetary values at some specified interest rate (such as the firm's cost of capital) to a present value at any designated point in time.

MINIMUM VALUE ANALYSIS

Minimum value analysis is a method of combining several criteria which may be based on both certain and uncertain factors [7]. For example, the present value cost, rate of return, and even intangible factors such as environmental impact of an investment, can be evaluated simultaneously.

For minimum value analysis an arbitrary scale such as a 0 to 1 scale (see Table 4-1) is designated and minimum values are objectively or subjectively decided upon for each criterion. The alternatives are judged (again, objectively or subjectively according to available data) against each criterion. Any alternatives that do not satisfy all minimums are eliminated and the alternative with the highest score is the most favorable.

TABLE 4-1 MINIMUM VALUE ANALYSIS (VALUE SCALE = 0 TO 1)

Criteria	Minimum value	Alt. *A*	Alt. *B*	Alt. *C*	Alt. *D*
Net present value	0.3	0.4	0.6	0.3	0.5
Adjusted rate of return	0.7	0.8	0.7	0.9	(0.6)
Labor relations effect	0.4	0.4	0.5	0.4	0.6
Environmental effect	0.3	0.5	(0.2)	0.8	0.3
Long-range growth	0.5	0.8	0.5	0.7	0.8
		2.9	xxx	3.1	xxx

Example 4-16

The data in Table 4-1 have been developed for four alternative projects with values assigned on a 0 to 1 scale. Rank the alternatives in order of desirability.

Solution

Alternatives *B* and *D* do not meet minimum criteria, as shown by the circled values, and are discarded. Alternative *C* is most favorable and *A* is next.

CONSIDERATIONS FOR MULTINATIONAL OPERATIONS

Multinational firms face some unique problems in managing foreign investments.[3] In this section we shall identify some of the most important financially based factors that influence operations in a foreign environment and take note of what procedures and techniques are currently most widely used to evaluate foreign investments.

ENVIRONMENTAL INFLUENCES IN MULTINATIONAL OPERATIONS

The environmental considerations that influence foreign operations from a financial standpoint have been identified by Bursk et al. in a study that was prepared for the Financial Executives Research Foundation [**2**:35–44]. Looking to the needs of those who design and use financial control systems in multinational operations, the study develops three classes of influences and groups them geographically, as shown in Table 4-2. The three classifications pertain to (1) those factors that affect financial transactions as part of the technical design of the formal control system, (2) those factors that are related to operating and financial risks, and (3) other

[3] An excellent reference on this is Multinational Business Finance, by David K. Eiteman and Arthur I. Stonehill, 2d ed., Addison-Wesley Publishing Company, Reading, Mass., 1978. Some of the following observations are drawn from this source.

TABLE 4-2 ENVIRONMENTAL CONSIDERATIONS EXTERNAL TO THE FIRM—RELEVANCE TO DESIGN OF CONTROL SYSTEM

		Western Europe	Middle East	Africa	Asia and Far East	Australia	Latin America	Canada
Technical implementation	Different currencies	H	H	H	H	H	H	S-H
	Taxation practices (U.S./foreign)	H	H	H	H	H	H	H
	Limited reliable market and economic indices	U-S	S-H	S-H	S-H	U-S	H	U-S
	Price-level changes	U	U-S	U-S	U-S	U	H	U
Risk considerations	Devaluation of currencies	H	H	H	H	H	H	S-H
	Expropriation risk	U	S	S	S	U	S-H	U
	Political instability	S	S	S	S	U	H	U
	Import-export controls	U-S	U-S	U-S	U-S	U	S-H	U
	Tight credit	U-S	S	S	S	U-S	S	U-S
	High credit costs	U-S	S	S	S	U-S	S	U-S
	Government regulation (U.S./foreign)	S	S-H	S-H	S-H	S	H	S
Administration implications	Personal value systems	U-S	S	S	S	U	S-H	U
	Cultural backgrounds	U-S	S	S	S	U	S-H	U
	Education levels	U-S	S	S	S	U-S	S	U-S

Source: [2]. Code H = highly significant; S = significant; U = unimportant.

(behavioral) factors that influence the effectiveness of the administration of the financial control system.

As can be seen from Table 4-2, the relative influence of the factors varies with the geographical area. The United States, Canada, Australia, and Western European countries are more akin to one another than are other countries in terms of economics, cultural background, and level of business sophistication.

The devaluation of currencies and expropriation (or takeover) of foreign properties by host-country governments have been two of the most significant risks in the past. However, even the day-to-day activities of maintaining balanced inventory and cash positions amid the fluctuating values of foreign (and domestic) currencies can be hazardous. For example, in their 1975 annual report, Tektronix, Inc., a multinational manufacturer of oscilloscopes based in Portland, Oregon, reported the impact of currency fluctuations on financial results as "a loss of $369,000. Not peanuts by any means, but well down from last year's $1 million-plus" [**12**: 9]. In 1974, the Du Pont company incurred foreign exchange losses of $12 million.

EVALUATION TECHNIQUES USED BY FOREIGN SUBSIDIARIES

Foreign subsidiaries of multinational organizations are almost always assigned profit responsibilities, rather than only manufacturing or sales responsibilities [**2**: 11]. Investment control by the parent company is then exercised on the basis of projects, instead of tight control over operations. Foreign projects are usually initiated because of a specific opportunity rather than as a broad search for foreign investment possibilities. As the investigation progresses from a rough, opinion-based start to more thorough on-the-spot studies, various financial criteria are used. One study has indicated that over 50 percent of the companies use some form of time-adjusted return, with 13 percent using an unadjusted rate of return, 25 percent using payback, and 10 percent not using any formal method at all [**2**: 24]. The analysts noted, however, that for the firms surveyed, discounted cash-flow methods were used more extensively in foreign operations than in domestic divisions. They attributed this to inflation and the attendant necessity of taking account of correspondingly higher discount rates.

As pointed out earlier in the chapter, the adjusted rate of return has a number of inherent advantages and they make it a widely used evaluation technique for foreign as well as domestic investment decisions. In addition to being a single figure that can reflect the overall financial success of a subsidiary, it would seem to be a good means of comparison among subsidiaries. It also gives parent-company management a one-figure measure of how well a subsidiary manager uses company resources to generate profits.

Despite these advantages, Bursk et al. [**2**: 107] report that "Basically, a single rate of return for each subsidiary is just too simple an economic model to base all trade-offs between investments and profits in a multinational firm." They point out that, in a given subsidiary, a dollar invested in inventory, receivables, cash, or fixed assets must earn the same rate of return. But although the tradeoff between investment and profit is the same for all investments within a given subsidiary, it will differ from one subsidiary to another because of differences in profit potential. A proposed investment yielding 12 percent may look good to a British subsidiary manager who has an after-tax profit objective of 10 percent, but may not even be proposed by a Dutch manager whose profit goal is 15 percent. If we carry this investment-profit equivalency a little further, it means that "a dollar invested in inventory in one subsidiary would be required to earn a different profit than a dollar invested in an identical type of inventory in another subsidiary" [**2**: 107].

To overcome these and other problems, a residual income method adjustment to the adjusted rate of return has been proposed [see **2**: 18]. This method allows the same rate of return to be used for similar assets in various subsidiaries and different rates of return for different assets within the same subsidiary. The method is not widely used, however, for most firms still rely upon traditional ways of analysis with which they are more familiar and which they use for domestic projects.

After a project has been undertaken, the final control element, involving correction of results that do not conform to plan, is often difficult, if not impossible, to achieve. There are at least three reasons for this [**2**: 13]. (1) The plan itself often hinges upon uncontrollable environmental variables. (2) Once an investment is made it usually represents a "sunk" cost that cannot be recovered or reduced. (3) It usually takes a long time for the effect of a given investment to be accurately measured and fed back for comparison to the plan. This inability to take corrective action simply means that foreign operations managers should place increased emphasis upon making sound decisions in the first place, as they participate in the evaluation of foreign investment projects.

COMPARISON AND SUMMARY

All organizations, whether private or public, operate on a limited supply of funds. Since there are many alternative ways to use funds in operations, capital investments should be carefully evaluated to ensure that the best choices are made. Several evaluation techniques exist, the most widely used methods being payback, present value, and adjusted rate of return. Many decisions justify the use of more than one technique, for each provides a slightly different perspective. And although we have worked through the various techniques more or less by hand, to gain an understanding of the methodology, most large firms have computer programs which can evaluate complex investment alternatives very rapidly.

Payback tells how long it takes for an investment to pay for itself. Its extensive use is probably attributable to its simplicity. Present value is more sophisticated in that it considers the time value of money. Net present value is the net result of all future incomes and outgoes of cash if they are discounted to a given point in time. Adjusted rate of return is similar in that it incorporates the compounding effect of interest over time. However, instead of yielding a net monetary advantage, as does present value, the adjusted rate of return represents an interest rate that equates the investment costs with future income resulting from the investment. It is really just another way of looking at the same advantage; we view it as a monetary amount under present value and as a compounding percentage under rate of return.

Equivalent annual cost and present value cost are even more similar since both are monetary amounts. The equivalent annual cost simply represents the amount of an annuity that is equivalent to the present value amount. It is sometimes advantageous to compare alternatives on an annual cost basis, and equivalent annual cost is ideal for this.

Average annual cost and unadjusted rate of return are somewhat similar to equivalent annual cost and adjusted rate of return respectively, but they involve approximations which limit their usefulness. With the widespread availability of hand calculators, the "ease-of-calculation" advantage of these methods is now being lost, and the time-adjusted methods of equivalent annual cost and adjusted rate of return are preferred. MAPI is used by some larger organizations but has not gained as widespread general usage.

Nearly all capital investment decisions involve assumptions about what will happen in the future. Very often these uncertainties are glossed over or compensated for by indirect means. A more scientific approach is to try to explicitly identify the uncertainty, evaluate its impact upon the alternative courses of action, and incorporate this into the decision. Simulation, decision trees, and various decision theory criteria are now being used to help evaluate investments under conditions of uncertainty. Simulation holds much promise for improving investment decisions as firms continue to develop their computer capabilities. Decision trees are a simple, but often very helpful, method of analyzing investment decisions. They are analyzed on an expected value basis and work is currently under way to extend this to an expected utility basis.

On the multinational level, firms face a variety of challenging problems ranging from unique features of the international capital environment to the necessities of making adjustments to the firm's own internal investment evaluation techniques. Foreign taxation practices, currency devaluations, expropriation risks, and less-direct forms of government regulation, such as local sourcing, are just a few of the environmental influences the foreign operations manager must be prepared to face.

SOLVED PROBLEMS[4]

CAPITAL AND INTEREST

1 Operating costs for a machine are estimated at \$500/yr for 10 years plus an additional \$1,000 for overhaul at the end of the fifth year. Assuming a 10 percent cost of capital, convert the maintenance and operating cost of the machine to a total present value amount.

Solution

We can depict the problem on the accompanying time-cost diagram.

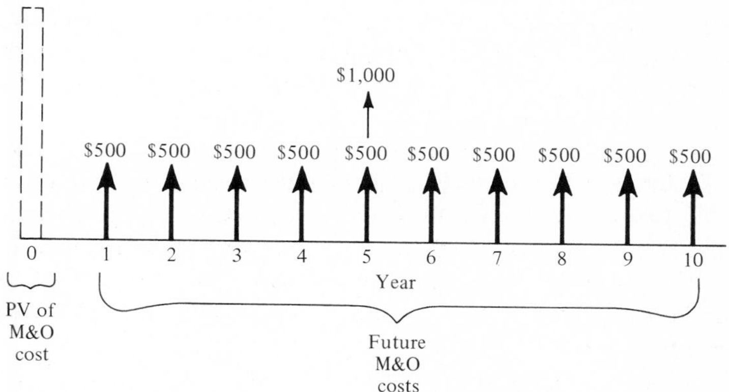

$$\begin{aligned} \text{PV M and O cost} &= \text{PV annual operating costs} + \text{PV maintenance cost} \\ &= \$500\,(\text{PV}_a)_{10\%}^{10\text{yr}} + \$1{,}000\,(\text{PV}_{sp})_{10\%}^{5\text{yr}} \\ &= \$500\,(6.145) + \$1{,}000\,(0.621) \\ &= \$3{,}072 + \$621 = \$3{,}693 \end{aligned}$$

[4] The solved problems in this chapter are classified according to the earlier chapter materials, with several problems illustrating ramifications of each evaluation technique. Present value and adjusted rate of return methods are now becoming widely used but, as pointed out, each of the techniques has its unique advantages and limitations.

CAPITAL INVESTMENT EVALUATION TECHNIQUES: PAYBACK

2 A \$40,000 extrusion machine is expected to be obsolete after 10 years, with no salvage value. During its lifetime, it should generate an \$8,000/yr operating advantage, of which \$3,000 must be paid in taxes. What is the payoff period?

Solution

$$\text{Payoff} = \frac{I - S}{\text{OA/yr}} = \frac{\$40{,}000 - 0}{\$8{,}000 - \$3{,}000} = 8 \text{ yr}$$

3 A proposed new \$16,400 automatic machine will have operating costs of \$0.30/unit produced whereas the existing machine costs are \$0.70/unit. The existing machine has a market value of \$8,700 now and has another 5 years of life. It would cost \$500 to remove the existing machine and install the new one. If the firm requires a 3-yr payout period, how many units must be produced annually to justify the new machine? Disregard taxes.

Solution

$$\text{Payout} = \frac{\text{investment}}{\text{OA/yr}}$$

where

Payout = 3 yr

Δ investment = \$16,400 − \$8,700 =		\$7,700
	Add installation cost:	500
	Total	\$8,200

OA/unit = \$0.70 − \$0.30 = \$0.40/unit

OA (total) = \$0.40 (N units/yr)

Therefore,

$$3 \text{ yr} = \frac{\$8{,}200}{\$0.40(N)}$$

$$\therefore N = \frac{\$8{,}200}{\$1.20/\text{unit}} = 6{,}833 \text{ units/yr}$$

CAPITAL INVESTMENT EVALUATION TECHNIQUES: AVERAGE ANNUAL COST

4 Coastal Printing Company has a typesetting machine that cost \$20,000 when new, 5 years ago, and now has a book value of \$10,000. The company could not get more than \$5,000 on the market for it now, as a used machine. The firm estimates the machine will last 5 more years and then have a salvage value of \$1,000.

(*a*) What has been the straight-line depreciation/yr charged against the machine in the past?

(*b*) For an economy study, what is I_{ave} over the next 5 years?

(*c*) What effect would writing off some machine book value as a loss have on current investment evaluation decisions?

Solution

(*a*) Straight-line depreciation $= \dfrac{I - S}{n}$ where S takes on the current book value

$$= \frac{\$20{,}000 - \$10{,}000}{5 \text{ yr}} = \$2{,}000/\text{yr}$$

(*b*) $$I_{ave} = \frac{I + S}{2} = \frac{\$5{,}000 + \$1{,}000}{2} = \$3{,}000$$

(*c*) None. The tax and other effects of the write-off will be realized regardless of the future action. The loss is a sunk cost and not relevant to future decisions except for suggesting faster depreciation rates in the future.

5 A public utility district (PUD) has found that it can lease a data processing service at an annual cost of \$9,100/yr for 5 years. This cost includes all maintenance and operating costs. Alternatively, it can purchase \$10,000 worth of equipment which will have a salvage value of \$3,000 in 5 years and will require \$7,000/yr in labor costs to operate. In addition, maintenance is expected to be \$500 the first year and increase by \$100/yr thereafter. The PUD is limited by the Federal Power Commission to 8 percent return on any investment. Using an average investment criterion, determine whether it is more economical for the PUD to lease the service or purchase the equipment. (Disregard taxes.)

Solution

Annual lease cost \$9,100/yr

Annual purchase cost:

$$\textit{Capital CR} = \frac{I - S}{n} = \frac{\$10{,}000 - \$3{,}000}{5 \text{ yr}} = \$1{,}400/\text{yr}$$

$$\textit{Return } R = (i)I_{ave} = (0.08)\frac{\$10{,}000 + \$3{,}000}{2} = 520/\text{yr}$$

Other OC: labor =	7,000/yr	
OC: maintenance =		
$\dfrac{\$500 + \$600 + \$700 + \$800 + \$900}{5\text{ yr}} =$	700/yr	\$9,620/yr
Net savings from leasing service		\$520/yr

The PUD should lease rather than purchase.

CAPITAL INVESTMENT EVALUATION TECHNIQUES: EQUIVALENT ANNUAL COST

6 Alaska Construction Company is purchasing a portable generator from Lyon Electric for \$5,026 and plans to finance the purchase from a local bank at 8 percent interest. The contract stipulates that Lyon Electric will pay the construction company \$1,000 for the used machine after 10 years. What is the equivalent annual purchase cost to Alaska Construction Company?

Solution

$$CR \text{ and } R = (I - S)\left[\frac{1}{(\mathrm{PV}_a)_{8\%}^{10\text{yr}}}\right]$$

$$= (\$5{,}026 - \$1{,}000)\left[\frac{1}{6.71}\right] = \$600/\text{yr}$$

$(i)S = (0.08)(\$1{,}000) =$		80/yr
Other costs: none considered		00/yr
	Total	\$680/yr

7 Porter & Fisher Ltd. plans to sign a 3-yr lease for automobiles for its production supervisors at a seafood plant in Norway. The company can obtain car *A* for \$1,000 plus \$.05/mile or car *B* for \$600 plus \$.10/mile. If funds cost 8 percent, how many miles must be driven before the use of car *A* is justified? Use the equivalent annual cost method.

Solution

$$CR \text{ and } R = (I - S)\left[\frac{1}{(\mathrm{PV}_a)_{8\%}^{3\text{yr}}}\right]$$

	car *A*	car *B*
	$(\$1{,}000)\dfrac{1}{2.577} = \$389/\text{yr}$	$\$600\,\dfrac{1}{2.577} = \$233/\text{yr}$
Interest on salvage:	no salvage	no salvage
Other: mileage charge	cost = \$.05*N*	cost = \$.10*N*
	Total \$389 + \$.05*N*	\$233 + \$.10*N*

Setting the total costs for car A equal to car B

$$\begin{aligned} TC_A &= TC_B \\ \$389 + \$.05N &= \$233 + \$.10N \\ \$.05N &= \$156 \\ N &= 3{,}120 \text{ miles} \end{aligned}$$

CAPITAL INVESTMENT EVALUATION TECHNIQUES: PRESENT VALUE

8 Computer Services, Incorporated, offers maintenance services at $1,000/yr for 5 years plus an additional $2,000 at the end of the third year for overhaul. If a firm contracts for 5 years of services, what is the net present value cost to the firm? The firm estimates its capital cost at 8 percent and has sales of $3.5 million/yr.

Solution

The sales data is not relevant to computing present value cost.

$$\begin{aligned} \text{Present value cost} &= \text{PV other costs} \\ &= \text{PV (maintenance cost)} + \text{PV (overhaul cost)} \\ &= \$1{,}000(\text{PV}_a)_{8\%}^{5\text{yr}} + \$2{,}000(\text{PV}_{sp})_{8\%}^{3\text{yr}} \\ &= \$1{,}000(3.993) + \$2{,}000(0.794) \\ &= \$3{,}993 = \$1{,}588 = \$5{,}581 \end{aligned}$$

9 An instrument transformer manufacturer in Long Island is considering purchase of an ultrasonic welding machine to replace an existing manually operated machine. The existing machine cost $12,000 two years ago and has been depreciated down to a $10,000 book value, using a 12-yr life and no salvage. However, the market value of the machine is only about $4,000 now. The ultrasonic welder would improve product quality enough to boost revenue from an existing $80,000/yr to $100,000/yr. It would cost $44,000 and have a 10-yr life. Any salvage value on it would be consumed in the removal expense. An advantage of the ultrasonic machine is that by reducing annual labor costs, it would cut operating expenses from $8,000 to $3,000 annually. The manufacturer is in a 50 percent tax bracket and estimates the firm's cost of capital at 12 percent. Use present value analysis to determine whether they should purchase the ultrasonic welder.

Solution

Determine the after-tax profit under each alternative and select the most favorable one. It will be most convenient to do calculations on an annual basis and then convert to present value.

Note the net PV gain AT from the ultrasonic machine installation exceeds the existing arrangement by $40,230 and thus the new machine should be installed.

Existing machine	
Revenue	\$80,000
Less:	
Operating costs	8,000
Depreciation	1,000
Income subject to tax	\$71,000
Income tax (@ 50%)	\$35,500

Cash inflow = revenue − operating costs − taxes
\$80,000 — \$8,000 — \$35,500 = \$36,500/yr

Present value of cash inflow (AT) $= R(PV_a)\,{}^{10yr}_{12\%} = 36{,}500\ (5.65)$
$= \$206{,}225$

Net PV gain after taxes = PV (cash inflow) − PV(I)
= \$206,225 − \$4,000 = \$202,225

New ultrasonic machine	
Revenue	\$100,000
Less:	
Operating costs	3,000
Depreciation	4,400
Income subject to tax	\$92,600
Income tax (@ 50%)	\$46,300

Cash inflow = \$100,000 − \$3,000 − \$46,300 = \$50,700
Present value of cash inflow (AT) = \$50,700(5.65) = \$286,455
Net PV gain after taxes = \$286,455 − \$44,000 = \$242,455

Note also that the relevant investment cost of the existing machine is the market value, *not the book value.* There is no relevant advantage to be gained from writing off some of the existing machine as a loss, since this write-off should take place whether the new machine is purchased or not. The write-off advantage is not relevant to the decision problem.

CAPITAL INVESTMENT EVALUATION TECHNIQUES: RATE OR RETURN (UNADJUSTED)

10 A metals brokerage firm has an opportunity to invest \$3,500,000 in uranium dioxide and make an immediate sale to a New England electric utility for \$4,350,000. What is the simple rate of return?

Solution

$$RR_s = \frac{\text{profit}}{\text{investment}}$$

where profit = \$4,350,000 − \$3,500,000 = \$850,000

$$= \frac{\$850{,}000}{\$3{,}500{,}000} = 24.3\%$$

11 A \$20,000 machine is expected to last 10 years and have a \$2,000 salvage. It will generate increased income (before depreciation) of \$4,000/yr but necessitate that \$1,100/yr be paid in taxes. What is the unadjusted rate of return? Assume straight-line depreciation.

Solution

$$(AT)\quad RR_u = \frac{\text{OA after tax}}{I_{\text{ave}}} = \frac{(\text{OA/yr} - \text{depreciation/yr} - \text{tax/yr})}{I_{\text{ave}}}$$

where

$$\text{OA} = \$4{,}000/\text{yr}$$

$$\text{depreciation/yr} = \frac{\$20{,}000 - \$2{,}000}{10\ \text{yr}} = \$1{,}800/\text{yr}$$

$$\text{tax/yr} = \$1{,}100$$

$$I_{\text{ave}} = \frac{\$20{,}000 + \$2{,}000}{2} = \$11{,}000$$

$$(AT)\quad RR_u = \frac{(\$4{,}000 - \$1{,}800 - \$1{,}100)}{\$11{,}000} = 10\%$$

Note that the figures in this problem are the same as those in Example 4-9, where the payback was found to be 6.2 years.

CAPITAL INVESTMENT EVALUATION TECHNIQUES: RATE OF RETURN (ADJUSTED)

12 An investment of \$5,650 is expected to yield an operating advantage (before depreciation and taxes) of \$4,000 at the end of the first year, \$2,000 at the end of the second year, and \$1,000 at the end of the third. What is the time-adjusted rate of return?

Solution

Set PV(income) = PV(I) = \$5,650.

Try 14 percent

$$\begin{aligned}
\text{1st yr earnings} &= F(\text{PV}_{sp})^{1\text{yr}}_{14\%} = \$4{,}000\ (0.877) = \$3{,}508\\
\text{2d yr earnings} &= F(\text{PV}_{sp})^{2\text{yr}}_{14\%} = 2{,}000\ (0.769) = 1{,}538\\
\text{3d yr earnings} &= F(\text{PV}_{sp})^{3\text{yr}}_{14\%} = 1{,}000\ (0.675) = \underline{675}\\
& \qquad\qquad\qquad\qquad\qquad\qquad\qquad \$5{,}721
\end{aligned}$$

Since PV(income) > PV(I), try higher rate.

Try 16 percent

$$\begin{aligned} \text{1st yr} &= \$4{,}000\ (0.862) = \$3{,}448 \\ \text{2d yr} &= \ \ 2{,}000\ (0.743) = \ \ 1{,}486 \\ \text{3d yr} &= \ \ 1{,}000\ (0.641) = \ \ \underline{\ \ \ 641} \\ & \qquad\qquad\qquad\qquad \$5{,}575 \end{aligned}$$

Since PV(income) < PV(I), try lower rate. Note that the 16 percent rate yields a PV(income) figure \$75 below the investment amount, whereas the 14 percent yields a figure \$71 above. Thus the correct value should be about midway between, or 15 percent.

Try 15 percent

$$\begin{aligned} \text{1st yr} &= \$4{,}000\ (0.870) = \$3{,}480 \\ \text{2d yr} &= \ \ 2{,}000\ (0.756) = \ \ 1{,}512 \\ \text{3d yr} &= \ \ 1{,}000\ (0.658) = \ \ \underline{\ \ \ 658} \\ & \qquad\qquad\qquad\qquad \$5{,}650 \end{aligned}$$

The $(BT)\ RR_A$ is 15 percent.

CAPITAL INVESTMENT EVALUATION TECHNIQUES: MAPI

13 An analyst is evaluating the replacement of an automatic grinder with a newer, numerically controlled machine. She has obtained MAPI calculation forms from the Machinery and Allied Products Institute. Upon following the calculation through, step by step, she has developed a MAPI value of "average net investment" of \$30,400, and an "available for return on investment" figure of \$8,200. What is the after-tax return (urgency rating) for the project?

Solution

$$UR = \frac{\text{amount available for return on investment}}{\text{average net investment}}$$

$$= \frac{\$8{,}200}{\$30{,}400} = 27\%$$

INVESTMENT EVALUATION UNDER UNCERTAINTY

14 Directors of Convalescent Care of Chicago, Incorporated, are considering a capital expansion program to meet the increased demand for health care facilities. They are proposing an expansion of either $A = 100$, $B = 200$, or $C = 300$ beds

and have estimated profits (losses) as shown in the accompanying table. Their estimate of demand for the various expansion alternatives is:

$$P(100 \text{ beds req'd}) = 0.2$$
$$P(200 \text{ beds req'd}) = 0.5$$
$$P(300 \text{ beds req'd}) = 0.3$$

Expansion alternatives	Profit ($000) for demand of 100 beds	200 beds	300 beds
$A = 100$	200	200	200
$B = 200$	000	400	400
$C = 300$	(200)	200	600

(*a*) How large an expansion should be planned under (1) maximax, (2) maximin, (3) maximum probability, (4) expected value criteria?

(*b*) Assume the profit figures are yearly annuity values that will continue for 5 years only. What is the net expected present value of the best alternative, assuming funds cost 10 percent?

Solution

(*a*) *Maximax* Choose 300-bed expansion where maximum profit of $600,000 is possible.

Maximin Choose 100-bed expansion where the least profit that can be obtained is the highest—$200,000.

Maximum probability Choose 200-bed expansion where $400,000 is the best gain under the most likely state of demand—200 beds.

Expected value

$$E(A) = 200{,}000(0.2) + 200{,}000(0.5) + 200{,}000(0.3) = 200{,}000$$
$$E(B) = 0\ (0.2) + 400{,}000(0.5) + 400{,}000(0.3) = 320{,}000$$
$$E(C) = -200{,}000(0.2) + 200{,}000(0.5) + 600{,}000(0.3) = 240{,}000$$

Therefore, choose 200-bed expansion where expected profit is $320,000.

(*b*) Where cash flows are in the future, they must be converted to present values before we take an expectation.

Therefore, *PV* of a 5-yr annuity at 10 percent for:

$$\$200{,}000/\text{yr} = \$200{,}000(\text{PV}_a)^{5\text{yr}}_{10\%} = 200{,}000(3.791) = \$758{,}200$$
$$400{,}000/\text{yr} = 400{,}000(3.791) = \$1{,}516{,}400$$
$$600{,}000/\text{yr} = 600{,}000(3.791) = \$2{,}324{,}600.$$

Expected present values

$$E(A) = 758{,}200(0.2) + 758{,}200(0.5) + 758{,}200(0.3) = \$758{,}000$$
$$E(B) = 0(0.2) + 1{,}516{,}400(0.5) + 1{,}516{,}400(0.3) = \$1{,}213{,}220$$
$$E(C) = -758{,}200(0.2) + 758{,}200(0.5) + 2{,}234{,}600(0.3) = \$925{,}840$$

Considering the extended flows and the time value of funds, the 200-bed expansion is still the best choice. Note, however, that the expected present value of \$1,213,200 is considerably less than the non-time-adjusted value would have been (\$320,000 × 5 yr = \$1,600,000). The \$387,000 difference is due to the time value of money at 10 percent.

MISCELLANEOUS PROBLEM

15 The Synco Steel production manager is evaluating two machines to determine which would be most economical. Both machines are capable of generating the same revenue. The firm's cost of capital is 8 percent.

	Machine A	Machine B
Initial cost	\$20,000	\$30,000
Maintenance and operating cost/yr	2,000	3,000
Economic life	4 yr	4 yr
Salvage value (estimated)	\$2,000	\$15,000

For machine A find (*a*) the net present value cost, (*b*) the average annual cost and (*c*) the equivalent annual cost. (*d*) Why is the equivalent annual cost more than the average annual cost?

Solution

(*a*) *Net present value cost*

Initial investment I	\$20,000
M and O: $R(\mathrm{PV}_a)^{4\mathrm{yr}}_{8\%} = (\$2{,}000)(3.312)$	6,626
Total	\$26,626
Less: PV(salvage) $= S(\mathrm{PV}_{sp})^{4\mathrm{yr}}_{8\%} = (\$2{,}000)(0.735) =$	−1,470
PV COST	\$25,156

(*b*) *Average annual cost*

Capital $\quad CR = \dfrac{I - S}{n} = \dfrac{\$20{,}000 - \$2{,}000}{4 \text{ yr}} =$ \$4,500/yr

Return $\quad R = (i)I_{\text{ave}} = 0.08\left(\dfrac{\$20{,}000 + \$2{,}000}{2}\right) =$ 880/yr

Other $\quad M$ and O = 2,000/yr

Total \$7,380/yr

(*c*) *Equivalent annual cost*

$$CR \text{ and } R = (I - S)\left(\frac{1}{\text{PV}_a}\right)$$

$$= (\$20{,}000 - \$2{,}000)\left(\frac{1}{3.312}\right) = \qquad \$5{,}435/\text{yr}$$

$$(i)S = (0.08)(\$2{,}000) = \qquad 160/\text{yr}$$

$$OC\text{: } M \text{ and } O = \qquad 2{,}000/\text{yr}$$

$$\text{Total} \quad \$7{,}595/\text{yr}$$

Since the equivalent annual cost is in fact a time-adjusted annuity, it can be calculated more directly from the net present value amount, if that has already been calculated. In this case it has been found to be $25,156 in (*a*). Therefore, from

$$P = R(\text{PV}_a)$$

we have

$$R = P\left[\frac{1}{\text{PV}_a}\right] P(CRF)$$

or

$$\text{Equivalent annual cost} = \text{PV cost } (CRF)$$

$$= \$25{,}156 \ \frac{1}{3.312}$$

$$= \$7{,}595/\text{yr}$$

(*d*) The equivalent annual cost value of $7,595 is greater than the average annual cost value of $7,380 because it takes compounding of interest values into account. Average annual cost is not a time-adjusted method and is not as accurate as equivalent annual cost, although it is often adequate.

QUESTIONS

4-1 How does the source of funds for a public organization differ from that of a private organization?

4-2 Suppose you were responsible for choosing between two capital investments, one of which was estimated to yield a 30 percent adjusted rate of return. What other information would you want before you make your decision?

4-3 Distinguish between the following: (*a*) PV_{sp}, (*b*) PV_a, (*c*) *CRF*, (*d*) MAPI.

4-4 In what respects are simple rate of return, RR_u, and RR_A similar? How do they differ?

4-5 Distinguish between interest rate i as used in present value calculations and as determined in the adjusted rate of return calculation.

4-6 If a firm wanted to adopt a depreciation policy that would give the greatest depreciation during the first year of an expected 5-year life, what method would it choose, straight line, declining balance, or sum-of-years digits?

4-7 Compare the equivalent annual cost method of evaluation with the present value cost. Which would you prefer and why?

4-8 Prepare a brief, concise table listing the traditional methods of capital investment evaluation along with two major advantages and disadvantages of each.

4-9 Upon discounting projected cash earnings to determine the rate of return on a proposed $20,000 investment, the present value, using a 12 percent discount rate, was found to be $19,072. Is the correct figure greater or less than 12 percent? Why?

4-10 Explain how simulation can be used to handle investment evaluation when uncertainties exist about future cash flows.

4-11 Discuss the advantages and limitations in the use of decision trees for evaluating capital investment.

4-12 Identify and discuss three factors that a multinational operations manager could expect to strongly influence the success of a foreign investment.

PROBLEMS

CAPITAL AND INTEREST

1 Ross Enterprises borrows $60,000 from Citizens Bank at 8 percent interest/yr. How much must they repay 2 years later?

2 What is the present value of a series of equipment rental costs of $1,000 each year for the next 10 years? Use an 8 percent discount factor.

3 Maintenance expense on a printing press is expected to be $300/yr over the next 6 years. If the owner must pay 12 percent to borrow money, what is the present value cost of the maintenance expense?

4 What is the appropriate capital recovery factor (CRF) for a $100,000 investment that is to be depreciated over 7 years when the capital cost is 14 percent?

DEPRECIATION AND TAXES

5 Vineyard Wines Ltd. invests $8,000 in a wooden tank which will have an estimated 20-yr life and no salvage value. Find (*a*) the amount of straight-line depreciation charged off during the third year, and (*b*) the book value of the tank during each of the first 3 years, assuming the maximum declining-balance rate is used.

CAPITAL INVESTMENT EVALUATION TECHNIQUES: PAYBACK

6 An investment of $20,000 in an automatic valve will yield savings in operating costs of $5,000/yr (before depreciation and after taxes). No salvage is expected. What is the payback?

7 A $20,000 machine will last 10 years, have no salvage, and generate a $4,000/yr operating advantage, of which $1,000 must be paid in taxes. Find the payoff period.

8 The Magnetic Tape Corporation has an opportunity to replace a machine with a new $10,000 unit that is expected to last for 10 years (no salvage) and save the firm $4,000/yr in labor and material costs. If taxes (at 50 percent rate) are taken into account in the calculation, what is the payback period?
Hint: Taxes must be paid on the savings less any expenses. Depreciation is an expense that should be deducted from the before-tax operating advantage of $4,000/yr.

CAPITAL INVESTMENT EVALUATION TECHNIQUES: AVERAGE ANNUAL COST

9 A $10,000 machine has a $4,000 salvage value at the end of 6 years. What is the average investment over the period?

10 A machine costs $15,000 installed and has a salvage value of $3,000 at the end of an 8-year economic life. Average operating and maintenance costs are $5,000/yr and the firm pays 10 percent for its capital. What is the average annual cost of the machine?

11 A leather-goods producer in San Francisco plans to modify his shop layout and is considering the alternatives shown in the accompanying table.

	Plan 1	Plan 2
New machinery cost	$22,000	$20,000
Installation labor cost	3,000	2,000
Annual savings expected	8,000	7,000

The new layout is expected to be suitable for 5 years operation. If the producer has an 8 percent cost of capital, (*a*) determine the average annual cost for plan 1 and plan 2, (*b*) determine the net savings under both plans, and (*c*) determine which plan should be adopted.

CAPITAL INVESTMENT EVALUATION TECHNIQUES: EQUIVALENT ANNUAL COST

12 A foreman at Georgia Paper Company has suggested a design modification on the roll-goods packaging machine which could save up to $8,000 in scrap over a year. Engineering estimates the modification would cost $11,000 to install and would require extra servicing costs of about $40 a month. The modification would be removed when the original equipment is replaced in 8 more years, and would have an estimated $1,000 salvage value at that time. Find the equivalent annual cost of this modification. Use an 8 percent cost of capital.

CAPITAL INVESTMENT EVALUATION TECHNIQUES: PRESENT VALUE

13 A new lead-casting furnace costs $30,000 installed and is expected to have a $4,000 salvage value at the end of an 8-year economic life. Operation and maintenance costs will run about $7,000/yr. Using 12 percent interest, what is present value cost of the furnace?

14 A US Forest Service supervisor is evaluating the use of new logging equipment which has an initial cost of $120,000. The supervisor expects the equipment will last 10 years and have a salvage value equal to 15 percent of the original purchase price. Annual operating and maintenance costs are estimated at $14,000. Using a 4 percent interest rate, find the net present value cost of this logging equipment investment.

***15** Given the data in Example 4-12, assume that the present value of income from the investment is $50,000 and the firm's tax rate is 50 percent. What is the net present value gain after taxes PV_{AT}?

16 An existing drill press valued at $1,000 will last two more years (zero salvage) and cost $4,000/yr to operate. If comparable 2-yr present value costs for a new machine are $7,000, what is the present value saving (using an 8 percent discount rate) from the new machine?

17 Monaghan Shoe Company wishes to decide between two automatic clicker machines. Machine X has a net present value cost of $25,000 (all costs considered). Machine Y has an initial cost of $14,000 and will have a salvage value of \$1,000. The annual labor cost is \$3,300 and annual taxes, insurance, and other costs are estimated at 5 percent of the initial cost. Both machines would have the same 4-year life under the heavy use expected. If Monaghan Shoe Company uses an 8 percent interest rate and uses the declining-balance method of depreciation, how would the net present value cost of machine Y compare with that of machine X?

CAPITAL INVESTMENT EVALUATION TECHNIQUES: RATE OF RETURN

18 What rate of return would be realized by a \$5,000 investment in an equity that was sold shortly thereafter for \$5,750?

19 A \$20,000 inventory storage building will last 10 years and have no salvage value. It is expected to generate \$4,000/yr savings in lost and damaged raw material over the next 10 years, of which \$1,500/yr will be lost in taxes. Find the unadjusted after-tax rate of return.

20 Repairs costing \$64,000 made to a baseball stadium are expected to increase returns (before depreciation and taxes) by \$20,000/yr over an economic life of 6 years. The club is allowed an 8-yr life and the tax rate is 50 percent. The club operations manager estimates their after-tax cost of capital at 12 percent and is trying to determine whether the repairs can be economically justified. Calculate the after-tax unadjusted rate of return and advise him.

21 A supervisor for Crescent City Gas Company has proposed that the company authorize \$40,000 for an on-line display unit in the customer services center. A study has indicated that after considering depreciation and other costs, the installation will generate a net advantage of \$4,000/yr of which \$1,500/yr will be lost in taxes. What is the company's unadjusted rate of return on this investment? Assume zero salvage value.

22 Koontz Korporation has an opportunity to invest \$7,680 in a plant modification which is expected to yield an operating advantage of \$5,000 at the end of the first year and \$1,000 at the end of each of the next 5 years. What is the before-tax adjusted rate of return?

CAPITAL INVESTMENT EVALUATION TECHNIQUES: MAPI

23 A MAPI analysis revealed an "available for return on investment" amount of \$4,000 on an "average net investment" figure of \$26,000. What urgency rating do these figures assign to the project?

INVESTMENT EVALUATION UNDER UNCERTAINTY

24 A firm has an opportunity to participate in a joint venture if they invest $700,000 in some specialized equipment. The amount of profit they will realize depends upon whether the venture partners are subsequently awarded a contract. Even if they do not participate in the joint venture they will receive a portion of the work if the other firms obtain the contract. A research study team estimates the probability of receiving a contract at 0.40. Given the payoff gains (and loss) shown in the accompanying table, (*a*) which course of action would be taken under a criterion of (1) maximax, (2) maximin, (3) maximum probability, (4) maximum expected value? (*b*) Show the decision situation schematically in the form of a decision tree. (*c*) Determine which decision theory strategy would probably be most appropriate for a small firm that does not enjoy a strong financial position.

	Contract ($p = 0.40$)	**No contract** ($p = 0.60$)
Participate	$2,000,000	$(700,000)
Not participate	$500,000	0

MISCELLANEOUS PROBLEMS

25 Forest Paper Company is considering purchase of a $10,000 paperbox press which would be used for 3 years and sold for $1,000 salvage. Operating costs are $400/yr and maintenance costs are $500 the first year and increase by $500 each year thereafter. Production volume is 1,000 units/yr and the firm operates on a 3-shift-per-day basis. They use straight-line depreciation, are in a 50 percent tax bracket, and estimate their cost of capital at 10 percent. (*a*) Determine the present value cost of owning and using the machine before tax is considered. (*b*) Determine what effect taxes have on the present value cost. (*c*) Assume the maintenance costs remain constant at $1,000/yr and all sales and administrative costs are included in the operating costs of $400/yr. If the firm achieves a paperbox sales revenue of $12,000/yr from the press, what is the unadjusted after-tax rate of return? (*d*) What is the after-tax payoff period?

26 Cascade Supply must decide whether (*A*) to lease a small production control computer for $7,000/yr (which includes all maintenance and operating costs) or (*B*) to purchase the computer for $15,000 installed. If purchased, it will have an 8-yr economic life and an expected salvage value of $3,000. Maintenance and operating costs are $5,000/yr and the cost of capital is 10 percent. Depreciation is straight line. For alternative *B*, what is (*a*) the average annual cost, (*b*) the equivalent annual cost, and (*c*) the net present value cost? (*d*) Should the firm *A* lease or *B* purchase the computer?

CASE: FACTHOMES, INCORPORATED

The time had come to reach a decision and Clint Sherwood knew it was not going to be easy. Clint was the domestic Shelter Products division manager of a large multinational firm. The company was financially sound and could afford to take risks, but headquarters had set a rate of 15 percent for their cost of capital so investments had to be scrutinized carefully. His division had recently entered the "instant housing" industry and was now producing complete, low-cost homes in a factory assembly line operation. Their FACTHOMES sold for $25,000 each and, at present costs, 8 percent of that selling price was profit (profit = $2,000 per home). Now Mr. Sherwood had to decide whether to shut down the plant for installation of some unique new equipment (UNE) that would put them in a better position to obtain a certain government housing contract. Unfortunately, they could not wait until after the contract was awarded to install the equipment, and it would not be usable on other contracts.

Mr. Sherwood finally called his production, marketing, and personnel managers into his office to help him reach the decision. Barbara Purvis (marketing) spoke first.

Purvis (marketing) I think we ought to really go after this one, Clint! I figure if we shut down and install UNE Model B equipment we'll have a 90 percent chance of getting that government contract for 100 homes.

Rowe (production) But the UNE Model B will cost us $60,000 to install, compared to only $20,000 for UNE Model A. And besides that, the minute we shut this plant down we automatically incur downtime costs of $25,000, regardless of the type of equipment we put in. How do you rate our chances of getting the contract if we have UNE Model A., Barbara?

Purvis I'd guess 40 percent. But remember the terms of the bidding competition. The government has stated in writing that even those bidders who are not awarded the 100-home contract will receive a contract for 10 homes. This was just to encourage bidding, of course, but at least it prevents us from coming out empty-handed.

Courtney (personnel) But, Barbara, there are advantages to not shutting down, too! Now I'm not too worried about the one-day layoff for changeover from the personnel standpoint. Jim Rowe tells me that most of our people can be temporarily used in other parts of the plant that day if they want to. But I understand we are assured of a private contract for 55 homes if we don't shut down to install the new equipment. We'd probably finish that job sooner, too.

Rowe That's debatable. The way I figure it, because the UNE will reduce production time, we would finish either the government or the private contract at the same time. In addition, as near as I can tell, our costs would all be payable at essentially the same time in either case, too. Only thing is the money from the private contract won't come in until a year after the government contract money does, but I'm not sure how significant that is. The company is sound though—no risk of them not paying.

Sherwood (division manager) I wonder if there isn't some way we could lay out these costs in a little more orderly fashion so we can get a better handle on them. Chuck, haven't you got something in your bag of tricks that could help us visualize these alternatives a little more easily, while still taking the uncertainties into account?

Rowe Right, boss! Suppose I see what I can do with this and we meet again tomorrow—same time but better prepared.

Sherwood Now you're making sense, and that's what profit dollars are made of. We'll meet here again at 10:00 A.M. tomorrow.

BIBLIOGRAPHY

[1] BUFFA, ELWOOD S.: *Modern Production Management*, 4th ed., John Wiley & Sons, New York, 1973.

[2] BURSK, EDWARD C., JOHN DEARDEN, DAVID F. HAWKINS, and VICTOR LONGSTREET: *Financial Control of Multinational Operations*, Financial Executives Research Foundation, New York, 1971.

[3] EITEMAN, DAVID K., and ARTHUR I. STONEHILL: *Multinational Business Finance*, 2d ed., Addison-Wesley Publishing Company, Reading, Massachusetts, 1978.

[4] *Federal Reserve Bulletin January 1976*, Board of Governors of the Federal Reserve System, Washington, D.C., January 1976.

[5] GARRETT, LEONARD J., and MILTON SILVER: *Production Management Analysis*, 2d ed., Harcourt, Brace & Jovanovich, New York, 1973.

[6] HERTZ, D. B.: "Risk Analysis in Capital Investments," *Harvard Business Review*, January–February 1964, pp. 95–106.

[7] KOTLER, PHILIP: *Marketing Decision Making*, Holt, Rinehart and Winston, New York, 1971.

[8] MAGEE, JOHN F.: "How to Use Decision Trees in Capital Investments," *Harvard Business Review, Statistical Decision Series III*, pp. 103–120.

[9] MOORE, FRANKLIN: *Production Management*, 6th ed., Richard D. Irwin, Homewood, Illinois, 1973.

[10] OLSEN, ROBERT A.: *Manufacturing Management: A Quantitative Approach*, International Textbook Company, Scranton, Pennsylvania, 1968.

[11] STONEHILL, ARTHUR, and LEONARD NATHANSON: "Capital Budgeting and the Multinational Corporation," *California Management Review*, Summer 1968.

[12] TEKTRONIX, INC.: *Annual Report, 1975*, Beaverton, Oregon, 1975.

[13] WESTON, J. FRED, and EUGENE F. BRIGHAM: *Essentials of Managerial Finance*, 2d ed., Holt, Rinehart and Winston, New York, 1971.

PART

2

Direction and Control of Operations

CHAPTER

5

Product and Process Analysis

RESEARCH AND DEVELOPMENT

TYPES AND ORIENTATION
MANAGING R&D TIME, COST, AND PRODUCTIVITY
UNCERTAINTIES IN R&D MANAGEMENT

PRODUCT DESIGN AND SELECTION

PRODUCT DESIGN AND DEVELOPMENT
PRODUCT SELECTION

PRODUCT-MIX DECISIONS VIA LINEAR PROGRAMMING

GRAPHIC METHOD OF SOLVING LINEAR PROGRAMMING PROBLEMS
SIMPLEX-ECHELON METHOD OF SOLVING LINEAR PROGRAMMING PROBLEMS
LINEAR PROGRAMMING APPLICATIONS

PROCESS PLANNING, SELECTION, AND ANALYSIS

TRANSFORMATION PROCESSES AND FACILITIES
PROCESS PLANNING AIDS: CHARTS, GRAPHS, AND QUANTITATIVE METHODS
LINE BALANCING
SIMULATING OPERATOR TIME VARIABILITY
GROUPING ASSEMBLY LINE ACTIVITIES
PROCESS AND PRODUCTIVITY ANALYSIS

SUMMARY
SOLVED PROBLEMS
QUESTIONS
PROBLEMS
CROSSWORD PUZZLE
BIBLIOGRAPHY

The labor, material, and capital inputs discussed in the previous chapters must eventually be integrated within a production process. In this chapter we blend the input resources into outputs that, hopefully, have more value than the individual labor, materials, and money that are used.

Value is, of course, in the eye of the consumer, so we find that the characteristics of demand begin to exert a stronger influence upon operations management decisions. Product and service desires of the consumer provide important guides to operations managers in their efforts to combine and mold the resources.

The transformation capabilities of a firm are, however, constrained by both their resource base and their existing levels of technology. So production managers are in effect challenged to satisfy a consumer demand on the one hand, but limited by their human, material, and capital resources and by associated levels of technology on the other. This challenge brings them many problems of both a technical and a human nature, and certainly keeps them "where the action is."

Although forecasting, scheduling, quality and other control efforts are the managers' means of meeting their challenge, we shall not attempt to discuss all of these efforts in this chapter. Instead, each of these major direction and control activities is reserved for a separate chapter that follows. Our immediate concern will be only with analysis of the product and process. We begin by examining how research and development activities help to translate consumer desires into feasible products. Then we consider the role of the operations manager with respect to product design and selection. Next we turn to an analysis of the production process; what kinds of production processes are appropriate and how can they best be planned and implemented? We conclude with some recommendations for analyzing ongoing processes to improve their overall effectiveness.

Throughout the chapter we shall endeavor to learn how operations managers might make better decisions with respect to product development and selection, and process selection and use. Where technological and resource constraints are relatively fixed we will find that some deterministic quantitative methods can be useful aids to decision making. Where consumer demand or worker variability inject major uncertainties into the decision situation, various statistical approaches and techniques of Bayesian analysis prove helpful.

RESEARCH AND DEVELOPMENT

Research is a consciously directed investigation to find new knowledge. It is the forerunner of an increasing number of products and processes ranging from transistors and synthetics to jet aircraft and nuclear fission. But as technology advances, it requires more and more research to generate further improvements. Since it involves a study of the unknown, its outcome is usually uncertain, and its cost can be high.

Research and development (R&D) expenditures in the United States grew from around $20 billion in 1965 to $35 billion in 1975, with about half of the country's R&D funds being provided by the federal government. Although government expenditures leveled off somewhat during the late 1960s, in the 1970s both government and industry's commitment to R&D has continued to grow.

Much of the R&D expenditure is nevertheless concentrated in a few industries. Over 75 percent of industry's expenditures are spent by firms in the fields of (1) aircraft and missiles, (2) electrical equipment and communication, (3) chemicals and allied products, (4) machinery, and (5) motor vehicles and transportation equipment [**3**: 597]. At the Du Pont Company, for example (which employs 135,000 people and has annual sales of around $7 billion), about 5,000 scientists and engineers spend some 5 percent of the total company sales revenue on research and development activities [**5**: 18]. Xerox spends about 6 percent of its revenues on research and development [**26**: 23].

While research often requires substantial capital investment and is certainly costly, it has become the hallmark of American industry and is vital to competitive firms in any free enterprise economy. About three-fourths of the R&D work in the United States is actually performed by private industry (although some of this is federally funded). Some major firms report that from 60 percent to as high as 90 percent of their current sales income is from products that did not exist 10 years ago.

TYPES AND ORIENTATION

Research efforts are usually classified into either "basic" or "applied" activities. *Basic Research* is simply a search for new knowledge without regard to any specific use. A considerable amount of basic research is carried on by universities and foundations, but even so this amount is nominal compared to the applied efforts. *Applied research* is directed toward specific problems, products, or processes. Being goal-oriented, the progress of applied research is (fortunately) more measurable and the efforts are perhaps more manageable than are those of basic research. Three major considerations in managing research are time, cost, and productivity. These considerations are discussed below.

MANAGING R&D TIME, COST, AND PRODUCTIVITY

Although research produces many a "necessary" innovation, studies of research projects have revealed that time and cost estimates are often understated [**21**: 227–231]. Cost and personnel overrun of around 50 percent have been found to occur surprisingly often—even when slippage was allowed for. One situation analysts have observed is that the most efficient research team size for cost minimization is frequently smaller than the optimal size for maximum productivity. This poses some difficult managerial problems when it comes to balancing time and cost.

A particularly useful scheduling and control device for R&D projects is PERT, which we shall consider in a later chapter. On a recent multimillion dollar air-to-ground missile system project, the Boeing Company found that PERT gave them exceptionally timely and accurate control. Their time and cost data were wholly computerized and were available at any time to both Boeing Company management and their customer (the U.S. Air Force) via duplicate video computer terminals.

By fast and accurate reporting of progress against preplanned milestones, R&D time, cost, and productivity can be improved. Nevertheless, there is an inherent element of uncertainty in any research that cannot be overlooked.

UNCERTAINTIES IN R&D MANAGEMENT

Basic research, by definition, has an uncertain outcome. Much applied research also has an uncertain outcome and often has to be written off as a loss. It is not uncommon for larger firms to invest up to $50 million or even more only to find their venture has been a failure. Some firms find that well over half of their research ideas ultimately prove unsuccessful. Sometimes the impracticability of a venture is not discovered until the development stage, which consumes the bulk of R&D funds. Yet many firms must depend heavily upon R&D to improve their existing products and to develop new ones.

While there is no way to guarantee the success of any research endeavor, research decisions can be facilitated if relevant data is collected, analyzed, and used in as complete and objective a manner as possible. In some cases the preliminary evaluations, pilot studies, and information-gathering activities are as consequential as the actual physical research itself. This is because these activities help to establish the economic (market) and technological feasibility which constitute two of the major uncertainties. Bayesian methods provide one means of placing a value on this decision information for purposes of analysis.

The Value of Information

We saw earlier that a decision-making situation under uncertainty is one where decision makers must select one alternative course of action and the consequence (or payoff) depends upon both the choice of action and the state of nature that ultimately prevails. *Uncertainty* refers to the decision makers' ignorance about which state of nature will prevail, for only one will occur and they are in no position to control that.

A number of criteria are available to them depending upon their attitude toward risk and their ability to estimate the payoffs that will occur under the various states. Thus we saw that they may choose on the basis of a maximax, maximin, maximum probability, or maximum expected monetary value (EMV) criterion. We found that an expected value criteria was useful in that it represented an unbiased long-run average outcome. Two additional concepts will now allow us to place a value on information which might improve upon a choice that was previously based solely upon an expected value criteria:

1 *Expected profit under certainty* (EPC) This is the profit that would result if no uncertainty existed with respect to the state of nature (the outcome of research). Thus, each state is presumed to exist in proportion to its probability of occurrence and the best act under a given state is always chosen.

2 *Expected value of perfect information* (EVPI) This is the incremental amount that can be justified to remove uncertainty (such as about the economic or technological feasibility of a project). It is the excess of value over the maximum expected monetary value (EMV) up to what would be the expected profit under certainty (EPC).

$$\text{EVPI} = \text{EPC} - \text{EMV} \tag{5-1}$$

The procedure for computing EVPI is:

1 Establish the decision matrix with actions, states of nature, and payoffs. Assign probabilities to each state.

2 Compute EMV by summing the payoff values times their probability of occurrence over each act.

3 Compute EPC by weighting the highest payoff under each state by the proportion of time (that is, the probability) that the state will occur and sum over the states.

4 Compute EVPI = EPC − EMV.

This difference, EVPI, is in effect a cost of uncertainty and the maximum value that perfect information would be worth. Applied to a research project, it could represent the maximum justified for a feasibility study or a pilot study to verify the desirability of a project [**13**].

Example 5-1

A major oil company is evaluating the prospect of developing nuclear fuel cells for automobiles. The cells would use spent (used) uranium fuel by-products and would revolutionize the automotive industry by replacing the internal combustion engine with a "clean" electric motor. As an alternative to financing the R&D by itself the firm is considering joining with an engineering consulting firm. Depending upon the success of the R&D, the oil company estimates its 10-yr present value profits (million $) as shown:

	Success of R&D		
	θ_1	θ_2	θ_3
	Highly successful	**Moderately successful**	**Not successful**
D = Develop on own	300	40	−60
J = Joint venture	200	30	−20

Based upon feasibility studies and consultations with development and marketing groups, the operations vice-president has assigned subjective probabilities of $\theta_1 = 0.2$, $\theta_2 = 0.4$, $\theta_3 = 0.4$. The vice-president feels that some prototype studies by his firm could perhaps give a better indication of success and thus modify these probabilities.

(*a*) Determine the expected profit of each course of action and the EMV.
(*b*) Determine the expected value of perfect information (EVPI).
(*c*) Explain the meaning of your EVPI figure.
(*d*) Depict this decision situation in the form of a decision tree.

Solution

(*a*) The expected value of each action, $E(A)$, can be determined by:

	$\theta_1 = 0.2$	$\theta_2 = 0.4$	$\theta_3 = 0.4$
D	300	40	-60
J	200	30	-20

$$E(A) = \sum \theta_{ij} P(\theta_j) \quad \text{where } i = \text{row and } j = \text{column}$$
$$E(D) = \$300\,(0.2) + 40(0.4) - 60(0.4) = \$52\text{m}$$
$$E(J) = \$200\,(0.2) + 30(0.4) - 20(0.4) = \$44\text{m}$$

$\therefore$ D is the optimal course and is designated EMV.

(*b*) EVPI = EPC − EMV. The EPC represents the expected profit under certainty and is the best course of action under each state weighted by the probability of occurence of that state:

(1) If state is known to be	**(2) Then the best action and profit would be**	**(3) And percent of time this occurs is**	**(4) Expected profit (2) × (3)**
θ_1	$D = 300$	0.2	\$60
θ_2	$D = 40$	0.4	16
θ_3	$J = -20$	0.4	-8
		EPC =	\$68

Expected profit with perfect information (EPC)	\$68 million
Expected monetary value of optional act (EMV)	−52 million
Expected value of perfect information (EVPI)	\$16 million

(*c*) This means it would be worth up to \$16 million to know how successful the R&D is likely to be before deciding between D or J. The firm's *expected profit* would increase by \$16 million if it had a perfect forecast of the success of the project. Note, however, that this is a long-range expected value concept and that the actual profitability may be more or less than \$16 million. Furthermore, perfect information may be unattainable in this situation.

(*d*) For the solution, see the accompanying diagram depicting the decision tree.

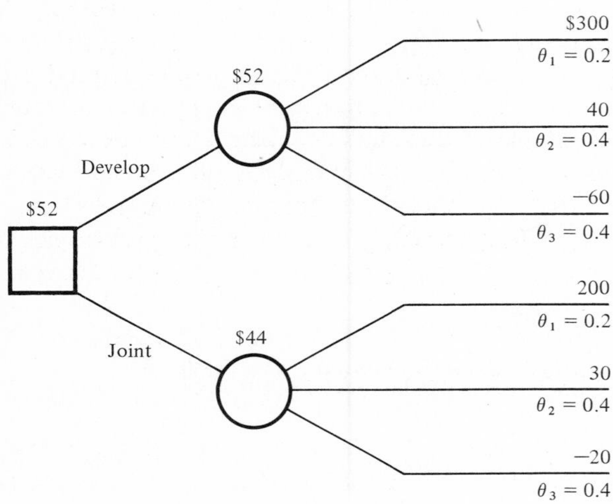

The Concept of Opportunity Loss

Research efforts are inherently attempts to innovate and to take advantage of opportunities. Although it is difficult to evaluate research performance, it would be desirable to judge performance against the opportunities available rather than simply on a total profit or loss basis. The accounting measure of monetary value overlooks courses of action that might have offered exceptional opportunities for the firm but that were not undertaken because of the risk or perhaps a managerial fear that failure of a project might jeopardize job security. As a result, management sometimes tends to be more conservative and less innovative than may be justified from the standpoint of the goals and financial strength of the organization.

Bayesian analysis provides a unique means of viewing managerial decisions from an expected opportunity loss (EOL) perspective [**9**]. The opportunity loss is incurred because of a failure to take the best economic action possible due to risk or uncertainty about which state of nature will prevail. Technically, this means it is the difference between the payoff of any given choice of action and the payoff that would have resulted if the best act had been chosen. Any standard payoff matrix may be restated as an opportunity loss matrix, but the mechanics of this is beyond our scope at this point.

PRODUCT DESIGN AND SELECTION

Product design is the structuring of component parts or activities so that as a unit they can provide a specified value. Products are normally thought of as physical goods, but services (such as medical care) are becoming increasingly significant products in our advanced and affluent society. In the United States, Canada, Japan, and several countries of Western Europe, about 50 percent or more of domestic outputs are now in the form of services (as opposed to manufacturing, construction, and agricultural products) [**6**: 9]. Since products constitute the major tangible output of an organization, and are normally its prime source of revenue, their design and selection should be closely identified with organizational objectives.

In this section we consider the competitive nature of products, some of their major design parameters, and how management might select appropriate products to produce. Whereas product design involves obvious engineering considerations, and selection entails obvious marketing considerations, we shall see that production capabilities exert a strong influence over both design and selection. In bridging the design and market aspects of a product, operations managers are in a position to make a meaningful contribution to the firm's objectives if they are willing and able to do so.

PRODUCT DESIGN AND DEVELOPMENT

Studies reveal that about 30 percent of the new product ideas come from research and development efforts. Marketing and customer inputs are another major source, while some firms have special departments for generating product suggestions [**1**]. Regardless of the source, the product design should be carefully specified, analyzed, and tested.

Product specification is typically an engineering function where exacting drawings are prepared giving dimensions, weights, volumes, tolerances, and so on. In service-related industries the product specification often consists of an environmental requirement to be maintained or a procedure to be followed. For example, a health care environment may be the product of a nursing home or a radiation film-developing procedure the product of a nuclear services firm. Design personnel should either be thoroughly familiar with production technology or should work with operations personnel to be sure that their design makes best use of the firm's production capabilities. In this way the product will emerge with the most desirable material, tolerances, finish, and service aspects.

Product analysis and testing is the exacting determination of how performance, cost, and other relevant parameters relate to design objectives. Customer requirements usually dictate basic performance levels and reliability measures. With the fundamental good or service as a base, the producing firm often adds special features or aesthetics that differentiate its product from competing products.

While the basic performance and aesthetic features all contribute to costs, value engineering efforts are usually undertaken to reduce costs by standardizing and simplifying products. Since the design dictates a majority of production costs, it deserves much attention, as noted in the following quotation from a corporate president [**11**]:

> The role of industrial design in product cost reduction is influenced by requirements for aesthetic value, customer appeal, product function, corporate prestige, and management's ability to implement cost reduction changes.
>
> Setting realistic goals requires good information and teamwork between management, marketing, engineering, production, and industrial design. No single department can achieve maximum cost reduction without the support and co-operation of all persons involved, including top management.

Successful products must ultimately satisfy both performance and cost criteria. If either is not met, the product should be quickly replaced by another. Many products have a "life cycle" in which they are introduced, blossom to maturity, and are eventually replaced by new and improved products. It is not uncommon for a large firm to be producing hundreds of products at a time, in various stages of their life cycles. Thus most firms have some choice as to which products to produce. We turn now to ways to improve the profit (performance or cost) by appropriate selection of products.

PRODUCT SELECTION

Product selection decisions are influenced by three major factors: (1) the firm's resources and technology, (2) the market environment, and (3) the (cultural) motivation to use the firm's capabilities to meet the needs of the marketplace. The cultural motivation is often economic, but it can also be social, political, religious, or other. These three factors are shown in Fig. 5-1, in which economic motivation is assigned a major role.

Some firms are very capital-intensive (for example, electric utilities), whereas others are more labor-intensive (such as clothing manufacturers), and some maintain sophisticated technologies whereas others do not. These resource and technological capabilities usually arise from corporate policy decisions related to the organization's line of business or industry. The most efficient firms within an industry use their resource and technological base to the fullest extent possible. Research and development is, of course, a primary method of expanding a firm's technological base so that it is in a more preferred position to compete.

From the market environment come both demand and competition. A firm is in for trouble unless consumers want the volume of goods and services being produced at the given time. Of course competitors can also foil a product selection if they are numerous or strong enough to dominate the market. In addition, society has established certain legal controls on competitive behavior. However, consumers, competitors, and society are all important sources of ideas concerning which products are most needed and are likely to be most successful.

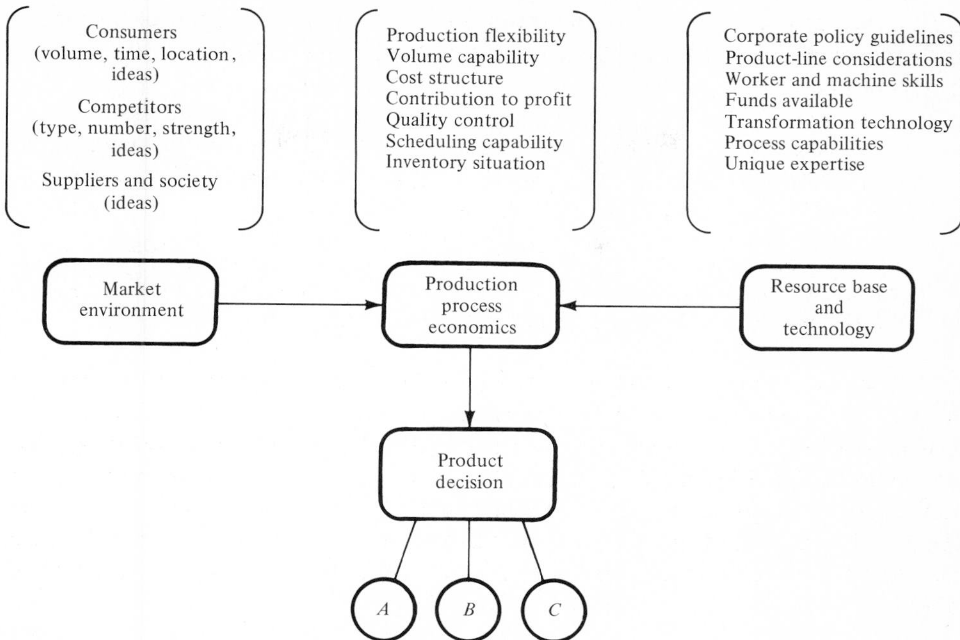

FIGURE 5-1 Factors relevant to product selection decision

The resource capabilities and market demands must be matched in the form of capability to produce at an economic or social advantage. For monopolistic or public agency organizations the profit concept is not so crucial, but economy and efficiency continue to be relevant criteria. Forecasts of demand from the market should be compared with existing inventory levels and forthcoming production schedules before any new product decisions are implemented. The operations manager is usually in the best position to evaluate inventory, scheduling, quality, and cost factors which are relevant to product selection decisions. Cost and capacity constraints often turn out to be critical determinants of product choice.

PRODUCT-MIX DECISIONS VIA LINEAR PROGRAMMING

The product selection decision can indeed be complex, and a clear and consistent understanding of organizational goals on the part of production, marketing, finance, and other subsystems of the firm is vital. Within the product line groupings, decisions must again be made with respect to which process to use or which mix of products to produce in view of cost, capacity, and other constraints that impose limits on the capability of the firm. Product-mix decisions typically involve major marketing concerns. But where marketing or other considerations are not overriding criteria, many firms have found that linear programming methods are useful techniques for assisting in the product mix decisions. Such a situation may arise, for example, when the firm has a current market for whatever quantities of two or more products it can produce. The selection of the least costly mix of raw materials or processes to use from among several available are more localized examples of the same type of mix decision.

Linear programming is a quantitative method of analysis that has found extensive application within the business system. It has been applied to capital budgeting problems, line balancing, product-mix determination, and numerous other operating situations. One of the earliest and most extensive uses has been in planning and scheduling. It is convenient to introduce graphic and simplex linear programming here for we shall be making reference to it throughout the remainder of the text. We encounter it in the context of product-mix determination situations that are closely related to short-term scheduling, and will refer the reader back to this section when we take up short-term scheduling in Chap. 9.

Linear programming, as we saw earlier with respect to distribution problems, is a technique for maximizing or minimizing an objective function subject to constraints. While it is the final solution that we seek, we must go through the mechanics of a solution to arrive at our goal. The graphic method is perhaps most enlightening, but for more complicated problems the simplex method is useful. Most large problems are solved by computer, however, so a basic understanding of the methodology, along with knowledge of how to set up a problem and interpret the results, is perhaps the most essential.

GRAPHIC-METHOD OF SOLVING LINEAR PROGRAMMING PROBLEMS

The graphic method of solution is satisfactory for problems involving two decision variables and consists of the following five steps:

1 Formulate the problem in terms of a linear objective function and linear constraints.

2 Set up a graph with one decision variable on each axis and plot the constraints.

3 Determine the slope of the objective function and indicate the slope on the graph.

4 Move the objective function in an optimizing direction until it is constrained.

5 Read off the solution values of the decision variables from the respective axes.

Example 5-2

A chemical firm produces automobile cleaner X and polisher Y and realizes \$10 profit on each batch of X and \$30 on Y. Both products require processing through the same machines A and B, but X requires 4 hr in A and 8 in B, whereas

Y requires 6 hr in A and 4 in B. During the forthcoming week machines A and B have 12 and 16 hr of available capacity respectively. Assuming demand exists for both products, how many batches of each should be produced to realize the optimal profit Z?

Solution

1 *Objective function*

$$\text{Max } Z = \$10X + \$30Y$$

Constraints

$$A \qquad 4X + 6Y \leq 12$$
$$B \qquad 8X + 4Y \leq 16$$

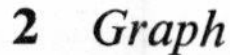

2 *Graph*

Variables are X and Y

Constraints are plotted as equalities.

$$A \qquad \text{If } X = 0,\ Y = 2$$
$$\qquad \text{If } Y = 0,\ X = 3$$

$$B \qquad \text{If } X = 0,\ Y = 4$$
$$\qquad \text{If } Y = 0,\ X = 2$$

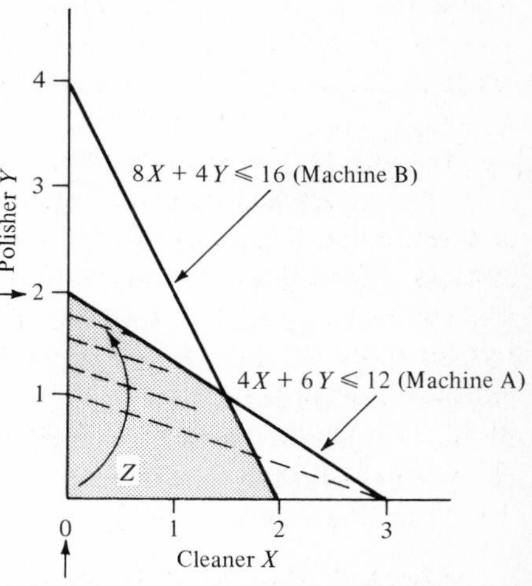

FIGURE 5-2 Graphic linear programming solution

Note that the graph (Fig. 5-2) establishes a feasible region bounded by the capacity constraints of A and B and the implicit constraints that production of $X \geq 0$ and $Y \geq 0$.

3 *Slope of objective function*

$$Z = 10X + 30Y$$

The standard slope-intercept form of a linear equation is

$$Y = mX + b \tag{5-2}$$

where m is the slope of the line (that is, change in Y per unit change in X) and b is the Y intercept.

Expressing our objective function in this form we have:

$$30Y = -10X + Z$$
$$Y = -\tfrac{1}{3}X + \frac{Z}{30}$$

Slope $= -\frac{1}{3}$, that is, a line decreasing one unit in Y for every three positive units of X. This is plotted at any convenient spot within the feasible region (shown dotted). The dotted line from $Y = 1$ to $X = 3$ illustrates this.

4 *Move objective function to optimize* The slope of the objective function is moved away from the origin until restrained by the furthermost intersection of constraint A and the implicit constraint $X \geq 0$. The solution will always be at a corner in the feasible region.

5 *Read solution values* The arrows point to the solution, which is determined by the X and Y coordinates at the corner. In this example $X = 0$ and $Y = 2$ so the firm should produce no cleaner and two batches of polisher for a profit of:

$$Z = \$10(0) + \$30(2) = \$60$$

As can be seen from the graph, the constraint imposed by machine B (that is, that $8X + 4Y \leq 16$) has no effect for it is the 12 hours of machine A (denoted by $4X + 6Y \leq 12$) that are constraining production of the more profitable polisher. The graph also reveals that profit would continue to increase if more hours could be made available on machine A up to the point of doubling output (to $X = 0$ and $Y = 4$). At this point the time available from machine B would become constraining.

The linear programming example described above assumed that demand was assured and profit contribution, processing time, and available machine time were known with certainty. In many cases there is enough certainty so that decisions can realistically be made with the aid of linear programming. Problem 2 in the solved problem section presents a problem with two decision variables and three constraint equations. The solution exists at the intersection of two explicit constraints and additional comments are made with respect to the sensitivity of the solution to changes in the constraints.

SIMPLEX-ECHELON METHOD OF SOLVING LINEAR PROGRAMMING PROBLEMS[1]

Many realistic linear programming problems have several decision variables and dozens of constraint equations. Such problems cannot be solved graphically and various algorithms, such as the simplex procedure, are used, usually in conjunction with a computer. The *simplex method* is an iterative procedure which progressively approaches and ultimately reaches an optimal solution. In the interest of gaining the capability of solving small problems we shall illustrate the solution to a simple problem using a simplex-echelon matrix method. A brief discussion of matrices will provide sufficient background.

[1] I am indebted to Professor Dave Carlson of the Oregon State University Department of Mathematics for suggesting this approach.

A *matrix* is simply a rectangular array of numbers, usually enclosed in brackets. Thus we can have matrices of several types, as shown.

$$A = \begin{bmatrix} 2 \\ 4 \\ -5 \\ 3 \end{bmatrix} \qquad B = [2 \quad 3 \quad 6] \qquad C = \begin{bmatrix} 3 & 7 & 4 \\ 5 & 2 & 1 \\ 6 & -3 & 7 \end{bmatrix} \qquad D = \begin{bmatrix} 1 & 0 & 0 \\ 0 & 1 & 0 \\ 0 & 0 & 1 \end{bmatrix}$$

The matrices are dimensioned by their number of rows times their number of columns. Thus A is a 4×1 and B is a 1×3 matrix. Compatible matrices can be added, subtracted, multiplied, and manipulated in various ways. Matrix D is unique to square matrices and is called an identity matrix since the product of another 3×3 matrix times D is simply the original matrix itself.

The solution matrix of a linear programming problem consists of a large matrix composed of various component matrices derived from the objective function, the constraints, an identity matrix, and a row matrix of zeros. It is of the form:

$$\begin{bmatrix} A & I & B \\ C & O & Z \end{bmatrix} \tag{5-3}$$

where

A = rectangular matrix consisting of the coefficients of the constraint equations
I = identity matrix
B = column matrix of the values on the right-hand side of the constraint equations
C = row matrix consisting of the coefficients of the objective function
O = row matrix of zeros
Z = negative value of the objective function

The solution methodology for maximization problems involves selecting a pivot column and row and using echelon operations to revise the matrix values until all values in the bottom row of the matrix are ≤ 0. We can follow it best by using the previous example.

Example 5-3

Use the simplex-echelon method to solve

$$\text{Max } Z = 10X + 30Y$$

subject to

$$4X + 6Y \leq 12$$
$$8X + 4Y \leq 16$$

Solution

The solution matrix is of the form

$$\begin{bmatrix} A & I & B \\ C & O & Z \end{bmatrix}$$

where

$$A = \begin{bmatrix} 4 & 6 \\ 8 & 4 \end{bmatrix} \qquad I = \begin{bmatrix} 1 & 0 \\ 0 & 1 \end{bmatrix} \qquad B = \begin{bmatrix} 12 \\ 16 \end{bmatrix}$$

$$C = [10 \quad 30] \qquad 0 = [0 \quad 0] \qquad Z = Z$$

Therefore, the first matrix is of the form:

$$\begin{bmatrix} 4 & \textcircled{6} & 1 & 0 & 12 \\ 8 & 4 & 0 & 1 & 16 \\ 10 & 30 & 0 & 0 & Z \end{bmatrix}$$

Revision steps

1 Select the column with the largest positive number in the bottom row (column 2).

2 Divide those column values into the last column and select the smallest number for a "pivot." (Use only positive numbers.)

$$\frac{12}{6} = 2 \qquad \frac{16}{4} = 4$$

∴ Row 1 (pivot is circled)

3 Divide each value in the pivot row by the pivot and enter new values in a second matrix.

$$\begin{bmatrix} \frac{2}{3} & 1 & \frac{1}{6} & 0 & 2 \\ & & & & \\ & & & & \end{bmatrix}$$

4 Use echelon operations to make all other elements in the pivot column = 0. Multiply the new values derived in step 3 (in the top row) by the negative of the selected element in the pivot column and add the result to the selected row. For example, to convert the 4 in the second row to zero: we multiply

$$-4(\tfrac{2}{3}) \qquad -4(1) \qquad -4(\tfrac{1}{6}) \qquad -4(0) \qquad -4(2)$$

to get values of

$$-\tfrac{8}{3} \qquad -4 \qquad -\tfrac{2}{3} \qquad 0 \qquad -8$$

which are added to

$$8 \qquad 4 \qquad 0 \qquad 1 \qquad 16$$

to get new values of

$$\tfrac{16}{3} \qquad 0 \qquad -\tfrac{2}{3} \qquad 1 \qquad 8$$

which are then entered in the second row in the new matrix (shown below). To convert the 30 to zero, we multiply row 1 in the second matrix by -30 and add this result to row 3.

Multiplying

$$-30(\tfrac{2}{3}) \qquad -30(1) \qquad -30(\tfrac{1}{6}) \qquad -30(0) \qquad -30(2)$$

gives values

$$-20 \qquad -30 \qquad -5 \qquad 0 \qquad -60$$

add row 3

$$10 \qquad 30 \qquad 0 \qquad 0 \qquad Z$$

new values

$$-10 \qquad 0 \qquad -5 \qquad 0 \qquad Z - 60$$

$$\begin{bmatrix} \tfrac{2}{3} & 1 & \tfrac{1}{6} & 0 & 2 \\ \tfrac{16}{3} & 0 & -\tfrac{2}{3} & 1 & 8 \\ -10 & 0 & -5 & 0 & Z - 60 \end{bmatrix}$$

5 Repeat steps 1 through 4 until all values in the bottom row are ≤ 0. Since all values are ≤ 0, the optimal solution is already reached. Variables in solution are identified by examining column locations corresponding to the decision variables X and Y (that is, columns 1 and 2 here). Columns that have one entry of 1 and remaining values of zero represent variables in solution and the solution values are given in the right-most column. The maximized function value is the negative of the value following Z.

$$\begin{array}{cc} X & Y \end{array}$$
$$\begin{bmatrix} - & 1 & - & - & 2 \\ - & 0 & - & - & - \\ - & 0 & - & - & Z - 60 \end{bmatrix} \qquad \begin{aligned} \therefore\ X &= \text{not in solution} \\ Y &= 2 \\ Z &= -(-60) = \$60 \end{aligned}$$

A careful examination of the solution matrices can reveal a good deal more than just the values of the variables in solution and the value of the objective function. The first matrix contained a basic feasible solution corresponding to the $X = 0$, $Y = 0$ point of the graphic solution of Fig. 5–2. In fact, the ones and zeros in the columns of the identity (and zero) portion of the first matrix indicated that neither X nor Y was in solution (being produced) and that both machines had unused or "slack" time. (The 1s in the identity matrix are often termed "slack" variables.) If 1s and zeros remain in this same portion of the final matrix, it indicates that there is still slack associated with a given constraint and therefore the constraint is not binding. In our final matrix the slack variable associated with the second constraint equation ($8X + 4Y \leq 16$) is in solution, indicating that machine B is "producing" unused (slack) time.

Another valuable bit of information can come from the numbers in the bottom row of the matrix. In our first matrix, the values 10, 30, 0, and 0 are associated with X, Y, machine A slack time, and machine B slack time respectively. The numbers associated with the decision variables X and Y (which were not yet in solution) indicate that the profit would be increased by \$10 for each unit of X (cleaner) produced, and by \$30 for each unit of Y (polisher) produced—up to a point. The values associated with the slack variables represent the amount of increase in the objective function that is associated with a one-unit increase in the respective constraint. From the initial matrix it is apparent that increasing the slack time associated with either machines A or B would net zero improvement.

Our first iteration resulted in introducing the production of as much polisher Y as could be achieved (two units) without violating any constraints. By dividing the machine hours available from A and B (that is, 12 and 16 respectively) by the number of hours per unit required for producing polisher (6 in A and 4 in B), we found that at most only two units of polisher could be produced. Selecting the smallest of these results as our pivot ensured that no constraints would be violated here.

The figures in the bottom row of the final matrix (-10, 0, -5, 0) reveal the following:

1 To produce one can of X (cleaner) would reduce profits by \$10 (because it would take machine time away from production of Y).

2 The first zero indicates Y is in solution (being produced). The next two values (—5 and 0) are referred to as *shadow prices*, and show the net effect of increasing the slack or idle time of machines A and B by one unit.

3 Since machine A is fully utilized, to take one hour out of production and "acquire" one hour of idle time would reduce profit by \$5 (profit from Y is \$30 for each 6 hours work on A, that is, a rate of \$5 per hour). Conversely, if another hour could be made available, say by shifting a current job from A, the time on A could be profitably utilized at a profit rate of \$5 per hour.

4 The zero corresponding to the constraint of machine B signifies that machine B already has slack time and increasing B's available time (or decreasing it) by one unit would have no effect on profits.

The graph of Fig. 5-2 is useful for visualizing the above observations.

LINEAR PROGRAMMING APPLICATIONS

Linear programming is a quantitative method that has gained increasingly wide use during the past 10 years. Examples [7] include applications in (1) farming to select crop types and amounts; (2) papermaking to allocate number of tons of a given grade on a given machine at minimum cost; (3) food processing to set levels of production by product and by period; (4) transistor manufacturing to establish production quantities that minimize cost while meeting inventory, assembly, and final demand constraints; (5) steelmaking to determine the mix of raw materials needed to produce 2,000 tons of alloy at minimum cost; (6) pharmaceutical testing to optimize payoff from five potential products; (7) electric power to establish power systems so as to minimize cost; (8) meat packing to optimize sausage (blending) mix; (9) oil-well production to set production schedules of highest profitability with known maximum well capacities, reservoir, and transportation cost. Numerous other examples exist in the petroleum, chemical, metal, agricultural, forestry, transportation, communication, medical, entertainment, information processing, and other goods and service industries. It is not uncommon for firms to report "savings of several thousand per month," "annual savings of over $32,000," "50 percent savings in time," "trim loss reduced by 30 percent," and so forth [7].

For minimization problems the simplex-echelon procedure is similar to maximization problems with some minor modifications. See [**18**: 274]. The solution steps require bringing in the variable with the largest negative number in the bottom row (step 1), and additional artificial variables must be introduced to account for the greater-than-or-equal-to constraints. References in the bibliography [**15**, **18**, **24**] provide additional information on minimization problems as well as on shadow prices, duality, and other conceptual foundations of linear programming.

PROCESS PLANNING, SELECTION, AND ANALYSIS

The transformation of resources into goods and services is the technological heart of a production operation. In this section we briefly review some of the transformation processes and examine means of process planning, selection, and analysis.

TRANSFORMATION PROCESSES AND FACILITIES

Our affluent society has come to accept sophisticated goods and services as almost necessities. Thus we expect to have electronic calculators, nylon carpets, and new automobiles when we want them, and we count on having electric power, jet aircraft transportation, and intensive care medical facilities being available when needed. These goods and services all result from basic transformations of a mechanical, chemical, electrical, nuclear, or informational nature. The transformation processes often require highly specialized complex equipment, such as vacuum melting furnaces, precisely controlled chemical reactors, computerized data systems, and the like. In each case, basic technologies (such as chemical) underlie the process which makes the goods and services valuable to us as consumers.

While the numerous processes are perhaps of interest to us individually, we shall make no attempt to try to describe the technology of metals processing or to study medical or nuclear technology. All operations managers must become acquainted with the unique capabilities and constraining technology of their individual operations. The same holds true to a greater or lesser degree for the company president and for all employees of an organization. Some organizational responsibilities require special engineering or technical training whereas others rely more upon managerial skills or on-the-job experience.

It might be ideal if all managers had the sum total capability of all those within their span of control, but this is not the case. Managers plan, organize, control, and direct the actions of others. The "others" may be cost accountants, engineers, operating technicians, process supervisors, and so on. And while we can appreciate the value of technical competence in these specific areas, our concern must remain with the decision making and managerial realm of responsibility. Managers should be skilled decision makers more than anything else. We focus now on some decision-making aids for process planning.

PROCESS PLANNING AIDS: CHARTS, GRAPHS, AND QUANTITATIVE METHODS

We saw earlier that product decisions are influenced by the market environment, the resource base and level of technology, and the production process economics of the individual firm. *Process planning* is concerned with designing and implementing a work system that will produce the desired product in the required quantities. The process planning activities are concerned with the *type of work flow* and the *design of work centers* [**22**: 303]. This is illustrated in Fig. 5-3. The figure reflects the strong influence of the original plant layout, which in turn depends upon the type of transformation technology used. Although many process planning decisions are made when an original layout is designed, most firms must continually adapt to product and volume changes, so that process planning really becomes a continuing activity.

Areas of frequent concern to operations managers relate to assembly and process procedures, equipment selection, and problems of balancing the workload. We shall turn now to these areas. Assembly charts, operations charts, and flow process charts (which were introduced in Chap. 3) are useful devices for planning and managing the various transformation processes. Equipment capacity concepts were introduced in Chap. 2. We shall now see how individual equipment capacity decisions can be facilitated by a break-even analysis similar in concept to that used for plant location decisions. Finally, we shall see how the approach to loading problems differs depending upon the type of layout. Algebraic methods and worker-machine charts (intro-

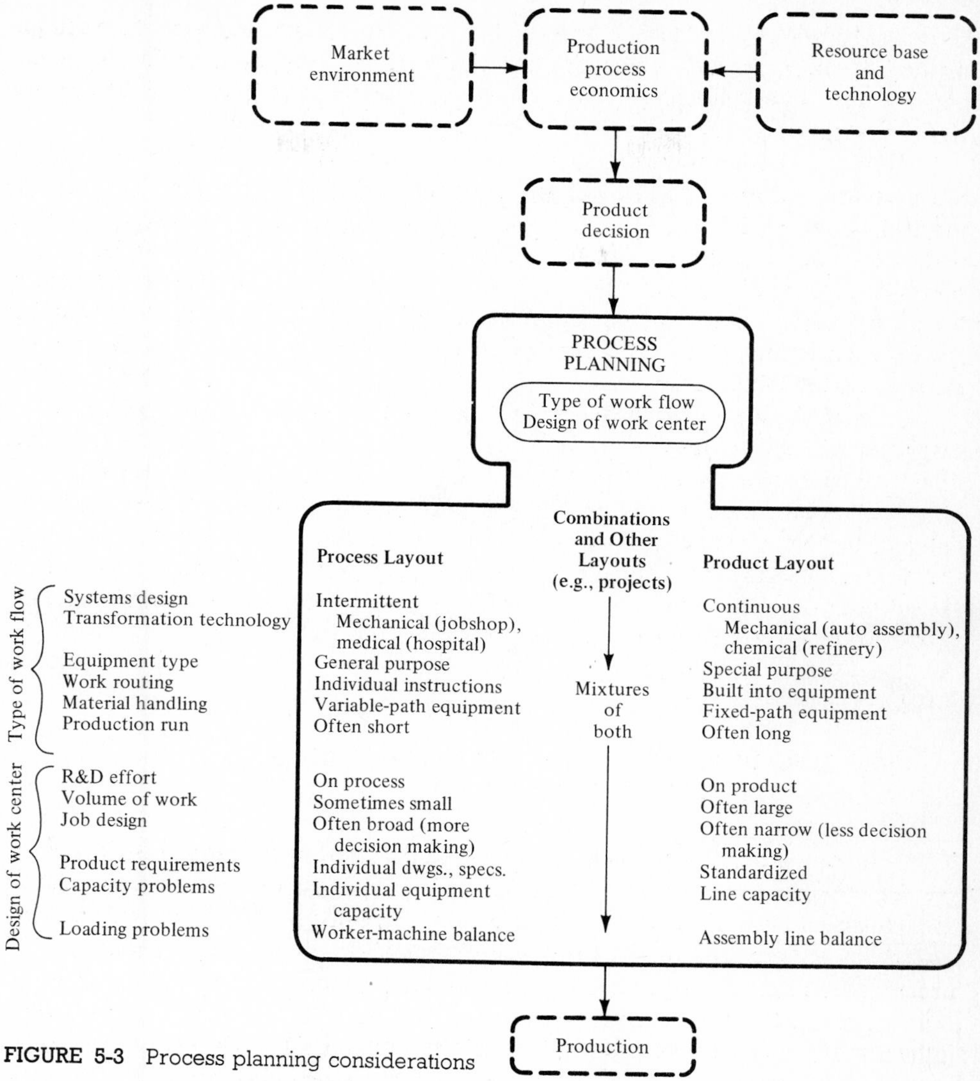

Market environment → Production process economics ← Resource base and technology

Production process economics → Product decision → PROCESS PLANNING

PROCESS PLANNING
Type of work flow
Design of work center

		Process Layout	Combinations and Other Layouts (e.g., projects)	Product Layout
Type of work flow	Systems design			
	Transformation technology	Intermittent Mechanical (jobshop), medical (hospital)		Continuous Mechanical (auto assembly), chemical (refinery)
	Equipment type	General purpose	Mixtures of both	Special purpose
	Work routing	Individual instructions		Built into equipment
	Material handling	Variable-path equipment		Fixed-path equipment
	Production run	Often short		Often long
Design of work center	R&D effort	On process		On product
	Volume of work	Sometimes small		Often large
	Job design	Often broad (more decision making)		Often narrow (less decision making)
	Product requirements	Individual dwgs., specs.		Standardized
	Capacity problems	Individual equipment capacity		Line capacity
	Loading problems	Worker-machine balance		Assembly line balance

→ Production

FIGURE 5-3 Process planning considerations

duced in Chap. 3) tend to be useful for planning process layout activities, but we must look to assembly line balancing techniques for solving the loading problems of product-line layouts.

Assembly and Process Charts

Assembly charts show the material requirements and assembly sequence of components that make up a mechanical assembly. Assembly charts use the standard symbols of ○ for operations and □ for inspections as illustrated in Fig. 5-4. The comparable aid for a chemical or nuclear transformation process would be a series

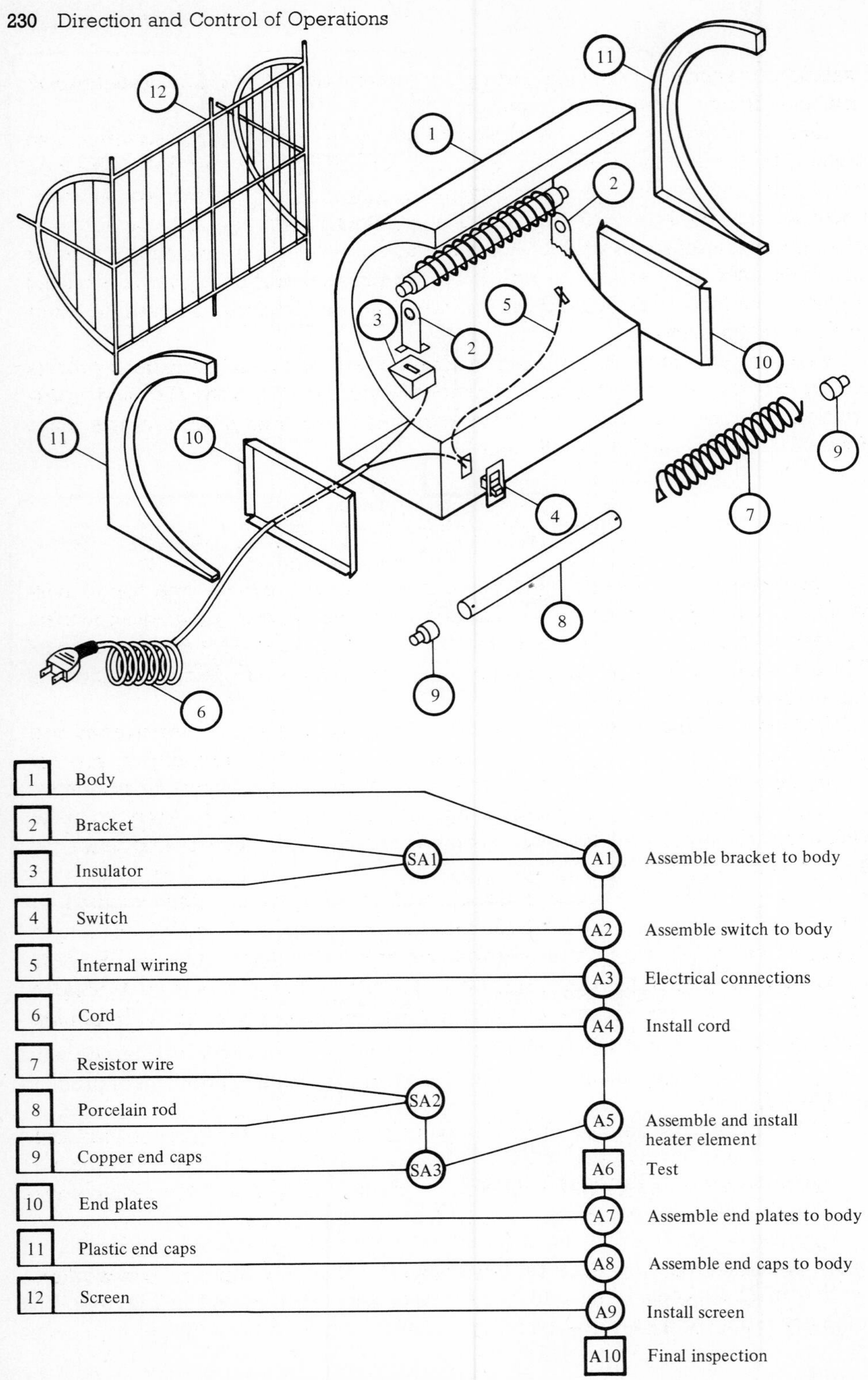
12
11
1
2
3
2
5
10
11
10
9
4
7
9
8
9
6
1 Body
2 Bracket
3 Insulator
4 Switch
5 Internal wiring
6 Cord
7 Resistor wire
8 Porcelain rod
9 Copper end caps
10 End plates
11 Plastic end caps
12 Screen
SA1
SA2
SA3
A1 Assemble bracket to body
A2 Assemble switch to body
A3 Electrical connections
A4 Install cord
A5 Assemble and install heater element
A6 Test
A7 Assemble end plates to body
A8 Assemble end caps to body
A9 Install screen
A10 Final inspection

FIGURE 5-4 Assembly chart for electric heater

of balanced chemical equations depicting the combination of raw chemicals to form a new and different compound or isotope.

Operations process charts are similar to assembly charts except they often also include specifications for the component parts as well as operating and inspection times. They thus provide more complete instructions on how to produce an item. Most firms that produce custom products in a process or jobshop-type layout summarize the operations and process routing information for a given item on a route sheet. The *route sheet* specifies precisely how to produce an item by identifying the equipment and tools to use, operations and sequence to follow, and the machine setup and run-time estimates.

Flow process charts, as described in Chap. 3, are similar to operations process charts except that the nonproductive activities of storage (▽), delay (D), and transportation (⇒) are also included. These additions make flow process charts more suitable for analysis of process efficiency.

Worker-Machine Charts and Activity Charts

We noted previously that *worker-machine charts* are graphic methods of portraying the simultaneous activities of a worker and the equipment he or she operates. A worker-machine activity is often characterized by a load-run-unload sequence. While the worker is working the machine is often stopped, and while the machine is running the worker may be idle.

Worker-machine charts can be used to show the activities of one worker and one machine, or several workers and several machines. They are useful in process planning to help ensure that the best use is made of these two important resources. If labor and machine time costs can be estimated, then the process planner can make an economic analysis of the alternative worker-machine combinations and select the best arrangement.

Worker-machine relationships are charted by showing the time required to complete various component tasks that make up a work cycle. A *cycle* is the length of time required to go through one complete combination of work activities. Whereas the product itself does not recycle, the relative position of the facilities or the degree of completion of a well-defined group of work activities is the same at the beginning of each cycle.

Example 5-4

An operator at Goodtire Rubber Company is expected to take 2 min to load and 1 min to unload a molding machine. There are several machines of this type, all doing the same thing, and the automatic run time on each is 4 min. Respective costs are $8/hr for the operator and $20/hr for each machine.

(*a*) Construct a worker-machine chart for the most efficient one-worker, two-machine situation.

(*b*) What is the cycle time?

(*c*) What is the idle worker-time per cycle?
(*d*) What is the total idle machine-time/cycle (both machines)?
(*e*) What is the total cost/hr?
(*f*) What is the total cost/cycle?
(*g*) What is the idle time cost/hr?

Solution

(*a*) If the operator begins by loading machine 1 the cycle does not reach an efficient steady state until the ninth min as shown in Fig. 5-5.
(*b*) CT = 7 min
(*c*) Worker idle 1 min/cycle.
(*d*) Machines not idle.
(*e*) Cost = worker + 2 (mach.) = \$8 + 2(\$20) = \$48/hr

(*f*) $$\text{Cost/cycle} = \frac{\$48}{60\text{ min}}\left(\frac{7\text{ min}}{\text{cycle}}\right) = \$5.60/\text{cycle}$$

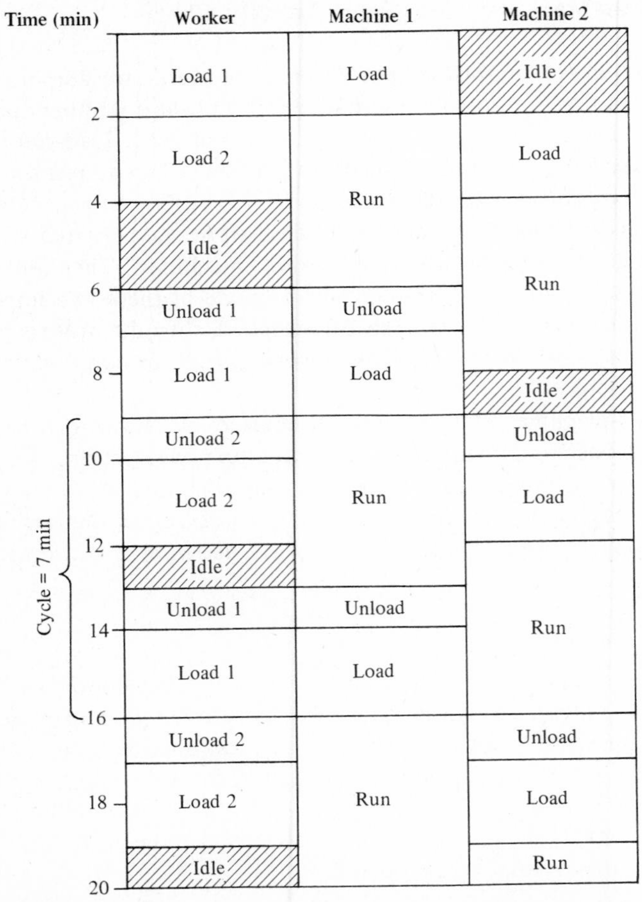

Time (min)	Worker	Machine 1	Machine 2
0–2	Load 1	Load	Idle
2–4	Load 2	Run	Load
4–6	Idle	Run	Run
6–7	Unload 1	Unload	Run
7–8	Load 1	Load	Run
8–9	Load 1	Load	Idle
9–10	Unload 2	Run	Unload
10–12	Load 2	Run	Load
12–13	Idle	Run	Run
13–14	Unload 1	Unload	Run
14–16	Load 1	Load	Run
16–17	Unload 2	Run	Unload
17–19	Load 2	Run	Load
19–20	Idle	Run	Run

Cycle = 7 min (from 9 to 16 min)

FIGURE 5-5 Worker-machine chart

$$(g)\ \text{Idle time cost/hr} = \frac{1 \text{ min}}{\text{cycle}}\left(\frac{60}{7}\frac{\text{min/hr}}{\text{min/cycle}}\right)\frac{\$8}{60 \text{ min}} = \$1.14/\text{hr}$$

The operation and control of complex or mobile equipment often restricts process activities to a one-worker-per-machine operation. Much construction and materials handling equipment falls into this category. These activities can be portrayed in an *activity chart*, which is similar to a worker-machine chart except that all components represent machines (or workers).

Selection via Economic Analysis

Many process planning decisions relate to equipment capacities required to produce a specified level of output. We were introduced to the concepts of use, efficiency, and output capacity in Chap. 2. These considerations are, in reality, continuing concerns for an operations manager. Often, the goods and services can be produced by more than one method or on alternative machines. For example, a construction firm may move dirt by dump trucks or by a carryall, or a machine shop may use either an automatic lathe or a numerically controlled machine to produce a part.

A choice of process equipment based upon economic analysis and comparison of alternative processes is one of the most fundamental and widely used criteria of selection. Some would even go so far as to say that if an economic analysis is not done, the venture itself is questionable. We have seen, however, that organizational objectives are overriding criteria and these may well include less-tangible social considerations. Very often though, the most favorable economic choice is also consistent with social and environmental objectives.

Example 5-5

Raleigh Furniture Company is redesigning its production process so that it is capable of producing 320 Early American chairs per work day. The firm plans to convert to new automatic cutting machines which can be purchased for \$10,500 each. Time estimates reveal that 72 hours of cutting work per day are required for the 320 chairs produced. In addition to the 72 hours, one job in every 20 is ultimately scrapped. The plant is expected to operate at 90 percent efficiency on a two-shift (8 hr/shift) per day basis. Derive an estimate of the cutting machines' cost.

Solution

$$\text{Scrap loss} = 1 \text{ in } 20 = 5\% \qquad \therefore \text{ Acceptable production} = 95\%$$

$$\text{Worker hr required/day} = \frac{72.0}{0.95} = 75.8 \text{ hr (assuming 100\% utilization)}$$

For 90 percent efficiency:

$$\text{Capacity} = \frac{\text{required output}}{\text{efficiency}} = \frac{75.8}{0.90} = 84.2 \text{ hr/day}$$

$$\text{No. machines required} = \frac{\text{hr capacity required}}{\text{hr available/machine}} = \frac{84.2}{16} = 5.26 \text{ machines}$$

$$\text{Cost} = (6 \text{ machines})(\$10{,}500) = \$63{,}500.$$

When the processing costs of alternative ways of doing a job can be broken down into their fixed and variable cost components, the most economical alternative is the one with the lowest total costs at the expected volume. A graph of the respective costs will show the machine breakpoints.

Example 5-6
Some brackets for a circuit breaker can be machined on any of three machines, as shown in the accompanying table.

	Fixed cost	**Variable cost/unit**
Machine *A*	\$10	\$0.30
Machine *B*	30	0.20
Machine *C*	60	0.10

What machines should be used for production volumes up to 400 units?

Solution (See Fig. 5-6.)
At 400 units:

$$TC_A = \$10 + 400(\$0.30) = \$130$$
$$TC_B = \$30 + 400(\$0.20) = \$110$$
$$TC_C = \$60 + 400(\$0.10) = \$100$$

For:

$0 < 200$ units use *A*
200–300 units use *B*
>300 units use *C*

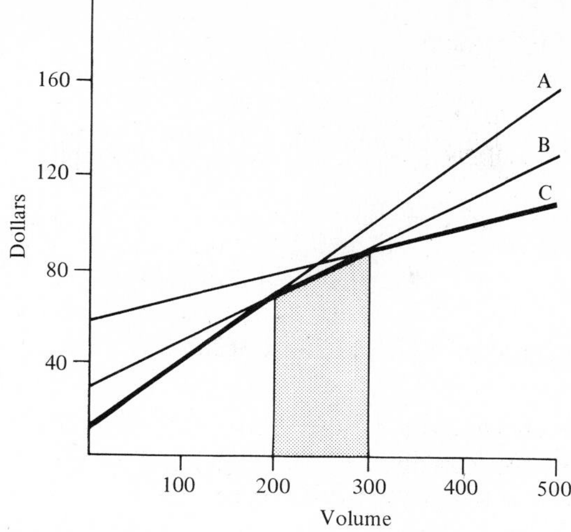

FIGURE 5-6 Machine breakpoints

In addition to equipment and process selection decisions, the process planning stage often generates make versus buy decisions. Many components or subassemblies of a firm's product can be either bought or produced and these decisions must be carefully analyzed as they arise during the process planning activities. We saw in Chap. 2 that make versus buy decisions can involve intangible factors, but it is important to establish economic feasibility before evaluating some of the less-tangible factors.

LINE BALANCING

We noted earlier that a production "line" is typically associated with a product type of layout where the same operations are repeated on each unit as it passes through a work station. Most production assembly lines use moving conveyors to bring the work units to the worker and then to carry them along to the next work station. Production lines are particularly appropriate for high-volume activities where a worker may have to spend anywhere from a fraction of a second up to perhaps half an hour per item. For example, we would find that a cannery line processing corn-on-the-cob requires a very short inspection and culling time per cob, whereas an upholstered furniture line may require 20 or 30 minutes of assembly time per sofa.

Line balancing is the apportionment of sequential work activities into work stations in an effort to gain a high utilization of labor and equipment facilities and to minimize idle time. When operations are wholly automated (that is, without workers interspaced between machine operations), the balancing of equipment capacities is largely achieved through engineering design. However, when production lines incorporate human workers, the operations manager is presented with balancing problems. Work activities must be subdivided or grouped so that there is an efficient and fair balance of work content for each laborer. Also, some allowance must be made for the fact that human output is inherently variable, whereas machine output is steady and mechanistically paced. From a design standpoint the allowance for time variability should be made first and then the work activities grouped according to allowances established.

The speed of an assembly line is determined by the output rate desired, spacing of products on the line, time requirements of the work stations, and pace considerations appropriate for the workers themselves. If the time requirements at one station are exceedingly large relative to other stations, the tasks at the station may have to be further subdivided, or additional personnel added to the station, or a parallel line section provided so that two or more units may be worked on simultaneously.

A considerable amount of theoretical effort has been devoted to constructing line balancing models. Many mathematical approaches assume that workers have constant operating times. Even with this assumption, the number of equations required and number of combinations to evaluate often make the solution infeasible, even for a computer. Models which attempt to incorporate the realities of industrial situations quickly become extremely complex. As a result, although some sophisticated models are under development, in practice a number of relatively simple simulation and heuristic methods are used. Fortunately, a computer can provide much assistance in the simulations and the heuristic search for alternatives. The heuristic approaches do not necessarily result in mathematically provable optimal balances, but they are likely to continue to be used for some time. Let us look briefly at the concepts behind simulating time variability and grouping work activities.

SIMULATING OPERATOR TIME VARIABILITY

Suppose it takes workers at a conveyor belt exactly 25 seconds to attach a switch to a television set and the workers have 30 seconds available. They should be able to complete all installations satisfactorily. However, if their time requirements vary from 24 to 32 seconds, depending upon parts availability or tolerances of the switch, then they will not be able to complete every unit. Allowing enough time (such as 32 seconds) for them to finish the installation *every* time may result in excessive idle time, whereas providing them with some lesser amount (such as 30 seconds) will mean some units will pass by without being completed. The "correct" time allowance depends upon the workers' time requirements as well as other objectives of the job design.

Economically, the designer would probably like to decrease the idle time of workers to the point where the idle time cost is just offset by the costs that would be incurred by allowing incomplete sets to leave the work station. Statistical and empirical data on the workers' performance time is useful to the job designer in establishing the necessary time availability for activities at each work station.

Psychological and other behavioral characteristics of workers must also be taken into account, however. As we noted earlier, problems of job satisfaction are especially prevalent in assembly line situations, and concerns arise over such things as monotony, safety, and even health. For example, many workers get nauseated simply

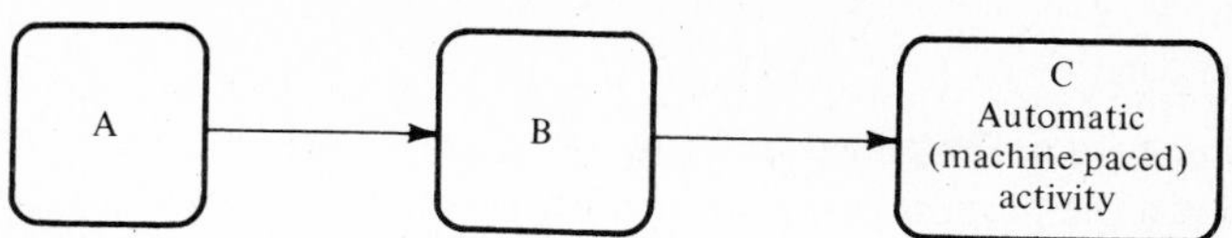

FIGURE 5-7 Work stations on paced assembly line

by having to work at a moving conveyor belt. Other concerns relate to the needs of workers to be able to communicate socially, vary their work rate, or gain some feeling of identification with the products they are producing. Thus, whereas we are concentrating here upon the more readily quantifiable factors of time and cost, we must recognize that less-tangible "human" considerations of job design may be overriding criteria.

Assume there are two work stations, A and B, in a line, followed by a rigidly paced activity C, as shown in Fig. 5-7. Operators A and B may have average performance times that are relatively close to each other, but their output rates are still likely to fluctuate because of the inherent variability of human operators. If B must deliver units to C at a specified rate, then either B's mean production rate must exceed the set rate of C or an in-process inventory must be maintained. The production rate of B is in turn affected by that of A and a similar requirement would hold for their interface.

If the time required to perform a work activity has a known statistical distribution, such as normal or Poisson, then the proportion of times that exceed some specified time can be easily computed using standard statistical methods (see Solved Prob. 7). Decisions can then be made as to the acceptability of a given work station design in relation to the production line.

When the time requirements for a work station cannot be identified by a specific statistical distribution, they may be analyzed by simulating empirical data manually or (preferably) by computer. Steps in performing the simulation include:

1 Collect actual (empirical) data on the distribution of assembly times (or estimate them from a pilot activity).

2 Develop a cumulative probability distribution and plot it, showing relative frequency on the vertical axis.

3 Using random numbers, determine simulated assembly times from the cumulative distribution.

4 From the simulated data, determine the effect of one work station on the next and the proportion of times that exceed some specified time.

A simplified example will illustrate how a few simulated times are derived from a cumulative distribution of empirical data [2]. A computer simulation could produce hundreds or thousands of such simulated times in a few seconds and the larger sample would, of course, lend more accuracy and be more desirable.

Example 5-7

Empirical data collected on the time required to weld a transformer bracket was recorded to the nearest one-half minute, as shown in the accompanying table.

Weld time (min)	Number of observations
0.5	24
1.0	42
1.5	72
2.0	38
2.5	14
3.0	10

(*a*) Formulate a cumulative distribution in percentage terms.
(*b*) Graph the frequency and cumulative distributions.
(*c*) A simulation is to be conducted using random numbers. What simulated weld times (to the nearest 0.5 min) would result from the random numbers 25, 90, and 59?
(*d*) What proportion of the times exceed 2.0 min?

Solution

(*a*) Cumulative distributions are usually formulated on either a scale where the cumulative percent is "more than" or "less than" a corresponding X axis amount. We shall use a "less than" ogive and so will need to identify the upper-class boundaries (UCB) as the Y coordinates for the cumulative distribution. In each case the weld times are assumed to represent midpoint values of a frequency distribution, and the class boundaries are half way between the midpoints.

Time in min (midpoint)	Frequency in numbers	Upper-class boundary (UCB)	Cumulative number of times <UCB	Cumulative percent of time <UCB
	0	0.25	0	0
0.5	24	0.75	24	12
1.0	42	1.25	66	33
1.5	72	1.75	138	69
2.0	38	2.25	176	88
2.5	14	2.75	190	95
3.0	10	3.25	200	100

(*b*) The frequency distribution is constructed by extending vertical lines from the class boundaries to the appropriate frequency level for the class.

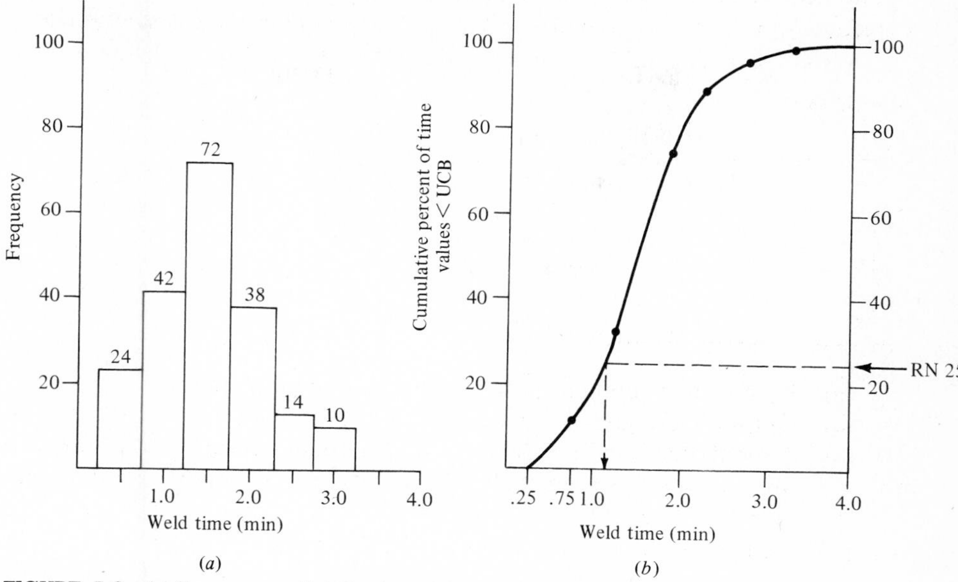

FIGURE 5-8 (**a**) Frequency distribution; (**b**) cumulative distribution

For the cumulative distribution, values of the cumulative percent of time < UCB are plotted at weld times corresponding to the UCB. For example, the frequency (12%) is plotted at UCB = 0.75.

(*c*) The simulated time for random number (RN) 25 is determined by entering the cumulative graph at 25 (as shown by the arrow) and proceeding horizontally to the curve and then down to the weld time. The resultant is a reading of 1.0 min (rounded to the nearest 0.5 min). Times for random numbers 90 and 59 are 2.5 and 1.5 min, respectively.

(*d*) From the cumulative distribution, about 12 percent of the times exceed 2 min.

Note that the empirical distribution preserves the probability of each class by virtue of the vertical distances on the graph, which correspond with the relative frequencies of the respective classes. Since all random numbers from 0 to 100 have an equal chance of occurring (that is, are uniformly distributed), this means that sections of the distribution with the greatest vertical rise will be the target of more random numbers than will other portions of the curve.

We carry on now with another example to illustrate how the simulated times can be used to gain knowledge of the interface of two assembly activities.

Example 5-8

In an aircraft assembly operation, activity A precedes activity B and inventory may accumulate between the two activities. Using random numbers, a simulated sample of performance times yielded the values shown (min) in the accompanying table.

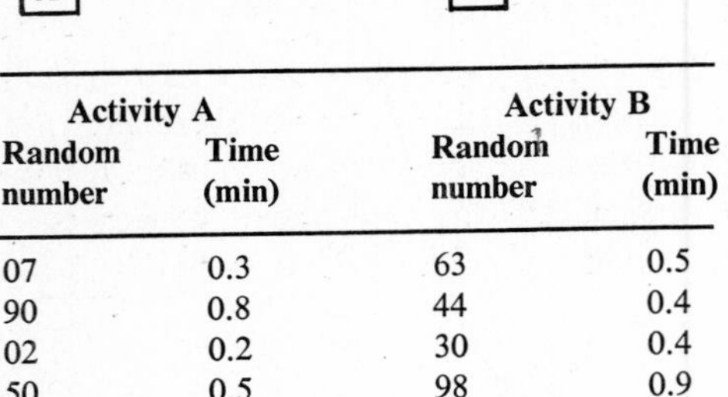

Activity A		Activity B	
Random number	Time (min)	Random number	Time (min)
07	0.3	63	0.5
90	0.8	44	0.4
02	0.2	30	0.4
50	0.5	98	0.9
76	0.6	30	0.4
47	0.5	72	0.6
13	0.3	58	0.5
06	0.3	96	0.9
79	0.7	37	0.4

(*a*) Simulate the assembly of six parts showing idle time in activity B, waiting time of each part, and number of parts waiting. *Note:* Omit the first random number of A so that activity B begins at time zero.

(*b*) What was the average length of the waiting line ahead of B (in number of units)?

(*c*) What was the average output/hr of the assembly line?

Solution

(*a*) Our interest lies in activity B so we can set up a table (below) to show

Part number	Part available for activity B at time	Activity B beginning time	Activity B ending time	Activity B idle time	Waiting time of part	Number parts waiting at B end time
1	—	0.0	0.5	0.0	0.0	0
2	0.8	0.8	1.2	0.3	0.0	1
3	1.0	1.2	1.6	0.0	0.2	1
4	1.5	1.6	2.5	0.0	0.1	1
5	2.1	2.5	2.9	0.0	0.4	2
6	2.6	2.9	3.5	0.0	0.3	2
7	2.9					
8	3.2					

when parts arrive at B, how long it takes B to work on them, and the resultant idle and waiting times. Activity B begins at 0.0 and it takes 0.5 min to complete the first part. B is then idle for 0.3 min until part 2 arrives from A at 0.8 min. Part 2 takes 0.4 min, so the ending time is 0.8 + 0.4 = 1.2 min. By this time part 3 has been waiting 0.2 min because it became available at 0.8 + 0.2 = 1.0 min, but work could not be begun on it until 1.2 min. However, before activity B is finished on part 3 at 1.6 min, part 4 has arrived (at 1.0 + 0.5 = 1.5 min) and so one part is waiting. We continue systematically in this manner through part 6, noting that when it is finished at time 3.5 min there are two parts waiting, for their availability times were 2.9 min and 3.2 min, respectively.

(*b*) To figure the average length of waiting line ahead of activity B, we see that the first six parts waited a total time of: 0 + 0 + 0.2 + 0.1 + 0.4 + 0.3 = 1.0 min.

Total time activity B was in operation = 3.5 min.

Note that if the total waiting time of the first six parts was 3.5 min, this would have been an average of *one assembly* waiting over the 3.5-min period. By ratio, then:

If a 3.5-min wait would be a 1-unit long waiting line
Then 1.0-min wait would be an X-unit long waiting line

$$3.5X = (1.0)(1)$$

$$X = \frac{1}{3.5} \cong 0.29 \text{ assemblies}$$

This can be stated in equation form as

$$\text{Ave. inv.} = \frac{\text{total waiting time}}{\text{total run time}} \tag{5-4}$$

Thus,

$$\text{Ave. inv.} = \frac{1.0}{3.5} = 0.29 \text{ assemblies}$$

(*c*) Average output per hour:

$$\text{units/hr} = \frac{6 \text{ units}}{3.5 \text{ min}}\left(\frac{60 \text{ min}}{\text{hr}}\right) = 102.9 \text{ units/hr}$$

GROUPING ASSEMBLY LINE ACTIVITIES

Line balancing activities are usually undertaken to meet a specified output. For example, if a conveyor speed is 4 feet per minute and units are placed at 4-foot intervals, the output rate will be one unit per minute, as illustrated in Fig. 5-9. Each work station will have one minute of available time. If the output is to be two units per minute, this could be accomplished by doubling the conveyor speed (to 8 feet per minute) or using a 2-foot spacing on the conveyor, rather than 4 feet. In either case, the time per unit available at each work station would be cut in half to half a minute per unit.

To produce at a specified rate, such as one unit per minute, as in some automobile assembly plants, the assembly sequence must be carefully delineated and the time requirements for each assembly task must be known. Most assemblies evidence a precedence relationship among the activities, as we saw in the assembly chart for the electric heater (Fig. 5-4). An efficient balance will complete the required assembly while maintaining the specified sequence and minimizing the idle time.

One heuristic method of balancing entails drawing a precedence diagram complete with activity times and then grouping the activities into work station zones that do not exceed the specified time availability per station. Assuming that activities may be combined within a given zone so long as precedence relationships are maintained, we can then designate work zones on the precedence diagram and move appropriate components into preceding zones (that is, to the left) until the times are as fully used as possible.

Example 5-9

An electric appliance assembly area is as shown in Fig. 5-10 with potential work stations A through F. The activities that must be done, along with their respective times, are indicated in the precedence diagram.

The machine scan is automatic and can come anytime after activity 2. The manufacturer desires an output of 367 units per 8-hr day and stops the line for a 20-min break in the middle of the morning and the afternoon. Group the assembly line activities into appropriate work stations and compute the balance efficiency.

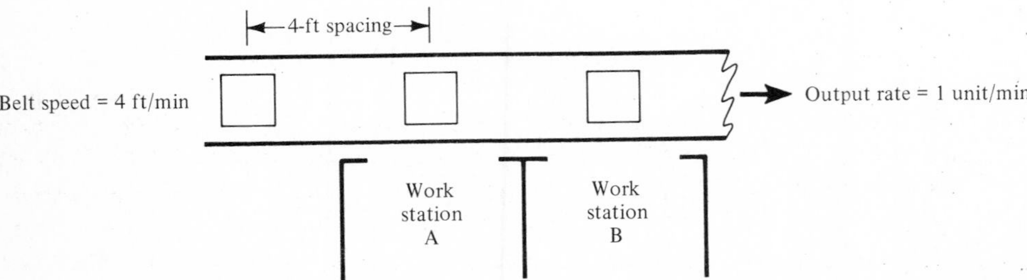

FIGURE 5-9 Conveyor speed and output relationship

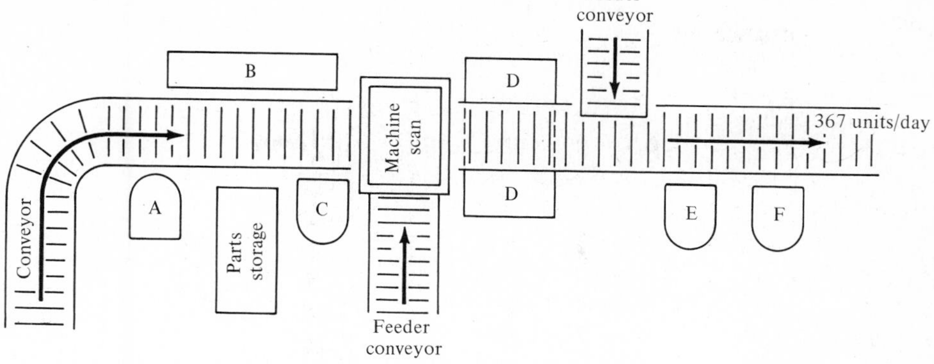

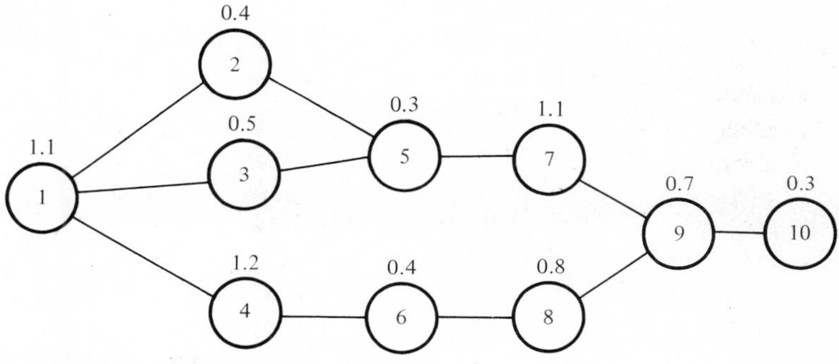

FIGURE 5-10 Appliance assembly layout

Solution

The precedence diagram is given complete with activity times. Time available per unit is:

$$\text{Min/day available} = 480 - 40 = 440 \text{ min}$$

$$\text{Output required} = \frac{367 \text{ units}}{\text{day}}$$

$$\frac{\text{Cycle time available}}{\text{unit}} = \frac{440}{367} = 1.20 \text{ min/unit.}$$

For reference, we can number the precedence diagram columns [**19**: 122]. Column 1 time at 1.1 min almost fully consumes a work station time (1.2 min) and there are no 0.1 min downstream activities that can be moved up so it is complete. (See Fig. 5-11.)

Activity 4 in column 2 requires the full 1.2 min available, but activities 2 and 3 add up to only 0.9 min and there appears to be sufficient time to bring

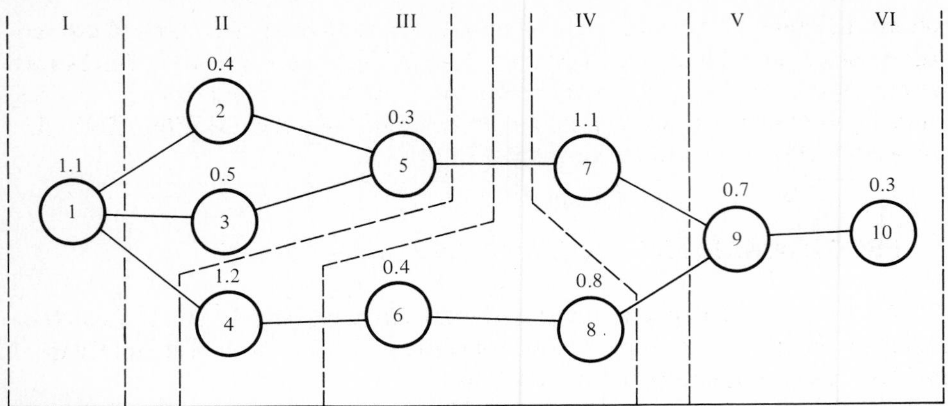

FIGURE 5-11 Precedence diagram time zones

activity 5 into the same work station zone. We proceed in this manner, marking off zones with dotted lines, until our ultimate grouping is as shown in the accompanying table.

Work station	Activities	Actual time (min)
A	1	1.1
B	2,3,5	1.2
C	4	1.2
D	6,8	1.2
E	7	1.1
F	9,10	1.0
		6.8

The balance efficiency [3: 126] may be computed by dividing the actual time utilization (Σt) by the station time available as determined by the number of stations n times the cycle time c.

$$\text{Eff}_B = \frac{\Sigma t}{nc} \tag{5-5}$$

$$= \frac{6.8}{(6)(1.2)}$$

$$= 94.5\%$$

For realistic large-scale line balancing problems, computerized routines can now search out and test a multitude of potential work station configurations much more efficiently than could ever be done by hand. And although these heuristics cannot evaluate the millions of possible combinations that often exist, they can rapidly converge upon a reasonably good balance by following logical decision rules. The balance that results will hopefully minimize the idle time cost of both workers and machines, within a job design that recognizes the physiological and psychological effects that arise from a close worker-machine interface.

PROCESS AND PRODUCTIVITY ANALYSIS

Analysis of ongoing activities constitutes an important means of improving production processes. The production operations model introduced in Chap. 1 provides a useful framework for this analysis.

An evaluation of the equipment use, efficiency, and output capacity of the process is an appropriate starting point. After reviewing layout suitability (perhaps using a flow process chart), materials handling, and make versus buy choices, the analyst can focus attention upon the labor input to the process. The human factors analysis will include consideration of the job design, work methods, and adequacy of the standards employed. From the perspective of using capital funds, the process should be the best alternative available, given the financial structure and earning power of the organization.

Process problems are often hidden under the guise of idle or overworked equipment, idle or overworked personnel, high inventories, frequent breakdowns or excessive maintenance, bottlenecks, poor quality, and an unsafe or unpleasant environment. The tools of analysis are the same charts, graphs, and analytical methods used in process planning. The analysis stage, however, has the advantage of usually having more operating data available for evaluation.

The analytical procedure for analyzing processes should involve a critical examination of the production process by questioning every step. In a manner similar to a methods improvement study (see Chap. 3) the analyst should question the purpose and necessity of each step, seeking out those activities that can be eliminated, combined, changed in sequence, or simplified in any way.

Although one may be inclined to isolate an equipment or personnel problem, the individual problems must ultimately be resolved in the context of the total operation. The most fruitful approach to analysis must therefore be from a systems perspective. Materials, labor, and capital should all be coordinated under a hierarchical goal structure and a systems approach will facilitate proper balance.

The level of productivity is one of the most widely quoted measures of production efficiency. Many industries and countries publish data that reveal changes in their output per worker-hour on an aggregate basis. Table 5-1 illustrates this with an estimate of the comparative increase in productivity for selected nations over a five-year period.

Although the United States has a high level of output per worker-hour (that is, of productivity), it has been difficult for it to maintain the same *rate of increase* in productivity as in other nations. United States industry is already highly automated and further advances depend upon breakthroughs in R&D and upon new technologies.

TABLE 5-1 COMPARATIVE GROWTH OF PRODUCTIVITY IN MANUFACTURING FOR VARIOUS NATIONS, 1965–1970

	Average annual increase, percent[a]		
Nation	Productivity (output per worker-hour)	Compensation per worker-hour	Unit labor cost
U.S.	2.1	6.0	3.9
Belgium	6.8	8.4	1.4
Canada	3.5	8.3	5.1
France	6.6	9.5	0.6
West Germany	5.3	8.7	4.7
Italy	5.1	9.1	3.8
Japan	14.2	15.1	0.8
Netherlands	8.5	11.1	2.5
Sweden	7.9	10.6	2.5
Switzerland[b]	6.2	6.2	0.0
U.K.	3.6	7.6	−0.2

[a] Source: [**6**: 9]
[b] Wage earners only.

Also, "Our successes are copied and our mistakes are avoided" [**6**: 9]. Finally, services (such as health care) now dominate the United States economy and productivity measurements in service industries are unreliable and misleading.

Table 5-1 also reveals that productivity fails to take the crucial element of wage costs into account. Note that, because of high labor costs, if American, Canadian, and West German goods are to be competitive in world markets, their productivity must substantially exceed that of other nations.

SUMMARY

Resource inputs to a production process usually undergo some type of technological transformation before eventually emerging as valuable goods and services. The management of this transformation process calls for knowledgeable leadership on the part of operations managers. They cannot be expected to have all the skills of those under their control, but they should be skilled decision makers. Key decision areas relate to research management, product design and selection, and process planning, selection, and analysis.

Research is classified as either basic or applied. All research involves an uncertainty of outcome, and it is desirable to place a cost (or value) on this uncertainty if possible. The expected value of perfect information (EVPI) is the incremental amount that can be justified to remove uncertainty. It is the difference between the expected profit under certainty (EPC) and the expected monetary value (EMV).

Another perspective is that of an opportunity loss, which is not simply an accounting loss, but rather the cost of foregone opportunities.

In addition to research, product and process ideas also come from customers and other sources. The product decision should take into account both the resource and technology base of the organization and the market environment. These factors must be merged in an economically feasible production process before a product alternative exists.

For selecting from among product and process alternatives, linear programming can be an effective means when cost and demand functions are known or can be assumed. In linear programming, we maximize or minimize an objective function subject to linear constraints. The graphic method is suitable for handling two decision variables, but the simplex-echelon method can handle many variables and constraints. The matrix is of the form

$$\begin{bmatrix} A & I & B \\ C & O & Z \end{bmatrix}$$

and is systematically revised until an optimal solution is reached. Complex problems should, however, really be done on a computer rather than manually.

Process planning aids include several types of charts: assembly, operations process, flow process, worker-machine, and activity. In addition, economic techniques, such as machine breakpoint analysis for equipment selection, are useful.

For product line layouts, a major problem consists of accounting for operator time variability and grouping work activities so that they most efficiently balance the production line. Simulation has proven to be a helpful technique for studying the effects of variable performance times. Simulation outputs reveal worker idle time, waiting time of parts, length of waiting line, and average output. Although work is progressing on sophisticated models to group assembly line activities into the optimal number of work stations, heuristic methods are still widely used.

Process analysis is a critical and questioning review of an ongoing process to eliminate problems or develop improvements. The techniques of analysis described in this and previous chapters should be used where applicable. The overall guide should be a systems perspective of the total operation. Productivity analysis can also be useful, but the problems of measurement limit the value of productivity comparisons to gross measures, such as output per worker-hour.

SOLVED PROBLEMS

RESEARCH AND DEVELOPMENT

1 A petrochemical company's R&D department has received corporate authorization to commence work on any or all of three potential pollution control products. Top management has agreed to allocate $20,000 each to all projects undertaken. If research efforts are not successful, the product will be scrapped after a year, but the patent rights on any successful development can be sold to a plastics firm for \$50,000, yielding a \$30,000 profit on each.

(*a*) Set up a payoff table.

(*b*) Determine how many projects should be undertaken to (1) maximize the maximum possible payoff; (2) maximize the minimum possible payoff.

(*c*) If the probabilities for success of 0, 1, 2, or 3 projects are 0.10, 0.30, 0.50, and 0.10 respectively, how many projects should be undertaken under an EMV criteria?

(*d*) What is the expected value of perfect information with respect to the success or failure of the project?

Solution (in \$000)

(*a*) The payoff from each successful project is \$30, whereas each unsuccessful project costs the firm \$20. Payoff table values are shown in the accompanying table.

Number projects undertaken	(Potential state) number of successes			
	0	1	2	3
0	0*	0	0	0
1	−20	30*	30	30
2	−40	10	60*	60
3	−60	−10	40	90*

(*b*) Maximax = undertake 3 projects in hopes of 3 successes.
Maximin = undertake 0 projects and limit monetary losses to zero.

(*c*) $E(0) = 0$

$E(1) = -20(0.1) + 30(0.3) + 30(0.5) + 30(0.1) = 25$

$E(2) = -40(0.1) + 10(0.3) + 60(0.5) + 60(0.1) = 35 \leftarrow \text{EMV}$

$E(3) = -60(0.1) - 10(0.3) + 40(0.5) + 90(0.1) = 20$

Undertake 2 projects for EMV = \$35,000.

(*d*) EVPI = EPC − EMV

where payoff values for computing EPC are starred

$$\text{EPC} = 0(0.1) + 30(0.3) + 60(0.5) + 90(0.1) = 48$$

$$\text{EVPI} = 48 - 35 = 13 \qquad \therefore \text{EVPI} = \$13{,}000$$

PRODUCT-MIX DECISIONS VIA LINEAR PROGRAMMING

2 An electronic goods manufacturer has distributors who will accept shipments of either transistor radios or electronic calculators to stock for Christmas inventory. Whereas the radios contribute \$10/unit and the calculators \$15/unit to profits,

both products use some of the same components. Each radio requires 4 diodes and 4 resistors while each calculator requires 10 diodes and 2 resistors. The radios take 12.0 min and the calculators take 9.6 min of time on the company's electronic testing machine and the production manager estimates that 160 hours of test time are available. The firm has 8,000 diodes and 3,000 resistors in inventory. What product or mix of products should be selected to obtain the highest profit?

Solution

The decision variables are radios R and calculators C, and we must determine how many of each should be produced to maximize profit Z.

1 *Objective function*

$$\text{Max } Z = \$10\text{R} + \$15\text{C}$$

Constraints

Diodes (8,000 available) R require 4 each, C require 10 each

$$\therefore\ 4\text{R} + 10\text{C} \leq 8{,}000$$

Resistors (3,000 available) R require 4 each, C require 2 each

$$\therefore\ 4\text{R} + 2\text{C} \leq 3{,}000$$

Testing (9,600 min available) R require 12.0 and C 9.6 min

$$\therefore\ 12.0\text{R} + 9.6\text{C} \leq 9{,}600$$

2 *Graph of variables and constraints*

Diodes $4\text{R} + 10\text{C} \leq 8{,}000$

Plotting this as an equality we have:

If R = 0, then C = 800
If C = 0, then R = 2,000

Resistors $4\text{R} + 2\text{C} \leq 3{,}000$
If R = 0, then C = 1,500
If C = 0, then R = 750

Testing $12.0\text{R} + 9.6\text{C} \leq 9{,}600$

Note that the resulting graph establishes a feasible region bounded by the time, diode, and resistor constraints and the implicit constraints that $\text{R} \geq 0$ and $\text{C} \geq 0$.

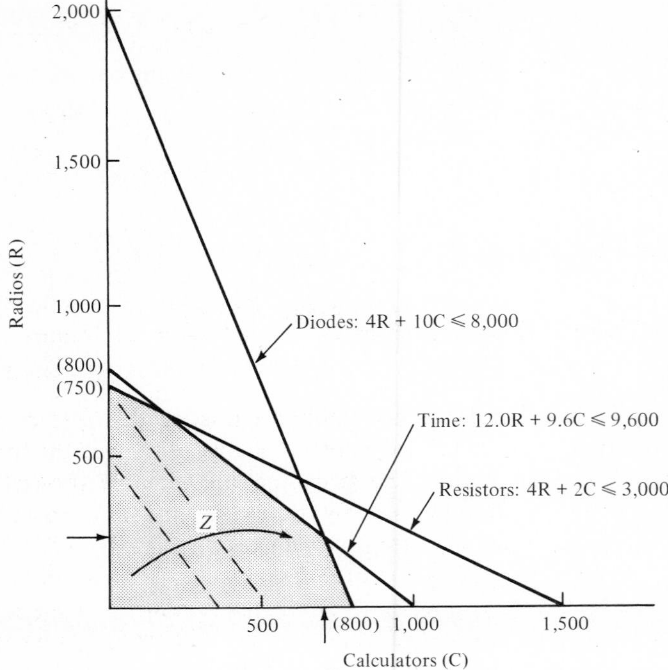

3 *Slope of objective function* We can express our objective function in slope-intercept form, where the Y axis corresponds to R and the X axis to C.

$$Z = 10R + 15C$$

or $10R = -15C + Z$

$$\therefore R = -\frac{15}{10}C + \frac{Z}{10} = -\frac{3}{2}C + \frac{Z}{10}$$

$\therefore$ Slope $= -\frac{3}{2}$, which means that for every 3-unit decrease in Y there is a 2-unit increase in X. This slope is plotted as a dotted line in the graph by marking off 3 units (negative) in R for each 2 units (positive) in C.

4 *Move objective function to optimize* The slope of the objective function (iso-objective line) is moved away from the origin until constrained. In this case the binding constraints are the diode inventory supply and testing machine time availability.

5 *Read solution values* The arrows point to the approximate R and C coordinates of the constraining intersection.

Number radios $\cong$ 240
Number calculators $\cong$ 700

Note that the simultaneous solution of the two binding constraint equations would lend more accuracy to the answer:

$$
\begin{aligned}
4R + 10C = 8{,}000 \rightarrow \text{times } (-3) = \quad -12R - 30C &= -24{,}000 \\
\text{add:} \qquad 12R + 9.6C &= 9{,}600 \\
-20.4C &= -14{,}400 \\
C &= 705 \text{ calculators}
\end{aligned}
$$

Substituting to solve for R:

$$4R + 10(705) = 8{,}000 \qquad \therefore\ R = \frac{8{,}000 - 7{,}050}{4} = 237 \text{ radios}$$

Comment: We had two decision variables (that is, products) to choose from and established a profit function Z and constraints and optimized the function by moving it away from the origin. The graph of this example showed that the resistor supply was not constraining, so only two constraints (diodes and test time) were binding. Similarly, there were two decision variables in the solution, that is, we ended up producing both radios and calculators. The number of variables in solution will always equal the number of explicit constraints that are binding.

The graphic linear programming solution gives an indication of the sensitivity of the solution to changes in the constraints. If, for example, additional diodes could be purchased from an outside supplier with no increase in cost, profit would be maximized by extending the iso-objective line to the next corner and producing 1,000 calculators and no radios. In this case we would have one explicit constraint (time) binding and only one decision variable (calculators) in the final solution.

3 A textile mill has received an order for fabric specified to contain at least 45kg wool and 25kg nylon. The fabric can be woven out of any suitable mix of two yarns (A and B). Material A costs \$2/kg and B costs \$3/kg. They contain the proportions of wool, nylon, and cotton (by weight) shown below.

	Wool percent	**Nylon percent**	**Cotton percent**
A	60	10	30
B	30	50	20

What quantities (kg) of A and B yarns should be used to minimize the cost of this order?

Solution

1 *Objective function*

$$\text{Min } C = \$2\text{A} + \$3\text{B}$$

Constraints

$$0.60A + 0.30B \geq 45\text{kg}$$
$$0.10A + 0.50B \geq 25\text{kg}$$

2 *Graph* (see accompanying sketch)

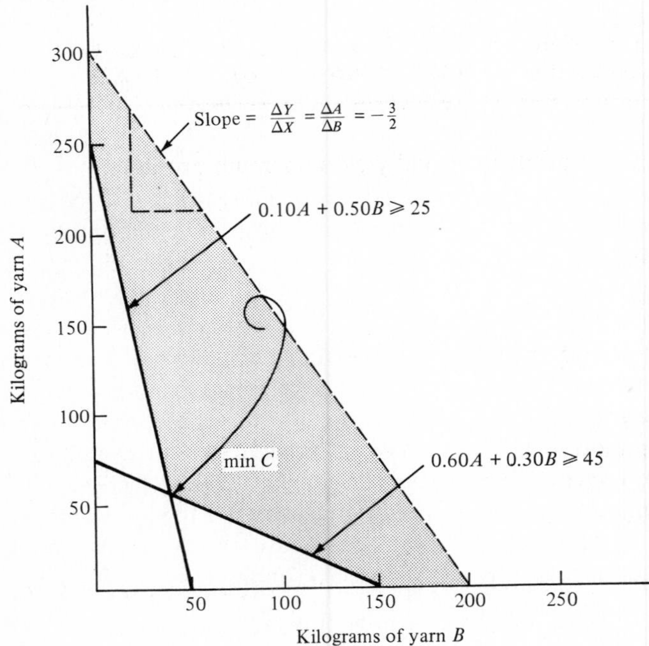

3 *Slope of objective*

$$2A = -3B + C$$

$$A = -\frac{3}{2}B + \frac{C}{2}$$

$$\therefore \text{Slope} = -\frac{3}{2}$$

4 and 5 *Optimize*

From graph, it appears:

$$A = 55\text{kg},\ B = 40\text{kg}$$

Simultaneous solution of the two constraint equations reveals:

$$A = 55\text{kg},\ B = 39\text{kg}$$

4 A commercial fertilizer manufacturer produces three grades, W, X, and Y, which net them \$40, \$50, and \$60 profits per ton respectively. The products require the labor and materials per batch that are shown in the accompanying table.

	W	X	Y	**Total available**
Labor hours	4	4	5	80 hr
Raw material A (lb)	200	300	300	6,000 lb
Raw material B (lb)	600	400	500	5,000 lb

What mix of products would yield maximum profits?

Solution

Objective function

$$\text{Max } Z = 40W + 50X + 60Y$$

Constraints

$$\begin{aligned} &\text{Labor} \quad 4W + 4X + 5Y \leq 80 \\ &\text{Material } A \quad 200W + 300X + 300Y \leq 6{,}000 \\ &\text{Material } B \quad 600W + 400X + 500Y \leq 5{,}000 \end{aligned}$$

Using the simplex-echelon method, the solution matrix is of the form:

$$\begin{bmatrix} A & I & B \\ C & O & Z \end{bmatrix}$$

where

$$A = \begin{bmatrix} 4 & 4 & 5 \\ 200 & 300 & 300 \\ 600 & 400 & 500 \end{bmatrix} \qquad I = \begin{bmatrix} 1 & 0 & 0 \\ 0 & 1 & 0 \\ 0 & 0 & 1 \end{bmatrix} \qquad B = \begin{bmatrix} 80 \\ 6{,}000 \\ 5{,}000 \end{bmatrix}$$

$$C = [40 \quad 50 \quad 60] \qquad O = [0 \quad 0 \quad 0] \qquad Z = Z$$

First table:

$$\begin{bmatrix} 4 & 4 & 5 & 1 & 0 & 0 & 80 \\ 200 & 300 & 300 & 0 & 1 & 0 & 6{,}000 \\ 600 & 400 & \textcircled{500} & 0 & 0 & 1 & 5{,}000 \\ 40 & 50 & 60 & 0 & 0 & 0 & Z \end{bmatrix} \begin{matrix} \\ \\ \leftarrow \\ \\ \end{matrix}$$

$$\qquad\qquad\uparrow$$

1 Pivot column is determined by the largest positive number in the bottom row.

$\therefore$ Column 3

2 Pivot row is smallest result of:

$$\frac{80}{5} = 16 \qquad \frac{6{,}000}{300} = 20 \qquad \frac{5{,}000}{500} = 10$$

$\therefore$ Row 3

3 Dividing values in the pivot row by 500 we have a new pivot row 3:

$$\left[\tfrac{6}{5} \quad \tfrac{4}{5} \quad 1 \quad 0 \quad 0 \quad \tfrac{1}{500} \quad 10\right]$$

4 Using echelon operations to get new values for row

no. 1: Multiply new row 3 by (−5) and add to row 1
no. 2: Multiply new row 3 by (−300) and add to row 2
no. 4: Multiply new row 3 by (−60) and add to row 4

Second table:

$$\begin{bmatrix} -2 & 0 & 0 & 1 & 0 & -\frac{1}{100} & 30 \\ -160 & 60 & 0 & 0 & 1 & -\frac{3}{5} & 3{,}000 \\ \frac{6}{5} & \textcircled{\frac{4}{5}} & 1 & 0 & 0 & \frac{1}{500} & 10 \\ -32 & 2 & 0 & 0 & 0 & -\frac{3}{25} & Z - 600 \end{bmatrix}$$
$$\uparrow$$

5 Since column 2 has a positive value in the bottom row, repeat.

6 Pivot column = column 2

7 Pivot row $\dfrac{30}{0} = \infty, \dfrac{3{,}000}{60} = 50, \dfrac{10}{\frac{4}{5}} = 12.5 \qquad \therefore$ Row 3

8 Dividing values in pivot row by $\frac{4}{5}$ we have a new pivot row

$$\left[\tfrac{3}{2} \quad 1 \quad \tfrac{5}{4} \quad 0 \quad 0 \quad \tfrac{1}{400} \quad \tfrac{25}{2}\right]$$

9 Using echelon operations to get new values for row

no. 1: Column value is already 0. Leave as is.
no. 2: Multiply new row 3 by (−60) and add to row 2

no. 4: Multiply new row 3 by (−2) and add to row 4

$$\begin{bmatrix} -2 & 0 & 0 & 1 & 0 & -\frac{1}{100} & 30 \\ -250 & 0 & -75 & 0 & 1 & -\frac{9}{20} & 2{,}250 \\ \frac{3}{2} & 1 & \frac{5}{4} & 0 & 0 & \frac{1}{400} & \frac{25}{2} \\ -35 & 0 & -\frac{5}{2} & 0 & 0 & -\frac{1}{8} & Z - 625 \end{bmatrix}$$

10 Since no values > 0 in bottom row, solution is complete. Only variable in solution is X and we produce 12.5 units. Profit = \$625.

Comment: The initial matrix was a feasible solution at the W, X, Y origin where no product was produced and the profit was zero. The \$60 in the bottom row indicated that for each unit of Y introduced the objective function would be increased by \$60. The next matrix called for production of 10 units of Y (only) for a profit coefficient of \$600. However, the positive 2 in the bottom row under the X variable column indicated that for every unit of X introduced the objective function would be increased by \$2 more. Our final solution called for 12.5 units of X, which raised our profit an additional \$25 to \$625 total. This is the best that can be obtained given the existing constraints.

PROCESS PLANNING, SELECTION, AND ANALYSIS

5 A production analyst estimated the following times for activities associated with a new casting process and came up with the information in the accompanying table. Show the activities in the form of a flow process chart.

Number	Classification	Time
1	Perform casting operation	12 min
2	Inspect casting	2 min
3	Wait for lift truck	13 min
4	Transport to warehouse	4 min
5	Store; await shipment	3 days

Solution

See the diagram at the top of page 256.

6 The accompanying portion of an activity chart is for an automatic loader mining operation. The loader, in the mine, requires 8 min to load a skip car. There are three skips and they take 9 min to travel loaded to the ore dump, 2 min to dump,

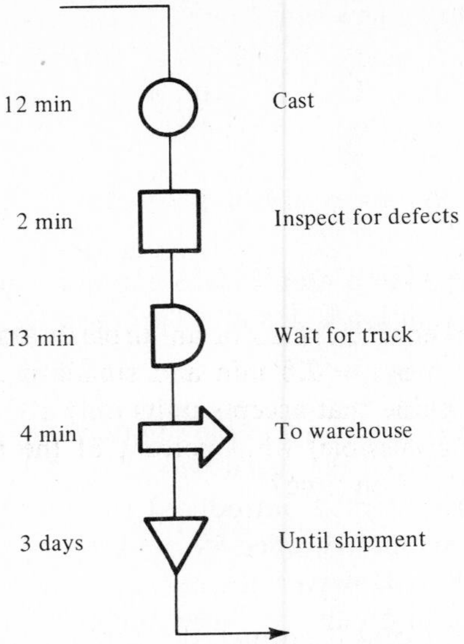

12 min — Cast

2 min — Inspect for defects

13 min — Wait for truck

4 min — To warehouse

3 days — Until shipment

and 7 min to return empty. The operating cost of each skip is \$200/hr and the automatic loader cost (including worker and machine) is estimated at \$350/hr.

(*a*) What is the length of the cycle?

(*b*) What is the idle time cost/hr?

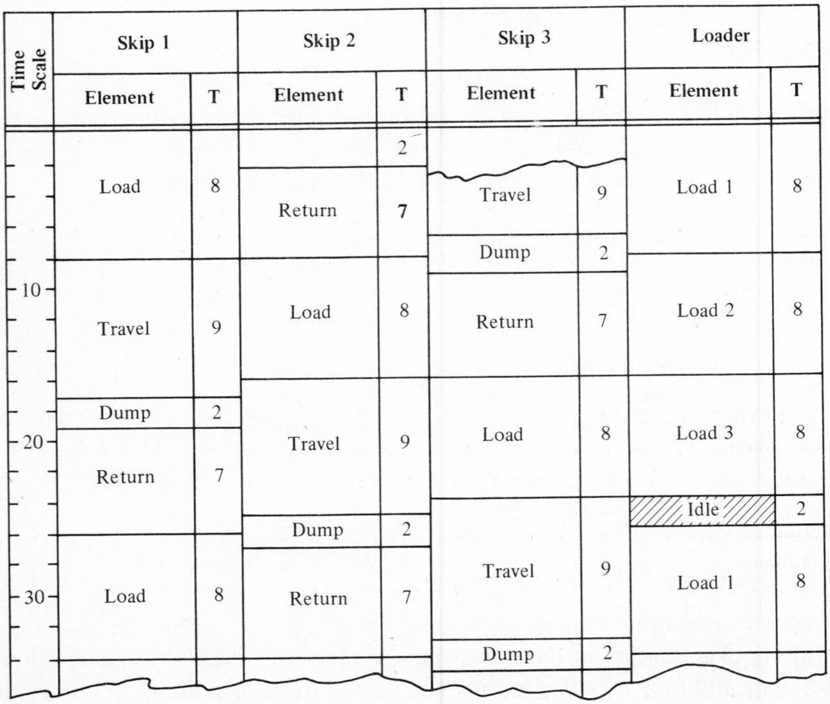

Time Scale	Skip 1		Skip 2		Skip 3		Loader	
	Element	T	Element	T	Element	T	Element	T
	Load	8		2	Travel	9	Load 1	8
	Travel	9	Return	7	Dump	2	Load 2	8
10	Dump	2	Load	8	Return	7	Load 3	8
20	Return	7	Travel	9	Load	8	Idle	2
30	Load	8	Dump	2	Travel	9	Load 1	8
			Return	7	Dump	2		

Solution

(*a*) Cycle length: The system is in a similar state at times 8 and 34.

$$\therefore \text{ Cycle length } = 34 - 8 = 26 \text{ min}$$

(*b*) Idle time cost: The loader is idle 2 min/cycle $= \frac{2}{26} = \frac{1}{13}$ of each hr

$$\therefore \text{ Cost/hr } = \tfrac{1}{13}(\$350) = \$26.92/\text{hr}$$

7 The time taken by worker A to perform an airplane assembly operation is normally distributed with mean = 2.8 min and standard deviation = 0.1 min. If this worker feeds a machine that accepts units only at 3.0 min intervals (and no inventory buildup is permissible) what percent of the time will the worker be unable to feed the machine on time?

Solution

Since the distribution of times is normal, the number of standard deviations is

$$Z = \frac{X - \mu}{\sigma} = \frac{3.0 - 2.8}{0.1} = 2.0$$

$\therefore$ Using the table of areas under the normal curve

$$P(X > 3.0) = 0.5000 - 0.4772 = 0.0228$$
$$\cong 3\% \text{ of the time}$$

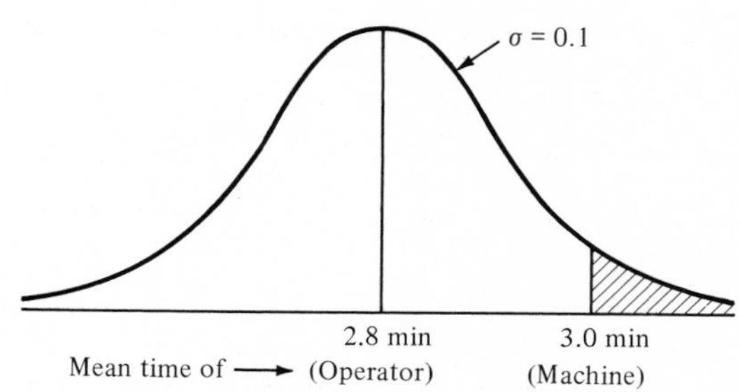

8 A Los Angeles producer of electronic equipment needs to add a component subassembly operation that can produce 80 units during a regular 8-hr shift. The operations have been designed for three activities with times as shown:

Operation	Activity	Standard time (min)
A	Mechanical assembly	12
B	Electric wiring	16
C	Test	3

(*a*) How many work stations (in parallel) will be required for each activity?
(*b*) Assuming that the workers at each station cannot be used for other activities in the plant, what is the appropriate percentage of idle time for this subassembly operation?

Solution

(*a*) With 480 min/day available to each activity the output capacities per single work station would be as shown in the accompanying diagram.

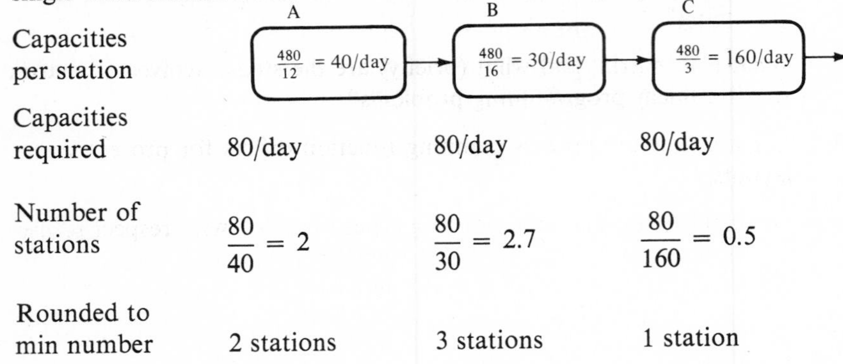

(*b*) Idle time can be determined by comparing the total time available with the standard time.

Time available at 480 min/day		Standard time for 80 units	
A: 2 stations at 480 min =	960	*A*: 80 units at 12 min =	960
B: 3 stations at 480 min =	1,480	*B*: 80 units at 16 min =	1,280
C: 1 station at 480 min =	480	*C*: 80 units at 3 min =	240
	2,880		2,480

$$\%\ \text{idle time} = \frac{\text{total available} - \text{standard}}{\text{total available}} = \frac{2{,}880 - 2{,}480}{2{,}880} = 14\%$$

QUESTIONS

5-1 What are the major advantages and disadvantages of doing industrial applied research? Is it necessary?

5-2 Distinguish between EMV, EVPI, and EPC.

5-3 Suppose you have responsibility for investigating the feasibility of producing a new product. It could be infeasible, feasible with minor modifications to your facilities, or feasible with existing facilities—you do not know which. The studies to establish feasibility could be very costly. How might you determine how much money would be justified to remove this uncertainty? Discuss.

5-4 What is meant by "opportunity loss"?

5-5 What major factors determine which products a firm should produce?

5-6 Why is linear programming a particularly suitable technique for product selection decisions? That is, how do the objectives and limitations of product selection decisions correspond with the assumptions underlying linear programming?

5-7 What is a matrix, and what (briefly) are the steps involved in matrix revision to solve linear programming problems?

5-8 Explain how the process planning function differs for process versus product layouts.

5-9 Distinguish between the following types of charts with respect to use:
(*a*) assembly
(*b*) operations process
(*c*) flow process
(*d*) worker-machine
(*e*) activity

5-10 In what respects is an equipment selection decision similar in concept to the initial steps in a break-even analysis?

5-11 What is the objective of line balancing activities?

5-12 Assume you are an operations analyst and are asked to look into a problem of machine idle time. You are told that workers A and B both have mean operating times of 53 seconds and machine *X* is set to perform an automatic welding

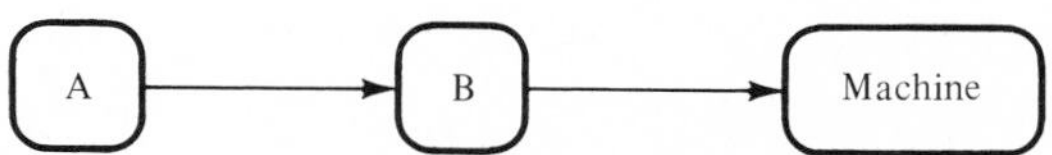

cycle every 55 seconds. However, the machine often goes through an "empty" cycle with a resultant loss of 55 seconds to all subsequent activities on the line. How would you go about resolving this problem?

5-13 What kinds of information can be obtained from the simulation of assembly line activities?

5-14 Of what use is a "precedence diagram" in grouping assembly line activities?

5-15 You have just been hired to fill a newly created position called "Process Analyst." The operations manager has asked you to identify some of the major analytical approaches you can use in your job of troubleshooting. The operations manager hopes to convince the personnel manager that your capabilities make you well worth your salary. Develop, in outline form, a brief summary for the operations manager.

PROBLEMS

1 The research department of an automobile firm has developed a new type of bicycle gear mechanism which could be very profitable if accepted nationally by teenagers. The firm must decide whether to go into production of the product themselves, enter into a lease agreement with a New England manufacturer, or sell the patent rights to the Swish Bicycle Company. It estimates its present value payoffs under the alternative actions as shown in the accompanying table.

	Market condition (values in $000)		
	Poor	**Good**	**Excellent**
Produce gears themselves	(80)	40	200
Lease production rights	20	50	100
Sell patent rights	50	50	50

The research department has also made a study of the market and feels it will most likely be either excellent ($p = 0.4$) or poor ($p = 0.4$) with only a 20 percent chance it can be classified as good.

(*a*) What course of action should be followed under a criterion of (1) maximax, (2) maximin, (3) maximum probability?

(*b*) For which course of action is the expected value highest and what is the EMV?

(*c*) What is the expected profit under certainty (EPC)?

(*d*) What is the EVPI?

***2** Given the data in problem 1:

(*a*) Construct an opportunity loss table.

(*b*) What is the value of the expected opportunity loss (EOL)?

(*c*) What is the EVPI?

(*d*) How is the EVPI value related to the EMV?

Note that this problem extends somewhat beyond the material covered in the text and solved problems. See, for example, reference [**9**].

3 Southern Oak Furniture Association (SOFA) must select one model of a chair to produce from their current line but they have no firm orders from distributors and are uncertain about demand. They have estimated the likelihood of demand and associated profits per day as shown in the accompanying table.

	Profit ($) if demand is		
	Low ($p = 0.3$)	**Medium** ($p = 0.5$)	**High** ($p = 0.2$)
Contemporary	2,500	6,000	10,000
Danish	500	5,000	15,000
Early American	−4,000	4,000	25,000

(a) What is the optimal choice and the EMV?
(b) Suppose the firm could send representatives around to all its distributors and establish with certainty what the actual demand would be. How much could the firm justify paying per day for this type of information?

4 Maximize $Z = 4X + 2Y$
subject to:
$$6X + 4Y \leq 12$$
$$2X + 8Y \leq 16$$

5 Precast Company can produce grade A material which yields a profit of \$1/unit and grade B material which yields a profit of \$2/unit. Each unit of A requires 2 hours of machining and 1 hour of finishing. Each unit of B requires 1 hour of machining and 3 hours of finishing. If 200 hours of machining capacity and 300 hours of finishing capacity are available (a) what amounts of A and B should be produced to maximize profits, and (b) what is the profit?

6 Minimize $C = \$10A + \$20B$
subject to:
$$5A + 20B \geq 25$$
$$15A + 5B \geq 30$$

(Use the graphic method.)

7 A company producing a standard and deluxe line of electric clothes dryers has the following time requirements (min) in departments where either model can be processed:

	Standard	**Deluxe**
Metal frame stamping	3	6
Electric motor installation	10	10
Wiring	10	15

The standard models contribute \$30 each and the deluxe \$50 each to profits. The motor installation production line has a full 60 min available each hour, but the stamping machine is available only 30 min/hr. There are two lines for wiring so the time availability is 120 min/hr. What is the optimal combination of output in units/hr? (Solve graphically.)

8 Solve the preceding problem using the simplex-echelon method.

9 The initial matrix of a maximization linear programming problem with all $\leq$ constraints was found to be:

$$\begin{bmatrix} 200 & 180 & 80 & 1 & 0 & 0 & 600 \\ 500 & 0 & 90 & 0 & 1 & 0 & 500 \\ 40 & 40 & 0 & 0 & 0 & 1 & 120 \\ 187 & 45 & 95 & 0 & 0 & 0 & Z \end{bmatrix}$$

(*a*) What is the objective function?
(*b*) What are the constraints?
(*c*) What is the initial pivot element value?

10 Southern Oak Furniture Association (SOFA) has a plant in Arkansas which produces three models of chairs with profit contributions per chair as follows:

C = Contemporary = \$10
D = Danish = 15
E = Early American = 25

The firm's dry kilns capacity for green lumber limits total production of any mix of chairs to 1,000 per day. If all production went into contemporary chairs and the dry kilns did not limit production, they could produce 1,500 chairs, but the Danish models take 1.5 times as long and the Early Americans' take twice as long as the contemporary chairs. Also, the Danish models require special inlaid backs which come from a single supplier who cannot supply more than 500 per day. Assuming their retailers would accept any mix of models, *set up* (only) the objective function and constraint equations that, if solved via linear programming, would result in an optimal selection of products to maximize profits.

11 Use the simplex-echelon method to solve the previous problem.

12 A building materials firm is reviewing its concrete mixing process activities. Prepare a flow process chart for the following activities.

(*a*)	Load bags of cement into truck at railroad dock.	3 hr
(*b*)	Wait for transport release from supervisor.	½ hr
(*c*)	Transport to covered storehouse by truck.	1 hr
(*d*)	Unload at storehouse.	2 hr
(*e*)	Inspect for damaged bags.	½ hr
(*f*)	Retain in storage until needed at plant 2.	1–10 days
(*g*)	Transfer to plant 2 via lift truck.	1 hr

13 The following operations must be performed on a housing which is part of a motor mounting bracket. The housings are then inspected before going on to the next assembly operation. This takes 6 sec each.

Operation	Machine	Output in parts/hr
Shear	Shear X-100	80
Form	Main press	400
Clean	Ultrasonic tank	150

(*a*) Construct an operations process chart showing the activities, appropriate symbols, and times in minutes.
(*b*) How many of each type of machine would be required for a production rate of 300 parts/hr assuming 80 percent utilization of the X-100 shear

machines, 100 percent utilization of the main press, and 50 percent utilization of the ultrasonic cleaning tanks. Assume 100 percent efficiency.

14 The manager of a plywood mill uses lift trucks to transport loads from a gluing operation to a railroad car for shipment to a finishing mill. At the gluing operation the lift trucks are loaded in 4.0 min by an overhead crane. They then travel 5.0 min to the rail siding and it takes 1.0 min to deposit the plywood and 4.0 min to return. The lift truck and driver cost is $15/hr and the cost allocated to the crane and operator is $28/hr.

(*a*) Given that there is only one crane operator, how many lift trucks (with drivers) are required to keep the crane operator busy full time?

(*b*) How many lift trucks should be used if the objective is to minimize idle time cost?

(*c*) Construct a multiple activity chart for the one-crane-and-three-lift-truck combination.

15 Skilled workers in one department of an aerospace plant work as a group to operate automatic machine tools which sequentially process a bearing bracket. This way each worker gains the ability to operate several machines and there are always adequate personnel to keep the machines in operation. In one area the following sequence takes place in the production process: *Lathe* (one in use): set-up time, 5 min; running time (automatic), 25 min; unloading time, 2 min. *Mill* (one in use): set-up time, 6 min; running time (automatic), 32 min; unloading time, 3 min. *Contour machine* (two in use): set-up time, 3 min; running time (automatic), 60 min; unloading time, 2 min.

(*a*) What is the cycle time in min?

(*b*) The contour machines are numerically controlled and an equivalent rental cost would be $100/hr each. At this costing rate, what is the idle time cost associated with these machines over an 8-hr period?

(*c*) Comment on the idea behind "group operation of the machine tools" as opposed to the principles put forth by Adam Smith.

16 Environmental Products Company is designing an automated process to meet a demand of 720 waste compactors per week on a 40 hr/week production schedule. Each compactor will require 10 min of automatic welder time, and with automatic control there will be zero scrap loss. Plant (system) efficiency is estimated at 75 percent. How much money should the process planning department budget for the welders if each one costs $23,000?

17 A production analyst is planning for the manufacture of valve fittings. Each fitting must be milled on any one of three milling machines, *X*, *Y*, or *Z*. The setup and operating costs for each are as shown.

	Set-up	Operating
X	$10	$0.30/unit
Y	30	0.10/unit
Z	40	0.05/unit

(*a*) Graph the cost structure for the three alternatives for volumes up to 250 units.

(*b*) For what *range* of outputs should the analyst specify the use of machine *Y*?

18 A Baltimore glass company can produce a certain insulator on any of three machines which have the charges shown. The firm has an opportunity to accept an order for either (1) 50 units at $20/unit, or (2) 150 units at $12/unit.

	Fixed cost	Variable cost
Machine *A*	$ 50	$4/unit
Machine *B*	200	2/unit
Machine *C*	400	1/unit

(*a*) Prepare a chart showing the machine breakpoints.

If the 50-unit order is accepted:

(*b*) Which machine should be used?

(*c*) What profit would result?

If the 150-unit order is accepted:

(*d*) Which machine should be used?

(*e*) What profit would result?

What is the:

(*f*) Incremental (profit) advantage of taking the 150-unit order over the 50-unit order?

(*g*) Break-even volume for machine *B* when revenue is $12/unit?

19 Flowmeter Company plans to use 100 type STN valve housings per month, which it could manufacture in its own plant using the idle time of an existing furnace (which is 4 hr of the 8-hr shift). The furnace cost $100,000 when new but is 10 years old now and has a remaining life of 10 years with no salvage value expected. Variable costs of the housings would be $70/unit and an average inventory of $6,000 would be required plus extra storage space rented at $100/month.

The firm has an opportunity to purchase the housings from a supplier at a cost of $72/unit, with delivery as required. The operations manager must decide whether the firm should *make* its own housings or *buy* them from the supplier. Compare the cost on a monthly basis and indicate the economic preference. Flowmeter Company has a 10 percent cost of capital, uses straight-line depreciation, and has no other known use for the idle furnace time.

20 A television cabinet assembly line is equipped with overhead carrier hooks at a spacing that is designed to carry a cabinet into a spray painting booth every 30 sec. The worker attaching the cabinets to the hooks has a normally distributed time with a mean of 24 sec and standard deviation of 4 sec. What proportion of the time will the worker fail to get a cabinet hooked to the overhead carrier before the carrier hooks move on to the painting booth?

21 Data were collected on the assembly times for 1,000 water valves, size 2-inch, 150 lb, at the Drain Company, as shown in the table.

Time LCB	Time UCB	Number valves
1.0	under 1.5 min	0
1.5	under 2.0 min	20
2.0	under 2.5 min	120
2.5	under 3.0 min	280
3.0	under 3.5 min	430
3.5	under 4.0 min	120
4.0	under 4.5 min	30
4.5	under 5.0 min	0
		1,000

(*a*) Graph the data as a cumulative distribution.
(*b*) What percentage of the assembly times exceed 4.0 min?
(*c*) What would be the simulated assembly time for a random number of 44? (Estimate to the nearest half-min.)

22 Operation *B* follows operation *A*. In a simulated operating time of 320 min, operator *B* was idle for 12.3 min and the total waiting time of assemblies before *B* was 1,120 min. If *B* completed 85 parts during the run, what was the average inventory of parts waiting for *B* in terms of number of assemblies?

23 In the meal preparation kitchens of New York International Airlines, dinners are prepared on an assembly line where there is limited space for inventory of partially filled plates. A simulation of two adjacent workers (where *Y* is dependent upon *X*) developed the random numbers and times shown (in sec).

X → Y →

Activity X Random number	Activity X Time	Activity Y Random number	Activity Y Time
72	22	84	32
18	10	26	12
77	23	13	8
84	27	60	24
5	7	53	22
20	11	22	12
46	27	90	36

(*a*) Simulate the preparation of 5 meals and determine idle time in activity *Y*; waiting time of each meal; number of meals waiting (omitting the first random number of *X*).

(*b*) What was the average length of the waiting line upstream of Y?
(*c*) What was the average output/min of the production line?

24 A toy manufacturer produces doll houses on a product line geared to an output of one/min. The assembly precedence relationships and activity times (min) are as shown in the diagram.

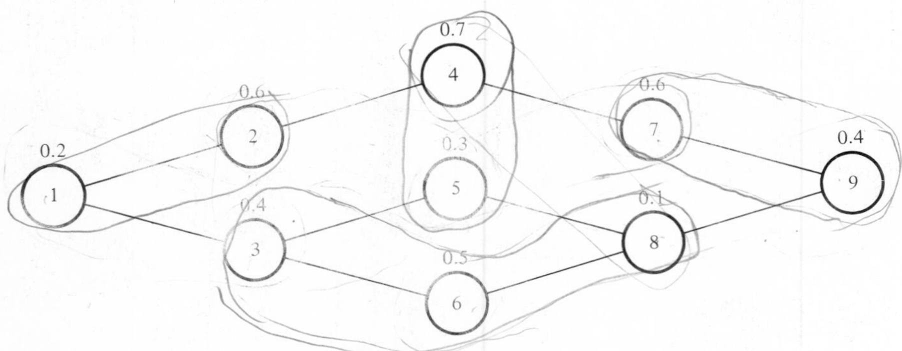

(*a*) Group the activities into the most efficient arrangement.
(*b*) What is the balance efficiency (Eff_B)?

CROSSWORD PUZZLE

Copy and complete the puzzle using the clues given below. The initial letter of each word is located by an r,c (row, column) designation.

Across

1-7 A new term you might coin to describe the simulation of an arrangement of components designed to accomplish an objective according to plan. Suffix is -sim.
2-2 The time parts spend in line, but not being transported or worked on.
3-3 A store on a military post.
3-6 A technique designed to duplicate the essence of an activity without actually achieving reality.
5-1 The expected loss incurred because of failure to take the best economic action possible. (*Hint:* Involves first letters of three words.)
5-5 The activity that goes on at a station along an assembly line. (Also defined as any human activity undertaken in a quest for extrinsic rewards.)
5-10 The state of parts in a job shop that end up being scrapped.
7-2 Process planners are concerned with the design of this place where work gets done.
7-13 Three letters describing the contents of the bottom row of an LP solution matrix.
8-10 The $\sum t \div nc$ describes the __________ of balance.
9-13 Production lines sometimes stop at noon so workers can do this.
10-2 A type of statistical analysis that uses expected values and opportunity loss concepts.
11-1 The human component of a chart portraying the simultaneous activities of a worker and the equipment the worker (male) operates.
11-7 A binary digit and the basic unit of information with which a computer works.

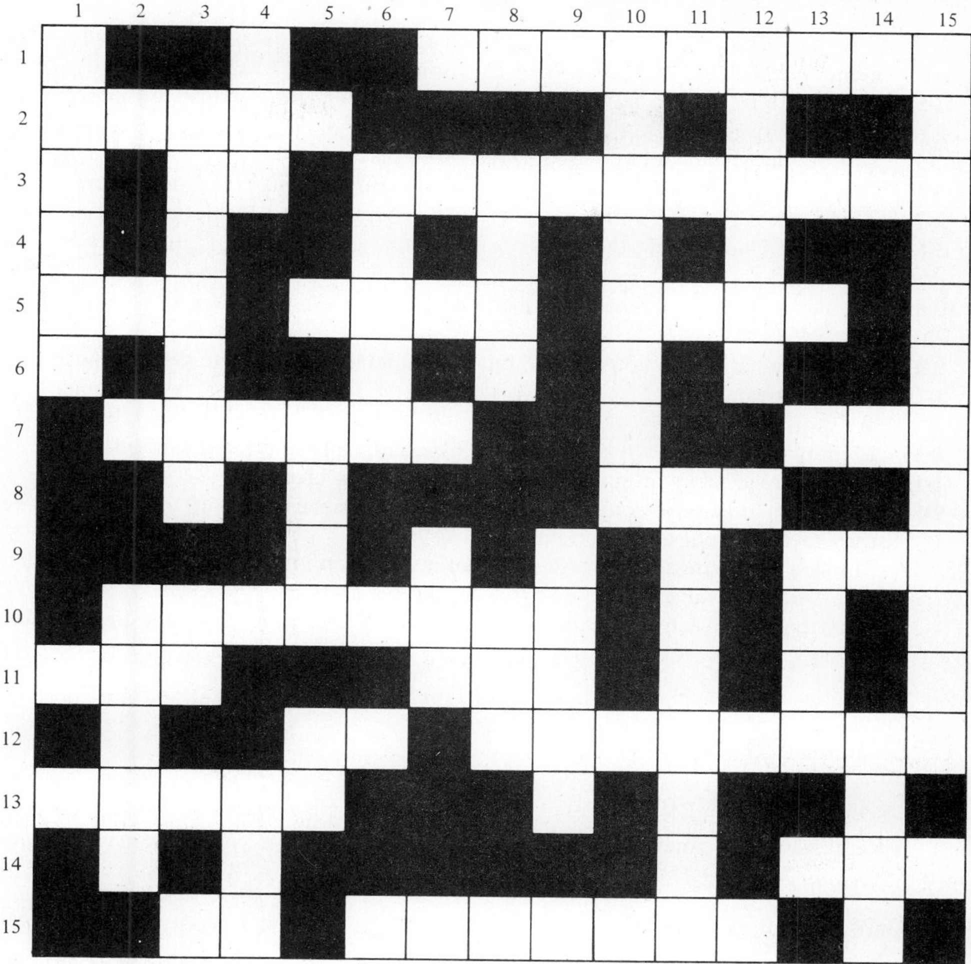

12-5 The location of work activities vis-à-vis a work station.

12-8 One approach to management concentrates upon this activity of managers and various criteria are used to facilitate these activities of theirs.

13-1 A key location that LP matrices and centers of basketball teams have in common.

14-13 The place to enter into a queue or leave a production line.

15-3 The initials for a technique used to maximize an objective function subject to constraints.

15-6 An iterative procedure which progressively approaches and ultimately reaches an optimal solution.

Down

1-1 One reason line balancing is a problem is because the time it takes a worker to do a job __________.

10-2 Research concerned simply with new knowledge.

2-3 Research directed toward specific products.

10-3 An article contained in the word "man."

1-4 LP techniques are useful in reaching product __________ decisions.

13-4 The first three letters of a word describing a type of loss that occurs as a result of uncertainty about which state of nature will prevail.
7-5 A measure of motion according to before and after and a major consideration in managing research.
12-5 A pronoun which could be used to refer to a machine.
3-6 In graphic LP, we graph only this aspect of the objective function (designated by *m*).
9-7 Three letters describing the contents of the top row of an LP solution matrix.
3-8 Assembly charts show the sequence necessary to __________ up a mechanical assembly.
10-8 A chart, graph, or quantitative method can be referred to as a process planning __________.
9-9 In a simulated production activity, this is what an item must do to get into the queue.
1-10 Some bosses will not __________ workers standing around idle, even though they are waiting for parts.
8-11 In graphic LP this is a region bounded by explicit and implicit constraints.
1-12 A rectangular array of numbers, usually enclosed in brackets.
9-13 The excess of value over the maximum expected monetary value up to what would be the expected profit under certainty.
12-14 The first four letters (in reverse order) of a word connoting knowledge of facts and data that have value.
1-15 What an LP objective function has undergone that is reduced to the lowest value possible.

BIBLIOGRAPHY

[1] BOOZ, ALLEN, and HAMILTON: "Management of New Products," Management Research Department, 1960. Cited in Lewis N. Goslin: *The Product Planning System*, Richard D. Irwin, Homewood, Illinois, 1967, p. 3.

[2] BUFFA, ELWOOD S.: *Modern Production Management*, John Wiley & Sons, New York, 1973.

[3] CHASE, RICHARD B., and NICHOLAS J. AQUILANO: *Production and Operations Management*, Richard D. Irwin, Homewood, Illinois, 1973.

[4] DI ROCCAFERRERA: *Introduction to Linear Programming Processes*, South-Western Publishing Company, Cincinnati, Ohio, 1967.

[5] *Du Pont Annual Report 1974:* E. I. Du Pont De Nemours & Company, Wilmington, Delaware, 1975.

[6] HAMILTON, H. RONALD, and ROBERT E. FREUND: "Productivity and the Viability of the U.S. Economy," *Battelle Research Outlook*, vol. 4, no. 3, 1972, Columbus, Ohio.

[7] IBM: "A Preface to Linear Programming and Its Applications," GE20-0350-0, White Plains, New York.

[8] INGALL, EDWARD J.: "A Review of Assembly Line Balancing," *Journal of Industrial Engineering*, vol. 16, no. 4, July–August 1965.

[9] JEDAMUS, PAUL, and ROBERT FRAME: *Business Decision Theory*, McGraw-Hill Book Company, New York, 1969.

[10] KILBRIDGE, M. D., and L. WESTER: "A Heuristic Method of Assembly Line Balancing," *Journal of Industrial Engineering*, vol. 13, no. 3, May–June 1962.

[11] KNAPP, J. G.: "Industrial Design: Its Role in Cost Reductions," *Mechanical Engineering*, ASME, New York, December 1971, pp. 23–26.

[12] MASTOR, ANTHONY A.: "An Experimental Investigation and Comparative Evaluation of Production Line Balancing Techniques," *Management Science*, vol. 16, no. 11, July 1970, pp. 728–746.

[13] MONKS, JOSEPH G.: "A Utility Approach to R&D Decisions," *R&D Management*, Manchester (England) Business School.

[14] MOORE, FRANKLIN G.: *Production Management*, 6th ed., Richard D. Irwin, Homewood, Illinois, 1973.

[15] NAYLOR, THOMAS H., EUGENE T. BYRNE, and JOHN R. VERNON: *Introduction to Linear Programming: Methods and Cases*, Wadsworth Publishing Company, Belmont, California, 1971.

[16] OLSEN, R. A.: *Manufacturing Management: A Quantitative Approach*, International Textbook, Scranton, Pennsylvania, 1968.

[17] ROBERTS, A. L.: *Production Management Workbook*, John Wiley & Sons, New York, 1962.

[18] SHAMBLIN, JAMES E., and G. T. STEVENS, JR.: *Operations Research*, McGraw-Hill Book Company, New York, 1974.

[19] SHORE, BARRY: *Operations Management*, McGraw-Hill Book Company, New York, 1973.

[20] SKINNER, WICKHAM: "Manufacturing-Missing Link in Corporate Strategy," *Harvard Business Review*, vol. 47, no. 3, May–June 1969.

[21] STARR, MARTIN K.: *Production Management, Systems and Synthesis*, Prentice-Hall, Englewood Cliffs, New Jersey, 1964.

[22] TIMMS, HOWARD L., and MICHAEL F. POHLEN: *The Production Function in Business*, Richard D. Irwin, Homewood, Illinois, 1970.

[23] TONGE, FRED M.: "Assembly Line Balancing Using Probabilistic Combinations of Heuristics," *Management Science*, May 1965.

[24] WAGNER, HARVEY M.: *Principles of Operations Research*, Prentice-Hall, Englewood Cliffs, New Jersey, 1969.

[25] WESTER, L., and M. D. KILBRIDGE: "Heuristic Line Balancing: A Case," *Journal of Industrial Engineering*, vol. 13, no. 3, May–June 1962.

[26] *Xerox Corporation 1974 Annual Report*, Xerox Corporation, Stamford, Connecticut, 1975.

CHAPTER

6

Forecasting

PURPOSE AND METHODS

PURPOSE OF FORECASTING ACTIVITIES
TYPES OF FORECASTS
TIMING OF FORECASTS
FORECASTING METHODOLOGY

CHARACTERISTICS OF DEMAND

OPINION AND JUDGMENTAL METHODS

TIME SERIES ANALYSIS

COMPONENTS OF A SERIES
FORECASTING PROCEDURE
METHODS OF ESTIMATING TREND
CHANGING THE ORIGIN AND SCALE OF EQUATIONS
SEASONAL INDEXES

REGRESSION AND CORRELATION METHODS

LINEAR REGRESSION
STANDARD DEVIATION OF REGRESSION
INTERVAL ESTIMATES
CORRELATION COEFFICIENTS: MEANING AND USE

EXPONENTIAL SMOOTHING

SIMPLE EXPONENTIAL SMOOTHING
SELECTION OF THE SMOOTHING CONSTANT
SEASONAL ADJUSTMENT TO EXPONENTIAL FORECAST
ADJUSTED EXPONENTIAL SMOOTHING

VALIDITY, CONTROL, AND USE OF FORECASTS

CONTROLS FOR SIMPLE AVERAGES
CONTROLS FOR ASSOCIATIVE FORECASTS
CONTROLS FOR EXPONENTIAL SMOOTHING FORECASTS

SUMMARY
SOLVED PROBLEMS
QUESTIONS
PROBLEMS
CROSSWORD PUZZLE
BIBLIOGRAPHY

Although the future holds uncertainties for everyone, human beings have become accustomed to facing an uncertain tomorrow. And in their organizations, whether they realize it or not, they make assumptions or predictions about the future. If they did not do so, they would have little basis for rational action in the present. The better we are able to anticipate the future, the more goal-oriented our current decisions can be.

Forecasts are basically estimates of the occurrence of uncertain future events or levels of activity. They are usually concerned with the timing, magnitude, or effects of events that are beyond immediate control. They play a key role in the management of operations because they can provide rational guidelines for activities that must be managed in a competitive and uncertain environment.

In this chapter we concentrate upon the uses and methodology of forecasting. Our purpose is to gain an appreciation of the value of forecasting, an understanding of some of the major techniques, and an insight into the selection of an appropriate technique for a given operations situation.

We begin by considering the need for forecasting and the types of forecasts that are made. Since forecasts often deal with demand for goods or services, we pay special attention to the uncertain nature of demand. The forecasting methods covered are of four main types: (1) judgmental, (2) time series, (3) regression and correlation, and (4) exponential smoothing. Examples of each method will be given and some refinements or extensions noted. We end the chapter with the reminder that the value of a forecasting technique lies in its ability to predict reliably and accurately. Thus it is important to measure forecast validity and control forecast error.

PURPOSE AND METHODS

PURPOSE OF FORECASTING ACTIVITIES

We have seen that management is typically charged with establishing organizational objectives and the policies to achieve them. Much of management's responsibility is solidly linked to its control over the use of resources. In particular, operations managers have significant responsibility with respect to the use of labor, materials, and capital. They must continually make decisions about employment levels, carrying inventories, purchasing new equipment, scheduling production, and so forth. Wise decisions in these areas depend upon a knowledge or prediction of future events. The purpose of forecasting activities is to make use of the best available present information to guide future activities toward system goals.

TYPES OF FORECASTS

System objectives are facilitated by a number of different types of forecasts. Some of them relate to demand, environmental or technological uncertainties, and others relate more specifically to cash flows, operating budgets, internal personnel requirements, inventory levels, and so on. Managers must select or develop those types of forecasts that will be most useful to them in planning and controlling their operations.

Forecasts of demand are an especially important input to operations management decision making because they serve as a vital input to the scheduling and production control activities, as we shall see in Chaps. 7, 8, and 9. Given a reliable forecast, managers must then formulate material and capacity plans directing how and to what extent the system will respond. The forecast itself may be generated in a number of ways, many of which rely heavily upon sales and marketing information.

Environmental forecasts are concerned with the social, political, and economic state of the environment. Environmental concerns, such as pollution control requirements, are much better managed from an anticipatory rather than an after-the-fact standpoint. *Economic forecasts* are valuable because they highlight current and expected economic fluctuations which may have an impact upon a firm's production plans.

Technological forecasts are concerned with new developments in existing technologies as well as the development of new technologies. They have become increasingly important to major firms in the computer, aerospace, nuclear, and many other technologically advanced industries. Sophisticated methods have been developed (such as envelope curves and delphi techniques) to extrapolate trends in innovation and synthesize the intuitive insights of experts in the field [**2**].

TIMING OF FORECASTS

Forecasts are often classified according to time period and use, as for example:

Short range—up to one year (typically 0–3 months)
Medium range—one to three years
Long range—five years or more

In general, short-range forecasts serve primarily as guides to current operations. Medium- and longer-range forecasts are often of a more comprehensive or aggregated nature. A three- to five-year forecast may be necessary to support plant capacity decisions whereas product line and plant location decisions may be of even longer-term considerations. As might be expected, short-term forecasts are typically more accurate than longer-term forecasts.

It is not uncommon for firms to maintain forecasts covering all three time periods or a combination of them. Electric utilities, for example, do hourly forecasting of load so that they will know in advance when to bring various generators on line to meet daily peaks of power use. They must also plan their system capacity 10 to 20 years in advance for it takes them several years to design and install new plants. They depend heavily upon forecasts of demand and have developed sophisticated exponential smoothing techniques to provide them with accurate projections of demand over the various time periods.

FORECASTING METHODOLOGY

Some organizations claim they do not forecast at all whereas others sport very sophisticated models. Companies that pay no attention to forecasting are implicitly assuming that what has happened in the past will continue in the future. This is not necessarily an irrational approach, but it could certainly be improved upon by anticipating future events that are known with a high degree of certainty.

The complexity of forecasting methodology sometimes tends to correspond with the extent to which future events are evaluated in an objective or professional manner. Subjective opinions are often adequate for less consequential or relatively certain situations. As the amount of uncertainty about future events increases, firms tend to rely more upon inferences and correlations based upon the present. When these inferences, in turn, come from analysis of data, the methodology becomes more objective but also more complex.

Complexity does not guarantee accuracy, however, for no forecasts can be expected to be 100 percent accurate. There is no such thing as a totally "reliable" forecasting technique [**18**: 147–167]. Even the sophisticated statistical techniques assume that the future will be like the past, and this is not always helpful. For some firms, effort spent on developing a more responsive production and inventory management system (such as the MRP system discussed in the next chapter) is likely to be more productive than efforts to increase the sophistication of existing forecasting techniques.

Some techniques are best suited to long-range or new-product forecasts whereas others are more appropriate for production and inventory control. Instead of any one ideal method, several techniques are in common use. *Opinion methods*, although subjective, are widely used, especially by small firms. To a large extent they rely upon personal insights, imagination, or perhaps even guesswork. Cost is low but accuracy is too. *Judgmental methods* are an improvement over opinion in that judgments call on past experience, consensus with others, or perhaps knowledge of historically analogous situations. They may be the most economically feasible methods for some long-range and new-product marketing situations.

Time series methods, which capitalize upon identification of trend and seasonal effects, are data-based and are likely to be more accurate than opinion methods. Nevertheless, they are based wholly upon time and do not base forecasts upon outside or related factors. The basic assumption is that history follows a pattern that will continue. *Exponential smoothing methods* are of this same type, for they are trajectory, or trend-based. They are, however, readily adaptive to current levels of activity and have become increasingly popular in production and inventory control applications during the past 10 years.

Regression and correlation methods are associative in nature and depend upon the causal relationship or interaction of two or more variables. They can be classified as statistical from an inferential standpoint, for we use one or more variables to infer something about the other.

Although econometric and simulation methods will not be covered in detail, we should note that they too are in promising stages of development. *Econometric methods* are statistically based but have a foundation of economic theory that helps to identify and explain causal relationships. *Simulation models* of a business system usually consist of numerous mathematical relationships between selected variables. Their formulation typically requires a good deal of systems analysis, computer programming skill, and large amounts of data. The models are not necessarily designed to provide specific estimates, but rather to demonstrate the effects of changing various levels of independent variables in the model. A major advantage of building a simulation model lies in the understanding it forces upon the model-builder.

CHARACTERISTICS OF DEMAND

A truly random variable is one that is not subject to control. Although we tend to think of numerous variables as random, many of them are only partly random. Sales for example, is a function of both controllable variables (advertising effort, inventory levels) and uncontrollable variables (competition, raw material cost). Individual firms operate under the assumption that astute management of the controllable variables will generate success for them, even though the uncontrollable variables may mitigate against it. Uncontrollable variables may have random and temporarily adverse effects, but, as a going concern, the firm strives to maintain viability and to reach long-run goals.

No forecasting technique could hope to predict the value of random components of an uncontrollable variable. If they follow a predictable pattern they are inherently not random! What the *forecasting methodologies* seek to do is to *allow for random components but base projections primarily upon the nonrandom trends and relationships* that the data exhibit. Thus we find that time series, regression, and exponential smoothing methods are all based primarily upon relationships that have been valid in the past.

Demand patterns that are not significantly affected by uncontrollable variables are relatively easy to forecast. When the patterns have uncontrollable elements, but they can be identified and isolated, this also facilitates forecasting. Similarly, if demand can be decomposed into identifiable trends, or cyclical or seasonal factors, this helps too. In general, the more the random effects can be isolated, the better the forecast will be.

Forecasts of product lines and groups of products take advantage of another aspect of randomness. Whereas individual product forecasts are strongly susceptible to error due to spontaneous random effects (which cannot be anticipated anyway), when several products are aggregated together the effect is dissipated throughout the group and compensating effects occur. One product's demand may exceed the forecast while another's may fail to meet it. But as a whole, the aggregative forecast generally tends to be more accurate than individual product forecasts. Production planners often take advantage of this knowledge by scheduling the use of production system capacities weeks before the specific end-item demand is firmed up.

OPINION AND JUDGMENTAL METHODS

One of the most simple yet widely used methods of forecasting consists of collecting the opinions and judgments of individuals who are expected to have the best knowledge of current activities or future plans. The employees with most immediate knowledge of demand trends and customer plans are often company marketing representatives and division or product line managers. Through regular contact with customers, the marketing and sales personnel are presumably knowledgeable of individual industrial customers or retail market segments. Division management usually maintains broader market information on trends by product line, geographic area, customer groups, and so on.

Judgmental forecasts often consist of one or more of the following:

1 Forecasts by sales representatives, which are made up individually and aggregated for various products.

2 Forecasts by top management at the division or product line level.

3 Forecasts based on the combined estimates of sales representatives and division or product line managers.

Some judgmental forecasts are largely intuitive whereas others integrate data and perhaps even some mathematical or statistical expectations into a judgmental framework. Large firms often have a good deal of systematically collected data available upon which to base judgments.

Judgmental forecasts have the advantage that they can incorporate intangible factors and subjective experience as inputs along with objective data, if that is also available. It is the amazing and unique structure of the human brain that permits assimilation of all types of information and the ultimate issuance of a prediction. No mathematical model or computer can duplicate this capability.

On the other hand, each human being has a different knowledge, experience, and perspective of reality. Thus, highly intuitive forecasts are likely to differ from one individual to the next. Furthermore, the less they are based upon facts and quantified data, the less they lend themselves to analysis and resolution of differences of opinion. The quantification of data gives them a more precise meaning than words and shadings in tone, which are inexact and are capable of being misunderstood [7]. Also, if the forecasts prove to be inaccurate there is a tangible, objective basis for improvement the next time around.

TIME SERIES ANALYSIS

A time series is a set of observations of some variable over time. The series is usually tabulated or graphed in a manner that readily conveys the behavior of the subject variable. For example, assume Fig. 6-1 presents the annual shipments (tons) of welded

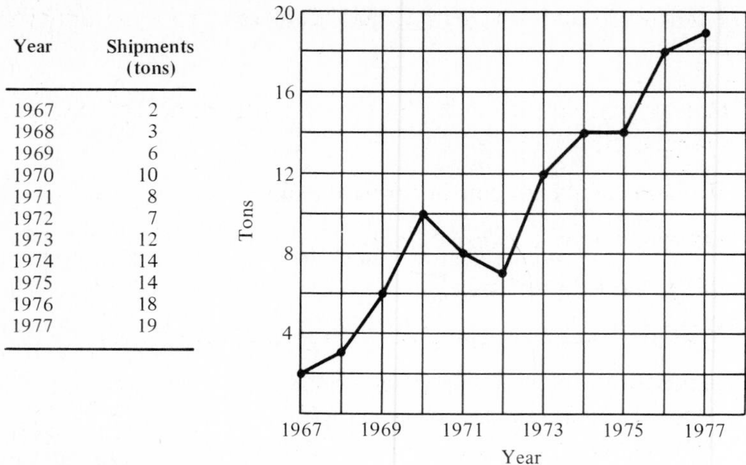

Year	Shipments (tons)
1967	2
1968	3
1969	6
1970	10
1971	8
1972	7
1973	12
1974	14
1975	14
1976	18
1977	19

FIGURE 6-1 Aluminum tube shipments

tube by an aluminum producer to machinery manufacturers. The graph suggests that the series is time dependent (but additional statistical tests such as runs tests and serial correlations could be made to verify this if desired). The forecaster is interested in determining *how* the series is dependent on time and in developing a means of predicting future levels with some degree of reliability. The nature of the time dependence is often analyzed by decomposing the time series into its components.

COMPONENTS OF A SERIES

The components of a time series are generally classified as trend (T), cyclical (C), seasonal (S), and random (R) or irregular. In the classical model of time series analysis, the forecast (Y) is a multiplicative function of these components:

$$Y = \text{TCSR} \tag{6-1}$$

The *trend* represents a long-term secular movement, characteristic of many economic series. *Cyclical* factors are long-term swings about the trend line and are usually associated with business cycles. *Seasonal* effects are similar patterns occurring during corresponding months of successive years. They can be hourly or weekly patterns as well, but are not usually evident unless the data are plotted on an appropriate time scale. *Random or irregular* components are sporadic effects due to chance and unusual occurrences.

FORECASTING PROCEDURE

Most forecasting procedures that use time series data abstract the trend and seasonal factors. Some methods attempt to go beyond this and express a cyclical component, but it is usually evasive and somewhat subjective. The random component is inherently not predictable, so the forecasting procedure results in the following:

1 Obtain historical data and plot it to confirm the type of relationship (for example, linear, quadratic)

2 Develop trend equation to describe data

3 Develop seasonal index (if desired)

4 Project trend into future

5 Multiply monthly trend values by seasonal index

6 Modify projected values by knowledge of:
(*a*) cyclical business conditions (C)
(*b*) anticipated irregular effects (R)

METHODS OF ESTIMATING TREND

Several methods of estimating the trend of a time series are available. Some of these methods simply portray or describe the data, such as freehand curves and moving averages. Other approaches describe the data *and* provide a trend equation, such as semiaverage and least squares. Let us refer to the data of Fig. 6-1 to illustrate.

Freehand

A freehand curve drawn smoothly through the data points is often an easy and perhaps adequate representation of the data. From Fig. 6-1 it appears that a straight line connecting the 1967 and 1977 shipments is a fairly good representation of the given data. The forecast can be obtained simply by extending the trend line. However, what appears to be a good fit for one individual may not be so for another and this method suffers from subjectivity.

Moving Average

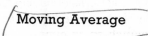

A moving average is obtained by summing and averaging the values from a given number of periods repetitively, each time deleting the oldest value and adding a new value.

$$\text{MA} = \frac{\sum X}{\text{number of periods}} \tag{6-2}$$

where one X value is exchanged each period.

Example 6-1

Compute a three-year moving average for the aluminum tube shipments of Fig. 6-1.

Solution

Year	Shipments (tons)	Three-year moving total		Three-year moving average
1967	2	—		—
1968	3	11	÷ 3 =	3.7
1969	6	19	÷ 3 =	6.3
1970	10	24		8.0
1971	8	25		8.3
1972	7	27		9.0
1973	12	33		11.0
1974	14	40		13.3
1975	14	46		15.3
1976	18	51		17.0
1977	19	—		—

Note that the moving average is recorded in the center position of the data it averages. The 3.7-ton figure in the above example would thus be centered on July 1, 1968. The average effectively smooths out fluctuations while preserving the general pattern of the data. A graph of the moving-average values superimposed upon Fig. 6-1 would reveal this smoothing effect. Of course, the more components in the average (that is, the longer the period), the smoother will be the curve. It has the additional advantage that it can be applied to any data, whether they fit a precise mathematical curve or not.

The adaptability of the moving average is also the source of a major disadvantage, however, for there is no equation for forecasting. In place of an equation we use the latest moving-average value as the forecast for the next period. In Example 6-1, the next period (1978) forecast would then be 17 tons, which would probably be low in view of the strong trend. Moving averages lose data values at each end of the series and can be strongly affected by extreme values.

An adjustment to the moving-average (MA) method allows one to vary the weights assigned to components of the moving average and in this way the most recent values can be emphasized.

$$\text{MA}_{\text{wt}} = \frac{\sum (\text{wt})\, X}{\sum \text{wt}} \tag{6-3}$$

This is often referred to as a weighted moving-average method. Weights can be percentages or any real numbers. In Example 6-1, if a weight of 3 is assigned to the 1977 shipments, 2 to 1976, and 1 to 1975, the weighted moving average is 17.8 tons.

Semiaverage

The semiaverage method permits the analyst to estimate the slope and intercept of the trend line quite easily if a linear function will adequately describe the data. The procedure is simply to divide the data into two groups and compute their respective means. The mean of the first group is the intercept value, and the slope is determined by the ratio of the difference in the means to the number of years between them, that is, the change per unit time. The resultant is a time series of the form

$$Y_c = a + bX \text{ (signature)} \tag{6-4}$$

The Y_c is the calculated trend value and a and b are the intercept and slope values respectively. The equation should always be stated complete with "signature," that is, the reference year where $X = 0$ and a decription of the units of X and Y.

Example 6-2

Use the semiaverage method to develop a linear trend equation for the data of Fig. 6-1. State the equation complete with signature and forecast a trend value for 1982.

Solution

Divide the data into two equal groups of 5 years (A and B) ignoring the middle year (1972). The first group (A) will then be centered upon 1969 and the second (B) on 1975.

$$\overline{Y}_A = \frac{2 + 3 + 6 + 10 + 8}{5} = 5.8 \text{ tons}$$

$$\overline{Y}_B = \frac{12 + 14 + 14 + 18 + 19}{5} = 15.4 \text{ tons}$$

$$\text{Slope} = b = \frac{\Delta Y}{\Delta X} = \frac{\text{change in tons}}{\text{number of years}} = \frac{15.4 - 5.8}{1975 - 1969} = \frac{9.6}{6}$$

$$= 1.6 \text{ tons/yr}$$

Intercept $= a = 5.8$ tons at 1969

Equation: $Y_c = 5.8 + 1.6X$ ($1969 = 0$, $X =$ years, $Y =$ tons)

Forecast for 1982: Since 1982 is 13 years distant from the origin (1969), we have

$$Y_c = 5.8 + 1.6(13) = 26.6 \text{ tons}$$

The semiaverage method of developing a trend equation is relatively easy to compute and may be satisfactory if the trend is linear, or very nearly linear. If the data deviate much from linearity, the forecast will be biased and less reliable.

Least Squares

Least squares is one of the most widely used methods of fitting trends to data because it yields what is mathematically described as a "line of best fit." This trend line has the properties that (*a*) the summation of all vertical deviations about it is zero, (*b*) the summation of all vertical deviations squared is a minimum, and (*c*) the line goes through the means $\bar{X}$ and $\bar{Y}$. For linear equations, it is found by the simultaneous solution for *a* and *b* of the two normal equations:

$$\begin{aligned} \sum Y &= na + b \sum X \\ \sum XY &= a \sum X + b \sum X^2 \end{aligned} \tag{6-5}$$

Where the data can be coded so that $\sum X = 0$, two terms in the above expressions drop out and we have:

$$\begin{aligned} \sum Y &= na \\ \sum XY &= b \sum X^2 \end{aligned} \tag{6-6}$$

Coding is easily accomplished with time series data for we simply designate the center of the time period as $X = 0$ and have an equal number of plus and minus periods on each side which sum to zero.

Example 6-3

Use the least-squares method to develop a linear trend equation for the data of Fig. 6-1. State the equation complete with signature and forecast a trend value for 1982.

Solution

Year	*X* year coded	*Y* shipments (tons)	$X \cdot Y$	X^2
1967	−5	2	−10	25
1968	−4	3	−12	16
1969	−3	6	−18	9
1970	−2	10	−20	4
1971	−1	8	−8	1
1972	0	7	0	0
1973	1	12	12	1
1974	2	14	28	4
1975	3	14	42	9
1976	4	18	72	16
1977	5	19	95	25
	0	113	181	110

Rearranging Eq. (6-6) we have:

$$a = \frac{\sum Y}{n} = \frac{113}{11} = 10.3$$

$$b = \frac{\sum XY}{\sum X^2} = \frac{181}{110} = 1.6$$

$\therefore$ The forecasting equation is:

$$Y = 10.3 + 1.6X \ (1972 = 0, X = \text{years}, Y = \text{tons})$$

Forecast for 1982: Since 1982 is 10 years distant from the origin,

$$Y = 10.3 + 1.6(10) = 26.3 \text{ tons}$$

The above example assumes that a linear equation adequately describes the data. *The appropriateness of a linear function should always be checked first*; this can be done simply by graphing the data and observing whether a straight line would provide a satisfactory fit. If not, higher-order normal equations can be used, and these may be obtained from any good statistical reference text. The solution procedure for developing parabolic or exponential equations is similar, but more tedious. Fortunately, linear equations often suffice, for even though the data may be nonlinear in the long range, over the short range much data approximates linearity.

CHANGING THE ORIGIN AND SCALE OF EQUATIONS

When a moving average or trend value is reported it is assumed to be centered in the middle of the month (fifteenth day) or the year (July 1). Similarly, the forecast value is assumed to be centered in the middle of the future period.

The reference point (origin) can be shifted, or the X and Y units changed to monthly or quarterly values if desired. To shift the origin, simply add or subtract the desired number of periods from X in the original forecasting equation. Changing the time units from annual values to monthly values is accomplished by dividing X by 12. To change the Y units from annual to monthly values, the entire right-hand side of the equation must be divided by 12.

SEASONAL INDEXES

A *seasonal index* (SI) is a ratio that relates a recurring seasonal variation to the corresponding trend value at that given time. We are all familiar with the peaking of retail sales at Christmas and the decline in heating fuel consumption in summer.

When data such as these are reported in monthly terms, and similar patterns occur during corresponding months of successive years, seasonal indexes of such patterns can be determined.

Several methods of computing seasonal indexes exist, but the most widely used is a ratio-to-moving-average method. The procedure is to tabulate the data in monthly terms and compute 12-month moving-average values over a period of several years. The 12-month moving average effectively dampens out all seasonal fluctuations. Actual monthly values are then compared to the moving average centered upon the actual month. For example, the 12-month moving average (that is, trend value) for heating fuel consumption for a plant in August 1974 may have been 40 gallons, but actual consumption only 32 gallons. The ratio to moving average for August of 1974 is then 32 divided by 40 = 0.80. Values for August of other years are similarly computed and all such values averaged to get one seasonal index value for the month of August. The same is done for other months. Some monthly index values will exceed 1.00 but the total for all 12 months will be made equal to 12.00.

After valid seasonal indexes have been determined, they can be applied to forecasted trend values to obtain seasonalized (adjusted) forecast values (Y_{sz}).

$$\text{Seasonalized forecast} = \text{seasonal index (trend forecast)}$$

$$Y_{sz} = (\text{SI})\ Y_c \tag{6-7}$$

Example 6-4

The production manager of a natural gas pipeline company has projected trend values for next August, September, and October of 2.1, 2.2, and 2.3 million cubic meters respectively. Seasonal indexes for the three months have been found to be 0.80, 1.05, and 1.20, respectively. What actual seasonalized (adjusted) production should the manager plan for?

Solution

$$Y_{sz} = \text{SI}\ (Y_c)$$

$$\text{For August:} \quad = (0.80)(2.1) = 1.68 \text{ million cubic meters}$$

$$\text{For September:} \quad = (1.05)(2.2) = 2.31 \text{ million cubic meters}$$

$$\text{For October:} \quad = (1.20)(2.3) = 2.76 \text{ million cubic meters}$$

After seasonal adjustments have been made, similar adjustments can be made for cyclical or irregular effects if data are available. For example, if a firm's business is closely tied to construction activity and economic indicators suggest a 20 percent drop in that activity over the next year, the firm may want to apply a 0.80 multiplier to its forecast of sales to the industry. Similarly, any irregular occurrence, such as a forthcoming strike, should be accounted for as much as possible.

REGRESSION AND CORRELATION METHODS

A time series equation describes the action of some variable over variable were a function of time. Although this is often a useful relationship, it is sometimes more meaningful to relate the variable we are trying to forecast to other variables that are more suggestive of a causal relationship. Regression and correlation techniques are means of describing the association between two or more such variables. They make no claim to establishing cause and effect, but instead merely quantify the statistical dependence or extent to which the two or more variables are related.

LINEAR REGRESSION

Regression means "dependence" and involves estimating the value of a *dependent variable* Y from an *independent variable* X. In simple regression only one independent variable is used whereas in multiple regression two or more independent variables are involved. The simple linear regression model takes the form $Y_c = a + bX$ where Y_c is the dependent and X the independent variable. A multiple linear regression equation may be of the form $Y_c = a + bX_1 + cX_2 + dX_3$ whereas a curvilinear relationship involving second- or higher-order functions might take the form $Y_c = a + bX + cX^2 + dX^3$. We shall limit consideration to simple linear regressions, which are often satisfactory for forecasting purposes, and refer the reader to a statistics text [**10, 13**] for multiple regression and curvilinear regression models.

The forecasting procedure using regression is similar to that of time series in that data are obtained and plotted to be sure the correct form of a model is chosen. A trend equation is then developed and the equation is used for forecasting. Since the variables are not necessarily related on a time basis, seasonal and cyclical adjustments are not usually made. However, the method of converting the data into a forecasting equation is the same in that the normal equations [see Equation (6-5)] are used. Since the equations are always solved for the values of the slope b and intercept a, they are often rewritten in the more convenient form:

$$b = \frac{\sum XY - n\overline{X}\overline{Y}}{\sum X^2 - n\overline{X}^2} \tag{6-8}$$

$$a = \overline{Y} - b\overline{X} \tag{6-9}$$

where $\overline{X} = (\sum X)/n$ and $\overline{Y} = (\sum Y)/n$ are the means of the independent and dependent variables respectively and n is the number of pairs of observations made.

Example 6-5

The general manager of a building materials production plant feels the demand for plasterboard shipments may be related to the number of construction permits issued in the county during the previous quarter. The manager has collected the data shown in the accompanying table.

Construction permits	Plasterboard shipments
15	6
9	4
40	16
20	6
25	13
25	9
15	10
35	16

(*a*) Graph the data to see whether it can be satisfactorily described by a linear equation.
(*b*) Use the normal equations of (6-5) to derive a regression forecasting equation.
(*c*) Confirm the values of (*b*) and (*a*) using Equations (6-8) and (6-9).
(*d*) Determine a point estimate for plasterboard shipments when the number of construction permits is 30.

Solution

(*a*) A scatter diagram (Fig. 6-2) shows the data are not perfectly linear but approach linearity over this short range.

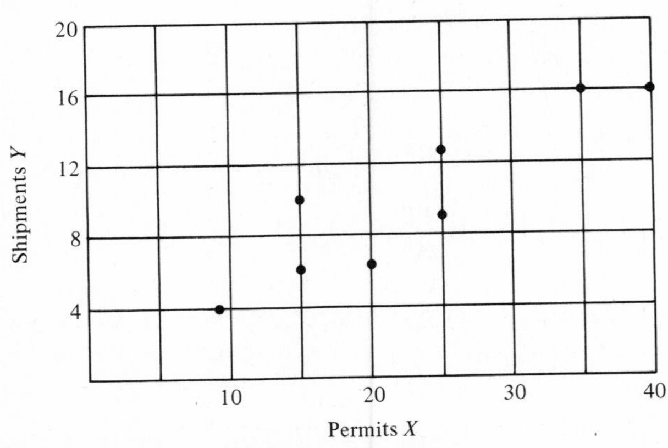

FIGURE 6-2 Plasterboard shipments and construction permits

(*b*) See the accompanying table and calculations.

X	Y	XY	X^2	Y^2
15	6	90	225	36
9	4	36	81	16
40	16	640	1,600	256
20	6	120	400	36
25	13	325	625	169
25	9	225	625	81
15	10	150	225	100
35	16	560	1,225	256
184	80	2,146	5,006	950

$n = 8$ pairs of observations

$$\bar{X} = \frac{184}{8} = 23$$

$$\bar{Y} = \frac{80}{8} = 10$$

$$\sum Y = na + b\sum X \rightarrow \quad 80 = 8a + 184b \quad (1)$$

$$\sum XY = a\sum X + b\sum X^2 \rightarrow \quad 2{,}146 = 184a + 5{,}006b \quad (2)$$

$$\text{multiplying (1) by } (-23)^1 \quad -1{,}840 = -184a - 4{,}232b \quad (3)$$

$$\text{adding (2) and (3)} \quad 306 = 774b \quad (4)$$

$$b = \frac{306}{774} = 0.395$$

substituting in (1)

$$80 = 8a + 184(0.395)$$

$$8a = 80 - 72.7$$

$$a = \frac{7.3}{8} = 0.91$$

Equation is

$$Y_c = 0.91 + 0.395X \ (X = \text{permits},\ Y = \text{shipments})$$

[1] Note that we are multiplying equation (1) by a number such that the coefficient for *a* will be of equal value (but opposite sign) as that in equation (2). The (23) is obtained from 184 ÷ 8 and assigned a negative value so that the *a* coefficient drops out upon addition.

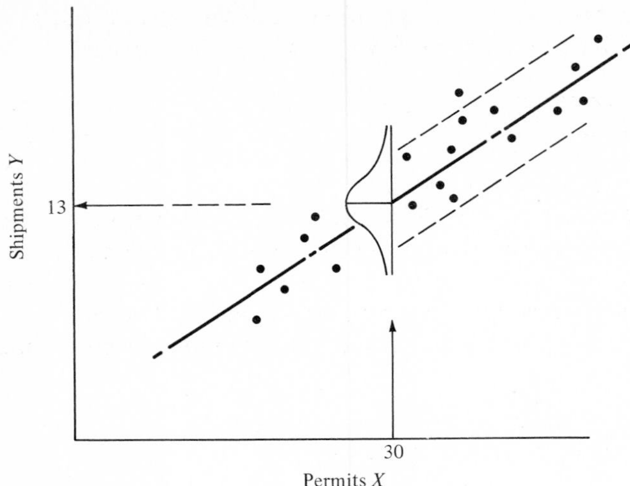

FIGURE 6-3 Regression line

(*c*) Alternatively,

$$b = \frac{\sum XY - n\overline{XY}}{\sum X^2 - n\overline{X}^2} = \frac{2{,}146 - 8(23)(10)}{5{,}006 - 8(23)(23)} = 0.395$$

$$a = \overline{Y} - b\overline{X} = 10 - 0.395(23) = 0.91$$

(*d*) Letting $X = 30$,

$$Y_c = 0.91 + 0.395(30) = 12.76 \cong 13 \text{ shipments}$$

The regression line developed via the use of the normal equations has the characteristics of a line of best fit so that the sum of the squares of the vertical deviations from this line is less than the sum of the squares of the deviations from any other straight line through the same points. Any regression curve essentially describes the relationship between a given value of the independent variable X and the mean $\mu_{Y.X}$ of the corresponding probability distribution of the dependent variable Y. Thus, for any value of X (such as 30 permits) there is a distribution of values of Y (many possible values) and our forecast, or point estimate of Y (the 13 shipments), is actually the mean of that distribution. See Fig. 6-3.

STANDARD DEVIATION OF REGRESSION

We can measure the dispersion around the regression line by subtracting the calculated trend value Y_c from each observation Y, squaring and summing the differences, and dividing by $n - 2$. If we take the square root of this we obtain the standard deviation of regression $S_{Y.X}$, read "S sub Y given X."

$$S_{Y.X} = \sqrt{\frac{\sum (Y - Y_c)^2}{n - 2}} \tag{6-10}$$

This conditional standard deviation is similar to other standard deviation computations in that observed values Y are subtracted from the mean (Y_c), squared, and summed. The $n - 2$ in the denominator reflects a loss of 2 degrees of freedom because in this bivariate case we are using sample statistics for both the X and Y variables. A more difficult-looking equation, but one that is easier to use, will provide the same answer:

$$S_{Y.X} = \sqrt{\frac{\sum Y^2 - a \sum Y - b \sum XY}{n - 2}} \tag{6-11}$$

Example 6-6

Given the data on permits and shipments in the previous example, compute the standard deviation of regression ($S_{Y.X}$).

Solution

$$S_{Y.X} = \sqrt{\frac{\sum Y^2 - a \sum Y - b \sum XY}{n - 2}}$$

$$= \sqrt{\frac{950 - (0.91)(80) - (0.395)(2{,}146)}{8 - 2}}$$

$$= 2.2 \text{ shipments}$$

INTERVAL ESTIMATES

We can use the standard deviation of regression to lend more precision to any point estimate of a forecast by stating the forecast as an interval. The interval estimate of the *mean* forecast value is

$$\text{Confidence interval } Y_c = Y_c \pm Z \frac{S_{Y.X}}{\sqrt{n}} \tag{6-12}$$

where Y_c is the calculated trend value and Z represents the confidence coefficient. This formulation recognizes that for any given value of X (permits), the *mean* value of Y (shipments) can be expected, with a specified confidence, to lie within the interval.

However, the interval estimate for an *individual* value of Y is usually of more interest to businesspeople because they are typically concerned with forecasting a specific number (of shipments) now, rather than the mean number usually made. The interval estimate for individual values will necessarily have a wider spread than that for mean values and is designated as a

$$\text{Prediction interval} \quad Y_c = Y_c \pm ZS_{Y.X} \tag{6-13}$$

This interval assumes that for a given X value, the Y values are normally distributed about the mean (that is, the regression line). Then, for example, 95.5 percent of the Y values are within $\pm 2S_{Y.X}$ of the regression curve as shown by the dotted lines in Fig. 6-3. If the standard deviation of regression has been computed from a sample size of less than one hundred, the t rather than the normal Z distribution should be used in both the confidence interval and the prediction interval equations and additional correction factors must be applied. Equations for these situations can be found in any good statistics reference [**13**].

CORRELATION COEFFICIENTS: MEANING AND USE

We have seen that a *regression* curve expresses the *nature* (that is, intercept and slope) of the relationship between two or more variables. The regression equation states how the dependent variable changes as a result of changes in the independent variables.

Correlation is a means of expressing the *degree* of relationship between two or more variables. In other words, it tells how well a linear—or other—equation describes the relationship. Unlike regression, in correlation all the variables enjoy equal "status," so we do not consider one as dependent on another. Like regression, though, correlations may also be simple or multiple, linear or nonlinear, depending on the data. The correlation *coefficient* r is a number between -1 and $+1$ and is designated as positive if Y increases with increases in X and negative if Y decreases with increases in X. If $r = 0$, this indicates the lack of any relationship between the two variables.

Figure 6-4 further illustrates the meaning of the correlation coefficient. If there were no correlation, our best estimate of Y, given any value of X, would probably be the mean of Y, or $\overline{Y}$. If X and Y were perfectly correlated we would expect all values to lie on the regression line. Then, for any given value of X, we could simply proceed up to the regression curve and over to the Y axis to read off the forecast value of Y. The regression line thus justifies, or explains why some value other than $\overline{Y}$ (the mean of Y) is to be expected when X takes on a specific value. The correlation coefficient is related to the percent of the variation in Y that is explained by the regression line. The figure on the right, which depicts only one of many possible points, relates the point to $\overline{Y}$ in terms of its deviation, or variation (that is, the summation of squared deviations):

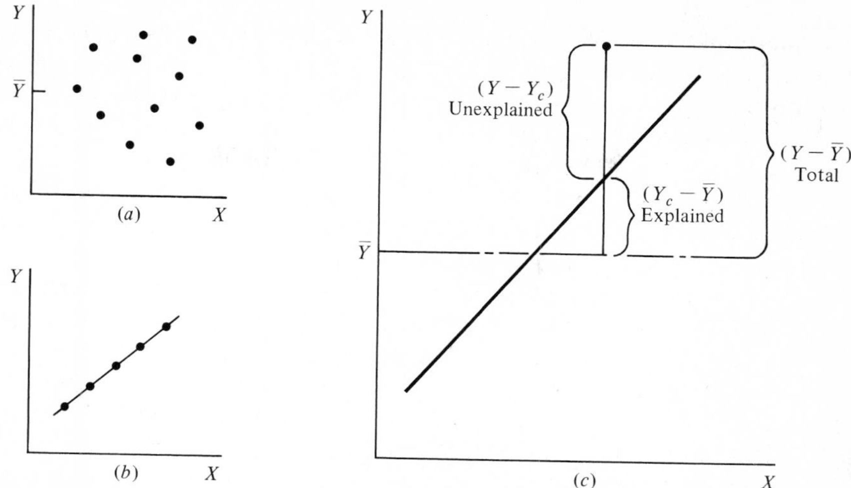

FIGURE 6-4 (a) No correlation; (b) perfect positive correlation; (c) deviation of dependent variable.

$$\text{Total variation} = \text{explained} + \text{unexplained}$$

$$\sum (Y - \overline{Y})^2 = \sum (Y_c - \overline{Y})^2 + \sum (Y - Y_c)^2$$

The ratio of explained to total variation is called the coefficient of determination, r^2. It is effectively the percent of variation in the dependent variable that is explained by the regression line.

$$r^2 = \frac{\sum (Y_c - \overline{Y})^2}{\sum (Y - \overline{Y})^2} \tag{6-14}$$

The square root of the coefficient of determination is the coefficient of correlation r:

$$r = \sqrt{\frac{\sum (Y_c - \overline{Y})^2}{\sum (Y - \overline{Y})^2}} \tag{6-15}$$

Since the explained variation as a percent of the total is equal to total minus unexplained variation, the correlation coefficient is sometimes more conveniently written in the form:

$$r = \sqrt{1 - \frac{\text{unexplained variation}}{\text{total variation}}} = \sqrt{1 - \frac{\sum (Y - Y_c)^2}{\sum (Y - \overline{Y})^2}} \tag{6-16}$$

Furthermore, if we divide variation by sample size n we get variance. Prior to (or ignoring) the correction for degrees of freedom, the correlation coefficient can also be expressed as

$$r = \sqrt{1 - \frac{S_{Y.X}^2}{S_Y^2}} \tag{6-17}$$

where $S_{Y.X}^2$ is the squared standard deviation of regression and S_Y^2 is the total variance of Y. When the sample size is large (e.g. >50), the value of r can also be computed more directly by the working equation:

$$r = \frac{n \sum XY - \sum X \sum Y}{\sqrt{[n \sum X^2 - (\sum X)^2][n \sum Y^2 - (\sum Y)^2]}} \tag{6-18}$$

so there are a number of ways of arriving at the same value. Fortunately, most of these "arrivals" are normally accomplished on the firm's computer, for the equations are tedious.

When all points lie on the regression line, the unexplained variation is zero and r takes on a value of 1. As the points deviate more and more, r gets closer to zero and the regression equation is less useful as an explanatory model. (The significance of any value of r can, however, be tested under a hypothesis that there is no correlation, that is, H_o: $r = 0$. The computed value of r is compared with a tabled value of r for a given sample size and significance level. If the computed value exceeds the tabled value, the hypothesis is rejected and the correlation is deemed significant at the specified level. Critical values of r for 5 percent and 1 percent levels of significance are given in most standard statistics texts [**13**].)

Example 6-7

A study to determine the correlation between plasterboard shipments X and construction permits Y revealed the following:

$$\sum X = 184 \qquad \sum X^2 = 5{,}006$$
$$\sum Y = 80 \qquad \sum Y^2 = 950$$
$$\sum XY = 2{,}146 \qquad n = 8$$

Compute the correlation coefficient.

Solution

$$r = \frac{n \sum XY - \sum X \sum Y}{\sqrt{[n \sum X^2 - (\sum X)^2][n \sum Y^2 - (\sum Y)^2]}}$$

$$= \frac{8(2{,}146) - (184)(80)}{\sqrt{[8(5{,}006) - (184)^2][8(950) - (80)^2]}}$$

$$= \frac{2{,}448}{\sqrt{7{,}430{,}400}}$$

$$= 0.90$$

The 0.90 appears to be a significant correlation but could be tested using values from any statistical table of correlation coefficients. (See [13]. For a sample size of $n = 8$ at the 5 percent level, the tabled value of r is only 0.707. Since the calculated r of 0.90 is greater than 0.707 we could conclude that such high correlation would have occurred by chance less than 5 percent of the time.)

The correlation coefficient may be very useful in confirming the closeness of the relationship of two or more variables used in forecasting demand, inventory requirements, accident rates, and so forth. Many firms have identified so-called leading economic indicators, such as freight car loadings or machine-tool orders, that tend to precede and are highly correlated with their own business. Government statistics such as these, covering the gross national product, disposable income, industrial production indexes, housing starts, and the like, are available in regular publications such as the *Survey of Current Business*, *Federal Reserve Bulletin*, *Monthly Labor Review*, and others.

EXPONENTIAL SMOOTHING

Exponential smoothing is a type of moving-average forecasting technique which weights past data in an exponential manner so that the most recent data carries more weight in the moving average. Simple exponential smoothing makes no explicit adjustment for trend effects whereas adjusted exponential smoothing does take trend effects into account.

SIMPLE EXPONENTIAL SMOOTHING

With simple exponential smoothing, the forecast is made up of the last period forecast plus a portion of the difference between the last period actual demand and the last period forecast.

$$F_t = F_{t-1} + \alpha(D_{t-1} - F_{t-1}) \tag{6-19}$$

where

F_t = current period forecast

F_{t-1} = last period forecast

α = smoothing constant

D_{t-1} = last period demand

Observe, from the equation, that each forecast is simply the previous forecast plus some correction for demand in the last period. If demand was above the last period forecast the correction will be positive, and if below it will be negative.

TABLE 6-1 MAGNITUDES OF EXPONENTIAL SMOOTHING COEFFICIENTS FOR TWO VALUES OF α

Coefficients	α	$\alpha(1-\alpha)$	$\alpha(1-\alpha)^2$	$\alpha(1-\alpha)^3$	$\alpha(1-\alpha)^4$
$\alpha = 0.1$	0.1	0.09	0.081	0.0729	0.06561
$\alpha = 0.9$	0.9	0.09	0.009	0.0009	0.00009

Source: [9]

The smoothing constant α actually dictates how much correction will be made. It is a number between 0 and 1 used to compute the forecast F_t which, in turn, is based upon previous forecasts where α was also used. By entering multiplicatively into all subsequent forecasts, an "exponential" weighting takes place which follows the form:

$$F_t = \alpha D_{t-1} + \alpha(1-\alpha)D_{t-2} + \alpha(1-\alpha)^2 D_{t-3} + \alpha(1-\alpha)^3 D_{t-4} + \cdots + \alpha(1-\alpha)^n D_{t-n}$$

where the weights sum to 1. The series thus extends indefinitely into the past but the influence of each period decreases the further it is from the current period.

When α is low, more weight is given to past data, and when it is high, more weight is given to recent data. The effect of different values is demonstrated in Table 6-1 [**9**]. When α is equal to 0.9, then 99.99 percent of the forecast value is determined by the four most recent demands. When α is as low as 0.1, only 34.39 percent of the average is due to these last 4 periods and the smoothing effect is equivalent to a 19-period arithmetic moving average [**12**].

If α were assigned a value as high as 1, each forecast would reflect a total adjustment to the recent demand and the forecast would simply be last period's actual demand. Since demand fluctuations are typically random and sporadic, however, the value of α is generally kept in the range of 0.005 to 0.30 in order to "smooth" the forecast. The exact value depends upon the response to demand that is best for the individual firm. We shall return to this consideration after an example.

Example 6-8

A firm uses simple exponential smoothing with $\alpha = 0.1$ to forecast demand. The forecast for the week of February 1 was 500 units whereas actual demand turned out to be 450 units.

(*a*) Forecast the demand for the week of February 8.
(*b*) Assume the actual demand during the week of February 8 turned out to be 505 units. Forecast the demand for the week of February 15. Continue on forecasting through March 15, assuming that subsequent demands were actually 516, 488, 467, 554, and 510 units.

Solution

(*a*)
$$F_t = F_{t-1} + \alpha(D_{t-1} - F_{t-1})$$
$$= 500 + 0.1(450 - 500) = 495 \text{ units}$$

(*b*) Arranging the procedure in tabular form, we have:

Week	Demand D_{t-1}	Old forecast F_{t-1}	Forecast error $(D_{t-1} - F_{t-1})$	Correction $\alpha(D_{t-1} - F_{t-1})$	New forecast (F_t) $F_{t-1} + \alpha(D_{t-1} - F_{t-1})$
Feb. 1	450	500	−50	−5	495
8	505	495	10	1	496
15	516	496	20	2	498
22	488	498	−10	−1	497
Mar. 1	467	497	−30	−3	494
8	554	494	60	6	500
15	510	500	10	1	501

In the accompanying example, an initial forecast value was available. If no previous forecast value is known, the "old forecast" starting point may be estimated or taken to be an average of some preceding periods.

SELECTION OF THE SMOOTHING CONSTANT

Some firms are in industries or produce products (such as style goods) that require a rapid and dramatic response to demand, whereas others are in more stable situations. A satisfactory value of α can generally be determined by trial-and-error testing of different smoothing constants to find one that has a good fit with past data. Some analysts recommend beginning with an α of 0.2 or 0.3 and watching the performance for a few months. Others suggest picking an α value that approximates "a length of moving average that makes sense" [**18**: 151]. The "correct" α value should facilitate scheduling by providing a reasonable reaction to demand without incorporating too much erratic fluctuation. An approximate equivalent to an arithmetic moving average, in terms of the degree of smoothing, can be estimated by [**12**]:

$$\alpha = \frac{2}{n + 1} \tag{6-20}$$

Thus, a seven-year moving average would correspond, roughly, to an α value of 0.25.

SEASONAL ADJUSTMENT TO EXPONENTIAL FORECAST

Where a seasonal pattern exists, it may be desirable to seasonally adjust an exponentially smoothed forecast, just as with a time series. The procedure is:

1 Deseasonalize the actual demand.

2 Compute a deseasonalized forecast.

3 Seasonalize (adjust) the forecast by multiplying by the seasonal index.

*ADJUSTED EXPONENTIAL SMOOTHING

The simple exponential smoothing model is highly flexible because the smoothing effect can be increased or decreased easily by lowering or raising the value of α. However, if a trend exists in the data the series will always lag behind the trend. Thus for an increasing trend the forecasts will be consistently low and for decreasing trends they will be consistently high. Simple exponential smoothing forecasts may be adjusted $(F_t)_{adj}$ for trend effects by adding a trend correction factor to the calculated forecast value (F_t):

$$(F_t)_{adj} = F_t + \frac{1 - \beta}{\beta} T_t \qquad (6\text{-}21)$$

where

$(F_t)_{adj}$ = trend-adjusted forecast

F_t = simple exponential smoothing forecast

β = smoothing constant for trend

T_t = exponentially smoothed trend factor

The value of the exponentially smoothed trend factor (T_t) is computed in a manner similar to that used in calculating the original forecast, and may be written as:

$$T_t = \beta(F_t - F_{t-1}) + (1 - \beta)T_{t-1} \qquad (6\text{-}22)$$

where T_{t-1} = last period trend factor.

* Although adjusted exponential smoothing is widely used, some firms prefer to use only simple exponential smoothing in conjunction with a tracking signal. If this section is specifically deleted (by your instructor on a prearranged basis), skip to the section on Validity, Control, and Use of Forecasts. Adjusted exponential smoothing problems in the problem section have been marked with an asterisk.

From Eq. (6-22), the trend factor (T_t) consists of a portion (β) of the trend evidenced from the current and previous forecasts ($F_t - F_{t-1}$) with the remainder $(1 - \beta)$ coming from the previous trend adjustment (T_{t-1}). An example will illustrate.

Example 6-9

Develop an adjusted exponential forecast for the firm in Example 6-8. Assume the initial trend adjustment factor (T_{t-1}) is zero and $\beta = 0.1$.

Solution

Week	D_{t-1}	F_{t-1}	F_t
Feb. 1	450	500	495
8	505	495	496
15	516	496	498
22	488	498	497
Mar. 1	467	497	494
8	554	494	500
15	510	500	501

The trend adjustment is simply an addition of a correction factor

$$\left[\frac{1-\beta}{\beta}\right] T_t$$

to the simple exponential forecast, so we will need the previously calculated forecast values. Letting the first $T_{t-1} = 0$ we have:

week 2/1:
$$T_t = \beta(F_t - F_{t-1}) + (1 - \beta)T_{t-1}$$
$$= 0.1(495 - 500) + (1 - 0.1)(0) = -0.50$$
$$(F_t)_{\text{adj}} = F_t + \frac{1-\beta}{\beta} T_t = 495 + \frac{1 - 0.1}{0.1}(-0.50) = 490.50$$

(The 490.50 is the adjusted forecast for week 2/8.)

week 2/8:
$$T_t = 0.1(496 - 495) + 0.9(-0.50) = -0.35$$
$$(F_t)_{\text{adj}} = 496 + 9(-0.35) = 492.85$$

Putting the remainder of the calculations in table form, the trend-adjusted forecast for the week of March 15 is $(F_t)_{\text{adj}} = 501.44$ compared to the simple exponential forecast of $F_t = 500$—not a large difference.

(1) Week	(2) Old forecast F_{t-1}	(3) Current trend $\beta(F_t - F_{t-1})$	(4) Previous trend $(1-\beta)T_{t-1}$	(5) Trend factor $T_t = (3) + (4)$	(6) Correction $\frac{1-\beta}{\beta} T_t$	(7) Adjusted forecast $F_t + \frac{1-\beta}{\beta} T_t$
Feb. 1	500	−0.50	0	−0.50	−4.50	490.50
8	495	0.10	−0.45	−0.35	−3.15	492.85
15	496	0.20	−0.32	−0.12	−1.08	496.92
22	498	−0.10	−0.11	−0.21	−1.89	495.11
Mar. 1	497	−0.30	−0.19	−0.49	−4.41	489.59
8	494	0.60	−0.44	0.16	1.44	501.44
15	500					

Simple and adjusted exponential smoothing are sometimes referred to as first-order and second-order smoothing, respectively. One reason they are widely used is that the forecast data can be computerized in a minimum amount of storage space and routinely updated. This advantage is important to firms with thousands of items in inventory. Since each current forecast value contains all past forecast and demand data in its properly weighted (exponential) manner there is no need to carry long records of historical data (as there is with arithmetic moving averages). It is an effective and efficient method of forecasting with a built-in means of tracking the average while discounting the erratic random fluctuations. Nevertheless, it is important to recognize that in some cases the sophistication gained by using adjusted exponential smoothing is simply not warranted. This is true if users (for example, shop schedulers) are *forced* to accept forecast values from a technique they do not understand.

VALIDITY, CONTROL, AND USE OF FORECASTS

One of the major concerns with any forecasting procedure relates to its reliability. While no methodology can do any better than utilize past and current information to estimate the future, some methods do a better job of minimizing forecast error than others. One common method of checking the validity of a forecasting model is to try it out on past data and see how well it would have predicted. A good fit to historical data does not, of course, guarantee accuracy in the future, but a bad fit should certainly be a warning signal.

There is some dispute as to what constitutes a valid model, but management is generally interested in results, and if a model yields reliable real-world forecasts it is a "good" model in their judgment. Figure 6-5 illustrates past use of selected forecasting models. The figure reports results of three surveys conducted over a 12-year period and represents 1,846 reporting firms in 1973. It reveals that the use of analytical and quantitative methods has increased over judgment and executive opinion. Although sales forecasters still make extensive use of managerial estimates and executive opinion, the use of exponential smoothing, correlation, and regression methods is increasing while the use of opinion methods is declining.

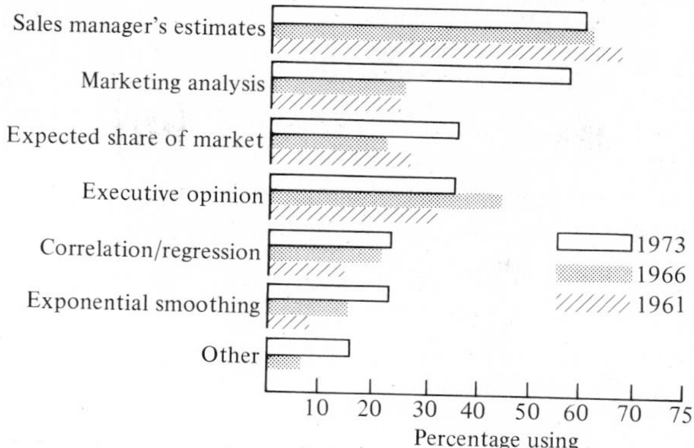

FIGURE 6-5 Past use of selected forecasting models

We noted previously that forecast accuracy is usually better for larger groups of items because the random variations of individual items are counterbalanced by offsetting variations of others. Measures of forecast accuracy are usually based on how much the actual demand values vary from predicted or average values. Both simple arithmetic totals and statistical measures of variation are commonly used to describe and control forecast error.

CONTROLS FOR SIMPLE AVERAGES

The time series and simple averages methods of forecasting basically track the one variable of interest (that is, these methods are univariate in nature). A simple measure of forecast error is to compute the deviation of the actual from the forecast values for that variable. The deviations will vary from plus to minus but they should tend to average out near zero if the forecast is on target.

A number of ways of establishing control limits about the forecast values have also been developed. Some of these are based on the range of difference and others on the standard deviation of values. Variations of actual values from the mean or average values can be quantified in terms of the standard deviation by:

$$S_F = \sqrt{\frac{\sum (\text{actual} - \text{forecast})^2}{n - 1}} = \sqrt{\frac{\sum (X - \overline{X})^2}{n - 1}}$$

where X is the actual individual demand value, $\overline{X}$ is the average or forecast demand value, and n is the number of periods in the average.

Much variation tends to be normally distributed about the mean, and if this is a reasonably valid assumption we might expect 95.5 percent of the actual demand values to be within two standard deviations of the average value, and 99.7 percent within three. When demand values occur outside these limits they may be indicative of an unusual event or a substantial change (or possibly an invalid model) and should be investigated. If the limits are based upon data from a sample of less than 30, the t rather than normal Z distribution applies. Values for the area under the t distribution are available in most statistical reference texts [**10, 13**].

CONTROLS FOR ASSOCIATIVE FORECASTS

The standard deviation of regression ($S_{Y.X}$) is the statistical measure of variation about the regression line and can be used as a means of control for forecasting methods involving two variables. In a manner similar to that used to establish reasonable limits for variation in demand about univariate averages, the probable limits for variation about the regression line can also be determined. Thus, we would expect 99.7 percent of the individual demand values to be within the control limits $Y_c \pm 3S_{Y.X}$ if the values are normally distributed about the regression line. When values fall outside these limits we assume the system is out of control, investigate, and take appropriate action.

CONTROLS FOR EXPONENTIAL SMOOTHING FORECASTS

Several control systems have been developed for exponentially smoothed forecasts. Some of the most straightforward and widely used systems make use of the same control concepts as used in other moving average forecasts. Often, however, the forecast error is measured in terms of the mean absolute deviation (MAD) rather than standard deviation. MAD is simply a measure of the average deviation of an actual from a forecast value, but it is easier to calculate than a standard deviation.

$$\text{MAD} = \frac{\sum |\text{actual} - \text{forecast}|}{N} \qquad (6\text{-}23)$$

where N is the number of periods.

MAD is related to the standard deviation by the approximation:

$$\sigma \cong 1.25 \text{ MAD} \qquad (6\text{-}24)$$

When the average deviation is divided into the cumulative deviation, the resultant is a "tracking signal."

$$\text{Tracking signal} = \frac{\text{cumulative deviation}}{\text{MAD}} \qquad (6\text{-}25)$$

The tracking signal tells how well the forecast is predicting actual values, for it yields a measurement of the consistent difference between actual and forecast values by expressing the cumulative deviation in terms of number of average deviations. If the cumulative deviation is, say, 1,500 units, whereas the average MAD is 200 units, then the tracking signal for the period is 1,500 divided by 200 = 7.5. Suppose next period's tracking signal is 7.6, then perhaps 7.8 in the following period. This would indicate that demand was consistently greater than the forecast. Similarly, a negative tracking signal would be indicative of demand that tended to be less than the forecast. A good forecast should have about as much positive (over) as negative (under) deviation, which would result in a low cumulative, or running sum of forecast error (RSFE).

Firms often set action limits for tracking signals so that when the tracking signal exceeds the limit the situation will be reviewed to determine if the forecast should be raised or lowered. If an action limit were set very low it would require too much review for items that were being satisfactorily forecast. A signal set too high would not provide timely response and would limit the usefulness of the forecasting system in managing inventories. An acceptable maxima for tracking signal values is from 4 to 8 (Plossl and Wight suggest 4 for high-value items and up to 8 for low-value items) [**12**: 107]. When the signal goes beyond this range, investigation and corrective action are called for.

The tracking signal is not only a practical control device but it is also a good measure of trends that deviate from a forecast. Oliver Wight, the noted inventory consultant, has pointed out that it is generally more useful to use a simple exponential smoothing model in combination with a tracking signal than it is to use the more complex trend-adjusted exponential smoothing model [**18**: 154].

The exponential smoothing technique also provides a means of continually updating the analyst's estimate of MAD. Thus, the current MAD_t is:

$$MAD_t = \alpha|\text{actual} - \text{forecast}| + (1 - \alpha)\,MAD_{t-1} \tag{6-26}$$

where α is a smoothing constant and higher values of α will make the current MAD_t more responsive to current forecast errors.

Other exponential smoothing systems also use a "smoothed-error" procedure, similar in concept to the forecasting procedure itself. The standard deviation of the smoothed error is sometimes related to the smoothed absolute error [**3**] or to the MAD value mentioned above. Control limits for the error are established and when they are exceeded the system can either signal the need for corrective action or switch to a more responsive level of smoothing [**8**]. Other systems for controlling the responsiveness of a forecasting system are based upon three levels of smoothing constants [**5**]. References in the chapter bibliography provide additional explanation of some of these methods [**3, 5, 8, 12, 15**]. The description of the Trigg and Leach model [**16**] and the comparison of adaptive forecasting techniques by Whybark [**17**] are worthy of special note. However, a discussion of them is beyond the scope of this text.

SUMMARY

Everyone anticipates the future, but some managers do a better job of forecasting it than others. The more reliable their forecasts, the better position they are in to guide future activities toward organizational goals.

Short-term and aggregate forecasts are generally more accurate than long-range and individual forecasts, but all types are important. They should incorporate the best judgments and information available. It is desirable to base forecasts upon objective and systematic analysis of data as much as possible, because this quantification forces more precision than do words or shadings in tone. On the other hand, quantification sometimes gives an illusion of accuracy which is unjustified and can be misleading.

Demand fluctuations present a firm with one of its greatest uncertainties and so they have received much attention in forecasting. While it is inherently impossible to forecast random fluctuations, various forecasting methodologies attempt to abstract trend and seasonal effects or patterns that can be associated with the action of related indicators.

Judgmental methods permit the incorporation of experience, but their subjectivity leaves little opportunity for analysis, control, or improvement. Time series methods chart the action of the subject variable (one variable *only*, such as demand) under the assumption that trend or seasonal patterns are a predictable function of time. Methods of deriving the trend component include (1) freehand curves, (2) moving average, (3) semiaverage, and (4) least squares. The semiaverage and least-squares methods yield forecasting equations which are valid insofar as past history is indicative of the future. When past data has a definite seasonal pattern, seasonal indexes should also be determined and applied to trend projections to render seasonalized (adjusted) trend values.

Regression and correlation methods rely upon the relationship of associated variables to make forecasts. A mathematical relationship is established via the normal equations or the coefficient of correlation. Then the action of an independent variable (in the case of regression) or associated variable (in the case of correlation) serves as a basis for prediction. Based upon an assumption (usually satisfactory) of normality, interval estimates can be made to add more precision to the forecasts of mean and individual values.

Exponential smoothing is a moving-average method but it includes exponential weighting which allows more recent data points to exert a stronger influence in the forecast. Simple exponential smoothing makes use of a smoothing constant (α) which essentially dictates how much weight should be given to the past versus the current demand; a small α value yields a strong smoothing effect. Adjusted exponential smoothing adds a trend correction factor which is again based upon a smoothed difference between the current forecast and the previous forecast. Exponential smoothing is widely used because it is readily adaptable and requires relatively little computer storage space.

Every forecasting system should have a means of tracking and controlling the forecast error. Common measures of variability are the standard deviation for univariate methods (that is, time series) and the standard deviation of regression for multivariate methods. Many firms using exponential smoothing have programmed their computers to calculate a tracking signal based upon mean average deviations (MADs) of actual from forecast values. When any variability or tracking signals exceed specified limits, investigative and corrective action should be taken.

Forecasts play a key role in determining material requirements that constitute inventories and in establishing production plans and schedules. We move on to these topics in the next three chapters.

SOLVED PROBLEMS

TIME SERIES ANALYSIS

1 A food processor uses a moving average to forecast next month's demand. Past actual demand (in units) is as shown in the accompanying table.

Month	Actual demand
43	105
44	106
45	110
46	110
47	114
48	121
49	130
50	128
51	137
52	

(*a*) Compute a simple five-month moving average to forecast demand for month 52.

(*b*) Compute a weighted three-month moving average where the weights are highest for the latest months and descend in order of 3, 2, 1.

Solution

(*a*)

$$\text{MA} = \frac{\sum X}{\text{number of periods}}$$

$$= \frac{114 + 121 + 130 + 128 + 137}{5} = 126 \text{ units}$$

(*b*)

$$\text{MA}_{\text{wt}} = \frac{\sum (\text{wt})(X)}{\sum \text{wt}}$$

where

wt		value		total
3	×	137	=	411
2	×	128	=	256
1	×	130	=	130
6				797

$$\therefore \text{MA}_{\text{wt}} = \frac{797}{6} = 133 \text{ units}$$

2 Given the demand data in Solved Prob. 1, use the semiaverage method
(*a*) to derive a trend equation centered on month 45, and
(*b*) to forecast the trend value for month 55.

Solution

(*a*) Dividing the data into two equal groups we compute means and slope.

$$\overline{Y}_A = \frac{105 + 106 + 110 + 110}{4} = 107.75$$

$$\overline{Y}_B = \frac{121 + 130 + 128 + 137}{4} = 129.00$$

$$b = \frac{\overline{Y}_B - \overline{Y}_A}{\text{no. years between}} = \frac{129.00 - 107.75}{5} = 4.25$$

$$Y_c = 107.75 + 4.25X \qquad \left(\begin{array}{l}\text{origin} = \text{1st day of month 45,} \\ X = \text{months, } Y = \text{monthly demand}\end{array}\right)$$

Note that since the average was computed from an even number of months it is centered between months 44 and 45. We can shift it to the middle of month 45 by adding one-half month to X:

$$Y_c = 107.75 + 4.25(X + 0.5)$$

$$Y_c = 109.87 + 4.25X \qquad \left(\begin{array}{l}\text{origin} = \text{month 45, } X = \text{months,} \\ Y = \text{monthly demand}\end{array}\right)$$

(*b*) Month 55 is now 10 units away from the origin:

$$Y_c = 109.87 + 4.25(10) = 152.0 \text{ units}$$

3 The following forecasting equation has been derived by a least-squares method to describe the shipments of welded aluminum tube.

$$Y_c = 10.27 + 1.65X \qquad (1972 = 0, X = \text{years}, Y = \text{tons/yr})$$

Rewrite the equation:
(*a*) shifting the origin to 1977
(*b*) expressing X units in months, retaining Y in tons/yr
(*c*) expressing X units in months, and Y in tons/month

Solution

(*a*) $Y_c = 10.27 + 1.65(X + 5)$

$= 18.52 + 1.65X \quad (1977 = 0,\ X = \text{years},\ Y = \text{tons/yr})$

(*b*) $Y_c = 10.27 + \dfrac{1.65X}{12}$

$= 10.27 + 0.14X \quad (\text{July 1, 1972} = 0,\ X = \text{months},\ Y = \text{tons/yr})$

(*c*) $Y_c = \dfrac{10.27 + 0.14X}{12}$

$= 0.86 + 0.01X \quad (\text{July 1, 1972} = 0,\ X = \text{months},\ Y = \text{tons/mo})$

REGRESSION AND CORRELATION

4 Given the following:

$$\sum X = 80 \qquad \sum Y = 1{,}200 \qquad n = 20 \qquad \sum (Y - Y_c)^2 = 7{,}200$$
$$\sum X^2 = 400 \qquad \sum Y^2 = 87{,}200 \qquad \sum XY = 5{,}600 \qquad \sum (Y - \bar{Y})^2 = 9{,}130$$

Find (*a*) linear regression equation, (*b*) $S_{Y.X}$, (*c*) r.

Solution

(*a*) $\sum Y = na \quad + b\sum X \rightarrow 1{,}200 = 20a + 80b$

$\sum XY = a\sum X + b\sum X^2 \rightarrow 5{,}600 = 80a + 400b$

$\therefore b = 10,\ a = 20$

$Y_c = 20 + 10X$

(*b*) $$S_{Y.X} = \sqrt{\frac{\sum (Y - Y_c)^2}{n - 2}} = \sqrt{\frac{7{,}200}{20 - 2}} = \sqrt{400} = 20$$

(*c*) $$r = \sqrt{1 - \frac{\sum (Y - Y_c)^2}{\sum (Y - \bar{Y})^2}} = \sqrt{1 - \frac{7{,}200}{9{,}130}} = \sqrt{0.21} = 0.46$$

EXPONENTIAL SMOOTHING

5 Lakeside Hospital has used a 9-month moving-average forecasting method to predict drug and surgical dressing inventory requirements. The actual demand

for one item is as shown in the accompanying table. Using the previous moving average data, convert to an exponential smoothing forecast for month 33.

Month	Demand
24	78
25	65
26	90
27	71
28	80
29	101
30	84
31	60
32	73

Solution

$$\text{MA} = \frac{\sum X}{\text{no. periods}} = \frac{78 + 65 + \cdots + 73}{9} = 78$$

$\therefore$ Assume $F_{t-1} = 78$

$$\text{Estimate } \alpha = \frac{2}{n+1} = \frac{2}{9+1} = 0.2$$

$$\begin{aligned} F_t &= F_{t-1} + \alpha(D_{t-1} - F_{t-1}) \\ &= 78 + 0.2(73 - 78) \\ &= 77 \text{ units} \end{aligned}$$

6 A shoe manufacturer, using exponential smoothing with $\alpha = 0.1$, has developed a January trend forecast of 400 units for a ladies' shoe. This brand has seasonal indexes of 0.80, 0.90, and 1.20 respectively for the first three months of the year. Assuming actual sales were 344 units in January and 414 units in February, what would be the seasonalized (adjusted) March forecast?

Solution [**12**: 40]

(*a*) Deseasonalize actual January demand:

$$\text{Demand}_{(D)} = \frac{344}{0.80} = 430 \text{ units}$$

(*b*) Compute the deseasonalized forecast:

$$\begin{aligned} F_t &= F_{t-1} + \alpha(D_{t-1} - F_{t-1}) \\ &= 400 + 0.1(430 - 400) = 403 \end{aligned}$$

(*c*) Seasonalized (adjusted) February forecast would be:

$$F_{t(sz)} = 403(0.90) = 363$$

Repeating for February we have,

(*a*) $$\text{Demand}_{(D)} = \frac{414}{0.90} = 460 \text{ units}$$

(*b*) $$F_t = 403 + 0.1(460 - 403) = 409$$

(*c*) $$F_{t(sz)} = 409(1.20) = 491$$

*7 (This problem is similar to Solved Prob. 1 except for exponential smoothing.) A food processor uses exponential smoothing (with $\alpha = 0.10$) to forecast next month's demand. Past (actual) demand in units and the simple exponential forecasts up to month 51 are shown in the accompanying table.

Month	Actual demand	Old forecast
43	105	100.00
44	106	100.50
45	110	101.05
46	110	101.95
47	114	102.46
48	121	103.61
49	130	105.35
50	128	107.82
51	137	109.84
52		

(*a*) Using simple exponential smoothing, forecast the demand for month 52.
(*b*) Suppose the firm wishes to start including a trend-adjustment factor of $\beta = 0.60$. If it assumes an initial trend adjustment of zero ($T_t = 0$) in month 50, what would be the value of $(F_t)_{\text{adj}}$ for month 52?
(*c*) Discuss the implications of a $\beta = 1.00$ trend constant.

Solution

Note that in this problem the smoothing constant for the original data ($\alpha = 0.10$) differs from the smoothing constant for the trend (0.60). We designate the trend constant as β.

(*a*) $F_t = F_{t-1} + \alpha(D_{t-1} - F_{t-1})$

$$= 109.84 + 0.1(137.00 - 109.84) = 112.56$$

(*b*) Forecast for month 51:

$$(F_t)_{\text{adj}} = F_t + \frac{1-\beta}{\beta} T_t$$

where

$$T_t = \beta(F_t - F_{t-1}) + (1 - \beta)T_{t-1}$$

$$= 0.6(109.84 - 107.82) + (1 - 0.6)0 = 1.21$$

$$(F_t)_{\text{adj}} = 109.84 + \left(\frac{1 - 0.6}{0.6}\right)(1.21) = 110.65$$

Forecast for month 52:

$$T_t = \beta(F_t - F_{t-1}) + (1 - \beta)T_{t-1}$$

$$= 0.6(112.56 - 109.84) + (1 - 0.6)(1.21) = 2.12$$

$$(F_t)_{\text{adj}} = F_t + \frac{1-\beta}{\beta} T_t$$

$$= 112.56 + \left(\frac{1 - 0.6}{0.6}\right)(2.12) = 113.98$$

(*c*) The trend correction T_t is based on the difference between the last two forecasts and not upon an independent evaluation of demand. Thus even though the trend correction is relatively large ($\beta = 0.6$), the initial smoothing ($\alpha = 0.1$) exerts a dominant effect. A value of $\beta = 1.0$ would correct the current simple exponential forecast by the total amount of the difference between the current (F_t) and previous (F_{t-1}) forecasts.

VALIDITY AND CONTROL OF FORECASTS

8 Use the Lakeside Hospital data of Solved Prob. 5 and compute:

(*a*) A three-month moving average (MA).

(*b*) The 90 percent control limits that could be expected for individual demand values (assuming a normal distribution).

Solution

(*a*) See the accompanying table.

Month	Actual demand	Three-month MA	Forecast demand	Deviation	(Deviation)^2
24	78				
25	65	77.7			
26	90	75.3			
27	71	83.3	78	−7	49
28	80	84.0	75	5	25
29	101	88.3	83	18	324
30	84	85.0	84	0	0
31	60	72.3	88	−28	784
32	73		85	−12	144
					1,326

(*b*) $S_F = \sqrt{\dfrac{\sum (\text{actual} - \text{forecast})^2}{n - 1}} = \sqrt{\dfrac{1{,}326}{6 - 1}} = 16.3$

Since $n < 30$, we must use the t distribution rather than the Z for the control limits. Referring to any standard statistics text we find that for $n - 1 = 5$ degrees of freedom at the 90 percent level, $t = 2.015$. The mean forecast value is:

$$\bar{X} = \frac{78 + 75 + 83 + 84 + 88 + 85}{6} = 82.1$$

$$\therefore \text{Control limits} = \bar{X} \pm tS_F$$

$$= 82.1 \pm 2.015(16.3)$$

$$= 48.9 \text{ to } 114.9$$

Note that the control limits explicitly recognize the variability in this data and, in turn, the uncertainty associated with trying to forecast it.

9 The moving average forecast and actual demand for a hospital drug is as shown in the accompanying table. Compute the tracking signal and comment on the forecast accuracy.

Month	Actual demand	Forecast demand	Deviation	Cumulative deviation
27	71	78	−7	−7
28	80	75	5	−2
29	101	83	18	16
30	84	84	0	16
31	60	88	−28	−12
32	73	85	−12	−24

Solution

The deviation and cumulative deviation have already been computed above:

$$\therefore \text{ MAD} = \frac{\sum |\text{actual} - \text{forecast}|}{N}$$

$$= \frac{7 + 5 + 18 + 0 + 28 + 12}{6}$$

$$= 11.7$$

$$\text{Tracking signal} = \frac{\text{cumulative deviation}}{\text{MAD}} = \frac{-24}{11.7} = -2.05 = |2.05|$$

The demand exhibits substantial variation but a tracking signal as low as 2.05 (that is, ≤ 4) would not suggest any action at this time.

QUESTIONS

6-1 Why are forecasts important to organizations?

6-2 Briefly summarize (in one or two sentences each) the *essence* of the following forecasting methodologies: (*a*) judgmental, (*b*) time series, (*c*) regression and correlation, and (*d*) exponential smoothing.

6-3 What determines whether a forecast should be short range or long range?

6-4 The manager of a local firm says, "The forecasting techniques are more trouble than they are worth. I don't forecast at all and I'm doing 20 percent more business than last year." Comment.

6-5 How do forecasting techniques predict the value of random fluctuations in demand? What effect do moving averages have on short-term fluctuations?

6-6 What do you see as the main problem with judgmental forecasts? Are they ever any better than "objective" methods?

6-7 Identify the classical components of a time series and indicate how each is accounted for in forecasting.

6-8 Regression and correlation are both termed "associative" methods of forecasting. Explain how they are similar in this respect and also how they are different.

6-9 A firm uses exponential smoothing with a very high value of α. What does this indicate with respect to the emphasis it places on past data?

6-10 Explain what is meant by "tracking" a forecast. How does tracking relate to the concept of forecast reliability?

PROBLEMS

TIME SERIES ANALYSIS

1 A sugar beet processing cooperative is committed to accepting beets from local producers and has experienced the following supply pattern (in thousands of tons/yr and rounded).

Year	Tons	Year	Tons
1968	100	1973	400
1969	100	1974	400
1970	200	1975	600
1971	600	1976	800
1972	500	1977	800

The operations manager would like to project a trend to determine what facility additions will be required by 1982.

(*a*) Graph the data and connect the points by straight-line segments.

(*b*) Sketch in a freehand curve and extend it to 1982. What would be your 1982 forecast based upon the curve?

(*c*) Compute a three-year moving average and plot it as a dotted line on your graph.

2 Use the data of problem 1 and the semiaverage method to develop a forecasting equation, centered upon 1970.

(*a*) State the equation, complete with signature.

(*b*) Use your equation to estimate the trend value for 1982.

3 Use the data of problem 1 and the normal equations to develop a least-squares line of best fit. Omit the year 1968.

(*a*) State the equation, complete with signature, when the origin is 1973.

(*b*) Use your equation to estimate the trend value for 1982.

4 A trend equation describing plastic-pipe shipments was derived by a semi-average method and found to be:

$$Y_c = 5.2 + 1.7X \qquad (1969 = 0, X = \text{years}, Y = \text{tons})$$

Convert the equation to a 1972 = 0 base.

5 A forecasting equation is of the form:

$$Y_c = 720 + 144X \qquad (1979 = 0, X \text{ unit} = 1 \text{ yr}, Y = \text{annual sales})$$

(*a*) Forecast the annual sales rate for 1979 and also for one year later.

(*b*) Change the time (X) scale to months and forecast the annual sales rate at July 1, 1979, and also at one year later.
(*c*) Change the sales (Y) scale to monthly and forecast the monthly sales rate at July 1, 1979, and also at one year later.

6 An analysis of past data on the use of capacitors in an assembly operation revealed the following time series equation.

$$Y_c = 144 + 72X \qquad \begin{pmatrix} \text{Origin} = 1979,\ X \text{ unit} = 1 \text{ yr} \\ Y = \text{annual consumption} \end{pmatrix}$$

(*a*) On what day is the equation now centered?
(*b*) State the equation that would correspond to a signature:

(Origin = July 1, 1979, X unit = 1 month, Y = monthly consumption)

(*c*) Modify the equation as required and use it to forecast the *annual* consumption rate (Y = annual consumption) during September 1979.

7 Data collected on the monthly demand for a housewares item were as shown in the accompanying chart.

January	100
February	90
March	80
April	150
May	240
June	320
July	300
August	280
September	220

(*a*) Plot the data as a one-month moving average.
(*b*) Plot a five-month moving average as a dotted line.
(*c*) What conclusion can you draw with respect to length of moving average versus smoothing effect?
(*d*) Assume the 12-month moving average centered on July was 231. What is the value of the ratio to moving average that would be used in computing a seasonal index?

8 An equation was developed to forecast demand for a chemical product as follows.

$$Y_c = 500 + 10X \qquad (1972 = 0,\ X = \text{years},\ Y = \text{units of annual demand})$$

The demand is seasonal and the indexes for October, November, and December are 0.80, 0.90, and 1.10 respectively.
(*a*) Forecast annual demand for 1982.
(*b*) Convert the X unit to months and the Y unit to monthly demand and

state the new equation complete with signature. (If necessary, shift the origin so that it is in mid-July 1972.)

(*c*) Forecast the trend value for November 1980.

(*d*) Forecast the seasonalized (adjusted) value for November 1980.

9 The data shown in the accompanying table gives the number of lost-time accidents for the Cascade Lumber Company over the past seven years. (*Note:* The number of employees is shown for reference only. You will not need it to solve this problem.)

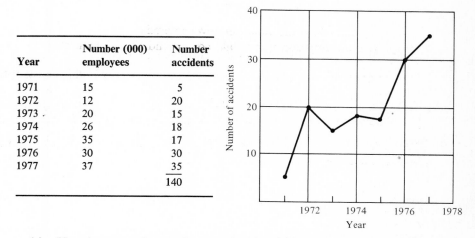

Year	Number (000) employees	Number accidents
1971	15	5
1972	12	20
1973	20	15
1974	26	18
1975	35	17
1976	30	30
1977	37	35
		140

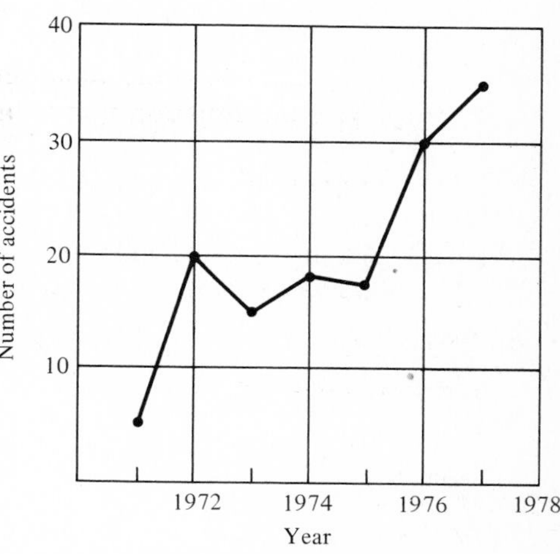

(*a*) Use the normal equations to develop a linear time series equation for forecasting the number of accidents. State the equation complete with signature.

(*b*) Use your equation to forecast the number of accidents in 1980.

REGRESSION AND CORRELATION

10 The data shown in the accompanying table gives the number of lost-time accidents for the Cascade Lumber Company over the past seven years. Some additional calculations are included to help you answer the following questions.

Year	X no.(000) employees	Y no. accidents	X^2	Y^2	XY	$(Y - \bar{Y})$	$(Y - \bar{Y})^2$	Y_c	$(Y - Y_c)$	$(Y - Y_c)^2$
1971	15	5	225	25	75	−15	225	13.38	−8.38	70.22
1972	12	20	144	400	240	0	0	11.40	8.60	73.96
1973	20	15	400	225	300	−5	25	16.68	−1.68	2.82
1974	26	18	676	324	468	−2	4	20.64	−2.64	6.97
1975	35	17	1,225	289	595	−3	9	26.58	−9.58	91.78
1976	30	30	900	900	900	10	100	23.28	6.72	45.16
1977	37	35	1,369	1,225	1,295	15	225	27.90	7.10	50.41
	175	140	4,939	3,388	3,873		588			341.32

(a) Use the normal equations to develop a linear regression equation for forecasting the number of accidents on the basis of the number of employees. State the equation.
(b) Use the equation to forecast the number of accidents when the number of employees is 33(000).

11 Given the data of problem 10, answer the following questions:
(a) What is the standard deviation of regression?
(b) What percent of the variation in number of accidents is explained by the employment level?
(c) What is the correlation coefficient between number of employees and number of accidents?
(d) (Optional) Is the correlation significant at the 5 percent level?

12 The two operations managers of a plastics firm have the responsibility of scheduling intermittent production runs of various grades of plastic pipe so as to maintain factory inventories at specified levels. They have formulated their own index (X)—from published construction and employment data—which they feel may be useful in anticipating demand (tons) of class 160 PVC pipe Y.

X **index**	Y **demand (tons)**
3	6
6	7
2	4
5	10
4	8

(a) Compute the regression equation.
(b) Determine the forecast values (Y_c) for each X and $\sum (Y - Y_c)^2$.
(c) Find $S_{Y.X}$.
(d) What percent of the variation in demand is explained by this index?
(e) Find r.

13 The Carpet Cleaner Company is attempting to do a better job of inventory management by predicting the number of vacuums the company will sell per week on the basis of the number of customers who respond to magazine advertisements in an earlier week. On the basis of a sample of $n = 102$ weeks the following data were obtained.

$$a = 25 \qquad \sum (Y - Y_c)^2 = 22{,}500$$
$$b = 0.10 \qquad \sum (Y - \bar{Y})^2 = 45{,}000$$

(a) Provide a point estimate of the number of vacuums sold per week when 80 inquiries were received in the earlier week.
(b) Calculate the 95.5 percent confidence limits for the *mean* number of vacuums sold per week when 80 inquiries were received earlier.

(*c*) State the value of the coefficient of determination.

14 A recreation operations planner has had data collected on automobile traffic at a selected location on an interstate highway in hopes that the information can be used to predict weekday demand for state-operated campsites 200 miles away. Random samples of 32 weekdays during the camping season resulted in data from which the following expression was developed:

$$Y_c = 18 + 0.02X$$

where X is the number of automobiles passing the location and Y is the number of campsites demanded that day. In addition, the unexplained variation $\sum (Y - Y_c)^2 = 1{,}470$ and the total variation $\sum (Y - \bar{Y})^2 = 4{,}080$.

(*a*) What is the dependent variable (in words)?
(*b*) What is the value of the standard deviation of regression, $S_{Y.X}$?
(*c*) Develop a point estimate of the demand for campsites on a day when 14,100 automobiles pass the selected location.

15 Given the data from the previous problem:

(*a*) What is the value of the coefficient of determination?
(*b*) Explain, in words, the meaning of the coefficient of determination.
(*c*) What is the value of the coefficient of correlation?

16 A management analyst has randomly selected 10 demand regions and determined population values in order to establish a relationship that will help to predict sales. The resultant linear regression equation is:

$$Y_c = 2.02 + 0.80X$$

In addition the analyst has determined that the unexplained variation is 0.76 and the total variation is 4.00. All population values are in ten thousands and sales in \$1,000.

(*a*) Identify (in words) the dependent and independent variables.
(*b*) Give a point estimate of demand for a region with a population of 60,000.
(*c*) Calculate the coefficient of correlation and explain its meaning.
(*d*) What relationship, in general, does *any* regression curve describe and how does regression differ from correlation?

17 Solved Prob. 4 shows the computation of $S_{Y.X}$ and r via the "definitional" type of equations. Use the data given to compute (*a*) $S_{Y.X}$ and (*b*) r, using alternate methods.

EXPONENTIAL SMOOTHING

18 The production supervisor at a fiberboard plant uses a simple exponential smoothing technique ($\alpha = 0.2$) to forecast demand. In April, the forecast was for 20 shipments and actual demand was for 20 shipments. Actual demand in May and June was 25 and 26 shipments respectively. Forecast the value for July.

19 A university registrar has adopted a simple exponential smoothing model ($\alpha = 0.4$) to forecast enrollments during the three regular terms (excluding summer) with the results shown in the accompanying table.

Year	Quarter	Actual enrollment (000)	Old forecast (000)	Forecast error (000)	Correction (000)	New forecast (000)
1	1st	20.50	20.00	0.5	0.20	20.20
	2d	21.00				
	3d	19.12				
2	1st	20.06				
	2d	22.00				
	3d					

(*a*) Use the data to develop an enrollment forecast for the third quarter of year 2.
(*b*) What would be the effect of increasing the smoothing constant to 1.0?

20 A firm producing photochemicals plans to use simple exponential smoothing to forecast weekly demand and has collected the past data shown. Assuming a first-week forecast of 20 units

Week	Demand
1	30
2	34
3	22
4	16
5	10
6	10
7	14
8	20
9	30
10	36
11	30
12	10
13	12
14	20
15	30

(*a*) Compute the forecast values for an $\alpha = 0.1$
(*b*) Compute the forecast values for an $\alpha = 0.5$.
(*c*) Plot the actual demand and the forecasted demands from (*a*) and (*b*) above.
(*d*) Comment on the difference in the reaction rate for $\alpha = 0.1$ and $\alpha = 0.5$.

Round each new forecast value to one digit beyond the decimal point.

21 A mattress company has been using a 12-month moving average to forecast monthly sales but wishes to convert to a simple exponential smoothing model. The current month's forecast is for 950 mattresses.

(*a*) If actual demand is 1,000, what should be the forecast demand for next month?

(*b*) If actual demand for the next month is 1,010, what should be the following month's forecast?

***22** A furniture company has developed a seasonal index where each month is expressed as a percent of total annual sales and March = 8.0 percent, April = 10.0 percent, May = 9.5 percent. The old forecast sales are for an average of 500 chairs per month, and the firm uses an alpha of 0.1. Prepare a seasonalized (adjusted) March forecast, then assume actual March sales were 420 and develop a seasonalized simple exponential forecast for April.

23 In Examples 6-8 and 6-9, assume the actual demand for the next three weeks in the sequence is March 22 = 561, March 29 = 587, April 5 = 615.

(*a*) Extend the simple exponential forecast to cover these periods.

*(*b*) Extend the adjusted exponential forecast to cover these periods.

***24** In using an adjusted exponential forecasting model, a government agency found the simple exponential forecast (F_t) for February to be equal to 500 units. The agency is using a trend-smoothing constant of $\beta = 0.3$ and has developed a trend-adjustment factor of $T_t = 120$ (based on actual January data). What is the appropriate adjusted demand forecast value for February?

25 A firm producing photochemicals has a weekly demand pattern as shown in problem 20. Using a smoothing constant of $\alpha = 0.5$ for both original data and trend, and beginning with week 1, (*a*) compute the simple exponentially smoothed forecast, and *(*b*) compute the trend-adjusted exponentially smoothed forecast for the first five periods.

26 Two "experienced" managers have resisted the introduction of a computerized exponential smoothing system, claiming that their judgmental forecasts are "much better than any impersonal computer could do." Their past record of prediction is as shown in the accompanying table.

Week	Actual demand	Forecast demand
1	4,000	4,500
2	4,200	5,000
3	4,200	4,000
4	3,000	3,800
5	3,800	3,600
6	5,000	4,000
7	5,600	5,000
8	4,400	4,800
9	5,000	4,000
10	4,800	5,000

(*a*) Compute S_X.
(*b*) Compute 95.5 percent control limits for the forecast, assuming the forecast errors are normally distributed.
(*Hint:* Since $n < 30$, the t rather than the normal distribution applies. When $n = 10$, for 95.5 percent limits, $t = 2.26$.)

27 Using the data from problem 26 above:
(*a*) Compute MAD.
(*b*) Compute the tracking signal.
(*c*) Based on your calculations, is the judgmental system performing satisfactorily?

CROSSWORD PUZZLE

Copy and complete the puzzle using the clues given below. The initial letter of each word is located by an r,c (row, column) designation.

Across

1-1 The type of equation that results from solving the two normal equations for a and b.
1-8 A time series factor that describes long-term swings about a trend line.
2-13 The number of dependent variables in a simple linear regression model.
3-1 When the exponential smoothing constant is low, ______ weight is given to past than to recent data.
3-9 The measure that results from computing the deviation of actual from forecast values. (Also, a mistake.)
5-5 Decisions concerning the purchase of materials, setting of inventory levels, and adjusting of employment all represent potential ______ of forecasts.
5-10 Simulation models demonstrate the ______ of changing various levels of variables in a model.
6-1 A term that is attributed to forecast data that is based upon factual, objective observation. (Also, one of three forms under which matter can exist.)
6-8 A preposition describing where a computer operator sits relative to a control console.
7-8 A word (with letters in reverse order) describing the type of deviation of regression designated by the symbol $S_{y.x}$.
8-1 The normal equations yield a line of best ______ through the data.
9-5 Letters describing a common measure of forecast error based upon absolute rather than standardized values.
9-9 The first three letters describing a type of factor that adjusts simple exponential smoothing forecasts for trend affects.
9-13 The kind of note an analyst gives the boss after the analyst loses the $20 bet that his or her forecast is correct.
11-1 The manner in which past data is weighted as it enters into an exponential smoothing forecast.
12-8 Symbols designating one who is qualified to care for managers who put *too* much faith in forecasting.
13-1 The abbreviation for the type of exponential smoothing that takes trend effects into account.

13-7 Correlation is a means of expressing the ______ of relationship between two or more variables.

14-12 In simple exponential smoothing, the smoothing constant is symbolized by ______ ______ (word, symbol).

15-1 Trend, cyclical, seasonal, and random are components of this kind of series.

15-6 The collective group of mathematical and/or statistical equations (such as simulation, regression) that describe the essence of a demand situation without actually duplicating reality.

15-12 The fact that simple exponential smoothing does not correct for trend should be evident from the equation which has ______ ______ (word, symbol).

Down

1-1 The points where action is called for when a tracking signal exceeds an acceptable maxima. Sometimes called action or control ______.

8-1 An estimate of the occurrence of uncertain future events or levels of activity.

6-2 An anagram for Oregon Technical Institute, where one can learn to use computerized forecasting programs.
1-3 The name given to a set of equations which yield a line of best fit.
8-3 What happens to a signal to cause it to generate action. (Also a journey, or to stumble.)
4-5 A widely used, but relatively subjective method of forecasting. (This spelling includes an "e" that is not usually included.)
2-7 What is done to time series data to simplify the calculation of coefficients a and b.
5-8 The emotional state of an analyst who fails to detect the seasonal component of a forecast (opposite of glad).
11-8 A long-term secular movement.
6-9 The kind of signal that results from dividing the cumulative sum of the (actual-forecast) values by MAD.
1-10 A freehand line drawn smoothly through a series of data points.
5-11 Forecasts can be useful to almost any competitive firm as well as to local, state, and ______ government organizations.
12-12 In the semiaverage method, data is divided into two groups and one of these is computed for each group.
1-13 A coefficient between -1 and $+1$ that tells how well a linear or other equation describes a relationship between two or more variables of equal status.
14-13 The answer to the question, "Is there any correlation?" when $r = 0$.
1-14 An article in the sentence, "Forecasting is not totally ______ art."
14-14 The two Greek symbols used in exponential smoothing models.
1-15 A method of fitting trends to data that yields a line of best fit.

BIBLIOGRAPHY

[1] ABRAMOWITZ, I.: *Production Management*, Ronald Press Company, New York, 1967.

[2] BRIGHT, JAMES R. (ed.): *Technological Forecasting for Industry and Government: Methods and Applications*, Prentice-Hall, Englewood Cliffs, New Jersey, 1968.

[3] BROWN, ROBERT G.: *Decision Rules for Inventory Management*, Holt, Rinehart and Winston, New York, 1967.

[4] BUFFA, ELWOOD S.: *Modern Production Management*, John Wiley & Sons, New York, 1973.

[5] CHOW, WEN M.: "Adaptive Control of the Exponential Smoothing Constant," *Journal of Industrial Engineering*, vol. 16, no. 5, September–October 1965, pp. 314–317.

[6] GARRETT, LEONARD J., AND MILTON SILVER: *Production Management Analysis*, Harcourt, Brace & World, New York, 1973.

[7] GRAYSON, C. JACKSON: *Decisions Under Uncertainty*, Harvard University Division of Research, Boston, Massachusetts, 1960.

[8] GROFF, GENE K., AND JOHN F. MUTH: *Operations Management: Analysis for Decisions*, Richard D. Irwin, Homewood, Illinois, 1972.

[9] HOFFMAN, THOMAS R.: *Production: Management and Manufacturing Systems*, Wadsworth Publishing Company, Belmont, California, 1971.

[10] NEWTON, BYRON L.: *Statistics for Business*, Science Research Associates, Palo Alto, California, 1973.

[11] OLSEN, ROBERT A.: *Manufacturing Management: A Quantitative Approach*, International Textbook Company, Scranton, Pennsylvania, 1968.

[12] PLOSSL, G. W., AND O. W. WIGHT: *Production and Inventory Control*, Prentice-Hall, Englewood Cliffs, New Jersey, 1967.

[13] RICHMOND, SAMUEL B.: *Statistical Analysis*, Ronald Press Company, New York, 1964.

[14] RIGGS, JAMES L.: *Production Systems: Planning, Analysis and Control*, John Wiley & Sons, New York, 1970.

[15] SHORE, BARRY: *Operations Management*, McGraw-Hill Book Company, New York, 1973.

[16] TRIGG, D. W., AND A. G. LEACH: "Exponential Smoothing With An Adaptive Rate," *Operations Research Quarterly*, March 1967, pp. 53–59.

[17] WHYBARK, D. CLAY: "A Comparison of Adaptive Forecasting Techniques," *The Logistics Transportation Review*, vol. 8, no. 3, January 1973, pp. 13–26.

[18] WIGHT, OLIVER W.: *Production and Inventory Management in the Computer Age*, Cahners Books, Boston, Massachusetts, 1974.

CHAPTER

7

Inventory Control

HANDLING UNCERTAINTIES VIA USE OF STANDARD STATISTICAL DISTRIBUTIONS

INVENTORY LEVELS UNDER NORMALLY DISTRIBUTED DEMAND
CORRECTIONS FOR DIFFERENT FORECAST AND LEAD TIME INTERVALS
INTERACTION OF DEMAND AND LEAD TIME UNCERTAINTIES
USE OF OTHER DISTRIBUTIONS AND UNCERTAINTY ADJUSTMENTS

MATERIAL REQUIREMENTS PLANNING (MRP) SYSTEMS

MRP FOR INVENTORIES AND SCHEDULING
PRIORITIES AND CAPACITY
HOW MRP SYSTEMS WORK

INVENTORY CONTROL SYSTEMS

ABC ANALYSIS
FIXED-ORDER QUANTITY SYSTEM
FIXED-ORDER INTERVAL SYSTEM
BASE STOCK SYSTEM
COMPUTERIZED MRP INVENTORY SYSTEMS

INTERNATIONAL INVENTORY MANAGEMENT

SUMMARY
SOLVED PROBLEMS
QUESTIONS
PROBLEMS
CASE: BEVERLY BROTHERS FURNITURE COMPANY
BIBLIOGRAPHY

Inventories are one of the major assets of most firms, ranging from perhaps 25 percent to 75 percent of their current assets, depending upon the firm and the type of industry. Along with plant and equipment, inventories often constitute the bulk of the asset value of an organization. The individual responsible for management of these assets is usually the operations manager.

Inventory management has been the key to the success of many firms and the cause of failure of numerous others. Insufficient inventories hamper production and fail to generate adequate sales, whereas excessive inventories adversely affect the firm's cash flows and liquidity position. From either perspective, poor inventory management can present a serious challenge to the viability of an organization and can sometimes have a disastrous effect on its solvency.

The problems of inventory management cannot simply be ignored in the hope that they will go away. Neither can one any longer rely on intuitive methods of establishing order quantities and setting inventory stock levels. The competitive business world and responsible public administrators will simply not permit this. Someone must intelligently set policies, establish guidelines for inventory levels, and ensure that appropriate control systems are functioning properly.

The purpose of this chapter is to gain an understanding of the basic theory of inventory control and, through examples, learn how this theory can be realistically applied to improve inventory management. We begin with the definition and purpose of inventories, look briefly at their cost components, and then take up the questions of what quantities to order (or to produce) and when to order them. The amount of inventory required (demand) and the delivery time (lead time) are two of the major uncertainties associated with inventory management and so we go into some depth in studying how to cope with these uncertainties. We conclude the chapter by examining the major types of inventory control systems, with special emphasis on material requirements planning (MRP) systems.

DEFINITION AND PURPOSE

INVENTORY

An *inventory* is an idle resource that possesses economic value [**4**: 377]. Inventories are usually in the form of raw materials, semifinished goods used in the production process, or finished products ready for delivery to consumers. We typically associate them with manufacturing and distribution activities. Service industries are often unable to inventory their final products, although they must manage their raw materials and supplies inventories just as any other organization. An airline company, for example, may have the seating capacity to provide a transportation service but lack the demand necessary to create the end product (final inventory) of a transportation service. Unused labor or capital is also an idle resource and in this sense it is essentially an inventory, although we do not normally refer to it as such.

Adequate inventories facilitate production activities and help to assure customers of good service. On the other hand, carrying inventories ties up working capital and can be costly. The major problem of inventory management thus consists of trying to achieve an optimal balance between the advantages of having inventories (or the losses that may be expected from not having adequate inventories) and the costs of carrying them.

Since the total supply of resources controlled by an organization is limited, the level of inventories of any specific resource (such as various materials, labor, capital) will necessarily affect levels of other resources. Thus, if inventories are necessary to provide a certain level of service, it is essential that this level be defined in accordance with organization's objectives and policy. Inventory levels and controls should therefore be managed from a systems perspective taking into account the total organizational framework.

ACCOUNTING FOR INVENTORIES

Because inventories constitute such a large part of the assets of an organization, the method of valuing them can have a significant effect upon stated profits. In the past, many companies have figured inventory value on a first-in, first-out (FIFO) basis, assuming that the oldest inventory (first in) is the first to be used (first out). Others use an average cost method, and some value inventories at the lower of cost or market value.

During the mid 1970s, the high rate of worldwide inflation pushed the value of inventories (and almost everything else) up so rapidly that firms realized significant "inventory profits" simply by selling lower-cost inventory at inflated prices. This tended to be misleading because it did not match current costs with current revenues. In order to report more realistic financial results, a number of firms switched to last-in, first-out (LIFO) accounting methods. LIFO assumes that the value of an item leaving inventory is its replacement cost and eliminates the otherwise taxable "phantom profits" of a company during inflationary periods.

PURPOSE OF INVENTORIES

Inventories serve a multitude of purposes including the following.

1 They aid continuous production by ensuring that inputs are always available and economic production runs can be made.

2 They facilitate intermittent production of several products on the same facilities (even though demand may be relatively constant for each product).

3 They decouple successive stages in processing a product so that downtime in one stage does not stop the entire process.

4 They help level production activities, stabilize employment, and improve labor relations by storing human and machine effort.

5 They provide a means of hedging against future price and delivery uncertainties, such as strikes, price increases, and inflation.

6 They provide a means of obtaining economic lot sizes and gaining quantity discounts.

7 They service customers with varying demands and in various locations by maintaining an adequate supply to meet their immediate and seasonal needs.

NATURE OF INVENTORIES: INDEPENDENT AND DEPENDENT DEMAND

If inventories are to achieve the purposes listed earlier, someone must decide *how much* to order and *when* the inventory is required. Those decisions are the responsibility of the inventory or production control manager, and we shall examine them both in this chapter.

The "how much" question is largely a function of costs, and our inquiry here will extend to the concept of an economic order quantity. The "when to order" question is a function of the firm's forecast or scheduled requirements. If the item is a finished product and has a demand that is "independent" of other items, an order point (or reorder point) technique can help to answer the question. On the other hand, most items brought into inventory in manufacturing firms are components or subassemblies of finished products. Their demand is "dependent" upon the finished product demand, and although the finished product demand may be uncertain, the requirements for components vis-à-vis other components are fixed by design. There is no need to consider each component as an entity with independent demand characteristics—in fact, it is better not to do so. In this situation, the "when to order" question is best answered by a material requirements planning (MRP) technique.

In the past, the economic order quantity and order point methodology was tried (sometimes disastrously) on about every type of inventory that existed. Only since the mid 1960s, when Dr. Joseph A. Orlicky of IBM proposed the "independent/dependent" principle, has a workable formal inventory planning system been feasible for high-volume dependent items [**6**]. As you may have surmised, this feasibility is linked directly to the availability of the digital computer.

We shall take up both the order point and MRP responses to the "when" question as we progress through this chapter. But first, we turn to the "how much" question, and this necessitates some knowledge of inventory costs. The "how much" question and its precise mathematical (EOQ) solution has been overemphasized in the past, for in many situations order quantity is not nearly as important as order timing. Nevertheless, an understanding of the costs associated with inventories is very important.

COSTS ASSOCIATED WITH INVENTORIES

The problem of balancing costs of less-than-adequate versus more-than-adequate inventory is a complex one due to the numerous and sometimes intangible costs that are relevant. Inadequate inventory can result in costs due to production delays and inefficiencies, as well as lost orders or even lost customers. These costs are often very difficult to measure. More-than-adequate inventories result in excessive expenditures to hold the inventory. The major tangible costs associated with inventory management are often classified as follows:

1. *Ordering and setup costs* These include the clerical costs of ordering inventory as well as setting up equipment for the firm to produce its own inventory. These costs/unit often decrease relative to the quantity ordered or produced.
2. *Carrying costs* These include the interest on invested capital, handling and storage, insurance and taxes, obsolescence, spoilage, and any system costs such as data processing.
3. *Purchase cost* This cost consists of the actual price paid for the item or the labor, material, and overhead charges necessary to produce it.

ECONOMIC ORDER QUANTITIES

An optimal inventory policy is one that would provide adequate inventory levels when needed at the minimum total cost of ordering, carrying, and purchase.

TOTAL COSTS AND THE EOQ EQUATION

The total cost (TC) of inventory is the sum of the cost of ordering, plus the cost of carrying, plus the purchase cost. If we let D = demand in units on an annual basis, C_o = cost to prepare an order, C_c = cost to carry a unit in stock for a given time period, P = purchase cost, Q = lot size, and $Q/2$ = average inventory, then the relationship can be expressed mathematically as:

Total cost = ordering cost + carrying cost + purchase cost

where

$$\text{ordering cost} = \left(\frac{C_o\ \$}{\text{order}}\right)\left(\frac{\text{order}}{Q\text{ units}}\right)\left(\frac{D\text{ units}}{\text{yr}}\right)$$

$$\text{carrying cost} = \left(\frac{C_c\ \$}{\text{unit-yr}}\right)\left(\frac{Q\text{ units}}{2}\right)$$

$$\text{purchase cost} = \left(\frac{P\ \$}{\text{unit}}\right)\left(\frac{D\text{ units}}{\text{yr}}\right)$$

$$\therefore \text{TC} = C_o \frac{1}{Q} D + C_c \frac{Q}{2} + PD \qquad (7\text{-}1)$$

Differentiating with respect to the order quantity Q yields the slope of the TC curve. (*Note:* Those whose calculus is a bit rusty may skip down to Eq. 7-2 or refer to Solved Prob. *1 for the differentiation explanation.)

$$\frac{d\text{TC}}{dQ} = -C_oDQ^{-2} + \frac{C_cQ^o}{2} + 0$$

Setting this first derivative equal to zero identifies the point where the TC is a minimum.

$$0 = -\frac{C_oD}{Q^2} + \frac{C_cQ^o}{2} + 0$$

$$\therefore Q = \text{EOQ} = \sqrt{\frac{2C_oD}{C_c}} \qquad (7\text{-}2)$$

Eq. (7-2) is known as the economic order quantity (EOQ) or economic lot size (ELS) equation. Note that although the purchase price P is an important component of total cost, the term drops out upon differentiating. Thus, so long as the purchase price does not vary with the quantity ordered, it should not directly affect the decision as to what is the most economical lot size to purchase. Figure 7-1 describes the relationship between the relevant ordering and carrying costs. Note also that the total cost curve is relatively flat in the area of the EOQ, so small changes in the amount ordered do not have a significant effect on total costs.

Once the economic order quantity Q has been determined, the minimum inventory cost can be computed by substituting this Q value into the total cost Equation (7-1). The number of orders per year required is:

$$\text{Orders/yr} = \frac{D \text{ units/yr}}{Q \text{ units/order}} = \frac{D}{Q} \qquad (7\text{-}3)$$

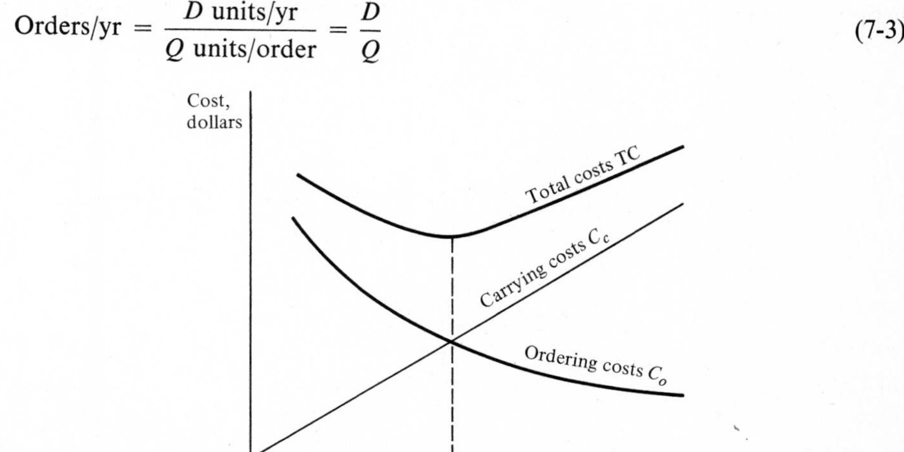

FIGURE 7-1 Economic order quantity curve

Example 7-1

Overland Motors uses 25,000 gear assemblies each year and purchases them at \$1.40 each. If it costs \$50 to process and receive an order and inventory can be carried at a cost of \$.10/unit-yr;

(*a*) How many assemblies should be ordered at a time?

(*b*) How many orders/yr should be placed?

Solution

(*a*) $$\text{EOQ} = \sqrt{\frac{2C_oD}{C_c}} = \sqrt{\frac{2(50)(25{,}000)}{0.10}} = 5{,}000 \text{ assemblies}$$

(*b*) $$\text{Orders/yr} = \frac{D}{Q} = \frac{25{,}000}{5{,}000} = 5 \text{ orders/yr}$$

ASSUMPTIONS OF THE EOQ MODEL

The EOQ equation is a convenient and widely used expression for determining optimal order quantities when the actual cost components and purchase conditions happen to coincide with the variables of the EOQ model. Order tables and nomographs have also been developed that offer a quick and even simpler means of determining the EOQ without necessitating calculations. However, it is well to keep in mind that in a manufacturing operation, obtaining an order at the right time (scheduling) is usually far more crucial than obtaining the exact order quantity. The enthusiastic and sometimes blind acceptance of the EOQ model has tended to obscure this fact in the past. Aside from the real-world problems of constantly changing requirements, expediting partial shipments, splitting lots, and so on, there are several assumptions underlying the basic EOQ model. Four of them are listed below.

1 Demand is known and constant.

2 Lead time is known and replenishment is instantaneous at the expiration of the lead time.

3 Ordering and carrying-cost expressions include all relevant costs and these costs are constant.

4 Purchase costs do not vary with quantity ordered.

The uncertainties associated with demand and lead time will be considered subsequently. With respect to the inclusion of all relevant costs, the addition of other costs can best be handled by going back to the original total cost equation [Eq. (7-1)]. Solved Prob. *1 shows how the EOQ formula changes when storage costs, based upon total rather than average inventory, are included. We turn now to the situation where purchase costs *do* vary with the quantity ordered.

QUANTITY DISCOUNTS

Manufacturers often provide a price discount for buyers who purchase in large volumes. A firm should take advantage of these quantity discounts to the point where the incremental increase in their annual carrying costs will just equal the savings in purchase cost. The assignment of a different purchase price, depending on the quantity purchased, now makes the price a function of lot quantity Q with the result that the total cost function becomes discontinuous, as shown in Fig. 7-2.

A mathematical expression for the optimal order quantity in a discount situation can be derived on the basis of minimizing incremental costs. However, the mathematics of this approach is unnecessary, for the technique of (1) determining the EOQ on the basis of the nondiscounted base price and (2) comparing the total cost at this EOQ point with that for price break points at *higher* volumes provides a most practical and expedient solution to the problem.

Referring to Fig. 7-2, the lot size designated EOQ represents the point of minimum slope on the total cost curve. Thus there is no more optimal order quantity of fewer units. However, because of the discontinuities in the TC curve, points to the right, representing larger lot sizes, may also represent lower total annual costs. The shape of the TC curve will obviously differ from one firm to another, depending upon the firm's cost of capital, ordering costs, and so on, as well as on the price discount rates. For the specific case in Fig. 7-2, calculation of the total costs [Equation (7-1)] at the initial EOQ point, as well as at the price break points Q_1, Q_2, and Q_3, would reveal that Q_2 has the minimum annual total cost. This may suggest, for example, that it is more economical to accept a 10 percent discount on a 5,000 unit purchase and carry a larger average inventory than it is to purchase a smaller EOQ lot size with no discount applied.

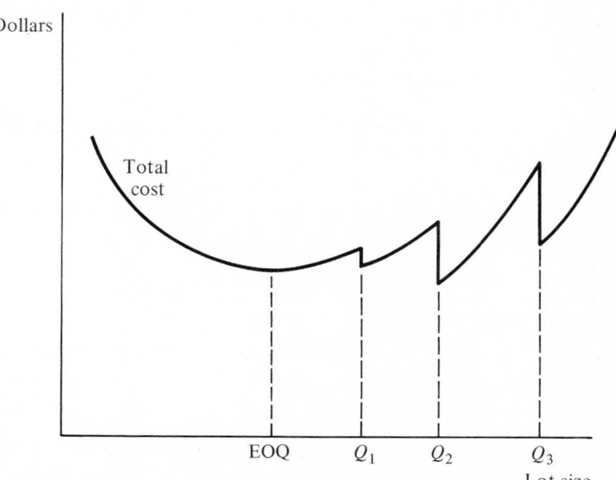

FIGURE 7-2 Quantity discount situation

Example 7-2

A producer of photo equipment buys lenses from a supplier at \$100 each. The producer requires 125 lenses/yr and the ordering cost is \$12.50/order. Carrying and storage costs per unit-yr (based on average inventory) are estimated to be \$5 each. The supplier offers a 4 percent discount for purchases of 100 lenses and a 6 percent discount for purchases of 250 or more lenses at one time. What is the most economical amount to order at a time?

Solution

Disregarding quantity discounts the EOQ amount would be:

$$\text{EOQ} = \sqrt{\frac{2C_oD}{C_c}} = \sqrt{\frac{2(12.50)(125)}{5.00}} = 25 \text{ lenses}$$

And the total annual cost associated with this EOQ is:

$$\begin{aligned} \text{TC} &= \text{ordering} + \text{carrying} + \text{purchase} \\ &= C_o \frac{1}{Q} D + C_c \frac{Q}{2} + D(P) \\ &= 12.50\left(\frac{1}{25}\right)(125) + 5.00\left(\frac{25}{2}\right) + 125(100) = \$12{,}625 \end{aligned}$$

For a 100-unit order, the purchase cost is reduced by 4 percent of \$100, or \$4. Assuming the ordering and carrying costs remain constant, the total annual cost associated with a 100 unit order is:

$$\text{TC} = 12.50\left(\frac{1}{100}\right)(125) + 5.00\left(\frac{100}{2}\right) + 125(100 - 4) = \$12{,}266$$

Similarly, the total annual cost associated with a 250-unit order is:

$$\text{TC} = 12.50\left(\frac{1}{250}\right)(125) + 5.00\left(\frac{250}{2}\right) + 125(100 - 6) = \$12{,}381$$

The 100-unit lot size results in the least total annual costs. Although the purchase price per unit is less with the 250-unit order, the carrying costs begin to outweigh such savings.

In the above example we assumed that carrying costs remained the same after the discount was applied. Since the discount reduces the amount of invested capital (that is, with the 4 percent discount the purchase price per unit is only \$96 instead of

\$100), the per unit carrying and storage cost (\$5 in this case) will likely be reduced by some small but proportionate amount. This correction should be accounted for if it is significant.

ECONOMIC RUN LENGTHS

When a firm is producing its own inventory rather than purchasing it, the same theory can be applied to minimize total inventory costs. However, the order costs are replaced by manufacturing setup costs. (Setup costs are of a fixed nature and represent the one-time costs for machine adjustments, paperwork, scheduling efforts, and the like, to begin production of a different item.) The EOQ equation must also be modified to account for the fact that only a portion of the production goes into inventory. The other portion is used concurrently in the production process or is sold as produced. The production rate p is, of course, noninstantaneous and must be greater than or equal to the demand rate d.

The modification to the EOQ equation thus does not affect C_o, which now becomes the setup cost, or the total demand D, but only acts to reduce the carrying cost C_c by deleting the carrying charge on that portion of the production run that does not go into inventory. (See Fig. 7-3.) If d = demand/day and p = production/day, the ratio (d/p) represents the proportion of production that is allocated to daily demand, and $[1 - (d/p)]$ represents that proportion of the production run that goes into inventory. If we take into account the decreased carrying cost of this reduced level of inventory, the economic run length (ERL) in number of units to produce per production setup is:

$$\text{ERL} = \sqrt{\frac{2C_oD}{C_c[1 - (d/p)]}} \tag{7-4}$$

where

C_o = setup cost in \$/setup
D = annual demand in units/yr
C_c = carrying cost in \$/unit-yr
d = demand rate, e.g., units/day
p = production rate, e.g., units/day

Note that when the demand rate just equals the production rate there is no carrying cost and the run length is continuous. Also, the two rates can be in other time period units so long as they are consistent units.

Example 7-3

A plastics molding firm produces and uses 24,000 teflon bearing inserts annually. The cost of setting up for production is \$85 and the weekly production rate is

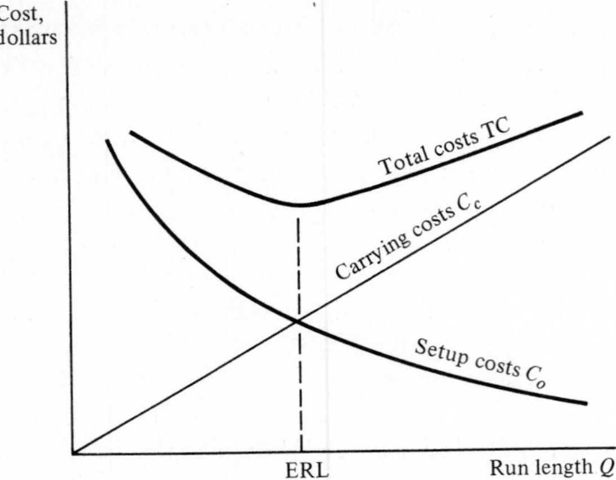

FIGURE 7-3 Economic run length curve

1,000 units. If the production cost is \$5.50/unit and the annual storage and carrying cost is \$.50/unit, how many units should the firm produce during each production run?

Solution

The demand and production rates must be in the same units, so we arbitrarily put both into annual terms, assuming a 52-week year.

$$\text{ERL} = \sqrt{\frac{2C_oD}{C_c[1 - (d/p)]}} = \sqrt{\frac{2(85)(24{,}000)}{0.50[1 - (24{,}000/52{,}000)]}} = 3{,}893 \text{ inserts}$$

At a production rate of 1,000 units per week each production run will last about one month, so the firm will be producing inserts about every other month. •

UNCERTAINTIES IN INVENTORY MANAGEMENT

Until now, we have assumed that demand for inventory was known and that lots were supplied when ordered. In reality this is often not the case, and firms must carry extra inventory, or safety stocks, to guard against these uncertainties. Safety stocks are not the panacea they once appeared to be (before the advent of MRP systems) but they are still the major hedge against uncertainties associated with independent demand items.

SOURCES OF UNCERTAINTY

Uncertainties due to varying demands from users and varying lead times from suppliers cause some of the most difficult problems in inventory management. The demand may be partly controlled by an effective advertising or marketing strategy, but it is often largely uncontrollable. And even though aggregate demand exhibits less variation than that for individual items, the firm must still produce individual items, so the aggregating effect does not alleviate the problem.

Lead time is typically of less concern for it is often a reasonably controllable variable. As a matter of fact, much (often most) of the lead time for a product made in a shop represents queue, or waiting, time which can potentially be "managed." Nevertheless, the uncertainty of not knowing when a necessary item will be received causes serious scheduling and production control problems for many firms. With both demand and lead time uncertainties, careful inventory management becomes more vital than ever.

INCREMENTAL COSTS OF INVENTORY UNCERTAINTIES

A firm could attempt to solve the problems of demand and lead time uncertainties simply by carrying such huge amounts of inventory for every item that it would never be out of stock. But of course the carrying costs on these idle resources might drive the firm into bankruptcy. Furthermore, there is usually no need to carry safety stock for dependent demand items so long as the supply schedule is properly time-phased.

A more scientific approach to the problem is to attempt to quantify and manage the uncertainties. Since the scale of probability constitutes a most useful measure of uncertainty, the problems of uncertain demands and lead times are often best analyzed on an expected value basis. This requires historical data and/or the formulation of probability distributions of demand and lead time. In each case, the concepts of incremental cost and marginal analysis apply. The organization should theoretically seek to adjust inventory levels to the point where:

$$\begin{pmatrix}\text{Incremental cost}\\ \text{of more inventory}\end{pmatrix} = \begin{pmatrix}\text{incremental gain}\\ \text{to production or sales}\end{pmatrix} (\text{probability of gain})$$

The incremental gain to production is realized by maintaining manufacturing inventories. Manufacturing inventory levels depend upon the production plan and are usually highly predictable (that is, they depend on demand inventories). When a product is completed, it becomes a distribution inventory item and enhances the possibility of an incremental gain through sales. Distribution inventories are typically finished products that have independent demands.

Stock levels can sometimes be most appropriately determined on the basis of an expected value of demand or lead time. Many perishable items and products that lose value if not immediately used or sold are particularly suitable for this type of analysis. The procedures for developing payoff and expected value tables, discussed in previous chapters, apply equally well to these inventory situations. In general the action (controllable) alternatives consist of the choice of how much inventory to stock and the state of nature (uncontrollable variable) is typically the demand or lead time.

In the case of uncertain and independent demand, finished goods inventory levels should be based upon specified levels of customer service, which, in turn, must be set with some knowledge of the probability distribution of demand. Similarly, if the firm is dependent upon suppliers with varying lead times, it must set its raw materials inventory levels in light of the best information available on lead time distribution. The "extra" amount of inventory carried to account for these uncertainties associated with customers and suppliers is part of the regular inventory but is designated as safety stock.

SAFETY STOCKS, ORDER POINTS, AND SERVICE LEVELS

Safety stocks (SS) constitute one of the major means of dealing with the uncertainties associated with variations in demand and lead time. They are amounts of inventory held in excess of regular usage quantities in order to provide specified levels of protection against stockout. Figure 7-4 illustrates a varying demand and lead time and the use of safety stock. The order point (OP) is the inventory level at which a replenishment order is placed. As illustrated in the figure, it should include a sufficient quantity to handle demand during the lead time (D_{LT}) plus a designated margin of safety stock.

$$\mathrm{OP} = D_{\mathrm{LT}} + \mathrm{SS} \tag{7-5}$$

Example 7-4

A nationwide trucking firm has an average demand of 10 new tires/week and receives deliveries from a Dayton, Ohio, tire company about 20 business days (5 days/week) after placing an order. If the firm seeks to maintain a safety stock of 15 tires, what is the order point?

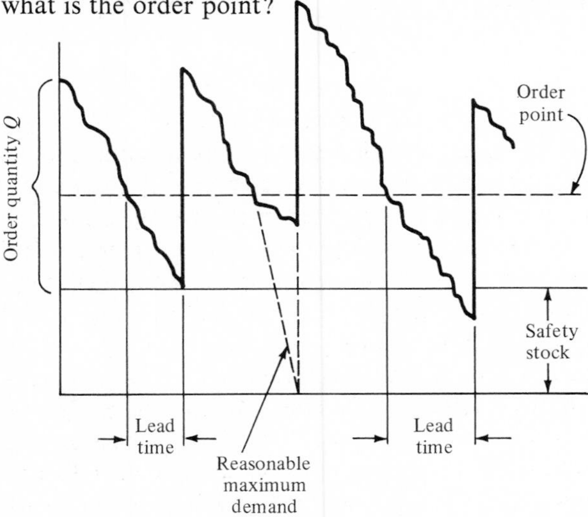

FIGURE 7-4 Inventory variables

Solution

$$\begin{aligned} \text{OP} &= D_{\text{LT}} + \text{SS} \\ &= (10 \text{ tires/week})(4 \text{ weeks}) + 15 \text{ tires} \\ &= 55 \text{ tires} \end{aligned}$$

When records are maintained on a computer, the computer simply keeps totals of current inventory levels and issues ordering instructions when the reorder point for any item is reached. This provides timely information for ordering and requires only a minimal amount of storage space on the computer. However, with today's relatively inexpensive direct-access computer files, many firms are finding it advantageous to maintain ordering information on a *time-phased basis* [**10**: 45–54].

Time-phasing the order point data has three major advantages: (1) it enables planners to predict more precisely *when* on-hand quantities are likely to go below safety stock levels so that immediate attention can be given to those orders, (2) it enables the firm to use a computer file format that is consistent with the MRP logic used for inventory control of items with dependent demand, (3) it facilitates planning priorities and scheduling (which we shall take up later in the text).

The following example will illustrate time-phasing the order point (TPOP) by using the same data as in the previous order point example.

Example 7-5

A firm has a demand rate averaging 10 units/week, carries a safety stock of 15 units, uses an order quantity of 80 units, and the lead time is 4 weeks. Assuming an on-hand inventory of 20 units (including safety stock) and a scheduled receipt of 80 units due during week 3, depict the use requirements in terms of a time-phased order point plan.

Solution

Our time-phased order point plan will show demand (projected requirements) on a weekly basis, along with scheduled order receipts and a running total of the inventory on hand over time (including safety stock). (See Table 7-1.) The order point is conveyed as a planned order release at a time that corresponds to the length of the lead time before the scheduled receipt of order.

It appears that this item already had a higher-than-expected usage during a recent period, for the projected demand of 10 units in week 1 will use up 10 of the 20 units on hand, leaving only 10 remaining at the end of the period. This is already 5 units into the safety stock. During week 2, the projected requirements will deplete on-hand inventory (including safety stock) and the chart signals that the 80-unit order scheduled for receipt by the beginning of week 3 will be needed right away, that is, early in week 3 without fail. Assuming that the order comes in on time, the inventory on hand goes to 80 − 10 = 70 at the end of week 3.

TABLE 7-1 TIME-PHASED ORDER POINT

Order quantity = 80
Lead time = 4 weeks
Safety stock = 15

		Week											
		1	2	3	4	5	6	7	8	9	10	11	12
Projected requirements		10	10	10	10	10	10	10	10	10	10	10	10
Scheduled receipts				80						80			
On hand at end of period[a]	20	10	—	70	60	50	40	30	20	90 ~~10~~	80	70	60
Planned order release						80							

[a] Including safety stock.

The 10-per-week usage rate would then reduce stocks down below the safety stock level of 15 units during week 9, so another scheduled receipt of 80 is needed in week 9. (The 80 units are not normally shown as a scheduled receipt until after the planned order for them is actually released. The entry is shown here in a dotted circle for illustrative purposes only.) Since the lead time is 4 weeks, an order release is scheduled for week 5, which is the week the order point is reached. Actually the projected order point will be reached when the on-hand inventory equals:

$$D_{LT} + SS = 40 + 15 = 55 \text{ units}$$

This corresponds to a time in the middle of week 5, for the on-hand inventory at the beginning and end of week 5 is 60 units and 50 units respectively. By receiving the 80-unit shipment by the beginning of week 9 the firm should not have to dip into safety stocks at that time, unless something unusual occurs again.

If no safety stock were carried and reorders were placed so that inventory was scheduled to arrive (on the average) when the previous inventory was used up, the organization would run out of stock about half the time. Costs of being out of stock include costs of expediting replacement inventory, loss of sales, loss of goodwill and various other intangible factors. The safety stocks help prevent stockouts from occurring by raising the order point.

The amount of safety-stock inventory necessary is generally considered to be that quantity necessary to meet any reasonable maximum demand during the lead time. This is shown in dotted lines in the second reorder cycle of Fig. 7-4. "Reasonable maximum demand" is, however, open to much interpretation. More precisely, the quantity should be determined on the basis of knowledge of the frequency distributions of demand and lead time. It is desirable to collect empirical data on the actual frequency distributions experienced by the given organization, but research has shown that many demand distributions conform to standard statistical distributions. In the next two sections of this chapter we shall deal first with setting safety stock levels on the basis of actual empirical data, and second with setting them on the basis of known statistical distributions. Before embarking upon that, however, we need one additional concept, that of service level.

The *service level* (SL) of an inventory is a number that represents the percent of order cycles in which all demand requests can be supplied from stock. The converse of service level is another percentage figure representing the stockout risk (SOR).

$$\text{SL} = 100\% - \text{SOR} \tag{7-6}$$

Customers would like 100 percent service, but production economics usually dictate that firms provide something less, perhaps in the range of 75–99.7 percent service. We shall return to the question of setting the stockout risk shortly.

HANDLING UNCERTAINTIES VIA USE OF EMPIRICAL DATA

We turn now to the methodology for setting safety stock levels on the basis of actual historical data on demand and lead-time variations. These techniques apply to finished products and components, such as spare parts, that have independent demands. It is not always possible (nor perhaps worthwhile) to collect the necessary data and make the required assumptions to determine safety stocks in this manner. But when it is feasible, it can represent a substantial improvement over intuitive or rule-of-thumb methods.

INVENTORY LEVELS UNDER UNCERTAIN DEMAND AND UNCERTAIN LEAD TIME

The procedure for establishing safety stock levels on the basis of knowledge of the demand requires an initial managerial decision as to what service level is desired. If the organization's policy is to limit the number of order cycles that cannot meet all demand from stock to 5 percent of the order cycles (SOR = 5 percent), this is obviously going to entail a greater cost than if the stockout risk is 10 percent. Once the SOR has been established, and past data on the actual pattern of demand requests have been collected, a cumulative distribution of demand can be formulated and the maximum demand for a given stockout risk (D_{SOR}) can be obtained directly from the cumulative distribution [**1**]. The required safety stock (SS) is then simply the difference between this maximum demand (D_{SOR}) and the average demand (D_{ave}).

$$\text{SS} = D_{\text{SOR}} - D_{\text{ave}} \tag{7-7}$$

Example 7-6

The data below represent weekly demand on a \$500 item. The firm has a 10 percent/yr cost for carrying inventory. Determine the safety stock level and carrying cost for providing a service level of (*a*) 90 percent, (*b*) 95 percent.

Weekly demand (number of units)	Frequency (number of weeks this demand occurred)	Cumulative frequency (number of weeks demand exceeded lower-class boundary)	Cumulative percent (percent of weeks demand exceeded lower-class boundary)
0 < 50	1	104	100.0
50 < 100	7	103	99.0
100 < 150	11	96	92.3
150 < 200	16	85	81.7
200 < 250	19	69	66.3
250 < 300	20	50	48.1
300 < 350	14	30	28.8
350 < 400	9	16	15.4
400 < 450	5	7	6.7
450 < 500	2	2	1.9
	104		

Solution

The 90 percent and 95 percent service levels represent stockout risks of 10 percent and 5 percent, respectively (per Equation 7-6). We can formulate a frequency distribution (histogram) and cumulative distribution (ogive) of demand as shown in Figs. 7-5 and 7-6.

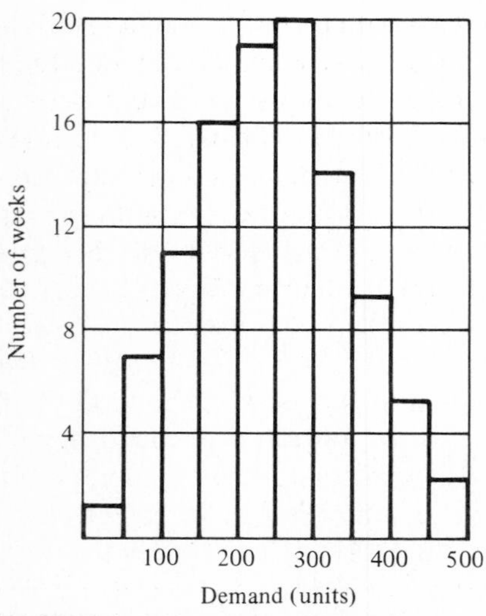

FIGURE 7-5 Frequency distribution of demand

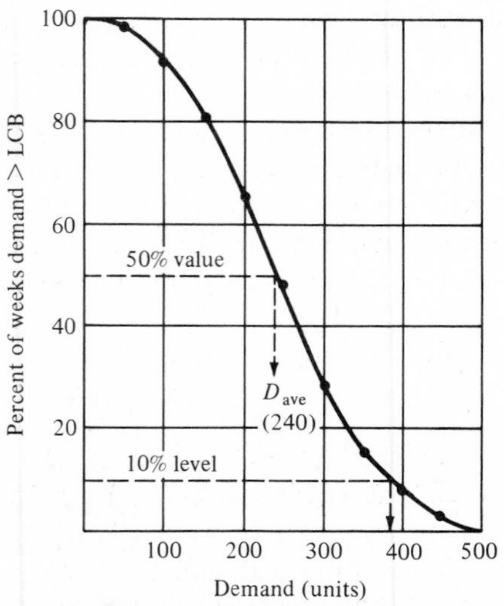

FIGURE 7-6 Cumulative distribution of demand

From the median (the 50 percent value) on the cumulative distribution:

$$D_{ave} = \text{average demand} \cong 240 \text{ units}$$

(*a*) 90 percent service level (10 percent SOR):

$$D_{SOR} = \text{demand level corresponding to 10 percent risk of stockout}$$

$$\cong 385 \text{ units (from graph)}$$

$$SS = \text{safety stock level} = D_{SOR} - D_{ave} = 385 - 240$$

$$= 145 \text{ units}$$

$$\text{SS cost} = \left(\frac{\$500}{\text{unit}}\right)\left(\frac{10\%}{\text{yr}}\right)(145 \text{ units}) = \$7{,}250/\text{yr}$$

(*b*) 95 percent SL (5 percent SOR):

$$D_{SOR} = \text{demand level corresponding to 5 percent risk of stockout}$$

$$\cong 430 \text{ units (from graph)}$$

$$SS = D_{SOR} - D_{ave} = 430 - 240 = 190 \text{ units}$$

$$\text{SS cost} = \left(\frac{\$500}{\text{unit}}\right)\left(\frac{10\%}{\text{yr}}\right)(190 \text{ units}) = \$9{,}500/\text{yr}$$

Variations in lead time are the second major cause of uncertainty in inventory management, although lead times are generally more controllable than demand. As with variations in demand, the lead-time uncertainty can be handled by developing cumulative frequency or probability distributions depicting the relative occurrence of different lead times for the given inventory item or group of items. By referring to the cumulative distribution, the safety stock level (as in weeks of usage) required to guard against this uncertainty can be determined. This is done by using the cumulative distribution to find the lead time required to limit the stockout risk to a given level (LT_{SOR}) and subtracting the average lead time (LT_{ave}) from LT_{SOR}.

$$SS = LT_{SOR} - LT_{ave} \tag{7-8}$$

DETERMINATION OF STOCKOUT RISK AND EFFECT UPON ORDER QUANTITIES

Because of the intangible nature of stockout costs associated with such concerns as loss of potential business or customer goodwill, management is often unprepared or reluctant to assign a cost to being out of stock. The above methods of setting safety stock levels in the face of uncertain demand or lead time approach the problem of stockout costs from a slightly different perspective. Instead of asking the manager, "What does it cost you to be out of stock?" the above approach seeks an answer to the question, "What would you be willing to pay *not* to be out of stock 90 percent of the time, or 95 percent of the time, or some other specified service level?" If, for example, the responsible manager is not willing to allocate as much as \$9,500 per year to ensure that there is stock on hand 95 percent of the order cycle times, the cumulative distribution curves can be used to identify the level of service a manager can expect for any lesser (or greater) carrying cost.

Example 7-7

Given the data from Example 7-6, suppose the manager is willing to allocate only \$3,000/yr to the carrying of safety stock for the \$500 item. What percent of order cycles can he or she expect to run out of stock?

Solution

We can compute how much safety stock the \$3,000 would fund by dividing the \$3,000 by the carrying cost/unit-yr.

$$\text{SS} = \frac{\$3{,}000 \text{ allocated/yr}}{\$500\text{/unit } (10\%\text{/yr})} = 60 \text{ units}$$

The stockout risk corresponding to SS = 60 units is:

$$\text{SS} = D_{\text{SOR}} - D_{\text{ave}}$$

$$\therefore D_{\text{SOR}} = \text{SS} + D_{\text{ave}} \qquad \text{where } D_{\text{ave}} = 240 \text{ units (from Fig. 7-6)}$$

$$= 60 + 240 = 300 \text{ units}$$

From the cumulative distribution (Fig. 7-6), a demand of 300 units corresponds to a percentage value of approximately 29 percent. Therefore the manager may expect to run out of stock on approximately 29 percent of the order cycles. That is, if the firm places an order each week, it may run out of stock on $(0.29)(52) \cong 15$ occasions. Knowing this, the manager may be willing to reconsider the \$3,000 allocation.

The effect of stockout costs on the order quantity is to tend to increase the order quantity so as to decrease the frequency of exposure to risk of stockout. If the stockout cost can be apportioned to the number of order cycles (exposures to a stockout), this cost C_e can be handled in the same fashion as an ordering cost using the expression:

$$Q = \sqrt{\frac{2D(C_o + C_e)}{C_c}} \tag{7-9}$$

As pointed out earlier, values for C_e can be difficult (if not impossible) to obtain. However, if a preliminary calculation of Q is made (without including C_e), an implied cost of C_e can be estimated by dividing the total annual carrying cost per year by the number of orders per year that would have to be placed. This yields an *implied cost per exposure* that may be taken as a reasonable starting point for adjusting the EOQ. The revised order quantity will then be greater than the original EOQ for it will be calling for fewer orders of larger quantity in order to reduce the frequency of exposure to stockout.

INTERDEPENDENCY OF INVENTORY VARIABLES

The order point, order quantity, demand, lead time, and safety stock levels are all interdependent variables. Each can influence the risk of stockout. The *order point establishes the amount of risk of stockout*, for it includes safety stock plus demand during lead time. Thus, the higher the order point the more inventory is carried in stock and the less the risk of stockout (although the greater the carrying cost). The *order quantity establishes the frequency of exposure to risk of stockout*, or number of trials to run out of stock. An order quantity equal to annual demand would limit the number of stockout risks, or trials, to one per year. On the other hand, carrying such a large average inventory for a long period of time could result in high carrying costs.

In terms of the EOQ model, ordering and stockout costs act to increase the quantity ordered so that the frequency of orders and exposures to stockout is reduced. Quantity discounts also tend to increase Q. Carrying and storage costs exert the opposite effect of tending to reduce order quantities.

We have seen how safety stock levels can be set using empirical data of actual demand or lead times. When the demand or lead-time pattern follows a known statistical pattern the problems of setting safety stock levels are simplified, for we need not go through the extra work of formulating cumulative distributions of actual data.

HANDLING UNCERTAINTIES VIA USE OF STANDARD STATISTICAL DISTRIBUTIONS

Sometimes the frequency pattern of demand or lead time follows a known statistical distribution such as the normal or Poisson. If, as with stock levels set using empirical data, a desired service level can be ascertained (a management decision), then the safety stock levels and appropriate order points can be determined quite easily.

INVENTORY LEVELS UNDER NORMALLY DISTRIBUTED DEMAND

If the distribution of demand is symmetrical and unimodal, the normal distribution may satisfactorily describe it.[1] In this case the standard deviation (σ) or mean absolute deviation (MAD) is a useful measure of deviation of individual demand values from the mean value. We have seen previously that:

$$\sigma = \sqrt{\frac{\sum (X - \mu)^2}{N}} \qquad \text{and} \qquad \text{MAD} = \frac{\sum |X - \mu|}{N}$$

$$\sigma \cong 1.25 \text{ MAD}$$

By expressing the service level as a percentage of area under the normal curve, the safety stock required to provide a given level of service can be calculated in terms of deviations from the mean. Conversely, if the number of units of safety stock is specified we can determine how much protection against stockout (that is, the percentage of service) the safety stock provides. A table of safety stock level factors (SF) for normally distributed variables is given in Table 7-2. The factors are simply the number of standard (and mean absolute) deviations required to include the specified percentage of area under the normal curve cumulated in the positive direction.

Example 7-8

Demand for a product during an order period is normally distributed with mean (μ) = 1,000 units and standard deviation (σ) = 40 units. What percent service can a firm expect to offer if (*a*) it provides for average demand only, (*b*) it carries 60 units of safety stock?

Solution

(*a*) Average demand (1,000 units) would include no safety stock.
∴ Service = 50 percent.

(*b*) With 60 units of SS:

$$SF_\sigma = \frac{SS}{\sigma} = \frac{60}{40} = 1.5$$

∴ From Table 7-2, the service level = 93.32 percent.

[1] The fit of data to a normal (or other) statistical distribution may, of course, be evaluated using the chi-square distribution.

TABLE 7-2 SAFETY STOCK LEVEL FACTORS FOR NORMALLY DISTRIBUTED VARIABLES

$$SS = SF_\sigma(\sigma) \quad \text{or} \quad SS = SF_{MAD}(MAD)$$

$$OP = D_{LT} + SS$$

Service level (percent of order cycles without stockout)	Safety factor using Standard deviation SF_σ	Mean absolute deviation SF_{MAD}
50.00	0.00	0.00
75.00	0.67	0.84
80.00	0.84	1.05
84.13	1.00	1.25
85.00	1.04	1.30
89.44	1.25	1.56
90.00	1.28	1.60
93.32	1.50	1.88
94.00	1.56	1.95
94.52	1.60	2.00
95.00	1.65	2.06
96.00	1.75	2.19
97.00	1.88	2.35
97.72	2.00	2.50
98.00	2.05	2.56
98.61	2.20	2.75
99.00	2.33	2.91
99.18	2.40	3.00
99.38	2.50	3.13
99.50	2.57	3.20
99.60	2.65	3.31
99.70	2.75	3.44
99.80	2.88	3.60
99.86	3.00	3.75
99.90	3.09	3.85
99.93	3.20	4.00
99.99	4.00	5.00

Source: Adapted from G. W. Plossl and O. W. Wight, Production and Inventory Control: *Principles and Techniques*, 1967, p. 108. Reprinted by permission of Prentice-Hall, Inc., Englewood Cliffs, N.J.

Note that the same result would be obtained from using any table of the normal distribution where

$$Z = \frac{X - \mu}{\sigma} = \frac{1{,}060 - 1{,}000}{40} = 1.5$$

The service level would correspond to the shaded area under the normal curve in Fig. 7-7.

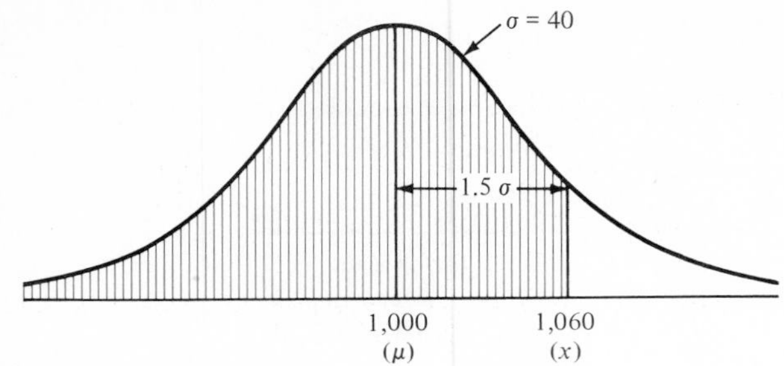

FIGURE 7-7 Service level shown as area under normal curve

Example 7-9 (using σ)

A firm has a normal distribution of demand during a (constant) lead time with $\sigma = 250$ units and desires to provide 98 percent service.

(*a*) How much safety stock should be carried?

(*b*) If the demand during the lead time averages 1,200 units, what is the appropriate order point?

Solution

(*a*) $\text{SS} = \text{SF}_\sigma(\sigma) = (2.05)(250) = 512$ units

(*b*) $\text{OP} = D_{\text{LT}} + \text{SS} = 1{,}200 + 512 = 1{,}712$ units

As indicated previously, the service level is a statement of the percentage of order cycles that do not experience a stockout. If the number of stockouts allowed per time period is designated, it can easily be expressed as a service level. We first estimate the number of reorder cycles. Then we express the number of cycles the stock is adequate as a percent of the total number of cycles. If, for example, a firm places an order about every week and wants to limit the number of stockouts to one per year, this means it must have sufficient safety stock to supply it during 51 of the 52 order cycles. The ratio 51/52 would then constitute a 98 percent service level.

Example 7-10 (using MAD)

A firm has a normally distributed forecast of usage with MAD = 60 units. It desires a service level which limits stockouts to one order cycle per year.

(*a*) How much safety stock should be carried if the order quantity is normally a week's supply?

(*b*) How much safety stock should be carried if the order quantity is five weeks' supply?

If the lead time is one week and expected usage is 500 units/week, what is the appropriate order point when the order quantity is:

(*c*) One week's supply, as in (*a*)?

(*d*) Five weeks' supply, as in (*b*)?

Solution

(*a*) $SS = SF_{MAD}\,(MAD)$

where SF_{MAD} depends upon service level:

1 week's supply/order = 52 orders/yr

$$1 \text{ stockout in } 52 = \frac{51}{52} \text{ in stock} = 98 \text{ percent service}$$

$\therefore SF_{MAD} = 2.56$ (from Table 7-2)

$SS = 2.56(60) = 154$ units

(*b*) For 5 weeks' supply/order $\frac{52}{5} \cong 10.4$ orders/yr

$$1 \text{ stockout in } 10.4 = \frac{9.4}{10.4} \text{ in stock} \cong 90 \text{ percent service}$$

$\therefore SF_{MAD} = 1.60$

$SS = 1.60(60) = 96$ units

(*c*) $OP = D_{LT} + SS$

where $D_{LT} = (500 \text{ units/wk})(1 \text{ week}) = 500$ units

$OP = 500 + 154 = 654$ units

(*d*) $OP = 500 + 96 = 596$ units

Note that the stockout limit of "one order cycle per year" translates into a higher service requirement when orders are placed weekly rather than every five weeks. This, in turn, is reflected in a higher order point to provide the added protection against stockout.

CORRECTIONS FOR DIFFERENT FORECAST AND LEAD-TIME INTERVALS

When the forecast interval is less than the lead-time interval, an adjustment must be made to σ and to MAD to account for the fact that the safety stock must increase as the lead time increases [7]. The increase required in safety stock is not, however, directly proportional to the increase in lead time. Various adjustment factors have been proposed [7, 9], with the observation that the best factors should theoretically be determined by simulation, using the company's actual demand data. Plossl and Wight [7: 112] have developed the empirical correction factors shown in Table 7-3, which have given reasonably good results.

TABLE 7-3 CORRECTION FACTORS FOR WHEN LEAD TIME EXCEEDS FORECAST INTERVAL

Ratio of lead time to forecast interval	Multiply σ or MAD by
2	1.63
3	2.16
4	2.64
5	3.09
6	3.51
7	3.91
8	4.29
9	4.66
10	5.01
15	6.66
20	8.14

Source: Adapted from G. W. Plossl and O. W. Wight, *Production and Inventory Control: Principles and Techniques*, 1967, p. 112. Reprinted by permission of Prentice-Hall, Inc., Englewood Cliffs, N.J.

Example 7-11

The forecast for next week is for 500 units, MAD = 60 units, and a service level of one stockout/yr is desired. What is the order point if the order quantity is five weeks' supply but lead time is three weeks (instead of one week, as in Example. 7-10)?

Solution

Note that the ratio $\dfrac{\text{Lead time}}{\text{Forecast}} = \dfrac{3\text{ weeks}}{1\text{ week}} = 3$

∴ Correction to MAD is required.

$$\text{OP} = D_{\text{LT}} + \text{SS}$$

where

$$D_{\text{LT}} = (500\text{ units/wk})(3\text{ weeks}) = 1{,}500\text{ units}$$

$$\text{SS} = \text{SF}_{\text{MAD}}\ (\text{correction for MAD})\ \text{MAD} \tag{7-10}$$

where

$$\text{SF}_{\text{MAD}} = \text{for 1 stockout in } \frac{52}{5} \text{ orders} = \text{for 10.4 orders}$$

$$= 9.4 \text{ services in 10.4 orders} = \frac{9.4}{10.4} = 90\%\ \text{SL}$$

∴ From Table 7-2, $\text{SF}_{\text{MAD}} \cong 1.60$.

$$\text{Correction for MAD (from Table 7-3)} = 2.16$$
$$\therefore \text{SS} = 1.60(2.16)(60) = 207 \text{ units}$$
$$\text{OP} = 1{,}500 + 207 = 1{,}707 \text{ units}$$

INTERACTION OF DEMAND AND LEAD-TIME UNCERTAINTIES

In the above discussions, using statistical techniques, we have concerned ourselves wholly with setting safety stocks and order points under conditions of uncertain demand. In effect we have assumed that a constant lead time prevailed. From a conservative standpoint we could make allowance for minor lead-time variations by taking as our lead time the "longest normal" lead time [**7**: 117]. However, if it is desirable to account for both demand and lead-time variation simultaneously, the combined effect of the two is:

$$\text{Combined standard deviation} = \sigma_c = \sqrt{(\sigma_D)^2 + (\sigma_{\text{LT}})^2} \tag{7-11}$$

where the variances under the radical represent the demand and lead-time values respectively, and must be in the same units. This equation reflects the fact that the demand and lead-time *deviations are not directly additive* (also, the longest lead time and maximum demands may not coincide), but the *variances of the two statistical distributions are additive.* Once the combined standard deviation (σ_c) has been determined it may be used in the above equations to determine safety stock levels and order points.

USE OF OTHER DISTRIBUTIONS AND UNCERTAINTY ADJUSTMENTS

When the demand for an item is infrequent, but the quantity of items per order is fairly constant, the Poisson distribution may be used to approximate the number of individual orders that will be received during a lead time [**7**: 119]. It cannot be used to directly describe demand (that is, the total number of units on the individual orders) but, with the use of appropriate service factors, order points can be calculated for Poisson order arrivals in a manner similar to those above using the normal. (See [**7**: 118].) The Poisson also has some applicability in estimating lead time.

Research has shown that many demands follow a normal distribution at the manufacturing plant level and a Poisson distribution at the retail level. Some demand distributions at the wholesale and retail levels also follow the negative exponential curve [**2**]. In other cases, the binomial or chi-square distribution may fit the data, depending upon the nature of the product and the distribution and marketing methods and institutions [**11**: 358]. When any uncertainty exists about the nature of the distribution of demand or lead time, it is desirable to collect empirical data first and check the statistical properties of the data using the chi-square goodness-of-fit test.

In addition to the statistical methods of handling uncertainty that have been discussed, several less-formal methods exist [**8**: 39]. Some of these include: (1) an *ultraconservative method* (based on the largest daily usage ever incurred multiplied by the longest delivery time); (2) *safety-stock percentage method* (where safety stock is equal to average demand times average lead time plus a 25–40 percent safety factor); and (3) a *square root of lead time usage method* (where safety stock is equal to the square root of average usage during the lead time). Combinations of these methods with the statistical methods described in this chapter are also used. In summary, numerous methods of handling uncertainties exist and it is up to operations managers to evaluate their own situations and to take action using whatever techniques are appropriate. If statistical techniques are not economically justified (or feasible), they should not be forced into application.

MATERIAL REQUIREMENTS PLANNING (MRP) SYSTEMS

Earlier in the chapter we noted that there is no need to manage each component of an assembled product as though it were an independent item. If uncertainty pertains only to finished products, then only the finished products require safety stocks. Assuming component parts are obtained at the proper time, they can be acquired and assembled on the basis of actual material requirements, with little or no excess stock. Of course, some safety stock can be carried to take care of scrap loss or contingencies, but even then, levels can often be drastically reduced from what independent statistical analysis would suggest.

MRP FOR INVENTORIES AND SCHEDULING

Material requirements planning (MRP) is a technique for determining *when to order* dependent demand items and *how to reschedule* orders to adjust to changing requirements. Although we take up the topic of MRP here, as a method of time-phasing inventory orders, it is really more of a scheduling technique than an inventory ordering guide [**10**: 269]. We shall return to the scheduling advantages of MRP in a later chapter.

Before the 1960s there was no satisfactory method available for handling the inventory of dependent demand items. A firm's formal inventory system was often patterned after order points, and was either misapplied or broken down into a maze of informal methods when it came to handling dependent items. There was no feasible method of keeping accurate records of the thousands of inventory items that went into finished products, so firms relied upon the safety stocks of the order point model to keep them out of too much scheduling trouble. Unfortunately they did not always achieve that objective, but they did always make a healthy contribution to the inventory carrying and storage costs. In essence, the manual and informal control systems in use before 1960 (and still in use in thousands of firms today) could not adequately cope with the multitude of items and complex activities that took place in an average-sized manufacturing concern.

During the 1960s the computer opened the door to MRP, an inventory ordering system that could—at one time—keep up-to-date records of the status of thousands of items in inventory. It also facilitated rapid rescheduling of jobs when planned order receipts got out of phase with planned requirements. MRP is not a highly theoretical, sophisticated inventory management technique. It is just something that works to handle the everyday problems of priority and capacity.

PRIORITIES AND CAPACITY

The noted inventory consultant Oliver Wight breaks production and inventory management down into two essential problems: *priorities* and *capacity* [**10**: 5]. *Priorities* refer to what material is needed and when it is needed. This is, of course, closely akin to the meaning of scheduling. *Capacity* refers to how much human and/or machine time is needed to meet the schedule. Since inventories are the quantities of materials that must be made available in the appropriate time schedule, it is perhaps obvious that inventory control and scheduling activities are thoroughly interdependent.

HOW MRP SYSTEMS WORK

MRP systems take their material requirements from the master schedule, which may indeed be based upon a forecast (and as such incorporates uncertainties). The master schedule typically specifies the individual end products and the time periods in which they are to be manufactured. Once the finished product requirements are set, schedules for the quantities of component materials are calculated and dates are set for releasing orders so that materials arrive when needed.

The planned order releases at one level in turn generate requirements at the next lower level. For example, consider a firm making wheelbarrows. Once the master schedule is set, for say 500 units, the quantity of steel plate, wheel assemblies, and handlebars required to produce the 500 units is well defined by the bill-of-materials specified on the wheelbarrow drawings. The need for wheel assemblies by a certain date will, in turn, generate a lower-level need for tires, rims, and bearings to be acquired and assembled earlier. MRP first emphasizes when the assemblies are required, and, as a result of that, when the materials to make up the assemblies must be ordered.

Table 7-4 illustrates a master schedule and some component part schedules designed to deliver 40 wheelbarrows in week 1, 60 in week 4, 60 in week 6, and 50 in week 8. Each wheelbarrow requires two handlebars so the projected material requirements for handlebars are double the number of end products. Apparently an order has recently been placed because 300 handlebars are scheduled to be received in week 2. With that receipt, the on-hand inventory will be adequate until week 8,

TABLE 7-4 MRP MASTER AND COMPONENT PLAN

End Item Master Schedule: Wheelbarrows

Week no.	1	2	3	4	5	6	7	8
Requirements	40			60		60		50

Component Materials Plan: Handlebars

Order quantity = 300
Lead time = 2 weeks

		1	2	3	4	5	6	7	8
Projected requirements		80			120		120		100
Scheduled receipts			300						300
On-hand at end of period	100	20	320	320	200	200	80	80	~~−20~~ 280
Planned order release							300		

negative amount (∴ place order in week 6)

Component Materials Plan: Wheel Assemblies

Order quantity = 200
Lead time = 3 weeks

		1	2	3	4	5	6	7	8
Projected requirements		40			60	90[a]	60		50
Scheduled receipts							200		
On-hand at end of period	220	180	180	180	120	30	~~−30~~ 170	170	120
Planned order release				200					

[a] Requirements from another product (garden tractor) which uses same wheel assembly.

negative amount (∴ place order in week 3)

Subcomponent Materials Plan: Tire for Wheel Assembly

Order quantity = 400
Lead time = 1 week

		1	2	3	4	5	6	7	8
Projected requirements				200					
Scheduled receipts				400					
On-hand at end of period	50	50	50	−150 250	250	250	250	250	250
Planned order release			400						

which at first glance will be 20 units short. To overcome this, a planned order release for the standard order quantity (300) has been scheduled for week 6 because handlebars have a two-week lead time. The scheduled receipt of 300 handlebars in week 8 will thus result in an end-of-period inventory of 280 units. Scheduled receipts are not normally shown on the plan until after someone actually authorizes the purchase or manufacture of the item. The scheduled receipts in the dotted circles are shown here for illustrative purposes only.

Moving on to the wheel assemblies, note that each end item requires one wheel assembly so the projected requirements coincide with end-product demand. In addition, 90 wheel assemblies are needed for a different order (for garden tractors) in week 5 and these are automatically incorporated into the projected requirements. The on-hand stock is adequate until week 6, when quantities will drop to −30 unless a planned order is released in week 3.

The bottom chart of Table 7-4 illustrates the material requirements plan for tires, which are a subcomponent of the wheel assemblies. Note that the planned order release of 200 units from the above wheel assemblies plan shows up as a projected requirement for 200 tires in the same week (3) on the subcomponents plan. Since on-hand inventory is inadequate to supply this need, a planned order release is scheduled for week 2. It should ensure that an order of 400 tires will be available by the beginning of week 3.

Key features of MRP systems are (1) the time-phasing of requirements, (2) planned order releases, (3) generation of lower-level requirements, and (4) the rescheduling capability provided. As each week passes, planned orders are (manually) released and any changes in requirements and due dates are entered into the computer data base as they occur. Most firms using MRP then "run" their MRP program once a week (over the weekend). The computer automatically explodes the material requirements to all lower-level components (subcomponents) and prints out the necessary planned order release dates. These are, of course, based upon the individual order quantities and lead times which have previously been specified for each item. The order quantity may, by the way, represent an EOQ or ERL amount, or simply a lot size that is convenient from a manufacturing standpoint.

The features of MRP systems have come about largely because of the availability of computers, which now intimately link inventory management with scheduling. This enables firms to reduce or eliminate the safety stocks that were formerly used to help overcome the uncertainties of trying to mesh two "distinct" activities.

Time-phased order point (TPOP) and MRP systems both utilize the same format; the chief difference is that TPOP was initially associated with independent demand items whereas MRP was identified with dependent demand items derived from end items. However, many analysts are now using the term MRP in a broader sense to include both, with the major focus being on the concept of time-phasing requirements.

MRP is not an automatic solution to all inventory problems nor has it elevated scheduling to a science. Machines still break down, parts get scrapped, and *people* must release and reschedule orders in line with customer requirements. But MRP helps, and it works. This simple but effective time-phasing concept is one of the little-noticed innovations that is currently revolutionizing production and inventory control. This in turn is supporting the continued growth of productivity in the United States and the world.

INVENTORY CONTROL SYSTEMS

Several other types of control systems have been in use for some time to achieve the various purposes of inventory cited at the beginning of this chapter. In this last section we look first at the ABC method of determining which inventory items deserve most attention, and then at three traditional inventory control systems: (1) fixed-order quantity, (2) fixed-order interval, and (3) base stock. These systems, by themselves, are essentially only "order launching" techniques for they basically only get an order issued but offer little in the way of follow-up control. They also tend to look *back* at historical average usage rather than ahead to a forecast of material requirements. Nevertheless, they are still widely used for they answer the basic questions of *how much* to order and *when*, although not in as effective a manner as MRP systems. We conclude the section with some final observations on computer-based MRP systems, pointing out some software programs that are available to potential users.

ABC ANALYSIS

The time and recordkeeping activities required to control inventories cost an organization money. Some items do not warrant as close and exacting control as others, for a small percentage of items usually accounts for a large percentage of an inventory investment. This widely recognized fact has led many firms to classify inventories into three groups designated A, B, and C:

A items include the 10–20 percent of items that typically account for 70–80 percent of the total dollar value.

B items include about 30–40 percent of the items that account for about 15–20 percent of the dollar value.

C items include about 40–50 percent of the items that account for about 5–10 percent of the dollar value.

This classification system reveals that for most inventories the bulk of items typically account for only 5–10 percent of the value and suggests that the firm have plenty of these low-value items on hand but concentrate the more costly control efforts on the high-value items. The implications of such a classification system upon ordering and control procedures are depicted in Table 7-5 [adapted from **7**: 60–61]. Class A and B items are sufficiently valuable or vital to warrant a close control under some type of perpetual or periodic monitoring system. Class C items are sometimes

TABLE 7-5 IMPLICATIONS OF ABC CLASSIFICATION

	Degree of control	Type of records	Order of priority	Ordering procedures
A items	Tight	Accurate and complete	High—to reduce inventory	Careful, accurate, and frequent review of EOQ and OP
B items	Normal	Good	Normal	Normal EOQ analysis
C items	Simple	Simple	Lowest	1- or 2-year supply reordered periodically

managed on a *two-bin system* basis. Items are withdrawn from one bin until the supply is depleted. Then a reorder card is sent to purchasing and the second bin goes into use. In practice, a simple periodic visual review of inventory levels tends to be easier to administer than a two-bin system [**10**: 53].

FIXED-ORDER QUANTITY SYSTEM

The *fixed-order quantity inventory control system* is a perpetual system which keeps a current record of the amount of inventory in stock. A fixed quantity Q is ordered when the order point is reached (that is, when the amount on hand, without using the safety stock, will just meet the average demand during the lead time). This type of system, illustrated in Fig. 7-8, lends itself to the use of EOQ purchasing methods. The system requires continuous monitoring of inventory levels, which can easily be done if the system is computerized. Because of this, it is often used for inventories that have large, unexpected fluctuations in demand.

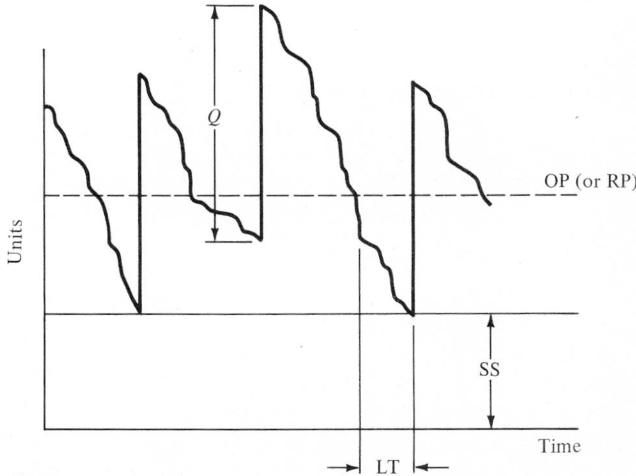

FIGURE 7-8 Fixed-order quantity system

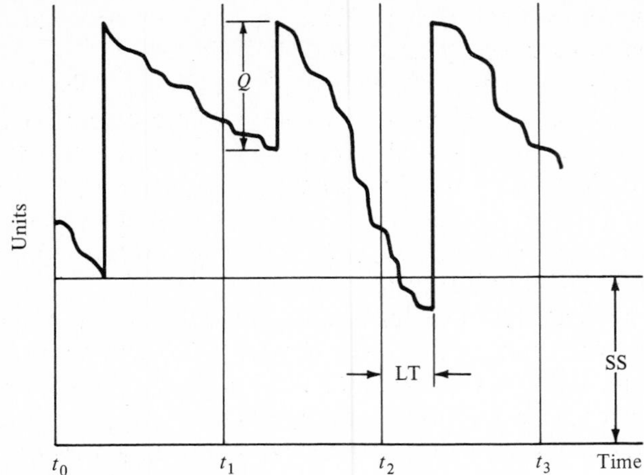

FIGURE 7-9 Fixed-order interval system

FIXED-ORDER INTERVAL SYSTEM

In the *fixed-order interval system* the amount of inventory in stock is reviewed at periodic intervals, such as weekly or monthly. A variable quantity Q is then ordered on a regular basis. The order quantity is adjusted to bring the inventory on hand and on order up to a specified level. Since the safety stock must provide protection over the entire cycle (such as from t_1 to t_2) it is typically larger than would be required under a fixed-order quantity system, where the safety stock must protect over the lead time only. This system does not, however, require continuous monitoring, and is especially useful for processes that call for a consistent use of material. It also lends itself to conditions where a single review period can identify several items which can then be ordered at one time, with a possible savings in the ordering cost.

BASE STOCK SYSTEM

The *base stock system* is one of many combinations of inventory systems and has elements of both the fixed-order quantity and fixed-order interval systems [**3**]. In this system, inventory levels are reviewed periodically, but orders are placed only when the stock is below some specified level. The system thus provides some of the control aspects of periodic review systems but would typically result in the placement of fewer orders, and orders of a more economic lot size.

COMPUTERIZED (MRP) INVENTORY SYSTEMS

Many firms have thousands of items of inventory which require some form of control. The usage calculations and recordkeeping chores would soon become overwhelming were it not for the computer and its unique information storage and retrieval capabilities. Inventory control is so ideally suited to computerization that it is usually one of the first and most important tasks to gain priority on an organization's computer. MRP systems are a prime example of this. MRP could really not be done if computers were not available to keep time-phased records on the multitude of items that typically constitute a firm's inventory.

Inventory control systems can be individually designed for the specific task or integrated into a total computerized management information system for the organization. Most computer manufacturers, such as IBM, Honeywell, and RCA, offer software packages of inventory control systems and will provide technical assistance to set up a computerized control system. As stressed in Chap. 1, however, it is important that the recipient firm participate fully and completely in the design and implementation of such a system.

Computerization of the inventory control system rests upon application of the inventory theory presented earlier in this chapter. The computer keeps a record of prices paid, quantities in stock, and so forth. The firm's management must specify service levels desired, stockout costs, carrying costs, usage expectations, and the like. From there on, the computer can calculate demand patterns, variances, and lead-time statistics, and can print out recommended order quantities on appropriate dates. It essentially does the busywork and tedious calculations for thousands of items which would be impractical to do by hand. In some cases its low-cost data storage capabilities have eliminated the need for traditional classifications of inventory, such as the ABC system. When working with families of items, simple EOQs may not result in the optimal number of orders or machine setups. Computerized methods have also been developed to determine the most economic lot sizes while staying within given setup hour limitations and still balancing ordering and inventory carrying costs [**7**: 75].

In the early days of computerized systems IBM introduced their Production and Inventory Control System (PICS), which has since been applied to many types of fabrication and assembly production systems [**5**]. In PICS, inventory control is one subsystem of a broader information system which includes forecasting, purchasing, scheduling, and some other functions. Inventory is analyzed on an ABC basis to identify which items need the tightest control. The user specifies either a safety stock level or a service level and the computation routine determines order quantities and minimum cost run sizes. The PICS system also produces reports of inventory on hand, in process, and on order, and has a feature whereby the data from an actual physical count of inventory in stock can be introduced.

Today, over 30 software packages are commercially available to users who wish to install MRP systems. Included are packages from IBM, Software International, Xerox, Honeywell, Martin Marietta, and Arista, to name just a few. Costs to put a complete MRP system on-line in an average-size firm may range from $200,000 to $500,000. Nevertheless, the success of MRP systems has been so favorable that such costs are often justified by savings within the first year or two.

INTERNATIONAL INVENTORY MANAGEMENT

For multinational firms, the purposes, costs, and uncertainties associated with carrying inventories in foreign locations generate additional concerns. While inventories serve many of the same functions, they often take on new dimensions such as in hedging (to protect against foreign price and delivery uncertainties) and in accommodating political instability. The level of inventories may be heavily influenced by tax rates, sourcing requirements, inflation, and expropriation risks.

Costs for ordering goods are sometimes higher because of the difficulty in finding suitable local suppliers. Carrying costs are likely to be higher due to the often higher capital costs. The risks of nonsuitability of items is greater, as are storage and obsolescence concerns. Purchase prices, of course, reflect foreign labor and material costs, as well as local shipping and market factors.

Unfortunately, the economic indicators and market information for many foreign locations are typically less reliable than for domestic locations. As we include price level changes, devaluation and expropriation risks, plus other political uncertainties such as import-export controls, credit costs, tax and sourcing policies, it becomes apparent that multinational inventory managers face a difficult task. A good understanding of inventory management principles, coupled with accurate data from an up-to-date information system, is essential to them.

SUMMARY

Inventories are idle resources that have economic value. They facilitate both continuous and intermittent production and effectively decouple processing activities. In addition, they can help to level production, to hedge against price and delivery uncertainties, and to enable more economic purchasing, as well as to provide service to customers. The major costs of inventories include (1) *ordering and setup*, (2) *carrying*, and (3) *purchase*, plus less-tangible costs such as those associated with stockout.

Inventory managers attempt to realize the benefits of inventory while minimizing the total costs necessary to provide for a specified level of service. The basic EOQ equation simply minimizes the ordering and carrying costs. When the purchase price is also a function of quantity, annual costs at the price break points must be compared with the EOQ to determine the optimal. The ERL equation is similar to the EOQ except that setup costs replace ordering costs, and the carrying charge is applied to only that proportion of production that goes into inventory.

Varying demands and lead times constitute the major uncertainties of inventory management. Firms carry extra inventory in the form of safety stocks to ensure that they can meet an independent demand a specified proportion of the time. The service level indicates what percent of order cycles the firm will be able to supply inventory from stock. Historical demand and lead-time data can be used to formulate cumulative distributions which reveal how much safety stock is needed to maintain a specified service level. The appropriate reorder point is then simply the average demand during the lead time plus the safety stock.

Many managers hesitate to attach a quantitative cost to being out of stock because it includes so many intangible factors. They may be more willing to indicate what they would agree to pay *not* to be out of stock a certain percent of the order cycles (to have, for example, 98 percent service). A first approximation to this cost can be implied from the carrying and storage cost, if it is apportioned into equal exposure costs for each order cycle. Given this, or some other suitable exposure cost, one can adjust the basic EOQ equation so that some measure of stockout cost is included.

When demand distributions follow a normal distribution, the calculations for setting safety stock levels are simplified, for we just compute the number of standard deviations (σ's) or mean absolute deviations (MADs) required to provide a given service level, and express this in units of inventory. A table of safety factors which can be multiplied by the σ or MAD values further simplifies this calculation. When the lead time exceeds the forecast interval, however, a correction must be applied. More conservative and less analytical methods of setting safety stocks and order points are also in use in industry.

In assembly activities where inventory requirements are dependent upon end-product demand, there may be little or no need to carry safety stocks providing the material requirements are time-phased (coordinated) with the production schedule. MRP systems determine when to order dependent demand items and how to reschedule to adjust to changing requirements. They take end-item requirements from the master schedule, generate lower-level requirements, and calculate planned order release dates which will enable the firm to meet projected requirements.

Inventory control can begin with an ABC analysis to determine which items merit what kind of control. Class A items typically include only 15–20 percent of the items but account for 75–80 percent of the dollar value of the inventory and deserve most attention. Fixed-order quantity and fixed-order interval are two of the most popular order launching systems in use today. Fixed-order quantity has continuous monitoring and can handle unexpected fluctuations in demand. It also permits use of EOQ ordering and lends itself to computerized control. Periodic systems are, however, more economical in some circumstances, and there are various combinations and ramifications of these two systems.

Firms with large inventories almost "need" a computerized inventory system if they are to maintain effective control at reasonable cost. Any well-integrated system will coordinate inventory levels with scheduling activities, and MRP systems tend to do this better than the traditional order launching systems.

SOLVED PROBLEMS

ECONOMIC ORDER QUANTITIES

***1** If carrying costs consist of two components (1) C_i = interest cost/unit-yr on the average inventory investment, and (2) C_s = storage space cost/unit-yr to accommodate Q units, set up an equation for total costs and derive an expression for the EOQ which includes both these terms.

Solution

$$\text{TC} = \text{ordering} + \text{interest} + \text{storage} + \text{purchase}$$

$$\text{TC} = C_o\left(\frac{1}{Q}\right)D + C_i\frac{Q}{2} + C_sQ + \text{PD}$$

The TC equation can be differentiated by standard calculus methods where the differential of $Y = X^n$ is:

$$\frac{dY}{dX} = nX^{n-1}$$

and, when a constant a is included, the differential of Y with respect to X is

$$Y = aX^n$$

$$\frac{dY}{dX} = naX^{n-1}$$

The differential of a constant (by itself) is, of course, equal to zero, so for example if $Y = 4 + 5X^3$

$$\frac{dY}{dX} = 0 + 15X^2$$

The differential of TC with respect to Q can be obtained most easily if we first move the Q's into the numerator (by adjusting to a negative exponent) so that:

$$\text{TC} = C_oDQ^{-1} + \frac{C_iQ}{2} + C_sQ + \text{PD}$$

Upon differentiating, the purchase cost is a constant and drops out:

$$\frac{d\text{TC}}{dQ} = -C_oDQ^{-2} + \frac{C_iQ^o}{2} + C_SQ^o + 0$$

Setting the first derivative equal to zero, the order quantity is now

$$\text{O} = -\frac{C_oD}{Q^2} + \frac{C_i}{2} + C_s$$

$$\frac{C_oD}{Q^2} = \frac{C_i + 2C_s}{2}$$

$$Q = \sqrt{\frac{2C_oD}{C_i + 2C_s}} \qquad \text{(7-12)}$$

2 An inventory manager is reviewing some annual ordering data for three years ago when the firm used only 2,000 cases and had carrying charges of only 6 percent of the $20/case purchase price. At that time it cost them only $10 to write up an order. The manager has come across the following equation.

$$Q = \sqrt{\frac{2(10)(2{,}000)}{1.20}} = \sqrt{\frac{2(\ \ )10(\ \ )2{,}000(\ \ )}{1.2(\ \ )}}$$

Identify the units associated with the numbers used in the equation and show what units Q results in.

Solution

$$Q = \sqrt{\frac{2\left(\begin{matrix}\text{pure}\\ \text{number}\end{matrix}\right)10(\ \$\ )2{,}000\left(\frac{\text{cases}}{\text{yr}}\right)}{1.20\left(\frac{\$}{\text{case-yr}}\right)}} = 183 \text{ cases}$$

Note that the ($) and (yr) units cancel leaving (cases)^2 so the answer is in cases.

3 A San Antonio stockyard uses about 200 bales of hay/month. They pay a broker $50/order to locate a supplier and handle the ordering and delivery arrangements, so their own storage and handling costs are only $.02/bale-month. If each bale costs $.78, what is the most economical order quantity?

Solution

The purchase price is not relevant and demand and carrying costs are already in the same units (months).

$$\text{EOQ} = \sqrt{\frac{2C_oD}{C_c}} = \sqrt{\frac{2(50)(200)}{0.02}} = 1{,}000 \text{ bales}$$

4 Far West Freeze Dry purchases 1,200 tins of tea annually in economic order quantity lots of 100 tins and pays $9.85/tin. If processing costs for each order are $10, what are the implied carrying costs of this policy?

Solution

$$Q = \sqrt{\frac{2C_oD}{C_c}}$$

∴ Solving for C_c we have:

$$C_c = \frac{2C_oD}{Q^2} = \frac{2(10)(1{,}200)}{(100)^2} = \$2.40/\text{tin-yr}$$

5 A manufacturer requires 600 printed circuit boards per year and estimates an ordering cost of \$20/order. Inventory is financed by short-term loans at approximately 10 percent which work out to a carrying charge of \$.10/unit-yr based upon the average inventory. Storage costs, based upon adequate space for maximum inventory, are \$.025/unit-yr, and the purchase price is \$1 unit. Find (*a*) the most economical order quantity, (*b*) the total annual cost of the inventory, (*c*) the number of orders placed per year.

Solution

(*a*) The EOQ can be determined from the total cost expression:

$$\begin{aligned} \text{TC} &= \text{ordering} + \text{interest} + \text{storage} + \text{purchase} \\ &= \frac{\$20(600)}{Q} + \frac{\$.10}{\text{unit-yr}}\left(\frac{Q}{2}\right)\text{units} + \frac{\$.025Q}{\text{unit-yr}} + \$1.00(600) \\ &= \frac{12{,}000}{Q} + 0.05Q + 0.025Q + 600 \\ &= \frac{12{,}000}{Q} + 0.075Q + 600 \end{aligned}$$

Differentiating we have:

$$\frac{d\text{TC}}{dQ} = \frac{-12{,}000}{Q^2} + 0.075$$

Setting the first derivative = 0

$$Q = \sqrt{\frac{12{,}000}{0.075}} = 400 \text{ units/order}$$

Alternatively, we could use Equation (7-12):

$$Q = \sqrt{\frac{2C_oD}{C_i + 2C_s}} = \sqrt{\frac{2(20)(600)}{0.10 + 2(0.025)}} = 400 \text{ units/order}$$

(*b*) Substituting $Q = 400$ into the TC expression we have:

$$\text{TC} = \frac{12{,}000}{400} + 0.075(400) + 600 = \$660$$

(*c*) Orders/yr $= \dfrac{D}{Q} = \dfrac{600}{400} = 1.5$ orders/yr $= 3$ orders every 2 yrs

ECONOMIC RUN LENGTH

6 The Finish Creamery Company produces ice cream bars for vending machines and has an annual demand for 72,000 bars. The company has the capacity to produce 400 bars per day. It takes only a few minutes to adjust the production set up (cost estimated at \$7.50/setup) for the bars, and the firm is reluctant to produce too many at one time because the storage cost (refrigeration) is relatively high at \$1.50/bar-yr. The firm supplies vending machines with its "Fin-Barrs" on 360 days of the year.

(*a*) What is the most economical number of bars to produce during any one production run?

(*b*) What is the optimal length of the production run in days?

Solution

(*a*) $$\text{ERL} = \sqrt{\frac{2C_oD}{C_c[1 - (d/p)]}}$$

where

C_o = setup cost = \$7.50

D = annual demand = 72,000 bars/yr

C_c = carrying cost = \$1.50/bar-yr

d = daily demand rate $= \dfrac{72{,}000}{360} = 200$ bars/day

p = daily production rate = 400 bars/day

$$\text{ERL} = \sqrt{\frac{2(7.50)(72{,}000)}{1.50[1 - (200/400)]}}$$

$$= 1{,}200 \text{ bars/run}$$

(*b*) Optimal number of days of the

$$\text{Number of days} = \frac{1{,}200 \text{ bars}}{400 \text{ bars/day}} = 3 \text{ days}$$

7 A firm has a yearly demand for 52,000 units of a product which it produces. The cost of setting up for production is \$80 and the weekly production rate is 1,000 units. The carrying cost is \$2.50/unit-yr. How many units should the firm produce on each production run?

Solution

$$Q = \sqrt{\frac{2C_oD}{C_c[1 - (d/p)]}} = \sqrt{\frac{2(80)(52{,}000)}{3.50[1-(1000/1000)]}} = \sqrt{\infty} = \infty$$

Note that the demand and production rates in this problem are equal and the equation (rightly) suggests they should have an infinite (continuous) run.

UNCERTAINTIES IN INVENTORY MANAGEMENT

8 A producer of SUN-STOP suntan lotion uses 400 gallons/week of a chemical which is ordered in EOQ quantities of 5,000 gallons at a quantity discount cost of \$3.75/gallon. Procurement lead time is two weeks and a safety stock of 200 gallons is maintained. Storage cost is \$.01/gallon-week. Find (*a*) the maximum inventory on hand (on the average), (*b*) the average inventory maintained, (*c*) the order point (in units).

Solution

(*a*) Maximum inventory: I_{max} = safety stock + EOQ

$$= 200 + 5{,}000 = 5{,}200 \text{ gal}$$

(*b*) Average inventory: $I_{ave} = \frac{I_{max} + I_{min}}{2} = \frac{5{,}200 + 200}{2} = 2{,}700$ gal

(*c*) Order point: OP $= D_{LT} + SS$

$$= (400)(2) + 200 = 1{,}000 \text{ units}$$

9 A firm has an annual demand of 1,000 units, ordering costs of \$10/order, and carrying costs of \$10/unit-yr. Stockout costs are estimated to be about \$40 each time the firm has an exposure to stockout. How much safety stock is justified by the carrying costs?

Solution

$$Q = \sqrt{\frac{2D(C_o + C_e)}{C_c}} + \sqrt{\frac{2(1{,}000)(10 + 40)}{10}} = 100 \text{ units}$$

$$\therefore \text{Orders/yr} = \frac{D}{Q} = \frac{1{,}000 \text{ units/yr}}{100 \text{ units/order}} = 10 \text{ orders/yr}$$

Stockout costs are (\$40/trial)(10 trials/yr) = \$400/yr

At carrying costs of \$10/unit-yr, the \$400 will fund:

$$\frac{\$400/\text{yr}}{\$10/\text{unit-yr}} = 40 \text{ units of safety stock}$$

Note that, given a cumulative distribution of demand, this SS could be used to find the corresponding level of service provided.

HANDLING UNCERTAINTIES VIA USE OF STANDARD STATISTICAL DISTRIBUTIONS

10 A firm producing portable typewriters has an average demand of 30/week ($\sigma_D = 8$ units). The firm mounts the typewriters in leatherette cases which are purchased from a supplier who delivers them about two weeks after receipt of order ($\sigma_{LT} = 1$ week). Both demand and lead time are normally distributed. The firm would like to provide sufficient safety stock of cases to limit the stock-out risk to 10 percent. How many cases should be carried as safety stock?

Solution

We must express both demand and lead time in common units and combine them per Equation (7-11).

Demand	Lead time
$\mu = 30$ units	$\mu = 2$ weeks at 30 units/week $= 60$ units
$\sigma_D = 8$ units	$\sigma_{LT} = 1$ week at 30 units/week $= 30$ units

$$\sigma_c = \sqrt{(\sigma_D)^2 + (\sigma_{LT})^2} = \sqrt{(8)^2 + (30)^2} = 31 \text{ units}$$

For SOR $= 10\%$, SL $= 100\% - 10\% = 90\%$

$\therefore$ $SF_\sigma = 1.28$ (per Table 7-2)

$$SS = SF_\sigma(\sigma_c)$$
$$= 1.28(31) = 39.74, \text{ say } 40 \text{ units}$$

***11** An inventory control analyst has determined that the lead time on a certain item is distributed as Poission with a mean $\mu = 1.8$ weeks. Each week the firm uses 200 of these items and the analyst wishes to establish a safety stock level that gives 99 percent assurance that the item will be in stock when it is needed. How many units of safety stock should be kept on hand to provide this level of service? (Round any fractional weeks of lead time to the next highest number, for example, >7 weeks $= 8$ weeks.)

Solution

Using a cumulative Poisson distribution we need to find a numerical value for X such that

$$P(X \geq ? \mid \mu = 1.8) = 0.01 \quad \text{where } 0.01 \text{ is the SOR}$$
$$1.8 \text{ is the mean } \mu$$

From the Poisson distribution table, Appendix F, we find

$$P(X > 5 \mid \mu = 1.8) = 0.01$$

$\therefore$ maximum value (i.e., >5) $= 6$

Thus, the lead time that will be exceeded only 1 percent of the time is 6 weeks.

$$SS = L_{SOR} - L_{ave}$$

$$SS = 6.0 - 1.8 = 4.2 \text{ weeks}$$

$$\text{Number of items} = (4.2 \text{ weeks}) \left(\frac{200 \text{ items}}{\text{week}} \right) = 840 \text{ items of SS}$$

QUESTIONS

7-1 Why do firms carry inventories? Would the reasons differ for a sawmill (with an inventory of logs) as opposed to a hospital (with an inventory of drugs)?

7-2 What are the major tangible and intangible costs associated with inventories?

7-3 Two members of the board of directors are upset by their firm's loss of a large military order because the firm was unable to ship a sufficient number of items from stock. In a top management meeting they have criticized the general manager's inventory management policies, pointing out that whereas sales have doubled over the past 10 years, the inventory levels have failed to increase a proportional (linear) amount. Comment.

7-4 Explain how the various assumptions of the basic EOQ model are recognized and/or accounted for.

7-5 The standard "cookbook" EOQ formula does not include the purchase price of an item. Why is this so? When is it important to consider purchase price in computing the most economic lot size?

7-6 In the economic run-length equation, what is the effect of letting the production rate get increasingly faster than the demand rate to the point where goods are produced almost instantaneously?

7-7 Identify the two major uncertainties encountered in managing inventories. What is usually done to compensate for these uncertainties?

7-8 How does the basic methodology for setting safety stock levels differ depending upon the characteristics and/or knowledge of the distribution of demand?

7-9 Suppose you are assigned the task of setting up safety stocks for generator spare parts for a municipal light and power company. How might you go about establishing a stockout cost?

7-10 Contrast the fixed-order quantity and fixed-order interval inventory control systems, pointing out (*a*) what the interrelated variables are, (*b*) briefly how each system functions, and (*c*) what kinds of uncertainties the systems are designed to cope with.

7-11 Using the accompanying diagram, identify the following by letter:

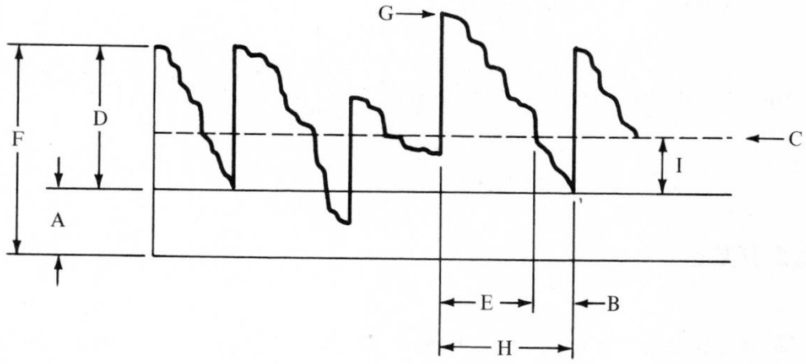

(*a*) ______ reorder point
(*b*) ______ lead time
(*c*) ______ order cycle
(*d*) ______ order quantity
(*e*) ______ safety stock

7-12 Distinguish between dependent and independent demand and explain why MRP systems are more appropriate under one type rather than under the other.

7-13 Indicate whether the following statements are true or false.

(*a*) The EOQ model is based upon minimizing the costs of storing goods versus carrying goods.

(*b*) According to the EOQ model, under constant ordering and carrying costs a doubling of demand will require a doubling of inventory.

(*c*) Quantity discounts cause steps (discontinuities) in the total cost curve.

(*d*) Total inventory costs are relatively insensitive to small changes in order quantities.

7-14 Indicate whether the following statements are true or false.

(*a*) An order point is a periodic (equal) time interval when orders are placed to bring inventories up to a specified level.

(*b*) It is common practice to include safety stock inventory when calculating order points.

(*c*) As the desired level of service increases, the amount of safety stock required increases in direct linear proportion.

(*d*) Stockout costs can be estimated by subtracting the carrying costs from the ordering cost.

7-15 Indicate whether the following statements are true or false.

(*a*) In the base stock system, inventory levels are reviewed on a periodic basis but orders are placed only when inventories have fallen below a predetermined level.

(*b*) In fixed-order quantity systems, the usual procedure is to place orders when the safety stock level is reached, rather than before or after.

(*c*) Fixed-order quantity systems require some form of continuous monitoring of inventory levels.

(*d*) MRP systems do not lend themselves to use of ordering by EOQ amounts.

PROBLEMS

1 The hospital operations manager at Mercy General has asked the stores department to begin ordering inventory on an economic lot size basis. They use 500 electrocardiogram tape rolls/yr, have an ordering cost of $10/order, and estimate carrying costs at $.25/unit-yr. How many tapes should be ordered each time?

2 An appliance distributor has an annual demand represented by the probability distribution shown.

Demand	Probability
200	0.10
400	0.20
600	0.30
800	0.40

The distributor operates 250 days/yr and carries a safety stock of 30 toasters. Each toaster costs $8.75, but ordering costs are $15/order so it is not profitable to order a few toasters. In addition, carrying and storage costs are $2.00 per toaster per year. Lead time for the supplier is approximately 10 days. What is the most economical number of toasters to order at one time?

3 Factory Built Homes, Incorporated (FBH), purchases paneling components from a nearby western New York mill for \$5/unit. They expect to use about 6,000 units during the coming year. FBH estimates it costs them \$15 to place an order and \$.50/unit-yr for carrying and storage costs. The mill can provide FBH with immediate delivery of any reasonable quantity.

(*a*) What is the most economical quantity for FBH to order?
(*b*) How many orders/yr should be placed?
(*c*) What is the total yearly cost associated with ordering, carrying, and purchasing the EOQ amount?

4 A farm machinery manufacturer requires 7,000 air filters/yr as replacement parts on mechanical harvesters. The filters cost \$3 each and are stored in rented facilities at a cost of \$.35/unit-yr, with storage requirements based upon the maximum number of units purchased at one time Q. The interest (carrying) costs, based upon average inventory, are \$.30/unit-yr and the firm uses \$35/order as the ordering cost. What is the most economical order quantity? (*Hint:* See Solved Prob. 1.)

5 Golden Valley Cannery uses 64,000 size no. 7X cans annually and can purchase any quantity up to 10,000 cans at \$.040/can. At 10,000 cans the unit cost drops to \$.032/can and for purchases of 30,000 it is \$.030/can. Costs of ordering are \$24/order, interest costs are 20 percent of the price/can and apply to the average inventory. Storage costs are \$.02/can-yr and are based upon maximum inventory. (Disregard safety stock costs.)

(*a*) What is the EOQ, disregarding the quantity discounts?
(*b*) What is the most economical order quantity considering the quantity discounts?

*6 Derive an equation for the most economic lot size when the following costs apply:

Ordering: C_o\$/order
Stockout: C_e\$/exposure (where each order cycle constitutes an exposure)
Interest: C_i\$/unit-yr (based upon average inventory)
Storage: C_s\$/order (based upon maximum inventory)
Purchase: P\$/unit (based upon annual demand D)

7 An electronics firm produces calculators at a rate of 100/week (5-day week and 50 weeks/yr). Each calculator requires two nickel-cadmium batteries (10,000/yr total) which are also produced internally at a rate of 500/day. Setup costs for battery production are estimated at \$230/run and the production analyst estimates carrying and storage costs for each battery at \$.20/unit-yr. What is the most economical run length for batteries?

8 A soft drink producer receives bottles in economic lot quantities of 8,000 units/order and uses them at a rate of 400/day. If the lead time is 15 working days and they carry a safety stock of 2,000 bottles, what is the appropriate order point?

9 A commercial airline has determined that 10 spare brake cylinders will give them a stockout risk of 30 percent whereas 14 will reduce the risk to 15 percent, and 16 to 10 percent. It takes four months to receive the cylinders from a Pittsburgh supplier and the airline uses an average of four cylinders per month. At what stock level should they reorder, assuming they wish to maintain an 85 percent service level?

10 Food-Mart chain purchases fresh bread in large quantity lots (thousands of loaves) from O'Sullivan's Bakery. The bread is delivered daily to its stores throughout the city, which have a demand characterized by the probability distribution shown. Purchase price is $250/thousand and the bread sells for $.35/loaf. All leftover (day-old) bread is disposed of the next morning at $.20/loaf. What is the most economical (profitable) amount to stock on an expected value basis?

Demand (loaves in 000)	**Probability of demand $P(X)$**
8	0.1
9	0.3
10	0.4
11	0.2

11 A Kansas City feedlot operator supplies beef to several meat packing plants. The steers have an average value of $450 and the operator finances them through a local bank, paying 10 percent interest on the borrowed funds. The data given represents the weekly demand over the past 100 weeks.

Weekly demand (no. steers)	**Frequency (no. weeks)**
0 < 100	10
100 < 200	35
200 < 300	40
300 < 400	10
400 < 500	5
	100

(*a*) Prepare a histogram of the frequency distribution of demand.
(*b*) Graph the cumulative distribution of demand.

The feedlot operator wishes to keep enough stock in the lot to supply weekly demand 90 percent of the time. Feed costs to "maintain" a steer at a prescribed weight are $5/week.

(*c*) What level of safety stock (that is, how many steers) should the operator carry to provide the 90 percent service level?
(*d*) What is the annual cost of carrying this safety stock?

12 Demand for a particular type of transformer bushing varies according to the schedule shown. The manufacturer purchases bushings from an outside supplier at $200/bushing and estimates that it costs 20 percent of the purchase price to carry a bushing in stock for a year.

Weekly demand (no. bushings)	Frequency (no. weeks)
0 < 10	5
10 < 20	10
20 < 30	35
30 < 40	20
40 < 50	15
50 < 60	10
60 < 70	5

(*a*) Compute the cumulative distribution of demand and plot the curve.

(*b*) What is the median number of bushings needed per week and the cost/yr of carrying this amount (that is, the median amount) on a continuing basis?

(*c*) Estimate the service level provided by carrying a safety stock of 30 units.

(*d*) What is the total carrying cost ($/yr including average inventory and safety stock) required to limit the risk of stockout to 5 percent of the order cycles?

(*e*) How many units of safety stock are required to provide the firm with a 50 percent service level?

13 Data on the distribution of lead times for a pump component were collected as shown. Management would like to set safety stock levels that will limit the stockout risk to 10 percent.

Lead time (weeks)	Frequency of occurrence
0 < 1	10
1 < 2	20
2 < 3	70
3 < 4	40
4 < 5	30
5 < 6	10
6 < 7	10
7 < 8	10
	200

(*a*) Graph the cumulative distribution.

(*b*) How many weeks of safety stock are required to provide the desired service level?

***14** A producer of cake and biscuit mixes purchases flour in 100 lb bags and has the following costs and usage rates:

Price	\$10/bag	Ordering cost	\$20/order
Annual usage	3,125 bags	Carrying cost/yr	20 percent of price

(*a*) What is the basic EOQ amount?

In order to obtain 90 percent service against stockout, the firm maintains a safety stock of 90 bags of flour.

(*b*) What is the carrying cost on the safety stock?
(*c*) What stockout cost per exposure does this carrying cost imply?
(*d*) Assuming the stockout cost is an acceptable approximation to management, what would be the revised EOQ?
(*e*) How many orders/yr will be placed under this revised EOQ?

***15** The Browne and Chocolate Candy Company supplies customers in the Nashville area with 60,000 boxes of "Brunchie" candy/yr at a rate of 200/day. The plant can produce 400/day but management hesitates to build up too large an inventory for the spoilage, storage, and carrying costs run to \$1.50/box-yr. The changeover cost to produce "Brunchies" is only \$25/setup and management feels a cost of \$75 is incurred in loss of goodwill each time the company runs out of stock and must tell customers they have to wait for their candy. What is the most economical number of boxes to produce during any one production run?

16 Demand for a piping component during its two-week lead time is normally distributed with a mean of 500 units and standard deviation of 20. The firm wishes to limit stockouts to an average of one in every 20 reorder cycles. What order point should be used?

17 A manufacturer of water filters purchases components in EOQs of 850 units/order. The total need (demand) averages 12,000 components/yr and MAD = 32 units/month. If the manufacturer carries a safety stock of 80 units, what service level does this give the firm?

18 A franchised restaurant drive-in operation in Chicago operates 50 weeks/yr and is closed 2 weeks for vacation. The restaurant gets its hamburger directly from a meat packer but must order a week in advance of shipment. The current forecast of demand is 600 lb/week, and the mean absolute deviation (MAD) is 40 lb/week. The operations manager wishes to carry enough hamburger to limit the stockouts to two times/yr.

(*a*) If the order quantity is 600 lb/order, how many extra pounds of hamburger (safety stock to the nearest pound) should be carried?
(*b*) What is the appropriate order point?
(*c*) Estimate the standard deviation (σ) of demand.

19 The same restaurant mentioned in the previous problem has just come up against an unexpected beef shortage that has increased the lead time to 4 weeks. (The manager still forecasts—weekly—a need for 600 lb/week). Approximately how much safety stock should now be carried to have the same level of protection as before?

20 (*a*) Complete the accompanying time-phased order point plan.

Order quantity = 500
Lead time = 4 weeks
Safety stock = 125

		Week 1	2	3	4	5	6	7	8
Projected requirements		150	150	150	150	200	200	180	320
Scheduled receipts				500					
On-hand at end of period	300	150	—	350	200				
Planned order release									

(*b*) What is the expected average amount of inventory on-hand at the *end* of the periods? (Do not include the initial 300 units in your end-of-period average.)

21 (*a*) Complete the accompanying material requirements plan (MRP).

Order quantity = 500
Lead time = 4 weeks

		Week 1	2	3	4	5	6	7	8
Projected requirements		150	150	150	150	200	200	180	320
Scheduled receipts				500					
On-hand at end of period	300	150	—	350	200				
Planned order release									

(*b*) What is the expected average amount of inventory on hand at the *end* of the periods? (Do not include the initial 300 units in your end-of-period average.)

22 The inventory manager of Office Fixtures, Incorporated, is attempting to plan material requirements for the production of one of the firm's desk lamps over the next eight weeks. Each lamp consists of a metal base, tube steel frame, and two light assemblies. The light assemblies are, in turn, each made up of a switch and tube holder. Details on the end-item requirements and component parts are given below. Develop a material requirements plan (MRP) for the various inventory components showing (1) the time-phased requirements, (2) the scheduled receipts, (3) the on-hand inventory, and (4) the planned order release information.

End-item requirements Week	Number
1	120
3	80
6	100
8	120

The component part data are shown in the following table:

	Base	Frame	Light assembly (complete)	Light assembly components Switch	Tube holder
Order quantity	200	350	150	500	600
Lead time (weeks)	5	3	4	2	2
On hand	250	200	420	340	550

23 The Hotel-Restaurant Supply Company orders potatoes in units of 500 bags/order and receives them 10 days later. Their deliveries and usage averages 20 bags/day and they maintain an extra rotating stock of 40 bags to be sure they do not run out of stock. Assuming their demand is normally distributed with $\sigma = 16$, (*a*) What is the lead time? (*b*) What is the order point? (*c*) What service level does the safety stock provide? (*d*) Suppose the firm management felt that running out of stock during two order cycles of the year was acceptable. By how much could the safety stock be reduced? Assume a 250-working-day year.

24 In an attempt to establish an ABC classification, a firm analyzed its inventory of 5,000 items in terms of number of items and value of items as shown [9].

	Number			Value		
$ Value class (usage × cost)	Number of items	Cumulative total items	Cumulative percent of items	Total value	Cumulative value ($)	Cumulative percent value
I (high)	250	250	5.0	490,000	490,000	50.0
II	50	300	6.0	65,000	555,000	56.6
III	300	600	12.0	180,000	735,000	75.0
IV	450	1,050	21.0	88,200	823,200	84.0
V	45	1,095	21.9	19,600	842,800	86.0
VI	865	1,960	39.2	31,360	874,160	89.2
VII	290	2,250	45.0	27.440	901,600	92.0
VIII (low)	2,750	5,000	100.0	78,400	980,000	100.0
		5,000	100.0		980,000	100.0

Following the usual rules for ABC breakdown indicate (*a*) the value classes that would be included, (*b*) the percentage of items, and (*c*) the percentage of value, respectively, in the A classification, B classification, and C classification.

25 A lumber distributor orders plywood sheets in economic lot sizes of 2,000 sheets/order and it takes 10 days before the mill delivers the plywood. The distributor sells roughly 40 sheets/day (12,000/yr) and maintains a safety stock of 300 sheets.

(*a*) What type of inventory control system could the distributor be using?
(*b*) What is the lead time?
(*c*) What is the appropriate order point?
(*d*) If it costs the firm $30 to place an order, what is the implied holding (including storage) cost?

26 Swensen Supply Company distributes 31,200 electric switches/yr and orders in economic lot sizes of 6,000 switches/order. A safety stock level of 4,000 has been set by management. Lead time is typically 10 calendar days and the firm operates 6 days/week, 52 weeks/yr.

(*a*) Under a fixed-order size system, what is the appropriate order point?
(*b*) If the firm switched to a fixed-order interval system, would it still order an economic lot size amount each time?
(*c*) What would be the reorder interval under a periodic system (assuming the same safety stock of 4,000 were maintained)?

CASE: BEVERLY BROTHERS FURNITURE COMPANY

Since one hundred years ago, when it was founded, Beverly Brothers Furniture Company had grown to claim a respectable share of the Midwestern furniture market. Bertrand Beverly, the president, attributed this partly to the competitive quality of their lines but mostly to their policy of "unexcelled customer service." He frequently repeated his claim that Beverly Brothers had never really lost any customers due to inability to ship on time, preferably from stock. Some customers had, of course, gradually shifted to other suppliers, but they still came back to Beverly for bits and pieces or less popular items because they "knew they could count on Beverly." As a result, Beverly had a large clientele.

Business had grown steadily until about 10 years ago when profits leveled off, and for the past 5 years they had declined. To remedy the situation (as well as appeal to more customers), 3 years ago Beverly took decisive action. As a marketing strategy, the company undertook a program which by now had nearly doubled its number of lines. To economize in production, it went to basic EOQ purchase amounts for all inventory items except where quantity discounts were available. In those cases it purchased the largest lot size available, or a one-year supply, whichever was less. Also, since service was a hallmark of company policy, it maintained a stock equivalent to the largest daily usage multiplied by the average delivery time for each item used in the construction of its furniture.

Despite these improvements, the financial situation at Beverly Brothers had deteriorated rapidly in the past two years and Bertrand Beverly was searching desperately for the cause. Marketing was ruled out as the problem area because sales had not only kept up fairly well but had even increased by 3 percent over the two years. Sales were also diversified across more lines and included an increasing number of one-shot replacement items which were shipped directly from stock and resulted in satisfied customers. Production had now fully converted to the planned EOQ–quantity discount program and the shop appeared to be in a constant flurry of activity. There was even some talk of a need for expansion.

Mr. Beverly concluded the problem must be one of financial management. The amount of current assets had grown substantially and yet the firm was, for the first time, experiencing real difficulty finding sufficient cash to pay off current liabilities. Yet the comptroller claimed that due to favorable long-term financing years ago, the firm's capital cost was very low. She pointed out that the right moves eight years ago enabled her still to quote an overall 6 percent cost of capital whereas some of their most recent short-term financing was double that amount. So financial mismanagement was also ruled out.

In exasperation Mr. Beverly sought out a management consultant who, for one day's work and a $500 fee, left him with a 30-page unintelligible report containing terms and symbols like "dependent-independent," ERL, SOR, MRP, and so forth. He slapped it on the desk of his assistant (a recently hired graduate) with the plea, "Look here, will you *please* tell me what this says in *layman's English*? How's about writing a one-page summary for me? If you can't understand it either, just *tell me what you think it should say*. I've got to do something even if it's wrong!"

Prepare the analysis requested by Mr. Beverly.

BIBLIOGRAPHY

[1] ABRAMOWITZ, IRVING: *Production Management*, Ronald Press Company, New York, 1967.

[2] BUCHAN, J., AND E. KOENIGSBERG: *Scientific Inventory Control*, Prentice-Hall, Englewood Cliffs, New Jersey, 1963.

[3] BUFFA, ELWOOD S.: *Modern Production Management*, 4th ed., John Wiley & Sons, New York, 1973.

[4] GARRETT, LEONARD J., AND MILTON SILVER: *Production Management Analysis*, 2d ed., Harcourt, Brace & World, New York, 1973.

[5] IBM: *The Production Information and Control System*, GE20-0280-2.

[6] ORLICKY, JOSEPH: *Material Requirements Planning: The New Way of Life in Production and Inventory Management*, McGraw-Hill Book Company, New York, 1975.

[7] PLOSSL, G. W., AND O. W. WIGHT: *Production and Inventory Control*, Prentice-Hall, Englewood Cliffs, New Jersey, 1967.

[8] RIGGS, JAMES L.: *Production Systems: Planning, Analysis, and Control*, John Wiley & Sons, New York, 1970.

[9] VOLLMAN, THOMAS E.: *Operations Management*, Addison-Wesley Publishing Company, Reading, Massachusetts, 1973.

[10] WIGHT, OLIVER W.: *Production and Inventory Management in the Computer Age*, Cahners Books, Boston, Massachusetts, 1974.

[11] YEOMANS, K. A.: *Statistics for the Social Scientist*, vol. 2, Penguin Education, Middlesex, England, 1968.

CHAPTER

8

Production Planning and Control: Aggregate Planning

Most firms would not attempt to follow completely the random ups and downs of actual demand. On the other hand, firms cannot afford to ignore them either. To what extent *should* a firm respond to demand? More precisely, how many units should it produce and when should it produce them? What will be the effect on employment and inventory levels? Once a production plan has been developed, how do the production activities get scheduled, authorized, and actually begun? And how is the production volume controlled? We focus upon these fundamental and crucial concerns of operations managers in this chapter and the next. This chapter is concerned with aggregate planning and the next one with detailed scheduling. But the chapter materials are intimately related and should be considered as a unit even though they have been separated for study purposes.

Before getting into the specifics of aggregate planning, we shall use the first half of this chapter to gain a quick overview of production planning and control. To do this, we first identify the "controllable" variables management has available to work with and examine the topics of aggregate planning and detailed scheduling as an integrated activity. We shall note how production control problems differ for continuous, intermittent, and project-type systems. In the same vein, some production systems must be adjusted for the effects of a learning phenomenon, so we shall recognize that also.

After the overview we concentrate on the major topic of this chapter, aggregate planning. Some general guidelines for planning are presented and we go into some detail on graphical, charting, and mathematical methods of adjusting the aggregate levels of production, employment, and inventory in response to demand. Planning techniques range from simple charts, through transportation linear programming models, to some of the more sophisticated nonlinear and heuristic computer search methods.

Following our study of aggregate planning in this chapter, we zero in on the management of specific day-to-day scheduling activities in the next chapter. The master schedule is really the link between aggregate planning and detailed scheduling, and, although it is introduced in this chapter, we shall be referring to it in both chapters. The next chapter begins with a review of scheduling philosophies and identifies a number of graphic, mathematical, heuristic, and computerized aids available to management. It includes consideration of jobshop systems, where individual worker or machine assignments must be scheduled. In addition to other techniques, the assignment method of linear programming is a useful method for assigning workers to jobs, jobs to machines, and so on, and will be included there.

After the aggregate planning and detailed scheduling have been done, system operations must be monitored to ensure that the correct quantities of output are produced at the right times. The last section of Chap. 9 discusses some appropriate control models, including basic output control. Whereas much of the detailed scheduling methodology will have pertained to continuous and intermittent systems, that section will provide a more in-depth study of PERT, a planning and control technique which has proven to be especially useful to project managers.

OBJECTIVES OF PRODUCTION PLANNING AND CONTROL

In this section we examine the need for controlling production, the variables subject to control, and finally define production control in terms of how it satisfies the need by managing the variables.

NEED FOR CONTROLLING PRODUCTION

We noted in an earlier chapter that forecasts of demand enable managers to plan future levels of production more intelligently than they otherwise could. But even with some smoothing, the forecasts often evidence variations in terms of trends or seasonal factors. Actual demands bring additional fluctuations.

In reality, demands cannot always be met, nor can all orders be accepted. Ultimately some authoritative decisions must be made specifying what the quantity of production will be for the forthcoming time periods. These critical decisions are the responsibility of planners and schedulers. These are the people who must also decide when and how the master schedule should be revised if it turns out that materials or capacity are inadequate to complete the planned activities.

The volume decision is, however, not as simple as something like adjusting the rate of flow from a water faucet for several reasons. *First*, each system is composed of an intricate and interdependent mix of labor, materials, and equipment. When the rate of output is changed, the previous balance is lost and a new "optimal" mix must be sought by readjusting the usage rate of the various resources. *Second*, the problem is further complicated by the fact that the plant, inventories, and human resources are investments that cost money to maintain—even (especially) if they are idle! *Third*, intangible constraints apply. Goals are not always clear and firms are increasingly recognizing a moral obligation (or perhaps even a contract commitment) to provide their workers with the security of reasonably stable employment.

Production control is perhaps the most integrative responsibility that operations managers have. The decisions of how, what, when, and how much to actually produce lie at the heart of organizational activity and send repercussions throughout the firm to the personnel, finance, marketing, and other areas. For this reason production controllers must maintain a systems perspective which reconciles subsystem objectives, such as level of employment, low inventory investment, high level of customer service, and so forth, within the framework of broader organizational goals.

In short, production control is needed to control both the *quantity* of output (production) and the *timing* of output (scheduling). But it is a complex problem that must be tackled with a thorough knowledge of the existing mix of inventory and personnel, accurate information on costs, and full cognizance of system and subsystem goals.

VARIABLES SUBJECT TO CONTROL

The variables subject to control are fundamentally the labor, materials, and capital inputs described in our production system model of Chap. 1. More labor effort will theoretically generate more volume of output, so the *employment level* and use of *overtime* are highly relevant variables. Materials can also be used to regulate the flow of output by storing and depleting *inventories*, *back-ordering*, and *subcontracting* items to other firms (the make versus buy decision). Finally, in addition to funding employment and inventory levels, the capital input represents a variable controlling the overall *plant capacity* in a longer-range sense.

In a more specific sense, the controllable variables become the actual jobs scheduled for production, the men and women assigned to jobs, and the machines as well as processes available for use. Someone must ultimately make detailed preparations and place the production machinery in motion.

WHAT IS PRODUCTION PLANNING AND CONTROL ?

Production planning and control is a staff activity that plans aggregate levels of production, employment, and inventories, and controls the combination activities by scheduling, authorizing, and monitoring how many and what kind of items to produce, and how, when, and where to produce them. Figure 8-1 depicts some of the many interrelationships of the production planning and control function. Note that the forecasts and long-term (aggregate) planning supply data for the master schedule, which in turn dictates requirements for short-term scheduling activities.

We can relate the major production planning and control activities more specifically to our topics of study by referring to Fig. 8-2. The figure extends the process planning considerations discussed earlier (from Fig. 5-3 and shown here as dotted) into the planning and control activities discussed in this chapter and the next. Our immediate concern is with *master planning*, which we shall define to encompass both development of the production plan and the master schedule.

A *production plan* is a statement of production goals, based on forecasts of demand and resource availability, that consciously attempts to manage employment and inventory levels to attain organizational objectives. As can be seen from Fig. 8-2, the forecast (Chap. 6) provides basic guidance for the production plan. Another input comes from a rough assessment of the firm's resource base and technological capabilities. The production plan then establishes how many units will be made during the forthcoming periods and projects the impact of this upon inventories, employment levels, customer service, and the like.

The *master schedule* (also shown in Fig. 8-2) flows from the production plan and is really what drives the entire production system. It is a high-level schedule that translates the production plan into specific product terms by specifying what end product or product modules are to be produced and the time periods during which they are to be made. It is the nerve center of the planning activities.

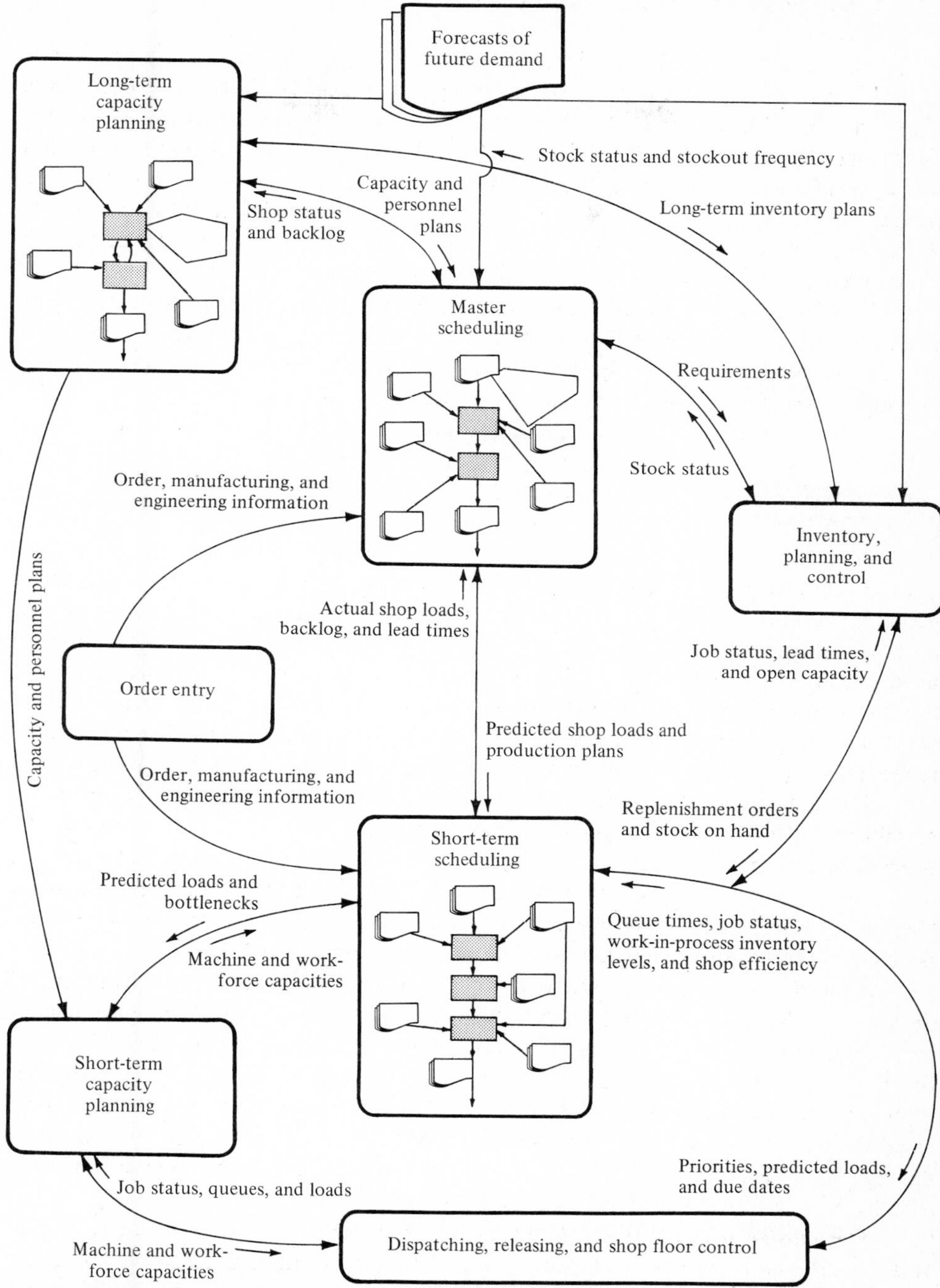

FIGURE 8-1 Interrelationships of production planning and control. Source: W. K. Holstein, "Production Planning and Control Integrated," *Harvard Business Review*, vol. 46, no. 3, May–June 1968.

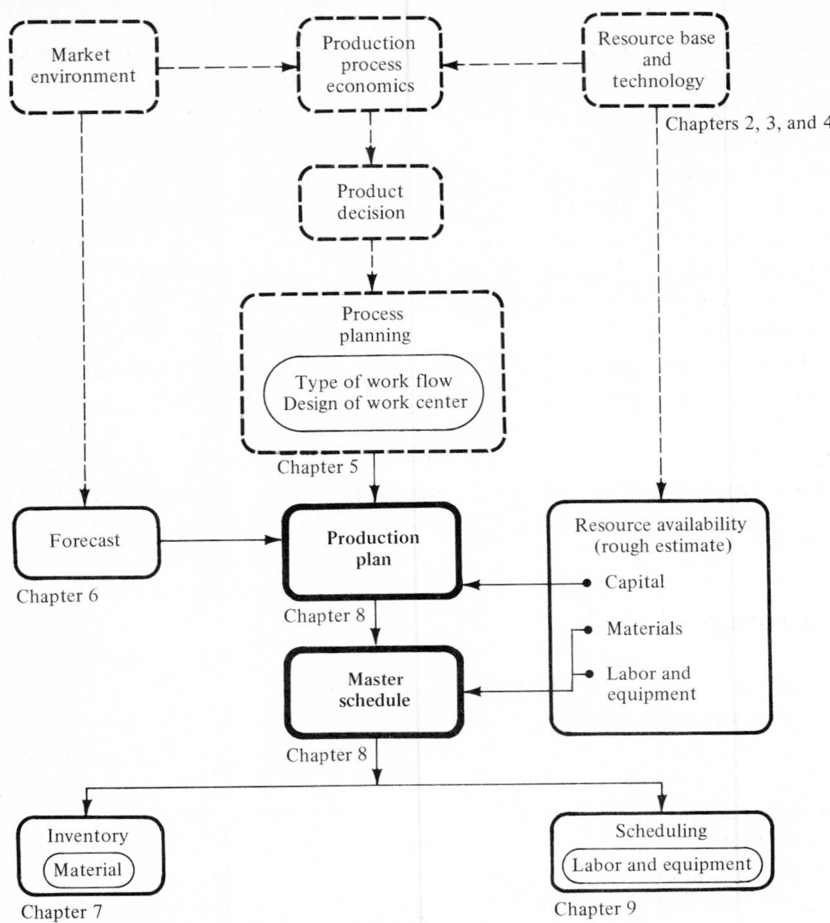

FIGURE 8-2 Production plan and master schedule

From the master schedule are derived the component inventory and scheduling requirements. Although the inventory and scheduling subsystems are highly integrative and interdependent, it is conceptually helpful to analyze each separately. The inventory component has already been described in Chap. 7 and the detailed (or assembly) scheduling activities will be taken up in Chap. 9. The *detailed schedule* is a low-level schedule specifying precisely what must be produced and the starting and/or completion dates. It generally covers a shorter time horizon (such as a few days) than the master schedule or the production plan.

The Production Planning and Control Department

The specific functions of production control departments vary widely among different industries and firms as indeed does even the existence of such departments. Some firms simply equate production control with quantity control whereas others empower it with countless associated functions. In essence, production control is concerned with anything that directly affects the *quantity* or *timing* of output.

Production planning and control activities may be carried out under the name of a production department, a production planning group, or perhaps even a scheduling department. In any case, production control is generally a staff activity, leaving to line management the actual exercise of authority to perform the work. Some organizations maintain a highly centralized control (where the production control office keeps detailed records of the daily progress of jobs) whereas others place more discretion in the hands of line management and foremen, letting them decide when and where to do the jobs and what records to keep [**15**: 444].

As mentioned earlier, the central aspects of production planning and control are master planning (*aggregate planning* and *master scheduling*) and *detailed scheduling.* To illustrate the interdependence of these activities we shall first view them sequentially, noting their role in the overall context of production planning and control. Following this, we shall return for a more in-depth consideration of aggregate planning methods.

Aggregate Planning

Aggregate planning consists of efforts to plan a desired output over the longer range by adjusting the production rate, employment, inventory, and other controllable variables. These controllable variables in effect constitute pure strategies by which fluctuations in demand and uncertainties in production activities can be accommodated [**1, 18**]. The strategies are illustrated in Table 8-1.

The first strategy suggests a firm might simply vary the size of the work force by hiring and laying off in direct proportion to demand. A second pure strategy would be to maintain a stable work force but to permit idle time (undertime) when demand is slack and to go to overtime when demand is strong. The third strategy would have a constant work force and level production but carry sufficiently large amounts of inventory to absorb all demand fluctuations. A back-order strategy assumes that customers are willing to wait for delivery and this effectively smooths out production too—otherwise this strategy results in stockout costs. In essence, it is the strategy of

TABLE 8-1 PURE AGGREGATE PLANNING STRATEGIES

Strategy	Vary work-force size	Use over- and idle time	Carry large inventories	Incur stockout costs	Use sub-contractors	Adjust capacity
1 Employment	(Yes)	No	No	No	No	No
2 OT and IT	No	(Yes)	No	No	No	No
3 Inventories	No	No	(Yes)	No	No	No
4 Back orders	No	No	No	(Yes)	No	No
5 Subcontracting	No	No	No	No	(Yes)	No
6 Plant capacity	No	No	No	No	No	(Yes)

negative inventory that acknowledges that some demands will not be satisfied. The subcontracting strategy would again permit level production, pushing the fluctuations off onto subcontractors. Finally, plant capacities can be adjusted over the longer run. In some cases the peak loads on facilities, for example, on electric power plants, can also be regulated by differential pricing or other marketing efforts.

Every strategy has countervailing costs associated with it. Varying employment levels results in hiring and training costs, severance and unemployment insurance costs, as well as adverse intangible effects upon the work force and the community. Idle time per se is obviously a waste, and overtime and shift work usually command a premium. Inventories have the usual carrying, storage, tax, and obsolescence costs. Firms that adopt a back-ordering strategy are likely to incur stockout costs, for many customers will simply seek other suppliers. Subcontracting costs are typically higher than in-house production, and additional capacity is, of course, usually a major capital expenditure.

The most favorable solution, however, does not usually result from a choice of one of the pure strategies. Indeed, the pure strategies are often infeasible from a practical standpoint. Instead, a combination, or mix, is typically used. Very often the intention, and result, is not to respond totally to the random fluctuations, but rather to generate a modified response that is judged to be best for the firm over the long run. So the mix may very well include some anticipated stockout costs (strategy 4). We will go into some examples of the uses of these strategies later in the chapter when we take up aggregate master planning methods.

Top management should (but sometimes does not) provide guidance to the aggregate planning activity because these planning decisions often involve basic company policy. Along with the responsibility for adjusting these aggregate levels, production control has the commensurate authority to specify them as operating parameters, and this specification is effectively embodied in the master schedule. The master schedule projects activity levels for some extended period, such as a 13-week quarter or perhaps even longer. As we have seen, it is typically justified on the basis of forecasts plus current orders and other demand information.

Master Scheduling, Priority, and Capacity Planning

Some analysts use the terms "master scheduling" and "aggregate planning" interchangeably, although master scheduling is more specific. Master schedule items are referred to as "end items" and comprise the highest level (or "level zero") in the hierarchy of products, assemblies, subassemblies, components, and so on, that constitute the bill of material for an item.

The master schedule is the vehicle that formalizes the production plan and translates it into specific material and capacity requirements. Figure 8-3 describes these activities in terms of the increasingly popular language being used in industry: *priority planning* and *capacity planning* [**22**: 73]. The meaning of these terms is very important.

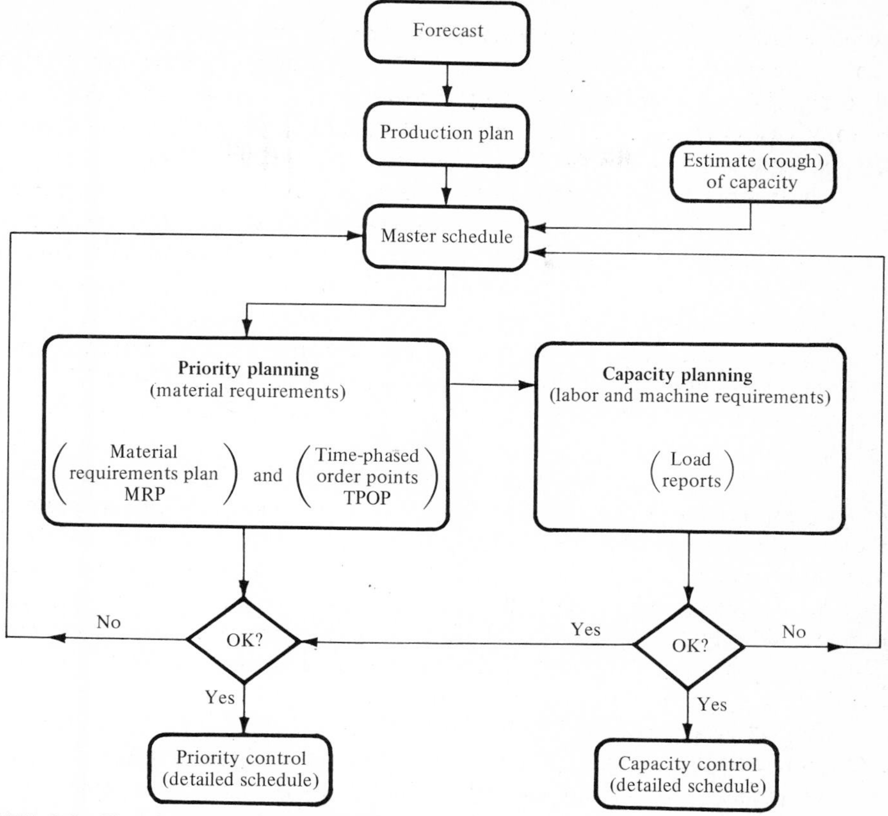

FIGURE 8-3 Planning and control flowchart

Priority planning relates to material requirements and consists of determining what material is required and when it is required. Being material-oriented, priority planning activities are concerned with the adequacy and timing of raw materials, in-process components, and finished inventory flows, as suggested in Fig. 8-2. This attention to inventory flows logically leads to implementation of the time-phased order point (TPOP) and material requirements planning (MRP) systems described in Chap. 7.

The term "priority planning" has come into wide use only since computers have become available to keep priorities up to date. Now, by using TPOP and MRP techniques (including the firm order features discussed below), the priority planning system can effectively handle large volumes of both independent and dependent demand items.

Computerized systems can also override the forecast of demand by incorporating the concept of a "firm planned order" [**22**: 62]. For example, suppose a toy manufacturer is faced with a seasonal peak in December and is trying to build up inventory in July and August to anticipate the demand. However, the December demand is beyond the 13-week planning horizon of their master schedule. Without firm planned orders, the system would automatically delay production of end items and components since the seasonal demand would not be present in the summer planning period. In lieu of any current shipping requirements, it would automatically reschedule items to a later date.

Firm planned-order capability allows schedulers to move a firm planned order into a given time period with the stipulation that the system will not automatically reschedule it. (The system may, however, generate a reschedule message, which the planners can ignore if they choose.) This feature accomplishes two key objectives: (1) it allows planners to generate planned orders at a rate that can help level the production plan, and (2) it permits this to be done within the normal operating constructs of the formal production and inventory control system. The lack of such flexibility and the resulting "forced informality" was one of the major causes of the breakdown of production control systems before the 1970s.

Capacity planning relates to labor and equipment requirements and consists of determining what labor and equipment capacity is required and when it is required. Capacity is usually planned on the basis of labor or machine hours available within the plant. This is typically more accurate than a detailed schedule of individual orders.

Recognizing that most (if not all) materials and components must be processed by the labor and machinery available within the plant, the material requirements constitute an input to the capacity planning function. (See Fig. 8-3.) Capacity planning must then assess the workload at the work centers and determine whether the proposed master schedule is practical.

The process of formulating and revising a master schedule can be complex. Gross requirements are first determined by translating the production plan into end items or modules (such as subassemblies) that are common to more than one end item. Net requirements are then determined by adding any safety stock requirements and adjusting for inventory already on hand or items in process.

The net requirements are then lot-sized into a time-phased schedule of planned orders; that is, they are set up as planned order releases of a predetermined lot size. These orders are then converted into capacity terms and summarized into load reports for the key work centers. The reports constitute the capacity requirements plan. If the planned orders fit within the firm's capacity during each of the forthcoming periods, orders can be released by the material requirements plan, and detailed schedules generated on a daily basis.

If capacity is inadequate, a human decision must be made directing how to revise the master schedule. Perhaps scheduled orders can be rescheduled within a one- or two-month planning horizon without too much harm to any one customer. In other cases, if the marketing decision is to accept more orders than plant capacity can deliver, marketing should be prepared to specify whose orders are to be delayed and should inform customers accordingly. Sometimes planned orders can be rescheduled into firm planned orders to achieve the required load leveling.

Returning to Fig. 8-3, the loop from the "OK?" under the capacity planning block back to the master schedule signifies the trials (and tribulations) the scheduler must sometimes undergo in order to derive a realistic master schedule. The resulting schedule of planned and released orders is the master schedule, which is then used by the MRP system to calculate the requirements for subassemblies and all manner of lower-level components.

Once the master schedule is firmed up, detailed schedules are formulated, work orders dispatched, activities commenced, and controls are expected to function. Control over the production activities is further classified into priority and capacity control as depicted in Fig. 8-3. As noted earlier (Chap. 1), control refers to the conformance of activities to plan and involves measurement, feedback, comparison, and correction. Priority control is concerned with keeping material priorities up to date. This includes monitoring in-process components that are subassemblies to other end products, and involves adjusting needs up *and down* as requirements change and items are rescheduled. (One of the most serious shortcomings of the hectic and unworkable expediting systems of the past has been their failure to downgrade priorities of components not urgently needed with a resultant loss of credibility in the entire formal system.)

Capacity control refers to actions to achieve the production plan by controlling production output rates and lead times. These controls are exercised over the capacity by adjusting labor and machine utilization. Capacities in key work centers are continuously monitored and reported in manageable units, such as standard hours of labor. If some capacities are inadequate, the information is fed back to the master scheduler so that the master schedule can be revised. It is this constant monitoring, rescheduling, and correcting that enables the modern computerized production control systems to function in a formal and effective manner. We shall take up this aspect of production control in more detail in the next chapter.

To carry out its responsibility, production control must maintain close communication with other areas of the organization. For example, the most current information on demand will come from marketing. The difficult task of hiring and training workers rests with personnel, and labor adjustments must be carefully coordinated. Inventory control responsibility (especially finished goods inventory) sometimes rests with other departments. In reality, it is so intimately related to production control that even if there are two departments they must effectively function as one. In essence, the various components must function as an integrated system, and production control plays a key role in making sure that this happens.

Short-term Scheduling

Short-term scheduling usually refers to the specific production plans for the next day, week, or perhaps month. Production control has prime responsibility for controlling the work load on the plant. In this capacity it authorizes and issues production orders specifying precisely how many and what kind of items to produce and how, when, and where to produce them.

Production control has the responsibility of ensuring that all raw materials, supplies, and semifinished parts are available in the right place at the right time. It must also ensure that the correct number of workers with appropriate skills have been scheduled for the right time. Furthermore, where any special tools, drawings, or customer instructions are required to perform the job, production control must make sure they are available. It must assign jobs to work centers and schedule the use of major equipment.

Drawings or specifications for finished goods must usually be "exploded" into their numerous component parts so that component manufacture can be appropriately scheduled. Fifteen years ago this explosion process, as well as the subsequent scheduling of the individual parts, was an overwhelmingly time-consuming manual activity. The paperwork task associated with manufacturing several hundred (or thousand) parts became so complex that the formal system in a moderately sized firm almost inevitably broke down. Production controllers then turned to expeditors who cut through the formalized procedures. Unfortunately, in doing so they often upset the total system balance even more.

Today, with MRP systems functioning from a computerized data base, thousands of items can be handled simultaneously. One reason for this is the way in which the lists of components (the bills of materials) are now structured. Instead of attempting to forecast and control every component and end item, MRP systems use a modularized bill of materials as a basis for planning. The modules specify the product from an assembly sequence standpoint, clearly identifying the subassembly or parent/component relationships that represent levels of completion in the buildup of a product. Planning and control efforts can then be applied to components and subassemblies common to several end products rather than trying to manage each end item as through it were a unique product from beginning to end. In this way the system becomes responsive, flexible, and can still offer the thousands of end-product combinations that arise from a product structure that includes optional features. The automotive industry is an example of one manufacturing group that has capitalized on this feature of MRP systems. It makes no attempt to identify specific option combinations at the master schedule level, but instead relies upon MRP and time-phased order point systems to ensure an appropriate inventory of modules covering the various options available to its dealers.

The computerization of inventory and scheduling activities is one of the most significant advances in the field of operations management in the almost 200 years since factory systems have been in use. Computers can handle the massive amounts of routine work very quickly and MRP systems will even automatically reschedule planned orders to adjust to current requirements. Nevertheless, human schedulers must still release orders to the shop and make the key decisions. Wight points out that some people make the "mistake of trying to generate an automatic master schedule," noting that it is still human beings that must control the master schedule [**22**: 75]. The computer cannot yet satisfactorily deal with price negotiations, delivery delays, strikes, preferential treatment, and the wide realm of employee and environmental concerns.

The decisions and action demanded of schedulers necessitate that they have a broad range of skills and psychologically stable personalities. Schedulers should know how to read engineering drawings, do "take-offs" of bills of materials, and formulate process charts and route sheets. In some firms the details of specifying how the products shall be made are strictly engineering functions, so schedulers may have to work closely with engineers. They must also maintain cost data and are sometimes asked to provide price and delivery estimates to the sales department for bidding purposes. Coordination with other subsystems of the organization is a vital aspect of their job.

We can begin to appreciate the magnitude of the production control task when we realize that the aforementioned functions must sometimes be done for hundreds of jobs at one time. Or perhaps thousands of items must be scheduled into one complex final assembly, such as a nuclear reactor or a spacecraft. It is not unusual for an average-size firm to carry 20,000 different items in inventory. However, the real difficulties come with customer changes, breakdowns, mistakes, or other unexpected delays to the schedule. Modifying or delaying one job can affect a multitude of others. Fortunately, much of the parts and personnel information, work-order instructions, job progress and inventory data is now computerized in large firms, so some of the paperwork burden is reduced. Nevertheless, this nerve center of the organization's activities continues to provide one of the great challenges to operations managers.

HOW PRODUCTION CONTROL DIFFERS DEPENDING UPON THE TYPE OF SYSTEM

Not all firms perform the same production control functions. Indeed, many service industries function entirely without production control departments, for as mentioned in the chapter on inventory control, some services simply cannot be inventoried. There is also a striking difference between the production control activities in continuous, intermittent, and project-type operations. All three types of systems can benefit from the results of aggregate planning of activity levels, although it may take slightly different forms—especially in project planning. However, a good deal of the individual job control that is required in intermittent systems has been designed and built into the continuous systems. Thus we find considerable difference in what have generally been regarded as the traditional production control functions of routing, scheduling, dispatching, and monitoring. The process planning considerations chart in Chap. 5 points out some contrasts between process and product-line layouts which help to account for this difference, and it would be worthwhile to review Fig. 5-3 at this time.

CONTINUOUS SYSTEMS: FLOW CONTROL

Continuous systems are designed to produce large volumes of a single item (or relatively few items) on specialized, fixed-path equipment. They often utilize assembly lines (as television or automobile producers) or continuous-processing equipment (as oil refineries or electric utilities). Most consumer goods and many industrial supplies are sufficiently standardized to warrant this type of system. Raw materials and component parts are common to each unit produced, labor operations are repetitive, and the transformation technology used is the same in each case. All units are *routed* along a fixed path and *scheduling* consists primarily of establishing a production rate (as, for example, in terms of units per day). The production line is put into operation (*dispatched*) by a simple release of authority to produce and is *monitored* in terms of the rate of acceptable units.

High-volume, line-assembled products are typically controlled by a "flow control" system. This means that emphasis is placed on control of the rate of flow of raw materials and subassemblies to the line, balancing the capacities of workers and machines along the line, and the smooth flow and shipment of items off the line. Assembly instructions and reports are relatively simple, for each worker repeats a specified task during each time interval.

Although line-type systems simplify production control, they do not eliminate it. "Behind all the smooth flow of final assembly lines lies a still bigger job; making subassemblies, and making parts for subassemblies" [**15**: 486]. Parts are often made in lots rather than continuously, and inventories of parts, supplies, and subassemblies must be in exactly the right place precisely when needed. Accommodating variety in a production line, such as is done in the automotive industry, becomes a real challenge. The concerns over assembly line balancing, studied previously, become very relevant here.

Continuous systems producing large volumes of similar products are typically found in what are called *make-to-stock* companies. These companies work more from a forecast of demand than, say, from a backlog of customer orders. Since their end-product demand is uncertain, and they intentionally carry a stock of finished items, their master schedule is established from the order points of items in their end-product inventory. This explains the presence of the time-phased order point component of the priority planning block in Fig. 8-3.

A time-phased order point system works from a forecast and will automatically generate planned orders to replenish inventory without regard for any planned production rates [**22**: 62]. Thus, in order to build up inventory for seasonal demands, make-to-stock firms often incorporate a firm planned-order feature into their computer-assisted scheduling programs.

INTERMITTENT SYSTEMS: ORDER CONTROL

Intermittent or job-order-type systems are designed to produce small quantities of many items on relatively general-purpose equipment. Layout and work flow is arranged according to the process and nature of the work to be performed. Many custom-made products, such as commercial jet aircraft, large power transformers, specialized air-handling equipment, and other fabricated assemblies are produced on a job-order basis.

The traditional production control functions require considerable attention in process-oriented jobshops. *Routing* completely specifies the path and sequence of an order through the system. The route sheet may well specify all materials to use, machine assignments, setup and operating times, and the detailed sequence of each manufacturing step. The paperwork for these instructions and associated monitoring can be voluminous unless automatic data processing systems are used. The *scheduling* activity specifies when each operation will be done and detailed analysis is often necessary to determine which equipment is best in view of cost and delivery commitments. *Dispatching*, or actually sending out instructions to perform the work, involves much more than a simple authorization to begin, as in line-type layouts. In jobshops, all the specifications, drawings, special tools, and job tickets or forms for reporting the status of jobs must be collected and released as a package. When some jobs get behind schedule it may be necessary to reschedule hundreds of other jobs. The *monitoring* effort is similarly more complex, for data on the status of all shop orders in process is often fed back to a common control center.

In many plants, expeditors are still assigned to particularly critical jobs to cut through the "red tape" paperwork, expedite materials and tooling, or circumvent other delays in order to give preferred treatment to "hot" items. Theoretically, expeditors operate in a suboptimizing manner and should not be required, but from a practical standpoint they have been deemed necessary in the past. Part of the reason for this is that until the advent of the computer no one had developed a feasible technique that would cope with the uncertainties of controlling the simultaneous production of numerous items requiring different processing times and subject to changes in design and quantity, delays from materials, breakdowns of equipment, and so forth.

The problems mentioned above still exist, but now the computerized MRP systems are providing a flexibility and rescheduling response rate that is finally beginning to alleviate them. Many firms have not yet converted to computer-assisted scheduling, but the number that have is growing rapidly.

Intermittent systems that produce *make-to-order* goods often have a high backlog (several months worth) of customer orders which gives them a fairly certain assessment of demand. In these situations, formal MRP systems generally offer a substantial improvement over the traditional but informal expediting systems. These firms do not have to rely very heavily on a forecast and so their master scheduling is relatively straightforward [**22**: 63].

Firms that are not fortunate enough to have a large backlog must depend upon forecasting over the longer term and then upon matching their forecasts up with customer orders in the short term. Where scheduling can be done on the basis of modules rather than in terms of specific end items, the firm gains a more realistic measure of priorities and load on the plant while still retaining the flexibility of handling last-minute changes that inevitably arise.

Low-volume, process-oriented facilities are typically controlled by an "order control" system. Each job or lot is assigned a number and a high degree of individual control is exercised over the materials, quantity, quality, and processing details. As indicated above, these customized products are often made in response to specific orders already received from customers, rather than for stock.

Orders are usually placed on the basis of a firmly quoted price, so as soon as customers have ordered an item their concern typically turns to, "How soon can you deliver?" Production control is then faced with loading the plant in an economical and expedient manner. This involves scheduling equipment, assigning individual jobs, and setting priorities in the processing of various orders and use of equipment. We shall take up these considerations in more detail in the section on scheduling methodology in the next chapter.

PROJECTS: PROJECT CONTROL

Projects are usually designed to produce a specific output and are often done by bringing workers and materials to the job site. They consist of a complex set of interdependent activities that take place over several weeks, months, or even years. Examples include construction of a building, design and construction of a ship, and refueling of an atomic power plant. The one-time or infrequent nature of these activities mitigates against the use of traditional routing, scheduling, dispatching, and monitoring methods. Some of these functions must be performed, but techniques, such as PERT and CPM, go a long way toward integrating many of the planning and control activities in a project environment.

The project organization typically puts a systems philosophy solidly into practice, for it is organized on a more explicit goal-oriented basis than most organizations. During the past 10 or 15 years numerous firms have used project management approaches to the point where project control is now an effective mechanism, deserving of equal status with flow control and order control.

LEARNING-CURVE EFFECTS

Planners must anticipate a multitude of influences, and one of the most significant impacts arises from the phenomenon of learning. The time per unit required to complete certain labor-intensive activities often decreases in relation to the number of times the job is performed. At the Boeing Company, for example, the assembly time required to produce numerous commercial jet aircraft components decreases in accordance with well-defined rates. This improvement in efficiency (or productivity) as a function of output is referred to as a *learning-curve effect*. Production control must allow for and take advantage of this improvement. Otherwise the benefits of the learning will be lost and instead, scheduling imbalances will occur, with attendant inventory, material flow, storage, and idle resource problems.

The improvement phenomenon has been empirically documented in a number of applications, such as aircraft assembly, machine shops, construction projects, and maintenance activities. Later units of an order, such as of airframes, will tend to be finished more quickly than earlier units. The improvement arises from such factors as individual skill development, better organization and planning of work, methods improvements, more sophisticated tools and fixtures, and work environment incentives.

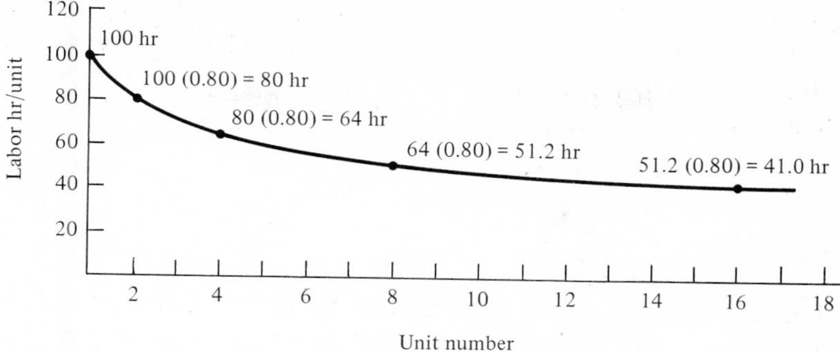

FIGURE 8-4 Eighty percent learning curve

The improvement effect is normally expressed in terms of the percentage of time it takes to complete the unit which represents a doubling of output.[1] For example, if an activity followed an 80 percent learning curve and required 100 hours for the first unit, the second would take 80 hours, the fourth 64 hours, and the eighth 51.2 hours, as shown in Fig. 8-4.

Mathematically, the number of direct labor hours required to produce the Nth unit of a product Y_N is exponentially related to the time to produce the first unit Y_1 by the expression [**4**: 488]:

$$Y_N = Y_1 N^X \tag{8-1}$$

where

Y_N = time to produce Nth unit

Y_1 = time to produce first unit

N = unit number

$$X = \frac{\log \text{ of learning } \%}{\log 2}$$

Example 8-1

An activity that follows an 80 percent learning curve requires 100 direct labor hours to complete the first unit. Estimate the time required for the fourth unit.

[1] This approach to the learning-curve effect is based on the Boeing formula which states that each time the production quantity doubles, the *unit worker-hours* is reduced at a constant rate. Another commonly used approach states that each time the production quantity doubles the *cumulative average unit worker-hours* is reduced at a constant rate. The two formulas yield similar but not identical results.

Solution

$$Y_N = Y_1 N^X$$

where

$$Y_1 = 100$$

$$N = 4$$

$$X = \frac{\log 0.80}{\log 2} = -0.322$$

$$Y_4 = 100(4)^{-0.322} = \frac{100}{(4)^{0.322}} = 63.9 \text{ hr (say, 64 hr)}$$

The exponential nature of the function suggests it would appear as a straight line on log-log paper, which it does. Calculations involving exponentials can become tedious, but fortunately coefficients of learning percentages in the common range of 70 percent to 98 percent have been developed [5] which minimize the computational effort required. Selected values from such tables are provided in Appendix J. To use the tables, first express the desired unit number as a percentage of a base unit with known time:

$$\text{Percent base} = \frac{\text{desired unit number}}{\text{known base number}} \tag{8-2}$$

Then enter the table row corresponding to the percent base, go over to the column relevant to the specified learning percentage, and read off the learning coefficient L. The time to produce the desired unit Y_N is then:

$$Y_N = Y_B(L) \tag{8-3}$$

where

$$Y_B = \text{base unit time}$$

$$L = \text{learning coefficient}$$

Example 8-2

The labor component of a ship construction activity required 12,000 worker days for the first project and the firm has now received an order for three additional ships. Assuming a 90 percent learning curve applies, how many worker days may be expected for the third unit?

Solution

Express the unknown unit as a percentage of the base unit:

$$\text{Percent base} = \frac{\text{desired unit number}}{\text{known base number}} = \frac{\text{unit 3}}{\text{unit 1}} = \frac{3}{1} = 300\%$$

Determine the appropriate coefficient from Appendix J and multiply it by the base unit time.

$$Y_N = Y_B(L)$$
$$= (12{,}000)(0.8492)$$
$$= 10{,}190 \text{ worker days}$$

As indicated previously, the learning (or improvement) curve tends to evidence itself primarily in labor-intensive applications, such as assembly work. Although one might expect a leveling off of the curve after an extended period, the normal result is to experience continued improvement over an indefinite time. In special cases the curve does level off, however, and it may even begin to turn upward. This might occur, for example, toward the end of a project, as skilled workers are shifted off onto new jobs and less attention is paid to improvements in efficiency.

When substantial changes are introduced to the routine work pattern, they may also cause changes in the curve and temporarily increase time (and costs) as shown in Fig. 8-5. The expectation here is that the cost of changes and methods improvements will generate savings which will outweigh the learning cost before the end of the job life.

Before production planners take it upon themselves to compensate for learning effects they should, insofar as possible, substantiate the phenomenon with empirical evidence from their own firm or industry. Some industries, such as the aircraft industry, already have well-documented data, and learning-curve effects are ordinary and expected occurrences. Others have never recognized the learning effect in such a formal way.

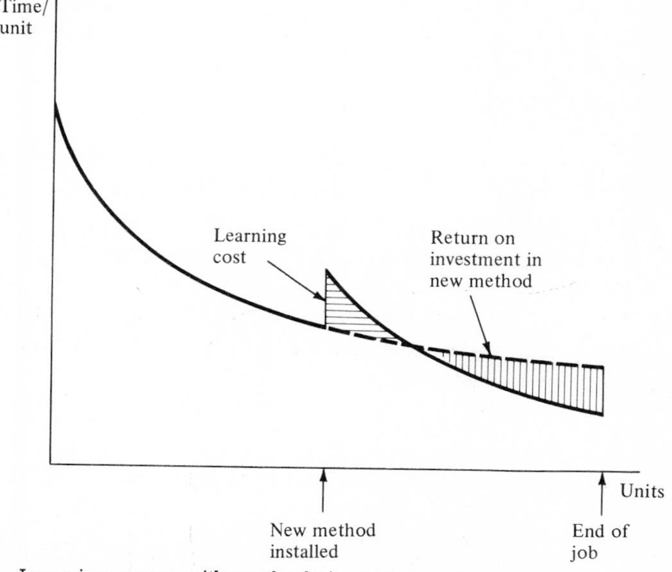

FIGURE 8-5 Learning curve with methods improvement

The impact of improvement over the course of extended production actually penetrates the entire organization, from schedulers and financial planners to marketing representatives negotiating price and delivery contracts for production two and three years hence. As might be expected, purchasing agents and government buyers are also well aware of learning effects. Pioneering customers hesitate to pay the early high costs of learning whereas the later consumers of units produced farther out on the learning curve hope to benefit from the reduced labor costs by obtaining a better price. The competitive firm must recognize this production phenomenon in its scheduling and pricing or eventually yield to those more alert firms that do take advantage of it. The effects are most likely to show up on aggregate plans but can also have an impact on detailed charts or schedules that extend over any significant period.

AGGREGATE PLANNING

Aggregate planning consists of formulating output plans that will adjust production activities to provide a rational response to demand. It begins with a forecast, takes account of any long-range capacity modifications, and focuses on making adjustments in the levels of controllable variables. In the remainder of this chapter we discuss some guidelines for aggregate planning and some methods of planning.

AGGREGATE PLANNING GUIDELINES

While we cannot attempt to go into detail on the job of aggregate planning, some selected guidelines are given in Table 8-2 and are discussed below.

Corporate Planning Policy

All aggregate planning activities should rest firmly upon underlying corporate objectives, for they effectively direct organization activities and dictate items of vital importance to employees, such as whether they will have steady work or will be laid off. Guides for such decisions should properly flow from corporate policy.

TABLE 8-2 AGGREGATE PLANNING GUIDELINES

1	Determine corporate policy regarding controllable variables.
2	Use a good forecast as a basis for planning.
3	Plan in appropriate units of capacity, not monetary units.
4	Maintain as stable a work force as is practical.
5	Maintain as much control over inventories as is needed.
6	Maintain as much flexibility to change as is practical.
7	Respond to demand fluctuations in a controlled manner.
8	Evaluate planning adequacy on a regular basis.

Unfortunately many firms have not given sufficient attention to the hierarchical structure of their organizational goals (see Chap. 1). In many cases their institutionalized value system has not emerged to the point where the value aspect of planning decisions is clearly recognized (see Chap. 3). This not only compels aggregate planners to imply and infer what the structure of goals and values is, but it also forces them to defend against and attempt to reconcile conflicting (and perhaps suboptimal) positions held by marketing, finance, engineering, and other groups. The consequence of this lack of a delineated policy or operating standards is that a difficult job becomes even more difficult.

Planners must make some of the most value-laden decisions within an organization. Whether or not corporate policy explicitly recognizes the full interests of employees, society, stockholders, and others, their own personal value system usually demands that they take relevant interests into account. This means that planning decisions may sometimes appear to be at variance with apparent standards of, say, short-term profits. Learning to live with and fostering the development of broadly based policy guidelines is an important aspect of the planners' job.

Forecast as a Basis for Planning

As shown in Fig. 8-3, a good forecast of demand constitutes the basis for aggregate planning. Although the forecast will not likely be accurate, nor will the firm very likely produce the exact amount of the forecast, the forecast still serves as a target, or adjusting mechanism. It is the basis for firm planned orders designed to help level the workload on a plant. In other words, the firm should develop a good forecast (using methods described in Chap. 6) and then place some faith in it, recognizing that random fluctuations in demand are to be expected. The forecast period, and planning horizon, should be sufficiently long so that decisions such as hiring and laying off are optimal in the long run, and not only on a period-to-period basis [**3**: 539]. Forecast controls and validity checks should also be constantly maintained to justify the faith in this system.

Appropriate Units of Capacity

Plant capacity is a relatively fixed asset which is often not fully utilized. As was noted earlier (Chap. 2), individual equipment capacities are not always balanced and the product mix may have characteristics that limit output of the system. Thus, aggregate planning decisions should be based on *system capacities* rather than individual unit capacities. In addition, allowance must be incorporated for normal system inefficiencies and learning effects. Plans themselves should be expressed in units of production, worker hours of production time, or other units that are directly manageable, rather than in monetary units.

Work-force Stability

Work-force stability has become an increasingly important goal as firms have begun to accept a greater responsibility for their role in society. As pointed out earlier (Chap. 3), besides being a most valuable asset of an organization, the human resource has a unique intrinsic value that warrants special consideration. Employees give life to an organization, dedicate their work efforts to it, and are deserving of a just share of the benefits and the security it can provide. Again, a delineated and forthright organization policy would seem to be desirable here. Then, for example, if workers were hired to satisfy a seasonal or demand peak they would fully realize the temporary nature of their employment before being engaged.

Effective Control over Inventories

Control over inventories is necessary if production control is to use them as an effective controllable variable. Items falling within the B and C classifications (see Chap. 7) may, of course, require less control than A items. But the authority to specify aggregate levels of raw materials, in-process, and finished goods inventory is essential. One of the best ways to exercise control is, of course, to first have the type of information that is available from computerized time-phased order point systems and MRP systems.

Flexibility to Change

Flexibility is a key concept for production control because in the business realm change is inevitable. Systems should be designed to provide a fast reaction to change with as little disruption to the plant as possible. Some firms are, of course, better equipped for this than others. Subcontracting is one way of shifting fluctuations to the external environment. Internally, inventory fluctuations generally cause less disruption than does employee turnover. From a process planning standpoint (see Chap. 5) a firm can improve its flexibility by making extensive use of standardized subassemblies [**15**: 484] and not committing component parts to a particular end item until as late in the process as possible [**21**: 578]. This type of flexibility is inherent in MRP systems, for common components are grouped and managed on a total requirements basis—thanks to the recordkeeping abilities of computer storage files.

Controlled Response to Demand

The controlled response to demand is an acknowledgment that demand fluctuations are in fact random deviations and should not be permitted to generate similar (or perhaps even amplified) fluctuations in the production rates at a manufacturing plant. Simulation studies by Forrester [6] and others have revealed that production distribution systems that involve factory, distributor, and retailer inventories have substantial lag and pipeline effects when an order-point system is used. A 10 percent increase in retail sales, followed by normal inventory adjustments, can appear as a 40 percent increase by the time the demand information gets back to the factory.

Amplified reactions often arise because the order points at the wholesaler and retailer levels are adjusted when they should not be. For example, a random increase in demand will generate a reorder at the retail level and cause a temporary overload on the production system, resulting in extended lead times. If the order clerk at the retail level adjusts the order point upward to compensate for the extended lead time, the result is more orders, more overload on production, and even longer lead times. The production department may deem it necessary to go on overtime or increase employment to meet the outstanding orders and bring lead times back down to reasonable levels.

The increased production eventually leads to an inventory buildup, for the initial demand increase was only random and not sustaining. With high inventories at the factory, the order clerk at the retail level enjoys a very short lead time and accordingly readjusts the order point down. This means that for some time there are practically no orders coming into the factory, so workers must be laid off and demand is met almost exclusively from inventory. As stocks are used up the retail branches place orders again and the cycle continues, or perhaps gets worse.

The rapid response to demand and overcorrection caused by adjusting the order points can amplify demand fluctuations. Production controllers must guard against such effects by developing a good information base, assisting wholesalers and retailers with inventory control and production information, and making a controlled, or modified, adjustment to demand.

The principle of modified response applies more to items produced for stock than to custom products made to order. A mathematical model using a modified response has been developed by Magee [13] and will be presented in a later section.

Evaluation of Planning Adequacy

Planning efforts are of no value unless the plans are implemented and do the job they are designed for. Control should be built into the aggregate planning system so that actual levels of activity are measured, the data are fed back to production control in a timely and accurate manner, comparisons are made of actual and planned levels, and corrections are authorized and made. This control effort is facilitated by a well-designed information system where checks can be carried out on a continuing basis.

Production planning and control requires a broad knowledge of production operations, as illustrated by the frequent reference to previous chapter materials in the above guidelines. We now turn to some useful planning methods.

GRAPHIC AND CHARTING METHODS

Because of the interdependency and intangible nature of the variables involved, no aggregate planning methods yield truly "optimal" rates of production, levels of personnel, and so forth, in all respects. The graphic and charting techniques basically work with a few variables at a time on a trial-and-error basis. Some mathematical approaches also follow this pattern whereas others begin with limiting (and sometimes unrealistic) assumptions and achieve a theoretical optimality. The problem then remains to reconcile this with the real-world situation.

Planning Charts and Workload Projections

An initial understanding of the essence of an aggregate planning problem is often best conveyed by means of production requirements charts and cumulative workload projections.

Example 8-3

A firm has developed the following forecast (units) for an item which has a demand influenced by seasonal factors.

Jan.	220	Apr.	396	July	378	Oct.	115
Feb.	90	May	616	Aug.	220	Nov.	95
Mar.	210	June	700	Sept.	200	Dec.	260

(*a*) Prepare a chart showing the daily demand requirements. (*Note:* Available workdays per month are given below.)

(*b*) Plot the demand as a histogram and as a cumulative requirement over time.

(*c*) Determine the production rate required to meet average demand and plot this as a dotted line on the graphs.

Solution

For (*a*), see Table 8-3. For (*b*), see Figs. 8-6 and 8-7.

$$(c)\quad \text{Average requirement} = \frac{\text{cumulative demand}}{\text{cumulative prod. days}} = \frac{3{,}500}{250} = 14 \text{ units/day}$$

The histogram and cumulative graphs illustrate the nature of the aggregate planning problem for they show how the forecast deviates from average requirements. Some alternative means of meeting the forecast requirement are suggested by the pure strategies listed in Table 8-1. One plan might consist of varying the size of the work force by hiring and laying off as required. The production rate would then exactly follow the forecast requirement as shown by the solid line in Fig. 8-6. Another

TABLE 8-3 CHART OF PRODUCTION REQUIREMENTS

Month	(1) Forecast demand	(2) Production days	(3) Demand/day (1) ÷ (2)	(4) Cumulative production days	(5) Cumulative demand
January	220	22	10	22	220
February	90	18	5	40	310
March	210	21	10	61	520
April	396	22	18	83	916
May	616	22	28	105	1,532
June	700	20	35	125	2,332
July	378	21	18	146	2,610
August	220	22	10	168	2,830
September	200	20	10	188	3,030
October	115	23	5	211	3,145
November	95	19	5	230	3,240
December	260	20	13	250	3,500
		250			

alternative might be to follow strategy 3 and attempt to meet the requirement by inventory adjustments. In this case production could be at a steady rate, shown by the dotted line in Fig. 8-6. A third plan might follow strategy 5 and produce at some low, steady rate, perhaps five units per day, and subcontract all excess demand to other firms. Numerous other plans, consisting of other pure strategies (such as overtime, undertime, and back-ordering) and mixed strategies could be proposed.

Example 8-4

Use the data of Example 8-3 and determine the monthly inventory balances required to follow a plan of letting the inventory absorb all fluctuations in demand (strategy 3 of Table 8-1). In this case we have a constant work force, no idle or overtime, no back-orders, no use of subcontractors, and no capacity adjustment. Assume the firm does not use safety stock to meet the demand.

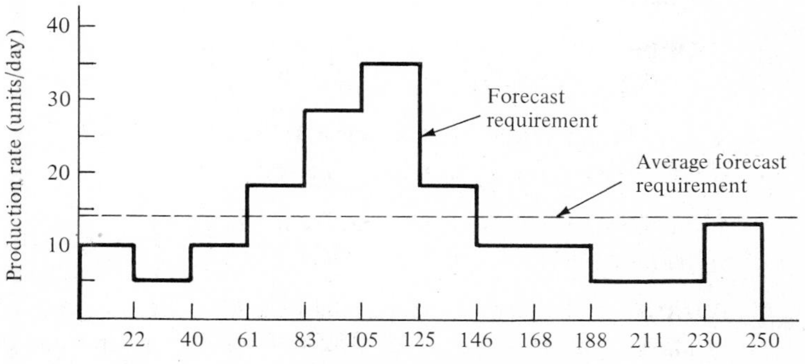

FIGURE 8-6 Histogram of forecast and average requirement

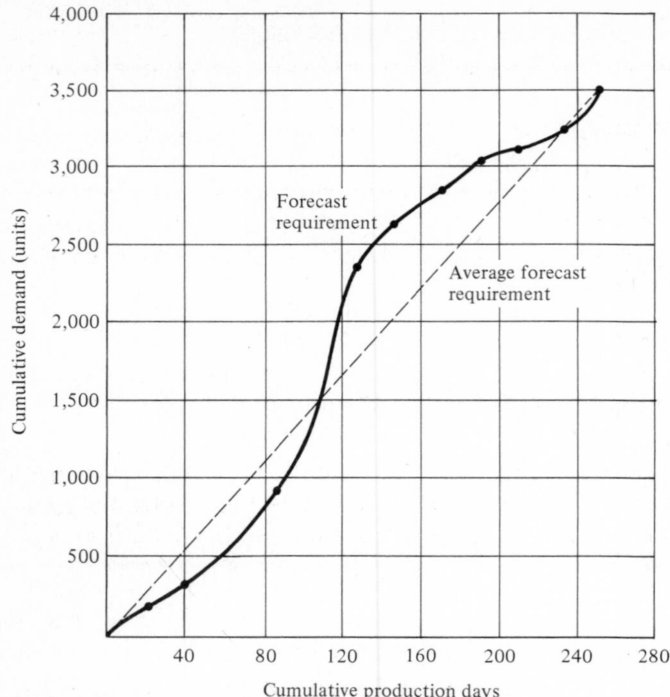

FIGURE 8-7 Cumulative graph of forecast and average requirement

Solution

The firm can satisfy demand by producing at an average requirement (14 units/day) and accumulating inventory during periods of slack demand (periods

Month	AVE. X PROD. DAYS (1) Production at 14/day	(2) Forecast demand	(3) Inventory change	(4) Ending inventory balance	(5) Ending balance with 566 on Jan. 1
January	308	220	+88	88	654
February	252	90	+162	250	816
March	294	210	+84	334	900
April	308	396	−88	246	812
May	308	616	−308	−62	504
June	280	700	−420	−482	84
July	294	378	−84	−566	0
August	308	220	+88	−478	88
September	280	200	+80	−398	168
October	322	115	+207	−191	375
November	266	95	+171	−20	546
December	280	260	+20	0	566
		3,500			

below the dotted line in Fig. 8-6) and depleting it during periods of strong demand. Disregarding any safety stock, the inventory balance is:

$$\text{Inventory balance} = \sum (\text{production} - \text{demand}) \tag{8-4}$$

The pattern of demand is such that column 4 reveals that a maximum negative balance of 566 units exists at the *end* of July, so 566 additional units must be carried in stock if demand is to be met. Column 5 shows the resulting inventory balances required.

Cost Computation for Pure Strategies

The above example requires that a substantial amount of inventory be carried, since it peaks at 900 units at the end of March and goes to zero in July. Knowing the inventory requirements, the carrying costs can be weighed against the costs of other alternative plans.

Example 8-5

Given the data of Example 8-3, the firm has determined that to follow a plan of meeting demand by varying the size of the work force (strategy 1) would result in hiring and layoff costs estimated at \$12,000. If the units cost \$100 each to produce, carrying costs/yr are 20 percent of the average inventory value, and storage costs (based upon maximum inventory) are \$.90/unit, which plan results in the lesser cost, varying inventory or varying employment?

Solution

From Example 8-4:

Maximum inventory requiring storage = 900 units (from column 5)

$$\text{Average inventory balance} \cong \frac{654 + 816 + 900 + \cdots + 566}{12}$$

$$\cong 460 \text{ units}$$

Plan 1 (varying inventory):

$$\text{Inventory cost} = \text{carrying cost} + \text{storage cost}$$

$$= (0.20)(460)(\$100) + (\$.90)(900) = \boxed{\$10,010}$$

Plan 2 (varying employment) = $\boxed{\$12,000}$

∴ Varying inventory is the lesser cost strategy

Cost Computation for Mixed Strategies

The above example compared the costs of two pure strategies only. Other alternatives might be to make use of overtime, subcontract work out, or follow a back-order strategy. In each case, the relevant costs of each alternative should be computed and compared. The best solution, however, will most likely come in the form of a mixed strategy. Unfortunately there are (theoretically) thousands of mixed strategy combinations that could be investigated. The realities of the situation will, however, generally help reduce the alternatives to a more manageable number. Example 8-6 carries forward with a simplified example of a mixed strategy.

Example 8-6

Given the data from the previous examples, suppose the firm wishes to investigate two other alternatives. A third plan is to produce at either 10 units/day or, by adding a second shift, at 20 units/day. Each time a shift is added or laid off it costs the firm an estimated \$3,500. The fourth plan is to produce at a steady rate of 10 units/day and subcontract the additional requirements out at a delivered cost of \$107/unit. Any accumulated inventory is carried forward.

Solution

Plan 3 (produce at either 10 or 20 units/day and carry inventory):

At a shift-change cost of \$3,500 this plan will permit a maximum of two changes (\$7,000), for with any additional changes it will automatically exceed the cost of plan 1 (\$10,010). From a long-range planning standpoint, since each year represents a cycle, we can assume the firm will want to enter the next year at the same respective level as the present, so two changes is also a minimum.

Referring to the forecast of Fig. 8-6, we must construct a new chart to reflect an increased production of 20 units/day for a continuous number of days N where:

$$\text{Total production} = N \text{ days @ } 20/\text{day} + (250 - N) \text{ days @ } 10/\text{day}$$

$$3{,}500 = N(20) + (250 - N)(10)$$

$$N = 100 \text{ days}$$

Allocating this increased rate to the block of months with the largest demand places it in the April to July period. Since the June demand rate markedly exceeds the 20 unit/day production rate, we should begin production at this faster rate in March in order to build up inventory for the June peak. (A more precise placement of the 100-day period could be determined by formulating and minimizing an expression for carrying costs.)

Month	(1) Production * = at 10/day ** = at 20/day	(2) Forecast demand	(3) Inventory change	(4) Ending inventory balance	(5) Ending balance with 150 on Jan. 1
January	* 220	220	0	0	150
February	* 180	90	+90	90	240
March	** 420	210	+210	300	450
April	** 440	396	+44	344	494
May	** 440	616	−176	168	318
June	** 400	700	−300	−132	18
July	{15 days @ ** 300; 6 days @ * 60}	378	−18	−150	0
August	* 220	220	0	−150	0
September	* 200	200	0	−150	0
October	* 230	115	+115	−35	115
November	* 190	95	+95	60	210
December	* 200	260	−60	0	150

$$\text{Maximum inventory} = 494 \text{ units (from column 5)}$$

$$\text{Average inventory balance} \cong \frac{150 + 240 + \cdots + 150}{12}$$

$$\cong 179 \text{ (from column 5)}$$

$$\text{Inventory cost} = \text{carrying cost} + \text{storage cost}$$

$$= (0.20)(179)(\$100) + (\$.90)(494) = \quad \$4{,}025$$

$$\text{Shift-change cost} = (\$3{,}500)(2) = \quad \$7{,}000$$

$$\text{Total cost of plan 3} = \quad \boxed{\$11{,}025}$$

Plan 4 (produce at 10 units/day, carry inventory and subcontract):

Referring to Fig. 8-6, we see that at a production rate of 10 units/day production exceeds demand during only three months (February, October, and November). The inventory accumulated during these periods must be carried at a cost of 20 percent (\$100) ÷ 12 months = \$1.67/unit-mo. Units are carried until they can be used to help meet demand in a subsequent month.

Month	Demand	Production at 10/day	Inventory to carry	Inventory carried until	Number months	Cost at \$1.67 per unit-month
February	90	180	90	90 units to April	2	\$300
October	115	230	115	60 units to Dec.	2	200
				55 units to April	6	551
November	95	190	95	31 units to April	5	259
				64 units to May	6	641
				Inventory cost		\$1,951

Inventory cost (from above) $1,951

Add marginal cost of subcontracting:

$$\begin{aligned} \text{Number of units} &= \text{demand} - \text{production} \\ &= 3{,}500 - 10(250) \\ &= 1{,}000 \text{ units} \\ \text{Cost/unit} &= \$107 - 100 = \$7/\text{unit} \\ \text{Marginal cost} &= 1{,}000 \text{ units } (\$7/\text{unit}) = \end{aligned}$$

$7,000

Total cost of plan 4 = **$8,951**

Comparison of plans:

	Plan	Cost
1	Vary inventory (pure strategy)	$10,010
2	Vary employment (pure strategy)	12,000
3	Vary employment and carry inventory (mixed strategy)	11,025
4	Subcontract and carry inventory (mixed strategy)	8,951

On the basis of this limited comparison, plan 4 is the best.

Additional exercises in formulating aggregate plans via the use of graphs and charts are provided in the problem sections at the end of the chapter. Whereas these approaches are relatively straightforward and useful, they are not evolutionary and they are not inherently optimizing. In other words the charts and graphs are useful means of evaluating previously proposed plans but they do not necessarily suggest better plans nor do they give any guarantee that a proposed plan is necessarily optimal. One must simply keep trying new plans, or revisions to plans, until a satisfactory one is obtained. In this sense they are trial-and-error approaches.

MATHEMATICAL PLANNING MODELS

The methods discussed previously certainly require mathematical computations and, conversely, the forthcoming methods can also be facilitated by diagrammatic or chart representations. So it would be incorrect to place too much emphasis upon the distinction between charting and mathematical approaches. In general, however, the mathematical models attempt to refine or improve upon basic trial-and-error approaches. Some approaches are of an optimizing character. In this section we shall consider a modified response model, linear programming approaches, and the linear decision rule.

Magee's Modified Response Model

The modified response model [**13**: 174] is designed to help stabilize production activity by limiting the firm's response to erratic fluctuations of demand. In this sense it is an approach to strategy 4 by inherently accepting stockout penalties. The

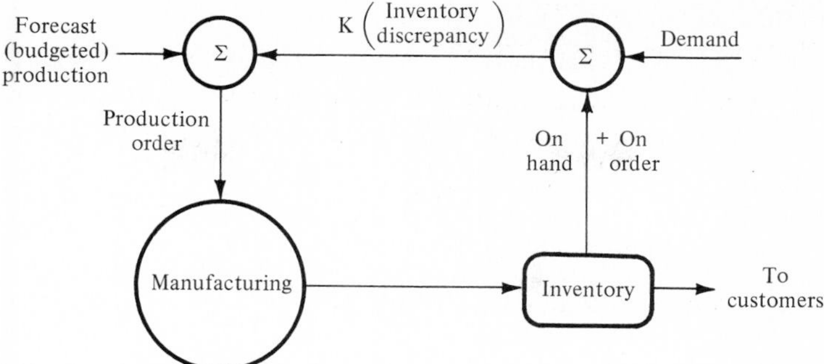

FIGURE 8-8 Modified response model

model essentially bases the production order on a forecast, or budgeted, amount which is modified to make a partial adjustment for current demand and inventory levels. Figure 8-8 is a schematic representation.

The model uses a control number K between zero and one which in effect directs that some portion of the production order is determined by current demand. It works like this. Inventory on hand and on order is matched against demand to determine how much additional production would seem to be warranted. However, only a fraction K of the resultant discrepancy is used. It is combined with a budgeted amount which has already been predetermined by the forecast. These two components constitute the production order which is issued to manufacturing for goods that ultimately go into inventory and to customers.

The value of K is, of course, a key determinant, and should be based upon experience in the industry, a knowledge of costs and other operating parameters of the firm, and an appreciation of the market environment. It is essentially a smoothing factor which, if set equal to zero, would simply disregard demand and give total weight to the forecast. If set equal to one, it directs that production respond 100 percent to demand fluctuations. A value of $K = 0.10$ would thus provide a damped response yielding a mild adjustment to the random fluctuations of demand.

A simplified mathematical statement of the model [7: 555] is shown below, where Δ represents a difference between planned versus actual.

$$\text{Production level} = \text{plan or forecast production} + K[\Delta\ \text{demand} + \Delta\ \text{inventory} + \Delta\ \text{deliveries}] \tag{8-5}$$

Computations are simplified if delivery requirements are automatically deducted from inventory and further simplified if the demand is essentially placed on the firm's inventory, as is often the case. The expression for the production level is then simply:

$$\text{Production level} = \text{plan or forecast} + K(\Delta D) \tag{8-6}$$

where ΔD is the difference between planned and actual demand.

In general, the incremental (Δ) amount of demand, inventory, or delivery is assigned a positive or negative sign in accordance with whether the compensating adjustment to production should be an increase or decrease in the level.

Example 8-7

An industrial chemicals producer has developed the accompanying forecast. The firm uses a modified response model (with a control number of $K = 0.8$) to set actual production levels. Since it takes almost 30 days lead time to adjust production, the incremental response is effective after an intervening month.

	Forecast	Actual
April	12,000	11,500
May	16,000	
June	14,000	
July	10,000	

If the actual demand (which includes inventory and delivery changes) is 11,500 units in April, what "modified" production quantity should be scheduled for June?

Solution

$$\text{Production level} = \text{forecast} + K(\Delta D)$$

where

$$\Delta D = \text{actual} - \text{planned}$$

$$= 11{,}500 - 12{,}000 = -500$$

$$= 14{,}000 + 0.8(-500)$$

$$= 14{,}000 - 400 = 13{,}600 \text{ units}$$

Linear Programming Approaches

If we view the aggregate planning problem as one of allocating capacity (supply) to meet forecast (demand) requirements it can be structured and solved in a linear programming format. Both distribution and standard matrix approaches can theoretically be useful [**4, 9, 18**], but we shall concentrate upon the former for illustrative purposes. In this case the supply consists of the inventory on hand and units that can be produced via regular time (RT), overtime (OT), and subcontracting (SC). Demand consists of the individual month (or period) requirements plus any desired ending inventory. Costs associated with producing units in the given period or producing and carrying them in inventory until a later period are entered in the small boxes inside the cells in the matrix, as we did previously with distribution linear programming problems (see Chap. 2).

Example 8-8

Given the accompanying supply, demand, cost, and inventory data for a firm that has a constant work force and wishes to meet all demand (that is, with no back orders). Allocate production capacity to satisfy demand at minimum cost.

Supply capacity (units)

Period	Regular time	Overtime	Subcontract
1	60	18	1,000
2	50	15	1,000
3	60	18	1,000
4	65	20	1,000

Demand forecast

Period	Unit
1	100
2	50
3	70
4	80

Cost data
Regular time cost/unit = \$100
(labor = 50 percent of the cost)
Overtime cost/unit = \$125
Subcontract cost/unit = \$130
Carrying cost/unit-period = \$2

Inventory data
Initial = 20
Final = 25

Solution

The initial linear programming matrix in units of capacity is shown in Table 8-4 with entries determined as explained below. Note that since total capacity exceeds demand, a "slack" demand of unused capacity is added to achieve the required balance in supply versus demand.

Initial inventory 20 units available at no additional cost if used in period 1. Carrying cost is \$2/unit per period if units are retained until period 2, \$4/unit to period 3, and so on. If the units are unused during any period, the result is a \$6/unit cost.

Regular time Cost/unit is \$100 if units are used in the month produced; otherwise a carrying cost of \$2/unit-month is added on for each month the units are retained. Unused regular time costs the firm 50 percent of \$100 = \$50.

Overtime Cost/unit is \$125 if the units are used in the month produced; otherwise a carrying cost of \$2/unit-month is incurred similar to the regular time situation. Unused overtime has zero cost.

Subcontracting Cost/unit is \$130 plus any costs for units carried forward. This latter situation is unlikely, however, for any reasonable demand can be obtained when needed, as indicated by the arbitrarily high number (1,000) assigned to subcontracting capacity. There is no cost for unused capacity here.

TABLE 8-4 LINEAR PROGRAMMING FORMAT FOR SCHEDULING

Supply, units from	Period 1	Period 2	Period 3	Period 4 and final	Unused capacity	Total capacity available
	Demand, units for					
Initial inventory	0	2	4	6	6	20
1 Regular	100	102	104	106	50	60
Overtime	125	127	129	131	0	18
Subcontract	130				0	1,000
2 Regular		100	102	104	50	50
Overtime		125	127	129	0	15
Subcontract		130			0	1,000
3 Regular			100	102	50	60
Overtime			125	127	0	18
Subcontract			130		0	1,000
4 Regular				100	50	65
Overtime				125	0	20
Subcontract				130	0	1,000
Demand	100	50	70	105	4,001	4,326

Note that if the initial allocations are made so as to use regular time as fully as possible, the solution procedure is often simplified. Overtime and subcontract amounts can also be allocated on a minimum cost basis.

Final inventory The final inventory requirement (25 units) must be available at the end of period 4 and has been added to the period 4 demand of 80 units to obtain 105 units total.

Since no back orders are permitted, production in subsequent months to fill demand in a current month is not allowed. These unavailable cells, along with the cells associated with carrying forward any subcontracted units, may therefore be blanked out since they are infeasible. The final solution, following normal methods of distribution linear programming, is shown in Table 8-5.

The optimal solution values can be taken directly from the cells. Thus in period 2, for example, the planners will schedule the full 50 units to be produced on regular time plus 12 units on overtime to be carried forward to period 4. This leaves 3 units of unused overtime capacity and no subcontracting during that period. Due to the similar carrying cost for units produced on regular or overtime, it does not matter which physical units are carried forward, once overtime production is required.[2]

The distribution linear programming approach can be extended to include back-order costs by entering them in the blanked-out portion of the matrix in the lower left corner. In this way, production in a later month can be allocated to supply a back-ordered demand from an earlier month at whatever stockout cost premium the firm chooses to assign. The planner must, of course, fill the back-ordered demand in subsequent periods. The format will still guarantee an optimal solution, but of course the solution is only as valid as the stockout cost assumptions that go into the matrix formulation.

The distribution linear programming model illustrated above assumed a constant work force so no hiring or layoff costs were involved. These and other costs can be expressed in the format of a standard or integer-type linear programming model. In theory, an aggregate plan might be expressed as shown below, where the following symbols refer to the costs shown:

RT = regular time	OT = overtime	SOC = stockout
H = hiring	IT = idle time	SC = subcontract
L = layoff	I_{cc} = inventory carrying	Cap = capacity change

$$\text{Min } C = \underset{(1)}{(RT + H + L)} + \underset{(2)}{(OT + IT)} + \underset{(3)}{I_{cc}} + \underset{(4)}{SOC} + \underset{(5)}{SC} + \underset{(6)}{Cap}$$

subject to contraints of:

Meeting demand unless stockout costs are justified
Limitations on regular time, hiring, layoff, overtime, subcontracting, and capacity

[2] This is reflected in the fact that different solutions (but with identical costs) may be obtained. Thus, the regular and overtime quantities for demand periods 3 and 4 may be rearranged as shown.

From

100 / 60	102 /
125 / 10	127 / 8

To

100 / 52	102 / 8
125 / 18	127 / 0

Note that the row and column totals still agree and it is simply a matter of physical designation. The situation arises from a degeneracy since the number of rows plus number of columns minus one (13 + 5 − 1 = 17) does not equal the number of entries (16) and could be remedied by assigning a zero to one of the cells, as we saw earlier in Chap. 2 and as shown in this footnote.

TABLE 8-5 MATRIX FOR PLANNING DECISION

Supply, units from	Demand, units for: Period 1	Period 2	Period 3	Period 4 and final	Unused capacity	Total capacity available
Initial inventory	[0] 20	[2]	[4]	[6]	[6]	20
1 Regular	[100] 60	[102]	[104]	[106]	[50]	60
Overtime	[125] 18	[127]	[129]	[131]	[0]	18
Subcontract	[130] 2				[0] 998	1,000
2 Regular		[100] 50	[102]	[104]	[50]	50
Overtime		[125]	[127]	[129] 12	[0] 3	15
Subcontract		[130]			[0] 1,000	1,000
3 Regular			[100] 60	[102]	[50]	60
Overtime			[125] 10	[127] 8	[0]	18
Subcontract			[130]		[0] 1,000	1,000
4 Regular				[100] 65	[50]	65
Overtime				[125] 20	[0]	20
Subcontract				[130] 0	[0] 1,000	1,000
Demand	100	50	70	105	4,001	4,326

Costs associated with production, employment, inventory, stockout, subcontracting, and changing capacity

The numbers in parenthesis above the objective function correspond with the pure strategies of Table 8-1.

The interdependency of the controllable variables makes it difficult, if not impossible, to use the above linear programming model on most realistic problems. Relevant portions of the model have, however, been abstracted and formulated. Shore [**18**: 339–346] has developed a model with an objective function of the general

$$\text{Min } C = r\sum_{i=1}^{k} P_i + h\sum_{i=1}^{k} A_i + f\sum_{i=1}^{k} R_i + v\sum_{i=1}^{k} T_i + C\left[\sum_{i=1}^{k}\sum_{j=1}^{i}(P_j + T_j - D_j)\right]$$

- r: Regular time cost/unit
- P_i: Regular time units
- h: Hiring cost/unit
- A_i: Number of units increased
- f: Layoff cost/unit
- R_i: Number of units reduced
- v: Overtime cost/unit
- T_i: Overtime units
- C: Inventory carrying cost/unit
- P_j: Regular time units
- T_j: Overtime units
- D_j: Demand during period

form as shown. The model essentially minimizes costs of employment, overtime, and inventories subject to meeting demand in each period i by regular time, overtime, or carrying inventory forward to the next period. The double summation in the brackets arises from this inventory carryforward.

The model includes the major parts of the first three pure strategies listed in Table 8-1. Other models have been developed which also include an idle time cost and a back-order mechanism for handling demand variations [**9**]. Although the simplex formulation of an aggregate planning situation may tend to increase the computational effort (over some distribution linear programming approaches) it does facilitate more generalizations, such as the inclusion of: "(1) cost parameters which vary with time; (2) warehouse capacity and production rate limitations; (3) planning production for more than one product, with joint production facilities; (4) materials and component purchases, together with materials and work-in-process inventories; (5) back orders and idle time; and (6) costs associated with changes in the size of the work force" [**8**: 420]. Nevertheless, the necessary assumptions severely limit the practical use of the standard linear programming model in aggregate planning situations.

Linear Decision Rules

One of the most widely publicized techniques for determining an optimum *production rate* and *work-force size* is the linear decision rule (LDR) developed by Holt, Modigliani, Muth, and Simon [**11**]. Like many other models, the LDR depends upon first quantifying the relevant tangible (and less tangible) variables in terms of costs. But unlike many other models, the LDR requires that cost functions be in quadratic form (and therefore include one or more squared terms).

The relevant costs are depicted in Fig. 8-9 with solid lines representing the presumed actual cost functions and dotted lines the assumed functions under the LDR assumptions. Relevant costs include regular payroll, hiring and layoff, overtime, and inventory-associated costs of holding, back-ordering, and setup. Other necessary inputs include a forecast for the forthcoming periods, the current size of the work force, and the inventory level during the last period. The model works by differentiating the quadratic cost functions with respect to each variable to ultimately

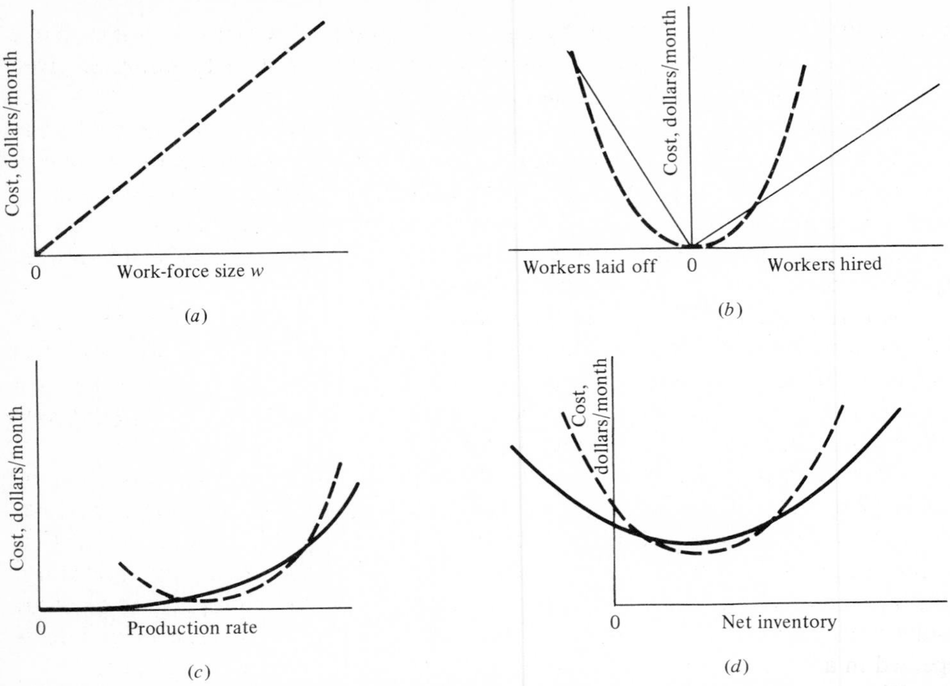

FIGURE 8-9 Linear decision rule relevant costs. (a) regular payroll cost: (b) changing work-force size cost; (c) overtime cost; (d) inventory, back order, and setup costs.

derive two linear decision rules for computing:

W_t = work-force size required for forthcoming period

P_t = number of units to produce in forthcoming period

The authors of the LDR applied the method to a paint company by reconstructing costs for a six-year period of actual operation. They found the quadratic cost structure and resultant LDRs gave them better (theoretical) performance than the actual company performance.

The assumptions behind the model do severely limit its application to industry, however. Aside from the cost quantification problem common to most models, many analysts hold that a quadratic function does not accurately represent the relevant costs, even though it may hold over a limited range. Often it appears that actual costs increase in a linear or step fashion. Also, there are no constraints on work-force size, overtime amount, inventory, and capital amounts. So the rule may yield impractical solutions. It has, nevertheless, helped focus attention on relevant cost relationships and has constituted a step forward toward understanding the aggregate planning problem.

Heuristic and Computer Search Models

Numerous heuristic, simulation, and computer search models have also been developed for production planning. The heuristics tend to simplify (or perhaps oversimplify) a complex situation by the use of guidelines or decision rules. While not necessarily optimizing per se, some heuristic methods tend to optimize given some basic cost and operational assumptions.

Bowman has proposed a *management coefficients model* [**2**] whereby decision rules for planning levels of production are based on past performance of the managers. The model attempts to minimize the erratic or variable behavior of the managers by using regression analysis of their past behavior in similar situations to develop coefficients for each variable in the model. It is a unique way of incorporating experience or sensitivity into a formalized model.

A *parametric production planning model* developed by Jones [**12**] is concerned with the same variables as the LDR (production rate and work-force size) and also assumes quadratic costs and develops two linear decision rules. However, it uses a heuristic search technique to develop coefficients and defines the model parameters in terms of both central tendency and deviation.

Other approaches include a *simulation and search* procedure developed by Vergin [**20**] and a *heuristic search procedure* designed to find minimizing cost coefficients by Taubert [**19**]. Taubert's computer search method requires formulation of cost equations for work-force changes, overtime, back orders, and inventory. Costs are then evaluated over a forecast period and the result is compared to previous results with different personnel, inventory levels, and so forth. The procedure is repeated in a systematic way until no better cost function can be determined.

The complexities of aggregate planning are great but the potential benefits also loom large. As a result, much theoretical effort has gone into the development of various models to cope with the real-world environment. Unfortunately, many of the models are still largely academic, although they are reaching a stage of being positively beneficial. Much of the benefit thus far has arisen from the detailed attention and careful analysis given to the relevant production parameters. In the future we may expect to see an increasing number of specialized models developed for the unique situations of individual organizations. Much of this work is now being coordinated with and incorporated into management information systems which (appropriately) view the planning problems from a total systems perspective.

SUMMARY

Production planning and control entails setting aggregate levels of production, employment, and inventories, and controlling the combination activities by scheduling, authorizing, and monitoring how many and what kind of items to produce, and how, when, and where to produce them. Control of intermittent systems (order control) is more involved than control of continuous systems (flow control) because of the individualized attention necessary in the jobshop environment. Projects are of an even more specialized nature.

Aggregate planning involves long-range (such as monthly or quarterly) adjustments of controllable variables in order to respond to forecast and demand fluctuations in a rational manner. Planning guidelines emphasize the importance of a systems approach that initially recognizes the need for clearly delineated and consistent corporate goals. A reliable forecast is essential to planning, and work-force stability, control over inventories, and flexibility to change are generally desirable. Planning should be done in units of capacity and should be evaluated on a regular basis.

Master scheduling follows aggregate planning and is somewhat more specific in that it leads to specification of specific material requirements (priority planning) as well as labor and machine requirements (capacity planning).

The controllable variables in aggregate planning include (1) employment, (2) overtime and idle time, (3) inventories, (4) back orders, (5) subcontracting, and, in the longer term, (6) plant capacity. Each variable constitutes a pure strategy which can for the most part be evaluated on an economic basis by computing costs for alternative production plans, such as for varying employment, carrying inventories, and the like. Most realistic situations will, however, call for a mix of strategies. The number of alternative combinations may indeed be large and there is no guarantee that any particular plan is optimal. Nevertheless, the realities of the situation will (hopefully) limit the alternatives.

Linear programming approaches have been devised that yield optimal production plans when a selected number of controllable variables are employed and linear assumptions are not violated. Distribution linear programming methods have been applied to optimize production plans over several time periods when the controllable variables are regular and overtime employment levels, and subcontracting and stockout (back-order) costs. In theory a simplex linear programming model could be extended to include all the variables, but in practice that is not yet feasible.

Linear decision rules, heuristic models, and numerous computer search and simulation approaches have also been developed to solve the aggregate planning problem, but it is extremely complex and the variables are highly interdependent. Much of the research is still largely theoretical and no single approach has yet emerged to provide an all-encompassing optimum. In the meantime, firms are identifying selected variables that are most relevant to their particular situation and are using some form of an economic, constrained optimization, or heuristic approach coupled with "judgment." We may expect to see more aggregate planning incorporated into management information systems in the future.

SOLVED PROBLEMS

LEARNING-CURVE EFFECTS

1 Interplanetary Tranportation Company is preparing a bid on 10 space shuttles, the first of which is estimated to take 300 work days to produce. Assuming the work follows a 78 percent learning curve, how much production time should be scheduled for the tenth unit?

Solution

$$\text{Percent base} = \frac{\text{desired unit number}}{\text{known base number}} = \frac{\text{10th}}{\text{1st}} = 1{,}000\%$$

Using the 78 percent column for 1,000% of base in Appendix I,

$$Y_N = Y_B(L) = 300(0.4381) = 131 \text{ days}$$

2 Emerald Electric has a new plant for producing home freezers. They have gone through a preliminary manufacturing period and believe they are experiencing an 88 percent learning curve. The 200th unit has required 1.40 labor hours for an assembly activity. Estimate the comparable time for the (*a*) 100th, (*b*) 500th, (*c*) 1,000th, (*d*) 5,000th unit.

Solution

(*a*) The 100th unit has already been completed, but we can estimate its time as a percentage of the base 200 as:

$$\text{Percent base} = \frac{\text{desired unit number}}{\text{known base number}} = \frac{\text{100th}}{\text{200th}} = \frac{100}{200} = 50\%$$

$$Y_N = Y_B(L) = 1.40(1.1364) = 1.5910 \text{ hr}$$

(*b*) $\text{Percent base} = \dfrac{\text{500th}}{\text{200th}} = 250\%$

$$Y_N = 1.40(0.8445) = 1.1823 \text{ hr}$$

(*c*) $\text{Percent base} = \dfrac{\text{1,000th}}{\text{200th}} = 500\%$

$$Y_N = 1.40(0.7432) = 1.0405 \text{ hr}$$

(*d*) $\text{Percent base} = \dfrac{\text{5,000th}}{\text{200th}} = 2{,}500\%$

Note that our table of learning coefficients does not go to this high a percentage of the base so we must establish a new (higher) base to operate from. The time for the 1,000th unit, developed in (*c*), will work satisfactorily, so we can designate 1.0405 hr for the 1,000th unit as the new base (100%) point.

$$\text{Percent base} = \frac{\text{5,000th}}{\text{1,000th}} = 500\%$$

$$Y_N = 1.0405(0.7432) = 0.7733 \text{ hr}$$

AGGREGATE PLANNING

3 High Point Furniture Company maintains a constant work force (no overtime, back orders, or subcontracting) which can produce 3,000 tables per quarter. The annual demand is 12,000 units and is distributed seasonally in accordance with the quarterly indexes: $Q_1 = 0.80$, $Q_2 = 1.40$, $Q_3 = 1.00$, $Q_4 = 0.80$. Inventories are accumulated when demand is less than capacity and are used up during periods of strong demand. To supply the total annual demand:

(*a*) How many tables must be accumulated during each quarter?

(*b*) What inventory must be on hand at the beginning of the first quarter?

Solution

Quarter	**(1) Production at 3,000/Q**	**(2) Seasonal demand $(SI)Y_c = Y_{sz}$**	**(3) Inventory change**	**(4) Inventory balance**	**(5) Balance with 600 on Jan. 1**
1st	3,000	(0.8)(3,000) = 2,400	600	600	1,200
2d	3,000	(1.4)(3,000) = 4,200	−1,200	−600	0
3d	3,000	(1.0)(3,000) = 3,000	0	−600	0
4th	3,000	(0.8)(3,000) = 2,400	600	0	600

(*a*) Inventory accumulation is given in column 3.

(*b*) From column 4, largest negative inventory is 600 units; therefore 600 must be on hand on January 1. Column 5 shows resulting balance at the end of each quarter.

***4** Michigan Manufacturing produces a product which has a 6-month demand cycle, as shown. Each unit requires 10 worker hr to produce at a labor cost of $6/hr regular rate (or $9/hr overtime). The total cost/unit is estimated at $200 but units can be subcontracted at a cost of $208/unit. There are currently 20 workers employed in the subject department and hiring and training costs for additional workers are $300/person whereas layoff costs are $400/person. Company policy is to retain a safety stock equal to 20 percent of the monthly forecast and each month's safety stock becomes the beginning inventory for the next month. There are currently 50 units in stock carried at a cost of $2/unit-month. Stockouts have been assigned a cost of $20/unit-month.

	January	**February**	**March**	**April**	**May**	**June**
Forecast demand	300	500	400	100	200	300
Work days	22	19	21	21	22	20
Work hrs at 8/day	176	152	168	168	176	160

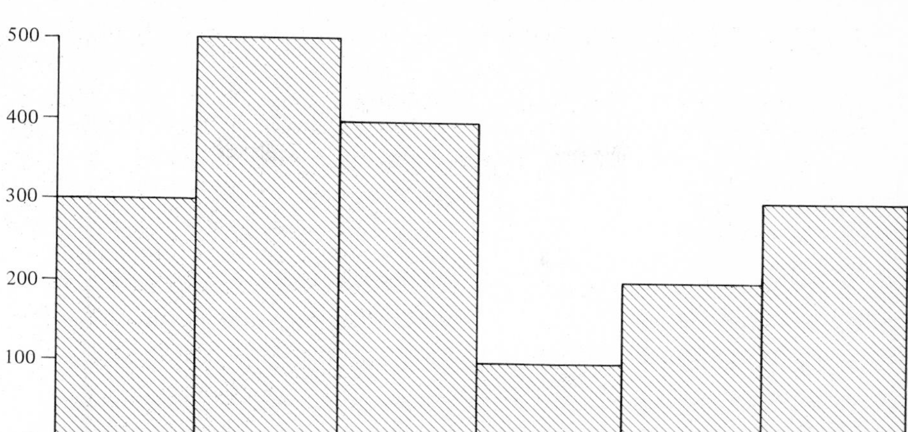

Three aggregate plans are proposed.

Plan 1 Vary work-force size to accommodate demand.

Plan 2 Maintain constant work force of 20 and use overtime and idle time to meet demand.

Plan 3 Maintain constant work force of 20 and build inventory or incur stockout cost. The firm must begin January with the 50-unit inventory on hand.

Compare the costs of the three plans.

Solution [form modified from **4**: 196]
We must first determine what the production requirements are as adjusted to include a safety stock of 20 percent of next month's forecast. Beginning with a January inventory of 50, each subsequent month's inventory reflects the difference between the forecast demand and the production requirement of the previous month.

	Forecast demand	**Cumulative demand**	**Safety stock at 20 percent forecast**	**Beginning inventory**	**Production requirement fcst. + SS − beg. inv.**
January	300	300	60	50	300 + 60 − 50 = 310
February	500	800	100	60	500 + 100 − 60 = 540
March	400	1,200	80	100	400 + 80 − 100 = 380
April	100	1,300	20	80	100 + 20 − 80 = 40
May	200	1,500	40	20	200 + 40 − 20 = 220
June	300	1,800	60	40	300 + 60 − 40 = 320

Plan 1 (vary work-force size):

	January	February	March	April	May	June	Total
1 Production required	310	540	380	40	220	320	
2 Production hours required (**1** × 10)	3,100	5,400	3,800	400	2,200	3,200	
3 Hours available per worker at 8/day	176	152	168	168	176	160	
4 Number of workers required (**2** ÷ **3**)	18	36	23	3	13	20	
5 Number of workers hired		18			10	7	
6 Hiring cost (**5** × $300)		$5,400			$3,000	$2,100	$10,500
7 Number of workers laid off	2		13	20			
8 Layoff cost (**7** × $400)	$800		$5,200	$8,000			$14,000

Plan 2 (use overtime and idle time):

	January	February	March	April	May	June	Total
1 Production required	310	540	380	40	220	320	
2 Production hours required (**1** × 10)	3,100	5,400	3,800	400	2,200	3,200	
3 Hours available per worker at 8/day	176	152	168	168	176	160	
4 Total hours available (**3** × 20)	3,520	3,040	3,360	3,360	3,520	3,200	
5 Number of OT hours required (**2** − **4**)		2,360	440			0	
6 OT prem.[a] (**5** × $3)		$7,080	$1,320			0	$8,400
7 Number IT hours (**4** − **2**)	420			2,960	1,320		
8 IT cost (**5** × $6)	$2,520			$17,760	$7,920		$28,200

[a] Incremental cost of OT = overtime cost − regular time cost = $9 − $6 = $3.

Plan 3 (use inventory and stockout based on constant 20-worker force):

	January	February	March	April	May	June	Total
1 Production required	310	540	380	40	220	320	
2 Cumulative production required	310	850	1,230	1,270	1,490	1,810	
3 Total hours available at 20 workers	3,520	3,040	3,360	3,360	3,520	3,200	
4 Units produced (**3** ÷ 10)	352	304	336	336	352	320	
5 Cumulative production	352	656	992	1,328	1,680	2,000	
6 Units short (**2** − **5**)		194	238				
7 Shortage cost (**6** × $20)		$3,880	$4,760				$8,640
8 Excess units (**5** − **2**)	42			58	190	190	
9 Inventory cost (**8** × $2)	$84			$116	$380	$380	$960

Note that plan 3 assumes a stockout cost is incurred if safety stock is not maintained at prescribed levels of 20 percent of forecast. The firm is in effect managing the safety stock level to yield a specified degree of protection by absorbing the cost of carrying the safety stock as a policy decision.

Summary:

Plan 1 $10,500 hiring + $14,000 layoff = $24,500
Plan 2 $8,400 overtime + $28,200 idle time = $36,600
Plan 3 $8,640 stockout + $960 inventory = $9,600

Plan 3 is the preferred plan.

5 Idaho Instrument Company produces calculators in a Lewiston plant and has forecast demand over the next 12 periods, as shown. Each period is 20 working days (approximately one month). The company maintains a constant work force of 40 employees and there are no subcontractors available who can meet its quality standards. The company can, however, go on overtime if necessary, and encourage customers to back-order calculators if they will. Production and cost data are as follows:

Period	Units	Period	Units	Period	Units
1	800	5	400	9	1,000
2	500	6	300	10	700
3	700	7	400	11	900
4	900	8	600	12	1,200

Production capacity:

Initial inventory: 100 units (final included in period 12 demand)
RT hours: (40 employees)(20 days/period)(8 hr/day) = 6,400 hr/period
OT hours: (40 employees)(20 days/period)(4 hr/day) = 3,200 hr/period
Standard labor hours/unit: 10 hr

Costs:

Labor: RT = $6/hr OT = $9/hr
Material and overhead: $100/unit produced
Back-order costs: apportioned at $5/unit-period
Inventory carrying cost: $2/unit-period

Option A Assume five periods constitute a full demand cycle and use the distribution linear programming approach to develop an aggregate plan based on the first five periods only. (*Note*: A planning length of five periods is useful for purposes of methodology, but in reality the planning horizon should cover a complete cycle, or else the plan should make inventory, personnel, and other such allowances for the whole cycle.)

Option B Determine the optimal production plan for the 12-period cycle using a distribution linear programming format. (*Note*: This more realistic option involves a substantial amount of calculation and should be done on a computer, using a distribution LP code if one is available.)

Solution (*option A*)

RT Cap. avail./period = 6,400 hr ÷ 10 hr/unit = 640 units
OT Cap. avail./period = 3,200 hr ÷ 10 hr/unit = 320 units
RT cost = (10 hr/unit)(\$6/hr) + \$100 mat'l. and OH = \$160/unit
OT cost = (10 hr/unit)(\$9/hr) + \$100 mat'l. and OH = \$190/unit

Note that the back orders are shown in the lower left portion of the matrix.

Demand, units for

Supply, units for	Period 1	Period 2	Period 3	Period 4	Period 5	Unused capacity	Total capacity available
Initial inventory	[0] 100	[2]	[4]	[6]	[8]	[8]	100
1 RT	[160] 640	[162]	[164]	[166]	[168]	[60]	640
OT	[190]	[192]	[194]	[196]	[198]	[0] 320	320
2 RT	[165] 60	[160] 500	[162] 60	[164] 20	[166]	[60]	640
OT	[195]	[190]	[192]	[194]	[196]	[0] 320	320
3 RT	[170]	[165]	[160] 640	[162]	[164]	[60]	640
OT	[200]	[195]	[190]	[192]	[194]	[0] 320	320
4 RT	[175]	[170]	[165]	[160] 640	[162]	[60]	640
OT	[205]	[200]	[195]	[190]	[192]	[0] 320	320
5 RT	[180]	[175]	[170]	[165] 240	[160] 400	[60]	640
OT	[210]	[205]	[200]	[195]	[190]	[0] 320	320
Demand	800	500	700	900	400	1,600	4,900

Solution (option B)

This solution is left as an exercise. See problem 15.

6 The High Point Furniture Company (of Solved Prob. 3) has decided to make a modified next-period response to demand fluctuations that deviate from the seasonalized forecast values, using a control number of $K = 0.4$. Actual demand during the four quarters turns out to be 2,800, 3,800, 3,500, and 2,200 units respectively. The firm begins the year with 600 units on hand, excess inventory is carried forward, but unfilled demand is lost.

(*a*) By how much does actual total demand differ from the forecast?

(*b*) Show the respective inventory balances at the end of each quarter and indicate how many unit sales are actually lost via stockout under this plan.

(*c*) Would the cost of such a plan be justified?

Solution

		Quarter				
		1st	**2d**	**3d**	**4th**	**Total**
1	Actual demand	2,800	3,800	3,500	2,200	12,300
2	Forecast demand	2,400	4,200	3,000	2,400	12,000
3	Difference ΔD	400	−400	500	−200	
4	$K(\Delta D)$, where $K = 0.4$	160	−160	200	−80	
5	Production adjustment	0	160	−160	200	
6	Actual production (3,000 + 5)	3,000	3,160	2,840	3,200	12,200
7	Difference (6 − 1)	200	−640	−660	1,000	
8	Balance with 600 January 1	800	160	−500[a]	1,000	

[a] No backlog allowed. ∴ These 500 units are lost sales.

(*a*) Actual − forecast = 12,300 − 12,000 = 300 units.

(*b*) Balances shown in row 8. The 500 units represent lost sales. Note that the production adjustments take one quarter to implement.

(*c*) More information is desirable to determine the full economic value of the plan. Average inventory on hand is 490 units and more units have been produced than forecast (12,200 versus 12,000). The costs of changing production levels, carrying inventory, stockouts, and the benefits of any additional profit should be compared with what would have occurred without modifying the response given the same actual demand.

QUESTIONS

8-1 Distinguish between aggregate production planning and scheduling on the basis of (*a*) time horizon and (*b*) scope of activities involved.

8-2 Define production planning and control. What are the two major activities associated with it?

8-3 What is the difference between (*a*) aggregate planning and master scheduling? (*b*) priority planning and capacity planning?

8-4 How do time-phased order point and MRP systems handle the problems of scheduling for seasonal demand?

8-5 Production planning and control can be viewed as concerned primarily with what: (*a*) quality and quantity, (*b*) place and timing, (*c*) place and price, or (*d*) quantity and timing?

8-6 Which of the controllable planning variables do you feel are most difficult to quantify in terms of cost? Explain.

8-7 Give an example of a situation where a pure planning strategy would be infeasible from a practical standpoint.

8-8 You are the operations manager of a large electronics jobshop producing power supplies for space vehicles. You must hire someone new to assume major responsibilities for short-term scheduling. Briefly, what type of individual would you seek?

8-9 An electrical manufacturer is producing a large custom-built generator for an electric utility and is four weeks behind schedule. Managers from both firms meet and the electric utility manager says the idea of any delay is "ridiculous, my firm never has production control problems like that, and if you had any sense your firm would eat humble pie and copy a good system from a firm like ours." Comment.

8-10 Distinguish between flow control and order control. Under which type of system would you be more likely to find an MRP system controlling scheduling and end-item inventory? Why?

8-11 How do the traditional production planning and control functions differ for continuous versus intermittent systems?

8-12 As an operations manager, would you prefer to see your activities on a 70 percent learning curve or a 90 percent curve? Why?

8-13 In what respect does the firm planned order of an MRP system accomplish a similar function as the fraction K in the modified response model?

8-14 What can happen to factory production and employment levels if the firm tries to respond directly to random fluctuations in demand as received through retailers and wholesalers? In what way does Magee's modified response model attempt to remedy this situation?

8-15 In relation to aggregate planning, how do the mathematical assumptions concerning costs differ with respect to linear programming techniques and the linear decision rule?

PROBLEMS

1 A manufacturer of radar assemblies has received a contract for 32 units and has produced the first one in 100 hours. If the activity follows a 90 percent learning curve, how long will it take to produce (*a*) the 2d unit, (*b*) the 4th unit, (*c*) the last unit?

2 Management is considering installing $20,000 worth of new equipment on an assembly operation that has been following a 90 percent learning curve. The firm has just completed the fourth assembly, which took 30 days, at direct labor costs of $1,000/day, and the contract calls for eight units total. The new equipment is expected to increase the time of the fifth unit to 31 days but would facilitate other improvements that would put the operation on a 70 percent learning curve.

(*a*) Show calculations to determine whether the new installation is economically justified.

(*b*) Sketch the situation in terms of the relevant portion of the two learning curves.

3 Rocket Control Incorporated, a Long Beach firm, does control panel wiring for solid-fueled rocket engines. The firm is currently preparing delivery estimates for a government contract for 80 panels. The first unit is expected to take 200 worker hours and the firm usually experiences an 84 percent learning curve for this type of work.

(*a*) What average time per unit can be expected for the first three units?

(*b*) How many worker hours should be scheduled for the 40th unit?

4 The Waterford Products planning department uses a forecasting equation of the form $Y = 320 + 10X$ (last quarter 1975 = 0, X = quarters, Y = units). The firm is currently studying production capacity requirements for the year 1980.

(*a*) Prepare a chart showing the quarterly production requirements for 1980.

(*b*) Determine the production rate required to meet average demand over the year and plot this as a dotted line on your chart.

5 Rainwear Manufacturing, Incorporated, produces outdoor apparel which has a demand projected to be as shown. The plant has a two-week vacation shutdown in July so the available production days/month respectively are 22, 19, 21, 21, 22, 20, 12, 22, 20, 23, 19, 21.

January	4,400	April	6,300	July	1,200	October	9,200
February	4,750	May	4,400	August	3,300	November	7,600
March	6,300	June	2,000	September	5,000	December	7,350

(a) Prepare a chart showing the daily production requirements.
(b) Plot the demand as a histogram and as a cumulative requirement over time.
(c) Determine the production rate required to meet average demand and plot this as a dotted line on your graph.

6 The Wexford Glass Company has a skilled work force capable of producing 2,000 sets of handcut crystal/month. The company has a highly seasonal annual demand of 24,000 sets with quarterly indexes of $Q_1 = 0.30$, $Q_2 = 0.80$, $Q_3 = 1.90$, $Q_4 = 1.00$. The company policy is to do all the work in house with its own steady work force on regular hours and it does not accept back orders. The firm absorbs demand fluctuations by carrying inventory at a cost of \$20/set-yr. To meet the demand, (a) what inventory balance must be on hand by the end of each quarter, (b) what is the average inventory balance, and (c) what is the cost for carrying the necessary inventory?

7 The Speedee Bicycle Company makes 10-speed bikes that sell for \$100 each. This year's demand forecast is as shown. Units not sold are carried in stock at a cost of 20 percent of the average inventory value/yr, and storage costs are \$2/bike-yr based upon maximum inventory.

Bike demand forecast

Quarter	**Units**
First	30
Second	120
Third	60
Fourth	70

(a) Plot the demand as a histogram on a quarterly basis and show the average requirement as a dotted line on your graph.
(b) Assume Speedee wishes to maintain a steady work force and to produce at a uniform rate (that is, with no overtime, back orders, subcontracting, or capacity changes) by letting inventories absorb all fluctuations. How many bikes must they have on hand on January 1 in order to meet the forecast demand throughout the year?
(c) For an incremental amount of \$400 in labor costs (total), Speedee can vary its work-force size so as to produce exactly to demand. Compare the costs of producing at a uniform versus variable rate and indicate which plan is less costly and the net difference in cost.

*8 Using the data from Solved Prob. 4, determine the comparative cost of a fourth plan which would be to reduce the work force, maintain it at a constant level of 10 workers, and subcontract all additional demand.

9 An aggregate planner at Duotronix has estimated the following demand requirements for forthcoming work periods, which represent one complete

demand cycle for them. It is a "going concern" and expects the next demand cycle to be similar to this one.

Period	Forecast	Period	Forecast	Period	Forecast
1	400	5	1,200	9	200
2	400	6	1,200	10	400
3	600	7	600		
4	800	8	200		

Five plans are being considered:

Plan 1 Vary the labor force from an initial capability of 400 units to whatever is required to meet demand.

Amount of change	Incremental cost to change labor force Increase	Decrease
200 units	$9,000	$9,000
400 units	15,000	18,000
600 units	18,000	30,000

Plan 2 Maintain a stable work force capable of producing 600 units/period and meet demand by overtime at a premium of $40/unit. Idle time costs are equivalent to $60/unit.

Plan 3 Vary inventory levels but maintain a stable work force producing at an average requirement rate with no overtime or idle time. The carrying cost per unit per period is $20. (The company can arrange to have whatever inventory level is required before period 1 at no additional cost.)

Plan 4 Produce at a steady rate of 400 units/period and accept a limited number of back orders during periods when demand exceeds 400 units. The stockout cost (profit, goodwill, and so on) of lost sales is $110/unit.

Plan 5 Produce at a steady rate of 200 units/period and subcontract for excess requirements at a marginal cost of $40/unit.

Graph the forecast in the form of histogram and analyze the relevant costs of the various plans. You may assume the initial (period 1) work force can be set at a desired level without incurring additional cost. Summarize your answer in the form of a table showing the comparative costs of each plan.

10 Two mixed strategy plans have been proposed for the Duotronix situation in the previous problem. Assume that the pattern inherent in the demand cycle given will be repeated in the next demand cycle.

Plan 6 (back orders and limited inventory) Produce at a steady rate of 400 units/period and carry inventory at $20/unit-period. Assume 200 units of excess demand can be satisfied by back orders placed in period 4 and filled in period 8. A 200-unit inventory is available at the beginning of period 1 and should also be available at the beginning of the next cycle.

Plan 7 (subcontracting and limited inventory) Produce at a steady rate of 400 units/period and subcontract for excess requirements at a marginal cost of $40/unit. A 400-unit inventory is available at the beginning of period 1 and should also be available at the beginning of the next cycle. Carry inventory at $20/unit-period.

Determine the comparative costs of the two plans.

11 A relay manufacturer uses a modified response method to plan production for the upcoming months and has found that a control number of 0.2 is satisfactory. Given the forecast shown, if actual demands in January and February were 5,600 and 4,300 units respectively, what modified production quantity should be scheduled for March? *Note*: Adjustments can be made almost instantaneously.

Forecast demand	
January	5,000 units
February	5,200 units
March	5,800 units

12 Burton Bag Company uses a modified response model with a one-month lead time and a K factor of 0.6 for aggregate planning. Its model includes adjustments for demand (orders received but not yet filled) and inventory levels. Forecast production for April was 10,000 units. If February inventories were 2,000 units higher than planned and unfilled demand was 1,000 less than estimated, how many units should be scheduled for production in April?

13 Sun Valley Ski Company, producers of the famous *Sun-Ski*, has a production cost of $60/pair during regular time and $70/pair on overtime. The firm's production capacity and forecast quarterly demands are shown below. Beginning inventory is 200 pairs and stock is carried at a cost of $5/pair-quarter. Demand is to be met without any hiring, layoff, subcontracting, or back orders. Unused regular time has a $20/pair cost.

(*a*) Develop the preferred plan and present it in the form of a solved matrix.
(*b*) What is the minimum total cost of the plan? [Adapted from **4**: 211.]

Supply, units from	Demand, units for: First quarter	Second quarter	Third quarter	Fourth quarter and Final	Unused capacity	Total capacity available
Initial inventory						200
1 Regular						700
Overtime						300
2 Regular						700
Overtime						300
3 Regular						700
Overtime						300
4 Regular						700
Overtime						300
Forecast demand	900	500	200	1,900	700	4,200

14 Set up and solve the following aggregate planning problem via the distribution linear programming method.

	Regular time	Overtime	Subcontracting
Production capacity/period	8,000 units	2,000 units	2,000 units
Production cost/unit	$7	$9	$10

Inventory: initial = 1,000 units. Carrying cost = $1/unit-period. Demand in units/period: (1) = 6,000; (2) = 18,000; (3) = 3,000; (4) = 10,000. Back orders are not allowed and unused regular time has a $4/unit cost.

(*a*) Show your solution matrix.

(*b*) Tabulate the total cost of your plan.

***15** Complete option B of Solved Prob. 5.

16 Using the data from Solved Prob. 6:

(*a*) Compute the number of units lost via stockout if the actual demand is as given and no modified response is made.

(*b*) Compute the number of units that are actually sold under the original (constant work force) plan versus the modified response plan.

CASE: RYDER MACHINE TOOL COMPANY

Fourteen years ago, Ryder Machine opened its doors as a small producer of two models of pneumatic and hydraulic controls. The controls were for machine tools used in the automotive industry. Within a few short years Ryder developed a high volume for these standardized products. Demand was strong and inventories were managed on an order point system which provided adequate stock to ensure all customers of prompt service.

During the next several years the Ryder shop gradually took on more aspects of machine tool production. By now the company has essentially moved from its initial status as a high-volume producer of two basic controls to a custom producer of large machine tools. The change had brought its share of problems and Bill Ryder, Jr., the company president, seemed to be unable to get a handle on them.

Bill had no formal education in business management, so two years ago he responded favorably when a college professor from Cleveland asked for permission to do a study at the Ryder factory. She wanted to do some analysis for possible application of a new planning technique called the linear decision rule (LDR). Ryder was already in the midst of growing scheduling problems so Bill agreed, thinking he would capitalize on some free consultation time. Bill never fully understood the model, but as the study progressed he could tell it was impractical for him, so as soon as the study team finished its project he abandoned the idea of mathematical aggregate planning and reverted to the more informal manual and verbal methods Ryder had developed over the years.

In the past, the backlog of orders had fluctuated from about 3 months to 24 months of work. Currently it was only 8 months, having been reduced from 14 months due primarily to some recent cancellations. During the last two years the backlog had never exceeded 18 months because the company had adopted a policy of automatically shunting off any backlog in excess of 18 months to subcontractors. No orders were turned down. This was probably a carry-over from William Ryder, Sr. (now chairman of the board) and his often-quoted statement, "Always accept an order. You may never get a second chance. We can always schedule it *and* get it done—somehow!"

The planning staff at Ryder recognized that with their backlog situation there was really no need for demand forecasting and master scheduling. As orders were received they went directly into a detailed schedule. Company policy was to hold rigidly to the schedule once an order was accepted, but this never occurred. As it turned out, expeditors had to champion almost every major order to get it through the shop, and overtime work to get them out was the normal routine. Even then, orders were likely to be three to six months late. These late deliveries had already caused some cancellations and, as word of them got out in the industry, were beginning to affect new business.

In addition to shipment problems, total costs had been getting more out of line over the past 18 months. Costs appeared to be soaring in some departments, although in others the reported costs were unbelievably static. While it was apparent that overall costs were climbing rapidly, it was impossible to relate them to specific jobs.

Nevertheless, this was one of the items on Bill's mind when he asked to meet with the production planning and control staff.

At the meeting, Bill learned that there were several "legitimate" reasons for the late shipments. First, much of the fault was not Ryder's at all but was due to subcontractors. In fact, most of the recent cancellations had been on orders that had been subcontracted out. Second, many of the in-plant delays at Ryder resulted from the inventory control department not doing its job properly. The inventory control manager always seemed to be short of one or two critical items when they were needed most. Third, engineering and marketing nearly always insisted on last-minute changes even though this was theoretically contrary to company policy. These changes created endless problems for the whole schedule and had even necessitated adding two more expeditors during the past six months, while at the same time the backlog was going down.

As Bill returned to his office, he thought, "There must be a better way. What are we doing wrong?"

Prepare an analysis for him, clearly addressing the following issues and proposing some recommended courses of action.

1 What factors are responsible for the rapid increase in costs?

2 What would your comment be on the firm's problems with respect to inventory management?

3 What changes would you recommend with respect to the firm's aggregate planning policy?

4 How "legitimate" are production control's reasons for late shipments? Make whatever suggestions you can to alleviate these problems.

BIBLIOGRAPHY

[1] ABRAMOWITZ, IRVIN: *Production Management*, Ronald Press Company, New York, 1967.

[2] BOWMAN, E. H.: "Consistency and Optimality in Managerial Decision Making," *Management Science*, vol. 4, January 1963, pp. 100–103.

[3] BUFFA, ELWOOD S.: *Modern Production Management*, 4th ed., John Wiley & Sons, New York, 1973.

[4] CHASE, RICHARD B., and NICHOLAS J. ACQUILANO: *Production and Operations Management*, Richard D. Irwin, Homewood, Illinois, 1973.

[5] CONWAY, R. W., AND ANDREW SCHULTZ, JR.: "The Manufacturing Progress Function," *The Journal of Industrial Engineering*, vol. 10, no. 1, January–February 1959, pp. 39–54.

[6] FORRESTER, JAY W.: *Industrial Dynamics*, M.I.T. Press, Cambridge, Massachusetts, 1961.

[7] GARRETT, LEONARD J., AND MILTON SILVER: *Production Management Analysis*, 2d ed., Harcourt, Brace, Jovanovich, New York, 1974.

[8] GROFF, GENE K., AND JOHN F. MUTH: *Operations Management: Analysis for Decisions*, Richard D. Irwin, Homewood, Illinois, 1972.

[9] HANSSMAN, F., AND S. W. HESS: "A Linear Programming Approach to Production and Employment Scheduling," *Management Technology*, vol. 1, January 1960, pp. 46–51.

[10] HOLSTEIN, W. K.: "Production Planning and Control Integrated," *Harvard Business Review*, vol. 46, no. 3, May–June 1968.

[11] HOLT, C. C., F. MODIGLIANI, J. F. MUTH, AND H. A. SIMON: *Production Planning, Inventories, and Work Force*, Prentice-Hall, Englewood Cliffs, New Jersey, 1960.

[12] JONES, CURTIS A.: "Parametric Production Planning," *Management Science*, July 1967, pp. 843–866.

[13] MAGEE, J. F.: *Production Planning and Inventory Control*, McGraw-Hill Book Company, New York, 1958.

[14] ———, AND D. M. BOODMAN: *Production Planning and Inventory Control*, 2d ed., McGraw-Hill Book Company, New York, 1967.

[15] MOORE, FRANKLIN G.: *Production Management*, 6th ed., Richard D. Irwin, Homewood, Illinois, 1973.

[16] ———, AND RONALD JOBLONSKI: *Production Control*, 3d ed., McGraw-Hill Book Company, New York, 1969.

[17] PLOSSL, G. W., AND O. W. WIGHT: *Production and Inventory Control*, Prentice-Hall, Englewood Cliffs, New Jersey, 1967.

[18] SHORE, BARRY: *Operations Management*, McGraw-Hill Book Company, New York, 1973.

[19] TAUBERT, WILLIAM H.: "A Search Decision Rule for the Aggregate Scheduling Problem," *Management Science*, February 1968, pp. 343–359.

[20] VERGIN, R. C.: "Production Planning Under Seasonal Demand," *Journal of Industrial Engineering*, May 1966, pp. 260–266.

[21] VOLLMAN, THOMAS E.: *Operations Management*, Addison-Wesley Publishing Company, Reading, Massachusetts, 1973.

[22] WIGHT, OLIVER W.: *Production and Inventory Management in the Computer Age*, Cahners Books, Boston, Massachusetts, 1974.

CHAPTER

Production Planning and Control: Scheduling and Control

Aggregate planning is vital, but it does not solve the immediate problems of deciding which job to work on when, or how to assign workers and machines in order to meet the plan. In this chapter we continue the transition from aggregate planning and master scheduling to more specific short-term scheduling activities. Beginning with an overview of scheduling philosophy, we examine some methods for scheduling and assigning work activities, and finish the chapter with a discussion of control models. As stated earlier, this chapter and the preceding chapter on aggregate planning are intimately related and should be studied as a unit.

SCHEDULING PHILOSOPHY

We saw earlier that aggregate planning conveys an overall picture of the workload assigned to facilities versus the productive capacity available. Capacity refers to the hours of labor and the machine time available (or to the ability to produce in terms of number of units). The cumulative workload projections developed through master scheduling provide an overall perspective of capacity utilization and help to identify potential delivery problems. They can also facilitate the more detailed scheduling of work which we shall take up in this chapter.

In Fig. 9-1 the shaded area represents a delivery requirement in excess of weekly capacity, suggesting that perhaps some of the specific jobs or output required during periods 3 and 4 be produced in an earlier period, say during periods 1 or 2. Alternatively, the deliveries might be delayed until later (back-ordered), or perhaps the firm could go on overtime to meet the excess requirement. The shaded area would then represent the specific number of hours that would have to be produced on overtime to meet the delivery requirements. As we begin relating these aggregate plans to immediate needs and specific jobs we are essentially moving into the realm of short-term scheduling. The overall levels of employment, inventories, and so on, begin to take on special meaning with respect to current requirements.

Another useful means of gaining a general perspective of the ensuing workload (that also conveys implications for current schedules) is by means of a Gantt progress chart of a production plan. An example of this is depicted in Fig. 9-2. By graphing activities on a sequential time scale the scheduler clearly specifies which activities must be completed before or concurrent with other activities. The Gantt chart of Fig. 9-2 shows all activities from the initial scheduling itself to the final packing and shipment of a specific order.

In a broad context, scheduling involves everything from the receipt of specific demand information, through the setting up of starting and stopping times for individual operations, issuing of shop orders, and routing of materials and work flow, to the actual authorization and completion of work activities.

Given some specific demand data, schedulers have several approaches open to them, depending upon the policy of the firm or organization. They can (*a*) simply schedule work on a cumulative or aggregate basis as we have seen above, (*b*) schedule on a detailed basis as jobs arrive, (*c*) use some combination of aggregative and detailed scheduling, or (*d*) not schedule at all. Each philosophy has its own merits and drawbacks.

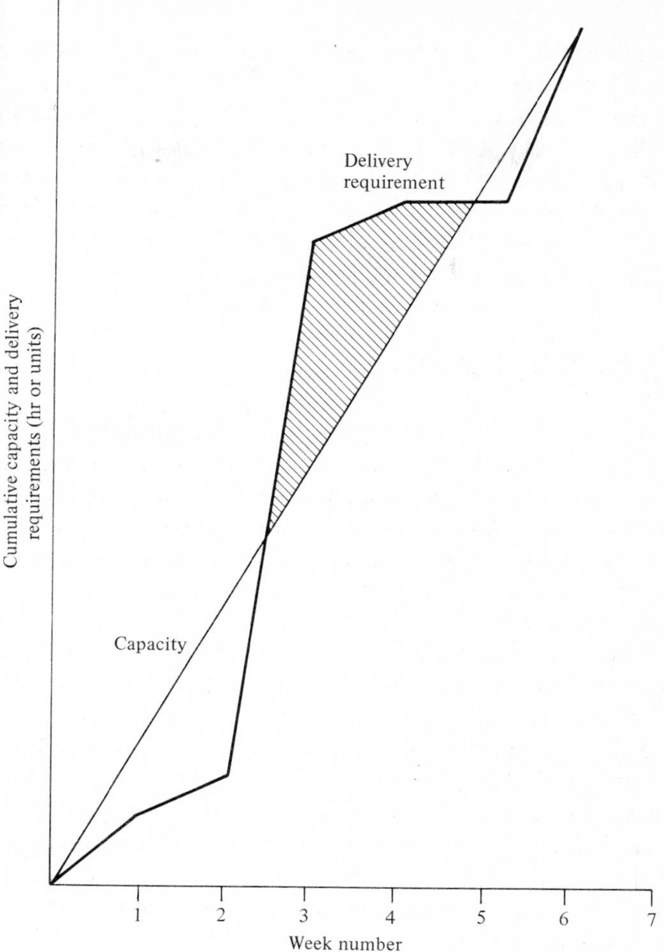

FIGURE 9-1 Cumulative workload

CUMULATIVE SCHEDULING

Cumulative scheduling only focuses primarily on aggregate capacity. It may suffice in some nonjobshop or highly decentralized systems, but in many cases it is not sufficiently definitive to be operationally satisfactory.

DETAILED SCHEDULING

Detailed scheduling as jobs come in also has one major shortcoming—it is often too definitive to work! In most job shops there are too many changes, breakdowns, and unexpected delays to presume that specific worker or machine assignments, on a daily (or even hourly) basis, can be made up more than one week in advance. As a result, the "published" schedule quickly breaks down to some sort of informal expediting system that is often out of control.

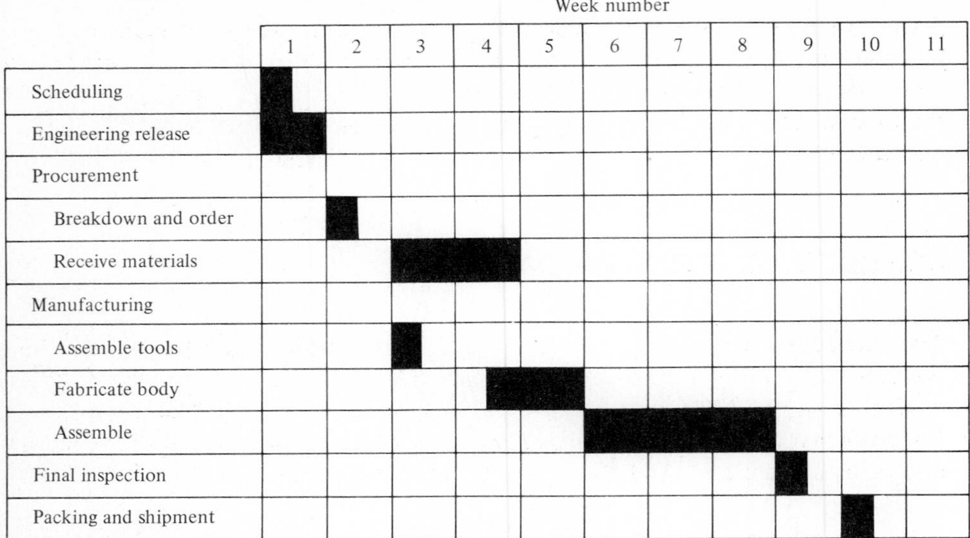

FIGURE 9-2 Gantt progress chart of production plan for 500 electric heaters

COMBINATION OF DETAILED AND CUMULATIVE SCHEDULING

The combination of cumulative workload projections as jobs come in, with more detailed scheduling as production time draws near, is usually a more satisfactory approach, especially now that computers are available to assist in the revision and updating of schedules. This approach focuses on material and capacity requirements, working as long as possible with modules common to many products rather than with specific end items. Job shops with MRP systems typically determine their material needs from a master schedule and material requirements plan, releasing orders only as needed, to arrive in time to produce the (master) scheduled end-product mix. Capacities are planned on a broad basis in terms of total labor and machine-hour requirements per week at key work centers rather than trying to schedule a specific job on specific equipment at a specific time. As changes occur during the weeks prior to manufacturing, the computer updates material and capacity requirements automatically. Capacity is then allocated to specific jobs as late as a week, or perhaps just a day or two before the actual work is performed. The actual time (capacity) allowed at each work center is then based on predetermined standard hour requirements for the job. However it usually does little good to try to specify which particular hour or minutes a worker shall work on a given job. Normally, one day is the shortest practical scheduling unit used in job shops.

NOT SCHEDULING AT ALL

The fourth alternative of *not scheduling at all* is, perhaps surprisingly, very widely used. Many job shops have found that the most practical way for them to decide when and where each work activity will be done is to not make any prior schedule at all, but instead to follow relatively simple dispatch decision rules. Examples of such rules are "first come first served," or "always work on items with the longest lead times." This way some of the problems of detailed scheduling are circumvented.

SCHEDULING METHODOLOGY

The scheduling methodology depends upon the type of industry, organization, product, and level of sophistication required. We shall examine three general classes of methodology: (1) charts, boards, and computers; (2) priority decision rules; and (3) mathematical programming methods. The methods are not mutually exclusive and many firms use a combination of scheduling techniques.

CHARTS, BOARDS, AND COMPUTERS

Gantt charts and associated scheduling boards have been extensively used scheduling devices in the past and continue to be widely used, although many firms are now going to computer-assisted scheduling. Gantt charts are extremely easy to understand and can quickly reveal the current or planned situation to all concerned. They are used in several forms including (*a*) *progress or scheduling charts*, which depict the sequential schedule, (*b*) *load charts*, which show the work assigned to a group of workers or machines, and (*c*) *record charts*, which are used to record the actual operating times and delays of workers or machines.

The production plan illustrated in Fig. 9-2 was a simplified progress chart. For more detailed scheduling, the symbols shown in Fig. 9-3 are also used.

Many schedulers find it desirable to maintain load charts in conjunction with progress charts. The load charts show the scheduled workload, maintenance, and idle time on key machines, and the accumulated backlog. In Fig. 9-4, the thin lines represent work scheduled for specific customer orders (the SOs) or inventory (the I 2A clips) and the thick lines constitute the cumulative workload.

Where two or more machines (such as lathes 7 and 8 in Fig. 9-4) are available and capable of doing the same job, the choice of machines may depend on setup and operating costs, operator skills required, and other jobs which must also be scheduled. An economic analysis, such as the machine breakpoint charting technique of Chap. 5, is often a good starting point for such equipment selection decisions. Other mathematical methods for assigning jobs will be discussed subsequently in this chapter.

Another (progress) chart is shown in Fig. 9-5, where the (V) indicates updating through July 7. The chart shows that the rod castings were delayed a day, probably due to extra maintenance on the casting furnace. The wires were completed half a day ahead of schedule and end-cap fabrication was two days late in getting started. With a planned three-day schedule, it appears the end caps will probably not be completed

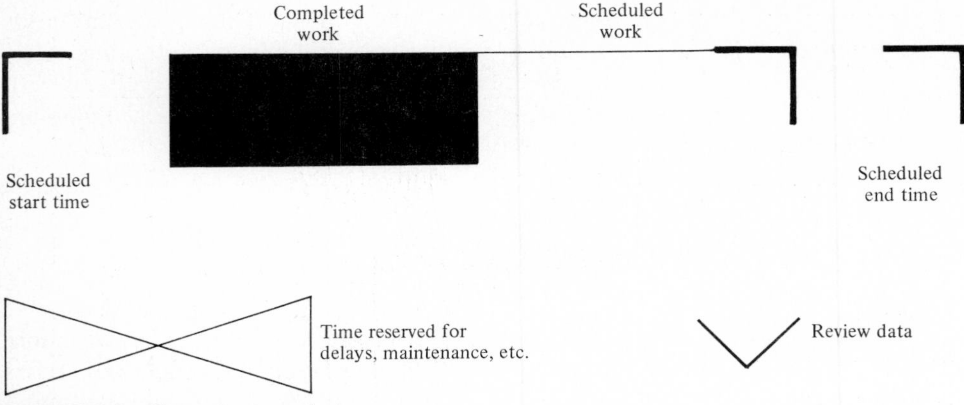

FIGURE 9-3 Gantt chart symbols

before the heater element assembly is begun on Monday, July 11, even though an extra day of slack was provided on July 8.

Keeping Gantt charts up to date has always been a major problem. Numerous mechanical and magnetic charts and boards are available to facilitate the revision process [**8**: 398]. A "Boardmaster" uses cards which snap into small grooves along the horizontal time scale. The "Sched-U-Graph," by Remington Rand, uses colored cards which are cut to a length corresponding to the scheduled time and inserted into a visible window. "Produc-trol" is another device which has a visible card window plus a tracking peg and cord to monitor progress of the job. Other systems make use of magnetic card holders. In general, however, reliance on graphic methods of control is diminishing in favor of the up-to-date reports that can be supplied by computers.

Many large firms have developed their own computerized scheduling system and their scheduling instructions are issued daily in the form of computer printouts. Current data on production capacities and requirements are fed into the computer and

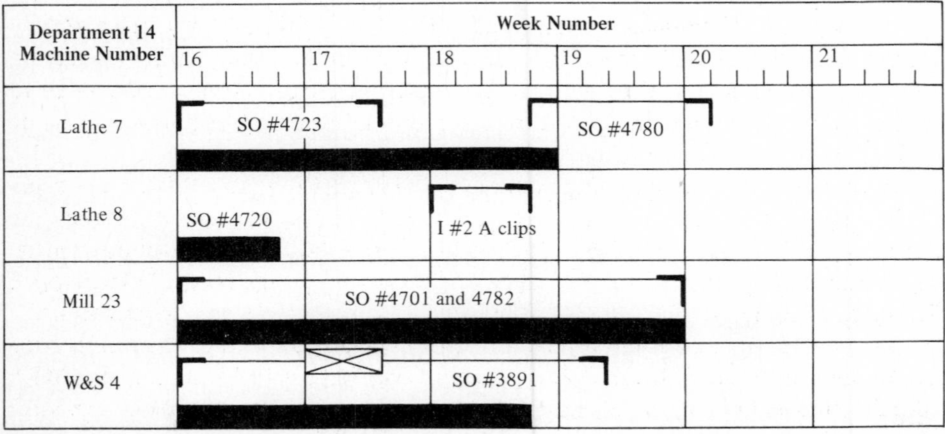

FIGURE 9-4 Load chart

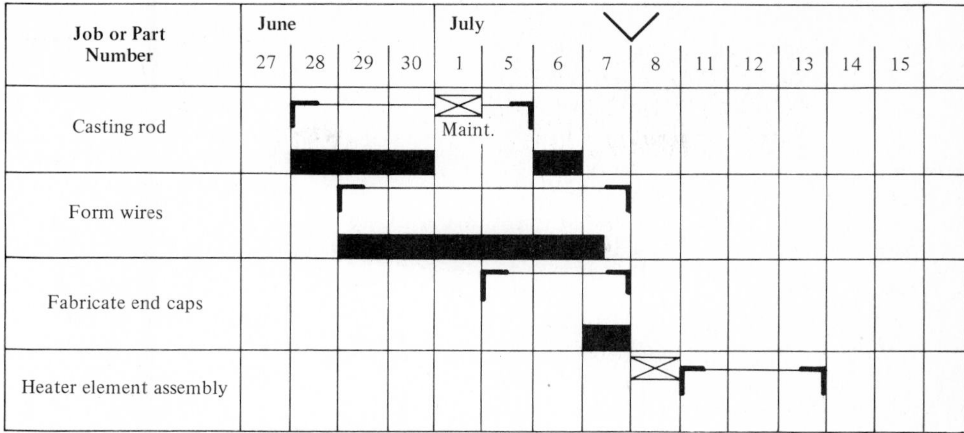

FIGURE 9-5 Progress (schedule) chart

production quantities, times, machine assignments, and the like, are provided as an output. For the most part, these scheduling systems are uniquely designed to suit the operating parameters of individual firms, although some generalized programs, such as the General Electric General Shop Scheduler (GJSCH$), are available. The scheduling problem is still just as complex, and the programs cannot guarantee the firm that it has an optimum schedule, but the computer can keep track of thousands of items of inventory and assist in generating revised schedules so quickly that the resultant schedules are nearly always an improvement over manual methods.

Scheduling and MRP Systems

In the two previous chapters we have noted that the computerization of inventory records, via time-phased order point (TPOP) and MRP systems, has naturally extended into the realm of scheduling. In fact, MRP is really more of a scheduling system than an inventory control system. Computer-assisted scheduling has proven so increasingly valuable over the past few years that it is worth examining in some additional depth at this point.

Both of the priority planning systems mentioned (TPOP and MRP) are time-conscious systems. That is, they try to ensure the availability of materials at the time required by the master schedule. In addition, they can be updated frequently. "Regenerative" MRP systems are typically updated weekly whereas the "net change" MRP systems being installed now are effectively updated daily or as changes occur.

Just as the master schedule drives an MRP system, signaling when purchased parts or internally manufactured components must be available, so too the MRP system in turn dictates what capacity of labor and machine hours must be available within the plant to meet the master schedule [**15**: 86]. This, of course, is the capacity requirements planning function, referred to in Fig. 8-3 as *capacity planning.*

Capacity Requirements Planning

Capacity requirements planning consists of loading the hours of work (from the proposed master schedule and priority planning phases) onto various key work centers to develop a plan showing what capacity is needed to meet the master schedule. It is a considerable extension of—and refinement over—the infinite loading procedures used in the past (and still in use in many firms today) where the total backlog was "loaded" on the work center, usually resulting in many orders showing up as "overdue."

Capacity requirements planning differs from infinite loading in that it proceeds from forecasts and planned orders via the master schedule and MRP system rather than working from backlogs only. Moreover, it is an iterative technique (that is, really a simulation) which recognizes that if capacities are inadequate, and confidence is to be maintained in the scheduling system, then schedule adjustments must be made [**15**: 86].

Figure 9-6 illustrates a simplified capacity requirements plan for a work center (shop 62) for the next eight weeks. The shaded portion represents actual scheduled customer orders whereas the unshaded area includes some planned orders (from the MRP system) plus perhaps up to 10 percent of the capacity for unplanned uses (such as breakdowns, emergency orders, and engineering use). The actual hours would be expected to vary from those shown in the plan, even after revision, for exact schedules are seldom maintained in a job shop. However, if the planner has an average of 200 hours per week available in shop 62, the chances are good that the schedule will be met.

If capacity is adequate in all the work centers, and the master schedule can be met, the MRP system can release orders to production (and to purchasing, as the case may be) and proceed to monitor their progress. If capacity is not adequate to meet the master schedule, either more hours must be obtained—through overtime, subcontracting, and so forth—or the master schedule must be revised.

In the past, the failure to recognize an overload situation and promptly revise the master schedule was one of the prime causes of the breakdown of formal scheduling systems. Perhaps this was because continuous revision of the master schedule and rescheduling of the detailed schedules posed an impossible data processing task. With hundreds of jobs, the charts, boards, and paperwork methods were unable to do the job.

A common but equally unsatisfactory solution to the scheduling problem was to assign priorities to certain jobs and to hire expeditors to push the "hot" jobs through the shop. Instead of solving the real problem, however, which was one of capacity, this solution endeavored to push more work through the shops. As numerous jobs became late, more of them required expediting, but few were ever "unexpedited" [**15**: 97]. The capacity problem was not solved, schedules were still not met, and confidence in the scheduling and control systems deteriorated.

Today, computerized systems are gradually restoring to managers the control they need to effectively manage schedules and production. These computer systems are electronically sophisticated but the logic of their scheduling operations is really

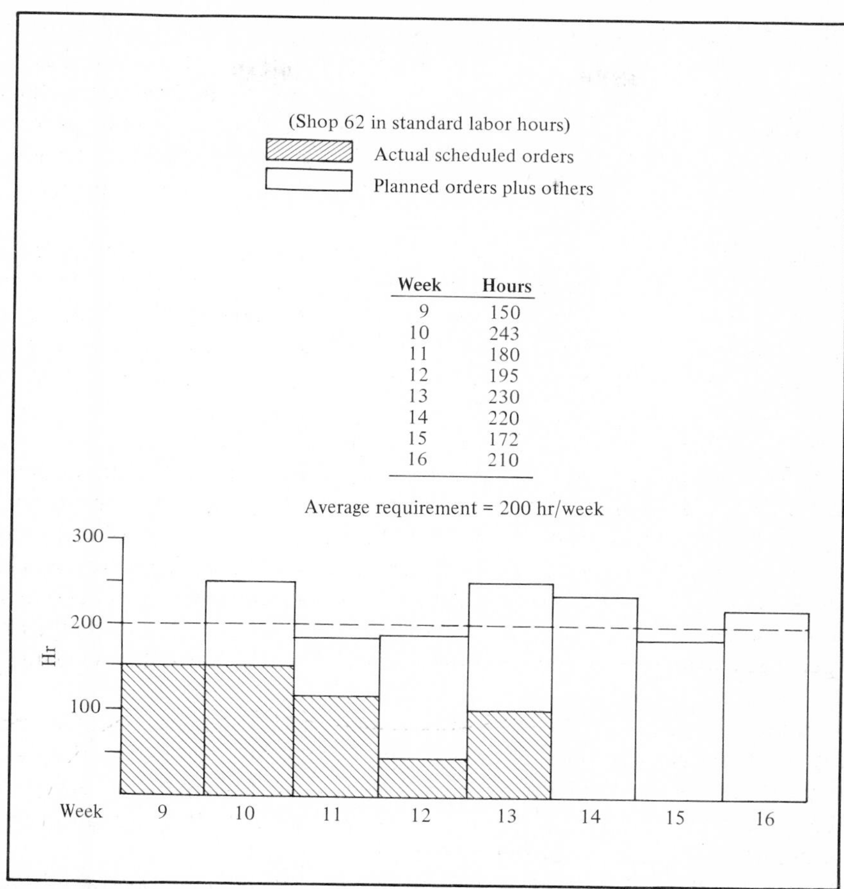

Week	Hours
9	150
10	243
11	180
12	195
13	230
14	220
15	172
16	210

FIGURE 9-6 Capacity requirements plan

quite straightforward. It consists basically of the master schedule, priority planning, and capacity planning features which have been discussed previously. In addition, controls are maintained to ensure that actual output does not deviate too far from scheduled output. We shall take up the subject of output control in a later section of this chapter, after considering some additional and more specific aids to scheduling.

In some cases, computerized scheduling is simplified by the use of formalized decision rules which take the place of complicated algorithms or intuitive rules of thumb used in manual systems. We turn now to some of these priority decision rules.

PRIORITY DECISION RULES

Priority decision rules are simplified guidelines for determining the sequence in which jobs will be worked on. In some firms these rules take the place of priority planning systems such as time-phased order point or MRP systems. In others, they are used in conjunction with some of these more advanced systems.

The search for "optimal" rules has generated a good deal of academic research having to do with assigning n jobs to m machines subject to various static and dynamic arrival patterns. Extensive simulations have been done to analyze effects on processing time, labor utilization, inventory carrying cost, and so on, of various decision rules.

Unfortunately, these studies have not always recognized the difference between dependent and independent items, nor have they faced the real-world problems that result from breakdowns of the formal priority systems. As a result, one consultant has claimed that the "studies of static priority rules have had almost no influence on manufacturing companies" [**15**: 122]. Nevertheless, priority decision rules are extensively used, so a number of them are discussed below. We lead off with some single criterion rules that are "static" in that they do not incorporate an updating feature. These are followed by one example of a combined heuristic rule and a description of Johnson's rule. Following that, we take up the critical ratio technique, a widely used priority system that permits regular updating and revision of priorities.

Single Criterion Rules

The simplest but sometimes most effective priority rules assign jobs on the basis of a single criterion. Some of these rules call for giving priority to jobs on the basis of:

1 First come first served

2 Earliest due date

3 Least slack (that is, time due less processing time remaining)

4 Shortest processing time

5 Longest processing time

6 Preferred customer order

7 Random order

One of the difficulties of selecting an appropriate rule, of course, lies in first deciding on the criterion. Rules which minimize flow time, or the average waiting time of orders, do not necessarily yield low in-process inventory costs or high labor or machine utilization. The rules listed above use only one criterion as a determinant for decision. The first come–first served order, for example, may appear desirable from a "fairness" standpoint, but customers in urgent need of a particular product may desperately need faster service on some occasions. None of the single-criterion rules takes the "big picture" into account.

Some priority rules are, however, generally better than others. Research has shown, for example, that the shortest processing-time rule has the lowest average flow time of numerous rules tested [**2**: 586]. This results in low in-process inventory cost. (On the other hand, consistently scheduling items with the shortest operation time will undoubtedly make some customers—with long processing times—quite unhappy!) A rule of giving priority to those jobs that have the least slack time per remaining operations (not listed above) has been reported to be effective for focusing upon the lateness of jobs [**12**: 419].

Combined Heuristic Rules

Combined loading rules often yield the best results, depending again upon the criteria of the individual firm. One very effective and efficient heuristic rule uses the shortest expected processing time as a base and combines this with two other rules.[1] These other two rules call for assigning priority to those items which may experience bottlenecks and to certain jobs with the longest total processing time remaining. An initial assignment on the basis of the shortest operating time helps get many machines into operation at the beginning of the scheduling period. Next, the scheduler gives special attention to the bottleneck machines and schedules jobs so as to get them into operation as quickly as possible and keep them running as steadily as possible, by scheduling the longest jobs first. Toward the end of the scheduling period a combination of the shortest and longest jobs appears to be effective, with the longest job rule having the effect of keeping critical machines in operation once they have begun. The bottleneck feature of this heuristic rule turns out to have a significant effect and the shortest processing-time component (which is the most effective single-loading rule) tends to be of least importance. But the rule depends upon consideration of all three individual rules simultaneously in order to break any ties.

Johnson's Rule

A simple rule which yields a minimum processing time for sequencing n jobs through two machines (A and B) has been developed by S. M. Johnson [**6**]. It works well for situations where the same processing sequence must be maintained on both machines and there are no in-process storage problems or overriding individual priorities.

Johnson's rule simply requires that all jobs be listed, showing the times each requires on each machine. The jobs are then scanned for the shortest individual activity time. If the shortest time lies with machine A, the job is placed as early in the schedule as possible, and if with machine B, it is placed as late as possible. Once one job has been scheduled it is eliminated from further consideration and the decision rule is applied to the remaining jobs. Ties are broken arbitrarily, for although they may yield a different sequence, the overall time is not affected. Furthermore, the one

[1] I am indebted to Professor Bruce Woodworth of the Management Science Department at Oregon State University for permission to use his research on this loading rule.

scheduling sequence that is derived then applies to both machines. By scheduling minimum-time jobs at the beginning and ending of the schedule the amount of concurrent operating time for machines *A* and *B* is maximized and thus the overall operating time to complete a specified number of jobs is minimized. The rule has also been extended to cover three machines.

Critical Ratio Technique

A priority scheduling technique that has been found effective for advance scheduling as well as for current review and revision of existing schedules is the critical ratio scheduling technique. In contrast to the "static" rules discussed earlier, critical ratio is dynamic in that it facilitates the constant updating of priorities. Although it is quite a simple system, it develops a comparative index for each job and, with data processing equipment, can be updated weekly or even daily to provide relatively close and timely control.

The critical ratio is designed to give priority to those jobs which most urgently need the work time in order to be shipped on schedule. As a job appears to be getting farther behind schedule its critical ratio becomes lower, and jobs with low critical ratios take precedence over others.

The critical ratio is:

$$\text{Critical ratio} = \frac{\text{estimated shipping date} - \text{today's date}}{\text{estimated shipping date} - \text{promised date}}$$

$$\text{CR} = \frac{\text{ED} - \text{TD}}{\text{ED} - \text{PD}} \tag{9-1}$$

where the numerator reflects the current total load on the firm's production facilities and the denominator reflects the firm's commitment to the customer or original schedule.

Example 9-1

Today is day 22 on the production control calendar and four jobs are on order as shown in the accompanying table.

Job	Promised (customer) date	Estimated shipping date
A	20	28
B	24	26
C	26	24
D	18	30

Determine the critical ratio for each job and assign priority rankings.

Solution

	Job *A*	Job *B*	Job *C*	Job *D*
ED − TD	28 − 22 = 6	26 − 22 = 4	24 − 22 = 2	30 − 22 = 8
ED − PD	28 − 20 = 8	26 − 24 = 2	24 − 26 = −2	30 − 18 = 12
	$CR = \frac{6}{8} = 0.75$	$\frac{4}{2} = 2.00$	$\frac{2}{-2} = -1.00$	$\frac{8}{12} = 0.67$
∴ Priority is	2	3	4	1

The priority decision rule in the above example would assign jobs in the order of *D*, *A*, *B*, and *C*. Both jobs *D* and *A* have critical ratios of less than one, meaning that they will not be shipped on time unless they are expedited. Note that job *C* is ahead of schedule, resulting in a negative index, which is assigned lowest priority.

Another version of the critical ratio [**13**: 585] calls for computation of the demand time for an item divided by the supply time. Then if, for example, an item is needed within 30 days and normal production time is 40 days, the critical ratio is 30/40 = 0.75. The implication here is that if demand is to be met on time it will be necessary to produce it in 75 percent of the expected time. This item (with a 0.75 critical ratio) would then take priority over all items with ratios greater than 0.75 as the job was routed from one machine center to the next.

Priority decision rules are often simple heuristics, but they can be relatively effective if carefully chosen and evaluated. On the other hand, where more sophisticated mathematical methods can be used, they hold out a theoretical potential of optimization that priority rules can never claim. We turn now to some of the mathematical methods of scheduling.

MATHEMATICAL PROGRAMMING METHODS

Scheduling is, in many respects, a complex resource-allocation problem. Firms possess capacity, labor skills, materials, and so forth, and seek to allocate their use so as to maximize a profit or service objective, or perhaps meet a demand while minimizing costs. The interdependencies, cost uncertainties, and assumptions that must be made, however, make a mathematical solution to the problem difficult. Nevertheless, as firms gain better productivity and cost data, the underlying assumptions become less restrictive. This, coupled with the availability of computers and advanced quantitative methods, has brought many of the scheduling problems closer to a logical, data based solution than they were previously. A brief review of applications will reveal that scheduling and production control are now very fertile areas for the use of standard simplex and distribution linear programming, assignment linear programming, and dynamic programming methods, all of which are discussed below.

Linear Programming: Graphic, Simplex, and Distribution Methods

We have already discussed the characteristics and solution methodologies for graphic, simplex-echelon, and distribution linear programming problems. Suffice it to point out that many scheduling and production control problems fit well into these frameworks.

Example 9-2

A firm can sell whatever quantities of three grades of steel it can produce. Each grade yields a different profit contribution and requires different times on common machines. The scheduling problem of designating which quantities to produce may be formulated as one of maximizing profit subject to machine time availability constraints. The solution can proceed via the standard simplex method of linear programming.

Example 9-3

A scheduler in a multiplant firm must direct the flow of raw materials from three peripheral supply points to five different mills in order to establish production quantities and operating times for each mill. The optimal allocation may be determined by setting up a distribution linear programming matrix covering supply and demand locations plus interconnecting transportation costs.

Example 9-4

Eight shop orders calling for different quantities must be assigned to production on five machines. Each machine has a limited number of hours available and may result in a different cost/piece. The assignment of jobs to machines can be made using the distribution linear programming method after the hours of machine time and units of demand are converted to common units of equivalent standard hours (ESH). To do this, an index of relative production capabilities is computed for the machines, with the best one assigned a value of 1. All machine time (supply) and demand is then expressed in terms of ESH. Costs in the body of the matrix are expressed as the amount of contribution (price − variable cost) per ESH. Normal methods of the distribution linear programming algorithm then apply [**5**, **11**].

Distribution linear programming methods were discussed in Chap. 2 and used again in the last chapter (Chap. 8) as methods of aggregate planning. Graphic and simplex-echelon methods of standard linear programming were introduced in Chap. 5 in a product-mix–short-term scheduling context. The reader may wish to review linear programming Examples 5-2 and 5-3 and Solved Probs. 2, 3, and 4 in Chap. 5 at this time. These product-mix and process selection examples further illustrate the comprehensiveness of the scheduling problem and the application of linear programming to help select raw material amounts and product quantities to schedule on a profit maximization or cost minimization basis.

Linear Programming: Assignment Method

The assignment method of linear programming is a variant of the distribution method. It is useful for assigning jobs to machines, workers to jobs, and so on, on the basis of some criterion such as cost, performance, quantity, time, or efficiency. Of course only one criterion can apply at a time and, in addition, the method requires that the number of items to be assigned equal the number of positions available. If the numbers are not equal, a dummy row or column is added and assigned a zero criterion coefficient (for example, to help identify which job to eliminate) or a high criterion coefficient (for example, to be sure the job never gets done). Similarly, if any worker-machine assignments are impractical or infeasible, the cell is blocked out or given an exhorbitant cost that will prohibit any assignment.

The solution method for minimization problems involves forming a square matrix of criteria values and systematically developing zeros in the cells until a zero exists for each row-column combination. As soon as there is at least one zero in each row and each column, an optimal solution has been obtained.

Step 1 Subtract the smallest number in each row from all others in the row and enter the results in the form of a new matrix.

Step 2 Using the new matrix, subtract the smallest number in each column from all others in the column, again forming a new matrix.

Step 3 Check to see if there is a zero for each row and column by drawing the minimum number of lines necessary to cover all zeros in the matrix.

Step 4 If the number of lines required is less than the number of rows, modify the matrix again by adding the smallest uncovered number to all values at line intersections and subtracting it from each uncovered number, including itself.

Step 5 Check the matrix again via zero covering lines and continue with the modification (step 3) until the optimal assignment is obtained.

Example 9-5

A scheduler has four jobs that can be done on any of four machines with respective costs ($) as shown. Determine the allocation of jobs to machines that will result in minimum cost.

	Machine			
Job	**1**	**2**	**3**	**4**
A	5	6	8	7
B	10	12	11	7
C	10	8	13	6
D	8	7	4	3

Solution

The five steps are as follows.

1 *Row subtraction*

	1	2	3	4
A	0	1	3	2
B	3	5	4	0
C	4	2	7	0
D	5	4	1	0

2 *Column subtraction*

	1	3	4	2
A	0	0	2	2
B	3	4	3	0
C	4	1	6	0
D	5	3	0	0

3 *Cover all zeros*

	1	2	3	4
A	0	0	2	2
B	3	4	3	0
C	4	1	6	0
D	5	3	0	0

4 *Modify matrix*

	1	2	3	4
A	0	0	2	3
B	2	3	2	0
C	3	0	5	0
D	5	3	0	1

5 *Cover zeros again*

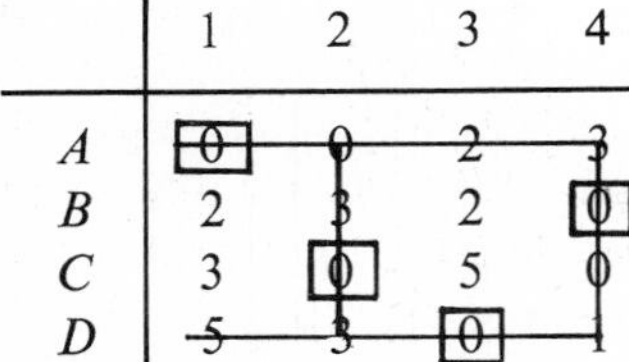

	1	2	3	4
A	0	0	2	3
B	2	3	2	0
C	3	0	5	0
D	5	3	0	1

Optimum assignments

Job *A* to machine 1 at $5
Job *B* to machine 4 at $7
Job *C* to machine 2 at $8
Job *D* to machine 3 at $4

Note that the final allocation (square boxes in step 5 above) should begin with those jobs that are limited to one machine (*B* and *D*), for once they are assigned this may constrain the assignment of the remaining jobs (*A* and *C*).

The assignment method described above encompasses the principle of opportunity cost which we encountered previously in Chap. 5. In the initial steps of the solution, the subtraction of the smallest row and column numbers from the remaining values essentially converted the other values in the rows and columns to opportunity costs. In our example they then represented the opportunity costs that would have resulted from not assigning the best job to the least costly machine.

Maximization problems can also be solved by using the same assignment algorithm [**11**: 199]. The only change required is that all the values that appear in the initial maximization matrix (such as profits) must first be subtracted from the largest number in the matrix. This action essentially converts all the values to "relative costs" and from there on the procedure is the same.

The assignment method has been extensively used for assigning jobs in machine shops, scheduling use of heavy equipment, and numerous other industrial settings where relatively accurate cost, profit, or time criteria have been available. As productive efforts in the economy gradually become more oriented toward services we may expect to see expanded use of this method in the assigning of personnel to service-oriented tasks.

Dynamic Programming

Dynamic programming is another optimization technique that has strong potential for increased application in both goods and services scheduling. It is designed to solve problems that can be partitioned into time-dependent stages. The solution procedure is based upon enumeration of the possible solution values at a given stage, partial determination of the objective function, and systematically working toward an overall optimum by carrying potential optimum values sequentially back to preceding stages.

In production scheduling, it is often convenient to begin with output requirements for periods at the end of the planning horizon and then work backward in time to determine what goods or services must be produced in current periods in order to optimize (for example, minimize costs or maximize profits) over the total horizon. Dynamic programming methods are particularly suitable to this approach for the cost or other functions may well be nonlinear and the problem lends itself to solution in "stages." The optimal production quantities, overtime arrangements, inventories, and so forth, are determined for the final period and then we work back to each preceding period to find what is the optimal combination to produce these subsequent results. By the principle of optimality we know that once an optimal arrangement has been achieved in a later stage, the arrangement will remain optimal regardless of the route taken to enter the stage [**14**: 207].

Although dynamic programming is an enumeration technique, not all possible combinations need be enumerated at each stage. Consideration is gradually restricted to those combinations possessing optimization potential. This can substantially reduce data processing effort. Together with the adaptability to nonlinear objective functions (and constraints), this makes dynamic programming a valuable tool for production scheduling as well as for other applications in inventory control, maintenance, and capital budgeting. In-depth coverage is beyond the scope of this text, but optional material is included in the Solved Problem section and additional references [**1**, **14**] are listed in the bibliography.

CONTROL MODELS

This final section of the chapter deals with controlling aggregate plans and detailed schedules. It applies to all three types of systems studied: intermittent, continuous, and project. Many of the intermittent and continuous scheduling methods we studied have their own inherent control features. This is especially true of computerized systems such as MRP that are designed to serve an integrated inventory and production control function. The line-of-balance is another technique for controlling continuous system and we will look briefly at it. The other "new" material in this section relates primarily to CPM and PERT, which are planning and control techniques especially suited to projects.

CHARTS, BOARDS, AND COMPUTERS

All planning and scheduling activities, including aggregate planning, should be evaluated periodically for effectiveness and accuracy. Aggregate planning is of special concern to top management for actual results influence policy decisions which in turn affect subsequent plans. Comparisons of planned versus actual performance should be made available to responsible management so that the organization can be positively guided toward planned goals rather than pursuing unrealistic objectives or simply responding to internal or environmental stimuli.

The elements of control cited in Chap. 1 are basic to any control system. Recall that these include measurement, feedback, comparison with standard, and correction where necessary. A sound control policy would thus necessitate some means of measurement, feedback, and comparison. Any significant deviations from the plans or schedule (especially in quantity or timing of output) should be investigated as to cause and likelihood of continued occurrence.

Although some form of statistical control of scheduling would seem theoretically desirable, it has not been extensively used in industry. In its absence, the Gantt charts (and various mechanical scheduling devices discussed earlier) essentially serve as scheduling *and control* devices. As such, they tend to satisfy the control need in many intermittent processing situations. Mechanical and magnetic boards are particularly suitable for discerning differences and can be updated (manually). In addition, many firms keep performance charts, have delivery targets, wall displays, and contests designed to motivate employees to improve and maintain close control over production.

Computer printouts of planned versus actual schedules provide one of the best sources of control data nowadays because of their timeliness and detail. Example 9-6 (below) illustrates a simple output control report covering the work done in shop 62. The planned work of 200 hours per week was derived from the capacity requirements plan described in Fig. 9-6. Although the individual weekly requirements depicted in the figure were not a smooth 200 standard hours per week, we can assume that the hours available were (approximately) adequate to meet the proposed master schedule and that the production supervisor agreed that a 200-hour average was a reasonable output to expect.

Example 9-6

Shop 62 has an average capacity requirement of 200 hours/week of work. Actual hours during weeks 9, 10, 11, and 12 were 180, 210, 170, and 160 respectively. Formulate an output control report showing cumulative deviation.

Solution

TABLE 9-1 OUTPUT CONTROL REPORT

	Week number				
	9	10	11	12	13
Planned hours	200	200	200	200	200
Actual hours	180	210	170	160	
Cumulative deviation	−20	−10	−40	−80	

Source: [15 (modified)].

The simple output control report shown in Example 9-6 can satisfy the basic elements of control mentioned repeatedly throughout this text. *Measurement* of actual hours typically flows from labor hours and variance reports. If labor data is logged into the computer via job number on a daily basis, the *feedback* process is greatly facilitated; otherwise it may have to be collected by cards or time forms. The *comparison* activity uses planned hours along with a maximum allowable cumulative deviation limit as a standard. The maximum deviation should be some prearranged cumulative amount such as one week's average (200 hours in this case) or perhaps one-half week's average. When the cumulative deviation exceeds this limit, *corrective action* in the form of overtime, subcontracting, or perhaps revision of the master schedule is called for. (In Table 9-1, the cumulative deviation at the end of week 12 is 80 hours and does not yet exceed a week's average.)

In some cases more sophisticated and meaningful control information can be obtained by adopting an input-output (I/O) reporting format rather than only an output format as described above. In I/O reports the planned input to a work center includes both released orders that have not yet arrived and unreleased "planned" orders. The planned output includes an adjustment for backlog, for it consists of the planned input plus or minus any desired change in the backlog at the particular work center.[2] By reporting both released and unreleased backlog separately, the production controller knows exactly what work is at the work center at any given time.

Control report formats vary, of course, from one firm to another. The important point is that they reflect capacity data. Reports that are based upon capacity requirements (and measure flows of planned work into and out of work centers over a given time horizon) are much more useful for control than the simple backlog tallys used in the old days (which are today for many firms). As with all management information, however, the key is to get current data to the responsible manager in decision-making form so that appropriate corrective action can be taken when required.

[2] A detailed description of these reports is beyond the scope of this text. The reader is encouraged to consult Wight's book [15] on production and inventory management for a discussion of I/O reports and shop floor controls.

MRP and time-phased order point systems, being computerized methods of scheduling and control, offer several unique advantages to production controllers. *First*, being computerized, they can easily and quickly accommodate a large volume of items. *Second*, they coordinate many of the vital activities by accepting inputs from the forecast via the production plan and master schedule. *Third*, they distinguish between dependent and independent demand and automatically adjust inventory levels accordingly. *Fourth*, they can incorporate firm planned orders which facilitate the leveling of load on the plant, thereby making the best use of capacity and minimizing costs of varying production rates. *Fifth*, they facilitate the production of optional items by working from a modularized bill of material which has well-defined parent/component relationships so that controls may be exercised over common modules rather than over each unit of product. *Sixth*, they lend themselves especially well to capacity planning and output control.

LINE OF BALANCE

Line of balance (LOB) is a control mechanism of slightly more complexity than Gantt charts and it is more suited to the monitoring of continuous systems. It is essentially a charting and computational technique whereby the progress of component and subassembly parts is monitored and compared to delivery date requirements by charting the lead times ahead of final assembly. Details of constructing the charts and graphs are included in the bibliography references [**5**, **7**].

In brief, LOB control begins with a cumulative delivery schedule, or objective. Purchased parts and subassembled components required to support the delivery schedule are then set out on a production plan which clearly identifies lead times required to meet the delivery schedule, as shown in Fig. 9-7. The lead times in turn reflect what quantities of items should be on hand or in process at various stages, such as at weekly intervals, in order to meet the final shipment schedule.

The LOB chart depicts the physical number of components and subassembly parts on hand at any given time. The actual "line of balance" is then a solid line drawn through the chart representing the quantities of items that should be on hand at that time if the delivery schedule is to be met. Figure 9-8 thus reveals that internal fabrication activities (items 1 and 3) are behind schedule, that purchased parts (item 2) are temporarily in excess of requirements, and that quantities of subassembled units (4) are also behind schedule. Furthermore, some final assembly has been completed that was not yet scheduled to start. Knowing this, production control would investigate the discrepancies and possibly initiate action to correct the situation if action were warranted.

The LOB is similar in concept to the time-phased order point and MRP systems with respect to time-phasing of component and subassembly requirements. Both approaches work backward to identify when materials and capacities must be available in order to meet delivery commitments. The LOB provides a chart or graph which helps visualize the problem but it does not offer the flexibility or responsiveness of an MRP system.

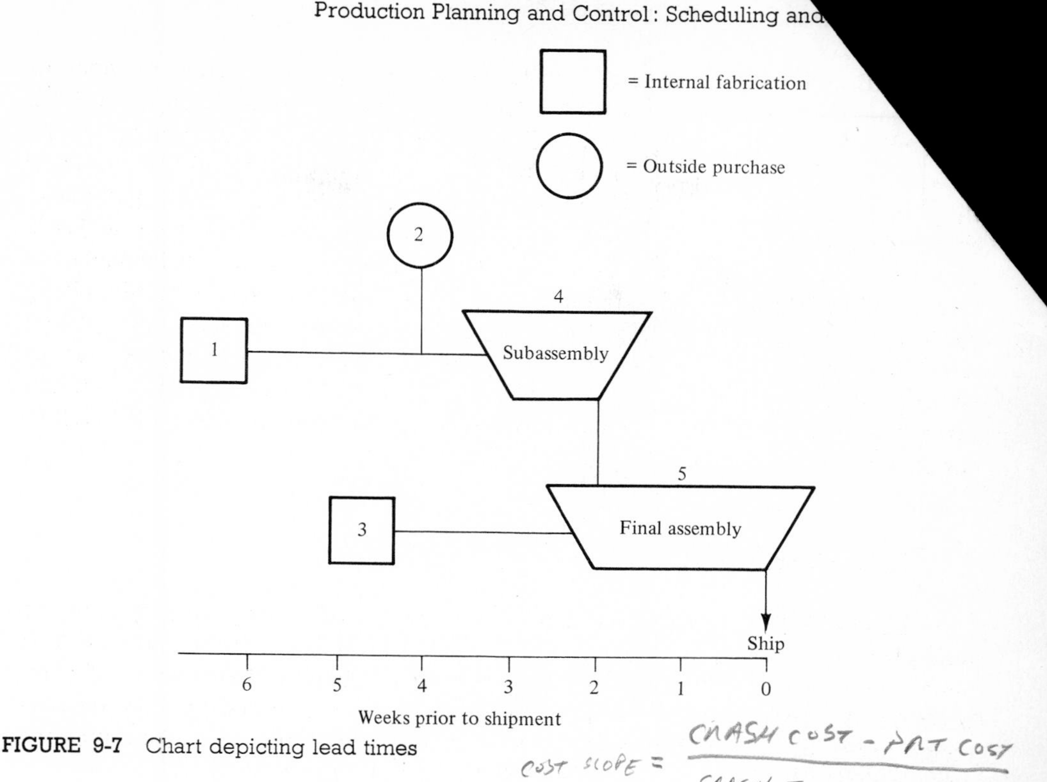

FIGURE 9-7 Chart depicting lead times

CPM AND PERT

Many organizations have found that their work objectives can best be met on a project basis. In effect, the project constitutes a system where the goal is specifically delineated, levels of available resources are well known, and a sequence of activities must take place that use the resources to achieve the goal. Such a system can often be described graphically in terms of a network of interdependent activities.

CPM (Critical Path Method) *and PERT* (Program Evaluation and Review Technique) are network techniques for analyzing a system in terms of activities and events that must be completed in a specified sequence in order to achieve a goal. Some activities can be done concurrently whereas others have precedence requirements. The *activities* are component tasks that take time and are designated by arrows (→). *Events* are points in time that indicate that some activities have been completed and others may begin. They are sometimes called *nodes* and are designated by circles (○). *A network diagram* consists of the activities and events in their proper relationship, as depicted in Fig. 9-9.

The figure shows, in network form, the work activities necessary to construct a licensed nuclear power plant (the objective). Preference relationships are indicated by the arrows and circles. For example, the plant design (activity 1-2) must be completed before anything else can take place. Then the selection of the site, vendor, and personnel can take place concurrently. The reactor plant installation (activity 5-7)

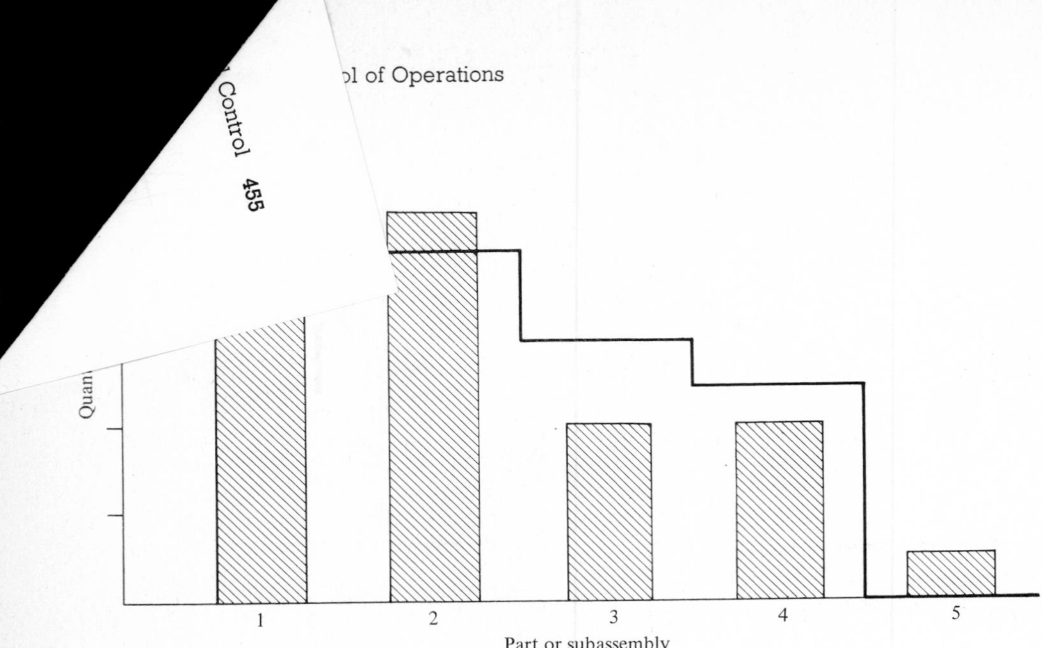

FIGURE 9-8 Line-of-balance chart

cannot begin until both the site has been prepared (3-5) and the reactor has been manufactured (4-5). Note that there are really four paths through the network from event 1 to event 8. The site preparation (3-5) and reactor manufacturing (4-5) are on different paths, but since they converge at event 5 either activity could delay the reactor installation.

Sometimes precedence relationships are needed even though no time-consuming activities are involved. For example, in Fig. 9-9, suppose the site preparation activity (3-5) cannot begin until the vendor is notified. This means that the vendor selection activity (2-4) must be completed before activity 3-5 can begin. We can indicate this preference requirement by means of a "dummy activity," drawn as a dotted line from event 4 to event 3 which would be assigned a zero time. This dummy activity would then create another unique sequential path (1–2–4–3–5–7–8) through the network.

Network analysis techniques can significantly improve the planning, scheduling, and control of complex projects. They force attention to aggregate planning by requiring specific delineation of work objectives, such as the construction of the plant in Fig. 9-9. Scheduling activities are facilitated by the preference relationships that must inevitably be identified. By attaching time or cost values to the component activities the network can become a plan or standard for resource allocation and control purposes. Given data on the current progress of component activities, managers can compare actual times and costs with planned values. Some activities may be short of time or funds whereas others may have excess resources. Adjustments can then be made by shifting personnel, materials, capital, and so on, if desired.

Critical Path

CPM is extensively used for project management in construction, R&D, product planning, and numerous other areas. Briefly, the steps involved in implementing CPM are:

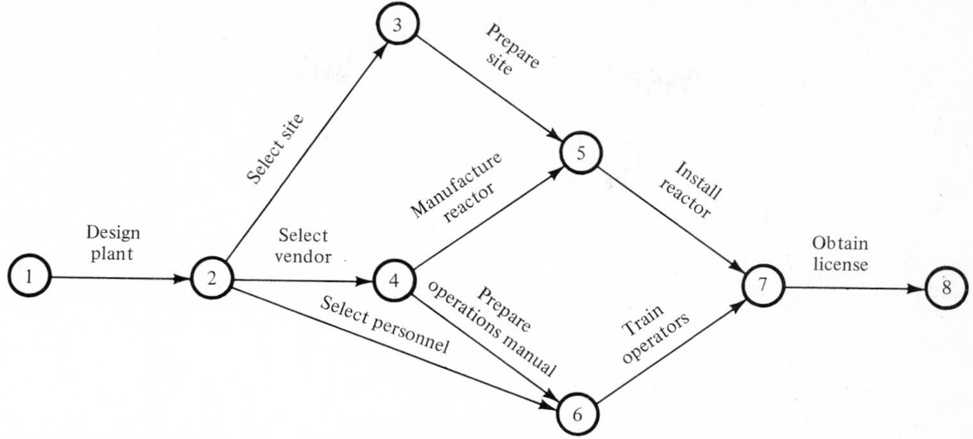

FIGURE 9-9 Network diagram of nuclear plant construction

1 Define the project in terms of activities and events.

2 Construct a network diagram showing the precedence relationships.

3 Develop a point estimate of each activity time.

4 Compute the time requirement for each path in the network.

5 Shift resources as warranted to optimize attainment of objectives.

The path with the longest time sequence as computed in step 4 is called the *critical path*, for the activity times of all items on this path are critical to the project completion date. The summation of these activity times is the expected mean time of the critical path (T_E). Other paths will have excess (or slack) time and the slack associated with any path is simply the difference between T_E and the time for the given path.

The completion time for any event on a path is, of course, dependent upon the time of the longest sequence of activities leading to that event. Thus, the earliest time (E) for occurrence of an event can be determined by computing the largest sum of activity times on paths leading to the event. Where two paths converge at a node, the time of the longest path (timewise) governs.

In opposite manner, the latest time (L) for occurrence of an event can be computed by starting at the end of the network and working backward. Beginning with the critical or ending time, each preceding activity time up to the specified event is subtracted from T_E. If two or more paths converge on one event en route, the figure developed from the path with the shortest total time governs because it has the least slack.

Example 9-7

The time estimates for completing the plant construction project of Fig. 9-9 are as shown (in months) on the accompanying network diagram (Fig. 9-10).

(*a*) Determine the critical path.

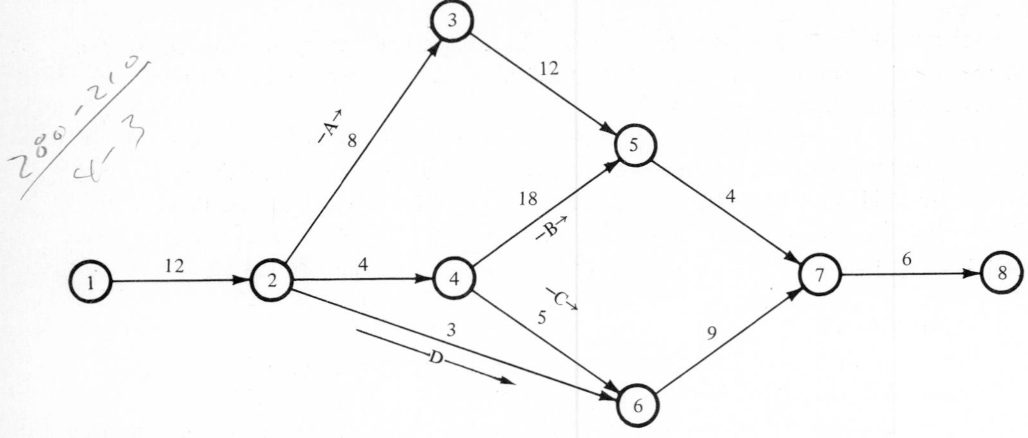

FIGURE 9-10 Network diagram with time estimates

(*b*) How much slack time is available in the path containing the operations manual preparation activity?

(*c*) What are the earliest and latest times for occurrence of event 6 such that the schedule will not be delayed?

Solution

	Path	Times
A	1–2–3–5–7–8	12 + 8 + 12 + 4 + 6 = 42
B	1–2–4–5–7–8	12 + 4 + 18 + 4 + 6 = 44
C	1–2–4–6–7–8	12 + 4 + 5 + 9 + 6 = 36
D	1–2–6–7–8	12 + 3 + 9 + 6 = 30

(*a*) Path *B* is critical with a time requirement of 44 months.

(*b*) The manual preparation activity is on path *C*:

$$\text{Slack} = \text{critical path } B - \text{path } C = 44 - 36 = 8 \text{ months.}$$

(*c*) Earliest time for 6: ($\sum$ times leading to (6))

$$\text{Via path } C = 12 + 4 + 5 = 21$$

$$\text{Via path } D = 12 + 3 = 15$$

$E = 21$ months since longest time governs

Latest time for 6: (T_E − preceding activity times)

$$\text{Via paths } C \text{ and } D = 44 - 6 - 9 = 29$$

$L = 29$ months

The slack in path *C* suggests that, other things remaining the same, the manual writing (activity 4-6) could fall behind by eight months before it would jeopardize the scheduled finish date for the project. This is confirmed by calculation of the earliest date (21 months) and latest date (29 months) for occurrence of event 6, the difference again representing slack.

If some of the personnel scheduled for activity 4-6 could be allocated to expediting reactor manufacturing (activity 4-5), the critical path time might be reduced to less than 44 months. The manual preparation activity would undoubtedly take longer, but the increase would not have any effect on the overall project completion time until it increased to the point where its own path became critical.

Example 9-8

The firm in Example 9-7 has determined that by shifting three engineers from manual writing (activity 4-6) to manufacturing assistance, activity 4-5 could be reduced to 15 months, whereas activity 4-6 would be increased to 10 months. What would be the net effect upon the schedule?

Solution

Path A remains the same, at 42 months

Path $B = 12 + 4 + 15 + 4 + 6 = 41$ months

Path $C = 12 + 4 + 10 + 9 + 6 = 41$ months

Path D remains the same, at 30 months

Path A would become critical and the new estimated completion time would be 42 months, a 2-month saving over the initial time.

PERT

PERT is, like CPM, also a time-oriented planning and control device. However, whereas CPM develops only one central measure of completion time for a project, PERT develops both a measure of central tendency (a mean) and a measure of dispersion (a standard deviation). Given these two parameters of the completion time distribution for a project, probabilities of finishing the project in any specified lesser or greater time than the mean time can be readily determined. There are other subtle differences between CPM and PERT, but this incorporation of statistical probabilities into the network is the basic difference.

PERT incorporates uncertainty (and probability) by including three time estimates for each activity rather than only one. These estimates are designated as:

a = *optimistic time* This is the best time that could be expected if everything went exceptionally well, and would be achieved only about 1 percent of the time.

m = *most likely time* This is the best estimate, or modal expectation.

b = *pessimistic time* This is the worst time that could reasonably be expected if everything went wrong, and would occur only about 1 percent of the time.

The expected mean time (t_e) and variance (σ^2) of each activity can then be determined on the basis of the beta statistical distribution[3] as:

$$t_e = \frac{a + 4m + b}{6} \tag{9-2}$$

$$\sigma^2 = \left(\frac{b - a}{6}\right)^2 \tag{9-3}$$

where

a = optimistic time estimate
m = most likely time estimate
b = pessimistic time estimate

Once the individual activity times have been estimated, they may be combined via summation over the respective paths. The path with the longest time is, again, the critical path. Variances of the component activity times along this path may also be summed because individual variances are additive (whereas standard deviations are not). The (theoretical) assumptions here are that the time estimates along the critical path are independent and that the resulting variation of project completion times about the mean completion time is normally distributed. These assumptions normally pose no problems from an applications standpoint.

The ending (normal) distribution of completion times for a project can then be depicted as shown in Fig. 9-11, where the mean completion time (T_E) equals the summation of activity times along the critical path,

$$T_E = \sum t_e \tag{9-4}$$

and the ending distribution standard deviation (σ) is the square root of the sum of the variances of activity times along the critical path:

$$\sigma = \sqrt{\sum \sigma_{cp}^2} \tag{9-5}$$

With this mean and standard deviation of the ending distribution, the probabilities of various completion times may be calculated using the normal distribution. For example, to determine the probability that a project would exceed time T_x in Fig. 9-11, we would compute

$$Z = \frac{T_x - T_E}{\sigma},$$

find the probability associated with that Z value from the normal distribution values in Appendix D (or a hand calculator) and subtract it from 0.5000. The resultant would represent the shaded area under the curve in Fig. 9-11.

[3] The beta distribution has been found to appropriately describe this type of data, has finite end points, and is relatively easy to calculate.

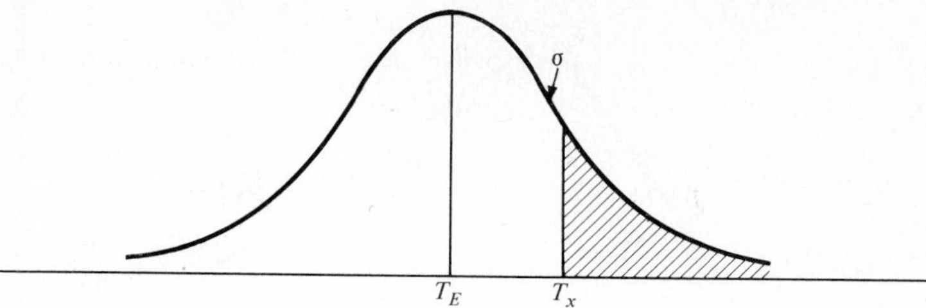

FIGURE 9-11 Ending time distribution

Example 9-9

Project planners have sought the experienced judgment of various knowledgeable engineers, foremen, and vendors and have developed the time estimates shown below for the plant construction project depicted in Fig. 9-9.

(*a*) Determine the critical path.
(*b*) What is the probability the project will be finished within four years?
(*c*) What is the probability that it will take more than 55 months?

Activity		Time estimates			t_e	σ^2
Description	Number	a	m	b	$\dfrac{a + 4m + b}{6}$	$\left(\dfrac{b - a}{6}\right)^2$
Design plant	1–2	10	12	16	12.33	1.00
Select site	2–3	2	8	36	11.67	32.11
Select vendor	2–4	1	4	5	3.67	0.44
Select personnel	2–6	2	3	4	3.00	0.11
Prepare site	3–5	8	12	20	12.67	4.00
Mfgr. reactor	4–5	15	18	30	19.50	6.25
Prepare manual	4–6	3	5	8	5.17	0.69
Install reactor	5–7	2	4	8	4.33	1.00
Train operators	6–7	6	9	12	9.00	1.00
License plant	7–8	4	6	14	7.00	2.78

Solution

(*a*) Values for t_e and σ^2 for the various activities have been calculated as shown in the example box. The t_e values are entered on the network diagram in Fig. 9-12. The critical path, as determined in the accompanying table, is now *A* and has been shown by a heavy solid line in the figure.

Path		Times
A	1–2–3–5–7–8	12.33 + 11.67 + 12.67 + 4.33 + 7.00 = 48.00
B	1–2–4–5–7–8	12.33 + 3.67 + 19.50 + 4.33 + 7.00 = 46.83
C	1–2–4–6–7–8	12.33 + 3.67 + 5.17 + 9.00 + 7.00 = 37.17
D	1–2–6–7–8	12.33 + 3.00 + 9.00 + 7.00 = 31.33

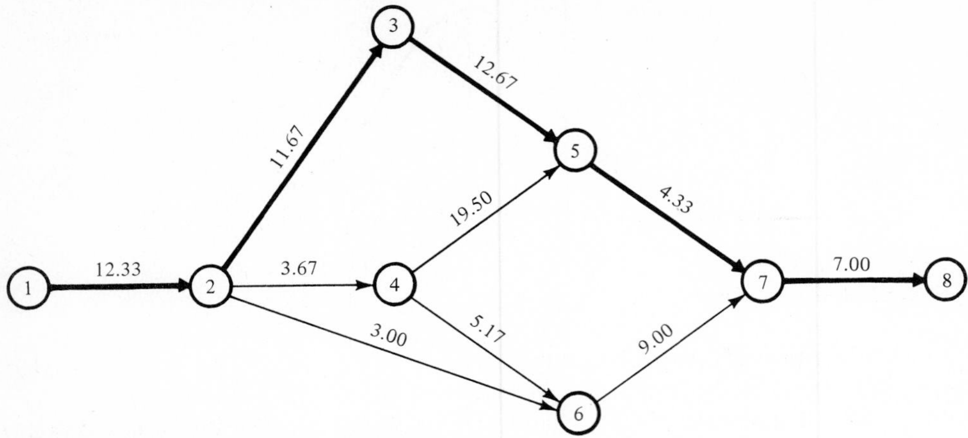

FIGURE 9-12 Network diagram showing critical path

(*b*) The best estimate of completion time is $T_E = 48.0$ months so there is a 50 percent chance it will be finished within the four-year time period.

(*c*) To determine any other completion time probabilities we must calculate the standard deviation of the distribution of completion times along the critical path.

$$\sigma = \sqrt{\sum \sigma_{cp}^{2}}$$

$$= \sqrt{1.00 + 32.11 + 4.00 + 1.00 + 2.78}$$

$$= 6.4 \text{ months}$$

$$Z = \frac{T_x - T_E}{\sigma} = \frac{55.0 - 48.0}{6.4} = 1.09$$

$$P(X > T_x) = 0.5000 - 0.3621 = 0.1379$$

$\therefore$ Probability $\cong 0.14$

It is interesting to note that although the most likely times used in the PERT example were identical to those used in the earlier CPM example, the critical paths turned out to be different. This is, of course, due to the fact that PERT incorporates a measure of uncertainty whereas CPM does not. A review of the individual activity variances in Example 9-9 reveals that although the site selection activity (2–3) has a most likely time estimate of 8 months, it has a pessimistic time estimate of 36 months, and $t_e = 11.67$, in contrast to the 8-month figure used in the CPM calculations. This estimate for the site selection probably reflects managerial awareness of public concern over the siting of nuclear plants. A strong feature of PERT is that these effects of uncertainty are incorporated into the standard deviation of the completion time distribution. (See Fig. 9-13.) This is because all variances of activities along the critical path, whether they represent much uncertainty (such as this 32.11 value) or much precision (as a value of 0 would), are summed to get the ending distribution variance.

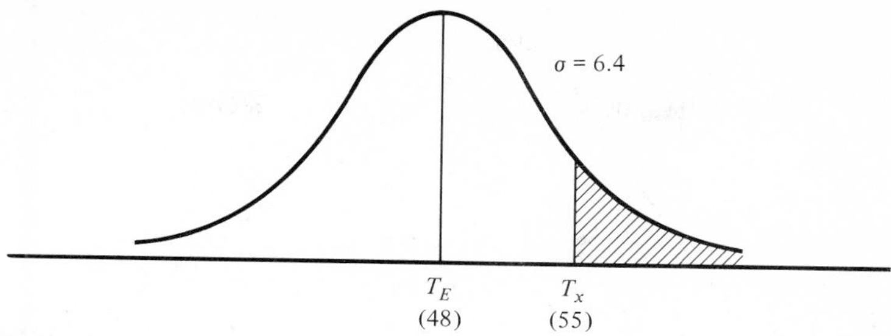

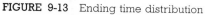

FIGURE 9-13 Ending time distribution

PERT and MRP Similarities

A brief comparison of PERT and MRP systems is useful at this point. We have seen that PERT is a planning and control technique particularly suitable for managing individual projects. It provides a means of time-phasing activities within a network format that permits the scheduler to handle uncertainties by incorporating optimistic, most likely, and pessimistic time estimates. These probabilistic estimates take account of both material and labor uncertainties.

Priority and capacity planning techniques accomplish these same functions for intermittent and continuous systems. However, instead of handling material (inventory) and labor (capacity) factors together, they are handled separately. Priority planning systems accomplish the time-phasing of material supplies and accommodate uncertainties by carrying safety stocks. Capacity planning activities further reduce the impact of uncertainties in scheduling by providing a flexibility that permits rapid adjustments in the schedule. The modern production planning system is designed for change by such things as modularizing the bills of material, deexpediting items that are not urgently needed, and in general speeding up rescheduling activities by means of the computer.

PERT SIMulation

Although basic PERT does take account of the variability of times on the critical path, as pointed out above, it is limited because the ending time distribution is based *only* upon the critical path activities. In an actual situation, a "noncritical path" whose path time is close to the critical path could quite possibly become the critical path, especially if it had a series of activities with large variances. PERT SIMulation (PERT-SIM) is an extension of basic PERT which allows us to take account of the near critical paths in a network as well as the critical path [**12**: 173–175].

In essence, PERT-SIM is much like the capital investment risk analysis via computer simulation described in Chap. 4. A network diagram is prepared, but rather than simply an optimistic, most likely, and pessimistic time estimate for each activity, a more comprehensive probability distribution can be used. It may be whatever subjective empirical distribution best describes the data, as exemplified in Fig. 9-14, where activities 1–2 and 2–7 have the estimated completion times as shown. Random numbers are then used to obtain a sample time for each activity where the

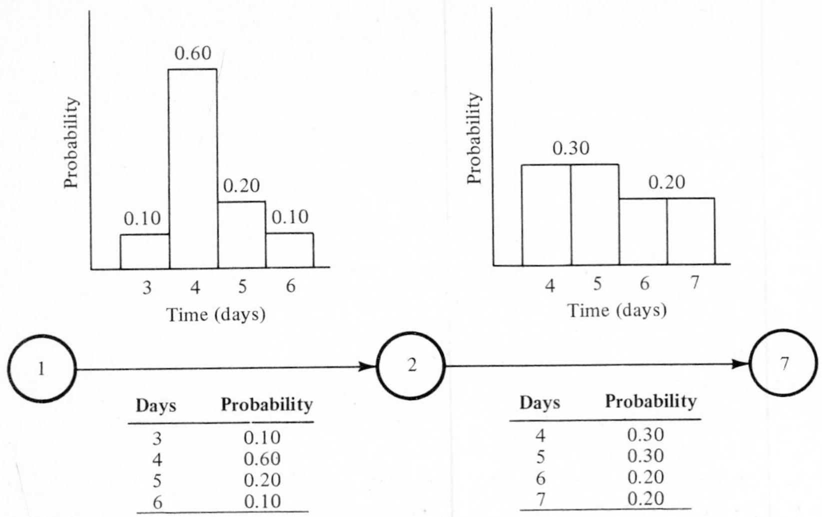

Days	Probability
3	0.10
4	0.60
5	0.20
6	0.10

Days	Probability
4	0.30
5	0.30
6	0.20
7	0.20

FIGURE 9-14 Distributions for simulated activity times

resultant times will occur in proportion to the probabilities expressed in the respective probability distributions. The critical path time for the network is then computed and recorded. Hundreds or thousands of such trials are run via computer and a distribution of simulated completion times developed as an output. This distribution, which reflects all empirical inputs to the network (and need not necessarily be normal) can then be used to estimate the probability of different completion times.

The output of a PERT-SIM computer run is not so much focused upon identification of a critical path, as upon a distribution of possible completion dates. Normally, the computer is also programmed to calculate and print out a critical index of the percent of time that each activity in the network was on the critical path. This type of data can alert project management to watch some activities more closely than others and in general facilitate better control over the total project.

PERT-COST

PERT-COST is an extension of basic PERT which focuses attention upon costs as well as time. It is designed to develop a minimum cost schedule or assist in maintaining tight control over costs.

The usual situation with a project is that the fixed and overhead expenses of supervision, facilities, and other indirect costs increase as the length of the project increases. If the overall time of the project could be shortened, these costs would be reduced. The project length can typically be shortened by reducing individual activity times through the use of more workers, better equipment, overtime, and so forth. But these actions generate higher direct costs for the individual activities. Time-cost models aim at finding the optimum reductions in such a time-cost tradeoff [**3**: 515]. We would like to shorten the length of a project to the point where the

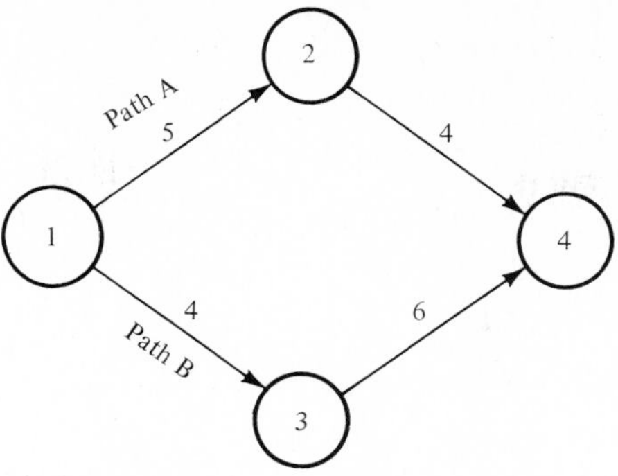

FIGURE 9-15 Network with original activity times

savings in indirect project costs are no longer justified because they become outweighed by the increased direct expenses incurred in the individual activities.

Example 9-10

A network has four activities (Fig. 9-15) with expected times as shown. The minimum feasible times and cost/day to gain reductions in the activity times are shown in the accompanying table.

Activity	Minimum time	Time reduction direct costs/day
1–2	2	$40 (each day)
1–3	2	35 (first), 80 (second)
2–4	4	(None possible)
3–4	3	45 (first), 110 (others)

If fixed project costs are $90/day, what is the lowest cost time schedule?

Solution

1 First we must determine the critical path (*) and critical path time cost.

	Path times	Total project cost
Path *A*	5 + 4 = 9	
Path *B*	4 + 6 = 10*	10 days × $90/day = $900

2 Next, we must select the activity that can reduce critical path time at the least cost.

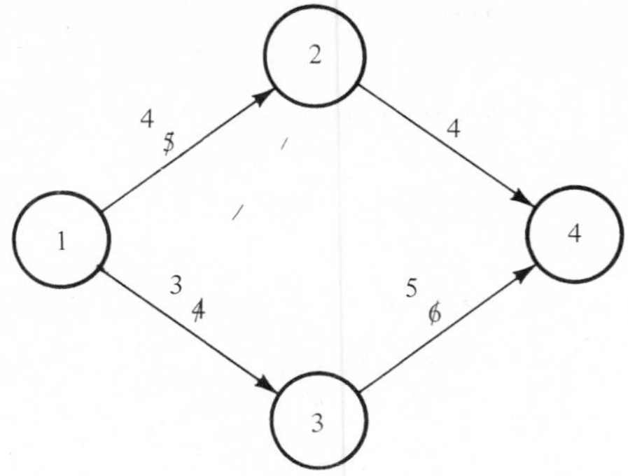

FIGURE 9-16 Network with reduced activity times

Select activity 1–3 at \$35/day which is < the \$90/day fixed cost.

Reduce activity 1–3 to 3 days (as shown in the figure above).

Revised path times	Total fixed cost	Savings over previous schedule
A 5 + 4 = 9	9 × 90 = \$810	900 − (810 + 35) = \$55
B 3 + 6 = 9		

3 Both paths are now critical so we must select an activity on each path.

Select activity 1–2 at \$40/day and 3–4 at \$45/day, where (\$40 + 45) < \$90.

Reduce activity 1–2 to 4 days, and 3–4 to 5 days.

Revised path times	Total fixed cost	Savings over previous schedule
A 4 + 4 = 8	8 × 90 = \$720	810 − (720 + 40 + 45) = \$5
B 3 + 5 = 8		

4 Again we must reduce the time of both paths (Fig. 9-16). Activity 1–2 is a good candidate on path *A* for it is still at 4 days and can go to 3 for a \$40 cost. But when combined with the \$80 cost for reducing activity 1–3 another day, this is > \$90 so further reduction is not economically justified. The lowest cost schedule is as shown.

In time-cost analysis, the shortest possible activity times are referred to as "crash times" and the costs associated with them are "crash costs." To use the time-cost approach, a standard network diagram is first developed. Then a sufficient

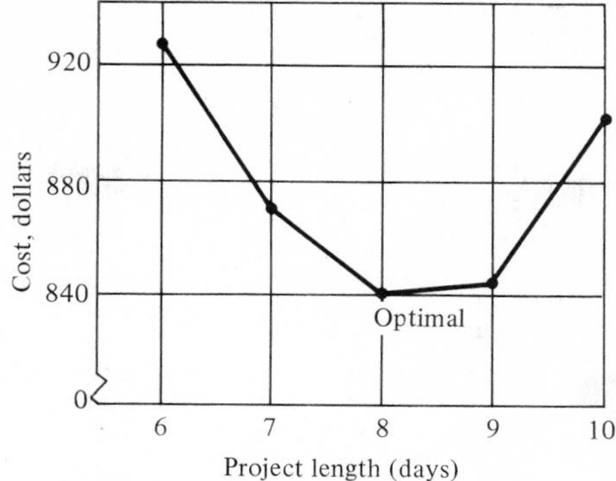

FIGURE 9-17 PERT-COST diagram for Example 9-11

number of intermediate schedules are computed such that the total of the direct and indirect (fixed) project costs over the relevant time span can be plotted. The minimum point on this total cost curve then represents the optimal time-cost tradeoff.

Example 9-11

Graph the total relevant costs for the previous example and indicate the optimal time-cost tradeoff value.

Solution

Project length (days)	Indirect cost	Activity reduced	Relevant direct cost	Relevant total cost
10	$900	none	$ 0	$900
9	810	1–3	0 + 35 = 35	845
8	720	1–2 and 3–4	35 + 85 = 120	840
7	630	1–2 and 1–3	120 + 120 = 240	870
6	540	1–2 and 3–4	240 + 150 = 390	930

PERT-COST has been used extensively in government contracts, at the request of various agencies in an effort to develop accurate project estimates and (hopefully) limit the amount of cost overrun. As the project progresses, actual costs are compared with budgeted costs to determine which activities are underrunning and which are overrunning the budget.

The cost collection and reporting system required for PERT-COST control can, however, become quite complex. Generally the network of activities is first subdivided into work packages of comparable length and dollar cost amount. But the accounting system must also be geared to project activities and events. In many (perhaps most) situations, new cost accounting systems must be devised for handling labor, material and various indirect costs on an activity basis. The firm adopting PERT-COST for control should therefore have good data processing capability and a thorough understanding of the impending accounting requirements before implementing the system.

LIMITED RESOURCE ALLOCATION

The PERT approach assumes that sufficient manpower and equipment resources are available as needed to keep a project on schedule. However, we know that the cost of acquiring and converting resources from one form to another can be significant. We noted the cost effect of changing levels of resources in the discussion on aggregate planning, and again in PERT-COST where additional resources were applied to certain activities in order to shorten the overall length of a project. This suggests that the balancing or leveling out of the need for resources would be desirable, which is indeed the case.

Numerous approaches can be taken to balance the workload and personnel requirements on project work. But the problems quickly become almost as complex as assembly line balancing, so it is not surprising that we again find that simple heuristics offer a most practical means of adjusting schedules. One such heuristic consists simply of locating the maximum and minimum resource requirements and attempting to shift activities into slack positions in order to smooth out the demand [**4**, **12**: 181].

The limited resource techniques can apply to any quantified resource, such as workers, machines, or even dollars, or to more than one resource at a time. However, when networks have many activities or when two, three, or four resources are involved, the solution soon becomes quite complex. Nevertheless, the approach does offer some insight into the theory and problems of allocating limited resources within the context of a network.

SUMMARY

In contrast to the broad and longer-range nature of aggregate planning, scheduling involves specific job assignments and detailed instructions for work flow in current periods. Fortunately, the cumulative workload projections and Gantt progress charts that provide an overall perspective for aggregate planning can also reflect current scheduling needs in terms of quantities and priorities. Depending upon the situation, a scheduler may (1) rely wholly upon these cumulative projections, (2) schedule on a detailed basis, (3) use a combination of aggregative and detailed scheduling, or (4) use simple priority decision rules.

Computer printouts of production schedules are gradually replacing the Gantt charts and scheduling boards that have been so popular in the past. The detail provided by the computer (practically upon demand) has helped overcome the perennial problems of manual charts—that is, of revision and updating. Time-phased order point and MRP systems appear to offer organizations the most effective means of scheduling material and capacity.

Many firms, especially those of a job-shop nature with numerous in-process orders, rely largely upon priority decision rules. Depending upon the organizational criteria, single loading rules, such as "earliest due date" or "shortest processing time," may suffice. Combined rules and special heuristics such as the critical ratio techniques are also common. Here again, computers often come to the rescue in handling the paperwork necessary to make assignments.

Whereas computerized schedules represent a gigantic improvement over manual methods in terms of number of trial schedules investigated and processing time for paperwork, they are not necessarily optimum schedules. Mathematical models offer this potential if the model assumptions are satisfied. Linear and dynamic programming scheduling techniques are now finding increased application. For specific assignment of jobs to machines and workers to jobs, the assignment method of linear programming has been in use for some time.

Intermittent processing firms often rely on the scheduling charts, boards, and computer printouts for control action as well as scheduling information. A well-designed MRP and time-phased order point system will tend to facilitate control by providing current data for output reports. For continuous processing activities, other techniques, such as line-of-balance controls, have been used in the past but they may be expected to gradually give way to MRP systems.

Project managers have come to rely heavily on CPM and PERT for both planning and control. By diagramming entire projects in terms of activity and event networks, critical paths can be determined and resources traded off to gain their most efficient usage. PERT-SIM and PERT-COST are extensions which have increased the usefulness of these techniques.

SOLVED PROBLEMS

SCHEDULING METHODOLOGY

1 Wonderloaf Bakery has orders for four specialty items that must be processed sequentially through baking and decoration activities that require the times shown (in hours).

	Time required (hours) for item			
	I	II	III	IV
Baking (B)	4	5	8	3
Decoration (D)	3	9	2	7

Determine the schedule sequence that minimizes the total elapsed time for the four items and present it in the form of a Gantt chart.

Solution

Using Johnson's rule we can:

Select the shortest activity and if it is a B activity, place job as early as possible. If it is a D activity, place job as late as possible. Repeat for remainder of items, breaking any ties between B and D activities by sequencing either one first.

(*a*) Shortest activity is under item III D (2 hr).

Place item III late

			III

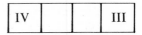

(*b*) Next shortest activities are under items I and IV (3 hr). Arbitrarily select item under IV B.

Place item IV early

IV			III

(*c*) Next shortest activity is under item I D (3 hr).

Place item I late

IV		I	III

(*d*) Last item goes into remaining opening

IV	II	I	III

So sequential times for B are	3	5	4	8
And sequential times for D are	7	9	3	2

Gantt chart for specialty items

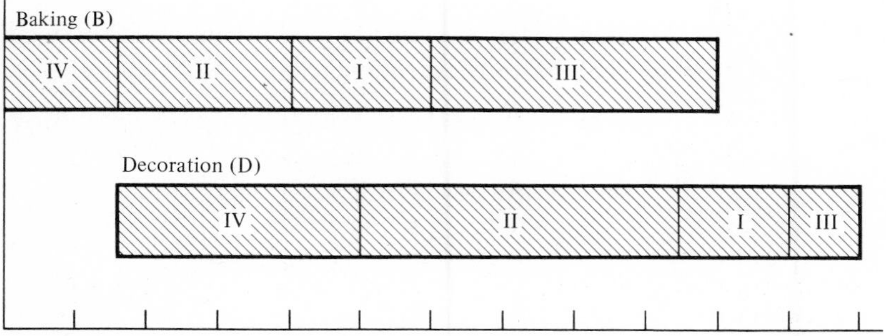

Baking (B)

IV II I III

Decoration (D)

IV II I III

Time (hr)

2 A bank operations manager has five tellers (T) whom he must assign to customer services of checking accounts (C), foreign exchange (F), notes (N), and savings (S) accounts. Three tellers are not yet qualified for foreign exchange and one teller cannot handle notes. Work-sampling studies have shown that, working under constant queues, the tellers can handle the number of customers/hr shown in the accompanying table. Assuming the manager wishes to serve as many customers as possible, what assignments should be made? The extra teller will be assigned a data processing task.

	Customers served/hr			
	Checking	Foreign	Notes	Savings
T-1	60	*X*	30	50
T-2	70	60	40	50
T-3	30	*X*	10	30
T-4	40	*X*	*X*	60
T-5	40	70	50	80

Solution

The number of workers does not balance the number of assignments so we must add an extra column (call it D = data processing) and assign it a low priority (zero service) so that it will absorb the poorest teller.

	C	*F*	*N*	*S*	*D*
T-1	60	*X*	30	50	0
T-2	70	60	40	50	0
T-3	30	*X*	10	30	0
T-4	40	*X*	*X*	60	0
T-5	40	70	50	80	0

Since this is a maximization problem, we must first convert the matrix values to relative costs by subtracting all values from the largest number, 80.

	C	*F*	*N*	*S*	*D*
1	20	*X*	50	30	80
2	10	20	40	30	80
3	50	*X*	70	50	80
4	40	*X*	*X*	20	80
5	40	10	30	0	80

We then follow the same steps as we did in solving Example 9-5.

1 *Row subtraction*

	C	*F*	*N*	*S*	*D*
1	0	*X*	30	10	60
2	0	10	30	20	70
3	0	*X*	20	0	30
4	20	*X*	*X*	0	60
5	40	10	30	0	80

2 *Column subtraction*

	C	*F*	*N*	*S*	*D*
1	0	*X*	10	10	30
2	0	0	10	20	40
3	0	*X*	0	0	0
4	20	*X*	*X*	0	30
5	40	0	10	0	50

3 *Cover zeros*

	C	F	N	S	D
1	0	X	10	10	30
2	0	0	10	20	40
3	0	X	0	0	0
4	20	X	X	0	30
5	40	0	10	0	50

4 *Modify matrix*

	C	F	N	S	D
1	0	X	0	10	20
2	0	0	0	20	30
3	10	X	0	10	0
4	20	X	X	0	20
5	40	0	0	0	40

5 *Cover zeros again*

	C	F	N	S	D
1	[0]	X	0	10	20
2	0	[0]	0	20	30
3	10	X	0	10	[0]
4	20	X	X	[0]	20
5	40	0	[0]	0	40

In step 5, it requires five lines to cover all zeros so a solution has been reached. Note that the maximum number of lines will never exceed the number of rows. Assigning tellers and tasks that have only one choice first, we assign *T*-4 to *S* and *T*-3 to *D*. We can then assign *T*-1 to *C*, *T*-2 to *F*, and *T*-5 to *N*.

Alternatively, we could assign *T*-2 to *C*, *T*-5 to *F*, and *T*-1 to *N* and have an equally optimal assignment as revealed by the total number of customers served/hr.

Solution	
T-1 at checking	= 60
T-2 at foreign	= 60
T-3 at data processing	= 0
T-4 at savings	= 60
T-5 at notes	= 50
Cust/hr	230

Alternate solution	
T-1 at notes	= 30
T-2 at checking	= 70
T-3 at data processing	= 0
T-4 at savings	= 60
T-5 at foreign	= 70
Cust/hr	230

DYNAMIC PROGRAMMING

***3** Precision Castings has 11 orders for custom castings to be supplied during the next four weeks. Their furnaces and casting facilities are normally used for regular production of standard castings but they can also be scheduled for use on up to four custom orders/week. Operating costs vary somewhat depending on the number of custom jobs the firm attempts to produce each week. This is because the mold preparation, furnace heats required, inventory, and overtime requirements tend to vary. If no custom work is performed, however, the facilities are assigned an idle time cost. Considering the various costs, as well as income from custom units, the accompanying profit matrix has been derived.

Number of units N produced in time period	Profit ($00) from producing N units in time period (week)			
	A	*B*	*C*	*D*
0	−4	−4	−4	−4
1	4	9	8	3
2	12	10	15	11
3	20	22	20	20
4	18	16	24	18

Use a dynamic programming approach to schedule the production of the 11 units over the four periods in such a way as to maximize profits.

Solution [adapted from **1**: 265–272]

We will first determine the optimal production plan for period *D* and then work backward following the principle that once an optimal plan has been achieved in a later period the plan will remain optimal regardless of the schedule preceding the period. The alternatives available for period *D* are taken from the profit matrix above (column *D*) and arranged diagonally in the table shown below. Other cells in the matrix are blocked out as infeasible, for in this last period we can (and must) accumulate only the number of units produced during the period. The asterisks indicate that any one of the production amounts is a potential optimum at this point.

Number of units produced in period *P*	Cumulative units from period *D*				
	0	1	2	3	4
0	−4*				
1		3*			
2			11*		
3				20*	
4					18*

Regressing back to include the previous period *C*, it is possible to accumulate up to 8 units in the two periods (by producing 4 in each). The feasible accumulations are only those combinations resulting from the two periods. Thus, for example, if only 1 unit were produced in period *C*, it would not be possible to accumulate 6 units from periods *C* and *D* together, for *D* can only contribute up to 4 units.

Number of units produced in period *C*	Cumulative units from periods *C* and *D*								
	0	1	2	3	4	5	6	7	8
0				16	14				
1				19*	28*	26			
2				18	26	35*	33		
3				16	23	31	40*	38	
4					20	27	35	44*	42*

Similarly, a minimum of 3 units must be accumulated in periods *C* and *D*, for the total requirement is 11, and the maximum capability is of 4 each (or 8 total) from periods *A* and *B*. Thus, the cumulative cells representing quantities less than 3 are also blocked out as infeasible.

The resultant profits are computed individually for each feasible combination. For example, consider the alternative ways shown in the accompanying table in which 3 units may be accumulated and the resulting profit possibilities.

Three units of production		Resultant profit		
period *C*	period *D*	from *C*	from *D*	total
0	3	−4	20	16
1	2	8	11	19*
2	1	15	3	18
3	0	20	−4	16

The optimum value(s) is marked with an asterisk and thereafter it is the only profit value (and way of accumulating 3 units) that is carried forward. The computations for accumulations of 4 through 8 are performed in similar manner with resultant profits as shown.

The continued regression back to periods *B* and *A* follows a similar pattern, using optimal values from the preceding matrixes. At least 11 − 4 = 7 units must be accumulated during the last three periods. If zero units are produced in period *B*, the optimal profit from accumulating the 7 units in periods *C* and

D of 44* (from the previous *C* and *D* table) is now combined with the profit of producing zero in period *B*(−4) given in the initial profit matrix, for a resultant

Number of units produced in period *B*	Cumulative units from periods *B*, *C*, and *D*				
	7	8	9	10	11
0	40	38			
1	49	53	51		
2	45	50	54	52	
3	50*	57*	62*	66*	64*
4	35	44	51	56	60

of 40, which is entered in the new period *B* table. Other values are similarly computed. For example, for 7 units, see the accompanying table.

Seven units of production		Resultant profit		
period *B*	period *C* and *D*	from *B*	from *C* and *D*	total
0	7	−4	44	40
1	6	9	40	49
2	5	10	35	45
3	4	22	28	50*
4	3	16	19	35

Finally, we continue until production during period *A* is included and derive the final table with an optimal profit of 77.

Number of units produced in period *A*	Profit from cumulative units from periods *A*, *B*, *C* and *D*
	11
0	60
1	70
2	74
3	77*
4	68

We can determine the schedule by going progressively from A to D. The optimum production in A is 3 units, leaving $11 - 3 = 8$ units for B, C, and D. Carrying the 8-unit requirement forward to period B, the optimum (57*) also happens to be 3 units. This leaves 5 units to be accumulated in stages C and D and the optimal period C production for 5 cumulative units is 2, leaving 3 units for period D. The resulting profit can be verified from the initial profit matrix shown in the accompanying table.

Period	Production	Profit
A	3	20
B	3	22
C	2	15
D	3	20
		77

Note that in some applications two or more cells may each exhibit a maximum (optimal) value. In these cases two or more paths, or production schedules, may yield the same optimal result.

4 Given the data shown in the accompanying table for a PERT network:

Preceding event	Event	Activity time *a*	*m*	*b*
1	2	5	6	13
1	3	2	7	12
2	4	1.5	2	2.5
2	5	1	3	5
3	5	4	5	6
3	6	1	1	1
4	7	2	3	10
5	7	4	5	6
6	7	3	5	7

(*a*) Draw the network and find the critical path.
(*b*) What are the parameters of the ending time distribution?
(*c*) Which activity has the most precise time estimate?
(*d*) Determine the earliest (E) and latest (L) times for all events in the system.
(*e*) Each day the project can be shortened is worth \$5,000. Should the firm pay \$12,500 to reduce activity 3–5 to 2 days?

Solution

(*a*)

Activity	$\frac{a + 4m + b}{6}$	$\left(\frac{b - a}{6}\right)^2$
1–2	7	1.78
1–3	7	2.77
2–4	2	0.02
2–5	3	0.44
3–5	5	0.11
3–6	1	0.00
4–7	4	1.78
5–7	5	0.11
6–7	5	0.44

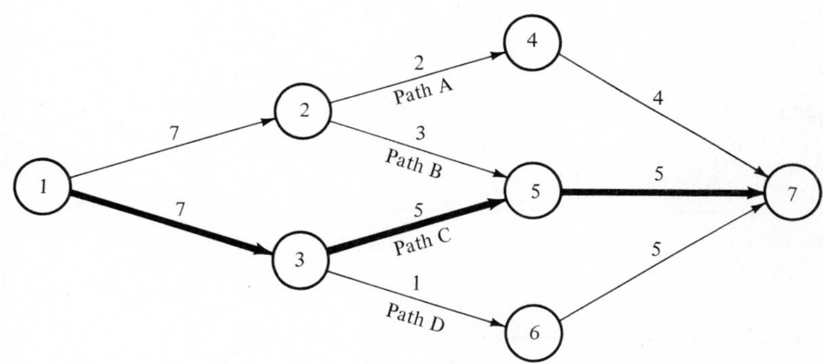

	Path	Times
A	1–2–4–7	7 + 2 + 4 = 13
B	1–2–5–7	7 + 3 + 5 = 15
C	1–3–5–7	7 + 5 + 5 = 17*
D	1–3–6–7	7 + 1 + 5 = 13

* Critical path.

(*b*) $T_E = 17$

$$\sigma_{cp} = \sqrt{\sum \sigma_{cp}^2} = \sqrt{2.77 + 0.11 + 0.11} = 1.73$$

(*c*) Most precise time is activity 3-6 with variance of zero.

(*d*) The earliest and latest dates for events on the critical path, *C*, are both the same and are simply cumulative totals of activity times. As shown in the accompanying chart, they are dominating values for they are

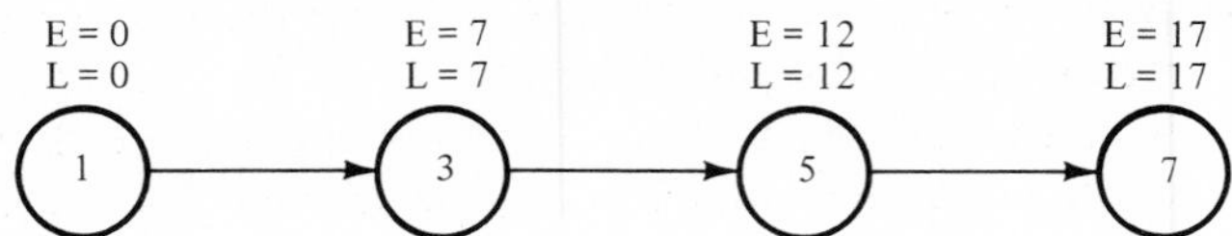

maximums in terms of computing earliest times (in the forward direction) and minimums in terms of computing latest times (in the reverse direction). In the chart, the competing paths at an event have been boxed together, and the dominating value, which is carried to the next event (forward or backward as the case may be), is marked by an asterisk.

Earliest time as determined from:	Event number in the network ①	②	③	④	⑤	⑥	⑦
Path *A*	0	7	—	7 + 2 = 9	—	—	9 + 4 = 13
Path *B*	0	7	—	—	7 + 3 = 10	—	12 + 5 = 17
Path *C*	0	—	7	—	7 + 5 = 12*	—	12 + 5 = 17*
Path *D*	0	—	7	—	—	7 + 1 = 8	8 + 5 = 13

Latest time as determined from:	①	②	③	④	⑤	⑥	⑦
Path *A*	9 − 7 = 2	13 − 2 = 11	—	17 − 4 = 13	—	—	17
Path *B*	9 − 7 = 2	12 − 3 = 9*	—	—	17 − 5 = 12*	—	17
Path *C*	7 − 7 = 0*	—	12 − 5 = 7*	—	17 − 5 = 12*	—	17
Path *D*	7 − 7 = 0*	–	12 − 1 = 11	—	—	17 − 5 = 12	17

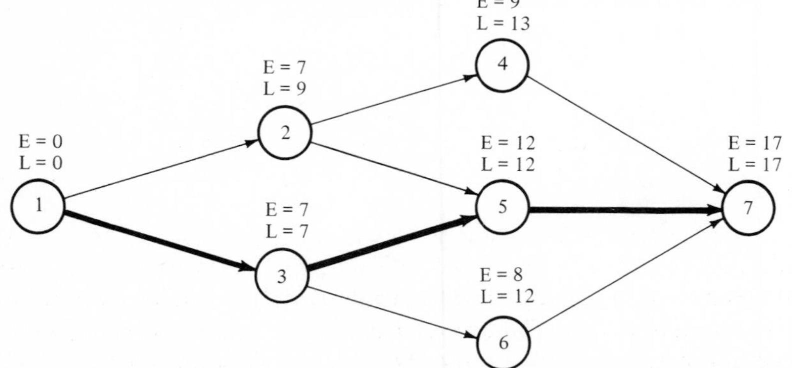

(*e*) Activity 3-5 is on the critical path and the reduction from 5 to 2 days would reduce the path *C* time to 17 − 3 = 14 days. However, path *B* would become critical at 15 days so the net reduction would be 2 days at \$5,000/day = \$10,000 savings versus the \$12,500 cost. The firm should not pay the \$12,500.

5 Worldwide Constructors, Incorporated, uses PERT and expected value techniques to prepare bids and manage construction jobs. Their bid price is set to give them 30 percent gross profit over expected costs. In calculating the PERT network for a bridge construction job, T_E was calculated to be equal to 60 days and total variance along the critical path was $\sigma_{cp}^2 = 36$. Total expenses for the project are estimated at \$335,000, but if the bridge is not completed within 70 days there is a penalty of \$50,000. Determine the appropriate bid price.

Solution

Bid price = expected costs + penalty allowance + profit

where

$$\text{expected costs} = \$335{,}000$$

$$\text{penalty allowance} = (\text{amount of penalty})(\text{probability of penalty})$$

$$Z = \frac{T_x - T_E}{\sigma} = \frac{70 - 60}{6} = 1.67$$

$$P(Z) = 0.4525$$

$$P(X > T_x) = 0.5000 - 0.4525 = 0.0475$$

$$\text{penalty allowance} = (\$50{,}000)(0.0475) = \$2{,}375$$

$$\text{profit} = 0.30(335{,}000 + 2{,}375) = 101{,}212$$

Bid price = \$335,000 + 2,375 + 101,212 = \$438,587.

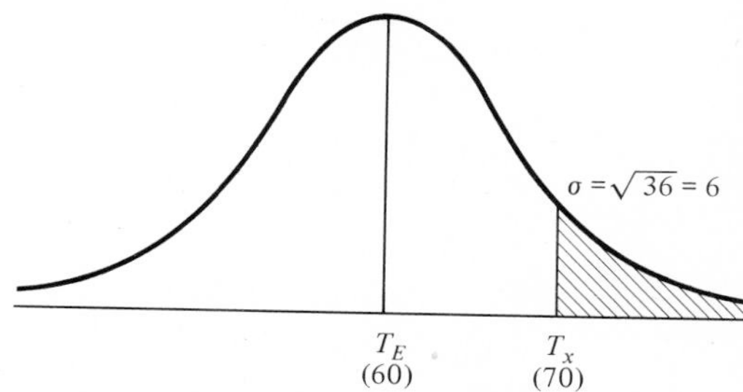

6 An electrical firm has developed a PERT plan for the electrical wiring activity of power plant control panels. They expect assembly operations will follow a 90 percent learning curve. The project team, composed of workers, electricians, and supervisors, feels the first assembly will most likely be completed in 14 days but could take as long as 24 days or, if everything went exceptionally well, would be finished in 10 days. What is the expected assembly time of the fourth unit?

Solution

$$t_e = \frac{a + 4m + b}{6} = \frac{10 + 4(4) + 24}{6} = 15$$

$$\text{Fourth unit \% base} = \frac{4}{1} = 400\%$$

Then, from Appendix J we have:

$$\therefore\ Y_N = Y_B(L) = 15(0.81) = 12.15 \text{ days}$$

LIMITED RESOURCE ALLOCATION

7 The accompanying schedule-time graph depicts a project with activity times (a through g) as shown on the horizontal axis and a critical path (a, b, e, g) of 7 days. Numbers above the activities represent personnel requirements. Develop an improved personnel balance [**12**: 181].

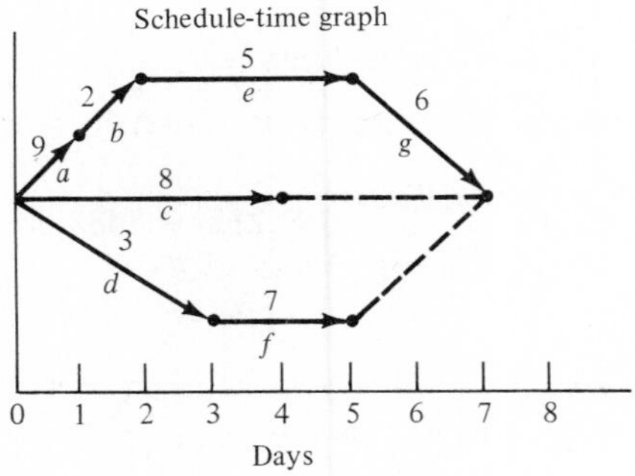

Solution
The dotted lines represent slack time and potential relocation zones for activities on the respective paths. Locate maximum and minimum resource requirements and try to shift activities into slack positions to smooth this demand. The personnel required for the original network is as shown. A revised network and personnel balance is shown below. The solution consists simply of shifting activities c and f, which reduces the range of personnel requirements from $20 - 6 = 14$ to $16 - 12 = 4$.

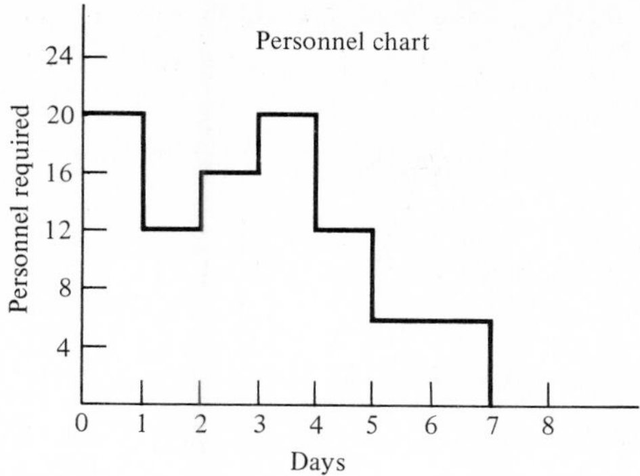

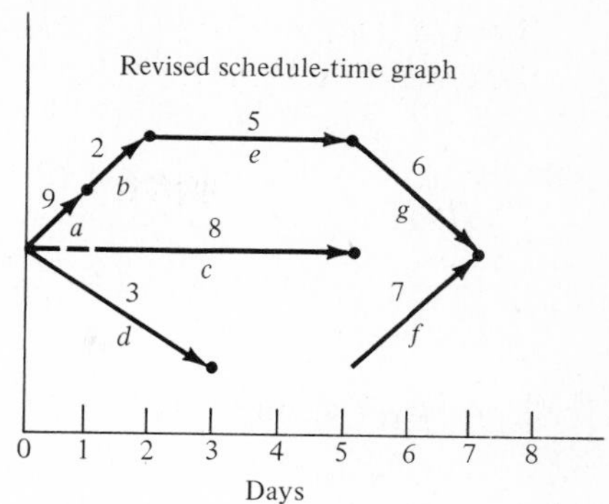

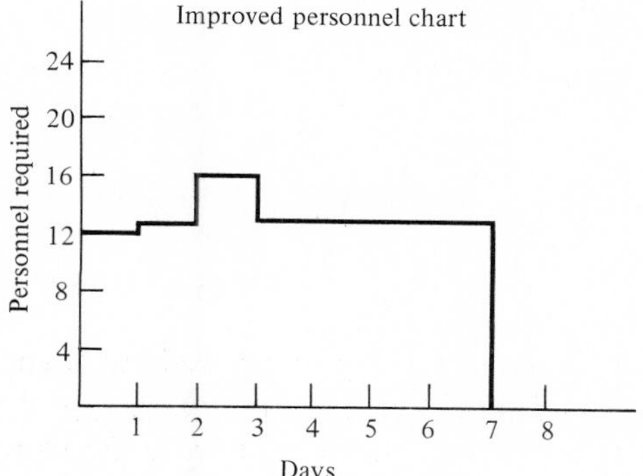

QUESTIONS

9-1 Scheduling seems to be a vital activity and yet some firms claim that they do not schedule work at all. Explain how this apparent contradiction could exist.

9-2 Distinguish between a Gantt progress chart and a Gantt load chart.

9-3 What has been a major shortcoming of Gantt charts and how has this been remedied?

9-4 What does capacity requirements planning consist of and what is the source of demand information for this planning activity?

9-5 It has been said that "in most factories, expediting is the real production control system" [**15**: 120]. Discuss the relative merits of this type of system and suggest any systems that might be preferred to an expediting system.

9-6 In what sense is the critical ratio technique a priority decision rule? What advantage does it hold over most other priority decision rules?

9-7 What single-criterion priority decision rule might you expect to find in use in:
(*a*) an airline ticket counter?
(*b*) a hospital emergency room?

(*c*) specification of security requirements for prison inmates?
(*d*) delivering milk to rural areas?
(*e*) repairing damaged missile launching sites?

9-8 What is a major distinction between mathematical programming methods of scheduling and heuristic methods?

9-9 In assignment linear programming, how can one tell when an optimal solution has been reached?

9-10 Briefly explain the concept of dynamic programming.

9-11 How would you rank the line of balance in complexity vis-à-vis Gantt charts and PERT? For controlling what type of systems is it best suited?

9-12 Identify the following terms pertaining to network diagrams and analysis:
(*a*) A task that "takes time" and is done as part of a total project
(*b*) The name given to the sequence of events that has the longest (controlling) time
(*c*) The chance that one of the optimistic or pessimistic times will occur
(*d*) The symbol for $\sum t_e$ along the longest path
(*e*) The kind of statistical distribution that is used to estimate mean times and variances of individual tasks within a network
(*f*) The name given to the difference between total time for jobs on the longest path and jobs on another path

9-13 To what extent does basic PERT analysis incorporate variance values for parallel but noncritical paths? How is this—or how could it be—accomplished?

9-14 In using PERT for project management, to what does "crashing" refer?

9-15 What, in general, are the objectives of limited resource allocation heuristics?

PROBLEMS

1 The Metric Instrument Company Limited uses an MRP system with output controls designated to signal corrective action when the cumulative deviation exceeds one-half of the forecast average per week. They have calculated capacity requirements/week for their testing laboratory over the next 8 weeks as shown.

Week	Hours	Week	Hours
1	400	5	420
2	380	6	410
3	210	7	500
4	530	8	350

(*a*) Formulate a capacity requirements plan showing the average requirement as a dotted line.
(*b*) Assume actual requirements for the first 5 weeks were 390, 460, 280, 510, and 550, and construct an output control report.
(*c*) Is corrective action warranted at this time?

2 The Ancient Maple Furniture Company has received five orders for chairs and tables that are estimated to require the production times shown. The plant is working two shifts/day. It can accommodate only one order in a given department at a given time and must follow a cutting-assembly-finishing sequence.

Order number	Cutting (hours)	Assembly (hours)	Finishing (hours)
75	40	32	24
76	16	24	8
77	24	24	40
78	8	32	24
79	24	32	16

(*a*) Prepare a daily Gantt chart schedule based upon a shortest total processing time/order criteria.
(*b*) How much sooner (or later) could the five orders be completed if they were scheduled on a first come–first served basis?

3 The following orders were received in a job shop where scheduling is done by priority decision rules. In what sequence would the jobs be produced according to the following priority rules? Assume operations are carried on seven days/week.

Job number	Date received	Date due	Production days required
870	3–17	5–7	20
871	3–19	5–13	30
872	3–20	4–23	10
873	3–26	5–12	25
874	4–2	4–15	15

(*a*) Earliest due date
(*b*) Shortest processing time
(*c*) Least slack
(*d*) First come first served

4 Data Processing Services has payroll and engineering jobs from five customers that must be processed first through its XL100 computer and then printed on a

PR70 printer in the same sequential order. The estimated time for each job is as shown.

	Estimated time (hours) for				
	Ajax Co.	B&B supply	Chico steel	D&M mtr.	EIMCO
XL100	8	4	11	4	9
PR70	10	9	4	2	7

(*a*) Develop a schedule sequence that will complete all work in the minimum amount of time and plot the schedule in the form of a Gantt chart. (*Hint:* Use Johnson's rule.)

(*b*) By how many hours would the overall time of the schedule be changed if the Ajax job required only 7 hr computer time and 12 hr printer time?

5 A defense contractor in Chicago has six different jobs in process with the delivery requirements shown. Today is day 70 and the contractor uses a critical ratio scheduling technique. Rank the jobs according to priority with number 1 = highest.

Job	Promised date	Estimated date
A	60	72
B	72	72
C	67	79

Job	Promised date	Estimated date
D	72	78
E	65	75
F	70	80

6 A sports equipment company has a large demand for tents and sleeping bags and must now schedule production for next month. The available and required times per unit are as shown. Each sleeping bag yields a profit contribution of $10/unit whereas the tents provide $40/unit. Use standard linear programming methods to determine (*a*) the number of bags and tents to produce, and (*b*) the total profit contribution from the two items.

	Time available	Time required/unit Bags	Tents
Material preparation	800 hr	1 hr	2 hr
Sewing	900 hr	3 hr	1 hr

7 Use linear programming to solve the scheduling problem 5 in Chap. 5.

8 Use linear programming to solve the scheduling problem 7 in Chap. 5.

9 Use linear programming to solve the scheduling problem 8 in Chap. 5.

10 Use linear programming to solve the scheduling problem 10 in Chap. 5.

11 Use linear programming to solve the scheduling problem 11 in Chap. 5.

12 Collins Heating Company has four central heating installations to design within an eight-week period (40 hr/week). They also have four capable designers, each of whom has been asked to estimate how long it would take to do each job. The work operations scheduler has compiled the estimates shown.

Designers	Hours to complete job 1	2	3	4
A	100	140	280	70
B	130	160	200	60
C	80	130	300	90
D	150	110	250	50

(*a*) Use assignment linear programming methods to determine how the jobs should be assigned so as to minimize the work time.
(*b*) Assuming the estimates are correct, can the jobs be completed within the eight-week period without planning for overtime?
(*c*) Assuming one designer per job and no overtime, could the work be completed in five weeks?
(*d*) In three weeks?

13 An electroplating shop scheduler has four jobs to schedule through a plating operation. Some jobs can be done in any one of five plating tanks, but some of the tanks are restricted to a specific use. The scheduling alternatives and variable costs of power, plating material, and labor are shown in the table. Which assignment of jobs to plating tanks will minimize cost?

Job	Plating tank cost ($) 1	2	3	4	5
A	120	n.a.	100	n.a.	200
B	80	70	50	130	300
C	40	70	90	n.a.	180
D	110	n.a.	150	n.a.	190

***14** *Dynamic programming* Verify the profit figures for four cumulative units produced in period *C* and *D* as shown in the dynamic programming Solved Prob. *3.

***15** *Dynamic programming* Surfside Swimming Pools has orders for six units to be produced on an overtime basis during the next three weeks. They must schedule at least one unit/week and can go up to three units/week. Considering their normal load, overtime costs, selling prices, and so forth, they would gain the profit shown in the accompanying table at the various production levels. Use dynamic programming to schedule production of the six units over the three-week period in such a way as to maximize profit from the order.

Number of units produced	Profits ($000) from producing N units in Week 1	Week 2	Week 3
1	4	3	5
2	7	10	6
3	12	12	9

16 In calculating the PERT network for a freeway construction job, the foreman optimistically felt a welding activity could conceivably be completed in 12 days whereas the welder, after citing all the possible delays, said it might take as long as 24 days. Both agreed that the most likely time was 15 days.

(*a*) What is the expected activity time (t_e)?

(*b*) What is the estimate of activity variance (σ^2)?

17 The expected completion time of a PERT project is $T_E = 15$ days and $\sigma_{cp}{}^2 = 4$ days. What is the probability that the project will take 18 or more days to complete?

18 A PERT network has expected times t_e in days as shown. The time estimates for activity 6–7 are $a = 1$, $m = 4$, and $b = 7$. For the network, what is the

(*a*) Expected completion time T_E?

(*b*) Completion time standard deviation σ?

(*c*) Probability the project will take more than 21.5 days to complete?

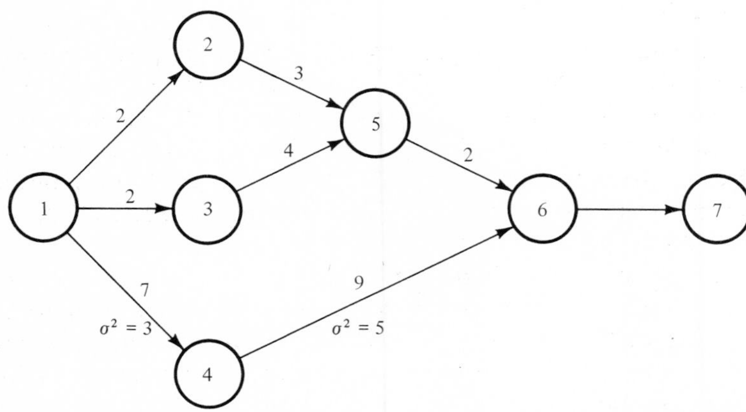

19 A microwave relay station construction project is being planned on a PERT basis with the data shown given in days.

Activity	a	m	b
1–2	2	3	10
1–3	8	12	20
1–4	10	14	16
2–5	6	10	12
3–5	14	20	26
3–7	3	5	7
4–6	8	12	20
5–7	1	1	1
6–8	6	10	12
7–8	1	3	7

(*a*) Construct a PERT network showing the expected mean time t_e for each activity.
(*b*) What is the critical path?
(*c*) What is the expected completion time T_E?
(*d*) How much slack exists in the path containing event 2?
(*e*) What is the latest day event 2 can be completed without delaying the project?
(*f*) Find σ_{cp}.
(*g*) What is the probability the project will take longer than 41 days to complete?

20 Given the data in the previous problem, assume that each day of improvement in the completion schedule results in a \$1,000 savings (or bonus). For a cost of \$1,500 the firm could do any one of the following:
(*a*) Reduce the t_e of activity 3–7 by 4 days.
(*b*) Reduce the t_e of activity 7–8 by 2 days.
(*c*) Reduce the t_e of activities 3–5 and 6–8 by 2 days each.
Evaluate the alternative choices and indicate which, if any, is preferable. (Adapted from [**5**:120].)

21 A building contractor company has bid on a job for a water reservoir that must be completed within 34 days ($T_L = 34$) or else it must pay a \$2,000 penalty. If finished within 28 days it will get a \$1,000 bonus. Expenses associated with the project are estimated to be \$30,000. The company has developed a PERT chart of the project and found that $T_E = 31$ days. The variance estimates of the five activities along the critical path are 1.3, 2.2, 2.1, 0.9, and 2.5 days respectively.
(*a*) What is the probability of obtaining the bonus (accurate to two digits)?
(*b*) Assuming the company wishes to adjust its bid price to allow for the expected bonus or penalty and come out with only a long run expected profit of \$5,000, for what contract price should it be willing to accept the job?

22 A PERT chart is to be used to estimate the assembly time for a new component which is later to be manufactured. Subsequent production is expected to follow an 80 percent learning curve. The optimistic, most likely, and pessimistic assembly times for the first assembly are estimated at 2, 4, and 12 hours respectively. What is the expected assembly time of the fourth unit?

23 The earliest (E) and latest (L) times for the occurrence of event 6 of a network are as shown. Determine appropriate values for all other events of the network and show them in a similar manner.

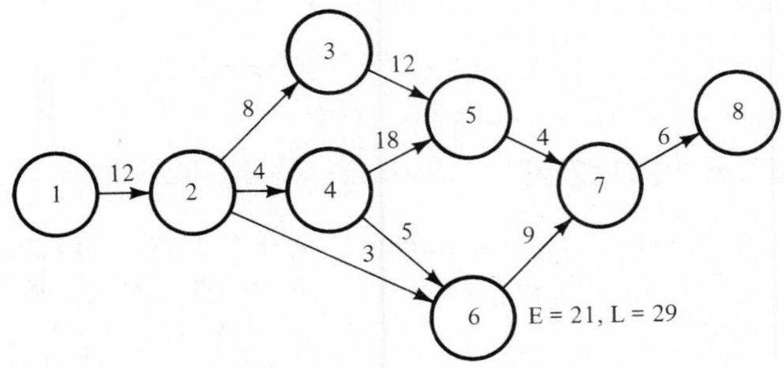

24 *PERT-COST* The minimum feasible times and cost/day to gain reductions in the activity times shown in the network are given in the accompanying table.

Activity	Minimum times (days)	Time reduction direct costs/days
1–2	3	$20 (first), $45 (second)
1–3	4	35 (first), 60 (others)
2–3	2	90
3–4	3	10 (first), 90 (second), 130 (third)

Assume indirect project costs are $100/day and develop a graph showing (*a*) the normal time-cost, (*b*) the crash time-cost, and (*c*) the optimal time-cost.

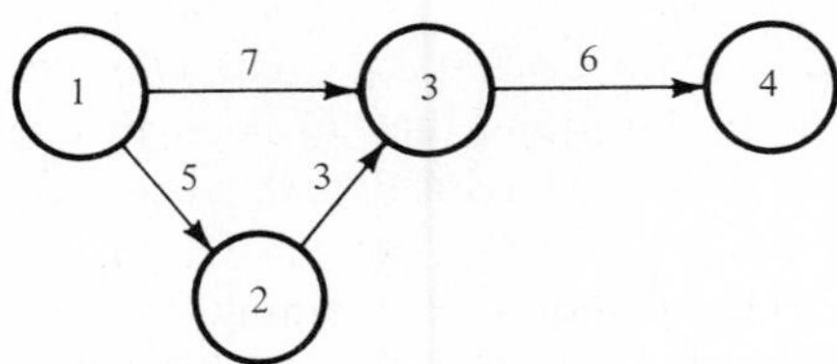

25 (Limited Resource Allocation) A government naval shipyard has received orders to proceed with a ship construction project and is using CPM. They have developed a schedule-time graph to show employment requirements over a portion of the project. The numbers above the activities indicate the number of shipfitters required for the respective activities. Develop an improved personnel balance that minimizes the range of the number of shipfitters required.

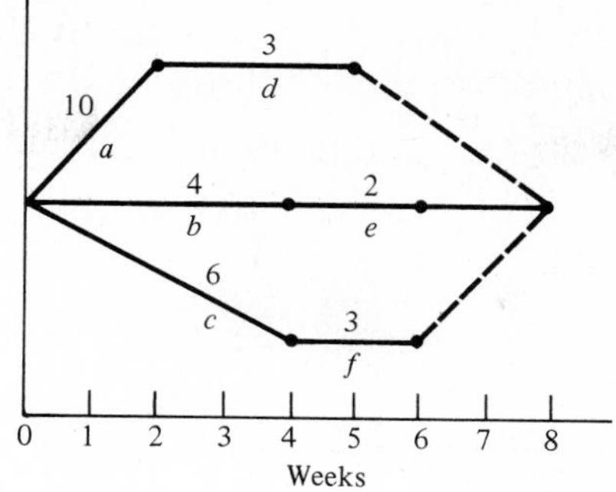

CROSSWORD PUZZLE

Copy and complete the puzzle using the clues given below. The initial letter of each word is located by an r,c (row, column) designation. This puzzle uses terms from both Chap. 8 and 9.

Across

1-1 A type of planning for output over the longer range by adjusting the levels of employment, inventories, and other controllable variables.

1-12 The statistical distribution used to compute t_e and σ^2 in PERT networks.

3-1 The value of the standard deviation of a PERT activity where $b = 70$ and $a = 10$.

3-5 A type of planning that relates to labor and equipment requirements.

5-3 A type of order point system that keeps priorities up to date so that order points are handled similar to MRP items.

6-7 An inventory control and scheduling system that treats items as if their priorities were dependent and signals when to order materials.

7-1 The aggregate planning strategies are basically ______ and error approaches since no one strategy is necessarily optimal.

7-8 A conjunction signifying the choice of one strategy ______ another.

7-11 An abbreviation sometimes used for "return on investment."

8-1 Slang for "yes."

9-2 To deal with inventories in a certain manner (as a verb). Also, to stand the cost of another's food or entertainment.

9-8 The first three and last letters (abbreviation) of a word which summarizes the planning strategy of varying the work-force size.

10-11 A point in time which indicates that some activities have been completed and others can begin.

11-1 A control mechanism of slightly greater complexity than Gantt charts that is more suited to the monitoring of continuous systems.

11-8 The branch of mathematics concerned with angles, sins, cosines, and identities.

12-13 The type of priority assigned to a job with the lowest critical ratio.

13-3 The action that ensures that production activities conform to priority and capacity plans. It involves measurement, feedback, calculation of deviation, and corrective action.

15-1 An acronym for resource allocation models.

15-6 A type of planning that relates to material requirements and consists of determining what is required and when.

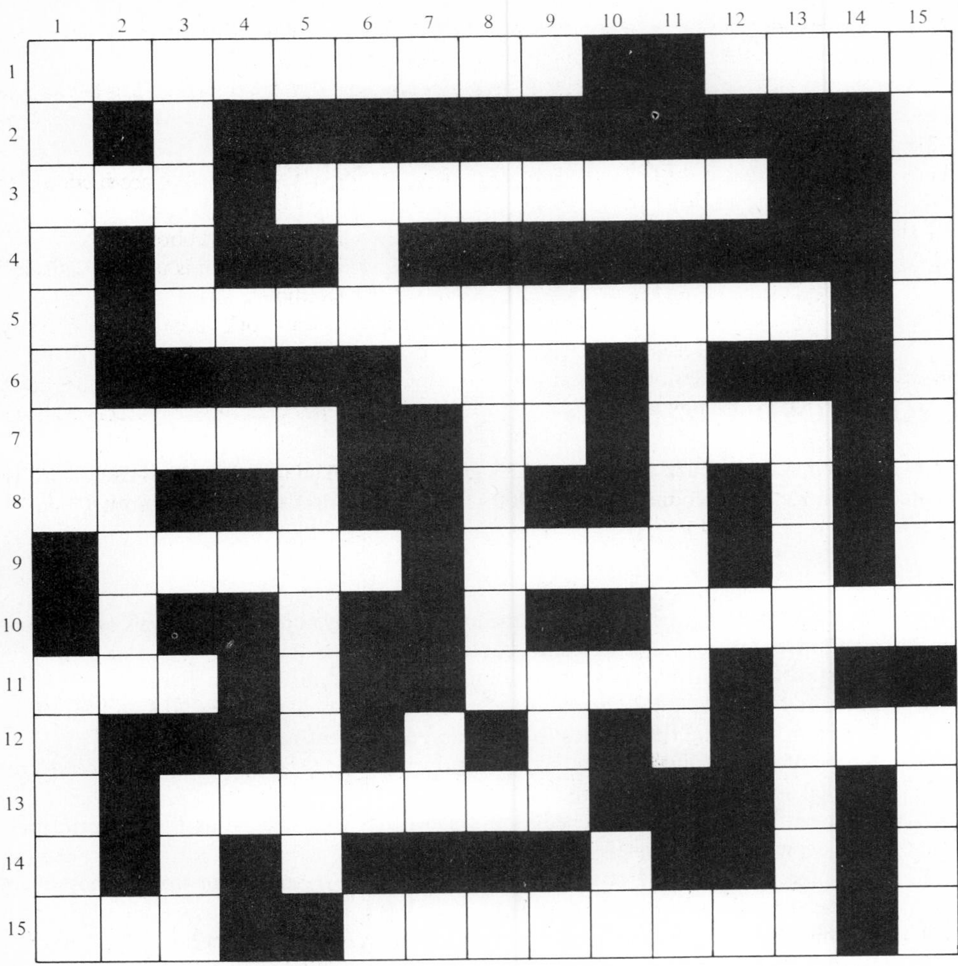

Down

1-1 An item in PERT networks that takes time and is designated by an arrow.

11-1 The type of hours in which capacities are normally expressed for capacity planning purposes.

7-2 The mathematical number that reflects the current total load on facilities in the numerator and the firm's commitment to the customer in the denominator is called a critical ______.

1-3 A type of bar chart still used extensively for scheduling, and named after a follower of Frederick Taylor.

13-3 A network technique for analyzing a system in terms of activities and events where only one time estimate per activity is used.

7-5 An improvement phenomenon (found mostly in labor-intensive assembly activities) that can effect scheduling.

3-6 A production rate that will satisfy both high and low demands as long as inventory levels are allowed to fluctuate as required (abbreviated).

12-7 Letters describing a priority scheduling technique that takes today's date, the promised date, and the estimated shipping date into account.

5-8 A complex set of interdependent activities that often takes place at a job site and frequently uses CPM and PERT for planning and control.

5-9 An anagram for a heuristic priority rule.

11-9 An abbreviation for a widely publicized decision rule that determines production rate and work-force size (letters are in reverse order).

14-10 A time unit that could be used for very short-term scheduling (abbreviated).

5-11 A plan or method of aggregate planning which can be "pure" but is usually "mixed." Employment, back orders, and subcontracting are examples.

7-13 The aggregate planning strategy that calls for a constant work force and sufficiently large amounts of inventories to absorb all demand fluctuations.

1-15 A quantitative method of linear programming that is particularly useful for allocating jobs to machines, workers to jobs, and so forth, on the basis of some predetermined criterion.

12-15 A network technique for planning and controlling projects where statistical estimates of completion times can be developed from the three time estimates of each activity along the critical path.

BIBLIOGRAPHY

[1] BEDWORTH, DAVID D.: *Industrial Systems*, Ronald Press Company, New York, 1973.

[2] BUFFA, ELWOOD S.: *Modern Production Management*, John Wiley & Sons, New York, 1973.

[3] CHASE, RICHARD B., AND NICHOLAS J. ACQUILANO: *Production and Operations Management*, Richard D. Irwin, Homewood, Illinois, 1973.

[4] DAVIS, E. W.: "Resource Allocation in Project Network Models—A Survey," *Journal of Industrial Engineering*, vol. 17, no. 4, April 1966, pp. 177–188.

[5] GARRETT, LEONARD J., AND MILTON SILVER: *Production Management Analysis*, Harcourt, Brace, Jovanovich, New York, 1973.

[6] JOHNSON, S. M.: "Optimal Two and Three Stage Production Schedules with Set-Up Time Included," *Naval Research Logistics Quarterly*, vol. 1, no. 1, March 1954.

[7] MOORE, FRANKLIN G.: *Production Management*, Richard D. Irwin, Homewood, Illinois, 1973.

[8] OLSEN, ROBERT A.: *Manufacturing Management: A Quantitative Approach*, International Textbook Company, Scranton, Pennsylvania, 1968.

[9] ORLICKY, JOSEPH A., GEORGE W. PLOSSL, AND OLIVER W. WIGHT: "Structuring the Bill of Material for MRP," *Production and Inventory Management*, vol. 13, no. 4, 1972.

[10] PLOSSL, G. W., AND O. W. WIGHT: *Production and Inventory Control*, Prentice-Hall, Englewood Cliffs, New Jersey, 1967.

[11] RIGGS, JAMES L.: *Production Systems: Planning, Analysis and Control*, John Wiley & Sons, New York, 1970.

[12] SHORE, BARRY: *Operations Management*, McGraw-Hill Book Company, New York, 1973.

[13] VOLLMAN, THOMAS E.: *Operations Management*, Addison-Wesley Publishing Company, Reading, Massachusetts, 1973.

[14] WAGNER, HARVEY M.: *Principles of Management Science*, Prentice-Hall, Englewood Cliffs, New Jersey, 1970.

[15] WIGHT, OLIVER: *Production and Inventory Management in the Computer Age*, Cahners Books, Boston, Massachusetts, 1974.

CHAPTER

10

Quality Control

Suppose you know the operations supervisor of a firm which produces 110-volt transformers in competition with other manufacturers. The transformers are expected to deliver current at a minimum voltage of 107 volts, but being very customer conscious your friend pushes his work force to install sufficient copper windings to make the transformers always deliver 110 volts or better. As a result of his relentless efforts the company's transformers finally average 115 volts with some reaching as high as 130 volts. Soon afterward, a customer buys several transformers, installs them on a multimillion dollar computer complex, and burns out $1 million worth of equipment. Your unemployed friend now comes to you explaining that throughout all these efforts to "improve quality" his boss always told him to "keep at it—things could be worse." So he kept at it—and sure enough! Now he hopes you can explain where he went wrong.

For many people, high quality simply means the best (or most) material, highest rating of performance, or most number of features that can be built into a good or service. But this is a very limited and suboptimizing perspective of the illusive entity labeled "quality." We shall try to be more specific, recognizing that quality is an inherently vital and often very competitive aspect of a product. As such, it deserves to be thoroughly understood and scientifically managed.

In this chapter we look first at the definition and objectives of quality control, considering the purpose, source of responsibility, and methods of controlling quality, the relevant costs, and the role of inspection. The two major methodologies in use today for controlling quality are then discussed; acceptance sampling and control charts. Both methods make extensive use of statistical techniques and we shall see how sampling plans and control charts are established and where they are best applied. We end the chapter by identifying some of the unique quality control problems faced by multinational firms.

OBJECTIVES OF QUALITY CONTROL

Unlike the understanding of quality held by the operations supervisor described above, high quality is not necessarily represented by the highest voltage, most features, longest life, or even the best design of a product. These attributes may or may not be indicative of quality. For example, a fuse that provides a long life of service by carrying a current overload is not as satisfactory as one that fails at a specified amperage level. Similarly, the added features (and gasoline consumption) of a larger V-8 engine would not represent higher quality to a self-employed taxi driver who ordered an economical six-cylinder compact. A businesswoman flying from Seattle to a meeting in Denver would probably not appreciate receiving the added "service" of a stopover in Poughkeepsie, New York.

Quality is a measure of how closely a good or service conforms to specified standards. The standards may relate to time, materials, performance, reliability, appearance, or any quantifiable characteristic of the product. The objective of quality control efforts is to ensure that specified standards are adhered to in the production of a firm's products and, where required, in its application. In nonindustrial situations, where the applications cannot be closely controlled, firms tend to rely more upon substitute measures of labeling and consumer-directed advertising to guide the product into proper applications.

Although we sometimes tend to associate quality with cost, the quality level for an inexpensive product may be "high" or "low" just as it may be "high" or "low" for an expensive product. It depends upon the extent to which the product meets specified or advertised characteristics. Unfortunately, we are not always careful to define the product line and specify the relevant standards of comparison. As a result, we sometimes use the word "quality" very loosely.

For example, if we speak of the quality of "automobiles" without being any more specific than that, our individual standards could be almost anything that happens to come to mind, such as appearance, performance, and so on. Since human preferences tend to be for "more" rather than "less," many persons would unconsciously associate high quality with the most expensive models in the product line. However, if our criteria related to specific variables such as surface finish, fuel consumption, maneuverability, and cost per mile, we could measure the extent to which a given automobile (such as a Volkswagen) met its standards. Volkswagens can be of high or low quality just as can Buicks, for both are produced to different specifications for different market segments.

Some customers prefer one product to another of equal quality on the basis of a subjective preference which varies with the individual. These subjective feelings are difficult to identify with quality for they reflect the utility value of a good or service to a specific consumer. The quality of a product per se is not changed by the preference of the individual who owns or uses it. Quality is more specific and definite than that. The quality variations management is concerned with normally occur within a product classification and often result from such things as defective raw materials, improper machine adjustments, substitute components, workers in search of shortcuts, and so forth. They constitute variations from a standard of material or performance that the firm is expected to deliver and the customer is entitled to expect.

PURPOSE, RESPONSIBILITY, AND METHODS OF CONTROLLING QUALITY

Organizations operate in a variety of noncompetitive as well as competitive environments, but in practically all situations the organization must supply a good or service desired by the consumer. Even the operation of hospitals and prisons arises from the aggregate desires of a society which includes potential "customers." Similarly, a business enterprise reflects consumer desires in their choice of product line and service goals. More specifically, the desired product characteristics and service levels must be translated into engineered specifications if the quality levels are to be controlled.

The purpose of quality control activities is to provide assurance that goods or services conform to specified standards. Like any other control activity the control of quality involves measurement, feedback, comparison with standards, and correction when necessary. It would be unreasonable to expect a product to have certain characteristics without having any way of measuring whether or not the product does in fact possess them. Similarly, an accurate and timely reporting of the measurement data is essential.

Quality standards often arise from design specification or service objectives. Where quantifiable standards are absent, quality becomes a matter of opinion and is not really controllable from a scientific standpoint. An abstract painting, for example, may appear exquisite to one person and detestable to another, depending upon their subjective impressions. Such a painting would be of questionable quality until such time as some recognized standard were established. In many cases interest groups within a culture develop surrogate standards, such as simply the name of an artist, composer, or performer. They then attempt to equate this substitute characteristic with quality. But cultural value systems differ widely, and the value attached to such a work is usually more a matter of subjective preference than it is of measurable characteristics. It properly belongs in the realm of art rather than science. When measurable characteristics can be developed and compared to quantified standards, then some logical basis for evaluation can be established. Only then can consistent decisions be made with respect to acceptance, rejection, or correction of a product. Only then can its quality be scientifically controlled.

From an organizational standpoint, the responsibility for controlling quality rests with everyone who is in a position to affect quality. However, the quality measurement function is often performed by a specific quality control—or quality assurance—group who has the responsibility for coordinating quality control activities. These activities are generally staff rather than line functions; but even though quality control technicians and inspectors report to their own line management, they often work informally in close cooperation with operating personnel. This method of operation preserves the autonomy of an inspector and yet expedites action on quality deficiencies.

The methods of controlling quality depend somewhat on where the control activities can most effectively and economically be implemented. Control activities can take place in either or all three of the input, transformation, or output phases of a production process. Control exercised over the incoming raw materials and outgoing finished products generally takes the form of acceptance sampling. Control of the actual process quality is often accomplished by means of control charts. Figure 10-1 depicts these two forms of control in the context of our general model of a production system.

Both methods involve statistical sampling techniques. However, the acceptance sampling methods rely upon estimating the levels of defectives before or after a process has been completed whereas control charts are more useful during a process to ensure that production is not outside of acceptable limits.

RELEVANT COSTS

Quality costs can be classified into the two major categories of inspection and control costs and defective product costs. As expenditures for inspection and control

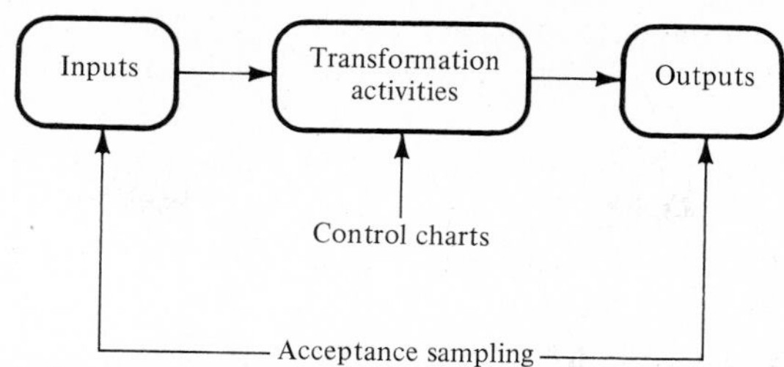

FIGURE 10-1 Statistical techniques for controlling quality

increase, the costs attributable to defective products decrease. The optimal level of expenditure on quality control activities occurs where the total costs are a minimum, as shown in Fig. 10-2.

Inspection and control costs include costs for training, administration, and operation of the quality control program as well as the labor and materials involved in inspection and testing activities. Defective product costs include those scrap and rework costs within the plant as well as the field repair and replacement costs and loss of goodwill after the product gets into the hands of the consumer.

To minimize the total quality costs, it is important to identify and control the relevant cost components as closely as possible. Although some managers may choose not to quantitatively assess all quality control costs (such as loss of goodwill) any real cost must nevertheless be paid in one way or another. Avoiding consideration of costs does not eliminate them; it simply means they are likely to be less scientifically managed. Where costs cannot be accurately measured, they should at least be carefully estimated to a precision consistent with the decision significance.

INSPECTION: WHEN, WHERE, AND HOW MUCH TO INSPECT

Measurement and inspection activities are designed to detect unacceptable quality levels before additional investment is added to a product. They cannot convert a defective item into an acceptable product, nor do they change a product or add any noticeable value to it. The timing, location, and amount of inspection should be governed by the expected cost or probable loss from passing defectives at any stage of a process. An optimal amount of inspection, in a theoretical sense, would be that amount where the cost of inspection and/or control would just equal the expected costs of not inspecting or controlling.

In an operational sense, when and where to inspect is a function of the type of process and the value added at each stage. A general guideline is to inspect when the cost of inspection at a given stage is less than the probable loss from not inspecting. Depending upon the process, some of the following times and/or places are often suitable [**8**: 406]. Inspect:

1 Incoming raw material (before payment for goods is authorized)

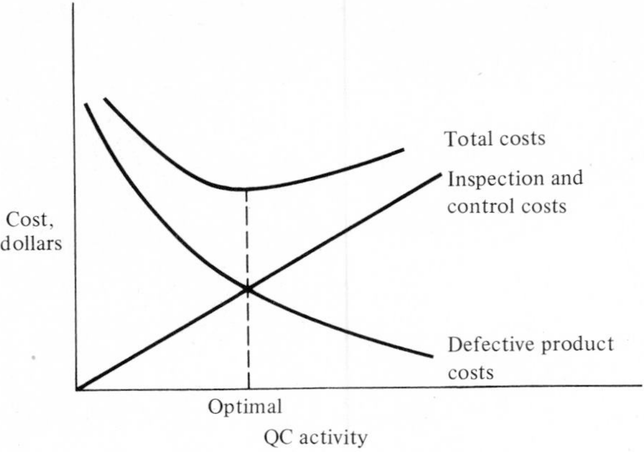

FIGURE 10-2 Quality costs

2 Before costly operations (to eliminate investment on defective items)

3 Before potential damage (where defectives could damage machines or cause substantial loss)

4 Before series of operations (where inspection is infeasible)

5 Before point of no return (where defectives cannot be reworked)

6 Before masking attributes (where defects would be hidden)

7 Before stocking (where investment is high or reliability important)

8 At point of responsibility transfer (where product control changes hands)

9 For quality incentives (where worker is paid on basis of quality)

10 Finished items (before delivery to consumer)

A problem sometimes arises, however, as to location of the inspection station. One heuristic rule [**8**: 409] for solution of this problem calls for comparison of the costs of locating (L_k) and costs of not locating (N_k) an inspection station at point k relative only to the next point in the line. The costs are then:

$$L_k = \begin{pmatrix}\text{cost of inspecting}\\ \text{at this station}\end{pmatrix} + \begin{pmatrix}\text{cost of inspection still}\\ \text{required at next station}\end{pmatrix} + \begin{pmatrix}\text{fixed cost}\\ \text{at this station}\end{pmatrix}$$

$$N_k = \begin{pmatrix}\text{cost of processing}\\ \text{defects}\end{pmatrix} + \begin{pmatrix}\text{cost of doing all inspection}\\ \text{at next station}\end{pmatrix}$$

For each potential inspection station, the estimated costs of locating and not locating an inspection station are then calculated and an inspection plan is set up on that basis. This heuristic rule may or may not be optimal, and other methods, including dynamic programming, are currently being employed to help solve this type of problem.

Components and products may ultimately be inspected many times during a production operation. One hundred percent inspection is sometimes justified for some products or processes. However, 100 percent inspection may also be uneconomical or unfeasible; some products are completely destroyed by testing. In these situations statistical samples can provide the basis for quality control decisions.

ACCEPTANCE SAMPLING OF INCOMING AND OUTGOING QUALITY

When 100 percent inspection is not practical, samples are usually the next best way of estimating the incoming or outgoing quality of a good or service. Random samples provide each element with an equal chance of being selected and permit logical inference to be made about the population quality on the basis of sample evidence. The parameters of most interest are usually the true mean μ and the standard deviation σ of the population, which are estimated from the sample mean $\bar{x}$ and sample standard deviation s.

We have noted previously that in a sampling situation any one sample mean may be expected to differ somewhat from the population mean due simply to variation among samples. Nevertheless the deviation of the sample means or standard error of the mean $s_{\bar{x}}$ can be estimated and controlled, for it is a function of the sample size n.

$$s_{\bar{x}} = \frac{s}{\sqrt{n}} \tag{3-16}$$

As the sample size approaches the population size N the standard error gets smaller to the point where it reduces to zero when the sample size is as large as the population.

Example 10-1

A quality control sample of $n = 100$ items is taken and the standard deviation calculated to be 0.250 inches.

(*a*) Estimate the standard error of the mean.

(*b*) What would be the standard error if the sample size were 1,000 instead of 100?

Solution

(*a*) $$s_{\bar{x}} = \frac{s}{\sqrt{n}} = \frac{0.250}{\sqrt{100}} = 0.025 \text{ inches}$$

(*b*) $$s_{\bar{x}} = \frac{0.250}{\sqrt{1{,}000}} = 0.008 \text{ inches}$$

The determination of the standard error of the mean is particularly important in quality control work for it facilitates statistical estimation and tests of hypothesis. Much of the inference made about the quality of large lots is based upon statistical theory which holds that regardless of the shape of the population distribution, the distribution of sample means (that is, the sampling distribution of the means) is approximately normal if the sample size is sufficiently large (greater than 30). Of course the same theory holds when we are making an inference based upon sample proportions except, as we saw in Chap. 3, proportions require a larger sample size (such as 50 or 100) and the standard error of proportion is:

$$s_p = \frac{\sqrt{pq}}{\sqrt{n}} \tag{3-7}$$

In practice we find that a good deal of acceptance sampling activities rely upon the comparison of actual sample means, or proportions, with what might theoretically be expected on the assumption of a normal distribution of means or proportions.

There are other situations in quality control work where the characteristics of the population are fairly well documented, and we wish to make deductive statements about specific items rather than inductive statements about the population as a whole. For example, we know that individual machined parts often have dimensions that follow a normal distribution, and failures of a machine often follow a Poisson distribution. If the variable of interest in a population is known to follow a normal, Poisson, or other statistical distribution, the probabilities of individual events can be deduced from our prior knowledge of the population itself. This use of probability theory represents an application of *deductive logic* whereas the inference about the population on the basis of sample evidence is an application of *inductive logic*. In this section we shall look first at some deductive situations, then at the inductive applications involving the use of operating characteristic curves, and finally at the economics of sampling.

STATISTICAL DISTRIBUTIONS FOR DEFECTIVES

We saw earlier that a frequency distribution is a quantitative description of a random variable. Very often the actual frequency distributions we encounter in quality control activities conform closely to theoretical probability distributions which have been mathematically defined. Those distributions most commonly encountered may be conveniently classified into the discrete and continuous categories as shown in the accompanying table. Recall that in *discrete distributions* the variable can assume a definite (countable) set of values, whereas in *continuous distributions* the variable takes on a measurable, or continuous, set of values.

Discrete distributions	Continuous distributions
Uniform	Normal
Hypergeometric	Student t
Binomial	Chi square
Poisson	F

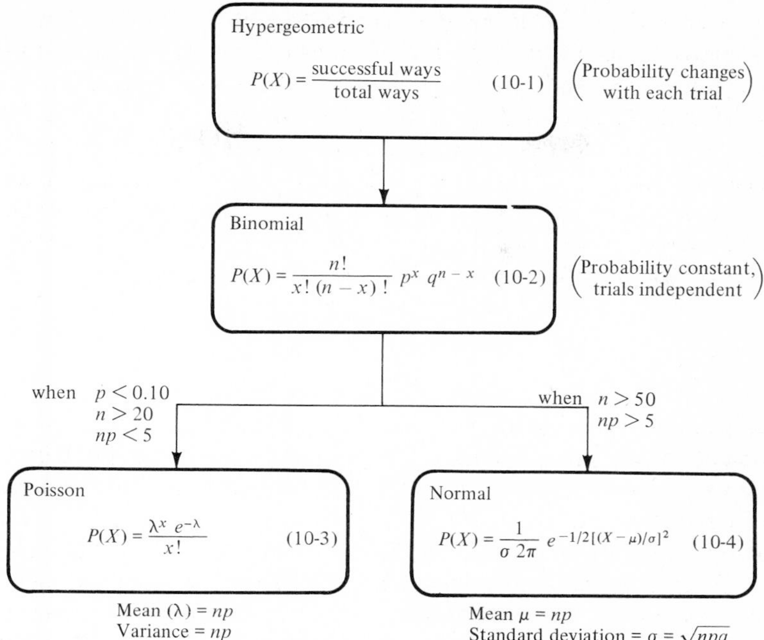

FIGURE 10-3 Probability distributions useful in quality control. Note that the normal and Poisson are useful approximations to the binomial depending upon the size of sample n and proportions of defectives p.

Although all of the mentioned distributions are useful in quality control work, the binomial, Poisson, and normal are often most appropriate for determination of the probability of defective goods or services. The appropriate distribution, of course, depends upon the specific situation. Some guidelines for use of some of the common distributions are shown in Fig. 10-3. Example problems which follow illustrate the applicability of some of these distributions to quality control situations.

Example 10-2 (hypergeometric)

A shipment of 20 transistors received six weeks ago was delivered to an assembly area without receipt inspection. Four of the transistors were installed in a space vehicle and the remainder were mixed with existing inventory. The supplier has just notified the firm that five of the transistors were defective.

(*a*) What is the probability that all four transistors installed in the vehicle were good?

(*b*) That there was one defective in the lot of four?

Solution

$$(a) \quad P(X = 4 \text{ good}) = \frac{\text{successful ways}}{\text{total ways}}$$

The successful and total number of ways of selecting 4 transistors from 20 must be computed recognizing that no transistor can be used more than once and that a different order of selection of the same 4 would not change anything. In this case we are concerned with *combinations* of x items chosen from $n = 20$:

$$C_x^n = \frac{n!}{x!\,(n-x)!} \tag{2-5}$$

(See Solved Prob. 2 for additional distinction between multiple choices, permutations, and combinations.) Note that the lot is known to have contained

$$\begin{array}{rl} 15 & \text{good} \\ +5 & \text{defective} \\ \hline 20 & \text{total} \end{array}$$

The number of successful ways to select 4 good from the 15 is the combinations of 4 in 15. $\Big\}$ C_4^{15}

For each of these ways

The number of successful ways to select 0 defectives from 5 is the combinations of 0 in 5. $\Big\}$ C_0^{5}

The total number of ways to select 4 transistors from 20 is the combinations of 4 in 20. $\Big\}$ C_4^{20}

$$\therefore\ P(X = 4) = \frac{C_4^{15} \cdot C_0^{5}}{C_4^{20}} = \frac{\dfrac{15!}{4!\,11!} \cdot \dfrac{5!}{0!\,5!}}{\dfrac{20!}{4!\,16!}} = 0.28$$

$$(b)\quad P(X = 3) = \frac{C_3^{15} \cdot C_1^{5}}{C_4^{20}} = \frac{\dfrac{15!}{3!\,12!} \cdot \dfrac{5!}{1!\,4!}}{\dfrac{20!}{4!\,16!}} = 0.47$$

Example 10-3 (binomial)

Ten percent of the fire bricks baked in an obsolete oven turn out to be defective in some way. What is the chance that exactly 2 will be defective in a random sample of 10?

Solution

The defective rate is given as a percentage and can be taken as constant. If we can assume each brick produced is independent of the previous brick, then the binomial distribution applies.

$$P(X = 2 \mid n = 10, p = 0.10) = \frac{n!}{x!\,(n-x)!}\,p^x q^{n-x}$$

$$= \frac{10!}{2!\,8!}(0.10)^2(0.90)^8 = 0.1937$$

Note that the solution value could also be obtained more directly from the table of binomial probabilities given in Appendix E.

Example 10-4 (Poisson approximation)

A very large shipment of textbooks comes from a publisher who usually supplies about 1 percent with imperfect bindings. What is the probability that among 400 textbooks taken from this shipment, exactly 3 will have imperfect bindings?

Solution

This problem could be solved by using the binomial expression for $P(X = 3 \mid n = 400, p = 0.01)$. However, unless one has a calculator that handles exponentials, the solution would be tedious. It can be closely approximated by the Poisson distribution since $p < 0.10$, $n > 20$ and $np < 5$.

$$P(X) = \frac{\lambda^x e^{-\lambda}}{x!}$$

where

$$\lambda = np = 400(0.01) = 4.0$$
$$x = 3$$
$$e = 2.718(\text{constant})$$

$$P(X = 3 \mid \lambda = 4.0) = \frac{\lambda^x e^{-\lambda}}{x!} = \frac{4^3 e^{-4}}{3!} = \frac{(64)(0.018)}{3.2} = 0.195$$

The solution value could also be obtained more directly from the table of summed Poisson probabilities given in Appendix F. Go down the λ column to $\lambda = 4$ and then right to the columns where the events are designated as $\leq c$ (rather than $\leq x$). Since we need $c = 3$, we must find the difference between $c \leq 3$ and $c \leq 2$ which is $0.433 - 0.238 = 0.195$.

Example 10-5 (normal approximation)

In a precious metals manufacturing process, 20 percent of the ingots contain impurities and must be remelted after inspection. If 100 ingots are selected for shipment without inspection, what is the probability 15 or more ingots will contain impurities?

Solution

This binomial problem $P(X \geq 15 \mid n = 100, p = 0.20)$ may be solved by using the normal approximation to the binomial since $n > 50$ and $np = 100(0.20) > 5$.

$$\mu = np = 100(0.20) = 20$$

$$\sigma = \sqrt{npq} = \sqrt{20(0.8)} = 4$$

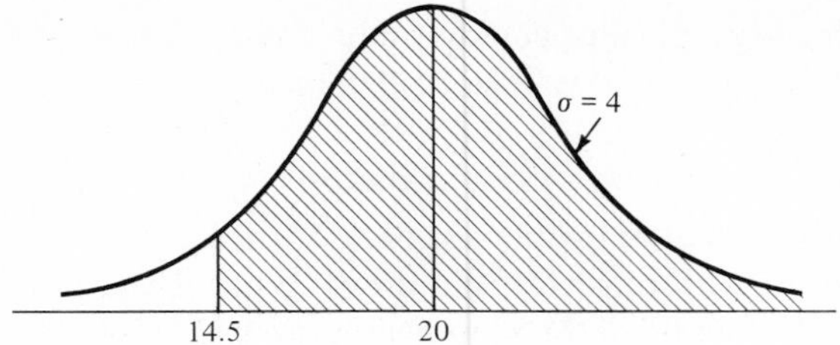

FIGURE 10-4 Normal approximation to binomial

Since we are using a continuous distribution to estimate discrete probabilities, the appropriate continuous value for ≥ 15 becomes 14.5

$$Z = \frac{x - \mu}{\sigma} = \frac{14.5 - 20}{4} = -1.375$$

$$P(Z) = 0.415 \text{ (from Appendix D)}$$

$$P(X > 14.5) = 0.415 + 0.500 = 0.915$$

The normal distribution is, of course, useful in its own right for continuous variables aside from its use as an approximation to the binomial probabilities.

Example 10-6 (normal)

Cans of corn at the Crescent Valley Cannery are filled by a machine which can be set for any desired average amount. If the fill is normally distributed with a standard deviation of 1.42 grams, where should the quality control supervisor recommend the machine be set (on the grams scale) so that 98 percent of the cans will contain 454.00 grams or more?

Solution

We wish to find the mean setting μ such that 48 percent of the cans containing less than the mean still contain 454 grams. Therefore we must enter the body of the normal distribution table (Appendix D) as close as possible to the value 0.480 and read off the corresponding number of standard deviations from the margin.

For $P(Z) = 0.480$, $Z \cong 2.05$

Then:

$$-Z = \frac{x - \mu}{\sigma}$$

where

$x = 454.00$ grams
$\sigma = 1.42$ grams

$$\therefore \mu = x + Z\sigma = 454.00 + 2.05(1.42) = 456.91 \text{ grams}$$

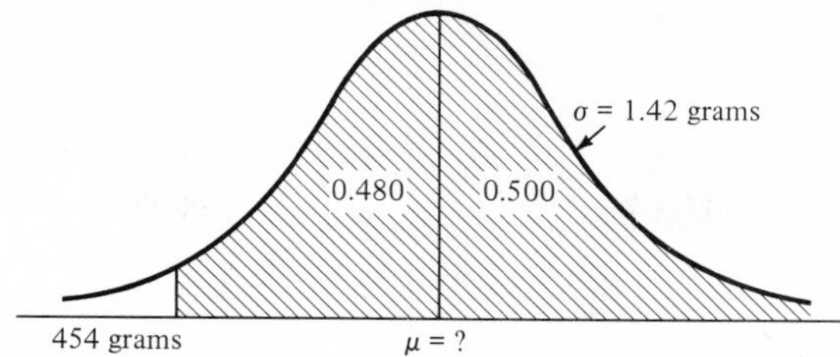

FIGURE 10-5 Normally distributed population

The preceding examples are all concerned with deducing something about the quality of individual items on the basis of statistical knowledge of the population or the production process. We proceed now to the use of individual or sample information to make statistical inference about the parent population.

SAMPLING PLANS FOR ATTRIBUTES AND VARIABLES

Quality control inspectors are often charged with the responsibility of making a decision as to whether an incoming or outgoing shipment is of acceptable quality or not. They are usually forced to decide on the basis of a limited sample because the inspection cost, or perhaps the destructive nature of testing activities, makes 100 percent inspection uneconomical or infeasible.

Since the decision to accept or reject a lot must be made on the basis of sample evidence, the firm's managers must be willing to accept some risks of rejecting good lots or accepting bad lots. Fortunately the amount of risk can be specified in terms of a sampling plan, so that its consequences can be evaluated. Then if the expected costs of making a wrong decision are too great, perhaps the risks of error can be shifted by mutual agreement between the producer and consumer, or even reduced in total by taking a larger sample.

A *sampling plan* is simply a decision rule which specifies how large a sample n should be taken and the allowable measurement, number, or percentage c of defectives in the sample. If the items to be inspected are classified *qualitatively* according to an attribute, such as good or bad, acceptable or not acceptable, and so on, then the sampling plan is referred to as an *attributes plan* and the probabilities of defectives in the parent population are estimated from discrete distributions such as the binomial and Poisson. An attributes sampling plan might read as follows: "Select a random sample of size $n = 40$ and count the number of defectives c. If the number of defectives, $c \leq 3$, accept the lot; otherwise reject it."

If the items to be inspected are classified *quantitatively* according to some measureable characteristic, they will require a *variables sampling plan*. Since variables plans necessitate the recording of actual measurements instead of simply a dichotomous classification (such as of good or bad), they provide more information and require fewer inspections for the same degree of assurance than do comparable attributes plans. Variables plans typically use the normal distribution and might be

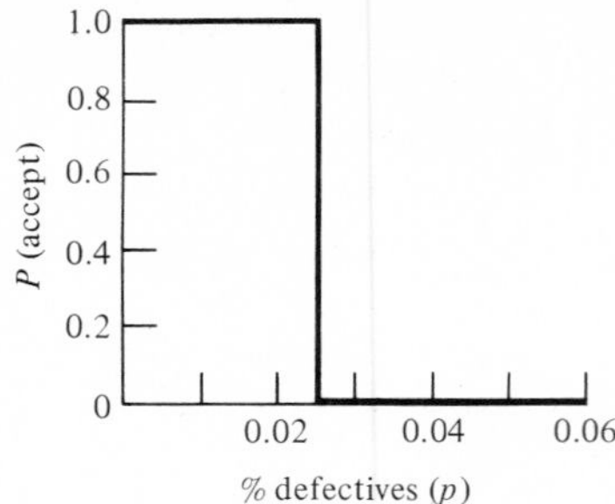

FIGURE 10-6 OC curve for 100 percent inspection

stated as follows: "Select a random sample of size $n = 40$ and determine the mean tensile strength $\bar{x}$. If $\bar{x} > 12{,}000$ psi, accept the lot; otherwise reject it."

The acceptance and rejection characteristics of both attributes and variables sampling plans can be described by *operating characteristic* (OC) curves. These curves always pertain to a specific plan, an n and c combination, and they show the probability that the given plan will accept lots of various (unknown) quality levels. Thus, the OC curve for a given sampling plan will indicate what percentage of lots of any (hypothesized or actual) quality may be expected to be accepted. We shall illustrate the determination of n and c values and the construction of OC curves in the forthcoming discussion on sampling plans for attributes.

Sampling Plans and OC Curves for Attributes

Suppose that an electronics producer supplies a consumer with miniaturized logic units that the consumer in turn uses in his own production process. The two have agreed on the price, delivery schedule, and quality level required for a proposed shipment of $N = 100$ units. If the shipment contains less than or equal to $2\frac{1}{2}$ percent defective units it is to be accepted, and if greater than $2\frac{1}{2}$ percent it is to be rejected and returned at the producer's expense. Now suppose further that an independent laboratory (that never makes mistakes) inspects all 100 items and accurately determines the percentage of defectives. Figure 10-6 shows that if the lot contains either 1 percent or 2 percent defectives the probability of acceptance by the consumer is 1.0—that is, there is no chance of rejecting the lot. Similarly, if the lot contains 3 percent or more defectives there is no chance it will be accepted. As shown on the operating characteristic curve for this plan, for a p value $\geq 2\frac{1}{2}$ percent, the $P(\text{accept}) = 0$.

The above plan called for 100 percent inspection of the population and, assuming it was accurately done, the plan entailed no risk of error to either the producer or the consumer. Let us assume now that the next shipment is much larger ($N =$ 1,000) and the producer and consumer are forced to adopt a sampling plan in order to reduce inspection costs. As with any decision based upon sample evidence each now incurs some risk of error:

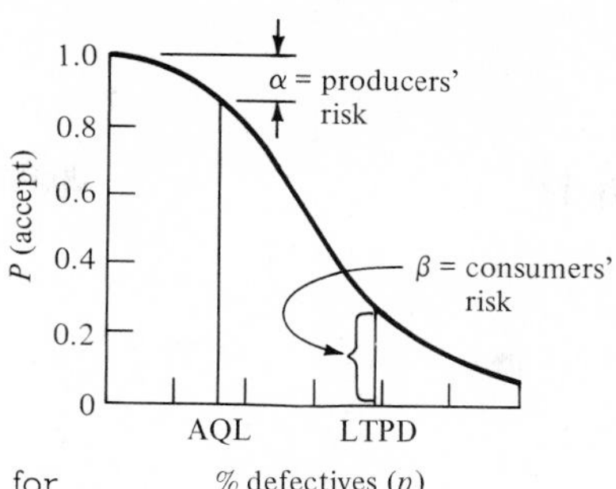

FIGURE 10-7 OC curve for less than 100 percent inspection

Producer's risk This is the risk of getting a sample which has a higher proportion of defectives than the lot as a whole, and rejecting a good lot. It is designated as the alpha (α) risk. Producers hope to keep this risk low, say at 1–5 percent. If a good lot is rejected, we refer to this as a type I error.

Consumer's risk This is the risk of getting a sample which has a lower proportion of defectives than the lot as a whole, and accepting a bad lot. It is designated as the beta (β) risk. Consumers want to keep this risk low. If a bad lot is accepted, we refer to this as a type II error.

To derive a sampling plan, the producer and consumer must not only specify the level of the α and β risk, but also the lot quality level to which these risks pertain. Thus we must further define "good lot" and "bad lot" in terms of the percent defective in the population.

AQL The *acceptable quality level* (AQL) is the quality level of a good lot. It is the percent defective that can be considered satisfactory as a process average, and represents a level of quality which the producer wants accepted with a high probability of acceptance.

LTPD The *lot tolerance percent defective* (LTPD) is the quality level of a bad lot. It represents a level of quality which the consumer wants accepted with a low probability of acceptance.

Lots which have a quality level between the AQL and LTPD are in an "indifferent" zone.

The relationship between α, β, AQL, and LTPD is shown in Fig. 10-7. The α risk at the AQL level and the β risk at the LTPD level establish two points from which the sample size n and acceptance number c are determined. Given these two points, the OC curve can then be drawn to describe the risk characteristics of the specific sampling plan.

The methodology of arriving at a sampling plan (given the α and AQL and the β and LTPD values) involves a trial-and-error process whereby different values of

n and c are tried in order to find the combination that most closely passes through the two points. For a small sample, the OC curve is likely to be rather flat, resulting in high risks to both the producer and consumer. Increasing the sample size makes the OC curve more discriminating between good and bad lots to the point where a 100 percent sample results in the curve shown in Fig. 10-6 where the respective risks have been reduced to zero. Changing the value of c shifts the risk from producer to consumer or vice versa. When the acceptance number c is zero, the OC curve is concave to the origin with, for example, relatively high α risk and relatively low β risk. As c is increased, the curve first takes on more of an S shape and then moves away from the origin in convex fashion becoming less discriminating. At high values of c the risk is shifted largely to the consumer.

The fact that both n and c values affect the shape of the OC curve makes the trial-and-error approach necessary. However, it is not necessary that quality control analysts repeat the calculations every time they wish to set up a sampling plan. Several tables of standard plans have been determined and printed, including the Dodge and Romig tables [**4**], the U.S. Military Standard MIL-STD-105 [**11**], and others. We will first illustrate the determination of an OC curve for a given plan in order to understand the underlying theory, and then see how predetermined plans can be selected more expediently from one of the most widely used standards, MIL-STD-105.

Example 10-7

A shipment of 1,000 semiconductors is to be inspected on a sampling basis. The producer and consumer have agreed to adopt a plan whereby the α risk is limited to 5 percent at AQL $=$ 1 percent defective and the β risk is limited to 10 percent at LTPD $=$ 5 percent defective. Construct the OC curve for the sampling plan $n = 100$, $c \leq 2$ and indicate whether this plan satisfies the requirements.

Solution

To construct the OC curve we must determine the probabilities of acceptance of the shipment for various possible values of the true percent defectives in the population. Since the shipment is accepted when there are ≤ 2 defectives in the sample, the probabilities we seek are $P(c \leq 2)$, given the alternative values of the population. If we were working with a binomial distribution, we could write this probability as

$$P(c \leq 2 \mid n, p) \qquad (10\text{-}5)$$

and obtain the values from a calculator or Appendix E. However, from Fig. 10-3 we note that the binomial probabilities of defectives can be approximated by a Poisson distribution here because the sample size (100) is >20, we appear to be working with a small percent defective of $p < 0.10$, and np looks to be

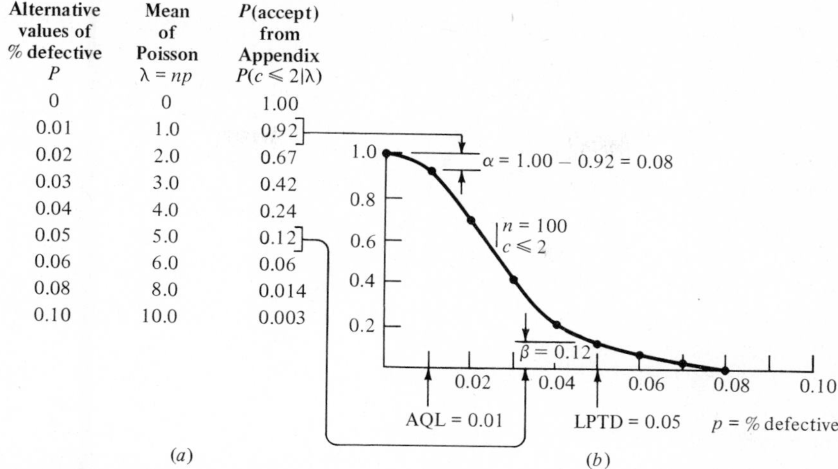

Alternative values of % defective P	Mean of Poisson $\lambda = np$	P(accept) from Appendix $P(c \leq 2 \mid \lambda)$
0	0	1.00
0.01	1.0	0.92
0.02	2.0	0.67
0.03	3.0	0.42
0.04	4.0	0.24
0.05	5.0	0.12
0.06	6.0	0.06
0.08	8.0	0.014
0.10	10.0	0.003

FIGURE 10-8 (a) OC curve values; (b) operating characteristic curve for sampling plan. $n = 100$, with $c \leq 2$.

in the neighborhood of 5. Using Appendix F we can obtain the Poisson probabilities as:

$$P(c \leq 2 \mid \lambda) \tag{10-6}$$

where

c = number of defectives in sample
λ = mean of Poisson distribution $= np$
p = (alternative) percent defectives in population

Thus, for the AQL percentage of $p = 0.01$, we can find the probability of acceptance of the lot as:

$$P(c \leq 2 \mid \lambda)$$

where

$$\lambda = np = (100)(0.01) = 1$$

$\therefore P(c \leq 2 \mid \lambda = 1) = 0.92$ (from Appendix F)

Probabilities for other possible values of the true mean are given in Fig. 10-8(*a*) and these values are plotted as an OC curve in Fig. 10-8(*b*).

Note that this plan ($n = 100$, $c \leq 2$) yields an α risk of 0.08 and a β risk of 0.12. Both exceed the respective limits of 0.05 and 0.10. Since both risks are exceeded, a larger sample size will be required and the calculations will have to be repeated.

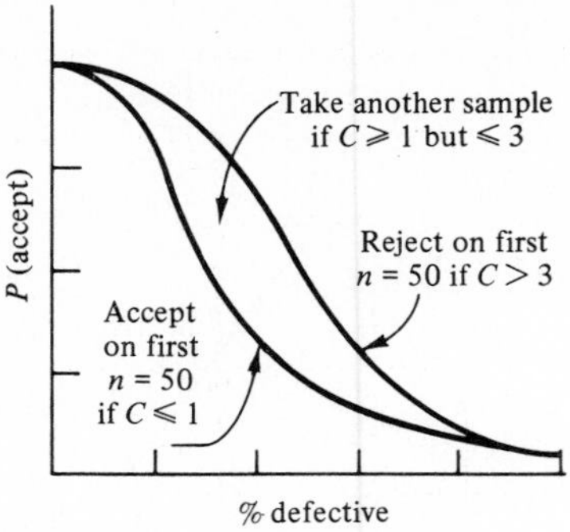

FIGURE 10-9 OC curves for double sampling

In the above example we assumed a sampling plan and then calculated the α and β risk to see if the plan satisfied them. In practice, an improved procedure calls for first establishing an OC curve which satisfies the α and AQL requirement and then substituting various values of n and c until the plan also satisfies β at the LTPD. The widely used MIL-STD-105 follows a different technique in that it identifies a sample size and the various levels of protection available to the producer and consumer depending upon the AQL level specified. Since the AQL does not describe the β risk to the consumer, the MIL-STD-105 makes it necessary to refer to the operating characteristic curves of the various plans to determine what protection the consumer will have. We shall examine the use of MIL-STD-105 after a brief look at double and multiple sampling.

Double and Multiple Sampling

Double or multiple sampling plans are sometimes used to reduce inspection costs. Figures 10-9 and 10-10 illustrate the underlying concepts. With *double sampling*, a smaller sample is drawn first, in hopes that if the lot is either very good or very bad a decision can be made on the basis of the smaller sample at a lesser cost. If the

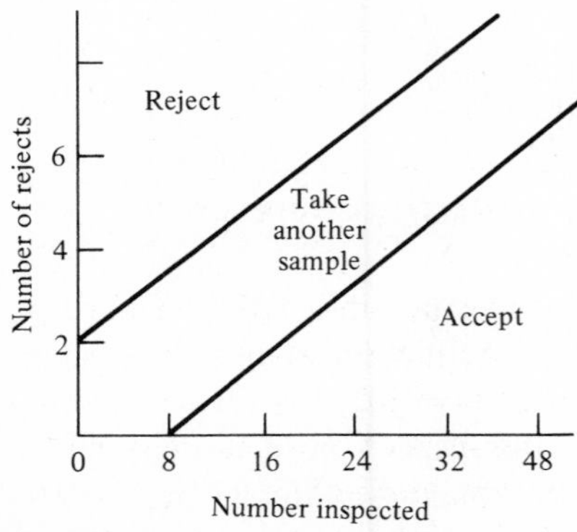

FIGURE 10-10 Sequential sampling

TABLE 10-1 SAMPLE SIZE CODE LETTERS

Lot or batch size			Special inspection levels				General inspection levels		
			S-1	S-2	S-3	S-4	I	II	III
2	to	8	A	A	A	A	A	A	B
9	to	15	A	A	A	A	A	B	C
16	to	25	A	A	B	B	B	C	D
26	to	50	A	B	B	C	C	D	E
51	to	90	B	B	C	C	C	E	F
91	to	150	B	B	C	D	D	F	G
151	to	280	B	C	D	E	E	G	H
281	to	500	B	C	D	E	F	H	J
501	to	1200	C	C	E	F	G	J	K
1201	to	3200	C	D	E	G	H	K	L
3201	to	10000	C	D	F	G	J	L	M
10001	to	35000	C	D	F	H	K	M	N
35001	to	150000	D	E	G	J	L	N	P
150001	to	500000	D	E	G	J	M	P	Q
500001	and	over	D	E	H	K	N	Q	R

Source: [11].

first sample is not decisive a second is drawn and the lot is either accepted or rejected on the basis of the total of the two samples. Figure 10-9 illustrates the preliminary situation in terms of two OC curves.

A *multiple, or sequential, sampling plan* would involve a number of OC curves. Multiple sampling plans use even smaller sample sizes than double sampling plans, for they allow for the drawing of whatever number of samples are necessary to reach a decision.

Figure 10-10 depicts a multiple sampling plan in terms closely related to a decision rule. Using Fig. 10-10, if inspectors found no rejects out of the first dozen items inspected, they would accept the lot. If, however, they had found two rejects by that time, they would continue sampling until the sample results placed the lot in either an "accept" or "reject" classification.

Using MIL-STD-105 Plans for Attributes

The Military Standard Sampling Procedures and Tables for Inspection by Attributes, MIL-STD-105, is available from the U.S. Government Printing Office in Washington, D.C. In addition to single sampling plans which use only one sample, this reference also contains plans for double and multiple sampling.

MIL-STD-105 also allows for three levels of inspection. Level II is for normal inspection, but tables are also provided for situations requiring less discrimination (level I, for cases where a supplier is known to be reliable) as well as for those requiring more discrimination than normal (level III). To illustrate the use of MIL-STD-105 we will need a familiarity with two tables and a chart. Table 10-1 is first

TABLE 10-2 SINGLE SAMPLING PLANS FOR NORMAL INSPECTION

Sample size code letter	Sample size	Acceptable quality levels (normal inspection)																									
		0.010	0.015	0.025	0.040	0.065	0.10	0.15	0.25	0.40	0.65	1.0	1.5	2.5	4.0	6.5	10	15	25	40	65	100	150	250	400	650	1000
		Ac Re	Ac Re	Ac Re	Ac Re	Ac Re	Ac Re	Ac Re	Ac Re	Ac Re	Ac Re	Ac Re	Ac Re	Ac Re	Ac Re	Ac Re	Ac Re	Ac Re	Ac Re	Ac Re	Ac Re	Ac Re	Ac Re	Ac Re	Ac Re	Ac Re	Ac Re
A	2	↓	↓	↓	↓	↓	↓	↓	↓	↓	↓	↓	↓	↓	↓	0 1	↓	↓	1 2	2 3	3 4	5 6	7 8	10 11	14 15	21 22	30 31
B	3	↓	↓	↓	↓	↓	↓	↓	↓	↓	↓	↓	↓	↓	0 1	↑	↓	1 2	2 3	3 4	5 6	7 8	10 11	14 15	21 22	30 31	44 45
C	5	↓	↓	↓	↓	↓	↓	↓	↓	↓	↓	↓	↓	0 1	↑	↓	1 2	2 3	3 4	5 6	7 8	10 11	14 15	21 22	30 31	44 45	↑
D	8	↓	↓	↓	↓	↓	↓	↓	↓	↓	↓	↓	0 1	↑	↓	1 2	2 3	3 4	5 6	7 8	10 11	14 15	21 22	30 31	44 45	↑	↑
E	13	↓	↓	↓	↓	↓	↓	↓	↓	↓	↓	0 1	↑	↓	1 2	2 3	3 4	5 6	7 8	10 11	14 15	21 22	30 31	44 45	↑	↑	↑
F	20	↓	↓	↓	↓	↓	↓	↓	↓	↓	0 1	↑	↓	1 2	2 3	3 4	5 6	7 8	10 11	14 15	21 22	↑	↑	↑	↑	↑	↑
G	32	↓	↓	↓	↓	↓	↓	↓	↓	0 1	↑	↓	1 2	2 3	3 4	5 6	7 8	10 11	14 15	21 22	↑	↑	↑	↑	↑	↑	↑
H	50	↓	↓	↓	↓	↓	↓	↓	0 1	↑	↓	1 2	2 3	3 4	5 6	7 8	10 11	14 15	21 22	↑	↑	↑	↑	↑	↑	↑	↑
J	80	↓	↓	↓	↓	↓	↓	0 1	↑	↓	1 2	2 3	3 4	5 6	7 8	10 11	14 15	21 22	↑	↑	↑	↑	↑	↑	↑	↑	↑
K	125	↓	↓	↓	↓	↓	0 1	↑	↓	1 2	2 3	3 4	5 6	7 8	10 11	14 15	21 22	↑	↑	↑	↑	↑	↑	↑	↑	↑	↑
L	200	↓	↓	↓	↓	0 1	↑	↓	1 2	2 3	3 4	5 6	7 8	10 11	14 15	21 22	↑	↑	↑	↑	↑	↑	↑	↑	↑	↑	↑
M	315	↓	↓	↓	0 1	↑	↓	1 2	2 3	3 4	5 6	7 8	10 11	14 15	21 22	↑	↑	↑	↑	↑	↑	↑	↑	↑	↑	↑	↑
N	500	↓	↓	0 1	↑	↓	1 2	2 3	3 4	5 6	7 8	10 11	14 15	21 22	↑	↑	↑	↑	↑	↑	↑	↑	↑	↑	↑	↑	↑
P	800	↓	0 1	↑	↓	1 2	2 3	3 4	5 6	7 8	10 11	14 15	21 22	↑	↑	↑	↑	↑	↑	↑	↑	↑	↑	↑	↑	↑	↑
Q	1250	0 1	↑	↓	1 2	2 3	3 4	5 6	7 8	10 11	14 15	21 22	↑	↑	↑	↑	↑	↑	↑	↑	↑	↑	↑	↑	↑	↑	↑
R	2000	↑	↑	1 2	2 3	3 4	5 6	7 8	10 11	14 15	21 22	↑	↑	↑	↑	↑	↑	↑	↑	↑	↑	↑	↑	↑	↑	↑	↑

↓ = Use first sampling plan below arrow. If sample size equals, or exceeds, lot or batch size, do 100 percent inspection.
↑ = Use first sampling plan above arrow.
Ac = Acceptance number.
Re = Rejection number.

Source: MIL-STD-105D, *Sampling Procedures and Tables for Inspection by Attributes*, Department of Defense, April 29, 1963.

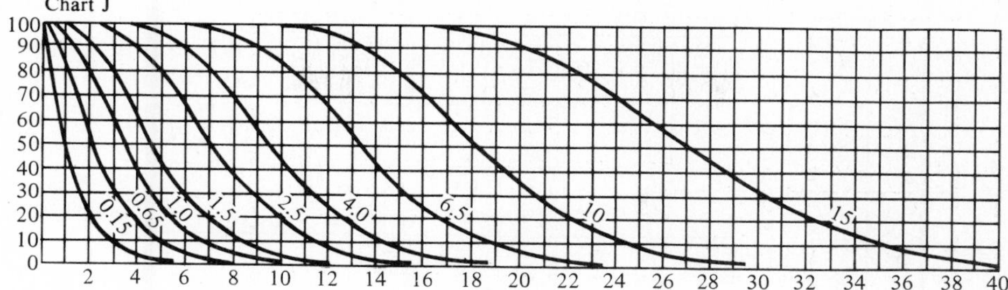

FIGURE 10-11 Operating characteristic curves for single sampling plans. Note that figures on curves are acceptable quality levels (AQLs) for normal inspection. *Source:* Department of Defense, *Sampling Procedures and Tables for Inspection by Attributes*, MIL-STD-105D, table X-J, chart J, April 29, 1963.

used to obtain a sample-size code letter which relates to the inspection level. The special inspection levels S-1 to S-4 are for relatively small sample sizes where large sampling risks can or must be tolerated. Our interest will lie primarily with the general inspection level II.

The code letter from Table 10-1 is then used as an entry point to Table 10-2. Table 10-2 gives the sample size, acceptance numbers (Ac), and rejection numbers (Re) that correspond to various AQL levels. AQL values of 10 and less are expressed in percent defective or in defects per 100 units. Those over 10 are expressed in defects per 100 units only.

Finally, MIL-STD-105 contains operating characteristic curves for each sample-size code letter. Figure 10-11 illustrates one such set of OC curves for code letter J. Note that the same information is given in tabular form in Table 10-3.

Example 10-8

A shipment of 1,000 semiconductors is to be inspected on a sampling basis. The producer and consumer have agreed to use a single sampling plan with an AQL of 1 percent.

(*a*) Select a plan from MIL-STD-105.
(*b*) Obtain the OC curve.
(*c*) For the given plan, what are the actual levels of α at AQL = 1 percent defective and β at a LTPD level of 5 percent defective?

Solution

From Table 10-1, for a lot size of 1,000 and general inspection level II, the sample-size code letter is J.

(*a*) From Table 10-2, for code letter J the sample size is $n = 80$. With a sample size of 80, and an AQL of 1 percent, the lot is accepted if the sample has ≤ 2 defectives and rejected if it has ≥ 3 defectives.

TABLE 10-3 TABULATED VALUES FOR OPERATING CHARACTERISTIC CURVES FOR SINGLE SAMPLING PLANS (CODE LETTER J)

	Acceptable quality levels (normal inspection)																					
P_a	0.15	0.65	1.0	1.5	2.5	4.0	X	6.5	X	10	0.15	0.65	1.0	1.5	2.5	4.0	X	6.5	X	10	X	15
	p (in percent defective)										*p* (in defects per hundred units)											
99.0	0.013	0.188	0.550	1.05	2.30	3.72	4.50	6.13	7.88	9.75	0.013	0.186	0.545	1.03	2.23	3.63	4.38	5.96	7.62	9.35	12.9	15.7
95.0	0.064	0.444	1.03	1.73	3.32	5.06	5.98	7.91	9.89	11.9	0.064	0.444	1.02	1.71	3.27	4.98	5.87	7.71	9.61	11.6	15.6	18.6
90.0	0.132	0.666	1.38	2.20	3.98	5.91	6.91	8.95	11.0	13.2	0.131	0.665	1.38	2.18	3.94	5.82	6.79	8.78	10.8	12.9	17.1	20.3
75.0	0.359	1.202	2.16	3.18	5.30	7.50	8.62	10.9	13.2	15.5	0.360	1.20	2.16	3.17	5.27	7.45	8.55	10.8	13.0	15.3	19.9	23.4
50.0	0.863	2.09	3.33	4.57	7.06	9.55	10.8	13.3	15.8	18.3	0.866	2.10	3.34	4.59	7.09	9.59	10.8	13.3	15.8	18.3	23.3	27.1
25.0	1.72	3.33	4.84	6.31	9.14	11.9	13.3	16.0	18.6	21.3	1.73	3.37	4.90	6.39	9.28	12.1	13.5	16.3	19.0	21.8	27.2	31.2
10.0	2.84	4.78	6.52	8.16	11.3	14.2	15.7	18.6	21.4	24.2	2.88	4.86	6.65	8.35	11.6	14.7	16.2	19.3	22.2	25.2	30.9	35.2
5.0	3.68	5.80	7.66	9.39	12.7	15.8	17.3	20.3	23.2	26.0	3.75	5.93	7.87	9.69	13.1	16.4	18.0	21.2	24.3	27.4	33.4	37.8
1.0	5.59	8.00	10.1	12.0	15.6	18.9	20.5	23.6	26.5	29.5	5.76	8.30	10.5	12.6	16.4	20.0	21.8	25.2	28.5	31.8	38.2	42.9
	0.25	1.0	1.5	2.5	4.0	X	6.5	X	10	X	0.25	1.0	1.5	2.5	4.0	X	6.5	X	10	X	15	X
	Acceptable quality levels (tightened inspection)																					

Source: MIL-STD-105D, *Sampling Procedures and Tables for Inspection by Attributes*, table X-J-1, Department of Defense, April 29, 1963.

(*b*) From Chart J (Fig. 10-11) the OC curve is the one designated 1.0.

(*c*) From the OC curve and tabulated values we can determine the α and β values for percent defective levels of approximately 1 percent and 5 percent. Table 10-3 gives us a fairly close estimate of the value for α and β. Usirg the column AQL = 1 percent, the nearest value to 1 percent defective is 1.03 and:

$$\text{At } p = 1.03, \ P_a = 95.0$$

$\therefore \alpha \cong 1.00 - 0.95 \cong 0.05$. Similarly, from the same column in Table 10-3 the nearest value to 5 percent is 4.84.

$$\text{At } p = 4.84, \ P_a = 25.0$$

$\therefore \beta < 0.25$ (from the OC curve, we might further refine the estimate of β by entering the chart at LTPD = 5 percent defective on the horizontal axis and proceeding up to the curve labeled 1.0 where we find that $\beta \cong 0.23$)

Probabilities given in the MIL-STD-105 tables of AQLs of less than 10 and sample sizes of 80 or less are based upon the binomial distribution. For sample sizes larger than 80 the Poisson approximation is used. The Poisson distribution is also used for all AQLs of greater than 10 regardless of the sample size.

Sampling Plans for Variables

Variables plans entail measurements, on a continuous scale, of how closely a given variable conforms to a specified characteristic. It is often reasonable to assume that these measurements follow a normal distribution, but even if they do not, the distribution of the means of samples of the measurements does approach normality, especially if they contain 30 or more observations.

The objectives and risks involved in variables sampling are similar to those in attributes sampling. However, in constructing the variables sampling plan we must determine sample size and some maximum or minimum measurement (reject limit c) or both, rather than simply an acceptable percentage of defectives. In this case, the reject limit c controls the producers α or consumers β risk or it controls both α and β. The problem is to determine a reject limit that is an appropriate number of standard deviations above or below a specified mean value such that the probabilities of rejecting good lots (if concerned with α only) or accepting bad lots (if concerned with β only), or both, are limited. In our first example, below, we shall specify a single quality level and determine the reject limit that is required to control the α risk, given a preassigned sample size. (We could alternatively have specified the reject limit and solved for the sample size, for the two are intimately related.) This will be followed by an example specifying two quality levels that results in control of both

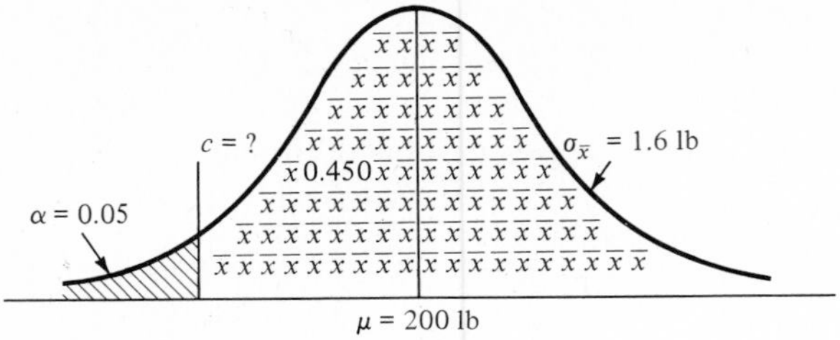

FIGURE 10-12 Sampling distribution of means (for samples of $n = 25$)

α and β risk. In this latter example, the specification of both risks will fully determine the reject limit c and the sample size n.

Example 10-9 (given α risk only: solving for c)

A metals firm produces titanium castings whose weights are normally distributed with a standard deviation of $\sigma = 8$ lb. Casting shipments averaging less than 200 lb are considered poor quality and the firm would like to minimize such shipments.

Design a sampling plan for a sample of $n = 25$ that will limit the risk of rejecting lots that average 200 lb to 5 percent.

Solution

The problem situation is described schematically in Fig. 10-12, which assumes that the distribution of sample means is approximately normal with mean $\mu = 200$ and standard error:

$$\sigma_{\bar{x}} = \frac{\sigma}{\sqrt{n}} = \frac{8}{\sqrt{25}} = 1.6\text{ lb}$$

The limit c is then:

$$c = \mu - Z\sigma_{\bar{x}}$$

where

$$\begin{aligned} Z &= \text{value corresponding to area of } 0.450 \\ &= 1.64 \text{ (from Appendix D)} \end{aligned}$$

$$\therefore c = 200 - 1.64(1.6) = 197.4\text{ lb}$$

Plan Take a random sample of $n = 25$ ingots and determine the mean weight. If $\bar{x} > 197.4$ lb accept the shipment; otherwise reject it.

In the preceding example, with the limit set at 197.4 lb, the risk of rejecting a lot that really averages 200 lb (a good lot) is limited to 5 percent. The plan was

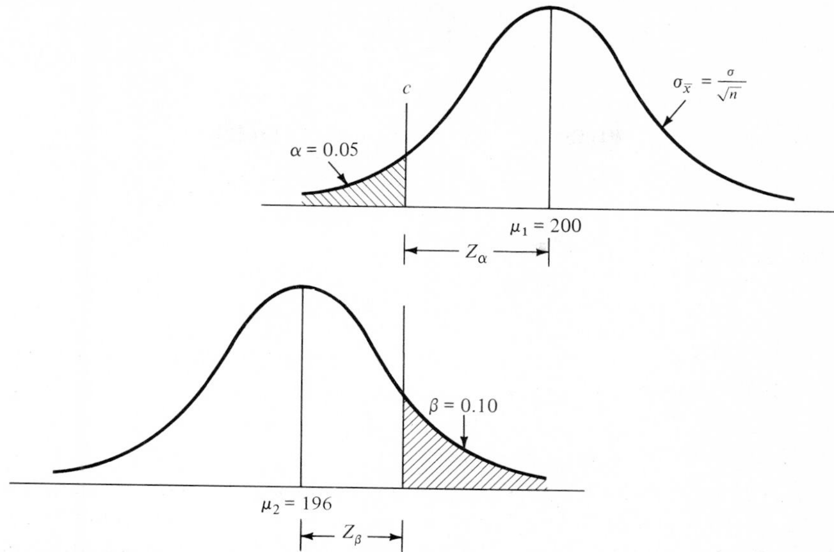

FIGURE 10-13 Sampling distributions where σ and β are specified

established wholly on the basis of the α risk and a given sample size. A larger sample size would, of course, be more discriminating. For example, with a sample of $n = 100$ the reject limit could be raised to 198.7 lb.

Example 10-10 (given α and β risk: solving for n and c)

A metals firm produces titanium castings whose weights are normally distributed with a standard deviation of $\sigma = 8.0$ lb. Casting shipments averaging 200 lb are good quality and those averaging 196 lb are poor quality. Design a sampling plan so that:

(*a*) The probability of rejecting a lot with an average weight of 200 lb is 0.05.
(*b*) The probability of accepting a lot with an average weight of 196 lb is 0.10.

Solution

The problem situation is described schematically in Fig. 10-13. The solution procedure is to first set up simultaneous equations defining the reject limit c in terms of Z standard errors. Then solve for n and substitute it back into either one of the equations to find c. The two equations locating c are:

$$(a) \quad \textit{From above: } c = \mu_1 - Z_\alpha \frac{\sigma}{\sqrt{n}} = 200 - 1.645 \frac{(8)}{\sqrt{n}}$$

$$(b) \quad \textit{From below: } c = \mu_2 + Z_\beta \frac{\sigma}{\sqrt{n}} = 196 + 1.28 \frac{(8)}{\sqrt{n}}$$

Setting the two equations for c equal to each other:

$$200 - 1.645 \frac{(8)}{\sqrt{n}} = 196 + 1.28 \frac{(8)}{\sqrt{n}}$$

$$n = \left(\frac{23.40}{4}\right)^2 = 34$$

$$\therefore c = 200 - 1.645 \frac{(8)}{\sqrt{34}} = 197.7 \text{ lb}$$

Plan Take a random sample of $n = 34$ ingots and determine the mean weight. If $\bar{x} > 197.7$ lb accept the shipment; otherwise reject it.

The above examples assumed that the shipment standard deviation σ was known. When σ is unknown, the sample standard deviation s is usually an acceptable substitute. However, some authorities [**5**] recommend that a larger sample size be used to compensate for the inherent uncertainty.

Just as MIL-STD-105 and other standard plans are available for attributes sampling, so too there are a number of standard plans available for variables. MIL-STD-414 is a widely disseminated standard for variables plans that contains plans for both situations where σ is known and where it is unknown [**12**, **3**: 436]. In the former case the sampling plan is based upon the sample mean, and in the latter upon the sample standard deviation. MIL-STD-414 also contains plans based upon the sample range. Like the attributes standard, MIL-STD-414 includes an option of several levels of inspection and yields an upper and lower specification limit for the measurement being controlled.

ECONOMICS OF SAMPLING: AOQ, ASN, ATI, AND BAYES

The sample size n and acceptance limits c are not the only characteristics of interest in a sampling plan. Often, when inspection activities reveal defects they are then removed. What then is the quality level of the resultant lot after the "purified" sample is returned? This and other questions can be answered by constructing other curves describing a sampling plan. Three such curves, the AOQ, ASN, and ATI are described briefly below [**3**: 430]. A more detailed discussion of these curves may be found in Burr [**2**].

The *average outgoing quality* (AOQ) curve shows the expected quality in all outgoing lots after the rejected lots from the sample have been 100 percent inspected and all defectives removed. The AOQ curve reflects the fact that incoming lots with a small percentage of defects will be passed with a resultant high outgoing quality.

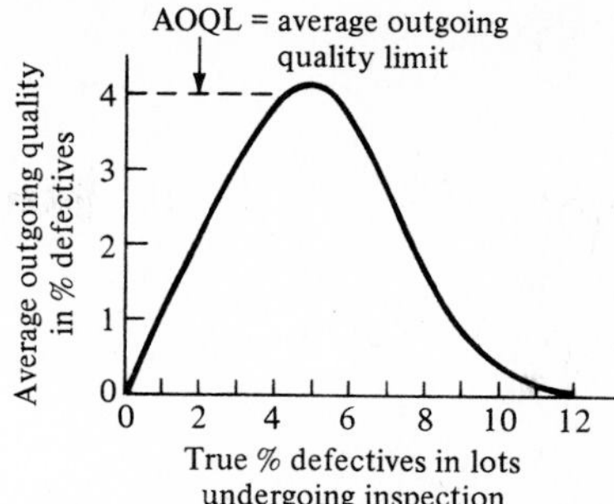

FIGURE 10-14 Typical AOQ curve

Those with a slightly larger proportion of defects will result in the worst level of outgoing quality because lots that have a large proportion of defects will end up undergoing 100 percent inspection with only the acceptable items being passed.

The shape of a typical AOQ curve is illustrated in Fig. 10-14. Values for the ordinate of the curve represent the percentage of defectives (P_D) in lots of size N after inspection. They can be computed from the equation.

$$\text{AOQ} = \frac{P_D P_A (N - n)}{N} \tag{10-7}$$

where P_A is the probability of accepting the lot for various values of the percent defective (from the OC curve) and n is the sample size.

Example 10-11

An OC curve reveals that lots with a true percentage of defectives of 2 percent have a probability of being accepted of $P_A = 0.67$. If the sampling plan for lots of $N = 1{,}000$ called for samples of size $n = 100$, what would be the average outgoing quality (AOQ) level?

Solution

$$\text{AOQ} = \frac{P_D P_A (N - n)}{N}$$

$$= \frac{(0.02)(0.67)(1{,}000 - 100)}{1{,}000}$$

$$= 0.012$$

In the above example, since the sample size is $n = 100$ and 2 percent of the items in the sample are defective (on the average), then the 2 defective items

> would be removed from the sample and replaced before the lot was allowed to continue on its way. For lots of $N = 1{,}000$ items, the number of defects would then be reduced to 2 percent of the 900 uninspected items. This amounts to 18 in 1,000, or 1.8 percent of the items. Since the probability of acceptance of a lot of 2 percent defectives is (from the OC curve) only 0.67, then the expected value or average outgoing quality level for lots (of 2 percent defective) is (0.67)(1.8 percent) or 1.2 percent defective.

In similar manner, numbers could be computed for other possible values of the true percent defectives. Upon plotting, these values would take a shape similar to that shown in Fig. 10-14. The highest (worst) percentage defective for outgoing quality is known as the average outgoing quality limit (AOQL).

The *average sample number* (ASN) curve applies to double and multiple sampling plans and also depends upon the quality of the incoming lot. This curve reveals the average number of items that must be inspected before a decision can be made to accept or reject the lot.

The *average total inspection* (ATI) curve shows the average total amount of inspection in a given lot, including both the original sample and follow-up 100 percent inspection required.

As we saw in Fig. 10-2, producers and consumers are often forced to accept the risks associated with decisions based upon samples in order to minimize the overall quality control costs. Whereas we have used statistical techniques to find the optimal sample size required to limit risks to a given level, we have not related the risk to a production or marketing cost of passing defectives, nor the sample size to a cost of sampling. In this sense, we have taken a classical approach of assuming a given risk (for example, $\alpha = 0.05$) and solving the problem from there, rather than asking how one might originally establish the risk level. In the past, many managers have set risk levels on an intuitive or judgmental basis. This has supposedly incorporated knowledge of the production process requirements, knowledge of costs, experience with suppliers and customers, etc. Today many organizations are still making judgmental decisions in this area, but Bayesian and other techniques of analysis are lending greater insight into such decisions. They are also introducing sampling costs into the analysis in a much more explicit manner. The Bayesian material is beyond the scope of this text, but for further development the reader is referred to a well-done text by Jedamus and Frame [**9**].

CONTROL OF PROCESS QUALITY

Control charts were introduced to industry by Walter Shewhart in the middle 1920s. They are statistically designed devices used to record selected quality characteristics of a production process over time. In contrast to acceptance sampling, control charts measure variation of the process during operation rather than the acceptability of materials or products before or after operations.

Control charts help to ensure that only acceptable goods or services are produced by monitoring the process average, which is expected to stay within the bounds of upper and lower statistical limits. If the process average falls outside the limits this indicates the process is out of control and suggests some identifiable cause is responsible. In effect, control charts are standards upon which measurements are recorded so that corrective action may be taken when necessary.

In this section we consider the problem of process variability and how control charts for variables and attributes can be designed and used to control quality.

TOLERANCE LIMITS OF A PROCESS

Almost any human or machine activity has some inherent variation. Consider anything around you—your own weight, the accuracy of your watch, even the exact dimension of the pages in this book. We tend to accept minor variations as inherent and consider them random, for although they obviously have a cause, we are not interested in or perhaps are not capable of assigning a cause to them. Variations in product quality that arise from random factors or so-called unassignable causes are usually not of major concern to quality control managers. Their interest lies primarily in identifying and correcting assignable causes, such as excessive tool wear, improper materials, and so forth.

Many production processes have empirically been found to exhibit a "natural" variability that is normally distributed. For example, the diameters of one-half-inch rods, when measured to an accuracy of one-thousandth of an inch, can be expected to vary in a normal manner about the mean dimension of 0.500 inches. When this is the case, we say the process has natural tolerance limits such that 99.7 percent of the individual items will lie within 3σ of their mean. The upper natural tolerance limit (T_{UN}) and lower natural tolerance limit (T_{LN}) are then:

$$T_{UN} = \mu + 3\sigma \tag{10-8}$$

$$T_{LN} = \mu - 3\sigma \tag{10-9}$$

Knowledge of the natural tolerance limits of a process can be useful to design engineers, production analysts, and marketing personnel for ensuring the proper application of a product. But natural tolerance limits are *not* the control limits used in a production process. *Control limits* do not rely upon the underlying normality of the production process for they *are based upon the distribution of sample means—and sample proportions*—not individual values. We now turn to an examination of the construction and use of control charts, looking first at charts for variables, and then at charts for attributes.

CONTROL CHARTS FOR VARIABLES

Control charts for variables are used to monitor processes by recording measurements of the central tendency (mean) and dispersion of the variable of interest. A

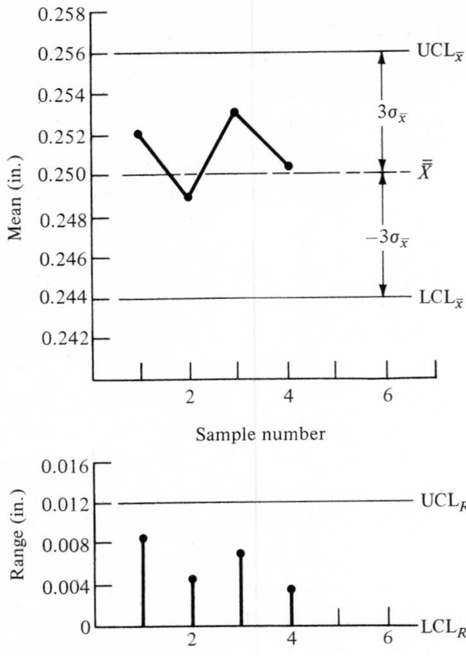

FIGURE 10-15 Control chart (variables)

control chart of means is called an $\bar{X}$ chart and the most common (and simplest) chart for dispersion is a range R chart. Many processes use both charts. Figure 10-15 illustrates a variables chart for both, where the means and ranges of four hypothetical samples have been recorded. Note that the control limits for the sample means are:

$$UCL_{\bar{X}} = \bar{\bar{X}} + 3\sigma_{\bar{X}} \tag{10-10}$$

$$LCL_{\bar{X}} = \bar{\bar{X}} - 3\sigma_{\bar{X}} \tag{10-11}$$

where $\bar{\bar{X}}$ is the mean of the sample means ($\bar{X}$'s). Since $\sigma_{\bar{X}}$ is often unknown, $s_{\bar{X}}$ serves as an estimator of $\sigma_{\bar{X}}$.

In practice, the calculation of control limits is simplified by the use of tables based upon range values rather than standard deviations [**2**]. For example, one factor (d_2) has been derived, which, when divided into the average sample range $\bar{R}$, serves as an approximation of the population standard deviation. This factor is then combined with other constants in the control limit equation to yield another factor (A):

$$UCL_{\bar{X}} = \bar{\bar{X}} + 3\frac{\sigma}{\sqrt{n}} = \bar{\bar{X}} + \frac{3}{\sqrt{n}}\frac{\bar{R}}{d_2} = \bar{\bar{X}} + A\bar{R}$$

In addition to the above A factor for means, other factors have been developed for the upper limit B and lower limit C of the range. These factors are given in Table 10-4.

TABLE 10-4 FACTORS FOR COMPUTING CONTROL LIMITS

Sample size n	Mean factor A	Upper range B	Lower range C
2	1.880	3.268	0
3	1.023	2.574	0
4	0.729	2.282	0
5	0.577	2.114	0
6	0.483	2.004	0
7	0.419	1.924	0.076
8	0.373	1.864	0.136
9	0.337	1.816	0.184
10	0.308	1.777	0.223
12	0.266	1.716	0.284
14	0.235	1.671	0.329
16	0.212	1.636	0.364
18	0.194	1.608	0.392
20	0.180	1.586	0.414
25	0.153	1.541	0.459

Source: Adapted from and used with permission of "Quality Control of Materials," Special Technical Publication 15-C, pp. 63, 72, American Society for Testing Materials, Philadelphia, 1951.

Using Table 10-4, control limits for means and ranges are:

$$\text{Mean:} \quad UCL_{\overline{X}} = \overline{\overline{X}} + A\overline{R} \tag{10-12}$$

$$LCL_{\overline{X}} = \overline{\overline{X}} - A\overline{R} \tag{10-13}$$

$$\text{Range:} \quad UCL_R = B\overline{R} \tag{10-14}$$

$$LCL_R = C\overline{R} \tag{10-15}$$

The procedure for establishing and using control limits is much like setting any other standard from empirical data:

1 Select the job to be controlled; identify the relevant characteristics and method of measurement.

2 Take approximately 20 samples of size n and compute the sample means $\overline{X}$'s and ranges R. Plot the $\overline{X}$ and R points on a chart. Note that sample sizes of $n = 4$ or 5 are frequently used. See [**5**].

3 Compute the mean and range control limits (per Equations 10-12 through 10-15) and plot them on the same chart.

4 Discard any samples with means or ranges outside the control limits and recalculate the mean and range control limits.

5 Evaluate the economic feasibility of the limits. If satisfactory, place them on standard forms for the job and begin regular sampling activities.

6 Investigate for assignable causes when the process is out of control as evidenced by:
   (*a*) An $\bar{X}$ or R point outside the control limits
   (*b*) A predominance of $\bar{X}$ points on one side of the center $\bar{\bar{X}}$ line
   (*c*) Any two points in a row at a location of $>\frac{2}{3}$ of the distance to a control limit

Example 10-12

A precision casting process is designed to produce blades having a diameter of 10.000 ± 0.025 centimeters. To establish control limits, 20 samples of $n = 5$ blades are randomly selected from the first 500 blades produced as follows:

Sample 1	Sample 2	...	Sample 20
10.010	10.018		10.004
9.989	9.992		9.988
10.019	9.996		9.990
9.978	10.014		10.019
10.008	10.005		9.983
50.004	50.025		49.984
$\bar{X}$ = 10.0008	10.0050	...	9.9968
R = 0.041	0.026	...	0.036

The grand mean $\bar{\bar{X}}$ of the sample means and mean of the sample ranges $\bar{R}$ were found to be:

$$\bar{\bar{X}} = \frac{\sum \bar{X}\text{'s}}{\text{no. samples}} = \frac{10.0008 + 10.0050 + \cdots + 9.9968}{20} = 10.002 \text{ cm}$$

$$\bar{R} = \frac{\sum R\text{'s}}{\text{no. samples}} = \frac{0.041 + 0.026 + \cdots + 0.036}{20} = 0.032 \text{ cm}$$

(*a*) Find the control limits for the sample means.
(*b*) Find the control limits for the sample ranges.

Solution

(*a*) Mean:

$$UCL_{\bar{X}} = \bar{\bar{X}} + A\bar{R} = 10.002 + 0.577(0.032) = 10.020 \text{ cm}$$
$$\text{Center} = \bar{\bar{X}} = 10.002 \text{ cm}$$
$$LCL_{\bar{X}} = \bar{\bar{X}} - A\bar{R} = 10.002 - 0.577(0.032) = 9.984 \text{ cm}$$

(*b*) Range:

$$UCL_R = B\bar{R} = (2.114)(0.032) = 0.068 \text{ cm}$$
$$\text{Center} = \bar{R} = 0.032 \text{ cm}$$
$$LCL_R = C\bar{R} = (0.000)(0.032) = 0.000 \text{ cm}$$

CONTROL CHARTS FOR ATTRIBUTES

Control plans for attributes typically rest upon classification of an item as defective or nondefective. The charts are referred to as "p charts for fraction defective." Since this dichotomous classification does not include any measurement of variation, attributes charts do not include anything comparable to the R charts derived from the range in variables sampling. In other respects, however, the attributes chart is similar to variables, for the control limits are set at three standard errors (σ_p's) away from the mean of all possible values of the fraction defective π. And again since σ_p and π are unknown, the estimators derived from the sample data s_p and p are used:[1]

$$UCL_p = p + 3s_p \tag{10-16}$$

$$LCL_p = p - 3s_p \tag{10-17}$$

where

$$p = \frac{\text{number of defectives}}{\text{total number of items}}$$

$$s_p = \sqrt{\frac{pq}{n}}$$

$$n = \text{sample size}$$

Example 10-13

A sportswear firm has set up for automated production of a line of sweaters. Twenty samples of size $n = 50$ are to be withdrawn randomly during the first week of production in order to establish control limits for the process. Defects remain in the shipment but bring less revenue for they eventually sell as "seconds." The defectives detected in the 20 samples are shown in Table 10-5. Compute the control limits for this process.

[1] Since p is often the mean value of the proportion from several samples, it is sometimes denoted as $\bar{p}$. However, it can simply be considered a proportion in its own right (but based upon more observations), and maintaining the symbol as p preserves the consistency with earlier portions of the text.

TABLE 10-5 DEFECTIVE ITEMS IN 20 SAMPLES OF $n = 50$ SWEATERS

Sample number	Number defectives	Percent defective
1	2	0.04
2	3	0.06
3	4	0.08
4	1	0.02
5	0	0.00
6	2	0.04
7	4	0.08
8	1	0.02
9	1	0.02
10	3	0.06
11	0	0.00
12	1	0.02
13	2	0.04
14	1	0.02
15	0	0.00
16	3	0.06
17	7	0.14
18	2	0.04
19	1	0.02
20	2	0.04
Total	40	

Solution

$$UCL_p = p + 3s_p$$

where

$$p = \frac{\text{number of defectives}}{\text{total number of items}} = \frac{40}{50 \times 20} = 0.040$$

$$s_p = \sqrt{\frac{pq}{n}} = \sqrt{\frac{(0.040)(0.960)}{50}} = 0.028$$

$$UCL_p = 0.040 + 3(0.028) = 0.124$$

$$LCL_p = p - 3s_p = 0.040 - 3(0.028) = 0.000$$

Using these limits, a preliminary chart is constructed and the data points plotted as shown in Fig. 10-16.

Note that the fraction defective in sample 17 is outside the upper control limit. Suppose the reason for this is investigated and the cause is found to be that a new machine was phased in at that point before receiving final adjustments

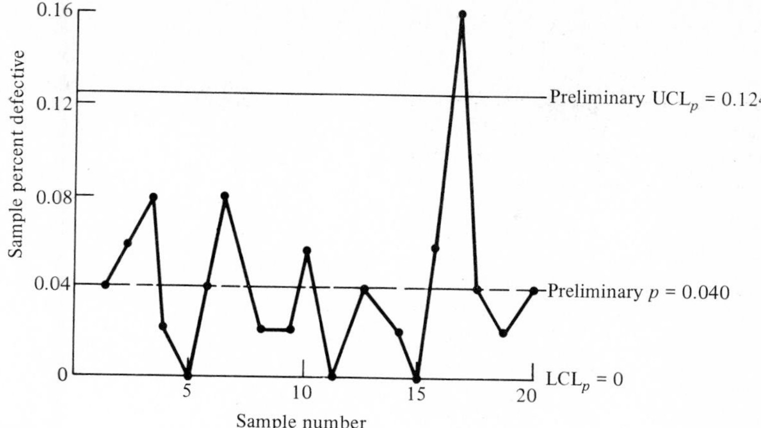

FIGURE 10-16 Control chart (attributes)

from a mechanic. This data point is then discarded and a new value for p and new control limits are calculated.

$$p = \frac{33}{50 \times 19} = 0.0347$$

$$s_p = \sqrt{\frac{(0.0347)(0.9653)}{50}} = 0.0259$$

$$UCL_p = 0.0347 + 3(0.0259) = 0.112$$

$$LCL_p = 0.0347 - 3(0.0259) = 0.000$$

None of the remaining sample values fall outside the new limits so these limits become the standard for controlling the process in the future.

QUALITY CONTROL IN MULTINATIONAL ORGANIZATIONS

From the initial pages of this chapter we have continuously related the concept of quality to the idea of specified standards. In some cases these standards result from competitive pressures and sometimes they are even embodied in state and national laws. For example some state laws control the quality of soft drink cans and our federal government has established national quality controls governing automobile exhaust.

Multinational firms producing for foreign markets must be keenly aware of local standards for they can vary widely from one country to another and from one year to the next. It is not prudent to assume that an outstanding product in one country can automatically be produced and sold in another country. Legal standards of quality may vary and the penalties for noncompliance may be severe. Product warranties are not enforced to the same extent. In summary, all quality control policies should receive careful review and thorough consideration before being implemented on an international basis.

SUMMARY

Quality is a measure of how closely a good or service conforms to specified standards. It is not changed by the location of the application or subjective preference of the consumer. Control activities over incoming raw materials and outgoing finished products generally take the form of acceptance sampling, whereas those performed during a process often use control charts. The optimal amount of control effort, from an economic standpoint, is where the total of inspection and control plus defective product costs is minimized.

Acceptance sampling activities rely heavily upon knowledge of the statistical properties of the population. Quality characteristics of individual items can often be deduced from a knowledge that the parent population is distributed as a hypergeometric, binomial, Poisson, or normal distribution.

Acceptance sampling procedures often take the form of a sampling plan (or decision rule) which specifies both how large a sample n to take and what the allowable measurement or percentage of defectives c in the sample is to be. Sampling plans for attributes are based upon classification of an item as defective or nondefective, whereas variables plans require a measurement of the characteristic in question. Both types of plans can be expressed as operating characteristic (OC) curves which show the probability that the given plan will accept a lot as a function of the actual (unknown) quality level.

To completely specify a sampling plan, the producer and consumer should agree on the producer's risk α at the acceptable quality level (AQL) and the consumer's risk β at the lot tolerance percent defective (LTPD) level. Varying the acceptance number c will change the shape of the OC curve and shift the risk, but the only way to reduce both α and β risks simultaneously is to increase the sample size. MIL-STD-105 is a widely used standard for selecting attributes plans. For a given sample size, it includes several OC curves, leaving it to the users to select the AQL level that will provide the most desirable limits of α and β risk.

Variables plans also offer the opportunity of controlling α and β risks by establishing a sample size n and reject limit c based upon the known normality of the distribution of sample means. The n and c values are determined by solving a pair of equations locating c from both the AQL point and the LTPD point.

Control charts are used to make inference about the current process quality on the basis of an ongoing series of random samples. Variables charts monitor processes by recording mean $\bar{x}$ and range R values, whereas attributes charts are set up to control the percent defective p. In both cases, the upper (UCL) and lower

(LCL) control limits are set at a distance of three standard errors ($s_{\bar{x}}$ or s_p respectively) away from the mean of the sample means $\overline{\overline{X}}$ or sample proportions p. A sample value outside the control limits suggests that some assignable cause of the variation exists and constitutes a call for identification and corrective action.

SOLVED PROBLEMS

OBJECTIVES OF QUALITY CONTROL

1 The marketing manager of Roller Bearings International (RBI) estimates that "defective bearings that get into the hands of industrial users cost RBI an average of \$20 each" in replacement costs and lost business. The production manager counters that "the bearings are only about 2 percent defective now, and the best a sampling plan could do would be to reduce that to 1 percent defective—but not much better (unless we go to 100 percent inspection)." Should RBI adopt a sampling plan if it cost

(*a*) \$.10/bearing?
(*b*) \$.25/bearing?
(*c*) How much/bearing can RBI afford to spend on inspection costs before it begins to lose money on inspections?

Solution

For purposes of illustration, assume all comparisons are based upon a lot of 100 bearings.

(*a*) Without inspection — Defect cost = 100(0.02)(\$20/brg) = \$40

With inspection — Inspect cost = 100(\$.10/brg) = \$10
Defect cost = 100(0.01)(\$20/brg) = \$20 → \$30
Advantage from inspection = \$10 = \$.10/brg

(*b*) Without inspection — Defect cost = \$40
With inspection — Inspect cost = 100(\$.25/brg) = \$25
Defect cost = \$20 → \$45
Disadvantage from inspection = \$ 5 = \$.05/brg

(*c*) Let x = the inspection cost per bearing. Then the minimum cost is where:

$$\text{Defect cost without inspect} = \text{inspect cost} + \text{defect cost with inspect}$$

$$100(0.02)(\$20/\text{brg}) = x(100) + (100)(0.01)(\$20/\text{brg})$$

$$x = \frac{40 - 20}{100} = \$.20/\text{brg}$$

ACCEPTANCE SAMPLING OF INCOMING AND OUTGOING QUALITY

2 Xistor Radio Company wishes to make performance tests on some finished radios. The quality control inspector has randomly selected five radios. In how many ways can radios be selected for three tests if:

(*a*) Any radio can be used for any or all of the tests so both duplication and different order of selection count as a different way (*multiple choices*)?

(*b*) No radio can be used for more than one test, but the order of selection makes a difference (*permutations*)?

(*c*) No radio can be used for more than one test and the order of selection of the radios does not count (*combinations*)?

Solution

Let $x = 3$ radios chosen from $n = 5$ radios.

(*a*) Multiple choices

$$N^x = 5^3 = 5 \cdot 5 \cdot 5 = 125 \text{ ways}$$

(*b*) Permutations

$$P_x^n = \frac{n!}{(n-x)!} = \frac{5!}{(5-3)!} = \frac{5 \cdot 4 \cdot 3 \cdot 2 \cdot 1}{2 \cdot 1} = 60 \text{ ways}$$

(*c*) Combinations

$$C_x^n = \frac{n!}{x!\,(n-x)!} = \frac{5!}{3!\,(5-3)!} = \frac{5 \cdot 4 \cdot 3 \cdot 2 \cdot 1}{3 \cdot 2 \cdot 1 \cdot 2 \cdot 1} = 10 \text{ ways}$$

3 A shipment of 10 items left the manufacturer with 3 defectives. The consumer's quality control department usually inspects two items from each shipment.

(*a*) In how many ways can it choose the sample of two?

(*b*) If it inspects the first two and finds only one defective, what is the probability of finding another defective if it inspects one more?

Solution

(*a*) $$C_2^{10} = \frac{n!}{X!\,(n-x)!} = \frac{10!}{2!\,(10-2)!} = \frac{10 \cdot 9 \cdot 8!}{2 \cdot 8!} = 45 \text{ ways}$$

(*b*) P(defective on 3d | defective on 1st, good on 2d)

$$P(D_3 \mid D_1G_2) = \frac{\text{successful ways}}{\text{total ways}} = \frac{\text{2 remaining defectives}}{\text{8 remaining items}} = \tfrac{1}{4}$$

4 Which probability distribution will yield an appropriate answer in a reasonable amount of time if we wish to know the probability of getting 10 or fewer defects in a sample of 400 from a population that is 1 percent defective?

(*a*) hypergeometric (*c*) normal (*e*) Student *t*
(*b*) binomial (*d*) Poisson

Solution

$$n = 400 = >20$$

$$np = (400)(0.01) = 4 = <5$$

$$p = 0.01 = <0.10$$

Poisson distribution is appropriate

$$P(X \leq 10 \mid \lambda = 4) = 0.997 \text{ (from Appendix F)}$$

5 In an industrial plant, the mean weight of a certain packaged chemical is $\mu =$ 82.0 kg and standard deviation is $\sigma = 4.0$ kg. If a sample of $n = 64$ packages is drawn from the population for inspection, find the probability that

(*a*) An *individual package* in the sample will exceed 82.5 kg. (Assume that the population is normally distributed for this part.)

(*b*) The *sample mean* will exceed 82.5 kg.

Solution

(*a*)
$$Z = \frac{x - \mu}{\sigma} = \frac{82.5 - 82.0}{4} = 0.125$$

$$P(Z) = 0.050 \quad \text{(Appendix D)}$$

$$P(X > 82.5) = 0.500 - 0.050 = 0.450$$

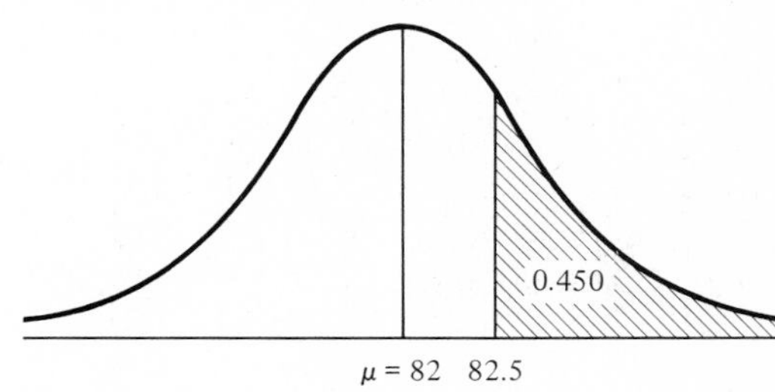

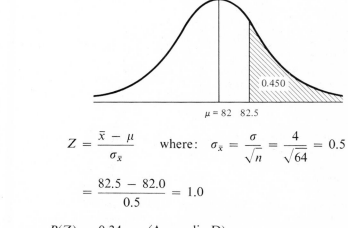

(*b*)
$$Z = \frac{\bar{x} - \mu}{\sigma_{\bar{x}}} \quad \text{where: } \sigma_{\bar{x}} = \frac{\sigma}{\sqrt{n}} = \frac{4}{\sqrt{64}} = 0.5$$

$$= \frac{82.5 - 82.0}{0.5} = 1.0$$

$$P(Z) = 0.34 \quad \text{(Appendix D)}$$

$$P(\bar{x} > 82.5) = 0.50 - 0.34 = 0.16$$

Note that this example illustrates the concept of a *sampling distribution* as used in quality control work. The probability of getting a sample mean more than one-half kg away from the true mean is substantially less than the chance of getting an individual value (a 16 percent versus a 45 percent chance).[2]

CONTROL OF PROCESS QUALITY

6 Nuclear Fuel Company manufactures uranium pellets to a specified diameter of 0.500 ± 0.005 cm. In 25 random samples of 9 pellets each, the overall mean of the means ($\overline{\overline{X}}$) and range $\overline{R}$ were found to be 0.501 cm and 0.003 cm respectively. Construct an $\overline{X}$ and R chart which includes the specified tolerances.

Solution

$$UCL_{\bar{x}} = \overline{\overline{X}} + A\overline{R} = 0.501 + (0.337)(0.003) = 0.502$$
$$LCL_{\bar{x}} = \overline{\overline{X}} - A\overline{R} = 0.501 - (0.337)(0.003) = 0.500$$
$$UCL_R = B\overline{R} = (1.816)(0.003) = 0.0054$$
$$LCL_R = C\overline{R} = (0.184)(0.003) = 0.0006$$

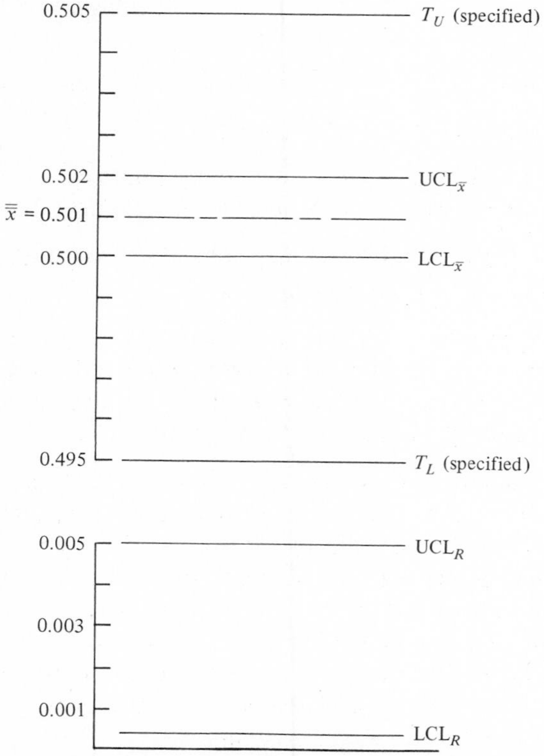

0.505 — T_U (specified)

0.502 — $UCL_{\bar{x}}$

$\overline{\overline{x}} = 0.501$

0.500 — $LCL_{\bar{x}}$

0.495 — T_L (specified)

0.005 — UCL_R

0.003

0.001

LCL_R

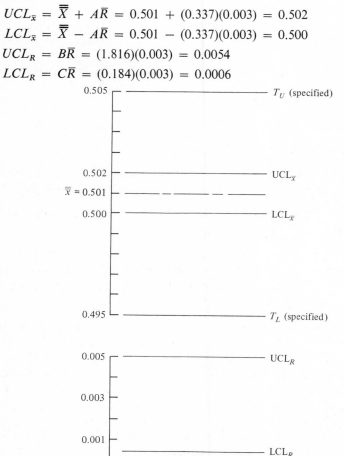

[2] For means, the standard error ($\sigma_{\bar{x}}$) is obtained by dividing the standard deviation (σ) by $\sqrt{n}$. Thus $\sigma_{\bar{x}} = \sigma/\sqrt{n}$. For proportions, the standard error (σ_p) is obtained by dividing the standard deviation ($\sqrt{npq}$) by n. Thus $\sigma_p = \sqrt{npq/n^2} = \sqrt{pq/n}$. Multiplying the standard error ($\sqrt{pq/n}$) by n yields a standard deviation in terms of number ($\sqrt{npq}$).

7 A daily sample of 30 items was taken over a period of 14 days in order to establish attributes control limits. If 21 defectives were found, what should be the LCL_p and UCL_p?

Solution

$$p = \frac{\text{no. of defectives}}{\text{total observations}} = \frac{21}{420} = 0.05$$

$$s_p = \sqrt{\frac{pq}{n}} = \sqrt{\frac{(0.05)(0.95)}{30}} = 0.04$$

$$UCL_p = p + 3s_p = 0.05 + 3(0.04) = 0.17$$

$$LCL_p = p - 3s_p = 0.05 - 3(0.04) = 0$$

QUESTIONS

10-1 Define quality. What is the purpose of quality control activities?

10-2 What constitutes a "quality" painting?

10-3 What major cost components make up the total costs associated with quality? Which components do you feel are the most difficult to quantify? Why?

10-4 Distinguish between quality control activities based upon deductive logic and those based upon inductive logic.

10-5 Discuss the role of statistical distributions in acceptance sampling. From an acceptance sampling standpoint, how do the hypergeometric, binomial, Poisson, and normal distributions differ? (Do not answer the question by simply expressing an equation for the distribution.)

10-6 A box containing 18 transducers (including 3 defectives) is stored on a spaceship before a long voyage. After getting under way, pairs of $n = 2$ are withdrawn and installed periodically. If only one defective is found in the first two pairs, which probability distribution would be suitable for calculating the probability of a defective transducer in the next pair? Why? Suppose the variable of interest were the number of flaws in the surface finish of the transducers (which is normally very few but could range from zero to several hundred). Now, which probability distribution would apply for predicting the number of flaws in the surface finish?

10-7 How do sampling plans for attributes differ from those for variables?

10-8 What does an operating characteristic curve show and what determines the shape of the curve?

10-9 Explain the type and location of the risks associated with a sampling plan by reference to an OC curve.

10-10 A producer and consumer agree to use a MIL-STD-105 single sampling plan for a specified lot size and general inspection level II. If the AQL is specified, how can the consumer's risk be determined?

10-11 The sampling distribution of means for a variables sampling plan is shown in Fig. 10-13. Copy the figure and then superimpose another plan with a substantially larger sample size using a dotted line. What is the effect upon the α and β risk?

10-12 What is meant by an "assignable cause"? Why are data from observations influenced by an assignable cause discarded before final control limits are calculated?

10-13 A newly promoted supervisor recently issued a directive calling for fraction defective p and range R charts on "every process in the plant where the percentage of defectives can be determined." Comment.

10-14 Briefly outline the steps involved in constructing an attributes control chart.

10-15 When is a process "out of control"?

PROBLEMS

OBJECTIVES OF QUALITY CONTROL

1 A cosmetics producer has established "QC activity levels" in units of equivalent worker hours of inspection and control effort devoted to a product per day. Each equivalent worker hour unit currently costs \$20. The firm estimates that with zero equivalent worker hour units, the defective product costs are \$400 and each additional unit reduces them by \$30. What is the optimal level of QC activity in terms of equivalent worker hours?

2 From a random sample of 100 x-ray films, 10 were found to be defective due to background exposure. What is the estimated standard error s_p in terms of proportions, and the standard deviation in terms of numbers? (*Hint:* See Example 10–5 and the footnote of Solved Prob. 5.)

3 A random sample of 400 items is drawn from a production process in order to test the hypothesis that the process has 10 percent defectives. Eighty defectives are found.

(*a*) What is the theoretical (hypothesized) standard error of proportion (σ_p)?
(*b*) What is the estimated standard error of proportion based upon the sample evidence only s_p?

STATISTICAL DISTRIBUTIONS FOR DEFECTIVES: HYPERGEOMETRIC

4 A furnace manufacturer has 10 used one-half HP motors in inventory; 2 of them are known to be burned out and 8 are known to be good. If a materials handling clerk randomly takes four motors out of inventory without checking any records or testing them, what is the probability that the four will contain one or more defective motors?

5 The operations manager of a metropolitan hospital has recorded 50 cases where health care time for a given illness exceeds the hospital standard. In 6 of the 50 cases the time was at least twice the allowable standard. If a management analyst randomly selects 5 of the 50 cases for investigation, what is the probability that exactly 2 of the 5 selected will reveal times at least twice the allowable standard? (Set up the expression only.)

STATISTICAL DISTRIBUTIONS FOR DEFECTIVES: BINOMIAL

6 A construction firm has found that 20 percent of the concrete blocks received from a certain supplier fail to meet an ASTM compression test standard. If three blocks are installed in especially critical locations where they will be subject to the full test load, what is the probability that exactly two of the blocks will fail?

STATISTICAL DISTRIBUTIONS FOR DEFECTIVES: POISSON

7 The operations department of a city-owned gas company has a quality service performance standard of no more than four complaints/hr. If the company averages four complaints/hr, what is the probability of 30 min passing with no complaints?

8 A manufacturer of clear glass tubes finds that the firm's product has an average of 0.2 bubbles/tube. What is the chance that a quality control inspector, examining the next three tubes, will find them to be bubble-free?

9 If defective components are coming off an assembly line at an average rate of 3.5/min, what is the probability that more than 5 defects will arrive in 1 min?

STATISTICAL DISTRIBUTIONS FOR DEFECTIVES: NORMAL

10 If $n = 36$ and $p = 0.5$, what are the mean and standard deviation of the normal distribution which approximates this binomial distribution?

11 The manufactured weight of boxes of laundry soap is known to be normally distributed with a mean of 20kg and a standard deviation of 0.4kg. Approximately what percent of the boxes in a carload shipment could be expected to weigh less than 19.5kg if an incoming receipt inspection is made?

SAMPLING PLANS FOR ATTRIBUTES AND VARIABLES

12 A producer and consumer agree that they want a sampling plan where $\alpha \leq 0.10$ at $p = 0.003$ and $\beta \leq 0.30$ at $p = 0.006$. The producer's QC "old timer" says the sampling plan ($n = 300$, $c \leq 2$) will be "just fine for both of us."
- (*a*) What is the specified AQL level?
- (*b*) What is the specified LTPD level?
- (*c*) What is the actual level of producer risk offered by this plan?
- (*d*) What is the actual level of consumer risk offered by this plan?
- (*e*) Should the plan be acceptable to both producer and consumer?

13 Northeast Paper Company packages a large volume of tissue under a brand name for a national food chainstore. Occasionally the packages are defective because they are from end cuts, the color is bleached, or they are not properly sealed. The paper company and food chain have agreed to adopt a sampling plan so that the risk to Northeast Paper Company of rejecting lots that are as good as 0.5 percent defective ($p = 0.005$) is limited to 2 percent and the risk of the food chain accepting lots as bad as 4 percent defective is no more than 5 percent.
- (*a*) Construct an OC curve for the sampling plan ($n = 200$, $c \leq 3$).
- (*b*) Does this plan satisfy the agreed-upon paper company risk?
- (*c*) Does this plan satisfy the food chain risk?

14 (*a*) Construct an OC curve for the attributes sampling plan $n = 50$, $c \leq 4$.
- (*b*) What is the value of α at AQL $= 0.04$?
- (*c*) What is the value of β at LTPD $= 0.16$?

15 Use MIL-STD-105 to find a single sampling plan for lots of size 800 and an AQL of 1.5 percent. Use general inspection level II.

16 Use MIL-STD-105 to find a single sampling plan for lots of size 1,150, and an AQL of 4 percent. Use general inspection level II.
- (*a*) What is the sample size n and acceptance number c?
- (*b*) What is the amount of β risk at an LTPD level of 12 percent defective?

17 How large a sample should be taken for acceptance-sampling of a lot containing 125 items if an AQL of 1 percent is desired? Use MIL-STD-105, assuming normal inspection.

18 A sampling plan is required for inspection of a lot containing 400 items where the AQL is set at 0.65 percent. Use MIL-STD-105 general inspection level II.
- (*a*) What size sample should be taken?

(*b*) What is the acceptance level?

(*c*) For the given plan, what is the level of alpha risk at $p = 0.666$ percent defective?

(*d*) For the given plan, what is the level of beta risk at $p = 8$ percent defective?

(*e*) At what process quality level may we expect to find 95 percent of the lots accepted?

19 A national bank has established quality standards for its branch banks and allocates a portion of its salary budget on this basis. One measure of service level is the time required to complete all arrangements for opening a checking account. A time of more than 12 min is considered "poor service" and times have a known standard deviation of 4.2 min.

Design a variables sampling plan, for a sample of $n = 36$ observations, that will allow the headquarters to sample branch banks so that the risk of rejecting a branch's claim (that it averages $\leq$ 12 min) is limited to 1 percent (when the true mean time is really 12 min).

20 A machine is supposed to produce only a small proportion of defectives. The quality control supervisor proposes to take a random sample of 100 units and recommend adjustment of the machine if the sample contains too many defects. If the machine is actually producing as high as 20 percent defectives, the supervisor wants the probability of adjustment to be 0.95. Design a decision rule for this quality control situation.

21 The QC supervisor at National Bakery has been asked to direct the receipt inspection of a carload shipment of flour. Each bag is supposed to weigh at least 50kg and the Chicago Mill has said the standard deviation is 4kg. Management wishes to limit the risk of rejecting a good lot to 2 percent. On the other hand, if the true mean weight of the bags is only 48kg, they desire to limit the chance of accepting the shipment to 5 percent.

(*a*) Diagram the situation in terms of a sampling distribution showing the α and β risks.

(*b*) How large a sample size is required?

(*c*) What is the critical value c of the sample mean that will satisfy the given conditions?

22 A carload of lead sheets has been received by a shipyard for use in shielding work. Each sheet is supposed to weigh *at least* 250 lb (Ho: $\mu \geq 250$) and it is known that the process producing them has a standard deviation of 20 lb. An inspection agreement is reached whereby the supplier's risk of type I error is limited to 0.05. On the other hand, if the true mean weight of the sheets is as low as 240 lb, the shipyard wants only a 10 percent chance of accepting the shipment. It seeks to determine the critical value (borderline weight) of the sample mean that will satisfy these conditions.

(*a*) What are the respective values of α, Z_α, β, and Z_B?

(*b*) How large a sample is required?

(*c*) What is the critical value c of the sample mean?

CONTROL CHARTS

23 In an effort to set up a control chart of a process, samples of size $n = 25$ are taken and it is determined that $\bar{\bar{X}} = 0.98$ centimeters and the standard deviation $s = 0.020$ centimeters. Find the control limits for the process.

24 In an aluminum production facility, a casting operation was sampled to establish variables control limits for a critical length. If 50 samples of $n = 5$ yielded an $\bar{\bar{X}} = 20$ inches with an average range ($\bar{R}$) of 0.3 inches, what are the (*a*) $UCL_{\bar{x}}$, (*b*) $LCL_{\bar{x}}$, (*c*) UCL_R, (*d*) LCL_R respectively?

25 The US Department of Testing (USDT) requires that the 100 lb bag shipments of the Prarie Seed Company do in fact average 100 lb or over. Sample data from $N = 10$ samples of $n = 6$ bags each showed the following weight deviations from 100 lb (over +, and under −).

Sample number	**1**	**2**	**3**	**4**	**5**	**6**	**7**	**8**	**9**	**10**
	2	3	4	1	6	0	2	−1	1	5
	−1	0	5	2	4	−2	3	−1	2	4
	4	3	6	2	3	2	2	2	0	5
	1	1	2	0	4	−1	2	0	0	2
	0	2	4	4	1	3	4	1	4	3
	2	1	2	2	4	0	6	−1	3	0
Σ	8	10	23	11	22	2	19	0	10	19
Mean $\bar{x}$	1.33	1.67	3.83	1.83	3.67	0.33	3.17	0	1.67	3.17
Range R	5	3	4	4	5	5	4	3	4	5

(*a*) What is the center line ($\bar{\bar{X}}$) and the upper and lower control limits for $\bar{X}$?
(*b*) What are the upper and lower control limits for the range? (Round your calculations to two significant digits beyond the decimal.)

26 In a rare metals production facility, a casting operation was sampled to establish attributes control limits. If one sample of size $n = 100$ revealed that 10 percent were defective, what should be the lower and upper control limits respectively?

27 A quality control policy requires setting up control limits on the basis of data from random samples of $n = 100$ per day taken from a 10-day pilot run of a plastics molding activity. A total of 200 defectives were found.
(*a*) What are the UCL_p and LCL_p for the process (in percent of defectives)?
(*b*) If samples of $n = 100$ continue to be taken, what would be the control limits in numbers of defectives (rather than in percent)?

CASE: TIMBERHILL POWER TOOL COMPANY

Timberhill Power Tool Company (TIPTOC) had manufactured a broad line of outdoor tools in its Lansing, Michigan, plant for nearly 30 years. With its recent plant expansion it now had 1,200 employees engaged in the production of over 40 different end products. The problem was that as volume increased, customer complaints about quality seemed to increase exponentially. President Kyle Thurmond was greatly worried that the company reputation, which rested heavily upon a quality image, was rapidly being shattered.

Until five years ago, TIPTOC was small enough so that a separate quality control department was not deemed necessary. The first QC manager had not worked out very well; his tight standards got the firm in trouble with suppliers and slowed up production.

Three years ago Marvin Reedy, who had been an outstanding field salesman, won the position of QC manager. This position did not give him the authority to stop production when a quality problem came up, but Marvin found he could function pretty effectively even without that authority. His forte was dealing with people, and he kept things running smoothly by doing his inspection on a relatively informal basis. He prided himself on being able to accomplish more by individualized persuasion than his predecessor had with mechanistic recordings on formal charts. Anyway, the TIPTOC operation was not part of a process industry and he did not feel it lent itself to the use of control charts.

Marvin had always been an outspoken advocate of "quality" and although he was not formally trained in QC methods he had faced quality problems where they were most difficult to handle—on the firing line with customers. Furthermore, he constantly talked up quality to management as well as employees—he always kept slogans and banners throughout the plant urging employees to "Keep TIPTOC Tops." No one could question Mr. Reedy's commitment to quality, and Mr. Thurmond was convinced he was doing a fine job personally, although the problems continued to intensify. He was thinking about giving Mr. Reedy more line responsibility so he could actually stop production operations when things got out of control.

To gain more insight into the problem, Mr. Thurmond invited Mr. Reedy, Tom Brocamp (production manager), and Jill Everly (engineering manager) to join him for an extended lunch so they could talk things over. The following conversation ensued:

Thurmond (president) I talked with Phil Carrier of Nationwide Distributors today. He said they have lost two more customers for our chain saws. They're still having problems of shearing with the saw teeth.

Everly (engineering) We rechecked our specifications on that last month and our metallurgists are really stumped. Those teeth are SAE steel with 45,000 psi shear strength.

Brocamp (production) Nationwide again, huh? I just can't fathom that Kyle—unless our heat-treating process temperature control isn't functioning. Marvin, you checked that last lot of material personally, didn't you?

Reedy (QC) You can say that again. Alloysteel Company is our supplier on that item, and I told purchasing to go all out for top-grade steel—not 40,000 psi, not 45,000 psi, no limitations at all. I told them we wanted the very best!

Everly You don't mean you told purchasing to disregard the engineering specifications, do you?

Reedy No, no! I just told them those specifications were a minimum but don't be afraid to get something better. You know, if we get a little higher-carbon steel I'm told we could run that strength up considerably.

Everly True, but we do get into ductility and brittleness problems then.

Reedy Of course, Jill.

Thurmond Well, I don't know. But Phil said one of their recent consumer tests showed our saw teeth sheared at 42,000 psi. He has had other reports that go as low as 38,000 psi. Nationwide is talking about dropping our entire line of power tools.

Reedy That's ridiculous—we'd never accept raw material that had a shear strength that low! In fact, I brought along the test data on the last shipment because I thought the question might come up again. I'm sure the strength was **over** 45,000 psi.

Mr. Reedy produced a folder which contained a report on a sample of 36 saw teeth that was taken from the last shipment of 5,000. The mean shear strength was 46,150 psi. The report was on Alloysteel Company stationery and confirmed the testing agreement which was that the risk of rejecting a good lot (of 45,000 psi) was to be limited to 5 percent and any unacceptable lots were to be replaced entirely at Alloysteel's expense within 10 days. Other data included the date, weight of shipment (105 lb), sample size (36), and standard deviation (18,840 psi).

Thurmond Then you don't think **that** lot could have been the one that had teeth that sheared at 42,000 psi?

Reedy No way! Not one chance in a thousand. We wouldn't even have accepted the steel in the first place if it tested out at 42,000 psi!

Thurmond I didn't think so either, but Phil insisted that was the case. (Turns to the other two.) What do you think, Jill?

Everly The engineering specifications are pretty well spelled out. Perhaps we should consider some finished product inspection program ourselves.

Reedy We've considered that before, but you know every chain we test is a lost sale. We'd soon be in the hole if we did much of that. But Jill may be right in doubting the Nationwide tests. They probably got a shipment of our chain mixed up with that from another supplier.

Brocamp How about some form of process control instead? I've been pushing for that for two years.

Reedy I've hesitated to do that because it's so mechanistic and I hate to be ruling out the use of good judgment. It's a little bit complex to set up but I could probably have some charts made up in two weeks or so. It involves setting up control limits at some distance away from the process average. (Reedy sketches a chart on the back of his placemat.)

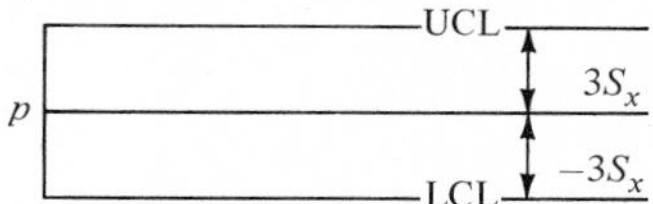

There are some statistics involved but I could set it up so that anybody could handle it. However, if we're going to the use of control charts I should have authority to start or stop the process when, in my judgment, it should be done.

Brocamp My foremen are going to fight that. Why can't you just work through them?

Reedy Oh I will, but I mean there's no need for them to try to understand everything and question my every decision. Know what I mean? That just holds things up even more.

Everly Wouldn't it be much faster and simpler to follow some standard plan to control our process? Seems to me we followed a military standard on a job three or four years ago and it worked out fine. MIL-STD-105, I think it was.

Reedy Yes, that's probably what it was. We could check into that, too. But you know I think if we're going to make any real progress here we've got to get our suppliers and employees thinking quality all the time. If everybody just did their best, as standard operating procedure, I think our quality problems would disappear overnight. We've got to push that quality image. Mr. Thurmond, I've been thinking about a contest that might just do the trick.

Thurmond Great idea! Why not jot down the details for me. In the meantime, would each of you please give me a one- or two-page summary of your thoughts on these issues? (Thurmond hands each person a previously prepared sheet containing the following questions.)

1 What are the strengths of our present quality control system?

2 Please document any weaknesses of our present quality control management system.

3 Is there any chance our sampling procedure would permit us to accept a lot as bad as 38,000 psi? How do you explain the difference in our shear strength data and the tests reported by Nationwide?

4 What specific recommendations would you make to improve our quality control situation?

BIBLIOGRAPHY

[1] BUFFA, ELWOOD S.: *Modern Production Management*, 4th ed., John Wiley & Sons, New York, 1973.

[2] BURR, IRVING W.: *Engineering Statistics and Quality Control*, McGraw-Hill Book Company, New York, 1953.

[3] DANIEL, WAYNE W., AND JAMES C. TERRELL: *Business Statistics*, Houghton Mifflin Company, Boston, Massachusetts, 1975.

[4] DODGE, HAROLD F., AND H. G. ROMIG: *Sampling Inspection Tables, Single and Double Sampling*, 2d ed., John Wiley & Sons, New York, 1959.

[5] DUNCAN, J. A.: *Quality Control and Industrial Statistics*, 3d ed., Richard D. Irwin, Homewood, Illinois, 1965.

[6] FREEMAN, H. A., et al. (eds.): *Sampling Inspection*, McGraw-Hill Book Company, New York, 1948.

[7] GARRETT, LEONARD J., AND MILTON SILVER: *Production Management Analysis*, 2d ed., Harcourt, Brace, Jovanovich, New York, 1973.

[8] GAVETT, J. WILLIAM: *Production and Operations Management*, Harcourt, Brace & World, New York, 1968.

[9] JEDAMUS, PAUL, AND ROBERT FRAME: *Business Decision Theory*, McGraw-Hill Book Company, New York, 1969.

[10] MOORE, FRANKLIN: *Production Management*, 6th ed., Richard D. Irwin, Homewood, Illinois, 1973.

[11] U.S. DEPARTMENT OF DEFENSE, MIL-STD-105D: *Sampling Procedures and Tables for Inspection by Attributes*, U.S. Government Printing Office, Washington, D.C., 1963.

[12] U.S. DEPARTMENT OF DEFENSE, MIL-STD-414, *Sampling Procedures and Tables for Inspection by Variables for Percent Defective*, U.S. Government Printing Office, Washington, D.C., 1957.

CHAPTER

11

Maintenance and Cost Control

COST STANDARDS

LABOR COSTS
MATERIAL COSTS
OVERHEAD COSTS

ANALYSIS OF COST VARIANCE

LABOR VARIANCE
MATERIAL VARIANCE
OVERHEAD VARIANCE

COST REPORTING AND CORRECTION

SUMMARY
SOLVED PROBLEMS
QUESTIONS
PROBLEMS
CASE: THE PLYWOOD MILL MAINTENANCE BUDGET
BIBLIOGRAPHY

Maintenance and cost control activities often make the difference between successful and unsuccessful managers. If the production system is not kept operable within reasonable cost limits, not only will the operations managers probably lose their jobs, but the whole organization will suffer, or perhaps even be forced to liquidate.

Although maintenance is primarily concerned with plant and equipment, whereas costs relate to funds, the two topics are grouped together for convenience in this chapter. Maintenance and cost control are in fact closely interdependent, for production continuity depends heavily upon the maintenance of production equipment, which in turn is typically justified on the basis of an analysis of relevant costs. Nevertheless, cost control activities extend beyond maintenance costs, which are usually part of overhead expense. Cost control includes the measurement and control of all direct labor and material costs as well as maintenance and other overhead costs. Many overhead costs are relatively fixed, but maintenance is one activity that offers some significant opportunities for astute control, so we place special emphasis upon it.

In this chapter we first define the objectives of maintenance and identify the manageable aspects of maintenance activities. We investigate the methods of determining the reliability against failure and the service rates and costs of handling breakdown situations. Then we extend the cost control concepts to budgets, standard costs, and the analysis of cost variance.

MAINTENANCE OBJECTIVES

Maintenance is any activity designed to keep equipment or other assets in working condition. Poorly maintained equipment can be unsafe to operate, and can create high costs in the form of delays and idle time. We often associate maintenance with servicing equipment, replacing wornout parts, doing emergency repairs, or perhaps performing building upkeep, and these are undoubtedly central concerns. But human resources also become exhausted, and even break down, so they too need care and maintenance—as we know all too well. Vacations, training programs, and company medical facilities are all personnel-oriented maintenance activities. In essence, any activity aimed at keeping or restoring any asset to satisfactory operating status can be considered a maintenance activity.

The objective of maintenance is to keep equipment and other assets in the condition that will best facilitate organizational goals. This does not necessarily mean that everything should be in the absolute best operating condition with all new parts so that breakdowns never occur. That would be nice from a theoretical standpoint, but unfeasible from a practical standpoint. It does, however, mean that maintenance activities should be evaluated in light of the total operating system, with decisions based upon criteria that are consistent with organizational objectives. In many cases these criteria are most conveniently satisfied by minimizing long-run maintenance costs. However, at other times employment stability, employee safety, reliability, or such things as short-term economic conditions may be overriding criteria. Like all other operations, maintenance activities should be managed from a total systems perspective with objectives clearly delineated and understood.

ADMINISTRATION AND RESPONSIBILITY

Maintenance responsibility may be assigned to a supervisor reporting to the production manager, to the plant engineer, or even directly to the plant manager. The maintenance staff normally includes craftspeople with sufficient skills to do routine service and repair work of a frequently occurring nature. In breakdown situations, equipment suppliers sometimes augment a firm's maintenance staff by supplying factory trained engineers or specialized technicians to supervise repair of highly technical industrial equipment they have sold.

Depending on the frequency of demand for maintenance services, the plant size (and travel time), and such things as the degree of specialization required, a firm will centralize or decentralize its maintenance department. Centralization usually results in better utilization of individual craftspeople, but decentralization of maintenance crews into different areas of the plant often results in faster service (at a slightly higher cost).

PREVENTIVE VERSUS BREAKDOWN MAINTENANCE

Maintenance activities are often classified into preventive and breakdown maintenance. *Preventive maintenance* involves a pattern of routine inspections and servicing. These activities are also designed to detect potential failure conditions and make minor adjustments or repairs which will help prevent major operating problems. *Breakdown maintenance* is usually of an emergency nature, where facilities or equipment are used until they fail to operate, and then are repaired—often at a cost premium.

An effective preventive maintenance program requires properly trained personnel, regular inspections and service, and an accurate records system. By planning maintenance activities on a scheduled basis (annually, monthly, or daily—perhaps during a second or third shift), management can make good use of skilled maintenance technicians and the lost production time is often less than if breakdowns are simply allowed to occur. The inspection records system should include equipment specifications and an inspection checklist, plus information on repair frequency, cost, and spare parts inventory availability [**9**: 1–2]. With computerized data files these records are more complete and more easily accessible today than they were 20 years ago.

MAINTENANCE COSTS

Equipment breakdowns idle men and machines, resulting in lost production time, delayed schedules, and expensive emergency repairs. These downtime costs

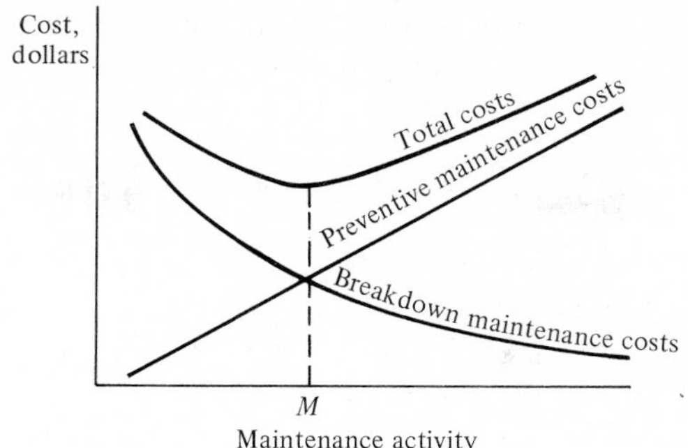

FIGURE 11-1 Maintenance costs

usually exceed the preventive maintenance costs for inspections, service, and scheduled repairs up to a point M as shown in Fig. 11-1. Beyond this optimal point an increasingly higher level of preventive maintenance is not economically justified and the firm would be better off waiting for breakdowns to occur.

Whereas the optimal level of maintenance activity M is easily identified on a theoretical basis, in practice this necessitates knowing a good deal about the various costs associated with both the preventive and breakdown maintenance activities. This includes knowledge of both the probability of breakdowns and the amount of repair time required. Although these data are not always easily obtained, good maintenance records will provide substantial help in estimating the probability distributions of breakdown and repair times.

The maintenance crew-size decision is a specific application of the concept of minimizing the total of preventive and breakdown maintenance costs. As illustrated in Fig. 11-2, when the crew size is increased the downtime costs tend to be decreased. These cost elements are, in effect, components of the more generalized situation depicted in Fig. 11-1 wherein crew costs are incorporated into overall preventive maintenance costs, and downtime costs constitute a part of the breakdown maintenance costs.

The maintenance models in the next section illustrate how the preventive and breakdown maintenance costs can be estimated and compared in order to help minimize total maintenance costs.

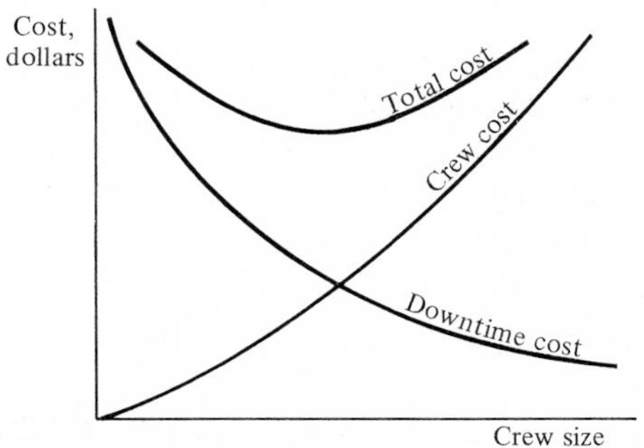

FIGURE 11-2 Crew size costs

MODELS FOR MAINTENANCE MANAGEMENT

Space does not permit us to examine the numerous sophisticated models for maintenance management that abound in the literature. However, it is useful to review both some expected value and simulation techniques for estimating breakdown cost and mention a relatively standardized probability model for selecting an appropriate preventive maintenance policy. We shall finish this section with some discussion of queuing models, because maintenance activities are often best analyzed from the standpoint of parts or equipment waiting for service or repair.

EXPECTED VALUE MODEL FOR ESTIMATING BREAKDOWN COST

Preventive maintenance is most effective when service requirements are well known or failures can be predicted with some degree of reliability. The following example assumes the firm has maintained good records of the frequency and cost of breakdowns in the past. By using the simple concept of expected value, the current breakdown policy can be compared to a given preventive maintenance policy.

Example 11-1

Worldwide Travel Services (WTS) has experienced the indicated number of breakdowns/month in its automated reservations processing system over the past two years.

Number of breakdowns	0	1	2	3	4
Number of months this occurred	2	8	10	3	1

Each breakdown costs the firm an average of $280. For a cost of $150/month WTS could have engaged a data processing firm to perform preventive maintenance which is guaranteed to limit the breakdowns to an *average* of one per month. (If the breakdowns exceed this limit, the firm will process WTS data free of charge.) Which maintenance arrangement is preferable from a cost standpoint, the current breakdown policy or a preventive maintenance contract arrangement?

Solution

Converting the frequencies to a probability distribution and determining the expected cost/month of breakdowns we have the information shown in the accompanying table.

Number of breakdowns (X)	Frequency (in months) $f(X)$	Frequency (in percent) $P(X)$	Expected value $X \cdot P(X)$
0	2	0.083	0
1	8	0.333	0.333
2	10	0.417	0.834
3	3	0.125	0.375
4	1	0.042	0.168
	24	Total	1.710

Breakdown cost per month

$$\text{Expected cost} = \left(\frac{1.71 \text{ breakdowns}}{\text{month}}\right)\left(\frac{\$280}{\text{breakdown}}\right) = \frac{\$478.80}{\text{month}}$$

Preventive maintenance cost per month Since the data processing firm guarantees to limit the cost to an "average" of one breakdown/month, and the expected number (1.710) is greater than one, we may assume that WTS will, in the long run, always incur the cost of one breakdown/month.

Average cost of one breakdown/month	\$280.00
Maintenance contract cost/month	150.00
Total	\$430.00

Preventive maintenance advantage = \$478.80 − \$430.00 = \$48.80/month

SIMULATION MODEL FOR ESTIMATING BREAKDOWN COST

Simulation techniques have been a godsend to maintenance managers, enabling them to "try out" numerous maintenance policies on a computer before actually implementing them. Many large firms simulate maintenance activities before shutting down a plant so that uncertainties can be carefully analyzed and downtime minimized. In one Western state, a management analyst was able to decide whether to centralize or decentralize maintenance services for two state mental health hospitals by first constructing and operating a GPSS simulation model of the activities.

The following example illustrates how simulated breakdown and repair time values could be used to estimate breakdown cost and help reach a decision on the appropriate crew size. Whereas only five breakdowns are simulated here to illustrate the methodology, in actual practice many thousands of trials would be analyzed via computer.

Example 11-2

A management analyst is attempting to study the total cost of the present maintenance policy for machinery in a decentralized section of a shoe manufacturing plant in Boston. The analyst has collected some historical data and simulated breakdowns of machinery over a 16-hr period as shown in the accompanying table.

Request for repair (arrival time)		Total repair time required (worker hours)
0100		1.0
0730		3.0
0800		0.5
1150		2.0
1220		0.5
	Total	7.0 hours

The firm has two maintenance technicians and charges their time (working or idle) at \$11.50/hr each. The downtime cost of the machines, from lost production, is estimated at \$120/hr. Determine:

(*a*) The simulated service maintenance cost
(*b*) The simulated breakdown maintenance cost
(*c*) The simulated total maintenance cost
(*d*) Would another technician be justified?

Solution

(*a*) Simulated service maintenance cost:

$$\text{Service cost} = (2 \text{ technicians})(\$11.50/\text{hr})(16 \text{ hr}) = \$368$$

(*b*) Simulated breakdown maintenance cost (note that we assume two technicians are twice as effective as one and reduce the downtime accordingly):

(1) Request arrival time	(2) Repair time required (2 technicians) Hr	Min	(3) Repair time begins	(4) Repair time ends	(5) Machine downtime hr (2 technicians)	(6) Machine downtime hr (3 technicians)
0100	0.50	30	0100	0130	0.50	0.33
0730	1.50	90	0730	0900	1.50	1.00
0800	0.25	15	0900	0915	1.25	0.67
1150	1.00	60	1150	1250	1.00	0.67
1220	0.25	15	1250	1305	0.75	0.33
	3.50 hr				5.00	3.00

The machine downtime is shown in the accompanying table, in hours, in column 5, as the decimal difference between the request arrival time (1) and the ending repair time (4). Note that on the 0800 breakdown the technicians were not available until 0900 when they finished the earlier job.

$$\text{Breakdown cost} = (\$120/\text{hr})(5\text{ hr}) = \$600$$

(*c*) Simulated total maintenance cost:

$$\begin{aligned}\text{Total cost} &= \text{service} + \text{breakdown} \\ &= \$368 + \$600 \\ &= \$968/\text{period}\end{aligned}$$

(*d*) The machine downtime hours for three technicians would have to be calculated in the same way as was done for two. The calculations are not included, but the final result is shown in column 6.

Service maintenance cost = (3)($11.50)(16) =	$552
Breakdown maintenance cost = ($120)(3 hr) =	360
Total	$912

There appears to be an advantage to adding a third technician.

The above examples use expected value and simulation concepts to help analyze the cost structure underlying Fig. 11-1. In Example 11-1 we simply converted the frequency distribution of breakdowns into a probability distribution and used it to compute a breakdown cost per month that was then compared to a preventive maintenance policy cost per month. Both policies were assumed to be fairly well fixed so the decision problem was one of a choice between two alternatives.

In Example 11-2 the firm again had established (simulated) breakdown and repair time distributions which determined the plant downtime, or breakdown, cost. In this example, however, the downtime cost could be reduced by providing additional service maintenance technicians. These service technicians are effectively a preventive maintenance cost which is incurred even if the technicians are idle, and the cost increases as the crew size increases. Our decision problem in this example was concerned with adjusting the crew size to where total maintenance costs were minimal. With three technicians the expected total cost per period was $56 per period less than with two technicians over a 16-hour period. Other less-tangible considerations might also be important factors in this situation, but the cost calculation at least establishes the economic preference for three technicians.

PROBABILITY MODEL FOR SELECTING PREVENTIVE MAINTENANCE POLICY

A more sophisticated cost tradeoff situation exists when the decision must be made as to not only whether a breakdown or preventive maintenance policy should be followed but also if a preventive maintenance policy is followed, how often service should be performed. The analysis proceeds as follows.

Data is collected on (1) the preventive maintenance servicing cost, (2) the breakdown cost, and (3) the probability of breakdown. The probability of breakdown reflects the fact that breakdowns will occur even if preventive maintenance is performed, but the chance of breakdown usually increases with time after a maintenance activity. The preventive maintenance cost for various policies, such as preventive maintenance every month, every two months, and so on, is then calculated by summing the servicing cost and the breakdown cost. Servicing cost is simply the number of units serviced multiplied by the service cost per unit. Breakdown cost is based on the expected number of breakdowns between services times the breakdown cost per unit. After these costs have been calculated for alternative policies, and the lowest cost policy determined, its cost is compared with the cost of a simple breakdown policy which is based on an average time between breakdowns. The best policy is then the one with the lesser cost.

This approach fully accounts for the uncertainties of breakdown by incorporating them probabilistically into each appropriate period and then determining expected costs. The computation process is tedious and a good candidate for help from the firm's computer. However, with a conscientious effort to obtain realistic data, and a willingness to apply an appropriate methodology, the analysis can suggest a preferable maintenance policy. True, there may be uncertainties in the data, but hopefully the model-building activities will bring them out into the open so they can be realistically evaluated. They should also help to identify deficiencies—which may be corrected with time. This is better than arbitrarily selecting some preventive maintenance policy, say a six-month policy, and blindly incurring unnecessarily high costs—perhaps much higher than competition. Optional Solved Prob. 2 illustrates this probability model.

QUEUING MODEL FOR ANALYZING MAINTENANCE SERVICE FACILITIES

A doctor's office and an electrical motor rewind shop may not appear to have much in common, but both are maintenance facilities. Although one services human resources whereas the other repairs electrical equipment, both are concerned with keeping productive assets in good working condition. In a general sense, both systems have objectives that are met by customers arriving and being served according to some predetermined rule. These parameters of (1) objectives, (2) arrival rate, (3) service order or discipline, and (4) service rate are distinguishing characteristics of queuing models. Queuing models offer a convenient and revealing means of analyz-

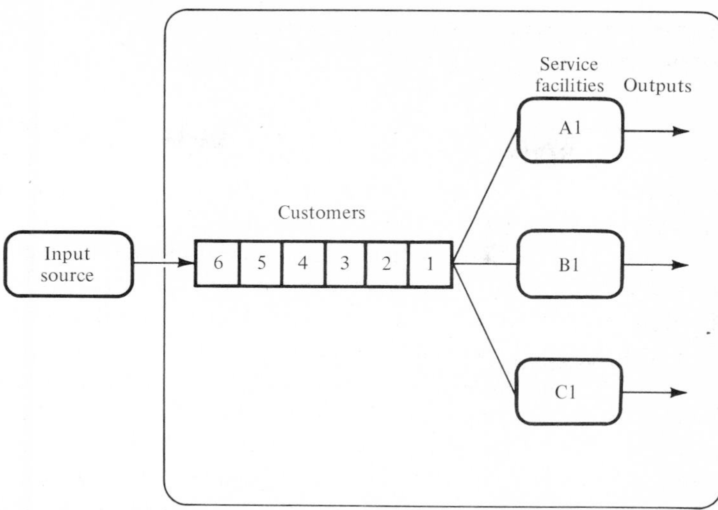

FIGURE 11-3 Structure of queuing problems

ing maintenance activities because arrival rates, service times, and waiting line lengths are often key considerations in maintenance decisions.

Queuing theory rests upon some rather complex mathematics, and all queuing problems do not necessarily justify the cost required for the analysis. However, many real-world situations can be modeled as simple systems without too much sacrifice of accuracy. We illustrate the methodology of queuing analysis by considering a simplified situation which satisfies the assumptions of an elementary queuing model. Our analysis will seek to determine such things as facility utilization, service rates, and waiting line length.

But first it will be helpful to examine the basic structure and some general terminology related to queuing situations. As illustrated in Fig. 11-3, a *queue* is simply a line of customers awaiting service. The *input source* is characterized by its size (finite or infinite) and the statistical pattern by which it generates arrivals. *Arrivals* to a service facility have been found (empirically) to often follow a Poisson distribution [**8**: 262]. The Poisson is a single-parameter, discrete distribution, that is particularly appropriate for describing the rate at which a statistically rare event, such as a breakdown, occurs. The number of *customers* arriving at any given time is expressed as a rate and is independent of the number that have already arrived. The *queue length* can theoretically be anything from zero to infinity, although in practice we know some individuals may choose not to enter a system rather than to enter a long queue. Customers are allocated to service facilities according to a *queue discipline*; the most common discipline is undoubtedly first-in first-out, but other rules such as last-in first-out, random choice, priority to emergencies, and the like, are also used.

Like arrival patterns, *servicing rates* also have a time dimension. Studies have found that the negative exponential distribution gives a reasonable approximation of many industrial servicing situations [**7**: 337]. The negative exponential probability function is concave on a time versus frequency axis with a slope that provides a greater probability of shorter times but also allows for an occasional task that far exceeds the average service time. Our forthcoming example will assume negative exponential service times, but we shall note the formula modifications necessary to accommodate constant service times later on.

In Fig. 11-3, if A1 were the only service facility, the structure would be designated as *single channel.* However, with facilities B1 and C1 it becomes *multiple channel.* If the customers required additional service facilities in series with the existing facilities, say A2, B2, and C2, the system would be considered *multiple phase* rather than *single phase* as is shown.

Calculations for multiple-channel, multiple-phase queuing systems quickly become very complex so we shall limit our inquiry to a maintenance system that can be described by a single-phase, single-channel queuing model. Other assumptions are an infinite number of customers and unlimited waiting-line length, Poisson arrivals, and negative exponential service times. The queue discipline shall be first-in first-out with no defections from the waiting line allowed. In addition we should note that in any queuing system the average service rate μ must be greater than the average arrival rate λ or else the waiting times and queue lengths could ultimately approach infinity. If every arrival and service time were an average value—that is, constant arrival and service times—a service facility could accommodate up to an equal rate of arrivals, but with statistically variable rates queues soon build up.

Example 11-3

A maintenance service facility has Poisson arrival rates, negative exponential service times, and operates on a first-come first-served queue discipline. Breakdowns occur on an average of λ = three per day with a range of zero to eight. The maintenance crew can service an average of μ = six machines per day with a range of from zero to seven. Find the

(*a*) Utilization factor (percent U) of the service facility
(*b*) Mean time T_s in the system
(*c*) Mean number N_s in the system in breakdown or repair
(*d*) Mean waiting time T_w in the system
(*e*) Probability P of finding $n = 2$ machines in the system
(*f*) Expected number N_q in the queue
(*g*) The percent of time the service facility is idle (percent I)

Solution

(*a*) Utilization factor:

$$\%U = \frac{\text{mean arrival rate}}{\text{mean service rate}} = \frac{\lambda}{\mu} \tag{11-1}$$

$$= \frac{3}{6} = 50\%$$

(*b*) Mean time in the system:

$$T_s = \frac{1}{\text{mean service rate} - \text{mean arrival rate}} = \frac{1}{\mu - \lambda} \tag{11-2}$$

$$= \frac{1}{6 - 3} = \frac{1}{3} \text{ day}$$

(*c*) Mean number in the system:

$$N_s = \text{(mean time in system)(mean arrival rate)}$$

$$= \left(\frac{1}{\mu - \lambda}\right)\lambda = \frac{\lambda}{\mu - \lambda} \tag{11-3}$$

$$= \frac{3}{6 - 3}$$

$$= 1 \text{ machine}$$

(*d*) Mean waiting time:

$$T_w = \text{total time in system} - \text{service time}$$

$$= \frac{1}{\mu - \lambda} - \frac{1}{\mu} = \frac{\lambda}{\mu(\mu - \lambda)} \tag{11-4}$$

$$= \frac{1}{6 - 3} - \frac{1}{6}$$

$$= \frac{1}{6} \text{ day}$$

(*e*) Probability of $n = 2$ machines in the system:

$$P_n = \text{(probability of none others)(probability of two)}$$

$$= \left(1 - \frac{\lambda}{\mu}\right)\left(\frac{\lambda}{\mu}\right)^n \tag{11-5}$$

$$= \left(1 - \frac{3}{6}\right)\left(\frac{3}{6}\right)^2$$

$$= 0.125$$

(*f*) Mean number in the queue:

$$N_q = \text{(mean number in system)} - \text{(mean number being served)}$$

$$= \frac{\lambda}{\mu - \lambda} - \frac{\lambda}{\mu} = \frac{\lambda^2}{\mu(\mu - \lambda)} \tag{11-6}$$

$$= \frac{3^2}{6(6 - 3)}$$

$$= \frac{1}{2} \text{ machine}$$

(*g*) Percent idle time:

$$\% I = \text{total} - \text{percent utilization}$$

$$= 100 - \% U \tag{11-7}$$

$$= 100\% - 50\% = 50\%$$

Data from the queuing model calculations can be used for analysis of costs, personnel usage, and so forth. For example, increasing the maintenance-crew size will increase service costs but will also decrease downtime costs by decreasing waiting time and service time in the system. Analysts may use the queuing model to experiment with these alternatives before selecting and actually implementing a course of action.

When service times are constant, rather than exponentially distributed, Eqs. 11-4 and 11-6 must be modified to reflect the improvement that results from a certain versus an uncertain time requirement in the system. The modified equations, designating constancy by c in the subscript, are the mean waiting time

$$T_{w(c)} = \frac{\lambda}{2\mu(\mu - \lambda)} \tag{11-8}$$

and the mean number in the queue

$$N_{q(c)} = \frac{\lambda^2}{2\mu(\mu - \lambda)} \tag{11-9}$$

Constant service times tend to occur when customers or equipment are processed according to a fixed, or mechanically timed cycle, as in some machine-paced services.

RELIABILITY AGAINST FAILURE

Preventive maintenance is worthwhile when it can increase the operating time of the asset by reducing the frequency or severity of breakdowns. It is often the unexpected

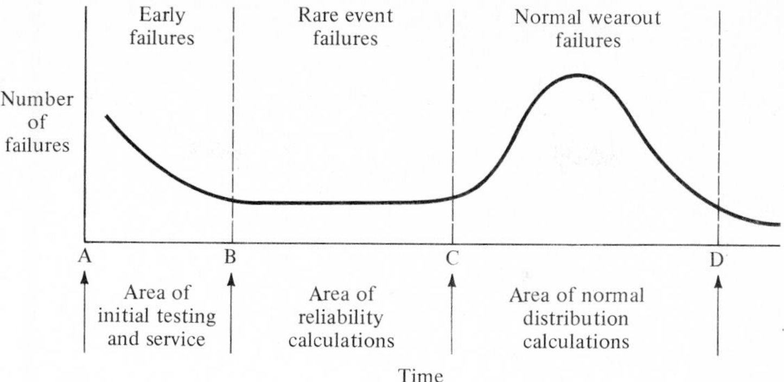

FIGURE 11-4 Product failure rates

and untimely nature of a breakdown that causes the greatest damage, disrupting operations when they seem to be most critical. Thus power plant managers strive to plan their maintenance for off-peak seasons rather than in midwinter when demand is high, and submarine commanders hope that their system reliability is adequately restored when the ship is in drydock, rather than having to deal with a failure while submerged under 400 feet of sea water.

Product reliability is the mathematical probability of a product performing a specific function in a given environment for a specific length of time or number of cycles. It is a characteristic of a product that is measurable on a probabilistic basis. Reliability measures are made more often than many of us realize. The reliability of such things as washing machine timers, automobile tires, electronic calculator components, and entire space systems are routinely determined. The Boeing Company, for example, makes thousands of reliability calculations in the form of a "fault-tree analysis" in order to combine the component reliabilities of thousands of items to determine the ultimate reliability of a total missile system for defense purposes. Airline companies are faced with the realities of transporting passengers in airplanes that have limited reliabilities. Each critical component is tested and evaluated quantitatively by the manufacturers to minimize the chance of some component, perhaps even a $2 item, causing the loss of several hundred lives and millions of dollars worth of equipment.

We noted earlier that product breakdowns often tended to follow a Poisson distribution; that is, failures occur on a "rare event" basis during the normal life of a product. Equipment manufacturers have found that the failure rate during the very early and late stages of product life often differs from that experienced during the normal operating life. This difference in failure rates is depicted in the form of the "bathtub" curve shown in Fig. 11-4.

Early failures may be due to improper assembly, incorrect adjustments, and the like. Manufacturers hope to detect these failures by a testing and shakedown period before the product gets into the hands of the consumer, but of course this does not always happen. Rare event failures are perhaps best analyzed as system reliability problems. These failures take place when one or two components of a system fail unexpectedly but the majority of the components remain in satisfactory operating condition. As a large number of components wear out and fail, we move into the normal wear-out period. Failures here may very well follow a statistical distribution such as the normal curve.

We might view the composite of Fig. 11-4 by tracing the life expectancy pattern of a simple product such as an installation of a group of fluorescent light tubes in a large plant. One would hope that factory testing had removed manufacturing defectives, although some early failures may result from such things as rough handling during transportation. During normal operation some failures could be expected, but probably not enough to warrant the time of a worker replacing tubes on an individual basis. Toward the end of the average life of the tubes, failures would probably begin to occur on a normally distributed basis. Group replacement could best be scheduled by taking this statistical wear-our failure rate into account.

Questions sometimes arise as to how many lights, bearings, transistors, and the like, to replace at one time, or what other items to replace when one component fails, causing an entire machine or system to break down. This decision should be analyzed on a cost basis taking labor and material costs plus downtime costs into account. A major unknown here is the length of service that can be expected after repair, depending upon what worn parts are replaced. Because subsequent failures involve statistical probabilities of failure, stochastic simulation models have been found to be useful for evaluating various alternatives in this type of maintenance decision situation [**3**: 617]. Optional Solved Prob. 7 illustrates one such application.

DETERMINING FAILURE RATES

A *failure* is simply an event that changes a product from an operational to a nonoperational condition. Manufacturers sometimes provide failure rate data on their equipment, especially in critical applications such as nuclear and space vehicles. Of primary interest to users are usually the failure rates and mean time between failures. The failure rate (FR) represents (1) a percentage of failures among the total number of products tested, or (2) a number of failures per given operating time.

1 $$\text{FR}_{\%} = \frac{\text{number of failures}}{\text{number tested}} \tag{11-10}$$

2 $$\text{FR}_{n} = \frac{\text{number of failures}}{\text{operating time}} = \frac{\text{F}}{\text{TT} - \text{NOT}} \tag{11-11}$$

where

F = number of failures

TT = total time

NOT = nonoperating time

Example 11-4

Fifty artificial heart valves were tested for 10,000 hr at a medical research center and 3 valves failed during the test. What was the failure rate in terms of

(*a*) Percent of failures?

(*b*) Number of failures per unit-yr?

(*c*) Based upon this data, how many failures could be expected during a year from installation of these valves in 100 patients?

Solution

(*a*) $$\text{FR}_{\%} = \frac{\text{number of failures}}{\text{number tested}} = \frac{3}{50} = 6.0\%$$

(*b*) $$\text{FR}_n = \frac{\text{number of failures during period}}{\text{operating time}} = \frac{F}{\text{TT} - \text{NOT}}$$

Note that the operating time is reduced by those units that failed. In lieu of actual data we assume failures are averaged throughout the test period.

$\therefore$ Total time = (10,000 hr) (50 units) = 500,000 unit-hr

Less: Nonoperating time of 3 failed units

for average of $\frac{10{,}000}{2}$ hr − 15,000 unit-hr

Operating time = 485,000 unit-hr

$$\text{FR}_n = \frac{3 \text{ failures}}{485{,}000 \text{ unit-hr}} = 0.0000062 \text{ failures/unit-hr}$$

$$= (0.0000062)\left(\frac{24 \text{ hr}}{\text{day}}\right)\left(\frac{365 \text{ days}}{\text{yr}}\right) = 0.0542 \text{ failures/unit-yr}$$

(*c*) From 100 units,

$$\left(\frac{0.0542 \text{ failures}}{\text{unit-yr}}\right)(100 \text{ units}) = 5.42 \text{ failures/yr}$$

The mean time between failure (MTBF) is another useful term in maintenance and reliability analysis. The MTBF is simply the reciprocal of FR_n:

$$\text{MTBF} = \frac{\text{operating time}}{\text{number of failures}} = \frac{\text{TT} - \text{NOT}}{F} \tag{11-12}$$

Example 11-5

Find the MTBF for the heart valves described in the previous example.

Solution

$$\text{MTBF} = \frac{\text{TT} - \text{NOT}}{F} = \frac{500{,}000 - 15{,}000}{3} = 161{,}666.67 \text{ unit-hr/failure}$$

$$= \frac{161{,}666.67}{(24)(365)} = 18.46 \text{ unit-yr/failure}$$

The 18.46 unit-year per failure figure represents the mean service time between failures that might be expected from a group of units during their several years of service. It is not necessarily indicative of the expected life of an individual unit. Recall, from Fig. 11-4, that we are dealing here with reliability calculations and rare event failures as opposed to normal wear-out failures. The 10,000-hour test time in the examples represented only slightly over one year of actual operating time and was not adequate to obtain data on normal wear-out failures.

RELIABILITY MEASUREMENT AND IMPROVEMENT

We indicated earlier that the reliability of individual components and systems is routinely measured and analyzed for many products. Factory and independent laboratory tests, such as illustrated by the heart valve example above, are used to establish mathematical reliability figures which in turn enable engineers and systems designers to improve total system reliability. Some ways to improve reliability are listed in Table 11-1.

Many of the suggested methods of improving reliability seem obvious, once they are delineated. Several of the ways mentioned will undoubtedly tend to increase production costs but, of course, these are preventive maintenance expenses that can often be justified by the alternative breakdown and downtime expense. There is also the possibility that design simplification and improvement in component design and

TABLE 11-1 WAYS TO IMPROVE RELIABILITY

1	Improve design of components
2	Simplify design of system
3	Improve production techniques
4	Improve quality control
5	Test components and system
6	Install parallel systems
7	Perform periodic preventive maintenance
8	Derate components and/or system

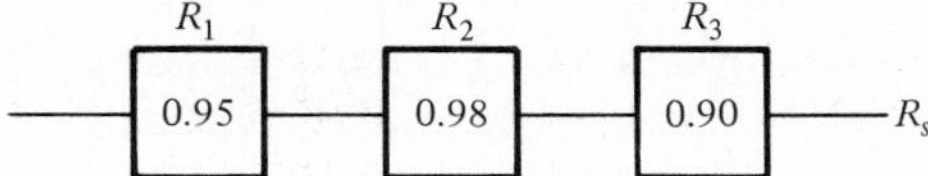

FIGURE 11-5 Series circuit

production techniques could reduce production costs. Derating the system so that it does not operate at full design capacity could also lessen product warranty costs.

The installation of parallel systems is a standard design procedure in many hazardous and capital intensive applications. Rapid transit systems, space vehicles, nuclear reactors, and other critical installations commonly have parallel or back-up systems that improve the overall system reliability at some cost of duplication. We can illustrate the improvement effect by taking an elementary example of series and parallel circuits in an electrical network. The reliability of components in series R_s is simply the multiplicative sum of the individual component reliabilities

$$\text{(Series) } R_s = R_1 \cdot R_2 \cdots R_n \tag{11-13}$$

For parallel circuits the reliability R_p of the system is determined by:

$$\text{(Parallel) } R_p = 1 - (1 - R_{s1})(1 - R_{s2}) \tag{11-14}$$

Example 11-6

An acid control system has three components in series with individual reliabilities R_1, R_2, and R_3 as shown in Fig. 11-5.

(*a*) Find the reliability of the system.

(*b*) What would be the reliability of the system if a parallel circuit were added?

Solution

(*a*) Series $R_s = R_1 \cdot R_2 \cdot R_3 = (0.95)(0.98)(0.90) = 0.84$

(*b*) The parallel system design would be as shown in Fig. 11-6, where R_{s1} and R_{s2} are the computed reliabilities of the respective series circuits.

$$\begin{aligned} \text{Parallel } R_p &= 1 - (1 - R_{s1})(1 - R_{2s}) \\ &= 1 - (1 - 0.84)(1 - 0.84) = 0.97 \end{aligned}$$

As can be seen, the installation of a parallel circuit renders a substantial improvement in the probability of the system functioning as planned without failure. Although parallel systems can be costly, when hundreds of items are series-dependent, as in some control circuits, the rapid deterioration in system reliability often necessitates the use of parallel systems.

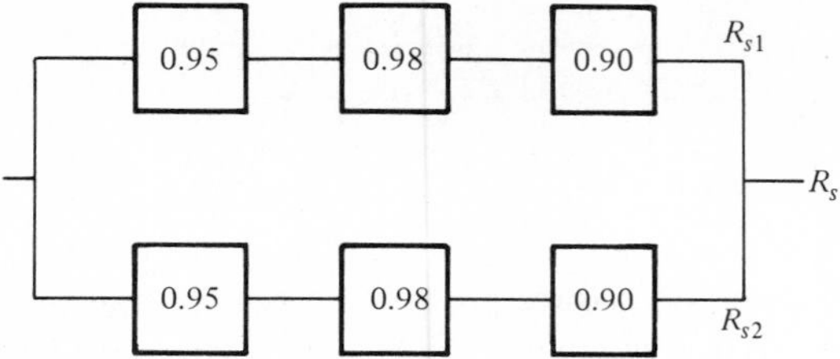

FIGURE 11-6 Parallel circuit

NORMAL STATISTICAL FAILURE

As a product moves along the time continuum of Fig. 11-4 from rare event failures to the area of normal wear-out failures, standard techniques of analysis using the normal statistical distribution often become appropriate. We illustrate this with an example concerning the fluorescent light tubes used to discuss Fig. 11-4.

Example 11-7

The manufacturing area in the plant of a New Jersey drug manufacturer requires 5,000 fluorescent light tubes. The lights have a normally distributed lifetime with a mean of 4,000 hr and a standard deviation of 120 hr. The plant manager has found that after 10 percent of the lights burn out, the quality and productivity of workers in the plant is affected. He would like to schedule maintenance activities so as to replace all lights when 10 percent fail. After how many hours of operation should the replacement activities be scheduled?

Solution

At the mean lifetime μ, 50 percent of the lights are still operating. (See Fig. 11-7.) We wish to find the earlier time x such that 40 percent more (or 90 percent total) are operating. Since the distribution is normal, we know (from Appendix D) that the number of standard deviations required to include an area of 0.40 is $Z = 1.28$.

Given the relationship:

$$-Z = \frac{x - \mu}{\sigma}$$

Then $x = \mu - Z\sigma$

$$= 4{,}000 - 1.28(120)$$

$$= 3{,}974 \text{ hr}$$

This concludes the material on maintenance. Having discussed objectives, some illustrative models for maintenance management, and the concept of reliability, we now move on to the topic of cost control.

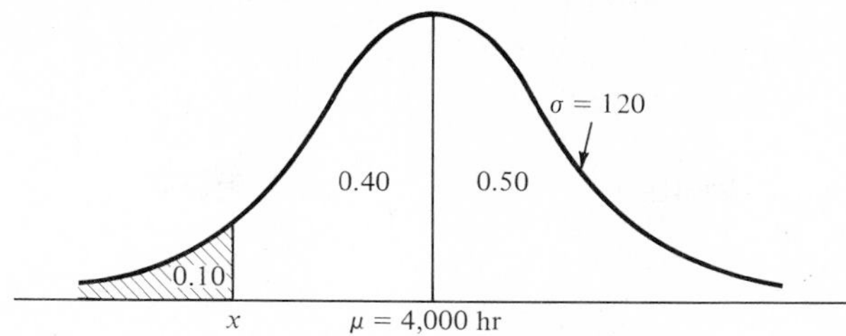

FIGURE 11-7 Distribution of lifetimes of fluorescent tubes

COST CONTROL CONCEPTS

Whether an organization is profit- or nonprofit-oriented, or concentrates upon the production of goods or services, costs form the basis for perhaps the greatest number of managerial decisions. They are one of the most important manageable aspects of an operation, so their control warrants special concern.

COST COMPONENTS

In nonprofit organizations, costs have to be kept within budgeted amounts.[1] Thus, welfare programs, public school operations, and even police and fire protection services all operate on limited budgets. In competitive profit-making organizations, unless the costs are kept below the revenues, no profit will result and, in the long run, the organization will fail. Figure 11-8 shows the cost composition of a typical manufacturing firm. Control of the total system costs clearly depends upon control of the individual component costs. For the operations manager, this usually means responsibility for control of the labor, materials, and overhead that make up the cost of goods sold.

COST TYPES

Cost collection and allocation into the various accounts is basically a cost accounting function. The method of collecting costs depends heavily upon the type of production system involved and is broadly classified into process and job costing.

Process costing Continuous systems charge costs directly to the responsible department or process and allocate costs to products by dividing them up into the units produced according to some logical apportionment procedure. Process costs nearly always represent some form of average costs.

[1] This does not always occur, however, as vividly exemplified by the New York City budget problems in 1975–1976 when the city turned to the federal government for help.

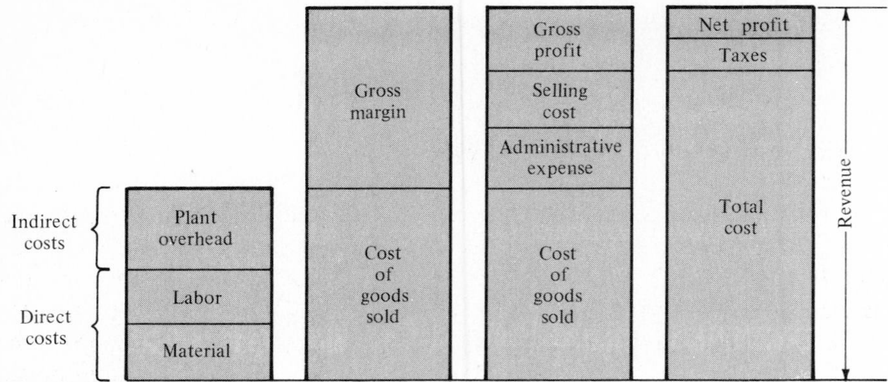

FIGURE 11-8 Cost components

Job costing Intermittent systems often use a job-order costing arrangement whereby costs are collected according to the job or customer. Project costs are also done on this basis.

Elements of both process costing and job costing are often found in the same organization. In addition, the cost elements are typically broken down into sub-elements or collected on a time-sequenced basis. Whatever the cost unit is, it should be chosen with a view toward providing information useful for management decision making. The cost units should also facilitate control by relating the costs to specific positions which are filled by individuals who can exercise control over the costs. Nothing (but frustration) is accomplished by holding people responsible for costs that they are not in a position to control.

A common classification of costs relates to their ability to be traced to a specific product. *Direct costs* are items such as labor and materials which can be directly identified with a given product. Since these costs vary directly with the volume of production they are also termed "variable" costs, and we have previously referred to them as such.

Indirect costs are legitimate costs of supporting activities which are not directly identifiable with specific products. They include overhead items such as depreciation, office supplies, and insurance, which (at least in theory) do not vary with production volume. We have referred to these as "fixed costs," recognizing that in the longer term many so-called fixed costs are at least semivariable. Total indirect costs are often two or three times as much as direct costs.

COST CONTROL

Effective control of costs requires all the elements common to any control system—only in this case they pertain to costs:

Measurement and allocation of actual labor, material, and overhead costs.

Feedback of actual cost data via cost summary and cost variance information system reports.

Comparison with standard (planned or budgeted) cost levels and standard costs.

Correction when costs differ from standards.

If any control elements are missing or defective, the whole cost control system will suffer. Thus, faulty measurement, slow feedback, inaccurate standards, or an inability to take corrective action will invalidate any cost control system. Whereas all these elements are important, the detailed operation of the cost accounting system is outside the scope of this text. We shall, however, pay special attention to the vital area of budgets and cost standards for they are very important to operations managers.

BUDGETS: FIXED AND FLEXIBLE

A *budget* is an operating plan which coordinates and summarizes individual estimates and plans for future periods. An organization may develop several types of budgets, including capital expenditures budgets, cash budgets, and operations budgets.

The operations budget is an important tool for cost control of production activities. This budget typically shows fixed, semivariable, and variable costs projected for the expected volume of production in a future period. The budgeted costs are derived from labor, material, and overhead standard costs. Subsequent performance reports may include room for both projected costs and actual costs, plus explanations as to why costs were greater than or less than budgeted values.

In addition to production cost control, budgets serve several other purposes. They (1) facilitate setting objectives, (2) help guide future activities, (3) provide measures of performance toward meeting objectives, (4) establish centers of responsibility for production activities and cost control, and (5) provide cost information for decision making with respect to financing, marketing, and other functional activities.

Budgets are generally classified as either fixed (static) or flexible (variable), depending upon whether they vary with the volume of production. The distinction is very important and Table 11-2 illustrates the two types. *Fixed budgets* are prepared for one chosen level of activity (such as 5,000 units) and comparisons of actual performance are always made against this initial plan. Thus, even if production turns out to be 6,000 units, basic comparisons would be made against the costs projected for a 5,000-unit budget. Fixed budgets are frequently used in association with long-range planning.

Flexible budgets project costs for a range of volume. Thus a firm may set up budgets for several possible levels of production and wait until after the time period is over to designate which budget applied. Since it is the variable costs and not the fixed costs which change with volume, flexible budgets are often referred to as "variable" budgets and are sometimes based on variable costs only. However, they

TABLE 11-2 FIXED AND FLEXIBLE BUDGETS, SHOP 62, FOR THE MONTH ENDING MAY 31, 19XX

	Fixed budget	Flexible budget		
Units	**5,000**	**4,000**	**5,000**	**6,000**
Direct labor	$75,000	$60,000	$75,000	$90,000
Direct materials	30,000	24,000	30,000	36,000
Variable overhead	20,000	16,000	20,000	24,000
Fixed overhead	160,000	160,000	160,000	160,000
Total	$285,000	$260,000	$285,000	$310,000

can and often do contain the fixed cost elements as well, as illustrated by the fixed overhead in the flexible budget of Table 11-2. By providing standards for what costs should be for various levels of output, flexible budgets provide reasonable and often more meaningful guides for cost control. This is because the underlying basis of comparison (the activity level) is common to both the budget and the actual cost figures.

Nevertheless, flexible budgets do not provide a stable measure of performance against a specified longer-range forecast production schedule. Volumes are important in the long run but the overall cost-revenue balance concerns may tend to be avoided or implicitly shifted to higher levels in the organization under flexible budgeting.

COST STANDARDS

A *cost standard* is a declaration of what a component or activity *should cost* under specified operating conditions. Standard costs are usually based upon attainable levels of performance rather than upon ideal levels (that may appear unreasonable to operating employees). Whereas the *budgeted costs typically refer to total amounts*, such as a budget for 50,000 units, *standard costs usually refer to unit costs*, such as material cost per unit and labor cost per unit or per hour. In the case of overhead costs, the individual unit costs are not always the most relevant for many decisions. Overhead costs, being composed of numerous items (many of which are not directly identifiable with the product), are often handled on a total (budget) basis rather than a unit (standard cost) basis.

Standard costs are used to establish budgets and production schedules. Thus it is important that all factors affecting the costs be properly weighted in the standards. The standards may be derived in different ways, such as from historical costs, from estimates of experienced estimators, or from more analytical approaches that stem from the buildup of costs based upon specifically defined materials and work methods. One method of determining cost standards for labor, material, and overhead is discussed next.

LABOR COSTS

Standard times, developed by predetermined time standards, time studies, or work sampling, often form the basis for labor cost standards. The most commonly used standards are set at a level where about 95 percent of the workers can meet the standard if they work at a normal pace (that is, a 100 percent rating factor). The standard labor cost for a particular unit of activity (C_l) is then the summation of the standard times (ST) multiplied by the base labor rate (LR).

$$C_l = \sum (\text{ST})(\text{LR}) = \sum (\text{hr/unit})(\$/\text{hr}) \tag{11-15}$$

MATERIAL COSTS

The efficient use of material is the concern of much design and value engineering effort, as well as production control effort. Material requirements for a given product are typically specified on engineering drawings or production control documents. Using the bills of material on the drawings (or the production control data files), purchasing and engineering personnel can determine standard material unit costs C_m.

OVERHEAD COSTS

Some elements of overhead cost, such as building depreciation, are fixed costs FC, whereas other components, such as supervision, maintenance, and factory supplies, are often classified as variable V, or perhaps semivariable SV.

Under flexible budgeting the overhead variable budget varies depending upon the projected volume. For example, in Table 11-2, if Shop 62 produces 4,000 units during May, the variable overhead cost standard will be \$16,000 (or \$16,000 ÷ 4,000 units = \$4/unit). For volumes of 5,000 and 6,000 units, the budget increases to \$20,000 and \$24,000 respectively (but of course the *per unit* standard amount remains at \$4) and intermediate amounts would be adjusted accordingly.

A convenient and popular method of expressing variable overhead standards is in terms of a cost per direct labor hour. Thus, for example, if the direct labor standard (the \$60,000 in Table 11-2) represents 10,000 direct labor hours, the variable overhead cost would be expressed as \$16,000 ÷ 10,000 direct labor hours, or \$1.60 per direct labor hour. Fixed overhead costs are usually retained as a total cost (such as \$160,000) rather than converting them to per-unit costs because they are typically analyzed on a total basis anyway.

With fixed budgets, the overhead standard cost C_{oh} does not differ depending upon the actual volume, so a single standard must be developed that is (hopefully) representative of all the overhead costs. This is often derived from an estimate of the overhead cost per unit at the midpoint of a likely volume range. One method of determining an overhead standard cost is by summing the FC + the mean of the V or SV overhead costs and dividing by the midpoint or expected volume. This over-

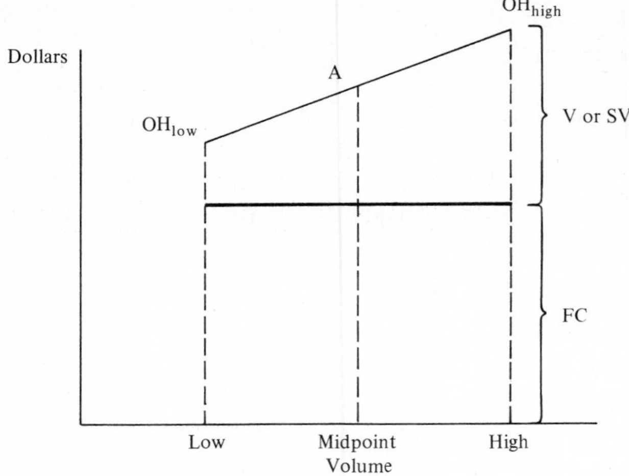

FIGURE 11-9 Overhead costs

head allocation is referred to as the *overhead liquidation* (*or absorption*) *rate* and is denoted by A in Fig. 11-9 [**3**: 696].

$$C_{oh} = \frac{\text{FC} + (\text{mean of } V_{oh} \text{ or } SV_{oh})}{(\text{midpoint volume})} \tag{11-16}$$

Example 11-8

A West Coast firm uses a fixed budget and produces legend plates for the instrument panels of aircraft. The legend plate operation has fixed costs of $50,000/yr and other overhead costs for administration, supervision, maintenance, and utilities of from $20,000 to $40,000 depending upon the volume, which may range from 35,000 to 45,000 units. Material costs for the Micarta average $.26/unit, with painting and sanding supplies and packaging materials at $.03/unit and $.01/unit respectively. A work-sampling study revealed the accompanying standard times (ST) with the respective labor rates (LR).

Activity	**ST (min)**	**LR ($/hr)**
Cutting	1.2	3.20
Engraving	9.0	3.20
Sanding	1.8	3.00
Inspection	0.6	3.00
Packaging	0.6	3.00

Find the

(*a*) Labor standard cost C_l
(*b*) Material standard cost C_m
(*c*) Overhead standard cost C_{oh}

Solution

(*a*) Labor standard cost C_l

$$C_l = \sum (\text{ST})(\text{LR})$$

Activity	ST(min)	ST(hr)	LR($/hr)	(ST)(LR)
Cutting	1.2	0.02	3.20	$.064
Engraving	9.0	0.15	3.20	.480
Sanding	1.8	0.03	3.00	.090
Inspection	0.6	0.01	3.00	.030
Packaging	0.6	0.01	3.00	.030
			Total = C_l	$.694/unit

(*b*) Material standard cost C_m

$$\begin{aligned} C_m &= \sum \text{material unit costs} \\ &= \text{Micarta} + \text{supplies} + \text{packaging materials} \\ &= \$.26 + \$.03 + \$.01 = \$.30/\text{unit} \end{aligned}$$

(*c*) Overhead standard cost C_{oh}

$$\begin{aligned} C_{oh} &= \frac{\text{FC} + (\text{mean of } V_{oh} \text{ or } SV_{oh})}{\text{midpoint volume}} \\ &= \frac{\$50{,}000 + \$30{,}000}{40{,}000 \text{ units}} = \$2.00/\text{unit} \end{aligned}$$

*ANALYSIS OF COST VARIANCE

The purpose of analyzing the deviation of actual costs from budgeted or standard costs is to identify causes of the variance and then make use of this information to capitalize on favorable variances or try to prevent unfavorable variances from occurring in future planning. Variance can usually be classified into one or more of three categories:

1 *Variance in volume* V_v where the actual is less than or greater than the forecast.

* This material extends to the important area of cost variance analysis that is normally covered in cost accounting texts. If this section is specifically deleted (by your instructor on a prearranged basis), simply read the first paragraph only; then skip to the next section on Cost Reporting and Correction. Otherwise continue on. All cost variance analysis problems in the problem section have been marked with an asterisk.

2 *Variance in rate* V_r or price V_p where the purchase cost per unit differs from standards.

3 *Variance in efficiency* V_e where the actual time or usage differs from standards.

If flexible budgeting procedures are used, the budget is adjusted to suit the volume produced and the volume variance may be eliminated. However, in the following examples, volume variance analysis is included in order to illustrate its calculation. (Flexible budget variance calculations are illustrated in Solved Prob. 9 and 10 at the end of this chapter.)

LABOR VARIANCE

Variance from labor standard costs rests upon computation of the difference (Δ) between budgeted and actual volume, rate, and hours.

Volume variance $$V_{v-l} = (\Delta \text{ vol})\, C_l \tag{11-17}$$

Rate variance $$V_{r-l} = (\Delta \text{ rate})\left(\text{actual } \frac{\text{time}}{\text{unit}}\right)(\text{actual vol}) \tag{11-18}$$

Efficiency variance $$V_{e-l} = (\Delta \text{ hr})\left(\text{std } \frac{\text{rate}}{\text{hr}}\right)(\text{actual vol}) \tag{11-19}$$

MATERIAL VARIANCE

As with labor costs, if flexible budgeting is used the volume variance for material may be eliminated. Otherwise, the volume, price, and efficiency variances can be calculated in a manner similar to that for labor.

Volume variance $$V_{v-\text{mtl}} = (\Delta \text{ vol})\, C_m \tag{11-20}$$

Price variance $$V_{p-\text{mtl}} = (\Delta \text{ price})\left(\text{actual } \frac{\text{mtl}}{\text{unit}}\right)(\text{actual vol}) \tag{11-21}$$

Efficiency variance $$V_{e-\text{mtl}} = (\Delta \text{ mtl})\left(\text{std } \frac{\text{price}}{\text{unit}}\right)(\text{actual vol}) \tag{11-22}$$

OVERHEAD VARIANCE

Variance from the overhead standard C_{oh} will be due primarily to volume V_{v-oh} and efficiency of the use of expenditures V_{e-oh}. Calculation of V_{v-oh} involves subtracting an adjusted standard overhead cost ($\text{OH}_{\text{adj std}}$) from the forecast overhead liquidation. (See Fig. 11-9.) The ($\text{OH}_{\text{adj std}}$) is composed of the minimum overhead

OH_{low} plus an incremental amount for each unit produced beyond the minimum. The adjusted standard thus reflects both fixed and variable or semivariable components over a range of volume, whereas the overhead liquidation rate C_{oh} is more representative of one (forecast) point in this range. The forecast overhead at point A in Fig. 11-9 is simply the forecast volume (midpoint) times the liquidation rate C_{oh}. If the actual volume turns out to be exactly as forecast, the volume variance is zero.

$$\text{Volume variance } V_{v-oh} = (\text{actual volume})\, C_{oh} - OH_{\text{adj std}} \tag{11-23}$$

where

$$OH_{\text{adj std}} = OH_{\text{low}} + \left(\frac{OH_{\text{high}} - OH_{\text{low}}}{\Delta \text{ volume}}\right) \times (\text{actual volume} - \text{low volume}) \tag{11-24}$$

$$\text{Efficiency variance } V_{e-oh} = OH_{\text{adj std}} - OH_{\text{actual}} \tag{11-25}$$

Since the $OH_{\text{adj std}}$ depends on total (such as annual) production, many firms compute and report overhead cost variance on an annual rather than individual job basis. (Again, if flexible budgeting procedures are used, the volume variance V_{v-oh} loses its significance.)

Example 11-9

An order from a commercial airline called for 1,000 legend plates. Data on actual production and production standards were as shown in the accompanying table. (Note that some dollar values have been rounded.)

	Actual	Standard
Number of plates produced	1,040	1,000
Time/unit (hr)	0.25	0.22
Wage rate ($/hr)	3.250	3.155
Labor hours	260	220
Labor cost (total job $)	845	694
Labor unit cost ($/unit)	0.813	0.694 (C_l)
Material price ($/oz)	0.50	0.50
Material consumption (oz/unit)	0.60	0.52
Material cost (except supplies, total job $)	313	260
Material unit cost ($/unit)	0.30	0.26 } (C_m)
Supplies and packaging ($/unit)	0.04	0.04 } (C_m)
For the year ending December 31:		
Annual production (units)	41,000	40,000
Annual fixed costs ($)		$50,000
Annual semivariable costs ($)		30,000
Annual total OH costs allocated		$80,000
Overhead liquidation rate		$2.00/unit ($C_{oh}$)
Annual total OH costs (41,000 volume)	83,100	82,000

The firm uses a fixed budget with the overhead standard costs based upon a \$75,000 overhead at 35,000 units and an \$85,000 overhead at 45,000 units. The overhead liquidation rate of \$2.00/unit is based upon allocating \$80,000 cost over 40,000 units. Find the

(a) Labor variance
(b) Material variance
(c) Overhead variance (annual basis)

Solution

(a) Labor variance:

$$\text{Volume} = V_{v-l} = (\Delta\ \text{vol})\ C_l$$
$$= (1{,}000 - 1{,}040)(0.694) \qquad = -\$27.76$$

$$\text{Rate} = V_{r-l} = (\Delta\ \text{rate})\left(\text{actual}\ \frac{\text{time}}{\text{unit}}\right)$$
$$\times\ (\text{actual vol})$$
$$= (3.155 - 3.250)(0.25)(1{,}040) = -24.70$$

$$\text{Efficiency} = V_{e-l} = (\Delta\ \text{hr})\left(\text{std}\ \frac{\text{rate}}{\text{hr}}\right)(\text{actual vol})$$
$$= (0.22 - 0.25)(3.155)(1{,}040) = -98.44$$
$$\text{Total} \quad -\$150.90$$

(b) Material variance:

$$\text{Volume} = V_{v-\text{mtl}} = (\Delta\ \text{vol})\ C_m$$
$$= (1{,}000 - 1{,}040)$$
$$\times\ (0.26 + 0.04) \qquad = -\$12.00$$

$$\text{Price} = V_{p-\text{mtl}} = (\Delta\ \text{price})\left(\text{actual}\ \frac{\text{mtl}}{\text{unit}}\right)(\text{actual vol})$$
$$= (0.50 - 0.50)(0.60)(1{,}040) = \qquad 0.00$$

$$\text{Efficiency}^2 = V_{e-\text{mtl}} = (\Delta\ \text{mtl})\left(\text{std}\ \frac{\text{price}}{\text{unit}}\right)(\text{actual vol})$$
$$= (0.52 - 0.60)(0.50)(1{,}040) = -41.60$$
$$\text{Total} \quad -\$53.60$$

[2] There is no reported variance in the amount or price of supplies and packaging which was used and was \$0.04 per unit. Therefore the calculation covers the materials only.

TABLE 11-3 COST VARIANCE ANALYSIS SUMMARY TABLE

	Volume variance	Price or rate variance	Efficiency variance	Total variance
Labor cost	\$−27.76	\$−24.70	\$−98.44	\$−150.90
Material cost	−12.00	0.00	−41.60	−53.60
Overhead cost	1,000.00	0.00	−2,100.00	−1,100.00
Total variance	\$+960.24	\$−24.70	\$−2,240.04	\$−1,304.50

(*c*) Overhead variance (annual basis):

$$\text{Vol} = V_{v-oh} = (\text{actual vol})\, C_{oh} - \text{OH}_{\text{adj std}}$$

where

$$\text{OH}_{\text{adj std}} = \text{OH}_{\text{low}} + \left(\frac{\text{OH}_{\text{high}} - \text{OH}_{\text{low}}}{\Delta \text{ volume}}\right) \times (\text{actual vol} - \text{low vol})$$

$$= \$75{,}000 + \frac{(85{,}000 - 75{,}000)}{10{,}000} \times (41{,}000 - 35{,}000)$$

$$= 75{,}000 + (1.00)(6{,}000) = \$81{,}000$$

$$V_{v-oh} = (41{,}000)(2.00) - 81{,}000 \qquad = +\$1{,}000$$

$$\text{Efficiency} = V_{e-oh} = \text{OH}_{\text{adj std}} - \text{OH}_{\text{actual}}$$

$$= \$81{,}000 - 83{,}100 \qquad = -2{,}100$$

$$\text{Total} \quad -\$1{,}100$$

The variances are summarized in Table 11-3.

The above example explains why the actual costs deviated from standard costs. For example, from the original labor cost data we see actual labor costs were \$845 − \$694 = \$151 more than budgeted. The summary table reveals that most (\$98) of this difference was due to inefficiency of labor, indicating that standard times are being exceeded and suggesting that they be rechecked. The largest contributor to inefficiency is, however, the overhead cost.

Note that the firm is using a budget where the overhead volume variance consists of the difference between the point estimate of actual volume (41,000) times the liquidation rate (\$2) and the adjusted OH standard, ($\text{OH}_{\text{adj std}}$). From the variance calculations we see that for a volume of 41,000 units our adjusted OH standard (\$81,000) was lower than the fixed-point liquidation rate allowed (\$82,000) and resulted in a \$1,000 favorable volume variance. However, actual overhead costs of \$83,100 exceeded the \$81,000 by \$2,100 which more than canceled the favorable effect of the volume variance.

COST REPORTING AND CORRECTION

Cost analysis requires feedback of cost and variance data from budgeted levels of expense. Since the purpose of cost reporting is primarily to facilitate future planning and control, only costs relevant to the present and future should be analyzed. Sunk costs are irrevocable and should not influence new decisions except to explain the current status of resources. Opportunity costs, which are gains that could be realized by placing capital in the best possible investment versus another alternative, are often overlooked because they do not fit nicely into an accounting system. However, insofar as possible, management should judge itself on the basis of opportunities as well as budgeted "problems."

Information from fixed budgets tends to be more useful for planning, while reports from flexible budgeting systems are more useful for control, but both are used. Regardless of the type of system used, the prime requirement of any cost reporting system is that the cost information be timely and relevant to decision making. Thus, those costs which are subject to control and which will influence future decisions (and only those costs) should be reported to the responsible management. With the availability of extensive cost data from an organization's centralized data processing system, special care should be taken to focus managerial attention on those costs which show large variance from budgeted levels. This is an application of the "management by exception" principle.

SUMMARY

Maintenance is any activity designed to keep or restore assets to a satisfactory working condition. Preventive maintenance consists of prior inspections and servicing whereas breakdown maintenance is often concerned with emergency repairs following some type of failure. From a cost standpoint, the optimal level of maintenance activity is attained when the total cost of preventive and breakdown maintenance is minimized.

Among the numerous models available for analyzing maintenance activities, four were discussed in this chapter.

1 The *expected value model* provided a simple means of comparing the cost of a given preventive maintenance policy with the expected cost of breakdowns over the same time period, where the breakdowns occur on an empirical probabilistic basis.

2 A *simulation model* was used to illustrate how simulated breakdown and repair time values can be used to estimate both the preventive (service crew) cost and the breakdown (downtime) cost so that the most economical crew size can be determined.

3 The *probability model* uses historical data on servicing costs, as well as breakdown probabilities (and costs) to help select the appropriate preventive maintenance policy to minimize maintenance costs. This model extends somewhat beyond the earlier models not only to choose between a breakdown versus a given preventive maintenance policy, but also to evaluate various preventive maintenance policies and discriminate among them on the basis of expected cost.

4 The *queuing model*, while resting upon some formidable mathematics, was seen to have realistic applications potential for analyzing the workload and utilization characteristics of maintenance facilities by accounting for the statistical patterns of arrival and service rates.

Failures of components during what might be classified as a normal operating lifetime occur on a rare event (Poisson) basis whereas those in the late stages of product life often occur on a normally distributed basis. The rare event failures present reliability problems and a number of ways exist to measure, analyze, and improve reliability, including such things as parallel systems. The wear-out distributions also lend themselves to statistical analysis.

Cost control is one of the most universal responsibilities of managers, and like other control activities it necessitates the development of reasonable standards. Cost standards specify what a component or activity *should* cost under normal operating conditions. Standards are typically established for labor, materials, and overhead costs. The analysis of cost variance is concerned with how much and why the actual costs differ from standards in terms of volume, rate (or price), and efficiency.

SOLVED PROBLEMS

MODELS FOR MAINTENANCE MANAGEMENT

1 A textile firm uses a \$10/hr cost for direct and indirect labor maintenance and estimates downtime costs on any of a large group of spinning machines at \$50/hr per machine. If breakdowns are distributed according to a Poisson distribution with a mean of four/hr, and the mean number of units a worker can service is six breakdowns/hr-worker (distributed exponentially), what is the optimal maintenance crew size?

Solution

In lieu of other information, estimate the total maintenance costs (crew + downtime) per hour beginning with one worker, and increase the crew size until total costs are minimized. The number of units in breakdown is the mean number in the system N_s:

$$(N_s) = \frac{\lambda}{\mu - \lambda}$$

where

λ = mean arrival rate = 4/hr
μ = mean service rate (varies depending upon crew size)

For crew size of 1:

$$\text{Crew cost} = 1 \text{ worker at } \$10/\text{hr} = \$10.00$$

$$\text{Breakdown cost} = (N_s)(\text{cost/hr})$$

$$= \left(\frac{4}{6 - 4}\right)(\$50/\text{hr}) = \underline{100.00}$$

$$\$110.00/\text{hr}$$

For crew size of 2:

$$\text{Crew cost} = 2 \text{ workers at } \$10/\text{hr} = \$20.00$$

$$\text{Breakdown cost} = \left(\frac{4}{12 - 4}\right)(\$50/\text{hr}) = \underline{25.00}$$

$$\$45.00/\text{hr}$$

For crew size of 3:

$$\text{Crew cost} = 3 \text{ workers at } \$10/\text{hr} = \$30.00$$

$$\text{Breakdown cost} = \left(\frac{4}{18 - 4}\right)(\$50/\text{hr}) = \underline{14.29}$$

$$\$44.29/\text{hr}$$

For crew size of 4:

$$\text{Crew cost} = 4 \text{ workers at } \$10/\text{hr} = \$40.00$$

$$\text{Breakdown cost} = \left(\frac{4}{24 - 4}\right)(\$50/\text{hr}) = \underline{10.00}$$

$$\$50.00/\text{hr}$$

The total costs for crew sizes of two and three are so close that other, non-economic factors should probably be deciding criteria.

*2 (Probability model) A copper refinery in Arizona has 40 flotation cells which can be serviced on a preventive maintenance schedule at $100 each. If the cells break down, it costs $500 to get them back into service (including unscheduled cleanout time and all breakdown costs). Records show that the probabilities of breakdown after maintenance are as shown in the accompanying table.

Months after maintenance	Probability of breakdown
1	0.2
2	0.1
3	0.3
4	0.4

Should a preventive maintenance (PM) policy be followed? If so, how often should the cells be serviced?

Solution

Determine cost of the alternative preventive maintenance policies and compare this with the cost of a breakdown policy.

(*a*) *Preventive maintenance every month*

$$\text{Cost} = \text{servicing cost} + \text{breakdown cost}$$

$$\text{Cost} = \begin{pmatrix}\text{number of}\\ \text{units}\\ \text{serviced}\end{pmatrix}\begin{pmatrix}\text{service}\\ \text{cost/}\\ \text{unit}\end{pmatrix} + \begin{pmatrix}\text{expected}\\ \text{number}\\ \text{of breakdowns}\\ \text{between}\\ \text{services}\end{pmatrix}\begin{pmatrix}\text{breakdown}\\ \text{cost/}\\ \text{unit}\end{pmatrix}$$

$$= (40\text{ cells})(\$100/\text{cell}) + (40\text{ cells} \times 0.2)(\$500/\text{cell})$$

$$= \$4{,}000 + 8(\$500) = \$8{,}000$$

(*b*) *Preventive maintenance every second month*

Note that a bimonthly policy involves a ($4,000) servicing cost plus the cost of individual breakdowns in *both* the first month and the second month. During the first month 40 × 0.2 = 8 machines are expected to break down. During the second month 40 × 0.1 = 4 machines are expected to break down. In addition, some of the machines (20 percent) that broke down in the first month (and were repaired on a breakdown basis) are expected to break down *again* in the second month (before the scheduled maintenance takes place).

$$\text{Cost} = \begin{pmatrix}\text{servicing}\\ \text{cost}\end{pmatrix} + \left[\overset{\text{expected number of breakdowns}}{\begin{pmatrix}\text{during}\\ \text{month}\\ 1\end{pmatrix} + \begin{pmatrix}\text{during}\\ \text{month}\\ 2\end{pmatrix} + (\text{repeats})}\right]\begin{pmatrix}\text{breakdown}\\ \text{cost/unit}\end{pmatrix}$$

$$= \$4{,}000 + (40 \times 0.2 + 40 \times 0.1 + 8 \times 0.2)\ \$500$$

$$\$4{,}000 + (\ 8 + 4 + 1.6\ )\ 500$$

$$= \$4{,}000 + 6{,}800 = \$10{,}800$$

$$\text{Cost/month} = \$10{,}800 \div 2 = \$5{,}400$$

(*c*) *Preventive maintenance every third month*

Beyond a two-month period it becomes more expedient to set up these calculations in a tabular format so that the expected number of breakdowns can be systematically determined before multiplying those values by the breakdown cost ($500). As shown in the accompanying table, a pattern for computing the expected number of breakdowns emerges wherein the 40 cells are assigned the respective probabilities of failure for one, two, three, or four months after maintenance as given in the original data. Note that each probability applies to the whole (40-cell) population and not just to the remaining units, thus preserving the full chance for all 40 units to fail anywhere throughout the four-month period. In addition, each time some cells fail in an earlier month, they are repaired and restored to a "renewed" status whereupon they regain their original probability (0.2) of failing again in the next period. Thus under the three-month PM policy, the eight units expected to break down in period 1 gain a renewed probability of 0.2 of breakdown in period 2 because period 2 then becomes their first month after maintenance. Adding their expected value of breakdown (1.6) to the original period 2 value (4.0) gives an expected breakdown total of 5.6 cells, which in turn is renewed and carried forward to period 3 resulting in a 1.12 expected value. Note that period 3 also contains an original allocation of breakdowns (12.0) plus the second-period probability of failure (0.1) associated with that portion of the (eight) cells which were renewed in period 1 and did not fail in period 2.

Type of PM policy	Determination of expected number of breakdowns during period: 1	2	3	4	Cumulative expected number of breakdowns during PM period
One-month PM policy	(40)(0.2) = 8.0	(same as period 1)	(same as period 1)	(same as period 1)	8
Two-month PM policy	(40)(0.2) = 8.0	(40)(0.1) = 4.0 (8)(0.2) = 1.6 5.6	(same as period 1)	(same as period 2)	8.0 5.6 13.6
Three-month PM policy	(40)(0.2) = 8.0	(40)(0.1) = 4.0 (8)(0.2) = 1.6 5.6	(40)(0.3) = 12.0 (8)(0.1) = 0.8 (5.6)(0.2) = 1.12 13.92	(same as period 1)	8.0 5.6 13.92 27.52
Four-month PM policy	(40)(0.2) = 8.0	(40)(0.1) = 4.0 (8)(0.2) = 1.6 5.6	(40)(0.3) = 12.0 (8)(0.1) = 0.8 (5.6)(0.2) = 1.12 13.92	(40)(0.4) = 16.0 (8)(0.3) = 2.4 (5.6)(0.1) = 0.56 (13.92)(0.2) = 2.78 21.74	8.0 5.6 13.92 21.74 49.26

The cumulative expected number of breakdowns B in M months may also be expressed by means of the equation:

$$B_n = N\sum_1^n P_n + B_{n-1}P_1 + B_{n-2}P_2 + \cdots + B_1P_{n-1} \qquad (11\text{-}26)^*$$

where

N = number of cells
P = probability of breakdown during a given month after maintenance
n = maintenance period

Thus:

$$B_1 = Np_1 = (40)(0.2) = 8.0$$

$$B_2 = N(p_1 + p_2) + B_1p_1 = 40(0.2 + 0.1) + 8(0.2) = 13.6$$

$$B_3 = N(p_1 + p_2 + p_3) + B_2p_1 + B_1p_2$$
$$= 40(0.2 + 0.1 + 0.3) + 13.6(0.2) + 8(0.1) = 27.52$$

$$B_4 = N(p_1 + p_2 + p_3 + p_4) + B_3p_1 + B_2p_2 + B_1p_1$$
$$= 40(1.0) + 27.52(0.2) + 13.6(0.1) + 8(0.3) = 49.26$$

The differences between the monthly cumulative totals then represent the individual period breakdowns. Thus the expected number of breakdowns during period 2 is 13.6 − 8.0 = 5.6, which agrees with the table. The following (preventive maintenance cost analysis) table carries forward the cost analysis to the determination of an expected total cost for the various preventive maintenance policies.

Preventive maintenance cost analysis—PM policy

	One month	Two months	Three months	Four months
Cumulative breakdowns during PM period	8.00	13.60	27.52	49.26
Cost at $500 each	$4,000	$6,800	13,760	$24,630
Add: PM cost at $100/cell	+4,000	+4,000	+4,000	+4,000
Total cost for M month PM policy	$8,000 (1$M$)	$10,800 (2$M$)	$17,760 (3$M$)	$28,630 (4$M$)
Monthly cost	$8,000	$5,400	$5,920	$7,158

The cost of following any PM policy (for example, \$5,400 for a two-month policy) must then be compared with the cost of a breakdown policy. The expected cost of following a breakdown policy C_p is simply the cost C_r of repairing all the cells N divided by the expected number of periods between breakdowns $\sum T_n(p_n)$:

$$C_p = \frac{NC_r}{\sum T_n(p_n)} \tag{11-27)*}$$

where

T_n = number of time period after repair
p_n = probability of breakdown during given time period n

Thus:

$$\sum T_n(p_n) = 1(0.2) + 2(0.1) + 3(0.3) + 4(0.4)$$
$$= 2.9 \text{ months between breakdowns}$$

$$C_p = \frac{NC_r}{\sum T_n(p_n)}$$
$$= \frac{(40 \text{ cells})(\$500/\text{breakdown-cell})}{2.9 \text{ month/breakdown}}$$
$$= \$6{,}897/\text{month}$$

Conclusion: Both the two-month and three-month preventive maintenance policies (at expected costs of \$5,400 and \$5,920 respectively) are preferred to the breakdown policy (\$6,897) with the two-month policy being most preferable.

3 Patients arrive at a medical clinic with an arrival rate that is Poisson-distributed with a mean of 6/hr. Treatment (service) time averages 8 min and can be approximated by the negative exponential distribution. Find the (*a*) mean waiting time, (*b*) mean number in the queue, and (*c*) percent of idle time.

Solution

$$\lambda = \text{arrival rate} = 6/\text{hr}$$

$$\mu = \text{service rate} = \left(\frac{\text{unit}}{8 \text{ min}}\right)\left(\frac{60 \text{ min}}{\text{hr}}\right) = 7.5/\text{hr}$$

(*a*) $$T_w = \frac{\lambda}{\mu(\mu - \lambda)} = \frac{6}{7.5(7.5 - 6)} = 0.53 \text{ hr} = 32 \text{ min}$$

(*b*) $$N_q = \frac{\lambda^2}{\mu(\mu - \lambda)} = 3.20 \text{ units}$$

(*c*) $$\%I = 100 - \%U = 100 - \frac{\lambda}{\mu} = 100 - \frac{6}{7.5} = 20\%$$

4 The time required to replace a filter on any of 500 industrial mixers can be considered a constant at 15 min/filter. Maintenance records show the failure rate of filters is distributed according to a Poisson distribution with a mean of 2/hr.

(*a*) Find the average number of mixers waiting.
(*b*) Find the average waiting time of a mixer for repair.

Solution

(*a*) $$N_{q(c)} = \frac{\lambda^2}{2\mu(\mu - \lambda)}$$

where

λ = arrival rate = 2/hr
μ = service rate

$$= \left(\frac{\text{filter}}{15 \text{ min}}\right)\left(\frac{60 \text{ min}}{\text{hr}}\right) = 4/\text{hr}$$

$$= \frac{2^2}{2(4)(4 - 2)} = 0.25 \text{ mixers}$$

(*b*) $$T_{w(c)} = \frac{\lambda}{2\mu(\mu - \lambda)} = \frac{2}{2(4)(4 - 2)} = 0.125 \text{ hr} = 7.50 \text{ min}$$

5 The housewares plant of a chemical company has 15 identical molding machines which produce a variety of molded products that generate a profit of $100/machine per day. The machines fail according to a Poisson distribution with an average of 2.2 machines down each day.

(*a*) What is the chance of having exactly three machines down on a given day?
(*b*) What is the expected amount of lost profit/day due to this Poisson failure rate of 2.2/day?
(*c*) If back-up machines could be maintained for a cost of $40 per machine per day, how many would be justified? [Adapted from **1**: 103.]

Solution

(*a*) Since failures follow the Poisson distribution, the probability of X machines failing on any given day is:

$$P(X) = \frac{\lambda^x e^{-\lambda}}{x!}$$

where

x = number of machines broken down = 3
λ = mean failure rate = 2.2/day
e = 2.718

$$P(X = 3) = \frac{(2.2)^3 e^{-2.2}}{3!} = 0.1966 = 20 \text{ percent chance}$$

(Note that the values may be calculated or taken from Appendix F.)

(*b*) The expected loss per day is:

$$E(X) = X \cdot P(X)$$

where

$$\begin{aligned} X &= \text{amount of loss} = \$100/\text{machine-day} \\ P(X) &= \text{mean value of distribution} \\ &= 2.2 \text{ machines/day} \end{aligned}$$

$$\begin{aligned} \therefore\ E(X) &= 100(2.2) \\ &= \$220/\text{day} \end{aligned}$$

Note that the expected loss could also be obtained by computing the sum of the loss amounts times the (Poisson) probability with which they occur as follows. Probability values are from Appendix F.

Number failed	Poisson $P(X)$	Amount of lost profit X	Expected loss of profit $X \cdot P(X)$
0	0.1108	0	$ 0
1	0.2438	100	24
2	0.2681	200	54
3	0.1966	300	59
4	0.1082	400	43
5	0.0476	500	24
6	0.0174	600	10
7	0.0055	700	4
8	0.0019	800	2
9	0.0005	900	0
10	0.0001	1,000	0
		Total	$220

(*c*) With no back-up machines, the lost profit is as indicated above. By having one back-up machine, there is no lost profit with either zero or one breakdown. With two breakdowns, the loss is only $100 and it occurs with a probability of 0.2681 so the expected loss is ($100)(0.2681) = $27. Similarly, with three breakdowns, the expected loss is ($200)(0.1966) = $39. As we go to two back-up machines, there is no loss until three machines have failed and the expected loss is ($100) × (0.1966) = $20. Remaining values are shown in the accompanying table. *Conclusion:* Two back-up machines minimize the loss of expected profit.

EXPECTED LOSS OF PROFIT

Number of machines broken down	Number of back-up machines				
	0	1	2	3	4
0	0	0	0	0	0
1	24	0	0	0	0
2	54	(100)(0.2681) = 27	0	0	0
3	59	(200)(0.1966) = 39	20	0	0
4	43	(300)(0.1082) = 32	22	11	0
5	24	(400)(0.0476) = 19	14	10	5
6	10	(500)(0.0174) = 9	7	5	3
7	4	(600)(0.0055) = 3	3	2	2
8	2	(700)(0.0019) = 1	1	1	1
9	0	(800)(0.0005) = 0	0	0	0
10	0	(900)(0.0001) = 0	0	0	0
Total expected loss	$220	$130	$67	$29	$11
Add cost of back-up machines at $40 ea.	+0	+40	+80	−120	−160
Total	$220	$170	$147	$149	$171

6 (*Replacement decision where operating life is known and constant.*) An automatic machine at an underground mine in Wyoming has two clutches that must be replaced periodically. Clutch *A* costs $40, can be installed for $50, and will operate satisfactorily for 300 hours. Clutch *B* costs only $30, can be installed for $35, and will operate for 400 hours. Both parts can be installed on one shutdown for $45. Compare the costs of replacing the clutches individually versus doing them together (use a cycle time of 3,600 hours).

Solution (See the sketch on the following page)

Individual replacement:

A: 9 times at $90 =	$810
B: 6 times at 65 =	390
A + *B*: 3 times at 115 =	345
Total	$1,545

All joint replacement: (every 300 hr)

A + *B*: 12 times at 115 = $1,380

Conclusion: Costs of individual replacement are $1,545 − $1,380 = $165 less per 3,600 hours.

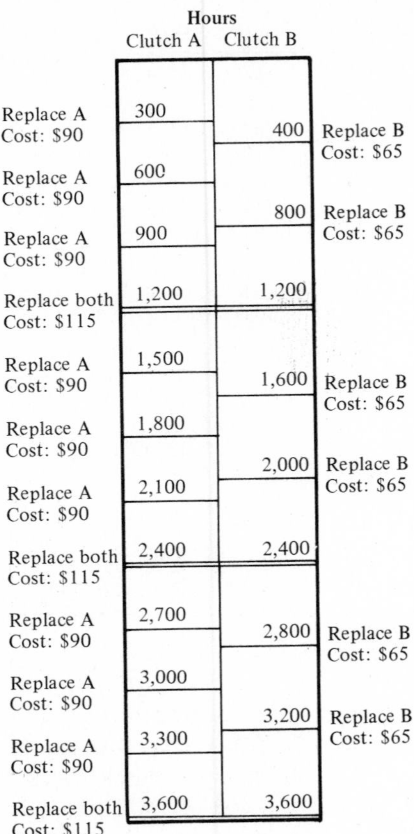

***7** (Replacement decision where operating life is variable.) Anodized Aluminum Incorporated has three heavily used circuit breakers which control electrolytic processing equipment in a large mill. The failure of any breaker stops operations with resulting downtime costs of $300/hr. The breakers cost $150 each and installation time is 30 min for replacing one, 45 min for two, and one hour for all three. Installation labor cost is $90/hr. Historical data on breaker life have been collected and simulated to help determine which maintenance policy to adopt:

(*a*) Replace each breaker after it fails.

(*b*) Replace all three breakers after any one fails. (Simulated service times until failure are as shown in the accompanying table.)

(*c*) Replace each breaker after it fails, plus any other breakers with 30 days or more operating time.

Days until failure		
Breaker A	Breaker B	Breaker C
18	3	28
2	30	11
46	24	33
13	42	20
42	21	38
25	22	13
2	21	29
16	14	45
12	20	20
27	31	35
15	12	20
20	22	19
32	38	32
9	31	15

Solution

For purposes of illustration we shall assume a cumulative operating time of 200 days is adequate for comparison of the policies. Thus we cumulate times until 200 days is reached.

(*a*) *Replace each breaker after it fails:*

Replacement period number	Individual and cumulative days until failure						
	Breaker A		Breaker B		Breaker C		
	Ind.	Cumul.	Ind.	Cumul.	Ind.	Cumul.	
1	18	18	3	3	28	28	
2	2	20	30	33	11	39	
3	46	66	24	57	33	72	
4	13	79	42	99	20	92	
5	42	121	21	120	38	130	
6	25	146	22	142	13	143	
7	2	148	21	163	29	172	
8	16	164	14	177	45	217	
9	12	176	20	197	20	237	
10	27	203	31	228	35	272	
11	15	218	12	240	20	292	
12	20	238	22	262	19	311	
13	32	270	38	300	32	343	
14	9	279	31	331	15	358	
Number of replacements by 200th day		9		9		7	(25 total)

$$\text{Material cost (breakers)} = \left(\frac{\text{number}}{\text{replaced}}\right)\left(\frac{\text{cost}}{\text{breaker}}\right) = (25)(\$150) = \$3{,}750$$

$$\text{Labor cost} = \left(\frac{\text{number}}{\text{replaced}}\right)\left(\frac{\text{number}}{\text{of hr}}\right)\left(\frac{\text{cost}}{\text{hr}}\right)$$

$$= (25 \text{ breakers})\left(\frac{0.5 \text{ hr}}{\text{breakdown}}\right)\left(\frac{\$90}{\text{hr}}\right) = 1{,}125$$

$$\text{Downtime cost}^{\dagger} = \left(\frac{\text{number}}{\text{replaced}}\right)\left(\frac{\text{number}}{\text{of hr}}\right)\left(\frac{\text{cost}}{\text{hr}}\right)$$

$$= (25)(0.5)(\$300) = 3{,}750$$

$$\text{Total cost} \quad \$8{,}625$$

(*b*) *Replace all three breakers after any one breaker fails*. With this policy, the first failure is breaker *B* at three days so *A* and *C* are also replaced at that time. The next failure is *A* at two days later so it, plus *B* and *C*, are replaced then. Continuing on we can determine the number of breakdowns for 200 hours of operation by always cumulating the shortest time of the three breakers as shown. (We reach 200 hours after breakdown number 13.)

Downtime number	Next failure time (days)	
	Incremental	Cumulative
1	3	3
2	2	5
3	24	29
4	13	42
5	21	63
6	13	76
7	2	78
8	14	92
9	12	104
10	27	131
11	12	143
12	19	162
13	32	194
14	9	203

$$\text{Material cost} = \left(\frac{\text{number of}}{\text{downtimes}}\right)\left(\frac{\text{breakers}}{\text{downtime}}\right)\left(\frac{\text{cost}}{\text{breaker}}\right)$$

$$= (13)(3)(\$150) = \$5{,}850$$

† No two breakers failed at the same time.

$$\text{Labor cost} = \left(\begin{matrix}\text{number of}\\ \text{downtimes}\end{matrix}\right)\left(\frac{\text{number of hr}}{\text{breakdown}}\right)\left(\frac{\text{cost}}{\text{hr}}\right)$$

$$= (13\ \text{breakdowns})\left(\frac{1\ \text{hr}}{\text{breakdown}}\right)\left(\frac{\$90}{\text{hr}}\right) = \quad 1{,}170$$

$$\text{Downtime cost} = \left(\begin{matrix}\text{number of}\\ \text{downtimes}\end{matrix}\right)\left(\begin{matrix}\text{number of hr}\\ \text{broke down}\end{matrix}\right)\left(\frac{\text{cost}}{\text{hr}}\right)$$

$$= (13)(1)(\$300) \qquad = \quad 3{,}900$$

$$\text{Total cost} \quad \$10{,}920$$

(*c*) *Replace each breaker after it fails, plus any other breakers with 30 days or more operating time.* The accompanying chart identifies additional replacements with dotted lines. The first joint replacement occurs on the seventh failure when *B* fails after 24 days of operation. By that time (day 57) breaker *A* has operated for 57 − 20 = 37 days so it is also replaced (even though it would have operated satisfactorily for another 9 days). Unfortunately the replacement for *A* fails in 13 days, but by this time *C* has operated for 31 days so it is then replaced along with *A*.

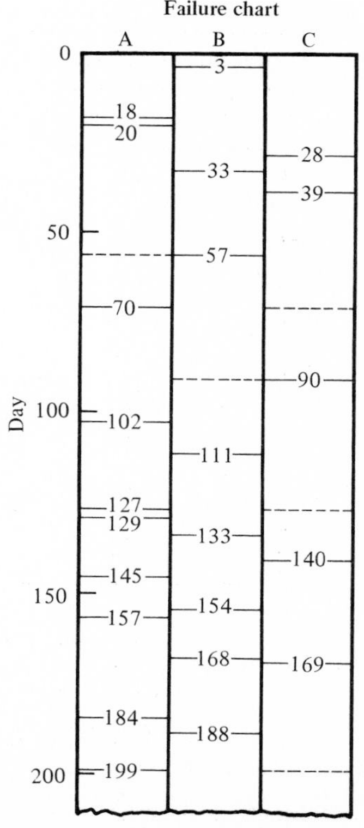

Material cost

$$= \left(\begin{matrix}\text{number of}\\ \text{breakers}\end{matrix}\right)\left(\frac{\text{cost}}{\text{breaker}}\right) = (28)(\$150) \qquad = \$4{,}200$$

Labor cost

$$\begin{aligned} = {} & 18 \text{ single replacements at } (0.5\text{ hr})(\$90/\text{hr}) && = \$810 \\ & 5 \text{ double replacements at } (0.75\text{ hr})(\$90/\text{hr}) && = \underline{\ \ 338} \\ & && \ 1{,}148 = 1{,}148 \end{aligned}$$

Downtime cost

$$\begin{aligned} = {} & 18 \text{ breakdowns at } 0.5\text{ hr} && = 9.00\text{ hr} \\ & 5 \text{ breakdowns at } 0.75\text{ hr} && = \underline{3.75\text{ hr}} \\ & \text{Total} && \ 12.75\text{ hr at } \$300 \qquad = \underline{3{,}825} \\ & && \text{Total cost} \quad \$9{,}173 \end{aligned}$$

The least-cost policy is to replace each breaker after it fails.

8 A cost accounting audit is to be taken of a file containing 30 orders, one of which has an incorrect calculation. What is the probability that in a random selection of two orders, one will be incorrect?

Solution

This is a hypergeometric probability problem.

$$P(X = 1 \text{ incorrect}) = \frac{\text{number of ways of choosing one incorrect}}{\text{total ways of choosing 2 from 30}}$$

$$= \frac{C_1^{29}C_1^{1}}{C_2^{30}} = \frac{\dfrac{29!}{1!\,(28)!}\cdot\dfrac{1!}{1!\,0!}}{\dfrac{30!}{2!\,28!}} = 0.033$$

*9 A toy manufacturer in Miami uses flexible budgeting procedures and has collected the following data on actual production and production standards for a toy hang-glider.

	Actual	Standard
Number toys produced	2,000	2,000
Direct labor (hr)	500	440
Wage rate ($/hr)	3.50	3.30
Material consumption (ft²)	1,200	1,040
Material price ($/ft²)	0.90	1.00
Variable overhead cost (total $)	2,000	2,200
Variable overhead cost ($/direct labor hour)	4.0	5.0

Find the (*a*) labor variance, (*b*) material variance, and (*c*) gross variable overhead variance.

Solution

Note that since "total" values are given for labor hours and material consumption, Eqs. 11-18, 11-19, 11-21, and 11-22 can be shortened accordingly.

(*a*) *Labor variance:*

$$\text{Rate} = V_{r-l} = \Delta \text{ rate (actual time)} = (\$3.30 - 3.50)(500)$$
$$= -\$100$$

$$\text{Efficiency} = V_{e-l} = \Delta \text{ hours (std rate)} = (440 - 500)(\$3.30)$$
$$= -\$198$$

(*b*) *Material variance:*

$$\text{Price} = V_{p-\text{mtl}} = \Delta \text{ price (actual mtl)}$$
$$= (\$1.00 - .90)(1{,}200) = \$120$$

$$\text{Efficiency} = V_{e-\text{mtl}} = \Delta \text{ mtl (std price)}$$
$$= (\$1{,}040 - 1{,}200)(\$1.00) = -\$160$$

(*c*) *Variable overhead variance* (simplified gross version):

$$\text{OH variance} = \text{standard} - \text{actual} = \$2{,}200 - 2{,}000 = \$200$$

***10** (Extension of Problem 9 above to more detailed analysis of variable overhead variance. [Adapted from **4**: 232.]) A toy manufacturer in Miami uses flexible budgeting procedures and has produced 2,000 hang-gliders in 500 direct labor hours whereas the standard called for 440 hours. The actual wage rate was $3.50/hr and the standard was $3.30/hr. Variable overhead was as shown in the accompanying table.

	Standard cost per direct labor hour	**Actual total cost incurred**
Indirect labor (inspection and rework)	$3.00	$1,100
Maintenance	.80	50
Setup and cleanup	1.00	840
Machine lubricants	.20	10
	$5.00	$2,000

Analyze the variable overhead according to (*a*) spending variance and (*b*) efficiency variance.

Solution

A common and useful method of analyzing flexible budget overhead variance is in terms of efficiency and spending variance [**4**: 234].

Efficiency variance is the amount expected to be incurred due to inefficient use of direct labor (that is, variable overhead costs are assumed to fluctuate in direct proportion to the direct labor hours). *Spending variance* is the amount unexplained by the efficiency variance and could be from, for example, use of higher-cost machine lubricants, or even increased inefficiency (or efficiency). The spending and efficiency variances are computed as shown in the accompanying table.

	(1) Actual costs incurred	(2) Budget based on 500 actual hours	(3) Budget based on 440 standard hours	(4) Total budget variance (3) − (1)	(5) Analysis of (4): Spending variance (2) − (1)	Efficiency variance (3) − (2)
Indirect labor	1,100	$1,500	$1,320	220	400	−180
Maintenance	50	400	352	302	350	−48
Setup and cleanup	840	500	440	−400	−340	−60
Machine lubricants	10	100	88	78	90	−12
		$2,500	$2,200	200	500	−300

Conclusion: The efficiency variance (an unfavorable $300) suggests some inefficiencies in the respective budget amounts that would have been allowed for 440 direct labor hours versus the 500 hours actually used. However, the spending variance (a favorable $500) reveals that actual costs were less than the flexible budget amount (based on 500 actual hours) in every category except setup and cleanup. It may be worthwhile to check those activities for possible improvement. In general, however, the favorable spending variances are also unexplained, and would merit some inquiry.

QUESTIONS

11-1 How are maintenance activities distinguished from other normal production activities?

11-2 Identify the major components of preventive and breakdown maintenance costs. Which do you feel are most significant?

11-3 Briefly summarize (in two or three sentences each) the purpose and methodology of the four models for maintenance management discussed in the chapter. In what respects are the models similar?

11-4 How would a breakdown probability distribution be obtained, what would it show, and how might it be useful to a maintenance manager?

11-5 Would preventive maintenance generally be more applicable to machines that have a high or low variability in their breakdown time distribution? Why? (*Note:* You may want to make a sketch similar to Fig. 11-4 to illustrate your answer.)

11-6 A maintenance manager has remarked to the plant manager that "the most important thing I've got to do in this plant, as I see it, is to do everything I can to minimize the total of all downtime costs. I work at that eight hours a day and you're still on my back! What more do you want?" Discuss.

11-7 Give an example of a single-channel, multiple-phase queuing situation and illustrate the structure of such a queuing situation by a simple diagram.

11-8 What assumptions underlie the basic queuing model discussed in the chapter?

11-9 Define product reliability. How is the reliability of a complex system determined?

11-10 Suppose you are in charge of reliability for a new interplanetary space ship and have also been selected to go along on the maiden voyage. What steps would you take now, while the system is being designed and made, to ensure that you are getting a round trip rather than a one-way passage?

11-11 Distinguish between failures distributed as Poisson and failures distributed normally. Which type of distribution is most closely associated with (*a*) maintenance activities, and (*b*) reliability concerns?

11-12 Define (*a*) cost standard, (*b*) job costing, (*c*) direct costs, (*d*) budget.

11-13 What is the difference between the overhead liquidation rate and the overhead adjusted standard?

11-14 Many very small firms make no cost variance analysis and still get by satisfactorily. Why is it done in larger firms?

11-15 Suppose you were asked to set up a cost control program for an established glass manufacturing firm. Briefly, what steps would you feel were absolutely vital to such a program?

PROBLEMS

1 Manchester (England) Woolen Mills has kept records of breakdowns on its carding machines for a 300-day work year as shown.

Number of breakdowns	Frequency (in days)
0	40
1	150
2	70
3	30
4	10
	300

They estimate that each breakdown costs \$65 and are considering adopting a preventive maintenance program that would cost \$20/day and limit the number of breakdowns to an average of one/day. What is the expected annual savings from the preventive maintenance program?

2 The following data were derived from a simulation of maintenance activities in the plant of a multinational book publisher in New Jersey. The firm has several machines but only one crew and occasionally (20 min/day—see accompanying table) there are two machines out of service at the same time.

Average number of service calls/day	5 calls/day
Average idle time/day of service crew	5 hr/day
Total delay time/day of machines awaiting service	20 min/day

The service call (repair) materials cost is essentially fixed at \$25/call and the operations manager uses a cost of \$120/hr-machine for each machine out of service. (Note that this applies to the 3 hr/day when a machine is being worked on plus the 20 min/day delay time when a second machine is also out of service and waiting to be worked on.) In addition to the \$120/hr-machine cost, the service crew cost is \$50/hr. For an eight-hr day, (*a*) what is the simulated crew idle-time cost, and (*b*) what is the simulated total maintenance cost? (*c*) Considering the crew cost of \$50/hr × 8 hr = \$400 as a preventive maintenance expense, comment upon the suitability of the crew size.

3 Cascade Plastics has a group of molding machines that require breakdown maintenance at a (Poisson-distributed) mean rate of six/day. Each maintenance technician can service an (exponentially distributed) average of eight/day. If downtime costs are \$400/eight-hr workday, what size maintenance crew will be the least costly? Maintenance labor costs are \$15/hr.

4 Machine breakdowns average 10/day and follow a Poisson distribution. Service rates are exponentially distributed and average 11/day with one maintenance worker, 15/day with two, 18/day with three, and 20 with four. If labor costs are \$150/day-worker and downtime costs are \$400/day-machine, what is the optimum crew size?

5 In a simulated operation, a firm's maintenance worker received requests for service and provided service during an 8-hr period, as shown.

Request arrival (clock) time	Required service time (hours)
0:00	1.5
1:00	0.5
3:30	2.0
4:00	0.5
7:00	1.0

The maintenance labor cost is \$14/hr and delay time (when machines are not being operated or repaired, but instead are simply waiting for service) is \$45/hr. Find (*a*) the idle-time cost for the maintenance worker, and (*b*) the delay-time cost for the machinery.

6 Requests for maintenance service made upon a centralized facility have been simulated for a typical eight-hr day with arrival and service time patterns as shown in the accompanying table.

Request (arrival time)	Repair (service time)
1:30	60 min
2:00	18 min
4:15	45 min
4:30	120 min
5:30	30 min
7:00	9 min

Labor attached to the maintenance center is charged at a rate of \$40/hr whether working or idle. The delay (waiting) time of operators and machinery that is broken down is costed at \$70/hr. Find (*a*) the idle-time cost of the maintenance facility, (*b*) the delay-time cost of the operators and machinery—the waiting-time cost only, not including actual repair, (*c*) the total facility idle-time and machinery delay-time cost. (*d*) Assume that for an additional cost of \$10/hr the maintenance center could add another worker and decrease the repair times by one-third. Would the additional cost be justified? (*e*) Show the effect of (*d*) by sketching Fig. 11-1 and locating two additional vertical dotted lines: line *A* should depict the \$40/hr maintenance center rate and line *B* the \$50 rate.

***7** Worldwide Construction Company has received a large contract for a highway construction project wherein they will be penalized \$2,500 per day for each day the project falls behind schedule. Each breakdown of a carryall during the day shift costs an average of \$50 in repair and service maintenance costs plus the loss of one-tenth day in completion time. The carryalls can be serviced on an overtime basis during an evening shift (with no loss of production time) at a cost of $80 each.

Weeks after maintenance	**Probability of breakdowns**
1	0.1
2	0.1
3	0.3
4	0.5

(*a*) What would be the expected cost of following a policy of simply waiting until carryalls break down to service them?
(*b*) How often should the carryalls be serviced?

8 A tool crib attendant receives requests for tools at a mean Poisson rate of 18/hr and can service an average of 20 requests/hr on a negative exponential basis. If requests are handled on a first-come first-served basis, what are (*a*) the mean number in the waiting line and (*b*) the mean waiting time?

9 A vegetable processing plant in the Sacramento Valley has one maintenance crew to service breakdowns in any one of several buildings on a first-call priority basis. Breakdowns occur on an average of λ = 5/week (Poissonly distributed) but the crew could service an average of μ = eight breakdowns/week (negative exponentially distributed). Find (*a*) $\%U$, (*b*) T_s, (*c*) N_s, (*d*) T_w, (*e*) N_q, (*f*) probability of finding the crew with three breakdowns to worry about at one time.

10 Freeway Auto Service Technicians Incorporated (FAST) advertises a (constant) standard time of 6 min to wash and lubricate passenger cars. Requests for service arrive according to a Poisson distribution with a mean of λ = four/hr.
(*a*) Express the standard time as a service rate.
(*b*) What is the mean waiting time (min) for service?

11 A large television service firm has Poisson arrival rates and negative exponential service times and serves customers 24 hr/day on a first-come first-served basis. If they receive service orders at a mean rate of 30/day and have the personnel and facilities to handle up to 35/day,
(*a*) How many sets, on the average, will they have in their shop at any one time?
(*b*) How many hours, on the average, will a customer have to wait *before the service firm starts work* on his set?
(*c*) How many hours, on the average, would the customer have to wait before the firm started work on his set if the firm had a *constant* service rate of 35/day.

***12** Green River Mills has 12 automatic machines that each do the work of several laborers for a net savings of $200/machine-day. The machines break down randomly at times corresponding to a Poisson distribution with a mean of $\lambda =$ two/day.

(*a*) What is the probability of more than one machine breaking down on any given day?

(*b*) Assume that manual labor can be substituted for machines that are down. Based on the average failure rate of two machines/day, what is the expected incremental (added) cost of the labor?

(*c*) The firm can maintain standby machines for an extra cost of $130/machine-day. How many standby machines are justified on an expected value basis?

13 Quick Freeze Foods has a corn line with two stripper saws operating in sequence to cut kernels from corn cobs. Blades on both the primary P and secondary S saws get dull and must be replaced periodically as shown in the accompanying table.

	Blade cost ($)	**Installation cost ($)**	**Operating life**
Primary	$60	70	80 hr
Secondary	40	60	100 hr
Both	100	90	

Should the blades be replaced individually at the end of their operating lives, or should both be replaced each 80 hr? Make your comparison over an 800-hr period.

***14** The Boulder Paper Company has three reversing motors in a high-temperature acidic environment where breakdowns occur frequently. The motors themselves cost $300 each and installation costs are $40 for replacing one, $60 for two, and $70 for all three. Downtime costs are estimated at $600/hr and the time to replace one, two, or three motors is 15 min, 25 min, and 30 min, respectively. The data shown are a representative simulation of failure times (in weeks) for the motors.

Motor 1	**Motor 2**	**Motor 3**
10	11	7
7	12	11
11	4	8
10	6	13
11	12	9
8	11	4
9	12	12
11	12	6
15	6	12
8	7	9

Based upon an analysis of this data for one year (through 52 weeks), show calculations and accompanying diagrams to determine the respective costs of the following maintenance policies:

(*a*) Replace each motor after it fails.

(*b*) Replace all three motors after any one fails.

(*c*) Replace each motor after it fails, plus any motor with ≥ 10 weeks of operating time.

Note: If two failures happen to occur during the same week, do not assume they occur simultaneously.

15 In response to a customer request for failure-rate data, an instrument manufacturer tested a group of 30 instruments over a 2,000-hr test period and found that 4 failed. Find (*a*) $FR_{\%}$, (*b*) FR_n (in failures/unit-yr).

16 A firm producing automobile exhaust filters was required to provide the Environmental Protection Agency with failure-rate data based upon a 10-hr test. If 200 units were tested and 8 failed, what is (*a*) the failure rate in failures/unit-yr and (*b*) the mean time between failures?

17 The purification system in a water treatment plant has three components in series (R_1, R_2, and R_3). The component reliabilities for a three-month period *remain constant* and are as shown. At the end of each three-month period all components are replaced regardless of the length of service. In the meantime, each time any component breaks down the cost of downtime and repair is $300. What is the annual expected cost of downtime and repair?

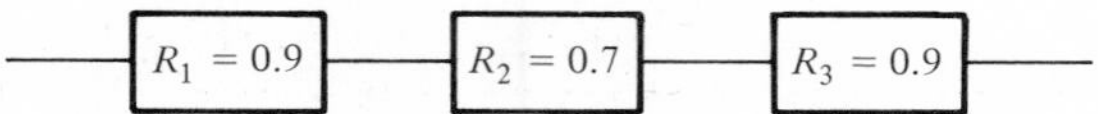

18 A firm with a processing system using machines X and Y in sequence has now installed another machine Z which performs an equivalent job. If the respective reliabilities of X, Y, and Z are 0.9, 0.8, and 0.7, what is the total reliability of the system?

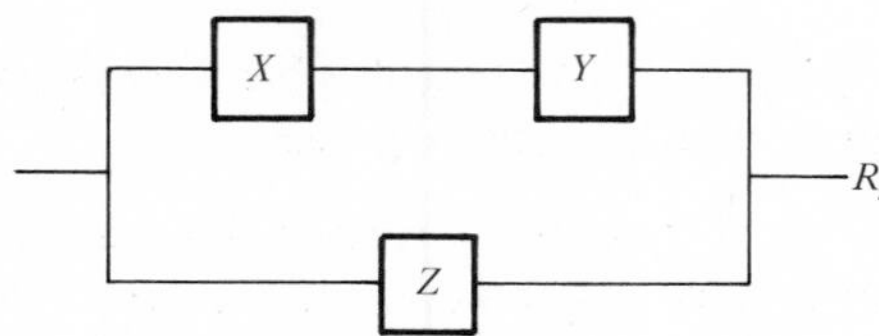

19 The maintenance manager for a nationwide trucking firm has found that a substantial savings in tire cost can be gained by contracting with a tire manufacturer to replace tires on the entire fleet of trucks at one time. For safety purposes, the manager feels this should be done at the time 15 percent of the tires are worn out. If tire life is normally distributed with a mean of 30 months and standard deviation of 3 months, when should the replacement take place?

20 A maintenance superintendent has determined that in a certain application, bearing life follows a normal distribution with a mean of 620 hours and standard deviation of 20 hours. What percent of the bearings should have lives between 600 and 660 hours?

21 The XRON Company has fixed costs of $180,000 and other variable overhead costs which range from $30,000 at a volume of 20,000 units to $50,000 at 60,000 units. They use a nylon material which costs $.30 per foot and each unit requires 4 feet of material. A work-sampling study revealed the following standard times for the manufacturing activity.

Activity	Standard time (hr/unit)	Standard labor rate ($/hr)
Cutting	0.06	6.50
Stamping	0.01	4.00
Cleaning	0.03	4.00
Inspection	0.01	5.00
Packaging	0.01	4.00

Find (*a*) the labor standard cost, (*b*) the material standard cost, (*c*) the overhead standard cost.

***22** A cost control study of direct labor in an appliance manufacturing plant revealed the information shown in the accompanying table.

	Actual	Standard
Heater units produced	1,000	900
Time/unit	15 min	10 min
Wage rate/hr (average)	$4.00	$3.60
Labor hours	250	150
Labor costs (total)	$1,000	$540
Labor cost/unit	$1.00	$.60

The firm operates on a fixed budget. What is (*a*) the volume variance, (*b*) the rate variance, (*c*) the efficiency variance?

***23** A firm producing weather barometers has a fixed cost of $10,000/yr and other overhead costs that vary at a constant rate/unit from $1,000 at 5,000 units to $3,000 at 7,000 units. The forecast volume for the past year was 6,000 units but the actual demand was 6,500 units and the actual total overhead cost was $13,000. Find the overhead cost variance due to (*a*) volume V_{v-oh}, (*b*) efficiency V_{e-oh}, and (*c*) the total overhead cost variance.

***24** The following data was collected for a variance analysis study of a firm using fixed budgeting procedures. Find (*a*) labor variance, (*b*) material variance, (*c*) overhead variance.

	Actual	Standard
Units produced	459	450
Time/unit	20 min	15 min
Wage rate	$5.00/hr	$4.80/hr
Labor hours	153	112.5
Labor costs	$765	$540
Labor cost/unit	$1.67	$1.20 C_l
Material price $/inch	$.30	$.25
Material consumption (in/unit)	0.18	0.15
Material costs (total)	$24.79	$16.88
Material unit cost	$.054	$.038 C_m
Annual production	22,000 units	20,000 units
Annual fixed cost		$30,000
Annual semivariable cost		$10,000
Total overhead cost	$42,000	$40,000
Overhead liquidation rate		$2/unit
Overhead low cost		$36,000
Overhead high cost		$44,000
Low volume		18,000 units
High volume		22,000 units

CASE: THE PLYWOOD MILL MAINTENANCE BUDGET

Andrew Tennyson, assistant manager of the Southern Plywood Mill, was on the spot, for he had to come up with a recommendation to general manager Frank Hawley. For the fifth time in six months maintenance expenses were over the budget and Mr. Hawley had promised that "next time heads will roll." This *was* the next time, and Mr. Hawley was relying on his assistant manager to recommend some corrective action—that is, whose head!

Andy Tennyson wanted the recommendation to be right for two reasons. First, he had some direct responsibility in this matter since the maintenance manager reported directly to him. Second, he had hoped to establish a reputation as an able, budget-conscious manager, and the last thing he needed to stifle his career was a second-rate maintenance problem.

Two years ago things had been different—perhaps even worse—but he felt he had been able to maneuver the department out of trouble quite skillfully. It was right after a plant expansion and the mill had seemed to be in one continuous nightmare of breakdowns. Patrick Shelton, the mill's maintenance manager, and his staff of eight repair workers simply could not cope with the breakdown situation. Each hour of downtime had been estimated to cost the firm $800 in profits, so after a few months the mill's problems began showing up in the parent company's profit and loss statement. Mr. Tennyson recalled that he had helped to bail Shelton out of that mess by insisting that, among other things, maintenance activities be decentralized.

Pat Shelton was an independent and resourceful jack-of-all-trades who had worked his way up through the ranks. He was capable and was willing to tackle almost any maintenance problem, but his solutions were not always conventional. Sometimes his jerry-rigging and bailing-wire techniques were a source of embarrassment when Mr. Tennyson brought visiting VIPs through the plant—but at least it was running.

Two years ago the budget had been no problem. Shelton's labor costs (which averaged $960 per day for the repair workers) were well within his budget. But there never seemed to be enough of the right kind of workers in the right place at the right time to keep the mill in running condition. Downtime averaged about 3 hours of each 24-hour day. (The mill usually operated three shifts per day with only one hour of scheduled downtime at midnight. The other 2 hours were unplanned shutdowns.)

Mr. Tennyson had successfully resisted efforts to increase the size of the repair crew until two years ago when Pat Shelton went directly to Mr. Hawley, pleading that he be permitted to hire "a couple more good maintenance technicians." Mr. Hawley agreed to have an operations analyst from the company headquarters come in and work under Mr. Tennyson to do a study of the situation. The analyst's report concluded as shown.

Our study has shown that with your present production program, simulated downtime hours are as follows:

No. of repair workers	6	8	10	12	14	16	18	20
Downtime hrs/24 hr	4.5	3.2	2.0	1.8	1.6	1.4	1.2	1.2

We recommend that (1) one of the experienced repair workers be reassigned full time to the development and supervision of a preventive maintenance program, (2) the existing repair crew size be augmented to reduce expected downtime, and (3) decentralization of maintenance activities should be investigated.

The report did not hold many surprises for Mr. Tennyson, and he remarked during its presentation that he had been after Mr. Shelton to improve the preventive maintenance program for nearly a year. Only the previous week he had directed him to begin decentralization of maintenance activities. With respect to the repair crew size, Mr. Tennyson observed that the analyst could easily recommend "larger crews and modernized test equipment" for he was not a line manager responsible for costs.

Mr. Hawley then spoke *strongly* in favor of an increase in the repair crew size. Mr. Tennyson observed that when one got into the report in depth and saw the printed comparisons with other divisions of the firm, it *did* seem like a reasonable move. He did, however, object that the report's conclusion of "an extremely weak maintenance situation relative to other divisions of the company" was an unnecessarily damaging (and permanent) indictment against Mr. Hawley and the mill's leadership in general.

The next day Mr. Tennyson recommended to Mr. Hawley that the repair crew size be doubled immediately, with an additional worker to supervise a preventive maintenance program. Mr. Hawley quickly authorized the increase on the basis of Mr. Tennyson's recommendation, but it took about six months to acquire and train the additional repair workers.

Pat Shelton had disagreed with some aspects of the operations analyst's report. He was against the decentralization of maintenance activities and the magnitude of the crew size adjustment, but the change had produced results. Downtime now (two years later) averaged only 1.2 hours per 24-hour day, which was only 12 minutes per day beyond the one hour of scheduled downtime. However, during the past year his problems had turned from breakdowns to budgets—and it appeared that the budget problems were even more threatening.

Southern Plywood operated on a fixed budget with each department charged for its own labor, materials, and fixed overhead, plus some variable overhead apportioned on the basis of expected volume. Monthly production over the past six months had been budgeted at 50,000 units per month, although actual production had varied as much as 20,000 units from this, and was currently averaging 45,000 units per month over the six-month period.

The labor budget for maintenance activities was based on a complex formula which incorporated a factor for actual downtime hours during the previous year. The formula had been developed by the comptroller, Ann Andrews, when she was in charge of cost accounting.

The budget had never presented any real problem to Pat Shelton before, although he had often questioned the fact that he was usually 20–30 percent under his budget. Ms. Andrews repeatedly explained that it was the total figure ("big picture" as she put it) that counted, and as long as it was in line Pat need not worry about the individual items in the budget.

In anticipation of his forthcoming meeting with Mr. Hawley, Mr. Tennyson planned to have Pat Shelton come to his office for an evaluation of Shelton's performance. He had not minded pulling Shelton out of an occasional jam, even though Shelton sometimes acted independently and did not always follow orders. But disregarding cost budgets was something else. It looked like a tough decision was called for.

Just as Mr. Tennyson finished convincing himself that he must talk with Mr. Shelton today, his phone rang. It was Mr. Hawley's secretary, asking him to come right over to a meeting in the general manager's office.

When Mr. Tennyson got to the meeting, two maintenance budgets were on the table: (1) the latest month, and (2) a corresponding month from two years earlier. The latest budget showed that Pat Shelton's department was 35 percent over budget on his labor costs and 80 percent over on the variable overhead. Material costs were slightly under the budgeted amount.

Mr. Hawley was just in the process of asking Ms. Andrews to explain the budget problem in detail. As Mr. Tennyson entered the room, Mr. Hawley turned to him and said, "Come right in Andy. Pat Shelton asked if we couldn't all get together and talk over his budget situation and I thought it was a good idea. Now let's try to get to the bottom of this and see who it is that's in trouble and what should be done about it."

1 In general, how were the earlier maintenance problems and later budget problems related?

2 What were the most serious mistakes made in handling the earlier maintenance problems and who should be held responsible for them?

3 Comment on the effectiveness of the mill's budgeting activities with respect to:
   (*a*) The appropriateness of the maintenance labor formula
   (*b*) The use of fixed budgeting data for control purposes
   (*c*) The job being done by Ms. Andrews.

4 Identify any organizational problems or value system incongruities that exist at the mill.

5 Prepare a list of specific recommendations (no more than 5) that you would make to Mr. Hawley for action at this time.

BIBLIOGRAPHY

[1] ABRAMOWITZ, IRVING: *Production Management*, Ronald Press Company, New York, 1967.

[2] BUFFA, ELWOOD S.: *Modern Production Management*, 4th ed., John Wiley & Sons, New York, 1973.

[3] GARRETT, LEONARD J., AND MILTON SILVER: *Production Management Analysis*, 2d ed., Harcourt, Brace, Jovanovich, New York, 1973.

[4] HORNGREN, CHARLES T.: *Cost Accounting: A Managerial Emphasis*, 3d ed., Prentice-Hall, Englewood Cliffs, New Jersey, 1972.

[5] MAYER, RAYMOND R.: *Production Management*, 3d ed., McGraw-Hill Book Company, New York, 1975.

[6] MOORE, FRANKLIN G.: *Production Management*, 6th ed., Richard D. Irwin, Homewood, Illinois, 1973.

[7] RIGGS, JAMES L.: *Production Systems: Planning, Analysis, and Control*, John Wiley & Sons, New York, 1970.

[8] VOLLMAN, THOMAS E.: *Operations Management*, Addison-Wesley Publishing Company, Reading, Massachusetts, 1973.

[9] WESTINGHOUSE ELECTRIC CORPORATION: *Maintenance Hints*, Westinghouse Electric Corporation, Pittsburgh, Pennsylvania, HB-6001-MM.

PART

3

Environmental Interface

CHAPTER

12

The Operating Environment

ENVIRONMENTAL IMPACTS

ENVIRONMENTAL OBJECTIVES
GOODS AND SERVICES
ECONOMIC IMPACTS
NONECONOMIC IMPACTS

THE ORGANIZATION AS A TOTAL SYSTEM

TOTAL SYSTEMS APPROACH
INTEGRATED OPERATIONS MANAGEMENT
INFORMATION: THE LIFEBLOOD OF OPERATING SYSTEMS

THE ORGANIZATION AS A DECISION-MAKING SYSTEM

DECISION METHODOLOGIES
ANALYTICAL METHODS FOR ENVIRONMENTALLY BASED DECISIONS
SYSTEMS ANALYSIS AND SYNTHESIS

MANAGEMENT INFORMATION SYSTEMS

INFORMATION FLOW CHARACTERISTICS
MIS SUBSYSTEMS
INTEGRATED MANAGEMENT INFORMATION SYSTEMS
CASE EXAMPLE: CITY PUBLIC SERVICE BOARD

A PHILOSOPHY OF MANAGEMENT

ENVIRONMENTAL MANAGEMENT AND RESPONSIBILITY
THE INDIVIDUAL AS DECISION MAKER
HUMAN VALUES IN DECISION-BASED SYSTEMS

SUMMARY
QUESTIONS
BIBLIOGRAPHY

The systems approach! How often have we stressed the importance of a total systems perspective throughout the text? Labor, inventory levels, quality control activities, maintenance efforts, and so forth, are all components of a total production system. This chapter seeks to integrate the components into a unified whole and to recognize the role of production systems within the total cultural environment. The essential link between components, subsystems, and environmental systems is, of course, information. Information flows, as well as physical flows, are truly vital aspects of any dynamic organization—and indeed of societies as a whole.

In earlier chapters, we discussed the major input, processing, and control activities of an organization. In this chapter, we first complete the input-processing-output model begun in Chap. 1 by examining the outputs, or environmental impacts, of a production process. Because many environmental influences are noncontrollable, or outside the decision responsibility of operations managers, our treatment of these factors shall be limited.

Next, we view (and review) the organization as a total system, noting the role of information as the lifeblood of the system. Information is used for making decisions, and we review the organization as a decision-making system and management information systems in general. Here we shall take a brief look at one of the most advanced information systems functioning today (in Texas). Finally, we end the chapter with some observations concerning the philosophy of management.

ENVIRONMENTAL IMPACTS

Anyone driving through a smog-filled city, or living within the reaches of a smelter or paper mill, can readily attest to the fact that firms produce more than they market. Years ago, the social by-products of production activities were unwittingly accepted as inevitable. Streams became polluted, smog filled the air, and bottles lined the highways. Today, managers must assume an increasing responsibility for the multitude of impacts their organizations have upon society.

Every organization that uses resources influences the environment—sometimes favorably, sometimes detrimentally. The judgment as to whether an effect is "good" or "bad" is a value-laden question, and one which we shall defer until later in the chapter. For the moment, however, let us be content to identify and classify the environmental impacts arising from an organization's use of resources.

ENVIRONMENTAL OBJECTIVES

In an earlier discussion of the human resource as an input to production systems we noted that all humans have the same essence but enjoy different levels of existence. As social beings, humans tend to group themselves into social units in order to achieve goals which raise their level of existence. In the past, these units often arose as a result of geographical boundaries, but political and ideological differences are also strong

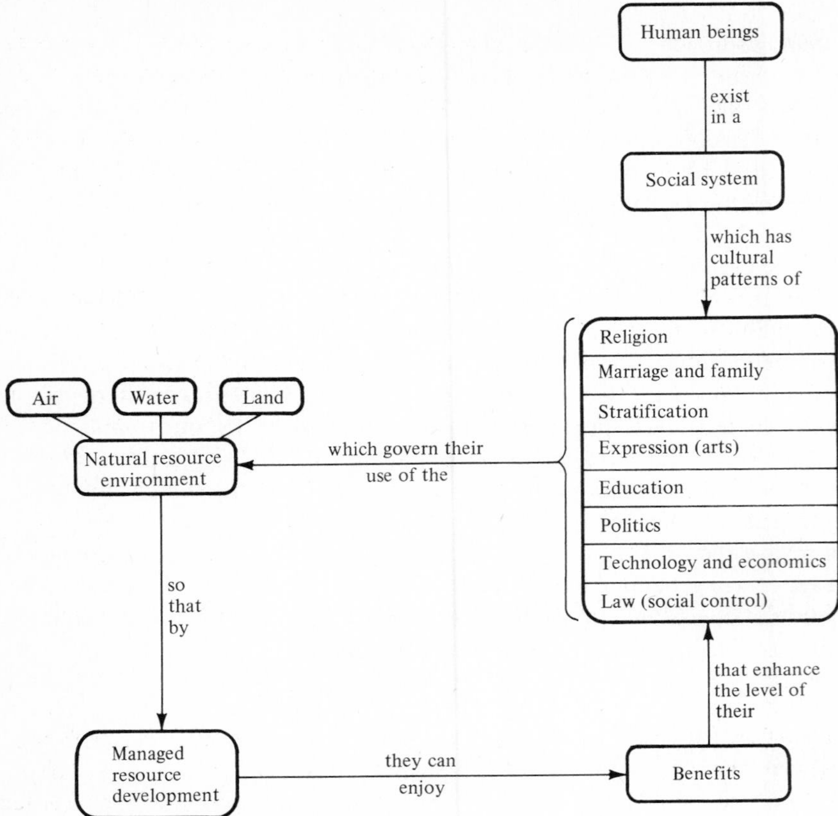

FIGURE 12-1 The use of resources by human beings

dividers. Figure 12-1 is a schematic conceptualization of how human beings in society use resources to give themselves a fuller existence.

People exist in a social system that has a number of identifiable cultural patterns, including religious, political, legal, and other components. As depicted in Fig. 12-1 the total cultural environment governs people's use of resources so that by effective utilization they can enjoy benefits that raise the level of existence of all (present and future) members of the society. This is society's objective in using environmental resources.

Productive activities using available technologies are only one component of human culture, although a very necessary one. Productive systems deliver the basic economic goods and services that humans need to survive in modern society. In addition, as noted earlier, they provide opportunities for socialization and the satisfaction of higher-level needs, including self-actualization.

Other subsystems of a culture are equally important, however. Social, political, and other patterns may influence the use of resources just as strongly as does technology. For example, even though nuclear breeder reactors are a technologically feasible means of using our abundant uranium-238 resource, social controls may limit their usefulness by dictating locations that are removed from the electrical load they are designed to serve. Artistic and esthetic factors also influence plant construction, product appearance (as of an automobile), and even use characteristics (such as highway locations). When powerful interests attempt to capitalize upon natural resources (or monopolize them) to the detriment of society at large, the political and legal subsystems of the culture respond with laws to limit such powers. Family patterns and educational levels exert wide-ranging influences over such things as the construction of multiple-dwelling units and allocation of public resources to research and development programs, mass transit, and the like. In effect, an organization's environment includes many interdependent cultural elements. Some of them are controllable, and others are beyond the control of the individual organization.

Productive organizations interface with the environment to deliver outputs that can be classified into three categories: (1) actual goods and services, (2) economic impacts, and (3) noneconomic impacts. The key to managing these environmental impacts lies in recognizing what factors are controllable, establishing realistic standards, and developing appropriate informational and corrective mechanisms.

GOODS AND SERVICES

The physical (and perhaps even intangible) goods and services that constitute the most obvious output of a productive system are largely controllable. Product structure flows from a conscious design, and product volume is a function of forecasting and production control efforts. Quality controls ensure that the product reaching the market environment has specified characteristics. Maintenance facilities and spare parts inventories can also be controlled to help guarantee the performance desired in the product. In summary, most organizations have some capability of controlling their primary outputs.

ECONOMIC IMPACTS

Goods and services increase the economic well-being of the society. Although one individual firm may have little economic impact nationally, in the aggregate the impacts are significant, and in local areas individual firms can generate strong influences on the economy. The United States economy depends heavily upon competitive factors to regulate the existence (or nonexistence) of economic units.

From an economic standpoint, organizations invest in resources, use available technology, and produce goods or services. The productive activity adds value, increases the level of local or national income, and provides desired end products which, at least theoretically, raise the level of existence of society. In many cases, the greatest benefits rest with the stockholders who have supplied the capital for the organization.

In the past, when the economic model of competition has been endangered by monopolistic or collusive threats, Congress has legislated to preserve competition.

The Sherman Anti-Trust Act (1890) ruled that combinations in restraint of trade and attempts to monopolize were illegal. This outlawed price-fixing and attempted to legislate competition by limiting market shares. The Clayton Act (1914) supplemented this by outlawing any mergers which might in the future tend to substantially lessen competition.

These major acts have been followed by the Fair Trade Law (dealing with brand name products), the Robinson-Patman Act (outlawing price discrimination), and others. The numerous legal regulations are societal measures to preserve and protect the competitive economic environment within which organizations function. To an individual firm they represent a largely uncontrollable variable, and it behooves the firm's management to be aware of these constraints.

NONECONOMIC IMPACTS

Noneconomic impacts impinge upon members of the organization and upon society as a whole. Let us illustrate these impacts by examples drawn from institutionalized value systems, unionism, and environmental quality control.

We noted earlier that organizations generate institutionalized values which influence the way of life of their members. One of the most publicized examples of the deterioration of an organizational value system was the Watergate incident in 1973-1974. Investigations revealed that numerous "responsible" officials from top United States presidential aids through lesser-known campaign workers were victims of a localized value system that lacked integrity and resorted to cover-up activities. The investigations vividly brought out the fact that values of superiors, when institutionalized within a bureaucratic framework, can exert strong pressures for conformity on (willing or unwilling) subordinates. As a result of the scandal, President Richard Nixon was forced to resign and numerous officials of lesser rank were convicted and sent to jail.

A second noneconomic (as well as economic) impact of an organization upon its own members is illustrated by the development and growth of unions. In the early 1800s the first unions were formed to improve wages and working conditions. By the mid-1800s employers were actively discouraging unionism by firing employees who were union members. A law in 1898 forbade employers from discharging workers because of union membership, but it was not until the early 1900s that the government and courts moved from an antiunionism position to one of neutrality. The Norris-LaGuardia Act (1932) forbade employers from getting injunctions to oppose union organization and was essentially the beginning of statute law on labor relations.

Labor's rise to power came during the 1930s and 1940s. In 1935, Congress, under President Roosevelt, passed the National Labor Relations Act (NLRA) which guaranteed labor unions the right to organize for the purpose of collective bargaining. This was essentially a "pro-labor" act which forbade unfair labor practices of employers. It was followed by the Taft-Hartley Act (1947), an "antilabor" piece of legislation which declared that unions also had an obligation to bargain in good faith. Since the early 1950s regulation and arbitration has generally prevailed, although a number of additional laws and amendments have been passed to refine the bargaining machinery.

Today the labor-management contracts are still "free" in that neither party (nor the government) unilaterally "dictates" the terms of agreement. Contract negotiations typically involve conditions in the working environment, employee facilities, safety, and so on. These improvements do have an economic impact upon the organization and society, but they also affect the noneconomic well-being of the employees and society. Union influence extends from the recognition of an individual's skill level to an impact on the stratification characteristics of society as a whole. Unions now have the legal and political power not only to improve working conditions in a given plant, but to stop production in an entire industry or even tie up the nation's transportation system. They can foster new technologies or stifle them. In essence, they are an environmental reality that management is forced to recognize and work with, but probably not control.

A third noneconomic impact of organizations upon society is in the realm of environmental quality. Both profit and nonprofit organizations exert significant impacts upon local communities and upon society in general. The growing awareness of these impacts is illustrated by the environmental statements which are now commonly published by both public and private organizations.

The Draft Environmental Statement covering the land use and timber management plan for the Willamette National Forest is a prime example of the awareness and concern by *public* officials over environmental impacts of their operations. The Willamette National Forest is the top timber producer among the nation's 154 national forests. It is essentially a "big business" for it produces well over $100 million per year in timber sales, employs over 600 full-time staff, and directly influences another 13,000 jobs. Development of their land-use plans involved public input at numerous stages along the way. Extensive analysis and computer simulation of possible land use was made, taking into account water quality, timber (sustained yield), visual quality, wilderness, wildlife, and recreation. Following this, Forest Supervisor John Alcock, in a forward to the Draft Environmental Statement, welcomed *additional* alternatives, stating [**20**: 2]:

> I cannot overemphasize the importance of receiving your input. This is a crucial phase of The National Forest land use and timber management planning process, and it needs thorough public discussion and review. My staff and I are available to help you understand the contents of the Draft Environmental Statement and the implications of various alternatives.

Profit-oriented enterprises also exert profound noneconomic impacts and are becoming increasingly aware of them. The broad range of effects is illustrated in Table 12-1, which lists the table of contents for a study describing the impact of moving a major electronics industry into a small, western Oregon city in 1976.

The project described in Table 12-1 involved impacting approximately 5,000 employees onto a city of approximately 35,000 people. The direct employment was expected to generate secondary employment effects estimated on the basis of a multi-

TABLE 12-1 TABLE OF CONTENTS FROM AN ENVIRONMENTAL IMPACT STUDY

List of Tables		i
List of Figures		v
Section 1	Introduction	1
Section 2	Background	2
Section 3	Socioeconomic Systems	6
	Plant development costs and timing	6
	Plant employment	16
	Plant payroll	37
	Local interindustry relations and spin-offs	40
	Projected secondary employment/payrolls	42
	Estimated population changes	51
	Estimated housing requirements	58
	Plant tax payments	62
	Local service charges	70
	Oregon state taxes	70
Section 4	Traffic and Related Environmental Considerations	76
	Home to work traffic patterns	76
	Environmental effects of traffic	82
	Other air emission considerations	84
	Service vehicles	85
	Other transportation requirements	85
	Mass transit	86
Section 5	Urban Systems Impact	87
	Water supply	91
	Waste treatment	93
	Solid waste	99
	Fire protection	99
Section 6	Unavoidable Adverse Effects and Suggested Mitigating Measures	103
	Site improvement considerations	103
	Air quality considerations	103
	Traffic considerations	104
Section 7	Project Alternatives	105
	Alternate sites	105
	Alternate development densities	105
	No project	106

Source: (15).

plier of 2.5 for employment and 2.8 for income [**15**: 50]. Needless to say, such significant changes cannot help but affect the way of life of existing residents.[1] A

[1] City residents generally favored strengthening their weak industrial base, although some were opposed to an influx of population. So far as location is concerned, the city is in the vicinity of the only two areas in the United States which received straight A's in a 1975 Environmental Protection Agency study of the ''quality of life'' in the United States [19: 33–36]. Quality categories included (1) economic, (2) political, (3) environment, (4) health/education, and (5) social.

small-town atmosphere was about to give way to the complexities of city life. The point of note, however, is that the firm's management undertook a conscientious study to discover the impacts well in advance, held open meetings with the residents to discuss potential problems and solutions to them, and recognized their corporate responsibility in managing the impact as smoothly and successfully as possible. Not all noneconomic impacts are controllable, but managers are being held increasingly responsible for careful control over any impacts that are.

THE ORGANIZATION AS A TOTAL SYSTEM

Having considered the goods and services, economic, and noneconomic impacts of an organization upon the environment (and vice versa), we shall find it useful to recall our original model from Chap. 1 in order to view now the total organization in perspective.

TOTAL SYSTEMS APPROACH

In the earlier chapters of the text, we followed an analytical approach of isolating components of the production system and analyzing them in considerable detail. In reality, breaking one component out of the production system was doing violence to the whole, for the whole system is more than simply a collection of parts. Individual components are important not only because of their own inherent characteristics, but also because of their position within the total system, that is, because of their relationship to other components and to system goals.

For example, inventory and maintenance activities are important in their own right. But their importance is enhanced as we recognize how vital these functions are to the achievement of organization goals. Moreover, their roles are interdependent. Insufficient inventories may delay necessary maintenance activities, whereas inadequate maintenance could prohibit the accumulation of desirable inventories. This is why we have repeatedly stressed viewing inventory, maintenance, quality, and other activities from a total-firm perspective, even though we had not yet analyzed all the components of the system to know exactly what the total perspective was. Having now considered the individual component activities and the surrounding environment we can take an integrated perspective of operations management.

INTEGRATED OPERATIONS MANAGEMENT

Figure 12-2 depicts, in schematic form, the total production system we have been developing and analyzing throughout the text. The reader will recognize that it is similar to the model introduced in Chap. 1. However, in Fig. 12-2 some components have been added, others amplified, and the role of each is more specifically delineated by referring to specific chapters wherein the given subject matter was studied. The

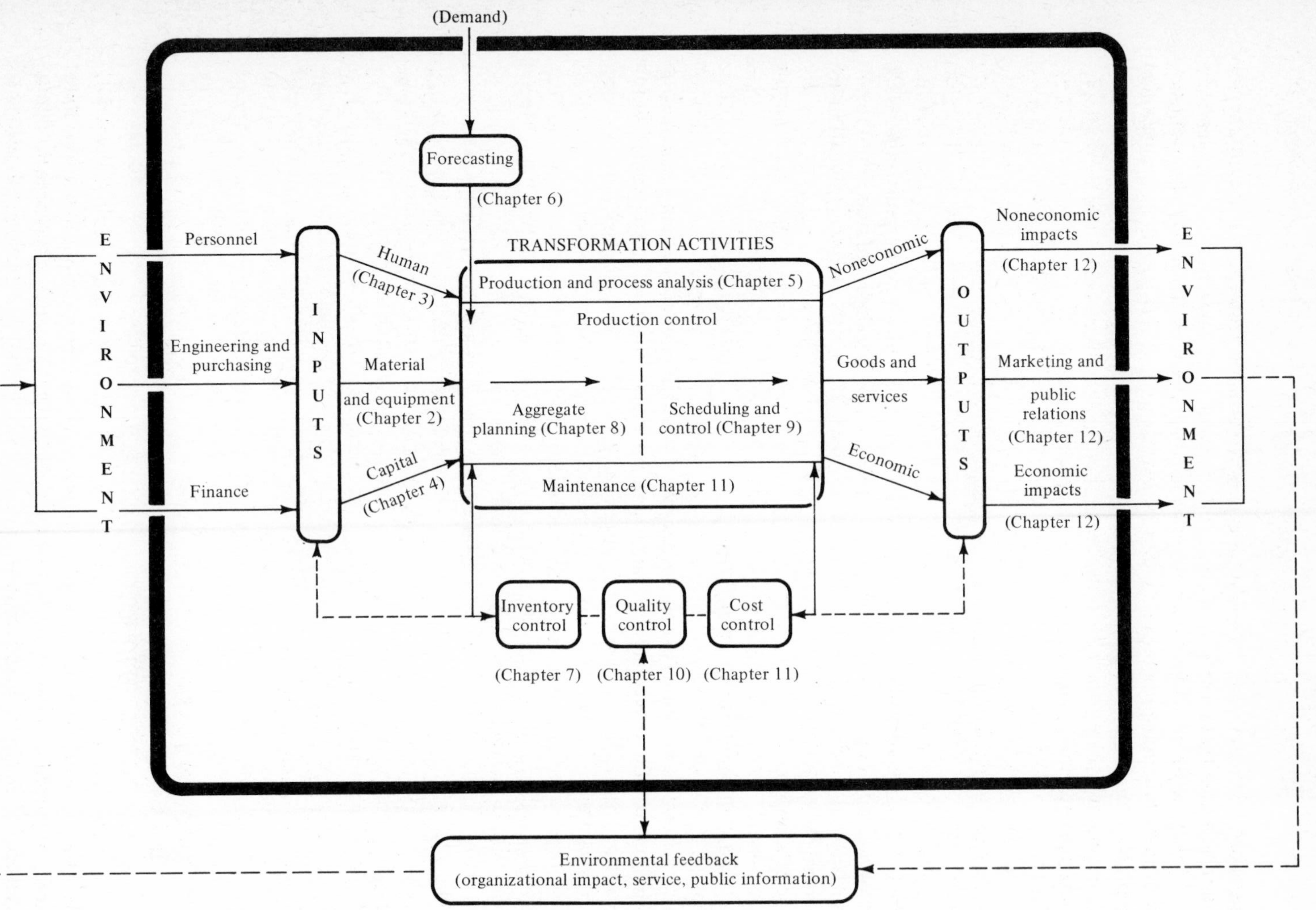

FIGURE 12-2 Physical and information flows in a production system

transformation activities have been expanded and feedback loops added for inventories, quality, and cost control.

We originally defined operations management as that activity whereby resources, flowing within a defined system, are combined and transformed in a controlled manner into outputs of higher value in accordance with policies communicated by management. From an integrated standpoint, the human resources (Chap. 3), material and equipment (Chap. 2), and capital (Chap. 4), are the inputs to the production process. The product and process are designed, selected, and analyzed (Chap. 5) as well as maintained (Chap. 11) in condition to deliver the required goods or services. Demand on the system is forecast (Chap. 6) and fed into the aggregate plan (Chap. 8) which is used to develop more detailed schedules (Chap. 9). They tell specifically what to produce, and when and where. Control of production activities rests firmly upon control of inventories (Chap. 7), quality (Chap. 10), and costs (Chap. 11). These control activities all incorporate measurement, feedback, comparison, and correction mechanisms to keep the total system in balance and aimed toward its goals. System outputs (Chap. 12) have both economic and noneconomic impacts on society as they flow into the same cultural and ecological environment from which the original resources were drawn.

Management of the total production system is heavily dependent upon information flows within and among the various components of the system. The flow of current, accurate, and relevant data is essential to sound decision making. Let us briefly review the types of decision information which should be available within the system.

INFORMATION: THE LIFEBLOOD OF OPERATING SYSTEMS

Information is the raw material for decisions, so the management of data collection and processing systems is very important [**12**: 6]. From an operations management standpoint, it is convenient to classify the information according to type or function as follows: (1) resource; (2) design, analysis, and maintenance; (3) forecasting, inventory, and production control; (4) quality and cost control; (5) environmental information.

Resource Information: Human, Material, and Capital Flows

In the early chapters of the text (Chap. 2, 3, and 4) we concerned ourselves with the human, material, and capital resources flowing into the production system. Many organizations maintain up-to-date data files for analysis and control of their resources. Personnel records include not only experience and skill classifications of all employees, but also time and productivity measurements.

Material and equipment records provide investment, depreciation, and usage data. Plant layouts and associated product flows are sometimes simulated and, of course, data is used for establishing least-cost production and distribution patterns, make versus buy decisions, and the like.

A number of organizations have now developed corporate financial models (simulations) which facilitate investment decisions in plant and equipment. Computerized investment analysis programs typically yield several measures of comparison including payback, net present value, and adjusted rate of return.

Information for Design, Analysis, and Maintenance of the Product and Process

Product and process analysis was discussed in Chap. 5 and maintenance in Chap. 11. While the design and product selection activities are often project- or problem-oriented and do not necessitate a high degree of continuous updating, this is not always the case. Some firms, for example, are using computerized PERT techniques for research and development of products over a three- or four-year period. Their project management is heavily dependent upon the information flow from regularly updated PERT charts. For proper maintenance, of course, accurate and accessible data on breakdown and preventive maintenance activities is essential, and information on planned shutdowns is a vital input to production planning.

Forecasting, Inventories, and Production Control Information

The most significant advances in operations management in recent years have come as a result of achieving timely, credible information flows in the forecasting, inventory, and production control areas (Chap. 6, 7, 8, and 9). Without computers the recent progress in time-phased order point and MRP systems would not have been possible.

Most major firms (and a number of government organizations) use computerized forecasting models to analyze demand and supply information for production control. Whereas time series and regression techniques have been around for some time, exponential smoothing methods have proven very useful to manufacturing firms.

Today's inventory systems now recognize the difference between dependent and independent demand, and use MRP systems for the former and time-phased order point systems for the latter. Economic order quantities and economic run lengths can be programmed into the system (where appropriate) and the need for safety stocks recognized (again, where appropriate).

Based upon the growth rate of MRP systems, well over a thousand firms have now successfully linked their inventory, aggregate planning, and scheduling systems in a time-phased format with priority and capacity *planning* and priority and capacity *control* features. These information subsystems are a particularly welcome addition because production control has always been one of the most complex activities to manage. In addition, many of the production processes are themselves computer-controlled as evidenced by the electrical, steel, and chemical industries.

Quality and Cost Control Information

Quality and cost control activities (Chap. 10 and 11) are key elements in many respects. Quality information is essential for designing acceptance sampling plans and maintaining process control charts. Firms also use acceptance sampling and vendor performance data to improve purchasing decisions.

Cost data is usually a product of the organization's cost accounting system. It is useful for preparing bids, estimating costs, and analyzing cost variance. Cost information is vital to the preparation of budgets for production and practically all other activities of an organization.

Environmental Information: Market, Economic, and Noneconomic

Many firms have extensive market information collection and processing programs, but as yet few firms carry this same coverage into the area of economic and noneconomic impacts. However, as society focuses more attention upon environmental impacts, the importance of these factors will skyrocket, and we may expect to see extensive data collection and analysis of environmental impacts in the future. Of prime importance will be the development of reliable techniques for gaining citizen input via such means as mail surveys, public meetings, electronically communicated surveys (over specially designed television sets), and so forth.

THE ORGANIZATION AS A DECISION-MAKING SYSTEM

Throughout the text, we have followed a decision making–systems approach to management, viewing a manager as a decision maker within an operating system. In using this approach we have called upon a wide range of analytical aids to decision making, many of which are equally applicable to the analysis of environmentally based decisions.

DECISION METHODOLOGIES

Beginning with the resource input decisions, we found that break-even analysis and expected-value concepts facilitated locational and capacity decisions. Next we encountered production and distribution situations and saw that distribution linear programming methods proved very useful for identifying the best production and distribution combinations. Statistical measures were found to be helpful in setting labor standards and analyzing human inputs, primarily because of the inherent variability among humans. Safety analysis called in the rules of probability. Capital investment analysis was facilitated by a number of investment criteria (payback, present value, annual cost, and rate of return methods) plus some decision-theory criteria (such as maximax, maximim). We also found that decision trees were useful there, especially when discounting techniques were incorporated in them. Simulation and minimum value analysis were additional tools.

Product and process analysts called into play some Bayesian concepts, linear programming, and simulation techniques. And for forecasting, we used time series, regression, correlation, and exponential smoothing methods.

In the area of inventory and production control, we again relied upon statistical tools to help set safety stock levels to accommodate the uncertainties of independent demand and lead time. For dependent demand and certainty (or assumed certainty) situations, techniques such as MRP and calculus approaches were found useful. Aggregate planning and scheduling was found to benefit from numerous analytical methods ranging from learning-curve analysis and critical ratio techniques to linear and dynamic programming, PERT, and CPM. But some of the most significant tools were the relatively simple priority and capacity requirements planning schemes identified as MRP and CRP.

Quality control methods relied very heavily upon statistical sampling plans and statistical control charts, for we were again concerned with variation there. In the maintenance area we found that, in addition to probability and reliability concepts, simulation and queuing theory were particularly relevant. Finally, cost control was facilitated by cost variance analysis of labor, materials, and overhead.

Each of these analytical models—and many others mentioned in the text—relies upon data for decisions. The "solution" to a problem is only as good as the data used in the analysis. If operations are to be managed on a scientific (or even quasiscientific) basis, the importance of good decision information cannot be overstressed.

ANALYTICAL METHODS FOR ENVIRONMENTALLY BASED DECISIONS

While we recognize that many environmental decisions are outside the decision capability of operations managers, the techniques discussed above, as well as other analytical methods, can be expected to find extensive application in the future. In particular, (1) benefit/cost, (2) simulation overlays, and (3) utility theory appear to hold much promise.

Benefit/Cost for Public Operations

The benefit/cost (B/C) approach is already required on many federally funded projects and has a solid base for expansion in the future. In this approach one simply discounts all future revenue and expense streams back to present value benefits and present value costs and computes the ratio of benefit to cost. If the ratio is greater than 1, benefits outweigh costs and the project is favorable (although possibly not as favorable as another alternative). For government projects the discount rate used is usually that specified by the Office of Management and Budget (OMB) in Washington, D.C.

The greatest difficulty in using a B/C approach is, as one might expect, determining appropriate values for benefits. Nevertheless, extensive work has already been done to establish empirical values. Dollar figures are available for such things as a visitor-day of fishing, an acre saved from flooding, and an animal unit-month of grazing. Such values are in everyday use by organizations such as the U.S. Bureau of Reclamation and the U.S. Forest Service, who are charged with responsible management of environmental resources.

Simulation Overlays

Modern societies such as the United States have been characterized by the term "social pluralism." This is a recognition of the fact that a multitude of interest groups (political, professional, religious, recreational, and so forth) exist within one democratic society. Each group has its own primary goals and, as one might expect, many of the goals are conflicting. For example, cross-country skiers treasure the serenity of a snow-clad forest while snowmobile clubs push to open the forests to the thrill of new and exciting trails. Farmers seeking to drain marshlands and use the soil for productive crops are countered by recreation groups fighting to preserve "these few remaining game habitats."

Goal conflicts in the use of environmental resources have posed some perplexing decision problems to corporate managers, city planners, land-use managers, and others. If objectives could be clearly delineated, techniques such as linear programming could be used to derive "optimal" solutions. However, because of the multiple and conflicting goal situations so commonly encountered in public decision making, some decision analysts are moving to the use of more sophisticated techniques such as goal programming and simulation overlays. For example, both government and private enterprise forest-management organizations have developed extensive computer simulation models of the resources existing on the forest lands they manage. Numerous management alternatives are generated by assigning different emphasis to timber production, fish and wildlife, grazing, recreation, and so forth, each time the simulation is run. These simulations, when overlaid onto the same geographic area, provide comparative data and help identify feasible management plans. They do not necessarily yield an "optimal" plan. But they do give the land-use manager factual and comparable data upon which to formulate decision alternatives, seek public input, and ultimately make decisions.

Utility Theory and Other Methods

The problems of environmental decision making are closely tied to societal and individual values. Because of the individualism and social pluralism existent in our society, many environmental values contain a strong subjective element. This causes decision making in the public sector to be more difficult than ever.

As society begins to hold corporate and governmental decision makers increasingly responsible for the environmental impacts of their decisions, it means decision makers cannot hide behind an institutionalized value system. Ultimately it is the individuals who are responsible—not organizations! This is why we may expect to see more value-based decision systems used in the future, especially where societal resources are being allocated.

Utility theory, benefit/cost analysis, and Bayesian techniques are some of the more value-based decision methodologies. These systems, in one way or another, allow the decision makers to inject their own experiences, judgments, or values, into a relatively formalized and systematized decision framework. One can certainly dispute the utility value, or the benefit assigned to an intangible good. Nevertheless, these systems take us a giant step forward by bringing this assignment out into the open where it can be discussed and reconciled. This is much better than hiding the intangible values under the guise of conservative monetary estimates or inaccurate probability estimates, as has been done in the past.

SYSTEMS ANALYSIS AND SYNTHESIS

Our approach to operations management has been somewhat of a *synthesis-analysis-synthesis* nature. In the first chapter we mentioned the importance of gaining a total systems perspective, that is, a synthesized perspective. But real-world problems relate to specific components of the total system—often to a selected few. Furthermore, it is usually more effective to tackle them by abstracting relevant variables and analyzing them in isolation with the aid of quantitative models. Thus, we developed specific analytical approaches to problems of inventory management, quality control, and so on. During this analysis phase, however, we strove to minimize the dangers of suboptimizing by following a decision framework which inherently recognized the hierarchical structure of goals, dictating that subsystem goals should always be consistent with organization goals.

Now, as we reemphasize the interdependencies of the component activities and the influence of environmental factors, we have returned to consideration of the total, or "macro" effects. We have effectively gone full-circle on the synthesis-analysis-synthesis approach.

One of the marks of a good information system is that it will give the decision maker both the specific data needed to analyze a problem and the summary type of data needed to put the problem into a total systems perspective. Having reviewed the kinds of information we have used throughout the text, and the types of decision methodologies this information supports, let us look more specifically at the information system as an entity in itself.

MANAGEMENT INFORMATION SYSTEMS

A *management information system* (MIS) is a formalized structure of equipment and/or personnel designed to collect, store, and process data in a time frame so that it is useful for decision making. The information then facilitates decision making by either reducing or removing uncertainties, or statistically summarizing data so that a more scientific decision process can be followed. Information systems do not make managerial decisions. However, they can automate many routine tasks and provide quantitative data for evaluation of the more complex situations.

Information systems are basically of four types: manual, mechanical, electromechanical, and electronic [**8**: 6]. Manual systems, such as file cabinets and written reports, are the simplest. But for large volumes of data, where manipulation, processing, and rapid retrieval are important, the electronic (computerized) systems are almost a necessity.

The objective of any information system is to get the information to the decision manager in the proper *form* at the right *time* and at a justifiable *cost*. Computerized systems are usually preferable because they can collect and synthesize data very quickly at a low cost per item. In addition, their storage and access capabilities enable different users (such as people from personnel or engineering) to simultaneously use data that was entered from one location and only once.

INFORMATION FLOW CHARACTERISTICS

The form and content of information should vary according to its use requirements. For example, top management should not be deluged with reams of detailed operating specifics. Nor should machine operators be given information to make policy decisions.

The bulk of computerized information flows generally supports day-to-day operations, such as payroll, accounting, inventory control, and the like. As one progresses up to higher levels of management, such as to the corporate planning levels, the difficulty of gaining and effectively using good information increases.

Figure 12-3 depicts the information flows as supporting the planning and operational hierarchy introduced in Chap. 1. Note that the entire management system rests upon a continuously updated data base. The data base provides routine, operational, strategic, and special request information. It, in turn, is modified as a result of new policies, operating results, and revised procedures.

Computerized systems typically store their data on magnetic tape, drums, or disks. Magnetic tape is relatively cheap per "byte" of storage capacity, but drums and disks have the advantage of direct access, eliminating the necessity of sequentially searching a tape for some desired information.

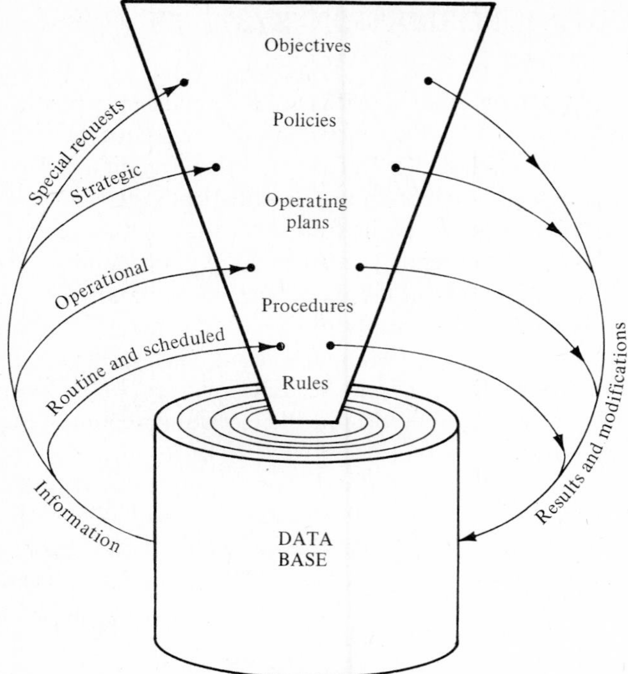

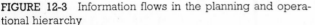

FIGURE 12-3 Information flows in the planning and operational hierarchy

MIS SUBSYSTEMS

Management information systems are often designed and implemented on a modularized (piecemeal) basis for several reasons. First, it is operationally feasible and useful to do so. Many organizational activities, such as accounting or personnel, can effectively function as subsystems. This means that organizations can start with small systems and progressively expand, integrate, and update their total information system over the years.

Second, an MIS is typically a major investment, often costing an organization well over $1 million. Expensive physical computer hardware must be accompanied by peripheral equipment to convert, communicate, store, and display the data. In addition, extensive programs (software) must be prepared for the specific functions to be performed. This can require a sizable staff of systems analysts and programmers. The risk associated with the investment in these facilities is reduced by getting selected activities on-line first, and capitalizing upon that experience while bringing other components into the system.

Third, a gradual installation helps orient employees to the fact that additional changes are to be expected. Good information systems should be flexible, for they must function in a dynamic environment. The recognition of an atmosphere of change facilitates acceptance and use of the system. Once part of the system is functioning

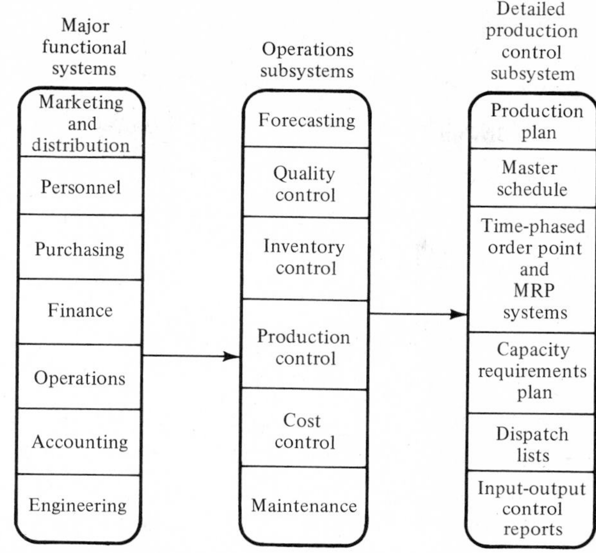

FIGURE 12-4 Management information systems and subsystems

effectively, other departments of the organization begin looking forward to the time they go "on-line," or become "updated."

The modular approach to information system design is not restricted to the master system subunits only. The concept can be effectively carried down to subsystem and lower levels of the organization, too. Figure 12-4 illustrates one means of modularizing the operations component of an information system. [Adapted from **12**: 350.] In this scheme, the major operations subsystems are forecasting, quality control, inventory control, production control, cost control, and maintenance. Data from these subsystem functions are not the "exclusive property" of operations, for they support other activities as well. For example, marketing both supplies and uses forecasting information, purchasing needs information on inventory levels, and accounting uses cost control data. In Fig. 12-4, one of the major operations subsystems, production control, is further modularized into the production plan, master schedule, MRP, CRP, dispatching, and input-output control subsystems. In a similar manner the other major subsystems, such as quality control, would be linked to different sets of detailed subsystems.

INTEGRATED MANAGEMENT INFORMATION SYSTEMS

Each of the detailed subsystems, major operations subsystems, and functional systems described in Fig. 12-4 has its own primary purpose, which of course should be supportive of the goals of the parent system. In addition, the various functional systems and subsystems are horizontally linked to and dependent upon each other in unique ways. It is these vertical and horizontal communications links that integrate the functional systems by supplying decision information that helps coordinate the activities into unified action.

One of the joys of working with a good information system is to witness the satisfaction employees have from participating in an organized and integrated system. Each employee sees where his or her efforts contribute to the organization as a whole. This understanding lends more purpose and importance to the individual's role and raises the level of satisfaction or self-actualization.

CASE EXAMPLE: CITY PUBLIC SERVICE BOARD[2]

City Public Service Board (CPSB) is a large gas and electric utility serving San Antonio, Texas, a metropolitan area of over 1 million inhabitants. In 1964, with full support from top management, and guidance from a consulting firm (EBASCO), a small study team spent approximately six months developing a five-year plan for installation of a management information system. The objectives of the system are depicted in Fig. 12-5.

The implementation schedule was modularized so that an orderly transition could be made to incorporate payroll, labor, distribution, construction budgeting, inventory control, and customer services functions. In 1965 a staff of 15 employees began carrying out the plans and by 1971 the staff had reached about 40 employees. The staff size of 40 to 45 was then maintained for the next several years. The accomplishments of this small staff, however, and CPSB in general, in designing and implementing such an advanced information system soon drew the respect and admiration of a number of other utilities and industries. As a result, CPSB developed joint working relationships with several other major utilities throughout the country, with whom they shared their knowledge and experience.

The hardware heart of CPSB's information system is now a Sperry Univac 1110 multiprocessor computer, which has two control processors and two input-output units, each of which can perform 1.7 million instructions per minute. The system has a main memory of 96,000 words and an extended memory of 262,000 words. This fourth generation multiprocessor has 10 times the speed and 5 times the memory capacity of an older Spectra 70/45 system installed previously [9]. The Univac 1110 was acquired in 1972, but the process of converting all the applications on the Spectra to the Univac took until late 1976 to complete. It was, nevertheless, a necessary transition. As stated by a staff specialist:

> It's not just a question of using the computer to handle work faster than it would be done manually. The magnitude of the data is so great that there is just no other way that we could get it integrated in time to make timely decisions without a multiprocessing capability [9].

[2] From personal conversations and correspondence with Donald S. Thomas, manager of the information services systems, James O. Timms, staff assistant, and sources (5, 6, 7, and 9).

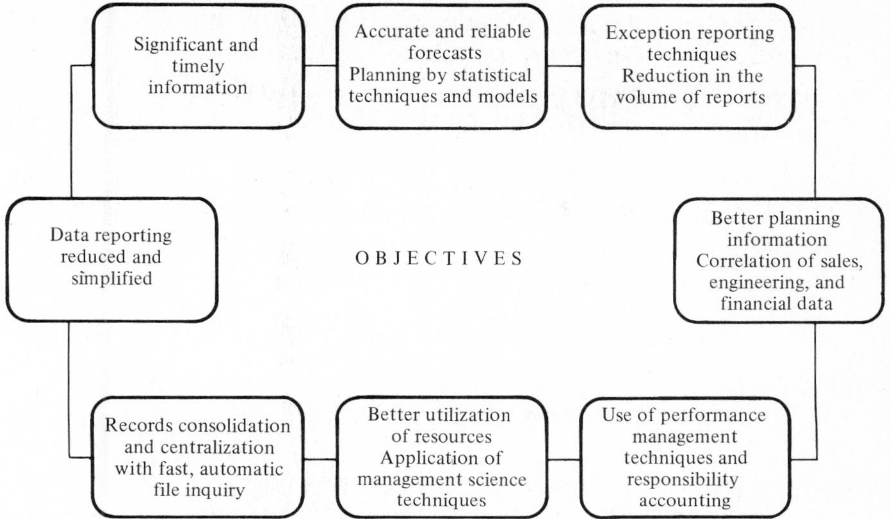

FIGURE 12-5 CPSB information system objectives. *Source:* City Public Service Board.

Integration and modularization have been keys to success in the CPSB system. During the initial 1965-1971 period, direct labor savings of over $5 million were achieved. This was somewhat offset by higher equipment costs, but in counter-balance, during that time the organization developed a "data base second to none, a highly trained group of professionals with strong computer backgrounds, and many other professionals in the organization ready to forge into the problems that lie ahead" [7].

A simplified schematic of the modular approach followed by CPSB is shown in Fig. 12-6. Customer services was one of the first modules on line. On a typical Monday, service representatives handle 2,500 to 2,800 customer inquiries [9]. Incoming calls are automatically routed to one of 28 service representatives seated at video terminals connected directly to the computer.

Upon receiving a call, the terminal operators first ask for the customer's address and type it into the terminal as the customer is talking. The computer responds immediately with a complete video display of the customer's account status. As the customer states his problem, the service representative has information to answer questions on the spot. For example, a customer may not understand why her electric bill seems high. The service representative might detect that it is a seasonal effect and that the bill is comparable to the amount during the same period a year ago. Or perhaps a customer wishes to report that a street light is out on his corner. The operator types the information into the computer, punches a transit key, and the computer compiles and prints out a work order in the appropriate one of four area service offices within minutes after the customer's call.

Other modules are equally sophisticated and integrated within the total system. The gas and electric operations system was the first computer-operated utility system in the United States to operate on-line. The system incorporates an exponentially

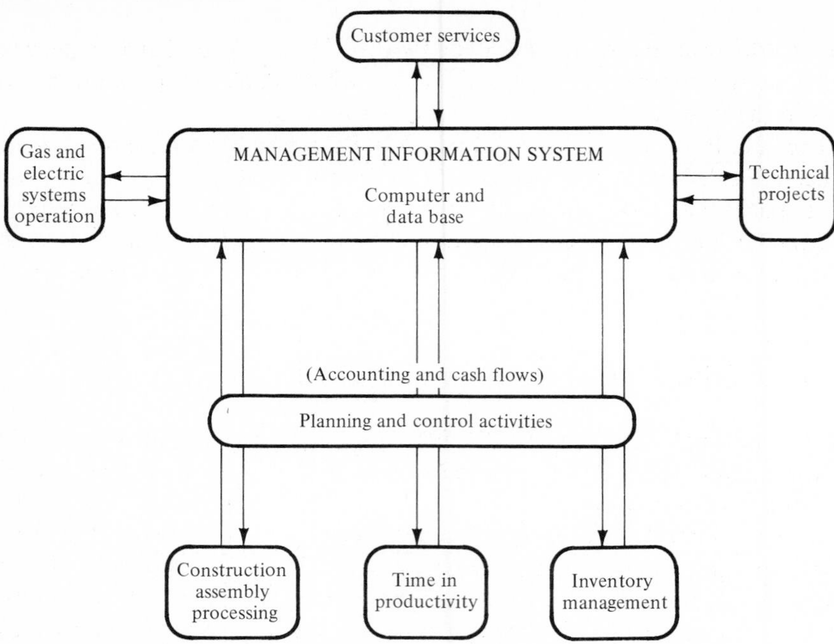

FIGURE 12-6 CPSB modular information flows. *Source:* City Public Service Board.

smoothed load-forecasting procedure which automatically signals when to bring energy supplies on line. Instead of the typical control room with hundreds of gauges, dials, and recorders to watch, CPSB operators employ a "management by exception" principle. The operator sits at a console containing three cathode-ray tubes and views an overall one-line diagram of either the gas or electric system. By means of light pen, the operator can call up details at any of 80 control points. Switches and valves can be operated remotely, with the computer providing options, performing the end action, and logging all data. Emergency signals and alarms are automatic and flashing symbols indicate trouble spots. The system has proven to be exceptionally efficient and reliable, and provides unusually clear operator comprehension [**5**].

The construction, productivity, inventory, and other modules are also of uniquely advanced design. Engineering packages have been modularized so that resource requirements and time and cost estimates can be readily obtained from the data base. Construction units are standardized as to the amount of labor, material, installation information, and the like that are required so that computer estimates can be made of worker hours (and workdays) required, and of start and completion dates for jobs. The actual scheduling is not fully automated, although labor and equipment summary reports tell the crew size needed and estimated hours required [**9**].

Inventory and purchasing systems have built-in EOQ and vendor performance features. If vendors supply defective products or fail to deliver on time, the computer keeps a record of this and soon suggests the buyer purchase from another supplier.

In addition to incorporating labor standard measures, the productivity module keeps a record of the classification of work done by each employee. Thus, if a programmer does systems design work for two weeks, that experience is permanently recorded in the computerized personnel file, which enhances promotional opportunities in the future.

The CPSB management information system has been developed under the guidance of skilled systems analysts and with the enthusiastic support of top management. It exemplifies what can be done with cooperative effort under good leadership. The dynamic nature of the system also attests to the fact that *integration* and *modularization* are key elements of a successful management information system.

A PHILOSOPHY OF MANAGEMENT

Any organizational system, whether private or public, utilizes cooperative efforts to achieve common goals. We might even say that a system has meaning only insofar as the components function cooperatively. To draw resources together, transform them in a productive manner, and deliver them to the environment, different individuals and groups become involved in cooperative efforts. Some supply labor or capital while others constitute the market, or perhaps only the market environment. In effect, numerous groups have legitimate interests in the activity of an organization: stockholders, workers, managers, suppliers, consumers, and even society as a whole. To rule out any group because its interest is difficult to quantify (or satisfy) would be shortsighted and probably unjust.

Although many groups are affected, one group holds the prime responsibility for carrying out an organization's role in society. That group is management. Management really sets the priorities and dispenses the rewards. Stockholders and bondholders supply the capital, but managers are the operating trustees—usually in full control. Employees can strike, and consumers shift their buying habits, but management must keep the organization a going concern. Society can pass restrictive legislation, but ultimately it is management that must make responsible decisions and direct the action.

Managers are the real leaders of the organization—the planners, organizers, and controllers. They set the pace of activity and distribute corporate justice. To do this wisely, they need an informed and balanced perspective of their organization's role in society. Furthermore, they must be capable of accurately translating that perspective into consistent operational goals at the various subsystem levels. In this final section of the chapter, we reemphasize the managerial requirements for both knowledge and values when dealing with the total system.

ENVIRONMENTAL MANAGEMENT AND RESPONSIBILITY

In the "early days," when our natural resources seemed abundant and manufactured goods were scarce, the traditional economic model played an important role in our country. Entrepreneurs, motivated by profits, rapidly built an industrial complex that was second to none. Expansion, growth, and abundance were the watchwords of the day. Few people expressed serious concern about the depletion of environmental resources.

Over the years many arguments have been advanced to isolate managers from environmental and social responsibility. Some hold that environmental responsibilities divert business people from their primary purpose, that they are not sufficiently skilled to deal with social problems, or that there is no basis in law for action or sanction. The major argument is, however, economic. Social and environmental projects do not often pay for themselves (at least in the short run) and this runs counter to the primary obligation firms envision of maximizing returns to stockholders.

In contrast to these arguments, *society today emphatically responds that managers are indeed responsible.* Their arguments counter that the problems must ultimately be solved, businesses have (and control) the resources to do this, and it is in their best long-run interests to accept responsibility voluntarily, rather than waiting for every situation to be "red taped" with legal regulations. As to the major argument, corporate stockholders are essentially only suppliers of capital. With today's stock exchanges they can shift their funds to another firm on a moment's notice. They carry no legal responsibility nor do they usually exert any control. Why should they claim a disproportionate share of rewards? They assume risks of loss (of capital) but so do employees (of jobs), and so do suppliers. And so does society.

Today's demands that managers act responsibly arise from a different environment than existed 50 or 100 years ago. We now have documented evidence that our natural resources are in short supply. We can look back and see that growth has not cured all our ills. A simple "profit maximization" mentality is too myopic a perspective for managing organizations in modern society. Profits, efficiencies, and economies are indeed key elements, but the concerns of employees and society have achieved legitimacy. It is not only in the stockholders' best interests to use scientific decision processes, quantitative techniques, and computerized information systems. Rather, it is in the best interests of the total organization.

Our free enterprise system, which stems from the time of Adam Smith, is only a tool (albeit a good one) for accomplishing the production and distribution of goods. Like a state-planned economy, the system is not inherently responsible for anything; it is amoral. Responsibility ultimately rests upon individuals—mostly managers.

THE INDIVIDUAL AS DECISION MAKER

As brought out earlier (Chap. 3), responsible actions stem from knowledge, values, and skills. Figure 12-7 depicts the knowledge-value requirement schematically. Here we see a decision situation impinging upon a managerial existence. The cognitive (intellect) and affective (will) domains go into action and a decision is reached which takes both knowledge and values into account.

Data supply the intellect with facts, which become knowledge. But data have no normative connotations, since they identify what *is* rather than what *should be.* Values affect the range of alternatives considered as well as the ordering of them

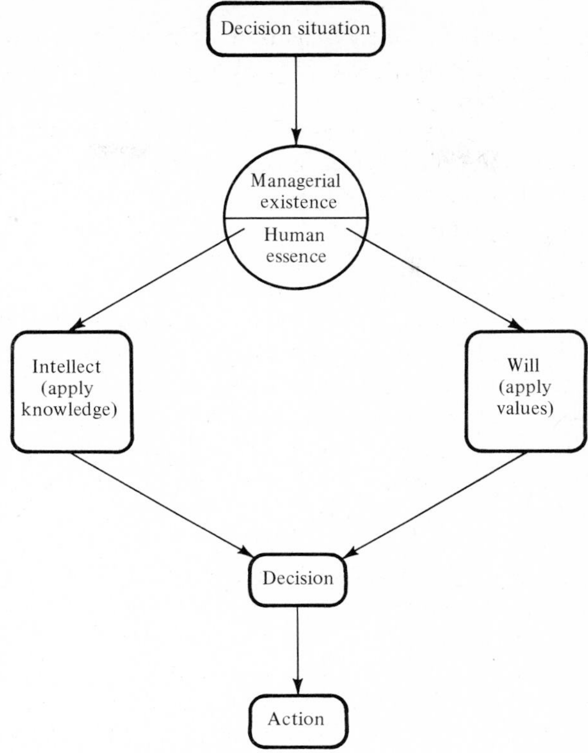

FIGURE 12-7 The individual as decision maker

[**2**: 161–169]. Waddell notes that "a science of management is thoroughly and maybe hopelessly enmeshed with values" [**21**: 35–36].

Decision theory clearly points to the fact that values are premises for decisions. C. West Churchman even urges that science be redefined so that the question of ethics can be tested by the scientific method [**4**: 380]. In *Challenge to Reason* he asks scientists and philosophers from diverse fields, such as theology and psychology, to view humanity as part of a total system [**3**: 216–217].

Figure 12-8 depicts the close relationship between knowledge and values by adding the value overhead to the information flow schematic of Fig. 12-3. Here we see that values influence objectives, policies, operating plans, procedures, and even rules by filtering down through the organizational structure (perhaps in a subtle way). The added link from knowledge to values suggests that the value base can be modified by factual evidence from the data base. This was brought out in Fig. 3-4 in reference to the individual decision process. Fig. 12-8 extends this same concept to an organizational base and relates it more specifically to the information system and institutionalized value system. As can be gleaned from the figure by the returning arrow from values to knowledge, value judgments often go so far as to dictate what type of information shall be collected in the data base. Surely the two are interdependent.

The importance of a good data (knowledge) base has long been recognized, but the development of sound value systems has received less attention in managerial

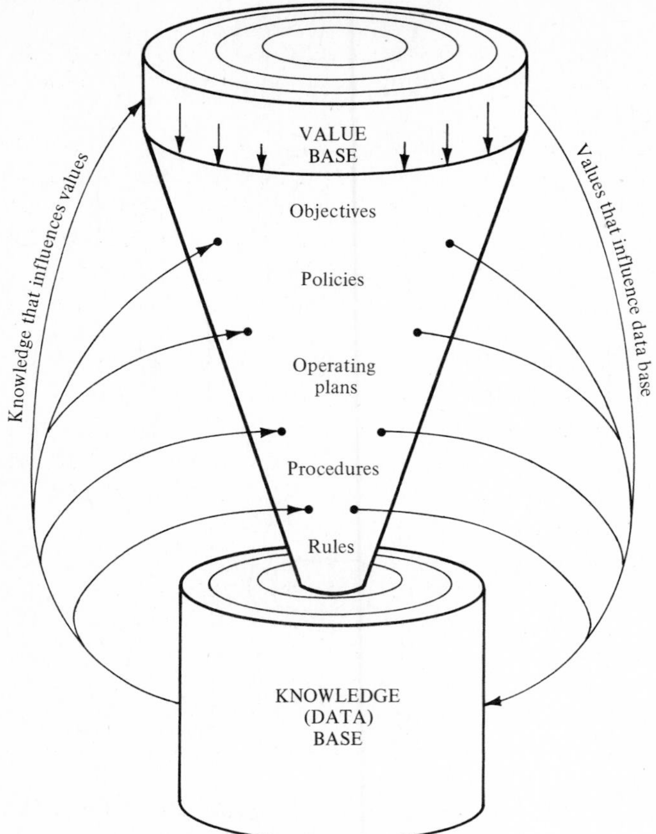

FIGURE 12-8 Knowledge and value base for decision systems

literature until recently. Nevertheless, the development of responsible value judgments represents one of our greatest challenges of the future. Warren Bennis has declared that "finding men with the right technical capability will not be nearly as difficult as finding men with the right set of values and attitudes" [**1**]. In response to the comment that it is more vital to have a manager who has an ethical sense than a manager with a knowledge of computers or blind ability to get things done efficiently, Professor William Scott has commented [**18**]:

> I think that if the major universities do not include these questions in their professional curricula, they have simply shirked their responsibilities. . . . The ethical and value questions must be implicit in the curriculum. . . . Students . . . must . . . learn values, ethical things, how to deal with ambiguities.

HUMAN VALUES IN DECISION-BASED SYSTEMS

We all recognize that values are a personal attribute and that our value systems are not necessarily modified by doing something like reading about them in a book.

Nor should they be. What then can be done to meet this challenge of the future? What values should a responsible manager be identified with, and how are such values to be developed?

Our response to the first question throughout this text has been to try to recognize the value-based situations as they arose in the context of studying operations. Waddell makes two recommendations [**21**: 38]. First, managers must have a better understanding of the effects of values (such as what values are behind the decision to hire the handicapped?). Second, managers should relate their decisions to the long-range consequences for both their organization and the environment in which it functions.

The choice of values is itself a value judgment and one that cannot be dictated to another. At the most basic level, however, we can observe that people seem to operate under a natural law which says they should "do good and avoid evil." But the interpretation of what is "good" or "evil" quickly leads to differences of opinion. Some of the differences are resolved by taking a "total systems" perspective of humans in their social and ecological environment.

We have seen that each person is a complex creature, sharing a common human nature with other people but leading a unique existence. Humans strive for a fuller existence (actualization) in terms of economic, artistic, religious, and other cultural norms. Yet they are limited in both their cognitive and effective domains. Intellectually, they cannot comprehend the vastness of space nor the simplicity of pure matter. Affectively, they have a natural love or respect for others of the same human nature, but their appetites for power, wealth, pleasure, and such things sometimes override that love and respect.

In short, human beings exist as limited beings, dependent upon one another and influenced by their environment. However, they are aware of these limitations and dependencies. This intellectual awareness, coupled with their natural concern for others, forms an important basis for their value system. When decisions must be made that affect others, they are conscious of their own limitations and of the equal value of others as human beings.

Any listing of specific values is likely to be challenged. A. M. Sullivan has listed seven values which he labels *senses* [**11**]. These are a sense of identity, order, purpose, power, love, dignity, and time. Robert Golembiewski has derived 11 meaningful "subordinate goals" from a study of the Judaeo-Christian ethic [**10**]. They are survival and physical well-being (productivity), fellowship, dignity and humility, enlightenment, aesthetic enjoyment, creativity, new experience, security, freedom, justice, and personality. In general, the preferred values seem to reflect purpose, integrity, and a continuing respect for the humanity of others.

The virtues inherent in a value system cannot be purchased or acquired in a quick and easy artificial manner. They arise from the religious and other cultural norms of society, from childhood training and mature reflection about the real purpose of life and the inherent value of one's self and of others. They are a product of our times—times which have taken from the slaughter of the American buffalo to the energy crisis to make us aware of Benjamin Franklin's simple concept of thrift.

Today managers allocate resources within the structure of a very complex cultural environment. An awareness of values does not promise to make their job any easier. It should, however, make their work more inherently satisfying to themselves and more equitable to society as a whole. It should make them better managers of our nation's limited resources.

SUMMARY

Our objective in using environmental resources is to raise our level of existence. The degree of use is largely determined by cultural patterns which include religious, political, technological, legal, and other components. Outputs from the productive (technology and economic) components are (1) goods and services, (2) economic impacts, and (3) noneconomic impacts. The economic impacts flow into a legislated competitive environment. Noneconomic impacts include such things as pressures from institutionalized value systems, effects of unionism, and impacts upon the environmental quality of life.

The framework for making environmentally conscious decisions is a total systems perspective. This approach recognizes the integration of internal operations with an environmental awareness. The linking mediums are information and values. Information flows are the lifeblood of an organization and values give it purpose and integrity.

Management information systems are formalized structures of equipment and/or personnel designed to collect, store, and process data in a time frame so that it is useful for decision making. The systems use a data base to provide managers with the knowledge necessary to set objectives and policies and to develop operating plans and procedures. Many information systems are modularized. For example, a production control subsystem may consist of modules comprised of the production plan, master schedule, MRP system, capacity requirements plan, dispatch system, and input-output control system.

A sound managerial philosophy must, however, recognize the prominent role of values, as well as of knowledge (data). Society demands that managers whose decisions affect environmental and social processes be aware of the values of others and operate from a sound value system of their own. The incorporation of values, such as justice and integrity, elevates the managerial decision process by extending the decision maker's perspective to total systems effects. Values raise managers from what might otherwise be the mechanistic level of their computers to the God-given level of their own humanity.

QUESTIONS

12-1 The United States consumes a large (and disproportionate) amount of the earth's environmental resources. Why is this so and what is the purpose of using these resources?

12-2 Which type of impact (physical good, economic, or noneconomic) is most important to society? Prepare an argument in support of your position.

12-3 Explain the role of legislation as a regulator of environmental impacts; that is, why is it used and how successful is it?

12-4 Silvester Penningford, a recent graduate of a 90-day wonder course in "Management by Similarity," claims he has a perfect management system that is guaranteed to work. Each department of the firm simply works toward its own objectives. Similar efforts automatically reinforce each other and contrary efforts cancel each other out. This can be expected to give the firm a direction and make the employees happy. Comment on Mr. Penningford's proposal.

12-5 A Chicago firm manufacturing C.B. radios has a maintenance superintendent and purchasing agent who both seem dedicated to convincing the general manager that their respective functions are the most essential to the firm and that they should be allocated additional personnel. How would you recommend the general manager approach this problem?

12-6 How are inventory, quality, and cost control activities similar with respect to the "control" aspect of each?

12-7 Some decisions are said to be more scientific than others depending upon the type and quantity of information. Explain how information influences both the analytical method (model) and the result associated with a decision.

12-8 President Phillip McCann of Bionics Unlimited has vetoed installation of purchasing and inventory information system modules because he has been told that with a "bits and pieces" approach to information systems he will continually be plagued with changes. He prefers to wait until the ultimate in a standardized total information system is developed (hopefully within 10 years), but has asked you for advice. Prepare a recommendation for him.

12-9 Explain how the value base and data base are related in the managerial planning and operating process.

12-10 Jack Perkins, the recently hired operations manager of a logging and timber company in Maine, has been told by the company president that he is expected to demonstrate "sound judgment and solid values" in his new managerial role. He has come to you, the general manager, saying, "But my job doesn't involve any value judgments—I just follow orders. Isn't that what he wants?" Write a paragraph suggesting some value-laden aspects of the job for Mr. Perkins to reflect upon.

12-11 Suppose you, as an operations manager of a multinational oil company, have the assignment of writing a job description outlining the knowledge, skill, and value characteristics for someone who is to be your new superior, the vice president of operations. How would you approach the problem, and what types of value characteristics would you want to see in your superior?

12-12 What changes do you anticipate will take place in the operations management field during the next 50 years? Prepare a paragraph or two discussing any trends that you feel will significantly influence the environment of operations.

BIBLIOGRAPHY

[1] BENNIS, WARREN: "Organizations of the Future," *Personnel Administration*, September–October 1967.

[2] BOULDING, KENNETH E.: "The Ethics of a Rational Decision," *Management Science*, vol. 12, February 1966.

[3] CHURCHMAN, C. WEST: *Challenge to Reason*, McGraw-Hill Book Company, New York, 1968.

[4] ———: *Prediction and Optimal Decisions*, Prentice-Hall, Englewood Cliffs, New Jersey, 1961.

[5] CITY PUBLIC SERVICE BOARD: "GEO," San Antonio, Texas, 1973.

[6] ———: "Information Services System 1974 Operational Plan," San Antonio, Texas, 1974.

[7] ———: "Information Services System 1972 Six Year Plan," San Antonio, Texas, 1972.

[8] DIPPEL, GENE, AND WILLIAM C. HOUSE: *Information Systems: Data Processing and Evaluation*, Scott, Foresman and Company, Glenview, Illinois, 1969.

[9] "Fourth-Generation Computer Powers First-Rate Management Info System," *Electric Light and Power*, May 26, 1975.

[10] GOLEMBIEWSKI, ROBERT T.: *Men, Management and Morality: Towards a New Organizational Ethic*, McGraw-Hill Book Company, New York, 1965.

[11] LAZARUS, HAROLD (ed.): *Human Values in Management: The Business Philosophy of A. M. Sullivan*, Thomas Y. Crowell Company, New York, 1968.

[12] MADER, CHRIS, AND ROBERT HAGIN: *Information Systems: Technology, Economics, Applications*, Science Research Associates, Palo Alto, California, 1974.

[13] MONKS, JOSEPH G.: "Water Resource Decision Making—How Effective Is the Public Input?" Institute of Environmental Sciences 1973 Proceedings, Mt. Prospect, Illinois, 1973, pp. 345–350.

[14] MOONEY, JAMES: *Principles of Organization*, Harper & Brothers, New York, 1947, pp. 5–8.

[15] MORELAND, UNRUH, SMITH, AND PARAMETRIX INC.: "An Assessment of the Impact of the Proposed Hewlett-Packard Facility on the City of Corvallis," Eugene, Oregon, September 1974.

[16] PARK, JAMES R., AND JOSEPH G. MONKS: "Ecology Decisions—Is Due Process Really Enough?" *Journal of Environmental Systems*, vol. 5, no. 1, 1975, pp. 1–11.

[17] POTLATCH CORPORATION: "The Company's Business Philosophy, Objectives, Values and Priorities: A Guide for Management," San Francisco, California, January 1976.

[18] SCOTT, WILLIAM G.: "New Values in Modern Management," an interview in *Economics/Business News*, Houghton Mifflin Company, Boston, April 1974.

[19] "The Best Places to Live in the USA," in *Changing Times*, December 1975, pp. 33–36.

[20] U.S. DEPT. OF AGRICULTURE: "Willamette National Forest," *Draft Environmental Statement: Land Use and Timber Management Alternatives*, Eugene, Oregon, 1975.

[21] WADDELL, WILLIAM C.: "Values: A Challenge to a Science of Management," *University of Washington Business Review*, Winter 1970.

APPENDIX

Answers to Odd-numbered Problems

CHAPTER 1

1 10,000 surveys
3 (*a*) \$6; (*b*) 0.75
5 (*a*) 800; (*b*) 10
7 (*a*) \$4; (*b*) 250 units
9 200,000 or more
11 \$23,600
13 \$1.5 million
15 EU [*A*] = 41, EU [*B*] = 36. Choose 20-person crew.

CHAPTER 2

1 33,300
3 (*a*) 8; (*b*) 50 percent; (*c*) 62.5 percent
5 (*a*) 75/hr; (*b*) 83.3 percent; (*c*) 33.3 percent
7 (*a*) Volume range 0–10,000; dollar range \$0–\$800,000; (*b*) city B; (*c*) 2,000 units
9 More than one solution may be optimal at transportation cost = \$7,400.
11 More than one solution may be optimal at production and distribution cost = \$10,000.
***13** (*a*) Dummy demand is required to supply 10 units; (*b*) \$700.
***15** There are at least 6 possible solutions involving no nonadjacent loads. Each is equally correct.

CHAPTER 3

1 Approximately 70 observations
3 13.10 min
5 (*a*) 120 percent; (*b*) 2.93 min/cycle
7 44.62 sec/cycle (45 sec/cycle rounded)
9 81
11 1.60 min/piece
13 (*a*) 0.0005; (*b*) 0.0245
15 0.70

CHAPTER 4

1 \$70,012 (answer may vary slightly due to rounding)
3 \$1,233
5 (*a*) \$400/yr; (*b*) first = \$8,000; second = \$7,200; third = \$6,480
7 6.7 yr
9 \$7,000
11 (*a*) \$6,000 and \$5,280; (*b*) \$2,000/yr and \$1,720/yr; (*c*) Plan 1
13 \$63,160
***15** \$5,768
17 PV cost of *Y* is \$1,513 more.
19 5 percent
21 12.5 percent
23 15.4 percent
25 (*a*) \$12,651. (*b*) Taxes reduce profits, but depreciation expenses can be deducted before taxes are computed. If depreciation = \$3,000/yr and taxes = 50 percent, tax = 0.50 (operating advantage before depreciation – \$3,000) and 0.50 (\$3,000) = \$1,500 less that is paid each year in taxes because of the depreciation expense. (*c*) 69.2 percent; (*d*) 1.3 years.

CHAPTER 5

1 (*a*) (1) produce, (2) sell, (3) either produce or sell; (*b*) Lease, EMV = \$58,000; (*c*) \$110,000; (*d*) \$52,000
3 (*a*) Early American with EMV = \$5,800; (*b*) \$2,950
5 (*a*) $A = 60$, $B = 80$; (*b*) \$220
7 Standard = 2, deluxe = 4
9 (*a*) Max $W = 187x + 45y + 95z$
(*b*)
$$\begin{aligned} 200x + 180y + 80z &\le 600 \\ 500x + 0y + 90z &\le 500 \\ 40x + 40y + 0z &\le 120 \end{aligned}$$
(*c*) 500

11 Solution is to produce 750 units of Early American for profit of $18,750.
13 (*a*) Shear = 0.75 min/part, form = 0.15 min/part, clean = 0.40 min/part, inspect = 0.10 min/part; (*b*) shear = 5 machines, form = 1 machine, clean = 4 machines.
15 (*a*) 82; (*b*) $332/day; (*c*) Group operation contrasts with specialization.
17 (*a*) Graph should show $ on Y axis, units on X; (*b*) $0 < 100$ use x, $100 < 200$ use Y, ≥ 200 use Z.
19 Making the product has a $50/month economic advantage.
21 (*a*) Graph should show assembly times (min) on X axis and cumulative percentages on Y axis; (*b*) 3 percent; (*c*) approximately 3 min
23 (*a*) Follow tabular format for simulation; (*b*) 0.47 meals; (*c*) 2.83 meals/min.

CHAPTER 6

1 (*a*) Graph should show time on X axis, tons on Y; (*b*) curves will differ, but forecasts will be around 1,200 (thousand) tons; (*c*) averages are: 133, 300, 433, 500, 433, 466, 600, 733.
3 (*a*) $Y = 489 + 75X$ (1973 = 0, X = years, Y = tons in thousands);
(*b*) 1,164,000 tons
5 (*a*) 720 units, 864 units
(*b*) $Y_c = 720 + 12X$ (July 1, 1979 = 0, X unit = 1 month, Y = annual sales rate in units)
720 units/year, 864 units/year
(*c*) $Y_c = 60 + 1X$ (July 1, 1979 = 0, X unit = 1 month, Y = monthly sales rate in units)
60 units/month, 72 units/month
7 (*a*) Graph should show time on X axis, units on Y axis; (*c*) longer average yields more smoothing; (*d*) 1.3
9 (*a*) $Y_c = 20 + 4X$ (1974 = 0, X = years, Y = number of accidents); (*b*) 44
11 (*a*) 8.3 accidents; (*b*) 42 percent; (*c*) 0.65; *(*d*) No
13 (*a*) 33; (*b*) 30 to 36; (*c*) 0.5; (*d*) 50 percent of the number of vacuums sold is explained by the magazine advertisements.
15 (*a*) 0.64; (*b*) it tells the percentage of variation in campsites demanded that is explained by (or associated with) automobile traffic at the selected site; (*c*) 0.80
17 (*a*) 20; (*b*) 0.46
19 (*a*) 20,800; (*b*) forecast would reflect the total amount of variation of previous demand from previous forecast—that is, no smoothing.
21 (*a*) 958; (*b*) 966
***23** (*a*) Simple exponential forecast for week of April 12 = 525; (*b*) adjusted exponential forecast for week of April 12 = 547.
25 (*a*) Forecast for week 6 is 15 units; (*b*) forecast for week 6 is 11 units.
27 (*a*) 570; (*b*) 0.53; (*c*) yes

CHAPTER 7

1 200
3 (*a*) 600; (*b*) 10; (*c*) 30,300
5 (*a*) 8,000; (*b*) 10,000 with total cost of $2,433.60
7 5,000 units
9 30 cylinders
11 (*a*) and (*b*) should be of sufficient size and accuracy to yield reasonably accurate values for the 50 percent and 10 percent demand levels. Values may vary, but should be around 130–150 steers for (*c*) and from $39,650 to $45,750 for (*d*).
13 (*a*) Graph should have weeks on *X* axis and the percentage of time the lower boundary is exceeded on the *Y* axis; (*b*) 3
***15** 4,000
17 97.72 percent
19 231 lb
21 (*a*)

OQ = 500 LT = 4		Week							
		1	2	3	4	5	6	7	8
Projected requirements		150	150	150	150	200	200	180	320
Scheduled receipts				500			500		500
On hand at end of period	300	150	—	350	200	—	300 ~~200~~	120	300 ~~200~~
Planned order release			500		500				

(*b*) 178 units
23 (*a*) 10 days; (*b*) 240 bags; (*c*) 99.38 percent; (*d*) 26 or 27 bags
25 (*a*) Fixed order quantity (or base stock or time-phased order point); (*b*) 10 days; (*c*) 700 sheets; (*d*) $0.18/sheet

CHAPTER 8

1 (*a*) 90 hr; (*b*) 81 hr; (*c*) 59 hr
3 (*a*) 173 hr/unit; (*b*) 79
5 (*a*) Chart should show January through December daily demands of 200, 250, 300, 300, 200, 100, 100, 150, 250, 400, 400, 350.
(*b*) Histogram should show cumulative production days on *X* axis, production rate (units/day) on *Y* axis. Cumulative requirement should show cumulative production days on *X* axis and cumulative demand (units) on *Y* axis.
(*c*) 255.4 units

7 (*a*) Histogram should show quarters on X axis and production rate (units/quarter) on Y axis; (*b*) 10; (*c*) variable rate is \$50/year less costly.

9 Graph shows period on X axis and demand level on Y axis. Plan costs are 1 = \$90,000; 2 = \$140,000; 3 = \$160,000; 4 = \$220,000; and 5 = \$160,000.

11 5,620 units

13 (*a*) One optimal solution is:

Initial inventory	Use in first quarter.
First RT	Use in first quarter.
Second RT	Use 500 in second quarter, 200 in fourth.
Third RT	Use 200 in third quarter, 500 in fourth.
Third OT	Use 200 in fourth quarter.
Fourth RT	Use 700 in fourth quarter.
Fourth OT	Use 300 in fourth quarter.

(*b*) \$208,500

***15** The solution should have the following entries in the row-column (r, c) matrix location:

Initial Inv – 1 = 100
1 RT – 1 = 640
2 RT – 1 = 60, 2 RT – 2 = 500, 2 RT – 3 = 60, 2 RT – 4 = 20
3 RT – 3 = 640
4 RT – 4 = 640
5 RT – 4 = 240, 5 RT – 5 = 400
6 RT – 6 = 300, 6 RT – 9 = 80, 6 RT – 10 = 60, 6 RT – 11 = 200
7 RT – 7 = 400, 7 RT – 9 = 240
8 RT – 8 = 600, 8 RT – 9 = 40
9 RT – 9 = 640
10 RT – 10 = 640
11 RT – 11 = 640
11 OT – 11 = 60, 11 OT – 12 = 240
12 RT – 12 = 640
12 OT – 12 = 320

The unused capacity column should show the remainder values from 640 RT and 320 OT.

CHAPTER 9

1 (*a*) Plan should show average requirement as dotted line at 400; (*b*) output control report should show cumulative deviations of –10, 50, –70, 40, and 190; (*c*) no.

3 (*a*) 874, 872, 870, 873, 871; (*b*) 872, 874, 870, 873, 871; (*c*) 874, 873, 872, 871, 870; (*d*) 870, 871, 872, 873, 874.

5 $A = 1$, $B = 6$, $C = 3$, $D = 5$, $E = 2$, $F = 4$

7 (*a*) A = 60 units, B = 80 units; (*b*) \$220

9 Standard = 2, deluxe = 4
11 Produce 750 units/day of Early American for a profit of \$18,750.
13 Assign: *A* to 3, *B* to 2, *C* to 1, *D* to 5, and *E* to 4.
15 The optimum schedule is:

Week 1	Produce 3 units for	\$12 (000) profit.
Week 2	Produce 2 units for	10 (000) profit.
Week 3	Produce 1 unit for	5 (000) profit.
		\$27 (000)

17 0.07
19 (*a*) Network should show activities as arrows and events as circles, beginning with event 1 and ending with 8; (*b*) 1–3–5–7–8; (*c*) 37 days; (*d*) 19 days; (*e*) day 23; (*f*) 3 days; (*g*) 0.0918
21 (*a*) 0.1587; (*b*) \$35,160
23 Event 1: $E = 0$, $L = 0$; event 2: $E = 12$, $L = 12$; event 3: $E = 20$, $L = 22$; event 4: $E = 16$, $L = 16$; event 5: $E = 34$, $L = 34$; event 7: $E = 38$, $L = 38$; event 8: $E = 44$, $L = 44$.
25 An improved allocation requires 14 shipfitters during periods 1 and 2, 10 during 3, 13 during 4, 11 during 5 and 6, 13 during 7 and 8, so the range is 14 − 10 = 4.

CHAPTER 10

1 8 equivalent worker hours
3 (*a*) 0.015; (*b*) 0.04
5 $(C_2{}^6\, C_3{}^{44})/C_5{}^{50}$
7 0.135
9 0.142
11 10.6 percent
13 (*a*) use Poisson; (*b*) yes; (*c*) yes
15 $n = 80$, $c \leq 3$
17 $n = 50$
19 If $\bar{x} \leq 13.63$ min, accept.
21 (*b*) 55 bags; (*c*) 48.88 Kg
23 UCL = 0.992 centimeters, LCL = 0.968 centimeters
25 (*a*) $\bar{x}$ = 102.30 lb, 104.39 lb, 100.21 lb; (*b*) 8.68 lb, 0 lb
27 (*a*) UCL = 0.32, LCL = 0.08; (*b*) 32 and 8

CHAPTER 11

1 \$1,800/yr
3 Two technicians

5 (*a*) \$35; (*b*) \$90
***7** (*a*) \$1,154; (*b*) every three weeks
9 (*a*) 62.5 percent; (*b*) 0.33 weeks; (*c*) 1.67 breakdowns; (*d*) 0.20 week; (*e*) 1.04; (*f*) 0.09
11 (*a*) 6; (*b*) 4.11 hr; (*c*) 2.06 hr
13 Replace both at 80 hr.
15 (*a*) 13.3 percent; (*b*) 0.625 failures/unit-yr
17 \$519.60
19 26.9 months
21 (*a*) \$0.64; (*b*) \$1.20/unit; (*c*) \$5.50/unit
***23** (*a*) \$−1,000; (*b*) \$1,000; (*c*) 0

APPENDIX

B

Random Number Table

27767	43584	85301	88977	29490	69714	94015	64874	32444	48277
13025	14338	54066	15243	47724	66733	74108	88222	88570	74015
80217	36292	98525	24335	24432	24896	62880	87873	95160	59221
10875	62004	90391	61105	57411	06368	11748	12102	80580	41867
54127	57326	26629	19087	24472	88779	17944	05600	60478	03343
60311	42824	37301	42678	45990	43242	66067	42792	95043	52680
49739	71484	92003	98086	76668	73209	54244	91030	45547	70818
78626	51594	16453	94614	39014	97066	30945	57589	31732	57260
66692	13986	99837	00582	81232	44987	69170	37403	86995	90307
44071	28091	07362	97703	76447	42537	08345	88975	35841	85771
59820	96163	78851	16499	87064	13075	73035	41207	74699	09310
25704	91035	26313	77463	55387	72681	47431	43905	31048	56699
22304	90314	78438	66276	18396	73538	43277	58874	11466	16082
17710	59621	15292	76139	59526	52113	53856	30743	08670	84741
25852	58905	55018	56374	35824	71708	30540	27886	61732	75454
46780	56487	75211	10271	36633	68424	17374	52003	70707	70214
59849	96169	87195	46092	26787	60939	59202	11973	02902	33250
47670	07654	30342	40277	11049	72049	83012	09832	25571	77628
94304	71803	73465	09819	58869	35220	09504	96412	90193	79568
08105	59987	21437	36786	49226	77837	98524	97831	65704	09514
64281	61826	18555	64937	64654	25843	41145	42820	14924	39650
66847	70495	32350	02985	01755	14750	48968	38603	70312	05682
72461	33230	21529	53424	72877	17334	39283	04149	90850	64618
21032	91050	13058	16218	06554	07850	73950	79552	24781	89683
95362	67011	06651	16136	57216	39618	49856	99326	40902	05069
49712	97380	10404	55452	09971	59481	37006	22186	72682	07385
58275	61764	97586	54716	61459	21647	87417	17198	21443	41808
89514	11788	68224	23417	46376	25366	94746	49580	01176	28838
15472	50669	48139	36732	26825	05511	12459	91314	80582	71944
12120	86124	51247	44302	87112	21476	14713	71181	13177	55292
95294	00556	70481	06905	21785	41101	49386	54480	23604	23554
66986	34099	74474	20740	47458	64809	06312	88940	15995	69321
80620	51790	11436	38072	40405	68032	60942	00307	11897	92674
55411	85667	77535	99892	71209	92061	92329	98932	78284	46347
95083	06783	28102	57816	85561	29671	77936	63574	31384	51924

Source: Paul G. Hoel, *Elementary Statistics*, 2d ed., John Wiley and Sons, Inc., New York, 1966. Reproduced by permission of the publisher.

90726	57166	98884	08583	95889	57067	38101	77756	11657	13897
68984	83620	89747	98882	92613	89719	39641	69457	91339	22502
36421	16489	18059	51061	67667	60631	84054	40455	99396	63680
92638	40333	67054	16067	24700	71594	47468	03577	57649	63266
21036	82808	77501	97427	76479	68562	43321	31370	28977	23896
13173	33365	41468	85149	49554	17994	91178	10174	29420	90438
86716	38746	94559	37559	49678	53119	98189	81851	29651	84215
92581	02262	41615	70360	64114	58660	96717	54244	10701	41393
12470	56500	50273	93113	41794	86861	39448	93136	25722	08564
01016	00857	41396	80504	90670	08289	58137	17820	22751	36518
34030	60726	25807	24260	71529	78920	47648	13885	70669	93406
50259	46345	06170	97965	88302	98041	11947	56203	19324	20504
73959	76145	60808	54444	74412	81105	69181	96845	38525	11600
46874	37088	80940	44893	10408	36222	14004	23153	69249	05747
60883	52109	19516	90120	46759	71643	62342	07589	08899	05985

APPENDIX

C Squares and Square Roots

N	N^2	$\sqrt{N}$	$\sqrt{10N}$
1	1	1.000 000	3.16227
2	4	1.414 214	4.47213
3	9	1.732 051	5.47722
4	16	2.000 000	6.32455
5	25	2.236 068	7.07106
6	36	2.449 490	7.74596
7	49	2.645 751	8.36660
8	64	2.828 427	8.94427
9	81	3.000 000	9.48683
10	100	3.162 278	10.00000
11	121	3.316 625	10.48809
12	144	3.464 102	10.95445
13	169	3.605 551	11.40175
14	196	3.741 657	11.83216
15	225	3.872 983	12.24745
16	256	4.000 000	12.64911
17	289	4.123 106	13.03840
18	324	4.242 641	13.41641
19	361	4.358 899	13.78405
20	400	4.472 136	14.14214
21	441	4.582 576	14.49138
22	484	4.690 416	14.83240
23	529	4.795 832	15.16575
24	576	4.898 979	15.49193
25	625	5.000 000	15.81139
26	676	5.099 020	16.12452
27	729	5.196 152	16.43168
28	784	5.291 503	16.73320
29	841	5.385 165	17.02939
30	900	5.477 226	17.32051
31	961	5.567 764	17.60682
32	1 024	5.656 854	17.88854
33	1 089	5.744 563	18.16590
34	1 156	5.830 952	18.43909
35	1 225	5.916 080	18.70829
36	1 296	6.000 000	18.97367
37	1 369	6.082 763	19.23538
38	1 444	6.164 414	19.49359
39	1 521	6.244 998	19.74842
40	1 600	6.324 555	20.00000
41	1 681	6.403 124	20.24846
42	1 764	6.480 741	20.49390
43	1 849	6.557 439	20.73644
44	1 936	6.633 250	20.97618
45	2 025	6.708 204	21.21320
46	2 116	6.782 330	21.44761
47	2 209	6.855 655	21.67948
48	2 304	6.928 203	21.90890
49	2 401	7.000 000	22.13594
50	2 500	7.071 068	22.36068
51	2 601	7.141 428	22.58318
52	2 704	7.211 103	22.80351
53	2 809	7.280 110	23.02173
54	2 916	7.348 469	23.23790
55	3 025	7.416 198	23.45208
56	3 136	7.483 315	23.66432
57	3 249	7.549 834	23.87467
58	3 364	7.615 773	24.08319
59	3 481	7.681 146	24.28992
60	3 600	7.745 967	24.49490
61	3 721	7.810 250	24.69818
62	3 844	7.874 008	24.89980
63	3 969	7.937 254	25.09980
64	4 096	8.000 000	25.29822
65	4 225	8.062 258	25.49510
66	4 356	8.124 038	25.69047
67	4 489	8.185 353	25.88436
68	4 624	8.246 211	26.07681
69	4 761	8.306 624	26.26785
70	4 900	8.366 600	26.45751
71	5 041	8.426 150	26.64583
72	5 184	8.485 281	26.83282
73	5 329	8.544 004	27.01851
74	5 476	8.602 325	27.20294
75	5 625	8.660 254	27.38613
76	5 776	8.717 798	27.56810
77	5 929	8.774 964	27.74887
78	6 084	8.831 761	27.92848
79	6 241	8.888 194	28.10694
80	6 400	8.944 272	28.28427

N	N^2	$\sqrt{N}$	$\sqrt{10N}$
81	6 561	9.000 000	28.46050
82	6 724	9.055 385	28.63564
83	6 889	9.110 434	28.80972
84	7 056	9.165 151	28.98275
85	7 225	9.219 544	29.15476
86	7 396	9.273 618	29.32576
87	7 569	9.327 379	29.49576
88	7 744	9.380 832	29.66479
89	7 921	9.433 981	29.83287
90	8 100	9.486 833	30.00000
91	8 281	9.539 392	30.16621
92	8 464	9.591 663	30.33150
93	8 649	9.643 651	30.49590
94	8 836	9.695 360	30.65942
95	9 025	9.746 794	30.82207
96	9 216	9.797 959	30.98387
97	9 409	9.848 858	31.14482
98	9 604	9.899 495	31.30495
99	9 801	9.949 874	31.46427
100	10 000	10.00000	31.62278
101	10 201	10.04988	31.78050
102	10 404	10.09950	31.93744
103	10 609	10.14889	32.09361
104	10 816	10.19804	32.24903
105	11 025	10.24695	32.40370
106	11 236	10.29563	32.55764
107	11 449	10.34408	32.71085
108	11 664	10.39230	32.86335
109	11 881	10.44031	33.01515
110	12 100	10.48809	33.16625
111	12 321	10.53565	33.31666
112	12 544	10.58301	33.46640
113	12 769	10.63015	33.61547
114	12 996	10.67708	33.76389
115	13 225	10.72381	33.91165
116	13 456	10.77033	34.05877
117	13 689	10.81665	34.20526
118	13 924	10.86278	34.35113
119	14 161	10.90871	34.49638
120	14 400	10.95445	34.64102
121	14 641	11.00000	34.78505
122	14 884	11.04536	34.92850
123	15 129	11.09054	35.07136
124	15 376	11.13553	35.21363
125	15 625	11.18034	35.35534
126	15 876	11.22497	35.49648
127	16 129	11.26943	35.63706
128	16 384	11.31371	35.77709
129	16 641	11.35782	35.91657
130	16 900	11.40175	36.05551
131	17 161	11.44552	36.19392
132	17 424	11.48913	36.33180
133	17 689	11.53256	36.46917
134	17 956	11.57584	36.60601
135	18 225	11.61895	36.74235
136	18 496	11.66190	36.87818
137	18 769	11.70470	37.01351
138	19 044	11.74734	37.14835
139	19 321	11.78983	37.28270
140	19 600	11.83216	37.41657

N	N^2	$\sqrt{N}$	$\sqrt{10N}$
141	19 881	11.87434	37.54997
142	20 164	11.91638	37.68289
143	20 449	11.95826	37.81534
144	20 736	12.00000	37.94733
145	21 025	12.04159	38.07887
146	21 316	12.08305	38.20995
147	21 609	12.12436	38.34058
148	21 904	12.16553	38.47077
149	22 201	12.20656	38.60052
150	22 500	12.24745	38.72983
151	22 801	12.28821	38.85872
152	23 104	12.32883	38.98718
153	23 409	12.36932	39.11521
154	23 716	12.40967	39.24283
155	24 025	12.44990	39.37004
156	24 336	12.49000	39.49684
157	24 649	12.52996	39.62323
158	24 964	12.56981	39.74921
159	25 281	12.60952	39.87480
160	25 600	12.64911	40.00000
161	25 921	12.68858	40.12481
162	26 244	12.72792	40.24922
163	26 569	12.76715	40.37326
164	26 896	12.80625	40.49691
165	27 225	12.84523	40.62019
166	27 556	12.88410	40.74310
167	27 889	12.92285	40.86563
168	28 224	12.96148	40.98780
169	28 561	13.00000	41.10961
170	28 900	13.03840	41.23106
171	29 241	13.07670	41.35215
172	29 584	13.11488	41.47288
173	29 929	13.15295	41.59327
174	30 276	13.19091	41.71331
175	30 625	13.22876	41.83300
176	30 976	13.26650	41.95235
177	31 329	13.30413	42.07137
178	31 684	13.34166	42.19005
179	32 041	13.37909	42.30839
180	32 400	13.41641	42.42641
181	32 761	13.45362	42.54409
182	33 124	13.49074	42.66146
183	33 489	13.52775	42.77850
184	33 856	13.56466	42.89522
185	34 225	13.60147	43.01163
186	34 596	13.63818	43.12772
187	34 969	13.67479	43.24350
188	35 344	13.71131	43.35897
189	35 721	13.74773	43.47413
190	36 100	13.78405	43.58899
191	36 481	13.82027	43.70355
192	36 864	13.85641	43.81780
193	37 249	13.89244	43.93177
194	37 636	13.92839	44.04543
195	38 025	13.96424	44.15880
196	38 416	14.00000	44.27189
197	38 809	14.03567	44.38468
198	39 204	14.07125	44.49719
199	39 601	14.10674	44.60942
200	40 000	14.14214	44.72136

APPENDIX

D

Areas under the Standard Normal Probability Distribution

Values in the table represent the proportion of area under the normal curve between the mean ($\mu = 0$) and a positive value of z.

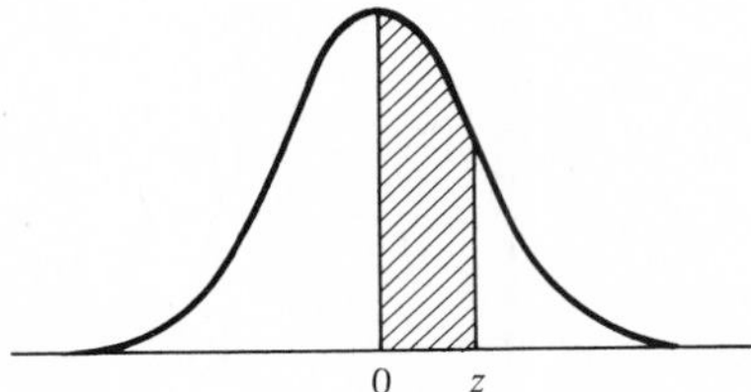

z	.00	.01	.02	.03	.04	.05	.06	.07	.08	.09
0.0	0.0000	0.0040	0.0080	0.0120	0.0160	0.0199	0.0239	0.0279	0.0319	0.0359
0.1	0.0398	0.0438	0.0478	0.0517	0.0557	0.0596	0.0636	0.0675	0.0714	0.0753
0.2	0.0793	0.0832	0.0871	0.0910	0.0948	0.0987	0.1026	0.1064	0.1103	0.1141
0.3	0.1179	0.1217	0.1255	0.1293	0.1331	0.1368	0.1406	0.1443	0.1480	0.1517
0.4	0.1554	0.1591	0.1628	0.1664	0.1700	0.1736	0.1772	0.1808	0.1844	0.1879
0.5	0.1915	0.1950	0.1985	0.2019	0.2054	0.2088	0.2123	0.2157	0.2190	0.2224
0.6	0.2257	0.2291	0.2324	0.2357	0.2389	0.2422	0.2454	0.2486	0.2517	0.2549
0.7	0.2580	0.2611	0.2642	0.2673	0.2703	0.2734	0.2764	0.2794	0.2823	0.2852
0.8	0.2881	0.2910	0.2939	0.2967	0.2995	0.3023	0.3051	0.3078	0.3106	0.3133
0.9	0.3159	0.3186	0.3212	0.3238	0.3264	0.3289	0.3315	0.3340	0.3365	0.3389
1.0	0.3413	0.3438	0.3461	0.3485	0.3508	0.3531	0.3554	0.3577	0.3599	0.3621
1.1	0.3643	0.3665	0.3686	0.3708	0.3729	0.3749	0.3770	0.3790	0.3810	0.3830
1.2	0.3849	0.3869	0.3888	0.3907	0.3925	0.3944	0.3962	0.3980	0.3997	0.4015
1.3	0.4032	0.4049	0.4066	0.4082	0.4099	0.4115	0.4131	0.4147	0.4162	0.4177
1.4	0.4192	0.4207	0.4222	0.4236	0.4251	0.4265	0.4279	0.4292	0.4306	0.4319
1.5	0.4332	0.4345	0.4357	0.4370	0.4382	0.4394	0.4406	0.4418	0.4429	0.4441
1.6	0.4452	0.4463	0.4474	0.4484	0.4495	0.4505	0.4515	0.4525	0.4535	0.4545
1.7	0.4554	0.4564	0.4573	0.4582	0.4591	0.4599	0.4608	0.4616	0.4625	0.4633
1.8	0.4641	0.4649	0.4656	0.4664	0.4671	0.4678	0.4686	0.4693	0.4699	0.4706
1.9	0.4713	0.4719	0.4726	0.4732	0.4738	0.4744	0.4750	0.4756	0.4761	0.4767

Source: From Paul G. Hoel, *Elementary Statistics*, 2d ed., John Wiley and Sons, Inc., New York, 1966. Reproduced by permission of the publisher.

z	.00	.01	.02	.03	.04	.05	.06	.07	.08	.09
2.0	0.4772	0.4778	0.4783	0.4788	0.4793	0.4798	0.4803	0.4808	0.4812	0.4817
2.1	0.4821	0.4826	0.4830	0.4834	0.4838	0.4842	0.4846	0.4850	0.4854	0.4857
2.2	0.4861	0.4864	0.4868	0.4871	0.4875	0.4878	0.4881	0.4884	0.4887	0.4890
2.3	0.4893	0.4896	0.4898	0.4901	0.4904	0.4906	0.4909	0.4911	0.4913	0.4916
2.4	0.4918	0.4920	0.4922	0.4925	0.4927	0.4929	0.4931	0.4932	0.4934	0.4936
2.5	0.4938	0.4940	0.4941	0.4943	0.4945	0.4946	0.4948	0.4949	0.4951	0.4952
2.6	0.4953	0.4955	0.4956	0.4957	0.4959	0.4960	0.4961	0.4962	0.4963	0.4964
2.7	0.4965	0.4966	0.4967	0.4968	0.4969	0.4970	0.4971	0.4972	0.4973	0.4974
2.8	0.4974	0.4975	0.4976	0.4977	0.4977	0.4978	0.4979	0.4979	0.4980	0.4981
2.9	0.4981	0.4982	0.4982	0.4983	0.4984	0.4984	0.4985	0.4985	0.4986	0.4986
3.0	0.4987	0.4987	0.4987	0.4988	0.4988	0.4989	0.4989	0.4989	0.4990	0.4990

APPENDIX

Binomial Distribution Values

$$P(X \mid n, p) = \frac{n!}{x!\,(n - x)!}\, p^x q^{n-x}$$

		p									
n	X	.05	.10	.15	.20	.25	.30	.35	.40	.45	.50
1	0	0.9500	0.9000	0.8500	0.8000	0.7500	0.7000	0.6500	0.6000	0.5500	0.5000
	1	0.0500	0.1000	0.1500	0.2000	0.2500	0.3000	0.3500	0.4000	0.4500	0.5000
2	0	0.9025	0.8100	0.7225	0.6400	0.5625	0.4900	0.4225	0.3600	0.3025	0.2500
	1	0.0950	0.1800	0.2550	0.3200	0.3750	0.4200	0.4550	0.4800	0.4950	0.5000
	2	0.0025	0.0100	0.0225	0.0400	0.0625	0.0900	0.1225	0.1600	0.2025	0.2500
3	0	0.8574	0.7290	0.6141	0.5120	0.4219	0.3430	0.2746	0.2160	0.1664	0.1250
	1	0.1354	0.2430	0.3251	0.3840	0.4219	0.4410	0.4436	0.4320	0.4084	0.3750
	2	0.0071	0.0270	0.0574	0.0960	0.1406	0.1890	0.2389	0.2880	0.3341	0.3750
	3	0.0001	0.0010	0.0034	0.0080	0.0156	0.0270	0.0429	0.0640	0.0911	0.1250
4	0	0.8145	0.6561	0.5220	0.4096	0.3164	0.2401	0.1785	0.1296	0.0915	0.0625
	1	0.1715	0.2916	0.3685	0.4096	0.4219	0.4116	0.3845	0.3456	0.2995	0.2500
	2	0.0135	0.0486	0.0975	0.1536	0.2109	0.2646	0.3105	0.3456	0.3675	0.3750
	3	0.0005	0.0036	0.0115	0.0256	0.0469	0.0756	0.1115	0.1536	0.2005	0.2500
	4	0.0000	0.0001	0.0005	0.0016	0.0039	0.0081	0.0150	0.0256	0.0410	0.0625
5	0	0.7738	0.5905	0.4437	0.3277	0.2373	0.1681	0.1160	0.0778	0.0503	0.0312
	1	0.2036	0.3280	0.3915	0.4096	0.3955	0.3602	0.3124	0.2592	0.2059	0.1562
	2	0.0214	0.0729	0.1382	0.2048	0.2637	0.3087	0.3364	0.3456	0.3369	0.3125
	3	0.0011	0.0081	0.0244	0.0512	0.0879	0.1323	0.1811	0.2304	0.2757	0.3125
	4	0.0000	0.0004	0.0022	0.0064	0.0146	0.0284	0.0488	0.0768	0.1128	0.1562
	5	0.0000	0.0000	0.0001	0.0003	0.0010	0.0024	0.0053	0.0102	0.0185	0.0312
6	0	0.7351	0.5314	0.3771	0.2621	0.1780	0.1176	0.0754	0.0467	0.0277	0.0156
	1	0.2321	0.3543	0.3993	0.3932	0.3560	0.3025	0.2437	0.1866	0.1359	0.0938
	2	0.0305	0.0984	0.1762	0.2458	0.2966	0.3241	0.3280	0.3110	0.2780	0.2344
	3	0.0021	0.0146	0.0415	0.0819	0.1318	0.1852	0.2355	0.2765	0.3032	0.3125
	4	0.0001	0.0012	0.0055	0.0154	0.0330	0.0595	0.0951	0.1382	0.1861	0.2344

Source: Adapted from R. S. Burington and D. C. May, *Handbook of Probability and Statistics with Tables*, 2d ed., McGraw-Hill Book Company, New York, 1970. Reproduced by permission of the publisher.

n	X	.05	.10	.15	.20	.25	.30	.35	.40	.45	.50
						p					
	5	0.0000	0.0001	0.0004	0.0015	0.0044	0.0102	0.0205	0.0369	0.0609	0.0938
	6	0.0000	0.0000	0.0000	0.0001	0.0002	0.0007	0.0018	0.0041	0.0083	0.0156
7	0	0.6983	0.4783	0.3206	0.2097	0.1335	0.0824	0.0490	0.0280	0.0152	0.0078
	1	0.2573	0.3720	0.3960	0.3670	0.3115	0.2471	0.1848	0.1306	0.0872	0.0547
	2	0.0406	0.1240	0.2097	0.2753	0.3115	0.3177	0.2985	0.2613	0.2140	0.1641
	3	0.0036	0.0230	0.0617	0.1147	0.1730	0.2269	0.2679	0.2903	0.2918	0.2734
	4	0.0002	0.0026	0.0109	0.0287	0.0577	0.0972	0.1442	0.1935	0.2388	0.2734
	5	0.0000	0.0002	0.0012	0.0043	0.0115	0.0250	0.0466	0.0774	0.1172	0.1641
	6	0.0000	0.0000	0.0001	0.0004	0.0013	0.0036	0.0084	0.0172	0.0320	0.0547
	7	0.0000	0.0000	0.0000	0.0000	0.0001	0.0002	0.0006	0.0016	0.0037	0.0078
8	0	0.6634	0.4305	0.2725	0.1678	0.1002	0.0576	0.0319	0.0168	0.0084	0.0039
	1	0.2793	0.3826	0.3847	0.3355	0.2670	0.1977	0.1373	0.0896	0.0548	0.0312
	2	0.0515	0.1488	0.2376	0.2936	0.3115	0.2065	0.2587	0.2090	0.1569	0.1094
	3	0.0054	0.0331	0.0839	0.1468	0.2076	0.2541	0.2786	0.2787	0.2568	0.2188
	4	0.0004	0.0046	0.0185	0.0459	0.0865	0.1361	0.1875	0.2322	0.2627	0.2734
	5	0.0000	0.0004	0.0026	0.0092	0.0231	0.0467	0.0808	0.1239	0.1719	0.2188
	6	0.0000	0.0000	0.0002	0.0011	0.0038	0.0100	0.0217	0.0413	0.0403	0.1094
	7	0.0000	0.0000	0.0000	0.0001	0.0004	0.0012	0.0033	0.0079	0.0164	0.0312
	8	0.0000	0.0000	0.0000	0.0000	0.0000	0.0001	0.0002	0.0007	0.0017	0.0039
9	0	0.6302	0.3874	0.2316	0.1342	0.0751	0.0404	0.0207	0.0101	0.0046	0.0020
	1	0.2985	0.3874	0.3679	0.3020	0.2253	0.1556	0.1004	0.0605	0.0339	0.0176
	2	0.0629	0.1722	0.2597	0.3020	0.3003	0.2668	0.2162	0.1612	0.1110	0.0703
	3	0.0077	0.0446	0.1069	0.1762	0.2336	0.2668	0.2716	0.2508	0.2119	0.1641
	4	0.0006	0.0074	0.0283	0.0661	0.1168	0.1715	0.2194	0.2508	0.2600	0.2461
	5	0.0000	0.0008	0.0050	0.0165	0.0389	0.0735	0.1181	0.1672	0.2128	0.2461
	6	0.0000	0.0001	0.0006	0.0028	0.0087	0.0210	0.0424	0.0743	0.1160	0.1641
	7	0.0000	0.0000	0.0000	0.0003	0.0012	0.0039	0.0098	0.0212	0.0407	0.0703
	8	0.0000	0.0000	0.0000	0.0000	0.0001	0.0004	0.0013	0.0035	0.0083	0.0176
	9	0.0000	0.0000	0.0000	0.0000	0.0000	0.0000	0.0001	0.0003	0.0008	0.0020
10	0	0.5987	0.3487	0.1969	0.1074	0.0563	0.0282	0.0135	0.0060	0.0025	0.0010
	1	0.3151	0.3874	0.3474	0.2684	0.1877	0.1211	0.0725	0.0403	0.0207	0.0098
	2	0.0746	0.1937	0.2759	0.3020	0.2816	0.2335	0.1757	0.1209	0.0763	0.0439
	3	0.0105	0.0574	0.1298	0.2013	0.2503	0.2668	0.2522	0.2150	0.1665	0.1172
	4	0.0010	0.0112	0.0401	0.0881	0.1460	0.2001	0.2377	0.2508	0.2384	0.2051
	5	0.0001	0.0015	0.0085	0.0264	0.0584	0.1029	0.1536	0.2007	0.2340	0.2461
	6	0.0000	0.0001	0.0012	0.0055	0.0162	0.0368	0.0689	0.1115	0.1596	0.2051
	7	0.0000	0.0000	0.0001	0.0008	0.0031	0.0090	0.0212	0.0425	0.0746	0.1172
	8	0.0000	0.0000	0.0000	0.0001	0.0004	0.0014	0.0043	0.0106	0.0229	0.0439
	9	0.0000	0.0000	0.0000	0.0000	0.0000	0.0001	0.0005	0.0016	0.0042	0.0098
	10	0.0000	0.0000	0.0000	0.0000	0.0000	0.0000	0.0000	0.0001	0.0003	0.0010

APPENDIX

Poisson Distribution Values

$$P(X \leq c \mid \lambda) = \sum_{o}^{c} \frac{\lambda^x e^{-\lambda}}{x!}$$

Note: The table shows 1000 times the probability of c or less occurrences of event that has an average number of occurrences of λ.

Source: Adapted from E. L. Grant, *Statistical Quality Control*, McGraw-Hill Book Company, New York, 1964. Reproduced by permission of the publisher.

Values of c

λ	0	1	2	3	4	5	6	7	8	9	10	11	12	13	14	15	16	17	18	19	20	21	22
0.02	980	1000																					
0.04	961	999	1000																				
0.06	942	998	1000																				
0.08	923	997	1000																				
0.10	905	995	1000																				
0.15	861	990	999	1000																			
0.20	819	982	999	1000																			
0.25	779	974	998	1000																			
0.30	741	963	996	1000																			
0.35	705	951	994	1000																			
0.40	670	938	992	999	1000																		
0.45	638	925	989	999	1000																		
0.50	607	910	986	998	1000																		
0.55	577	894	982	998	1000																		
0.60	549	878	977	997	1000																		
0.65	522	861	972	996	999	1000																	
0.70	497	844	966	994	999	1000																	
0.75	472	827	959	993	999	1000																	
0.80	449	809	953	991	999	1000																	
0.85	427	791	945	989	998	1000																	
0.90	407	772	937	987	998	1000																	
0.95	387	754	929	984	997	1000																	
1.00	368	736	920	981	996	999	1000																
1.1	333	699	900	974	995	999	1000																
1.2	301	663	879	966	992	998	1000																
1.3	273	627	857	957	989	998	1000																
1.4	247	592	833	946	986	997	999	1000															
1.5	223	558	809	934	981	996	999	1000															
1.6	202	525	783	921	976	994	999	1000															
1.7	183	493	757	907	970	992	998	1000															
1.8	165	463	731	891	964	990	997	999	1000														
1.9	150	434	704	875	956	987	997	999	1000														
2.0	135	406	677	857	947	983	995	999	1000														

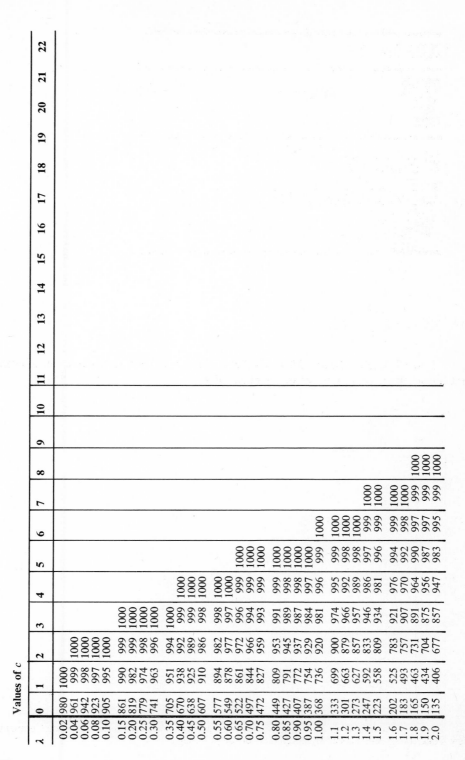

Values of c

λ	0	1	2	3	4	5	6	7	8	9	10	11	12	13	14	15	16	17	18	19	20	21	22
2.2	111	359	623	819	928	975	993	998	1000														
2.4	091	308	570	779	904	964	988	997	999	1000													
2.6	074	267	518	736	877	951	983	995	999	1000													
2.8	061	231	469	692	848	935	976	992	998	999	1000												
3.0	050	199	423	647	815	916	966	988	996	999	1000												
3.2	041	171	380	603	781	895	955	983	994	998	1000												
3.4	033	147	340	558	744	871	942	977	992	997	999	1000											
3.6	027	126	303	515	706	844	927	969	988	996	999	1000											
3.8	022	107	269	473	668	816	909	960	984	994	998	999	1000										
4.0	018	092	238	433	629	785	889	949	979	992	997	999	1000										
4.2	015	078	210	395	590	753	867	936	972	989	996	999	1000										
4.4	012	066	185	359	551	720	844	921	964	985	994	998	999	1000									
4.6	010	056	163	326	513	686	818	905	955	980	992	997	999	1000									
4.8	008	048	143	294	476	651	791	887	944	975	990	996	999	1000									
5.0	007	040	125	265	440	616	762	867	932	968	986	995	998	999	1000								
5.2	006	034	109	238	406	581	732	845	918	960	982	993	997	999	1000								
5.4	005	029	095	213	373	546	702	822	903	951	977	990	996	999	1000								
5.6	004	024	082	191	342	512	670	797	886	941	972	988	995	998	999	1000							
5.8	003	021	072	170	313	478	638	771	867	929	965	984	993	997	999	1000							
6.0	002	017	062	151	285	446	606	744	847	916	957	980	991	996	999	999	1000						
6.2	002	015	054	134	259	414	574	716	826	902	949	975	989	995	998	999	1000						
6.4	002	012	046	119	235	384	542	687	803	886	939	969	986	994	997	999	1000						
6.6	001	010	040	105	213	355	511	658	780	869	927	963	982	992	997	999	999	1000					
6.8	001	009	034	093	192	327	480	628	755	850	915	955	978	990	996	998	999	1000					
7.0	001	007	030	082	173	301	450	599	729	830	901	947	973	987	994	998	999	1000					
7.2	001	006	025	072	156	276	420	569	703	810	887	937	967	984	993	997	999	999	1000				
7.4	001	005	022	063	140	253	392	539	676	788	871	926	961	980	991	996	998	999	1000				
7.6	001	004	019	055	125	231	365	510	648	765	854	915	954	976	989	995	998	999	1000				
7.8	000	004	016	048	112	210	338	481	620	741	835	902	945	971	986	993	997	999	1000				
8.0	000	003	014	042	100	191	313	453	593	717	816	888	936	966	983	992	996	998	999	1000			
8.5	000	002	009	030	074	150	256	386	523	653	763	849	909	949	973	986	993	997	999	999	1000		
9.0	000	001	006	021	055	116	207	324	456	587	706	803	876	926	959	978	989	995	998	999	1000		
9.5	000	001	004	015	040	089	165	269	392	522	645	752	836	898	940	967	982	991	996	998	999	1000	
10.0	000	000	003	010	029	067	130	220	333	458	583	697	792	864	917	951	973	986	993	997	998	999	1000

APPENDIX

Present-Value Factors for Future Single Payments

Periods until payment	1%	2%	4%	6%	8%	10%	12%	14%	15%	16%	18%	20%	22%	24%	25%	26%	28%	30%
1	0.990	0.980	0.962	0.943	0.926	0.909	0.893	0.877	0.870	0.862	0.847	0.833	0.820	0.806	0.800	0.794	0.781	0.769
2	0.980	0.961	0.925	0.890	0.857	0.826	0.797	0.769	0.756	0.743	0.718	0.694	0.672	0.650	0.640	0.630	0.610	0.592
3	0.971	0.942	0.889	0.840	0.794	0.751	0.712	0.675	0.658	0.641	0.609	0.579	0.551	0.524	0.512	0.500	0.477	0.455
4	0.961	0.924	0.855	0.792	0.735	0.683	0.636	0.592	0.572	0.552	0.516	0.482	0.451	0.423	0.410	0.397	0.373	0.350
5	0.951	0.906	0.822	0.747	0.681	0.621	0.567	0.519	0.497	0.476	0.437	0.402	0.370	0.341	0.328	0.315	0.291	0.269
6	0.942	0.888	0.790	0.705	0.630	0.564	0.507	0.456	0.432	0.410	0.370	0.335	0.303	0.275	0.262	0.250	0.227	0.207
7	0.933	0.871	0.760	0.665	0.583	0.513	0.452	0.400	0.376	0.354	0.314	0.279	0.249	0.222	0.210	0.198	0.178	0.159
8	0.923	0.853	0.731	0.627	0.540	0.467	0.404	0.351	0.327	0.305	0.266	0.233	0.204	0.179	0.168	0.157	0.139	0.123
9	0.914	0.837	0.703	0.592	0.500	0.424	0.361	0.308	0.284	0.263	0.225	0.194	0.167	0.144	0.134	0.125	0.108	0.094
10	0.905	0.820	0.676	0.558	0.463	0.386	0.322	0.270	0.247	0.227	0.191	0.162	0.137	0.116	0.107	0.099	0.085	0.073
11	0.896	0.804	0.650	0.527	0.429	0.350	0.287	0.237	0.215	0.195	0.162	0.135	0.112	0.094	0.086	0.079	0.066	0.056
12	0.887	0.788	0.625	0.497	0.397	0.319	0.257	0.208	0.187	0.168	0.137	0.112	0.092	0.076	0.069	0.062	0.052	0.043
13	0.879	0.773	0.601	0.469	0.368	0.290	0.229	0.182	0.163	0.145	0.116	0.093	0.075	0.061	0.055	0.050	0.040	0.033
14	0.870	0.758	0.577	0.442	0.340	0.263	0.205	0.160	0.141	0.125	0.099	0.078	0.062	0.049	0.044	0.039	0.032	0.025
15	0.861	0.743	0.555	0.417	0.315	0.239	0.183	0.140	0.123	0.108	0.084	0.065	0.051	0.040	0.035	0.031	0.025	0.020
16	0.853	0.728	0.534	0.394	0.292	0.218	0.163	0.123	0.107	0.093	0.071	0.054	0.042	0.032	0.028	0.025	0.019	0.015
17	0.844	0.714	0.513	0.371	0.270	0.198	0.146	0.108	0.093	0.080	0.060	0.045	0.034	0.026	0.023	0.020	0.015	0.012
18	0.836	0.700	0.494	0.350	0.250	0.180	0.130	0.095	0.081	0.069	0.051	0.038	0.028	0.021	0.018	0.016	0.012	0.009
19	0.828	0.686	0.475	0.331	0.232	0.164	0.116	0.083	0.070	0.060	0.043	0.031	0.023	0.017	0.014	0.012	0.009	0.007
20	0.820	0.673	0.456	0.312	0.215	0.149	0.104	0.073	0.061	0.051	0.037	0.026	0.019	0.014	0.012	0.010	0.007	0.005
21	0.811	0.660	0.439	0.294	0.199	0.135	0.093	0.064	0.053	0.044	0.031	0.022	0.015	0.011	0.009	0.008	0.006	0.004
22	0.803	0.647	0.422	0.278	0.184	0.123	0.083	0.056	0.046	0.038	0.026	0.018	0.013	0.009	0.007	0.006	0.004	0.003
23	0.795	0.634	0.406	0.262	0.170	0.112	0.074	0.049	0.040	0.033	0.022	0.015	0.010	0.007	0.006	0.005	0.003	0.002
24	0.788	0.622	0.390	0.247	0.158	0.102	0.066	0.043	0.035	0.028	0.019	0.013	0.008	0.006	0.005	0.004	0.003	0.002
25	0.780	0.610	0.375	0.233	0.146	0.092	0.059	0.038	0.030	0.024	0.016	0.010	0.007	0.005	0.004	0.003	0.002	0.001
26	0.772	0.598	0.361	0.220	0.135	0.084	0.053	0.033	0.026	0.021	0.014	0.009	0.006	0.004	0.003	0.002	0.002	0.001
27	0.764	0.586	0.347	0.207	0.125	0.076	0.047	0.029	0.023	0.018	0.011	0.007	0.005	0.003	0.002	0.002	0.001	0.001
28	0.757	0.574	0.333	0.196	0.116	0.069	0.042	0.026	0.020	0.016	0.010	0.006	0.004	0.002	0.002	0.002	0.001	0.001
29	0.749	0.563	0.321	0.185	0.107	0.063	0.037	0.022	0.017	0.014	0.008	0.005	0.003	0.002	0.002	0.001	0.001	0.001
30	0.742	0.552	0.308	0.174	0.099	0.057	0.033	0.020	0.015	0.012	0.007	0.004	0.003	0.002	0.001	0.001	0.001	

APPENDIX

Present-Value Factors for Annuities

Years (*N*)	1%	2%	4%	6%	8%	10%	12%	14%	15%	16%	18%	20%	22%	24%	25%	26%	28%	30%
1	0.990	0.980	0.962	0.943	0.926	0.909	0.893	0.877	0.870	0.862	0.847	0.833	0.820	0.806	0.800	0.794	0.781	0.769
2	1.970	1.942	1.886	1.833	1.783	1.736	1.690	1.647	1.626	1.605	1.566	1.528	1.492	1.457	1.440	1.424	1.392	1.361
3	2.941	2.884	2.775	2.673	2.577	2.487	2.402	2.322	2.283	2.246	2.174	2.106	2.042	1.981	1.952	1.923	1.868	1.816
4	3.902	3.808	3.630	3.465	3.312	3.170	3.037	2.914	2.855	2.798	2.690	2.589	2.494	2.404	2.362	2.320	2.241	2.166
5	4.853	4.713	4.452	4.212	3.993	3.791	3.605	3.433	3.352	3.274	3.127	2.991	2.864	2.745	2.689	2.635	2.532	2.436
6	5.795	5.601	5.242	4.917	4.623	4.355	4.111	3.889	3.784	3.685	3.498	3.326	3.167	3.020	2.951	2.885	2.759	2.643
7	6.728	6.472	6.002	5.582	5.206	4.868	4.564	4.288	4.160	4.039	3.812	3.605	3.416	3.242	3.161	3.083	2.937	2.802
8	7.652	7.325	6.733	6.210	5.747	5.335	4.968	4.639	4.487	4.344	4.078	3.837	3.619	3.421	3.329	3.241	3.076	2.925
9	8.566	8.162	7.435	6.802	6.247	5.759	5.328	4.946	4.772	4.607	4.303	4.031	3.786	3.566	3.463	3.366	3.184	3.019
10	9.471	8.983	8.111	7.360	6.710	6.145	5.650	5.216	5.019	4.833	4.494	4.192	3.923	3.682	3.571	3.465	3.269	3.092
11	10.368	9.787	8.760	7.887	7.139	6.495	5.937	5.453	5.234	5.029	4.656	4.327	4.035	3.776	3.656	3.544	3.335	3.147
12	11.255	10.575	9.385	8.384	7.536	6.814	6.194	5.660	5.421	5.197	4.793	4.439	4.127	3.851	3.725	3.606	3.387	3.190
13	12.134	11.343	9.986	8.853	7.904	7.103	6.424	5.842	5.583	5.342	4.910	4.533	4.203	3.912	3.780	3.656	3.427	3.223
14	13.004	12.106	10.563	9.295	8.244	7.367	6.628	6.002	5.724	5.468	5.008	4.611	4.265	3.962	3.824	3.695	3.459	3.249
15	13.865	12.849	11.118	9.712	8.559	7.606	6.811	6.142	5.847	5.575	5.092	4.675	4.315	4.001	3.859	3.726	3.483	3.268
16	14.718	13.578	11.652	10.106	8.851	7.824	6.974	6.265	5.954	5.669	5.162	4.730	4.357	4.033	3.887	3.751	3.503	3.283
17	15.562	14.292	12.166	10.477	9.122	8.022	7.120	6.373	6.047	5.749	5.222	4.775	4.391	4.059	3.910	3.771	3.518	3.295
18	16.398	14.992	12.659	10.828	9.372	8.201	7.250	6.467	6.128	5.818	5.273	4.812	4.419	4.080	3.928	3.786	3.529	3.304
19	17.226	15.678	13.134	11.158	9.604	8.365	7.366	6.550	6.198	5.877	5.316	4.844	4.442	4.097	3.942	3.799	3.539	3.311
20	18.046	16.351	13.590	11.470	9.818	8.514	7.469	6.623	6.259	5.929	5.353	4.870	4.460	4.110	3.954	3.808	3.546	3.316
21	18.857	17.011	14.029	11.764	10.017	8.649	7.562	6.687	6.312	5.973	5.384	4.891	4.476	4.121	3.963	3.816	3.551	3.320
22	19.660	17.658	14.451	12.042	10.201	8.772	7.645	6.743	6.359	6.011	5.410	4.909	4.488	4.130	3.970	3.822	3.556	3.323
23	20.456	18.292	14.857	12.303	10.371	8.883	7.718	6.792	6.399	6.044	5.432	4.925	4.499	4.137	3.976	3.827	3.559	3.325
24	21.243	18.914	15.247	12.550	10.529	8.985	7.784	6.835	6.434	6.073	5.451	4.937	4.507	4.143	3.981	3.831	3.562	3.327
25	22.023	19.523	15.622	12.783	10.675	9.077	7.843	6.873	6.464	6.097	5.467	4.948	4.514	4.147	3.985	3.834	3.564	3.329
26	22.795	20.121	15.983	13.003	10.810	9.161	7.896	6.906	6.491	6.118	5.480	4.956	4.520	4.151	3.988	3.837	3.566	3.330
27	23.560	20.707	16.330	13.211	10.935	9.237	7.943	6.935	6.514	6.136	5.492	4.964	4.524	4.154	3.990	3.839	3.567	3.331
28	24.316	21.281	16.663	13.406	11.051	9.307	7.984	6.961	6.534	6.152	5.502	4.970	4.528	4.157	3.992	3.840	3.568	3.331
29	25.066	21.844	16.984	13.591	11.158	9.370	8.022	6.983	6.551	6.166	5.510	4.975	4.531	4.159	3.994	3.841	3.569	3.332
30	25.808	22.396	17.292	13.765	11.258	9.427	8.055	7.003	6.566	6.177	5.517	4.979	4.534	4.160	3.995	3.842	3.569	3.332

APPENDIX

Compound Interest Factors and Example Calculations for 10 Percent

In the following table, P is present worth, F is future sum, A is annuity amount, i is interest rate, and n is the year. In the example calculations, let i equal 10 percent and n equal 5 years.

To find	Compound interest factors		Example calculations		
F given P	$F = P(1 + i)^n$	$= P(F \mid P)_i^n$	If P = \$30,000	F = 30,000(1.611)	= \$48,330
P given F	$P = F\dfrac{1}{(1 + i)^n}$	$= F(P \mid F)_i^n$	If F = \$10,000	P = 10,000(0.6209)	= \$6,209
A given F	$A = F\dfrac{i}{(1 + i)^n - 1}$	$= F(A \mid F)_i^n$	If F = \$10,000	A = 10,000(0.16380)	= \$1,638
A given P	$A = P\dfrac{i(1 + i)^n}{(1 + i)^n - 1}$	$= P(A \mid P)_i^n$	If P = \$30,000	A = 30,000(0.26380)	= \$7,914
F given A	$F = A\dfrac{(1 + i)^n - 1}{i}$	$= A(F \mid A)_i^n$	If A = \$5,000	F = 5,000(6.105)	= \$30,525
P given A	$P = A\dfrac{(1 + i)^n - 1}{i(1 + i)^n}$	$= A(P \mid A)_i^n$	If A = \$5,000	P = 5,000(3.791)	= \$18,955

	To find F, given P: $(1+i)^n$	To find P, given F: $\frac{1}{(1+i)^n}$	To find A, given F: $\frac{i}{(1+i)^n-1}$	To find A, given P: $\frac{i(1+i)^n}{(1+i)^n-1}$	To find F, given A: $\frac{(1+i)^n-1}{i}$	To find P, given A: $\frac{(1+i)^n-1}{i(1+i)^n}$
n	$(F\mid P)_{10}{}^n$	$(P\mid F)_{10}{}^n$	$(A\mid F)_{10}{}^n$	$(A\mid P)_{10}{}^n$	$(F\mid A)_{10}{}^n$	$(P\mid A)_{10}{}^n$
1	1.100	0.9091	1.00000	1.10000	1.000	0.909
2	1.210	0.8264	0.47619	0.57619	2.100	1.736
3	1.331	0.7513	0.30211	0.40211	3.310	2.487
4	1.464	0.6830	0.21547	0.31547	4.641	3.170
5	1.611	0.6209	0.16380	0.26380	6.105	3.791
6	1.772	0.5645	0.12961	0.22961	7.716	4.355
7	1.949	0.5132	0.10541	0.20541	9.487	4.868
8	2.144	0.4665	0.08744	0.18744	11.436	5.335
9	2.358	0.4241	0.07364	0.17364	13.579	5.759
10	2.594	0.3855	0.06275	0.16275	15.937	6.144
11	2.853	0.3505	0.05396	0.15396	18.531	6.495
12	3.138	0.3186	0.04676	0.14676	21.384	6.814
13	3.452	0.2897	0.04078	0.14078	24.523	7.103
14	3.797	0.2633	0.03575	0.13575	27.975	7.367
15	4.177	0.2394	0.03147	0.13147	31.772	7.606
16	4.595	0.2176	0.02782	0.12782	35.950	7.824
17	5.054	0.1978	0.02466	0.12466	40.545	8.022
18	5.560	0.1799	0.02193	0.12193	45.599	8.201
19	6.116	0.1635	0.01955	0.11955	51.159	8.363
20	6.727	0.1486	0.01746	0.11746	57.275	8.514
21	7.400	0.1351	0.01562	0.11562	64.002	8.649
22	8.140	0.1228	0.01401	0.11401	71.403	8.772
23	8.954	0.1117	0.01257	0.11257	79.543	8.883
24	9.850	0.1015	0.01130	0.11130	88.497	8.985
25	10.835	0.0923	0.01017	0.11017	98.347	9.077
26	11.918	0.0839	0.00916	0.10916	109.182	9.161
27	13.110	0.0763	0.00826	0.10826	121.100	9.237
28	14.421	0.0693	0.00745	0.10745	134.210	9.307
29	15.863	0.0630	0.00673	0.10673	148.631	9.370
30	17.449	0.0573	0.00608	0.10608	164.494	9.427
31	19.194	0.0521	0.00550	0.10550	181.943	9.479
32	21.114	0.0474	0.00497	0.10497	201.138	9.526
33	23.225	0.0431	0.00450	0.10450	222.252	9.569
34	25.548	0.0391	0.00407	0.10407	245.477	9.609
35	28.102	0.0356	0.00369	0.10369	271.024	9.644
40	45.259	0.0221	0.00226	0.10226	442.593	9.779
45	72.890	0.0137	0.00139	0.10139	718.905	9.863
50	117.391	0.0085	0.00086	0.10086	1163.909	9.915
55	189.059	0.0053	0.00053	0.10053	1880.591	9.947
60	304.482	0.0033	0.00033	0.10033	3034.816	9.967
65	490.371	0.0020	0.00020	0.10020	4893.707	9.980
70	789.747	0.0013	0.00013	0.10013	7887.470	9.987
75	1271.895	0.0008	0.00008	0.10008	12708.954	9.992
80	2048.400	0.0005	0.00005	0.10005	20474.002	9.995
85	3298.969	0.0003	0.00003	0.10003	32979.690	9.997
90	5313.023	0.0002	0.00002	0.10002	53120.226	9.998
95	8556.676	0.0001	0.00001	0.10001	85556.760	9.999
100	13780.612	0.0001	0.00001	0.10001	137796.123	9.999

APPENDIX

J

Learning Curve Coefficients

% base	70%	74%	78%	80%	82%	84%	86%	88%	90%	94%	98%
2	7.486	5.469	4.065	3.523	3.065	2.675	2.343	2.058	1.812	1.418	1.121
5	4.672	3.674	2.927	2.623	2.358	2.125	1.919	1.738	1.577	1.307	1.091
10	3.270	2.718	2.283	2.098	1.933	1.785	1.651	1.529	1.419	1.228	1.069
20	2.290	2.012	1.781	1.674	1.585	1.499	1.420	1.346	1.277	1.155	1.048
30	1.858	1.687	1.540	1.473	1.412	1.354	1.300	1.249	1.201	1.113	1.036
40	1.602	1.489	1.389	1.343	1.300	1.259	1.221	1.184	1.149	1.085	1.027
50	1.429	1.351	1.282	1.250	1.220	1.190	1.163	1.136	1.111	1.064	1.020
60	1.300	1.248	1.201	1.178	1.158	1.137	1.118	1.099	1.081	1.047	1.015
70	1.201	1.167	1.137	1.121	1.108	1.094	1.081	1.088	1.056	1.032	1.010
80	1.122	1.101	1.083	1.074	1.066	1.058	1.050	1.042	1.034	1.020	1.007
90	1.056	1.047	1.039	1.034	1.031	1.027	1.023	1.020	1.016	1.010	1.003
100	1.000	1.000	1.000	1.000	1.000	1.000	1.000	1.000	1.000	1.000	1.000
110	0.9521	0.9593	0.9665	0.9696	0.9731	0.9764	0.9796	0.9827	0.9855	0.9916	0.9973
120	0.9105	0.9239	0.9369	0.9428	0.9492	0.9551	0.9610	0.9670	0.9726	0.9839	0.9947
125	0.8915	0.9076	0.9231	0.9307	0.9381	0.9454	0.9526	0.9552	0.9667	0.9803	0.9935
130	0.8737	0.8921	0.9104	0.9200	0.9279	0.9359	0.9447	0.9528	0.9609	0.9769	0.9923
140	0.8410	0.8640	0.8864	0.8974	0.9084	0.9188	0.9294	0.9399	0.9501	0.9704	0.9903
150	0.8117	0.8381	0.8645	0.8776	0.8905	0.9029	0.9156	0.9280	0.9402	0.9645	0.9882
160	0.7852	0.8152	0.8452	0.8595	0.8744	0.8885	0.9028	0.9170	0.9309	0.9590	0.9864
170	0.7611	0.7938	0.8270	0.8428	0.8591	0.8752	0.8910	0.9067	0.9225	0.9538	0.9847
175	0.7498	0.7842	0.8183	0.8352	0.8520	0.8687	0.8854	0.9020	0.9185	0.9513	0.9838
180	0.7390	0.7746	0.8103	0.8274	0.8452	0.8624	0.8798	0.8974	0.9144	0.9489	0.9830
190	0.7187	0.7568	0.7947	0.8133	0.8322	0.8510	0.8698	0.9885	0.9070	0.9443	0.9815
200	0.7000	0.7400	0.7800	0.8000	0.8200	0.8400	0.8600	0.8800	0.9000	0.9400	0.9800
220	0.6665	0.7098	0.7540	0.7759	0.7981	0.8201	0.8423	0.8646	0.8870	0.9321	0.9772
240	0.6373	0.6835	0.7306	0.7543	0.7783	0.8022	0.8265	0.8508	0.8754	0.9249	0.9748
260	0.6116	0.6602	0.7103	0.7349	0.7607	0.7863	0.8123	0.8384	0.8649	0.9182	0.9726
280	0.5887	0.6392	0.6915	0.7177	0.7447	0.7717	0.7992	0.8270	0.8550	0.9122	0.9704
300	0.5682	0.6203	0.6743	0.7019	0.7301	0.7586	0.7875	0.8161	0.8492	0.9066	0.9684
400	0.4900	0.5476	0.6084	0.6400	0.6724	0.7056	0.7396	0.7744	0.8100	0.8836	0.9604
500	0.4368	0.4970	0.5616	0.5956	0.6308	0.6671	0.7045	0.7432	0.7830	0.8662	0.9542
600	0.3977	0.4592	0.5261	0.5617	0.5987	0.6372	0.6771	0.7187	0.7616	0.8522	0.9491
700	0.3674	0.4294	0.4978	0.5345	0.5729	0.6129	0.6548	0.6985	0.7440	0.8406	0.9449
800	0.3430	0.4052	0.4746	0.5120	0.5514	0.5927	0.6361	0.6815	0.7290	0.8306	0.9412
900	0.3228	0.3850	0.4549	0.4929	0.5331	0.5754	0.6200	0.6668	0.7161	0.8219	0.9380
1000	0.3058	0.3678	0.4381	0.4765	0.5172	0.5604	0.6059	0.6540	0.7047	0.8142	0.9351

Source: R. W. Conway and Andrew Schultz, Jr., "The Manufacturing Progress Function," *Journal of Industrial Engineering*, vol. 10, no. 1, January–February 1959, pp. 39–54; and Thomas E. Vollman, *Operations Management*, Addison-Wesley Publishing Company, Reading, Massachusetts, 1973, pp. 381–384. Reproduced by permission of the AIIE and Addison-Wesley.

Index